THE OXFORD

Essential Guide
for Puzzle Solvers

Also available

THE OXFORD DESK DICTIONARY AND THESAURUS
THE OXFORD DICTIONARY OF AMERICAN USAGE AND STYLE
THE OXFORD ESSENTIAL DICTIONARY
THE OXFORD ESSENTIAL GUIDE TO THE U.S. GOVERNMENT
THE OXFORD ESSENTIAL GUIDE TO WRITING
THE OXFORD ESSENTIAL QUOTATIONS DICTIONARY
THE OXFORD ESSENTIAL SPELLING DICTIONARY
THE OXFORD ESSENTIAL THESAURUS
THE OXFORD FRENCH DICTIONARY
THE OXFORD GERMAN DICTIONARY
THE OXFORD GREEK DICTIONARY
THE OXFORD ITALIAN DICTIONARY
THE OXFORD RUSSIAN DICTIONARY
THE OXFORD NEW SPANISH DICTIONARY

THE OXFORD

Essential Guide
for Puzzle Solvers

BERKLEY BOOKS, NEW YORK

Some material in *The Oxford Essential Guide for Puzzle Solvers* was adapted from *The Oxford Puzzle Solver* (published in the U.K. by Oxford University Press, 1999) and from *The Oxford Word Challenge* by Tony Augarde (published in the U.K. by Oxford University Press, 1998).

THE OXFORD ESSENTIAL GUIDE FOR PUZZLE SOLVERS

A Berkley Book / published by arrangement with Oxford University Press, Inc.

PRINTING HISTORY
Berkley edition / July 2000

The Penguin Putnam Inc. World Wide Web site address is
http://www.penguinputnam.com

ISBN: 0-425-17599-5

BERKLEY®
Berkley Books are published by
The Berkley Publishing Group, a division of Penguin Putnam Inc.,
375 Hudson Street, New York, New York 10014.
BERKLEY and the "B" design are trademarks
belonging to Penguin Putnam Inc.

PRINTED IN THE UNITED STATES OF AMERICA

10 9 8 7 6 5 4 3

PREFACE

The Oxford Essential Guide for Puzzle Solvers is ideal for anyone who enjoys solving crosswords and word puzzles or playing word games. It was compiled to provide easy-to-find answers to general knowledge clues and quiz questions and to be useful in playing a wide variety of games.

The book contains lists of answers arranged first by general category (Famous People, Science and Technology, Sports, etc.), then by specific subcategories (within Geography one finds Countries of the World, Oceans and Seas, Major Deserts, Bridges, etc.). Answers are further organized by the number of letters, so that in the list of Mammals one sees *ai* and *ox* under **2 letters**, *ape*, *ass*, *bat*, etc., under **3 letters**, and so forth until the *scaly-tailed squirrel* is listed under **19 letters**. Note, however, that the preference has been to list more words of six, seven, or eight letters than very long answers, as these are more likely to be useful for the puzzle solver.

In addition to the handy reference information provided in these lists, the book contains an extensive appendix of word games, with the answers provided in the back of the book. The appendix is divided into three sections of increasing difficulty. Test yourself or take the book along so groups can play while traveling—*The Oxford Essential Guide for Puzzle Solvers* provides both information and entertainment.

STAFF

CONTENTS

FAMOUS PEOPLE

U.S. Presidents	1
Prime Ministers of the U.K.	1
Roman Emperors	3
Popes from 1492	4
Historical, Political, and Military Figures	5
Religious Figures and Theologians	39
Scientists and Inventors	48
Artists, Cartoonists, Designers, and Architects	67
Composers, Musicians, Singers, and Instrument Makers	82
People Involved in Movies, Theater, and Dance	95
Writers, Philosophers, and Scholars	111
Sports Figures	142

HISTORY, POLITICS, AND WAR

Tribes of the U.S. and Canada	153
Empires	155
Chinese Dynasties	156
Political Philosophies and Systems	156
Wars and Battles	157
Seven Wonders of the Ancient World	159
British Ranks of Hereditary Peerage	159
Military Ranks	160
Weapons	161

RELIGION AND MYTHOLOGY

Religions and Major Denominations	163
Religious Festivals and Dates	164
Christian Saints	166
The Twelve Tribes of Israel	168
Orders of Angels	168
Biblical Characters	168
Books of the Bible	169
Monastic Orders	170
Christian Ecclesiastical Officers	171
Names of God	172
Names for the Devil	172
Seven Virtues	173
Seven Deadly Sins	173
Parts of a Church	173
Greek Gods and Goddesses	174
Roman Gods and Goddesses	174
The Three Fates	175
The Nine Muses	175
Characters from Greek and Roman Mythology	175
The Labors of Hercules	176
Rivers of Hades	177
Egyptian Gods and Goddesses	177
Hindu Gods and Goddesses	177
Celtic Gods, Goddesses, and Heroes	178
Norse Gods, Goddesses, and Other Mythological Figures	178
Arthurian Legend	179
Monsters and Demons	180

GEOGRAPHY

Countries of the World	181
Capital Cities	183
U.S. States	186
U.S. Capitals	187
States and Territories of Australia	188
Provinces and Territories of Canada	189
Canadian Capitals	189
Mexican States	190
Provinces of New Zealand	190
Provinces of South Africa	191
Cities, Towns, and Villages	191
Oceans and Seas	210
Lakes and Reservoirs: U.S. and Canada	211
Lakes, Lochs, and Loughs: Outside of the U.S. and Canada	214
Rivers: U.S. and Canada	215
Rivers: Outside of the U.S. and Canada	220
Waterfalls	223
Mountains	224

GEOGRAPHY (*continued*)

Mountain Ranges	226	Bridges	233
Volcanoes	230	Dams	235
Major Deserts	232	Canals	236
Major Earthquakes	232		

TRANSPORT

Motor Vehicles	237	Naval Vessels	244
Motorless Vehicles	238	Sailing Ships and Boats	245
Vehicle Parts	238	Nautical Terms	245
Famous Locomotives and		Ports	246
Types of Locomotive	239	Aircraft	252
Railroads, U.S. and Canada	240	Military Aircraft	252
Ships and Boats	243	Major Airports	253

SCIENCE AND TECHNOLOGY

Units of Measurement	255	Metal Ores	263
Elementary Particles	256	Geological Ages, Eras, Periods,	
Chemical Elements	256	and Epochs	263
Mathematical Terms	257	Galaxies	264
Branches of Engineering	259	Constellations	264
Computer Programming		Planets	265
Languages	260	Satellites of the Planets	266
Computer Parts and		Comets	266
Peripherals	260	Winds	267
Rocks and Minerals	261	Clouds	267

MEDICINE AND THE HUMAN BODY

Human Bones	268	Diseases and Medical	
Parts of the Human Ear	268	Conditions	272
Human Glands	269	Surgical Operations	273
Parts of the Human Eye	270	Therapies	275
Human Muscles	270	Branches of Psychology	276
Medical Specialties	271	Phobias	277
Types of Medication and Drug	271		

ANIMALS, PLANTS, AND AGRICULTURE

Collective Names for Animals		Seashells	295
and Birds	280	Trees and Shrubs	296
Adjectives Relating to Animals		Flowers	297
and Birds	281	Parts of a Flower	299
Names for Male and Female		Fruits and Nuts	299
Animals	281	Vegetables	300
Young of Animals	282	Grasses, Sedges, and Rushes	301
Mammals	283	Fungi and Algae	302
Marsupials	285	Types of Farming	303
Birds	286	Breeds of Horse and Pony	303
Reptiles	288	Points of a Horse	304
Amphibians	289	Breeds of Cattle	305
Fish	290	Breeds of Sheep	305
Insects and Arachnids	292	Breeds of Fowl	307
Butterflies and Moths	293	Breeds of Dog	308
Invertebrates	294	Breeds of Cat	309

LITERATURE AND LANGUAGE

Literary Terms   310
Meters and Metrical Feet   311
Characters from Well-Known
  Works of Fiction   312
Characters from the Novels of
  Charles Dickens   321
Characters from the Plays of
  William Shakespeare   329

Rhetorical Devices   333
Theatrical Terms   333
Languages   335
Accents and Diacritical Marks   339
Phonetic Alphabet   339
Punctuation Marks   339
Grammatical Terms   340
Branches of Philosophy   341

SPORTS

Sports and Sporting Activities   342
Sports Terms   344
Gymnastic Events   346
Trophies, Awards, and Events   347
Stadiums and Venues   351
Baseball Stadiums   353
NFL Stadiums   354
Football Teams   355

Baseball Teams   356
Cricketing Terms and
  Expressions   356
Golf Terms   357
Rugby Positions and Roles   357
Boxing Weight Divisions   358
Fencing Terms   358

MISCELLANEOUS

Cooking Terms   359
Herbs   359
Spices   359
Cheeses   360
Types of Pasta   361
Beans and Peas   361
Desserts   362
Cakes   362
Wines and Varieties of Grapes   363
Champagne Measures   364
Beers   365
Games   365
Board Games   366
Card Games   367
Fabrics and Fibers   368
Sewing Techniques   369

Sewing Stitches   369
Knitting Terms   369
Knots   370
Ceramics   370
Types and Styles of Furniture   371
Gemstones and Semiprecious
  Stones   372
Colors   372
Birthstones   373
Signs of the Zodiac   373
Wedding Anniversaries   374
Tools   374
Currencies of the World   375
Economic Terms and Theories   378
Financial Terms   380
Roman Numerals   380

APPENDIX: WORD GAMES

FAMOUS PEOPLE

U.S. Presidents

(with dates in office)

4 letters

Bush, George Herbert Walker	1989–93
Ford, Gerald Rudolph	1974–77
Polk, James Knox	1845–49
Taft, William Howard	1909–13

5 letters

Adams, John Quincy	1825–29
Adams, John	1797–1801
Grant, Ulysses Simpson	1869–77
Hayes, Rutherford Birchard	1877–81
Nixon, Richard Milhous	1969–74
Tyler, John	1841–45

6 letters

Arthur, Chester Alan	1881–85
Carter, James Earl, Jr	1977–81
Hoover, Herbert Clark	1929–33
Monroe, James	1817–25
Pierce, Franklin	1853–57
Reagan, Ronald Wilson	1981–89
Taylor, Zachary	1849–50
Truman, Harry S	1945–53
Wilson, Thomas Woodrow	1913–21

7 letters

Clinton, William Jefferson	from 1993
Harding, Warren Gamaliel	1921–23

(continued)

Jackson, Andrew	1829–37
Johnson, Andrew	1865–69
Johnson, Lyndon Baines	1963–69
Kennedy, John Fitzgerald	1961–63
Lincoln, Abraham	1861–65
Madison, James	1809–17

8 letters

Buchanan, James	1857–61
Coolidge, Calvin	1923–29
Fillmore, Millard	1850–53
Garfield, James Abraham	1881
Harrison, Benjamin	1889–93
Harrison, William Henry	1841
McKinley, William	1897–1901
Van Buren, Martin	1837–41

9 letters

Cleveland, Stephen Grover	1885–89; 1893–97
Jefferson, Thomas	1801–1809
Roosevelt, Franklin Delano	1933–45
Roosevelt, Theodore	1901–1909

10 letters

Eisenhower, Dwight David	1953–61
Washington, George	1789–97

Prime Ministers of the U.K.

(with dates in office)

3 letters

Law, Andrew Bonar	1922–23

4 letters

Bute, Earl of	1762–63
Eden, Sir Anthony	1955–57
Grey, Earl	1830–34
Peel, Sir Robert	1834–35; 1841–46

5 letters

Pitt, William	1783–1801; 1804–07
Atlee, Clement	1945–51
Blair, Tony	from 1997
Derby, Earl of	1852; 1858–59; 1866–68

Prime Ministers of the U.K. *(continued)*

Heath, Edward	1970–74
Major, John	1990–97
North, Lord	1770–82

6 letters

Pelham, Henry	1743–54
George, David Lloyd	1916–22
Wilson, Harold	1964–70; 1974–76

7 letters

Asquith, Herbert Henry	1908–16
Baldwin, Stanley	1923–24; 1924–29; 1935–37
Balfour, Arthur James	1902–05
Canning, George	1827
Chatham, Earl of	1766–68
Grafton, Duke of	1768–70
Russell, Earl of	1846–52; 1865–66
Walpole, Sir Robert	1721–42

8 letters

Aberdeen, Earl of	1852–55
Disraeli, Benjamin	1868; 1874–80
Goderich, Viscount	1827–28
Perceval, Spencer	1809–12
Portland, Duke of	1783; 1807–09
Rosebery, Earl of	1894–95
Thatcher, Margaret	1979–90

9 letters

Addington, Henry	1801–04
Callaghan, James	1976–79

Churchill, Winston Spencer	1940–45; 1951–55
Gladstone, William Ewart	1868–74; 1880–85; 1886; 1892–94
Grenville, George	1763–65
Grenville, Lord William	1806–07
Liverpool, Earl of	1812–27
MacDonald, Ramsay	1924; 1929–35
Macmillan, Harold	1957–63
Melbourne, Viscount	1834; 1835–41
Newcastle, Duke of	1754–56; 1757–62
Shelburne, Earl of	1782–83

10 letters

Devonshire, Duke of	1756–57
Palmerston, Viscount	1855–58; 1859–65
Rockingham, Marquess of	1765–66; 1782
Wellington, Duke of	1828–30; 1834
Wilmington, Earl of	1742–43

11 letters

Chamberlain, Neville	1937–40

12 letters

Douglas-Home, Sir Alec	1963–64

18 letters

Campbell–Bannerman, Sir Henry	1905–08

Roman Emperors

(with dates of reign)

(Note that during the reign of Diocletian, the Roman Empire was divided into the Eastern Roman Empire and the Western Roman Empire, after which there were often two emperors, one ruling each part of the empire. Therefore, the dates for two emperors listed below may overlap [e.g., Arcadius and Honorius].)

4 letters

Geta	209–12
Leo I	457–74
Nero	54–68
Otho	69
Pius, Antoninus	138–61
Zeno	474–91

5 letters

Carus	282–83
Leo II	474
Nepos, Julius	474–75
Nerva	96–98
Titus	79–81
Verus, Lucius	161–69

6 letters

Avitus	455–56
Decius	249–51
Gallus	251–53
Jovian	363–64
Julian	360–63
Philip	244–49
Probus	276–82
Trajan	98–117
Valens	364–78

7 letters

Carinus	283–85
Florian	276
Gratian	375–83
Hadrian	117–38
Marcian	450–57
Maximin	310–13
Maximus	238
Maximus, Petronius	455
Severus	306–07
Severus, Alexander	222–35
Severus, Linius	461–67
Severus, Septimius	193–211
Tacitus	275–76

8 letters

Aemilian	253
Arcadius	395–408
Augustus	27 BC–AD 14
Aurelian	270–75
Aurelius, Marcus	161–80
Balbinus	238
Caligula	37–41
Claudius	41–54
Commodus	180–92
Domitian	81–96
Galerius	305–11
Gordian I	238
Honorius	395–423
Julianus, Didius	193
Licinius	308–24
Macrinus	217–18
Majorian	457–61
Maximian	286–305; 306–08
Numerian	283–84
Olybrius	472–73
Pertinax	193
Tiberius	14–37
Valerian	253–60

9 letters

Anthemius	467–72
Caracalla	198–217
Constans I	337–50
Gallienus	253–68
Gordian II	238
Hostilian	251
Maxentius	306–12
Procopius	365–66
Vespasian	69–79
Vitellius	69

10 letters

Augustulus, Romulus	475–76
Claudius II	268–69
Diocletian	284–305; abdicated
Gordian III	238–44

Roman Emperors *(continued)*

Magnentius	350–51	Heliogabalus	218–22
Maximinus I	235–38	Theodosius II	408–50
Quintillus	269–70	Valentinian I	364–75

11 letters
Theodosius I	379–95

12 letters
Constantine I (the Great)	312–37
Constantinus, Flavius Claudius	407–11
Constantius I	306–06

13 letters
Constantine II	337–40
Constantius II	337–61
Valentinian II	375–92

14 letters
Constantius III	421–23
Valentinian III	423–55

Popes from 1492

(with dates in office)

4 letters
Leo X	1513–21

5 letters
Leo XI	1605
Paul V	1605–21
Pius V	1566–72
Pius X	1902–14

6 letters
Leo XII	1823–29
Paul IV	1555–59
Paul VI	1963–78
Pius IV	1559–65
Pius VI	1775–99
Pius IX	1846–78
Pius XI	1922–39

7 letters
Leo XIII	1878–1903
Paul III	1534–49
Pius III	1503
Pius VII	1800–23
Pius XII	1939–58
Sixtus V	1585–90

8 letters
Adrian VI	1522–23
Clement IX	1670–76

Julius II	1503–13
Pius VIII	1829–30
Urban VII	1590

9 letters
Julius III	1550–55
Gregory XV	1621–23
Urban VIII	1623–44
Innocent X	1644–55
Clement IX	1667–69
Clement XI	1700–21
John XXIII	1958–63
John Paul I	1978

10 letters
Benedict XV	1914–22
Clement VII	1523–34
Clement XII	1730–40
Clement XIV	1769–74
Gregory XIV	1590–91
Gregory XVI	1831–46
Innocent IX	1591
Innocent XI	1676–89
John Paul II	from 1978

11 letters
Alexander VI	1492–1503
Benedict XIV	1740–58
Clement VIII	1592–1605

Clement XIII	1758–69	Benedict XIII	1724–30
Gregory XIII	1572–85	Innocent XIII	1721–4
Innocent XII	1691–1700		
Marcellus II	1555		

13 letters

Alexander VIII   1689–91

12 letters

Alexander VII   1655–67

Historical, Political, and Military Figures

3 letters

Ali, Muhammad See MUHAMMAD ALI

Cid, El (also **the Cid**) (born Rodrigo Díaz de Vivar), Count of Bivar (*c.* 1043–99) Spanish Soldier

FDR nickname of Franklin Delano Roosevelt

Ito, Prince Hirobumi (1841–1909) Japanese statesman, Premier four times between 1884 and 1901

Jay, John (1745–1829) American jurist, chief justice of the Supreme Court

Law, (Andrew) Bonar (1858–1923) Canadian-born British Conservative statesman, Prime Minister 1922–23

Lee, Henry (known as **Light-Horse Harry**) (1756–1818) American military leader

Lee, Robert E(dward) (1807–70) American general

Lie, Trygve Halvdan (1896–1968) Norwegian politician, first Secretary-General of the United Nations 1946–53

May, Curtis (1906–90) American military commander

Ney, Michel (1768–1815) French marshal

Rao, P(amulaparti) V(enkata) Narasimha (born 1921) Indian statesman, Prime Minister 1991–96

4 letters

Amin, Idi (full name **Idi Amin Dada**) (born 1925) Ugandan soldier and head of state 1971–79

Anne (1665–1714) queen of England and Scotland (known as Great Britain from 1707) and Ireland 1702–14

Ball, John (died 1381) English rebel

Benn, Anthony (Neil Wedgwood) ("**Tony**") (born 1925) British politician

Biko, Stephen ("**Steve**") (1946–77) South African radical leader

Blum, Leon (1872–1950) French statesman, Prime Minister 1936–37, 1938, 1946–47

Bond, Julian (born 1940) American civil rights leader

Burr, Aaron (1756–1836) American Democratic Republican statesman

Bush, George (Herbert Walker) (born 1924) American Republican statesman, 41st President of the U.S. 1989–93

Bush, George W. (born 1946) American politician

Byrd, Robert (born 1917) American politician

Cade, John ("**Jack**") (died 1450) Irish rebel

Cato, Marcus Porcius (known as **Cato the Elder** *or* **Cato the Censor**) (234–149 BC) Roman statesman, orator, and writer

Historical, Political, and Military Figures *(continued)*

Clay, Henry (1777–1852) American political leader

Cnut See CANUTE

Cook, Captain James (1728–79) English explorer

Cook, Thomas (1808–92) English founder of the travel firm Thomas Cook

Dias, Bartolomeu (also Diaz) (*c.* 1450–1500) Portuguese navigator and explorer

Diaz, Porfirio (1830–1915) Mexican general and statesman, President 1877–80 and 1884–1911

Dole, Elizabeth (born 1936) American government official

Dole, Robert Joseph ("Bob") (born 1923) American Republican politician

Earp, Wyatt (Berry Stapp) (1848–1929) American gambler and marshal

Eden, (Robert) Anthony, 1st Earl of Avon (1897–1977) British Conservative statesman, Prime Minister 1955–57

Edwy (also Eadwig) (died 959) king of England 955–57

Eyre, Edward John (1815–1901) British-born Australian explorer and colonial statesman

Fish, Hamilton (1808–93) American government leader

Foch, Ferdinand 1851–1929) French general

Ford, Gerald R(udolph) (born 1913) American Republican statesman, 38th President of the U.S. 1974–77

Ford, Henry (1863–1947) American motor manufacturer

Gama, Vasco da See DA GAMA

Giap, Vo Nguyen (born 1912) Vietnamese military and political leader

Gore, Al(bert), Jr. (born 1948) American politician, vice president

Grey, Charles, 2nd Earl (1764–1845) British statesman, Prime Minister 1830–34

Grey, Lady Jane (1537–54) queen of England July 9–19, 1553

Haig, Alexander (born 1925) American general, chief of White House staff under Nixon

Hale, Nathan (1755–76) American Revolutionary War soldier

Hare, William (*fl.* 1820s) Irish murderer

Hess, (Walther Richard) Rudolf (1894–1987) German Nazi politician

Hiss, Alger (1904–96) American public servant

Hyde, Edward See CLARENDON

Jehu (842–815 BC) king of Israel

John (known as John Lackland) (1165–1216) son of Henry II, king of England 1199–1216

Khan, Ayub See AYUB KHAN

Kidd, William (known as Captain Kidd) (1645–1701) Scottish pirate

King, Martin Luther (1929–68) American Baptist minister and civil–rights leader

King, William Lyon Mackenzie (1874–1950) Canadian Liberal statesman, Prime Minister 1921–26, 1926–30, and 1935–48

Knox, Henry (1750–1806) American general

Knut See CANUTE

Koch, Edward I. (born 1924) American politician, mayor of New York City

Kohl, Helmut (born 1930) German statesman, Chancellor of the Federal Republic of Germany 1982–90, and of Germany 1990–98

Long, Huey P. (1893–1935) American political leader

Lott, Trent (born 1941) American politician

Meir, Golda (born Goldie

Mabovich) (1898–1978) Israeli stateswoman, Prime Minister 1969–74

Mott, Lucretia (1793–1880) American women's rights activist

Nagy, Imre (1896–1958) Hungarian Communist statesman, Prime Minister 1953–55 and 1956

Nero (full name Nero Claudius Caesar Augustus Germanicus) (AD 37–68) Roman emperor 54–68

Offa (died 796) king of Mercia 757–96

Owen, Robert (1771–1858) Welsh social reformer and industrialist

Park, Mungo (1771–1806) Scottish explorer

Parr, Katherine (1512–48) sixth and last wife of Henry VIII

Peel, Sir Robert (1788–1850) British Conservative statesman, Prime Minister 1834–35 and 1841–46

Penn, William (1644–1718) English Quaker, founder of Pennsylvania

Pitt, William, 1st Earl of Chatham (known as Pitt the Elder) (1708–78) British Whig statesman

Pitt, William (known as Pitt the Younger) (1759–1806) British statesman, Prime Minister 1783–1801 and 1804–06

Polk, James Knox (1795–1849) American Democratic statesman, 11th President of the U.S. 1845–49

Polo, Marco See MARCO POLO

Reno, Janet (born 1938) American government official

Root, Elihu (1845–1937) American statesman

Ross, Sir James Clark (1800–62) British explorer

Saul (11th century BC) (in the Bible) the first king of Israel

Shah, Reza See PAHLAVI

Sven See SWEYN I

Taft, William Howard (1857–1930) American Republican statesman, 27th President of the U.S. 1909–13

Tito (born Josip Broz) (1892–1980) Yugoslav Marshal and statesman, Prime Minister 1945–53 and President 1953–80

Tojo, Hideki (1884–1948) Japanese military leader and statesman, Prime Minister 1941–44

Tone, (Theobald) Wolfe (1763–98) Irish nationalist

Tutu, Desmond (Mpilo) (born 1931) South African clergyman

Zog I (full name Ahmed Bey Zogu) (1895–1961) Albanian statesman and king 1928–39

5 letters

Abbas, Ferhat (1899–1989) Algerian nationalist leader, President of Algeria 1958–61

Akbar, Jalaludin Muhammad (known as Akbar the Great) (1542–1605)

Adams, John (1735–1826) American Federalist statesman, 2nd President of the U.S. 1797–1801

Adams, John Quincy (1767–1848) American statesman, 6th President of the U.S. 1825–29

Adams, Samuel (1722–1803) American patriot

Allen, Ethan (1738–89) American soldier

Arrow, Kenneth Joseph (born 1921) American economist

Asoka (died c. 232 BC) Indian emperor

Assad, Hafiz al- (born 1928) Syrian Baath statesman, President since 1971

Astor, Nancy Witcher Langhorne, Viscountess (1879–1964) American-born British Conservative politician

Babur (born Zahir al–Din Muhammad) (1483–1530) Mogul emperor of India c. 1525–30

Historical, Political, and Military Figures *(continued)*

Bacon, Francis, Baron Verulam and Viscount St. Albans (1561–1626) English statesman and philosopher

Bader, Sir Douglas (Robert Stuart) (1910–82) British airman

Banda, Hastings Kamuzu (1906–97) Malawian statesman, Prime Minister 1964–95 and President 1966–94

Beale, Dorothea (1831–1906) English educator

Begin, Menachem (1913–92) Israeli statesman, Prime Minister 1977–84

Benes, Edvard (1884–1948) Czechoslovak statesman, Prime Minister 1921–22, President 1935–38 and 1945–48

Beria, Lavrenti (Pavlovich) (1899–1953) Soviet politician and head of the secret police (NKVD and MVD) 1938–53

Blair, Anthony Charles Lynton ("Tony") (born 1953) British Prime Minister since 1997

Bligh, William (1754–1817) British naval officer

Blunt, Anthony (Frederick) (1907–83) British art historian, Foreign Office official, and Soviet spy

Boone, Daniel (*c.* 1734–1820) American pioneer

Botha, Louis (1862–1919) South African soldier and statesman, first Prime Minister of the Union of South Africa 1910–19

Botha, P(ieter) W(illem) (born 1916) South African statesman, Prime Minister 1978–84, State President 1984–89

Bowie, James ("Jim") (1799–1836) American frontiersman

Braun, Eva (1910–45) German mistress of Adolf Hitler

Brown, Edmund G., Jr. ("Jerry") (born 1938) American politician

Brown, John (1800–59) American abolitionist

Bruce, James ("the Abyssinian") (1730–94) Scottish explorer

Bruce, Robert the See ROBERT THE BRUCE

Bryan, William Jennings (1860–1925) American politician and orator

Burke, Edmund (1729–97) British man of letters and Whig politician

Burke, Robert O'Hara (1820–61) Irish explorer

Burke, William (1792–1829) Irish murderer

Cabot, John (Italian name Giovanni Caboto) (*c.* 1450–*c.* 1498) Italian explorer and navigator

Capet, Hugh (*or* Hugo) (938–96) king of France 987–96

Cecil, William See BURGHLEY

Chaka See SHAKA

Clark, William (1770–1838) American explorer

Clive, Robert, 1st Baron Clive of Plassey (known as Clive of India) (1725–74) British general and colonial administrator

Cyrus (known as Cyrus the Great) (died *c.* 530 BC) king of Persia 559–530 BC

Cyrus (known as Cyrus the Younger) (died 401 BC) Persian prince

David (died *c.* 962 BC) king of Judah and Israel *c.* 1000–*c.* 962 BC

Davis, Jefferson (1808–89) American political leader

Dayan, Moshe (1915–81) Israeli statesman and general

Derby, 14th Earl of (title of Edward George Geoffrey Smith Stanley) (1799–1869) British Conservative statesman, Prime Minister 1852, 1858–59, and 1866–68

Dewey, Thomas E. (1902–71) American politician

Diana, Princess (formally called Diana, Princess of Wales; born Lady Diana Frances Spencer) (1961–97) Former wife of Prince Charles

Drake, Sir Francis (*c.* 1540–96) English sailor and explorer

Edgar (944–75) king of England 959–75

El Cid See CID, EL

Elgin, 8th Earl of (title of James Bruce) (1811–63) British colonial statesman

Forbes, Malcolm, Jr. ("Steve") (born 1947) American publisher and politician

Frank, Anne (1929–45) German Jewish diarist

Fuad (1868–1936) king of Egypt, reigned 1922–36

Fuchs, Sir Vivian (Ernest) (born 1908) English geologist and explorer

Galba (full name Servius Sulpicius Galba) (*c.* 3 BC–AD 69) Roman emperor AD 68–69

Gaunt, John of See JOHN OF GAUNT

Getty, Jean Paul (1892–1976) American industrialist

Gowon, Yakubu (born 1934) Nigerian general and statesman, head of state 1966–75

Grant, Ulysses S(impson) (born Hiram Ulysses Grant) (1822–85) American general and 18th President of the U.S.1869–77

Hatch, Orin (born 1934) American politician

Havel, Václav (born 1936) Czech dramatist and statesman, President of Czechoslovakia 1989–92 and of the Czech Republic from 1993

Hawke, Robert James Lee ("Bob") (born 1929) Australian Labor statesman, Prime Minister 1983–91

Hayes, Rutherford B(irchard) (1822–93) American Republican statesman, 19th President of the U.S. 1877–81

Heath, Sir Edward (Richard George) (born 1916) British Conservative statesman, Prime Minister 1970–74

Helms, Jesse (born 1921) American politician

Henry (known as Henry the Navigator) (1394–1460) Portuguese prince

Henry, Patrick (1736–99) American patriot

Hoffa, James Riddle ("Jimmy") (1913–*c.* 1975) American trade union leader

Horsa (died 455) semi-mythological Jutish leader

Hoxha, Enver (1908–85) Albanian statesman, Prime Minister 1944–54 and First Secretary of the Albanian Communist Party 1954–85

Husák, Gustáv (1913–91) Czechoslovak statesman, leader of the Communist Party of Czechoslovakia 1969–87 and President 1975–89

Ivan I (*c.* 1304–41) ruler of Russia, grand duke of Muscovy 1328–40

James, Jesse (Woodson) (1847–82) American outlaw

John I (known as John the Great) (1357–1433) king of Portugal, reigned 1385–1433

Jones, John Paul (born John Paul) (1747–92) Scottish-born American naval officer

Kádár, János (1912–89) Hungarian statesman, First Secretary of the Hungarian Socialist Workers' Party 1956–88 and Prime Minister 1956–58 and 1961–65

Kelly, Edward ("Ned") (1855–80) Australian outlaw

Kelly, Petra (Karin) (1947–92) German political leader

Khama, Sir Seretse (1921–80) Botswanan statesman, Prime Minister of Bechuanaland 1965 and President of Botswana 1966–80

Khufu See CHEOPS

Klerk, F.W. de See DE KLERK

Historical, Political, and Military Figures (continued)

Krupp, Alfred (1812–87) German arms manufacturer

Lenin, Vladimir Ilich (born Vladimir Ilich Ulyanov) (1870–1924) the principal figure in the Russian Revolution and first Premier (Chairman of the Council of People's Commissars) of the Soviet Union 1918–24

Lewis, Meriwether (1774–1809) American explorer

Lodge, Henry Cabot (1850–1924) American senator

Major, John (born 1943) British Conservative statesman, Prime Minister 1990–97

Marat, Jean Paul (1743–93) French revolutionary and journalist

Mary I (known as Mary Tudor) (1516–58) daughter of Henry VIII, reigned 1553–58

Meade, George (1815–72) American military commander

Menes Egyptian pharaoh, reigned c. 3100 BC

Moses (fl. c. 14th–13th centuries BC) Hebrew prophet and lawgiver

Murat, Joachim (c. 1767–1815) French general, king of Naples 1808–15

Nehru, Jawaharlal (known as Pandit Nehru) (1889–1964) Indian statesman, Prime Minister 1947–64

Nerva, Marcus Cocceius (AD c. 30–98) Roman emperor 96–98

Ne Win (born 1911) Burmese general and socialist statesman

Ngata, Sir Apirana Turupa (1874–1950) New Zealand Maori leader and politician

Nixon, Richard (Milhous) (1913–94) American Republican statesman, 37th President of the U.S. 1969–74

Nkomo, Joshua (Mqabuko Nyongolo) (born 1917) Zimbabwean statesman

North, Frederick, Lord (1732–92) British Tory statesman, Prime Minister 1770–82

North, Oliver (born 1943) American government official

Obote, (Apollo) Milton (born 1924) Ugandan statesman, Prime Minister 1962–66, President 1966–71 and 1980–85

Olaf V (1903–91) king of Norway 1957–91

Omar I (c. 581–644) Muslim caliph 634–44

Orton, Arthur (known as 'the Tichborne claimant') (1834–98) English butcher

Otto I (known as Otto the Great) (912–73) king of the Germans 936–73, Holy Roman emperor 962–73

Palme, (Sven) Olof (Joachim) (1927–86) Swedish statesman, Prime Minister 1969–76 and 1982–86

Pašić Nikola (1845–1926) Serbian statesman

Paton, Alan (Stewart) (1903–88) South African writer and politician

Peary, Robert Edwin (1856–1920) American explorer

Percy, Sir Henry (known as "Hotspur" and "Harry Hotspur") (1364–1403) English soldier

Peres, Shimon (Polish name Szymon Perski) (born 1923) Israeli statesman, Prime Minister 1984–86 and 1995–96

Perón, Eva (full name Maria Eva Duarte de Perón; known as "Evita") (1919–52) Argentinian politician

Perón, Juan Domingo (1895–1974) Argentinian soldier and statesman, President 1946–55 and 1973–74

Perot, H. Ross (born 1930) American entrepreneur and politician

Perry, Oliver Hazard (1742–86) American naval officer

Rabin, Yitzhak (1922–95) Israeli statesman and military leader, Prime Minister 1974–77 and 1992–95

Reith, John (Charles Walsham) 1st Baron (1889–1971) Scottish politician, first director-general (1927–38) of the BBC

Sadat, (Muhammad) Anwar al- (1918–81) Egyptian statesman, President 1970–81

Scott, Dred (c. 1795–1858) American slave

Scott, Sir Robert Falcon (1868–1912) English explorer and naval officer

Shaka (also Chaka) (c. 1787–1828) Zulu chief

Smith, Ian (Douglas) (born 1919) Rhodesian statesman, Prime Minister 1964–79

Smuts, Jan Christiaan (1870–1950) South African statesman and soldier, Prime Minister 1919–24 and 1939–48

Solon (c. 630–c. 560 BC) Athenian statesman and lawgiver

Starr, Kenneth (born 1946) American attorney

Stuart, J.E.B. (1833–64) American military commander

Sucre, Antonio José de (1795–1830) Venezuelan revolutionary and statesman, President of Bolivia 1826–28

Sulla (full name Lucius Cornelius Sulla Felix) (138–78 BC) Roman general and politician

Tambo, Oliver (1917–93) South African politician

Timur See TAMERLANE

Titus (full name Titus Vespasianus Augustus; born Titus Flavius Vespasianus) (AD 39–81) Roman emperor 79–81, son of Vespasian

Tudor, Henry See HENRY VII OF ENGLAND

Tudor, Mary See MARY I OF ENGLAND

Tweed, William M. ("Boss") (1823–78) American politician

Tyler, John (1790–1862) American Whig statesman, 10th President of the U.S. 1841–45

Villa, Pancho (born Doroteo Arango) (1878–1923) Mexican revolutionary

Wales, Prince of See CHARLES, PRINCE

Wayne, ("Mad") Anthony (1745–96) American soldier

Weber, Max (1864–1920) German economist and sociologist

6 letters

Abiola, Moshood (Kashimawo Olawale) (1937–98) Nigerian politician

Abrams, Creighton (1914–74) American military commander

Addams, Jane (1860–1935) American social reformer and feminist

Aitken, William Maxwell See BEAVERBROOK

Alaric (c. 370–410) king of the Visigoths

Albert, Prince (1819–61) consort to Queen Victoria

Antall, Jozsef (1933–93) Hungarian statesman, Prime Minister 1990–93

Antony, Mark (Latin name Marcus Antonius) (c. 83–30 BC) Roman statesman and general

Arafat, Yasser (born 1929) Palestinian leader

Aragon, Catherine of See CATHERINE OF ARAGON

Arnold, Benedict (1741–1801) American military commander, traitor

Arthur traditionally king of Britain, historically perhaps a 5th or 6th-century Romano-British chieftain or general

Arthur, Chester Alan (1830–86) American Republican statesman,

Historical, Political, and Military Figures *(continued)*

21st President of the U.S.
1881–85

Attila (406–53) king of the Huns
434–53

Attlee, Clement (Richard)
(1883–1967) British statesman,
Prime Minister 1945–51

Austin, Stephen F. (1793–1836)
American politician

Baffin, William (*c.* 1584–1622)
English navigator and explorer

Balboa, Vasco Nunez de
(1475–1519) Spanish explorer

Barton, Sir Edmund
(1849–1920) Australian statesman and jurist, first Prime
Minister of Australia 1901–03

**Bayard, Pierre du Terrail,
Chevalier de** (1473–1524)
French soldier

Becket, St. Thomas à (*c.* 1118–
70) English prelate and statesman

Bering, Vitus (Jonassen)
(1681–1741) Danish navigator
and explorer

Bhutto, Benazir (born 1953)
Pakistani stateswoman, Prime
Minister 1988–90 and 1993–96

Bhutto, Zulfikar Ali (1928–79)
Pakistani statesman, President
1971–73 and Prime Minister
1973–77

Boleyn, Anne (1507–36) second
wife of Henry VIII and mother of
Elizabeth I

Bolger, James B(rendan) (born
1935) New Zealand statesman,
Prime Minister 1990–97

Bonney, William H. (**"Billy the
Kid"**) (1859–81) American outlaw

Borgia, Cesare (1476–1507)
Italian statesman

Borgia, Lucrezia (1480–1519)
Italian noblewoman

Brandt, Willy (born Karl Herbert
Frahm) (1913–92) German
statesman, Chancellor of West
Germany 1969–74

Brutus, Marcus Junius (85–42
BC) Roman senator

Buffet, Warren (born 1930)
American investor

Bunche, Ralph (1904–71)
American diplomat

Burton, Sir Richard (Francis)
(1821–90) English explorer,
anthropologist, and translator

Caesar See JULIUS CAESAR

Canute (also Cnut) (died 1035)
Danish king of England 1017–
35, Denmark 1018–35, and
Norway 1028–35

Capone, Alphonse ("Al")
(1899–1947) American gangster

Carter, James Earl ("Jimmy")
(born 1924) American
Democratic statesman, 39th
President of the U.S. 1977–81

**Castle, Barbara (Anne),
Baroness Castle of Blackburn**
(born 1911) British politician

Castro, Fidel (born 1927) Cuban
statesman, Prime Minister
1959–76 and President since 1976

Cavell, Edith (Louisa)
(1865–1915) English nurse

**Cavour, Camillo Benso, Conte
di** (1810–61) Italian statesman,
Prime Minister 1852–59,
1860–61

Cheops (Egyptian name Khufu)
(*fl.* early 26th century BC)
Egyptian pharaoh of the 4th
dynasty

Chirac, Jacques (René) (born
1932) French statesman, Prime
Minister 1974–76 and 1986–88
and President since 1995

Clovis (465–511) king of the
Franks 481–511

Cobden, Richard (1804–65)
English political reformer

Corday, Charlotte (full name
Marie Anne Charlotte Corday
d'Armont) (1768–93) French
political assassin

Cortés, Hernando (also Cortez) (1485–1547) first of the Spanish conquistadors

Cunard, Sir Samuel (1787–1865) Canadian-born British shipowner

Curtin, John (Joseph Ambrose) (1885–1945) Australian Labor statesman, Prime Minister 1941–45

Custer, George (Armstrong) (1839–76) American cavalry general

Da Gama, Vasco (c. 1469–1524) Portuguese explorer

Danton, Georges (Jacques) (1759–94) French revolutionary

David I (c. 1084–1153) king of Scotland, reigned 1124–53

Deakin, Alfred (1856–1919) Australian Liberal statesman, Prime Minister 1903–04, 1905–08, and 1909–10

Decius, Gaius Mesius Quintus Trajanus (c. 201–51) Roman emperor 249–51

Delors, Jacques (Lucien Jean) (born 1925) French socialist politician, president of the European Commission 1985–94

Dubček, Alexander (1921–92) Czechoslovak statesman

Dudley, Robert, Earl of Leicester (c. 1532–88) English nobleman

Dulles, John Foster (1888–1959) American Republican statesman, secretary of state under Eisenhower

Eadwig See EDWY

Edward, Prince of Wales See BLACK PRINCE

Egbert (died 839) king of Wessex 802–39

Fabius (full name Quintus Fabius Maximus Verrucosus, known as "Fabius Cunctator") (died 203 BC) Roman general and statesman

Farouk (1920–65) king of Egypt, reigned 1936–52

Fawkes, Guy (1570–1606) English conspirator

Franco, Francisco (1892–1975) Spanish general and statesman, head of state 1939–75

Fraser, (John) Malcolm (born 1930) Australian Liberal statesman, Prime Minister 1975–83

Frémont, John Charles (known as "the Pathfinder") (1813–90) American explorer and politician

Frisch, Ragnar (Anton Kittil) (1895–1973) Norwegian economist

Gandhi, Mahatma (born Mohandas Karamchand Gandhi) (1869–1948) Indian nationalist and spiritual leader

Gandhi, Mrs. Indira (1917–84) Indian stateswoman, Prime Minister 1966–77 and 1980–84

Gandhi, Rajiv (1944–1991) Indian statesman, Prime Minister 1984–89

Garvey, Marcus (Mosiah) (1887–1940) Jamaican political activist and black nationalist leader

Gaulle, Charles de See DE GAULLE

Godiva, Lady (died 1080) English noblewoman, wife of Leofric, Earl of Mercia

Greene, Nathanael (1742–86) American Revolutionary War general

Grivas, George (Theodorou) (1898–1974) Greek-Cypriot patriot and soldier

Harris, Sir Arthur (Travers), 1st Baronet (known as "Bomber Harris") (1892–1984) British Marshal of the RAF

Harrod, Charles Henry (1800–85) English grocer and tea merchant

Helena, St. (AD c. 255–c. 330) Roman empress and mother of Constantine the Great

Henry I (1068–1135) king of England, youngest son of William I, reigned 1100–35

Historical, Political, and Military Figures *(continued)*

Henry I (Henry the Fowler) (*c.* 876–936) king of the Germans, reigned 919–36

Henry V (1387–1422) king of England, reigned 1413–22

Henry V (1081–1125) king of the Germans (1099–1125, Holy Roman Emperor 1111–25

Hickok, James Butler (known as "Wild Bill Hickok") (1837–76) American frontiersman and marshal

Hitler, Adolf (1889–1945) Austrian-born Nazi leader, Chancellor of Germany 1933–45

Hoover, Herbert C(lark) (1874–1964) American Republican statesman, 31st President of the U.S. 1929–33

Hoover, J(ohn) Edgar (1895–1972) American lawyer and director of the FBI 1924–72

Hoover, William (Henry) (1849–1932) American industrialist

Howard, Catherine (*c.* 1521–42) fifth wife of Henry VIII

Howard, John (Winston) (born 1939) Australian Liberal statesman, Prime Minister from 1996

Hudson, Henry (*c.* 1565–1611) English explorer

James I (1566–1625) son of Mary, Queen of Scots, king of Scotland (as James VI) 1567–1625, and of England and Ireland 1603–25

James I (1394–1437) Stuart king of Scotland 1406–37, son of Robert III

James V (1512–42) Stuart king of Scotland 1513–42, son of James IV

Jinnah, Muhammad Ali (1876–1948) Indian statesman and founder of Pakistan

Joffre, Joseph Jacques Césaire (1852–1931) French Marshal

Juárez, Benito Pablo (1806–72) Mexican statesman, President 1861–64 and 1867–72

Julian (known as the Apostate) (full name Flavius Claudius Julianus) (AD *c.* 331–63) Roman emperor 360–63, nephew of Constantine

Kaunda, Kenneth (David) (born 1924) Zambian statesman, President 1964–91

Keynes, John Maynard, 1st Baron (1883–1946) English economist

Kruger, Stephanus Johannes Paulus (known as "Oom (= uncle) Paul") (1825–1904) South African soldier and statesman

Leo III (*c.* 680–741) Byzantine emperor 717–41

Louis I (778–840) king of the West Franks and Holy Roman Emperor (814–40), son of Charlemagne

Louis I (known as Louis the Great) (1326–82) king of Hungary 1342–82 and of Poland 1370–82

Louis V (967–987) king of France 979–987

Louis X (1289–1316) king of France 1314–16

Manley, Michael (Norman) (1923–97) Jamaican statesman, Prime Minister 1972–80 and 1989–92

Marion, Francis ("the Swamp Fox") (*c.* 1732–95) American Revolutionary War general

Marius, Gaius (*c.* 157–86 BC) Roman general and politician

Martel, Charles See CHARLES MARTEL

Mary II (1662–94) joint queen of England, Scotland, and Ireland (1989–94)

McCain, John, III (born 1936) American politician

Mellon, Andrew W(illiam) (1855–1937) American financier and philanthropist

Minuit, Peter (*c.* 1580–1638) Prussian-born American colonist

Mobutu, Sese Seko (full name
Mobutu Sese Seko Kuku Ngben-
du Wa Za Banga) (1930–97) Zare-
an politician; President 1965–97

Monash, Sir John (1865–1931)
Australian general

Monroe, James (1758–1831)
American Democratic Republican statesman, 5th President of
the U.S. 1817–25

**Mosley, Sir Oswald (Ernald),
6th Baronet** (1896–1980)
English Fascist leader

Mugabe, Robert (Gabriel) (born
1924) Zimbabwean statesman,
Prime Minister 1980–87 and
President since 1987

Nansen, Fridtjof (1861–1930)
Norwegian Arctic explorer

Nasser, Gamal Abdel (1918–70)
Egyptian colonel and statesman,
Prime Minister 1954–56 and
president 1956–70

Nation, Carry (1846–1911)
American temperance advocate

Necker, Jacques (1732–1804)
Swiss born banker

**Nelson, Horatio, Viscount
Nelson, Duke of Bronte**
(1758–1805) British admiral

Nevsky See ALEXANDER NEVSKY

Nimitz, Chester (1885–1966)
American admiral

Oakley, Annie (full name Phoebe
Anne Oakley Mozee) (1860–
1926) American markswoman

O'Neill, Thomas P., Jr. ("Tip")
(1912–94) American politican,
Speaker of the House

Orange, William of See WILLIAM

Ortega, Daniel (full surname
Ortega Saavedra) (born 1945)
Nicaraguan statesman, President
1985–90

Osman I (also Othman) (1259–
1326) Turkish conqueror,
founder of the Ottoman
(Osmanli) dynasty and empire

Oswald, Lee Harvey (1939–63)
American alleged assassin of John
F. Kennedy

Othman See OSMAN I

Pandit, Vijaya (Lakshmi)
(1900–90) Indian politician and
diplomat

Patton, George S. (1885–1945)
American military commander

Pelham, Henry (1696–1754)
British Whig statesman, Prime
Minister 1743–54

**Pétain, (Henri) Philippe
(Omer)** (1856–1951) French
general and statesman, head of
state 1940–42

Peter I (known as Peter the Great)
(1672–1725) czar of Russia
1682–1725

**Philby, Harold Adrian Russell
("Kim")** (1912–88) British
Foreign Office official and spy

**Philip, Prince, Duke of
Edinburgh** (born 1921) husband of Elizabeth II

Pierce, Franklin (1804–69)
American Democratic statesman,
14th President of the U.S.
1853–57

Pilate, Pontius (died AD c. 36)
Roman procurator of Judaea c.
26–c. 36

Pol Pot (born Saloth Sar) (1925–
98) Cambodian Communist
leader, Prime Minister 1976–79

Pompey (known as Pompey the
Great; Latin name Gnaeus
Pompeius Magnus) (106–48 BC)
Roman general and statesman

Powell, Colin (born 1937)
American military leader

Rahman See ABDUL RAHMAN,
MUJIBUR RAHMAN

Rákosi, Mátyás (1892–1971)
Hungarian Communist states-
man, First Secretary of the
Hungarian Socialist Workers'
Party 1945–56 and Prime
Minister 1952–53 and 1955–56

Ratana, Tahupotiki Wiremu
(1873–1939) Maori political and
religious leader

Reagan, Ronald (Wilson) (born
1911) American Republican

Historical, Political, and Military Figures *(continued)*

statesman, 40th President of the U.S. 1981–89

Revere, Paul (1735–1818) American patriot

Rhodes, Cecil (John) (1853–1902) British-born South African statesman, Prime Minister of Cape Colony 1890–96

Rob Roy (born Robert Macgregor) (1671–1734) Scottish outlaw

Rommel, Erwin (known as "the Desert Fox") (1891–1944) German Field Marshal

Romney, George W. (1907–95) American businessman and politician

Sanger, Margaret (Higgins) (1883–1966) American birth-control campaigner

Savage, Michael Joseph (1872–1940) New Zealand statesman

Seneca, Lucius Annaeus (known as Seneca the Younger) (*c.* 4 BC–AD 65) Roman statesman, philosopher, and dramatist

Seneca, Marcus (or Lucius) Annaeus (known as Seneca the Elder) (*c.* 55 BC–*c.* AD 39) Roman rhetorician, born in Spain

Seward, William H. (1801–72) American government leader

Shamir, Yitzhak (Polish name Yitzhak Jazernicki) (born 1915) Israeli statesman, Prime Minister 1983–84 and 1986–92

Sharma, Shankar Dayal (born 1918) Indian statesman

Sivaji See SHIVAJI

Somoza, Anastasio (full surname Somoza Garcia) (1896–1956) Nicaraguan soldier and statesman, President 1937–47 and 1951–56

Stalin, Joseph (born Iosif Vissarionovich Dzhugashvili) (1879–1953) Soviet statesman

Stopes, Marie (Charlotte Carmichael) (1880–1958) Scottish birth-control campaigner

Stuart, Charles Edward (known as "the Young Pretender" or "Bonnie Prince Charlie") (1720–88) pretender to the British throne, son of James Stuart

Stuart, James (Francis Edward) (known as "the Old Pretender") (1688–1766) pretender to the British throne, son of James II (James VII of Scotland)

Stuart, Mary See MARY, QUEEN OF SCOTS

Suzman, Helen (born 1917) South African politician, of Lithuanian Jewish descent

Sweyn I (also Sven; known as Sweyn Forkbeard) (died 1014) king of Denmark *c.* 985–1014, ruler of England 1013–14

Tasman, Abel (Janszoon) (1603–*c.* 1659) Dutch navigator

Taylor, Zachary (1784–1850) American Whig statesman, 12th President of the U.S. 1849–50

Thomas, Norman M. (1884–1968) American social reformer and politician

Trajan (Latin name Marcus Ulpius Traianus) (AD *c.* 53–117) Roman emperor 98–117

Truman, Harry S (1884–1972) American Democratic statesman, 33rd President of the U.S. 1945–53

Valera, Eamon de See DE VALERA

Vargas, Getúlio Dornelles (1883–1954) Brazilian statesman, President 1930–45 and 1951–54

Walesa, Lech (born 1943) Polish statesman, President 1990–95

Warren, Earl (1891–1974) American jurist, chief justice of the Supreme Court

Wilson, (James) Harold, Baron Wilson of Rievaulx (1916–95) British statesman, Prime Minister 1964–70 and 1974–76

Wilson, (Thomas) Woodrow
(1856–1924) American
Democratic statesman, 28th
President of the U.S. 1913–21
Wolsey, Thomas (known as
Cardinal Wolsey) (*c.* 1474–1530)
English prelate and statesman
Zapata, Emiliano (1879–1919)
Mexican revolutionary
**Zhukov, Georgi
(Konstantinovich)** (1896–1974)
Soviet military leader, born in
Russia

7 *letters*

Acheson, Dean Gooderham
(1893–1971) American states-
man
Aga Khan title of the imam or
leader of the Nizari sect of Ismaili
Muslims
Agrippa, Marcus Vipsanius
(63–12 BC) Roman general
Allende, Salvador (1908–73)
Chilean statesman, President
1970–73
Anthony, Susan B(rownell)
(1820–1906) American women's
rights activist
**Anyaoku, Eleazar
Chukwuemeka** (born 1933)
Nigerian diplomat
Ashmole, Elias (1617–92) English
antiquary
**Asquith, Herbert Henry, 1st
Earl of Oxford and Asquith**
(1852–1928) British Liberal
statesman, Prime Minister
1908–16
Atatürk, Kemal (born Mustafa
Kemal; also called Kemal Pasha)
(1881–1938) Turkish statesman
and general, President of Turkey
1923–38
Aung San (1914–47) Burmese
nationalist leader
Azikiwe, (Benjamin) Nnamdi
(1904–96) Nigerian statesman,
President 1963–66
Babbitt, Bruce (born 1938)
American politician

**Bakunin, Mikhail
(Aleksandrovich)** (1814–76)
Russian anarchist
**Baldwin, Stanley, 1st Earl
Baldwin of Bewdley** (1867–
1947) British Conservative
statesman, Prime Minister
1923–24, 1924–29, and 1935–37
**Balfour, Arthur James, 1st Earl
of Balfour** (1848–1930) British
Conservative statesman, Prime
Minister 1902–05
Barents, Willem (died 1597)
Dutch explorer
Batista, Fulgencio (full name
Fulgencio Batista y Zaldivar)
(1901–73) Cuban soldier and
statesman, President 1940–44
and 1952–59
Bokassa, Jean Bédel (1921–96)
Central African Republic states-
man and military leader,
President 1972–76, emperor
1976–79
Bolívar, Símon (known as "the
Liberator") (1783–1830)
Venezuelan patriot and statesman
Bormann, Martin (1900–*c.* 1945)
German Nazi politician
Bradley, Bill (born 1943)
American basketball player and
politician
Bradley, Omar (1893–1981)
American military commander
**Burgess, Guy (Francis de
Moncy)** (1911–63) British
Foreign Office official and spy
Cadbury, George (1839–1922)
English cocoa and chocolate
manufacturer and social
reformer
Canmore nickname of Malcolm
III of Scotland
Canning, George (1770–1827)
British Tory statesman, Prime
Minister 1827
Cartier, Jacques (1491–1557)
French explorer
Cassius, Gaius (full name Gaius
Cassius Longinus) (died 42 BC)
Roman general

Historical, Political, and Military Figures *(continued)*

Charles, Prince, Charles Philip Arthur George, Prince of Wales (born 1948) heir apparent to Elizabeth II

Chatham, 1st Earl of See PITT

Chifley, Joseph Benedict (1885–1951) Australian Labor statesman, Prime Minister 1945–49

Clinton, Hillary Rodham (born 1947) U.S. First Lady

Clinton, William Jefferson ("Bill") (born 1946) American Democratic statesman, 42nd President of the U.S. since 1993

Cochise (1815–74) Native American chief

Colbert, Jean Baptiste (1619–83) French statesman, chief minister to Louis XIV

Collins, Michael (1890–1922) Irish nationalist leader and politician

Crassus, Marcus Licinius ("Dives") (*c.* 115–53 BC) Roman politican

Crippen, Hawley Harvey (known as Doctor Crippen) (1862–1910) American-born British murderer

Croesus (6th century BC) last king of Lydia *c.* 560–546 BC

Darius I (known as Darius the Great) (*c.* 550–486 BC) king of Persia 521–486 BC

Darling, Grace (1815–42) English heroine

Darnley, Lord (title of Henry Stewart or Stuart) (1545–67) Scottish nobleman, second husband of Mary, Queen of Scots

de Klerk, F(rederik) W(illem) (born 1936) South African statesman, President 1989–94

Dirksen, Everett M. (1896–1969) American politician

Dowding, Hugh (Caswall Tremenheere), Baron (1882–1970) British Marshal of the RAF

Dreyfus, Alfred (1859–1935) French army officer, of Jewish descent

Dukakis, Michael (born 1933) American politician

Edward I (known as the Hammer of the Scots) (1237–1307) king of England 1272–1307, son of Henry III

Edward V (1470–*c.* 1483) reigned in England 1483 but not crowned, son of Edward IV

Eugénie (born Eugénia Maria de Montijo de Guzmán) (1826–1920) Spanish empress of France 1853–71 and wife of Napoleon III

Faisal I (1885–1933) king of Iraq, reigned 1921–33)

Farnese, Alessandro, Duke of Parma (1545–92) Italian general and statesman

Ferraro, Geraldine (born 1935) American politician

Forrest, John, 1st Baron (1847–1918) Australian explorer and statesman, Premier of Western Australia 1890–1901

Froebel, Friedrich (Wilhelm August) (1782–1852) German educator and founder of the kindergarten system

Gaddafi, Mu'ammer Muhammad al (also Qaddafi) (born 1942) Libyan colonel, head of state since 1970

Gemayel, Amin (born 1942) Lebanese President 1982–88

Gemayel, Pierre (1905–84) Lebanese political leader

George I (1660–1727) king of Great Britain and Ireland 1714–27

George V (1865–1936) king of Great Britain and Ireland 1910–36, (of the U.K. from 1920), son of Edward VII

Gilbert, Sir Humphrey (*c.* 1539–83) English explorer

Glyndwr See GLENDOWER

Göbbels See GOEBBELS

Godunov, Boris (1550–1605) czar of Russia 1598–1605

Goering, Hermann Wilhelm (1893–1946) German Nazi leader and politician

Gokhale, Gopal Krishna (1866–1915) Indian political leader and social reformer

Goldman, Emma (known as "Red Emma") (1869–1940) Lithuanian-born American political activist

Grafton, Augustus Henry Fitzroy, 3rd Duke of (1735–1811) British Whig statesman, Prime Minister 1768–70

Gromyko, Andrei (Andreevich) (1909–89) Soviet statesman, President of the U.S.S.R. 1985–88

Guevara, Che (full name Ernesto Guevara de la Serna) (1928–67) Argentinian revolutionary and guerrilla leader

Hadrian (full name Publius Aelius Hadrianus) (AD 76–138) Roman emperor 117–38

Hancock, John (1737–93) American patriot

Harding, Warren (Gamaliel) (1865–1923) American Republican statesman, 29th President of the U.S. 1921–23

Harold I (known as Harold Harefoot) (died 1040) king of England, reigned 1035–40

Hengist (died 488) semi-mythological Jutish leader

Henry II (1133–89) king of England, reigned 1154–89

Henry II (Saint Henry) (973–1024) king of the Germans, reigned 1002–24

Henry IV (Henry Bolingbroke) (1367–1413) king of England, reigned 1399–1413

Henry IV (known as Henry of Navarre) (1553–1610) king of France 1589–1610

Henry IV (1050–1106) king of the Germans 1056–1105, son of Henry III, Holy Roman Emperor 1084–1105

Henry VI (1421–71) king of England, reigned 1422–61 and 1470–71

Henry VI (1165–97) king of the Germans 1069–97, Holy Roman Emperor 1191–97

Hillary, Sir Edmund (Percival) (born 1919) New Zealand mountaineer and explorer

Himmler, Heinrich (1900–45) German Nazi leader, chief of the SS (1929–45) and of the Gestapo (1936–45)

Hotspur nickname of Sir Henry Percy

Houston, Samuel (1793–1863) American military leader

Hussein, Abdullah ibn See ABDULLAH IBN HUSSEIN

Hussein, ibn Talal (also Husain) (1935–1999) king of Jordan 1953–99

Hussein, Saddam (also Husain) (full name Saddam bin Hussein at–Takriti) (born 1937) Iraqi President from 1979

Jackson, Andrew (1767–1845) American general and Democratic statesman, 7th President of the U.S. 1829–37

Jackson, Jesse (Louis) (born 1941) American politician and clergyman

Jackson, Thomas Jonathan (known as "Stonewall Jackson") (1824–63) American general

James II (1633–1701) king of England, Ireland and (as James VII) of Scotland 1685–88

James II (1430–60) Stuart king of Scotland 1437–60, son of James I

James IV (1473–1513) Stuart king of Scotland 1488–1513, son of James III

James VI See JAMES I

John III (known as John Sobieski) (1624–96) king of Poland 1674–96

Historical, Political, and Military Figures *(continued)*

Johnson, Andrew (1808–75) American Democratic statesman, 17th President of the U.S. 1865–69

Johnson, Lyndon Baines (known as "LBJ") (1908–73) American Democratic statesman, 36th President of the U.S. 1963–69

Kalinin, Mikhail Ivanovich (1875–1946) Soviet statesman, head of state of the U.S.S.R. 1919–46

Karl XII See CHARLES XII

Keating, Paul (John) (born 1944) Australian Labor statesman, Prime Minister 1991–96

Kellogg, Will Keith (1860–1951) American food manufacturer

Kennedy, Edward Moore ("Teddy") (born 1932) American Democratic politician

Kennedy, John F(itzgerald) (known as "JFK") (1917–63) American Democratic statesman, 35th President of the U.S. 1961–63

Kennedy, Robert F(rancis) (1925–68) American Democratic statesman

Kossuth, Lajos (1802–94) Hungarian statesman and patriot

Kosygin, Aleksei Nikolaevich (1904–80) Soviet statesman, Premier of the U.S.S.R. 1964–80

La Salle, René-Robert Cavelier, Sieur de (1643–87) French explorer

Laurier, Sir Wilfrid (1841–1919) Canadian Liberal statesman, Prime Minister 1896–1911

Leghari, Farooq Ahme (born 1940) Pakistani statesman, President since 1993

Lepidus, Marcus Aemilius (died *c.* 13 BC) Roman statesman and triumvir

Lesseps, Ferdinand Marie, Vicomte de (1805–94) French diplomat

Lin Biao (1908–71) Chinese Communist statesman and general

Lincoln, Abraham (1809–65) American Republican statesman, 16th President of the U.S. 1861–65

Lin Piao See LIN BIAO

Louis II (846–879) king of France 877–879

Louis IV (921–954) king of France 936–954

Louis VI (1081–1137) king of France 1108–37

Louis IX (1214–70) king of France 1226–70, son of Louis VIII

Louis XI (1423–83) king of France 1461–83, son of Charles VII

Louis XV (1710–74) king of France 1715–74, great grandson and successor of Louis XIV

Ludwig I (1786–1868) king of Bavaria 1825–48

Luthuli, Albert John (also Lutuli) (*c.* 1898–1967) South African political leader

Macbeth (*c.* 1005–57) king of Scotland 1040–57

Maclean, Donald Duart (1913–83) British Foreign Office official and Soviet spy

Madison, James (1751–1836) American Democratic Republican statesman, 4th President of the U.S. 1809–17

Mandela, Nelson (Rolihlahla) (born 1918) South African statesman, President 1994–1999

Masaryk, Tomás (Garrigue) (1850–1937) Czechoslovak statesman, President 1918–35

Matilda (known as "the Empress Maud") (1102–67) English princess, daughter of Henry I

Mazarin, Jules (Italian name Giulio Mazzarino) (1602–61) Italian-born French statesman

Mazzini, Giuseppe (1805–72) Italian nationalist leader

Medicis, Marie de See MARIE DE
MÉDICIS
Mendoza, Antonio de (*c.*
1490–1552) Spanish colonial
administrator
Menzies, Sir Robert Gordon
(1894–1978) Australian Liberal
statesman, Prime Minister
1939–41 and 1949–66
**Molotov, Vyacheslav
(Mikhailovich)** (Born
Vyacheslav Mikhailovich
Skryabin) (1890–1986) Soviet
statesman
**Mubarak, (Muhammad) Hosni
(Said)** (born 1928) Egyptian
statesman, President since 1981
Muldoon, Sir Robert (David)
(1921–92) New Zealand states-
man, Prime Minister 1975–84
Murdoch, (Keith) Rupert (born
1931) Australian-born American
publisher and media entrepre-
neur
Neville, Richard See WARWICK
Nkrumah, Kwame (1909–72)
Ghanaian statesman, Prime
Minister 1957–60, President
1960–66
Noriega, Manuel (Antonio
Morena) (born 1940)
Panamanian statesman and general, head of state 1983–89
Novotný, Antonín (1904–75)
Czechoslovak Communist statesman, President 1957–68
Nyerere, Julius Kambarage
(born 1922) Tanzanian states-
man, President of Tanganyika
1962–64 and of Tanzania
1964–85
Onassis, Aristotle (Socrates)
(1906–75) Greek shipping mag-
nate and businessman
**Onassis, Jacqueline Lee Bouvier
Kennedy** (known as "Jackie O")
(1929–94) U.S. First Lady
Pahlavi, Muhammad Reza (also
known as Reza Shah) (1919–80)
shah of Iran 1941–79
Pahlavi, Reza (born Reza Khan)

(1878–1944) shah of Iran
1925–41
Paisley, Ian (Richard Kyle) (born
1926) Northern Irish clergyman
and politician
Parnell, Charles Stewart
(1846–91) Irish nationalist leader
Pearson, Lester Bowles
(1897–1972) Canadian diplomat
and Liberal statesman, Prime
Minister 1963–68
Philip I (1052–1108) king of
France 1059–1108
Philip I (known as Philip the
Handsome) (1478–1506) king of
Spain 1504–06
Philip V (known as Philip the Tall)
(1294–1322) king of France
1316–22
Philip V (1683–1746) king of
Spain 1700–24 and 1724–46,
grandson of Louis XIV
Photius (*c.* 820–*c.* 891) Byzantine
scholar and patriarch of
Constantinople
Pizarro, Francisco (*c.* 1470–
1541) Spanish conquistador
Profumo, John (Dennis) (born
1915) British conservative politi-
cian
Pyrrhus (*c.* 318–272 BC) king of
Epirus *c.* 307–272
Qaddafi See GADDAFI
Raffles, Sir (Thomas) Stamford
(1781–1826) British colonial
administrator
Raleigh, Sir Walter (also Ralegh)
(*c.* 1552–1618) English explorer,
courtier, and writer
Rameses See RAMSES
Ramses I (14th cent. BC) Egyptian
pharaoh of the 19th dynasty
1320–18 BC
Ramses V (12th cent. BC) Egyptian
pharaoh 1160–56 BC, son of
Ramses IV
Ramses X (12th cent. BC)
Egyptian pharaoh 1121–13 BC
Rayburn, Sam (1882–1961)
American politician, Speaker of
the House

Historical, Political, and Military Figures *(continued)*

Russell, John, 1st Earl Russell
(1792–1878) British Whig statesman, Prime Minister 1846–52
and 1865–66

**Saladin (Arabic name Salah-ad-
Din Yussuf ibn-Ayyub)**
(1137–93) sultan of Egypt and
Syria 1174–93

Salazar, Antonio de Oliveira
(1889–1970) Portuguese
statesman, Prime Minister
1932–68

Selkirk, Alexander (also called
Alexander Selcraig) (1676–1721)
Scottish sailor

Severus, Septimius (full name
Lucius Septimius Severus
Pertinax) (146–211) Roman
emperor 193–211

Seymour, Jane (*c.* 1509–37) third
wife of Henry VIII and mother of
Edward VI

Shabaka (known as Sabacon)
(died 698 BC) Egyptian pharaoh
of the 25th dynasty

Sherman, William Tecumseh
(1820–91) American general

Shivaji (also Sivaji) (1627–80)
Indian raja of the Marathas
1674–80

Simpson, O(renthal) J(ames)
(born 1947) American football
player and murder suspect

Simpson, Wallis (*née* Bessie Wallis
Warfield) (1896–1986) American
wife of Edward, Duke of Windsor
(Edward VIII)

Soliman See SULEIMAN I

Solomon king of ancient Israel *c.*
970–*c.* 930 BC

Solyman See SULEIMAN I

Stanley, Sir Henry Morton (born
John Rowlands) (1841–1904)
Welsh explorer

Stanton, Elizabeth Cady
(1815–1902) American women's
rights activist

Stephen (*c.* 1097–1154) grandson

of William the Conqueror, king of
England 1135–54

Sukarno, Achmad (1901–70)
Indonesian statesman, President
1945–67

Sun King nickname of Louis XIV
of France

Thomson, Roy Herbert, 1st
Baron Thomson of Fleet
(1894–1976) Canadian-born
British newspaper publisher

Toynbee, Arnold (1852–83)
English economist and social
reformer

Trotsky, Leon (born Lev
Davidovich Bronstein)
(1879–1940) Russian revolutionary and Marxist theorist

Trudeau, Pierre (Elliott) (born
1919) Canadian Liberal statesman, Prime Minister of Canada
1968–79 and 1980–84

Ulyanov, Vladimir Ilich See
LENIN

Wallace, George (1919–98)
American politician

Wallace, Sir William (*c.* 1270–
1305) Scottish national hero

Walpole, Horace, 4th Earl of
Orford (1717–97) English writer
and politician

Warwick, Earl of (title of Richard
Venille; known as "the Kingmaker")
(1428–71) Englilsh statesman

Willard, Emma (1787–1870)
American educational reformer

Windsor, Duke of title conferred
on Edward VIII on his abdication
in 1936

Xerxes I (*c.* 435–*c.* 354 BC) Greek
historian, writer, and military
leader

Yeltsin, Boris (Nikolaevich)
(born 1931) Russian statesman,
President of the Russian
Federation 1991–99

Zenobia (3rd century AD) queen of
Palmyra *c.* 267–272

8 letters

Abdullah, Sheikh Muhammad (known as "the Lion of Kashmir") (1905–82) Nationalist leader in Kashmir

Aberdeen, 4th Earl of (title of George Hamilton Gordon) (1784–1860) British Conservative statesman, Prime Minister 1852–55

Adenauer, Konrad (1876–1967) German statesman, first Chancellor of the Federal Republic of Germany 1949–63

Agricola, Gnaeus Julius (AD 40–93) Roman general and governor of Britain 78–84

Albright, Madeleine K. (born 1937) U.S. secretary of state

Amundsen, Roald (1872–1928) Norwegian explorer

Andropov, Yuri (Vladimirovich) (1914–84) Soviet statesman, General Secretary of the Communist Party of the U.S.S.R. 1982–84 and President 1983–84

Atkinson, Sir Harry (Albert) (1831–92) New Zealand statesman, Prime Minister 1876–77, 1883–84, and 1887–91

Augustus (born Gaius Octavianus; also called [until 27 BC] Octavian) (63 BC–AD 14) the first Roman emperor

Aurelian (Latin name Lucius Domitius Aurelianus) (c. 215–75) Roman emperor

Aurelius, Marcus (full name Caesar Marcus Aurelius Antoninus Augustus) (121–80) Roman emperor 161–80

Ayub Khan, Muhammad (1907–74) Pakistani soldier and statesman, President 1958–69

Ben Bella, (Muhammad) Ahmed (born 1916) Algerian statesman, Prime Minister 1962–63 and President 1963–65

Berenice (3rd century BC) Egyptian queen, wife of Ptolemy III

Bismarck, Otto (Eduard Leopold) von, Prince of Bismarck, Duke of Launburg (known as "the Iron Chancellor") (1815–98) German statesman

Boadicea See BOUDICCA

Boethius, Anicius Manlius Severinus (c. 480–524) Roman statesman and philosopher

Bothwell, 4th Earl of (title of James Hepburn) (c. 1536–78) Scottish nobleman and third husband of Mary, Queen of Scots

Boudicca (also Boadicea) (died AD 62) queen of the Britons, ruler of the Iceni tribe in eastern England

Brezhnev, Leonid (Ilich) (1906–82) Soviet statesman, General Secretary of the Communist Party of the U.S.S.R. 1966–82 and President 1977–82

Buchanan, James (1791–1868) American Democratic statesman, 15th President of the U.S. 1857 61

Buchanan, Pat (born 1938) American journalist and presidential candidate

Bukharin, Nikolai (Ivanovich) (1888–1938) Russian revolutionary activist and theorist

Bulganin, Nikolai (Aleksandrovich) (1895–1975) Soviet statesman, Chairman of the Council of Ministers (Premier) 1955–58

Burgoyne, John ("Gentleman Johnny") (1722–92) English general and dramatist

Caligula (born Gaius Julius Caesar Germanicus (ad 12–41) Roman emperor 37–41

Cambyses (died 522 BC) son of Cyrus, king of Persia 529–522 BC

Carnegie, Andrew (1835–1919) Scottish-born American industrialist and philanthropist

Carville, James, Jr. (born 1944) American political consultant

Casanova, Giovanni Jacopo (full surname Casanova de Seingalt) (1725–98) Italian adventurer and librarian

Historical, Political, and Military Figures *(continued)*

Catiline (Latin name Lucius Sergius Catilina) (*c.* 108–62 BC) Roman nobleman and conspirator

Charles I (1500–58) king of Spain, reigned 1516–56 and Holy Roman emperor

Charles I (1600–49) king of England, Scotland, and Ireland, reigned 1625–49

Childers, (Robert) Erskine (1870–1922) Irish writer and political activist, born in England

Chrétien, (Joseph-Jacques) Jean (born 1934) Canadian Liberal statesman, Prime Minister since 1993

Claudius (full name Tiberius Claudius Drusus Nero Germanicus) (10 BC–AD 54) Roman emperor 41–54

Columbus, Christopher (Spanish name Cristóbal Colón) (1451–1506) Italian-born Spanish explorer

Coolidge, (John) Calvin (1872–1933) American Republican statesman, 30th President of the U.S. 1923–29

Crichton, James (known as "the Admirable Crichton") (1560–*c.* 1585) Scottish adventurer

Crockett, David ("Davy") (1786–1836) American frontiersman, soldier, and politician

Cromwell, Oliver (1599–1658) English general and statesman

Cromwell, Thomas (*c.* 1485–1540) English statesman, chief minister to Henry VIII

de Gaulle, Charles (André Joseph Marie) (1890–1970) French general and statesman, President 1959–69

de' Medici, Catherine See CATHERINE DE MEDICI

de Valera, Eamon (1882–1975) American-born Irish statesman, Prime Minister 1932–48

Disraeli, Benjamin, 1st Earl of Beaconsfield (1804–81) British Tory statesman, of Italian Jewish descent; Prime Minister 1868 and 1874–80

Dollfuss, Engelbert (1892–1934) Austrian statesman, Chancellor of Austria 1932–34

Domitian (full name Titus Flavius Domitianus) (AD 51–96) Roman emperor 81–96

Duvalier, Francois (known as "Papa Doc") (1907–71) Haitian statesman, President 1957–71

Edward II (1284–1327) king of England 1307–27, son of Edward I

Edward IV (1442–83) king of England 1461–83, son of Richard, Duke of York

Edward VI (1537–53) king of England 1547–53, son of Henry VIII

Eichmann, (Karl) Adolf (1906–62) German Nazi administrator

Ericsson, Leif (also Ericson) (*fl. c.* 1000) Norse explorer, son of Eric the Red

Faisal II (1935–1958) king of Iraq, reigned 1939–58

Farragut, David (1801–70) American admiral

Fillmore, Millard (1800–74) American Whig statesman, 13th President of the U.S. 1850–53

Francis I (1494–1547) king of France 1515–47

Franklin, Benjamin (1706–90) American statesman and scientist

Galtieri, Leopoldo Fortunato (born 1926) Argentinian general and statesman, President 1981–81

Garfield, James A(bram) (1831–81) American Republican statesman, 20th President of the U.S. March–September 1881

George II (1683–1760) king of Great Britain and Ireland 1727–60, son of George I

George IV (1762–1830) king of
Great Britain and Ireland
1820–30, son of George III

George VI (1895–1952) king of the
U.K. 1936–52, son of George V

Geronimo (*c.* 1829–1909) Apache
chief

Gingrich, Newt (born 1943)
American politician, Speaker of
the House

Giolitti, Giovanni (1842–1928)
Italian statesman, Prime Minister
five times between 1892 and 1921

Giuliani, Rudolph (born 1944)
American politician, mayor of
New York City

Gloriana nickname of Elizabeth I
of England and Ireland

Goebbels, (Paul) Joseph (also
Göbbels) (1897–1945) German
Nazi leader and politician

Gracchus, Tiberius Sempronius
(*c.* 163–133 BC) Roman tribune

Griffith, Arthur (1872–1922)
Irish nationalist leader and states-
man, President of the Irish Free
State 1922

Hallowes, Odette (born Marie
Celine) (1912–95) French heroine of World War II

Hamilcar (*c.* 270–229 BC)
Carthaginian general and father
of Hannibal

Hamilton, Alexander (*c.* 1757–
1804) American Federalist politician

Hamilton, Lady Emma (born
Amy Lyon) (*c.* 1765–1815)
English beauty and mistress of
Lord Nelson

Hannibal (247–182 BC)
Carthaginian general

Harefoot, Harold See HAROLD

Harold II (*c.* 1022–66) king of
England 1066

Harrison, Benjamin (1833–
1901) American Republican
statesman, 23rd President of the
U.S. 1889–93

Harrison, William Henry
(1773–1841) American Whig

statesman, 9th President of the
U.S. 1841

Hastings, Warren (1732–1818)
British colonial administrator

Hathaway, Anne (*c.* 1557–1623)
the wife of Shakespeare, whom
she married in 1582

Henry III (1207–72) king of
England, reigned 1216–72

Henry III (1017–56) king of the
Germans 1039–56, Holy Roman
Emperor 1046–56

Henry VII (Henry Tudor)
(1457–1509) king of England,
reigned 1485–1509

Henry VII (*c.* 1275–1313) king of
the Germans 1308–13, Holy
Roman Emperor 1312–13

Hirohito (born Michinomiya
Hirohito) (1901–89) emperor of
Japan 1926–89

Honecker, Erich (1912–94) East
German Communist statesman,
head of state 1976–89

**Humboldt, Friedrich Heinrich
Alexander, Baron, von**
(1769–1859) German explorer
and scientist

Humphrey, Hubert H. (1911–78)
American senator

Ikhnaton See AKHENATEN

Iron Duke nickname of Wellington

Iron Lady nickname of Margaret
Thatcher

James III (1451–88) Stuart king of
Scotland 1460–88, son of James II

James VII See JAMES II

Jeffreys, George, 1st Baron (*c.*
1645–89) Welsh judge

**Jellicoe, John Rushworth, 1st
Earl** (1859–1935) British admiral

Jugurtha (died 104 BC) joint king
of Numidia *c.* 118–104

Kenneth I (known as Kenneth
MacAlpine) (died 858) king of
Scotland *c.* 844–58

Kenyatta, Jomo (*c.* 1891–1978)
Kenyan statesman, Prime
Minister of Kenya 1963 and
President 1964–78

Historical, Political, and Military Figures *(continued)*

Khomeini, Ruhollah (known as Ayatollah Khomeini) (1900–89) Iranian Shiite Muslim leader

Leopold I (1790–1865) first king of Belgium 1831–65

Louis III (863–882) king of France 879–882, son of Louis II

Louis VII (*c.* 1120–80) king of France 1137–80

Louis XII (1462–1515) king of France 1498–1515

Louis XIV (1638–1715) (known as the Sun King) king of France 1643–1715

Louis XVI (1754–93) king of France 1774–92, grandson and successor of Louis XV

Ludwig II (1845–86) king of Bavaria 1864–86

Lysander (died 395 BC) Spartan general

McCarthy, Joseph R(aymond) (1909–57) American Republican politician

McGovern, George (born 1922) American politician

McKinley, William (1843–1901) American Republican statesman, 25th President of the U.S. 1897–1901

Maecenas, Gaius (*c.* 70–8 BC) Roman statesman

Magellan, Ferdinand (Portuguese name Fernao Magalhaes) (*c.* 1480–1521) Portuguese explorer

Malcolm I (died 954) king of Scotland, reigned 943–54

Malcolm X (born Malcolm Little) (1925–65) American political activist

Malenkov, Georgy (Maksimilianovich) (1902–88) Soviet statesman, born in Russia

Margaret, Princess, Margaret Rose (born 1930) only sister of Elizabeth II

Marshall, George C(atlett) (1880–1959) American general and statesman

Marshall, John (1755–1835) American jurist, chief justice of the Supreme Court

Marshall, Thurgood (1908–93) American jurist, Supreme Court justice

Mata Hari (born Margaretha Geertruida Zelle) (1876–1917) Dutch dancer and secret agent

Michelin, André (1853–1931) and **Édouard** (1859–1940) French industrialists

Mirabeau, Honoré Gabriel Riqueti, Comte de (1749–91) French revolutionary politician

Mitchell, George (born 1933) American politician

Montcalm, Louis Joseph de Montcalm-Gozon, Marquis de (1712–59) French general

Montfort, Simon de (*c.* 1165–1218) French soldier

Muhammad, Mahathir (born 1925) Malaysian statesman, Prime Minister since 1981

Mulroney, (Martin) Brian (born 1939) Canadian Progressive Conservative statesman, Prime Minister 1984–93

Nehemiah (5th century BC) Hebrew leader who supervised the rebuilding of the walls of Jerusalem *c.* 444 and introduced moral and religious reforms *c.* 432

O'Connell, Daniel (known as "the Liberator") (1775–1847) Irish nationalist leader and social reformer

Octavian See AUGUSTUS

O'Higgins, Bernardo (*c.* 1778–1842) Chilean revolutionary leader and statesman, head of state 1817–23

Papineau, Louis Joseph (1786–1871) French-Canadian politician

Perceval, Spencer (1762–1812) British Tory statesman, Prime Minister 1809–12

Pericles (*c.* 495–429 BC) Athenian statesman and general

Pershing, John (1860–1948) American military leader

Philip II (known as Philip Augustus) (1165–1223) king of France 1180–1223, son of Louis VII

Philip II (1527–98) king of Spain 1556–98, son of Charles I

Philip IV (known as Philip the Fair) (1268–1314) king of France 1285–1314, son of Philip III

Philip IV (1605–1665) king of Spain 1621–65

Philip VI (known as Philip of Valois) (1293–1350) king of France 1328–50

Pinochet, Augusto (full name Augusto Pinochet Ugarte) (born 1915) Chilean general and statesman, President 1974–90

Pompidou, Georges (Jean Raymond) (1911–74) French statesman, Prime Minister 1962–68 and President 1969–74

Porsenna, Lars (also Porsena) (6th century BC) legendary Etruscan chieftain

Pulitzer, Joseph (1847–1911) Hungarian-born American newspaper publisher

Quaddafi See GADDAFI

Ramses II (14th–13th cent. BC) Egyptian pharaoh of the 19th dynasty 1304–1237 BC, son of Seti I

Ramses IV (12th cent. BC) Egyptian pharaoh 1166–60 BC, son of Ramses III

Ramses VI (12th cent. BC) Egyptian pharaoh 1156–48 BC

Ramses IX (12th cent. BC) Egyptian pharaoh 1140–21 BC

Ramses XI (12th cent. BC) last Egyptian pharaoh of the 20th dynasty 1113–1085 BC

Rasputin, Grigori (Efimovich) (1871–1916) Russian monk

Red Baron, the See RICHTHOFEN

Rehoboan king of ancient Israel *c.* 930–c. 915 BC

Reynolds, Albert (born 1933) Irish Fianna Fáil statesman, Taoiseach (Prime Minister) 1992–94

Reza Shah See PAHLAVI

Richard I (known as Richard Coeur de Lion or Richard the Lionheart) (1157–99) king of England, reigned 1189–99

Rickover, Hyman (1900–86) American admiral

Robinson, Mary (Terese Winifred) (born 1944) Irish stateswoman, President 1990–97

Rosebery, 5th Earl of (title of Archibald Philip Primrose) (1847–1929) British Liberal statesman, Prime Minister 1894–95

Rowntree, Benjamin Seebolm (1871–1954) English entrepreneur and philanthropist

Sargon II (died 705 BC) king of Assyria 721–705

Selcraig See SELKIRK

Sheridan, Philip (1831–88) American military leader

Sihanouk, Norodom (born 1922) Cambodian king 1941–55 and since 1993

Sobieski, John See JOHN III

Stanhope, Lady Hester Lucy (1776–1839) English traveler

Thatcher, Margaret (Hilda), Baroness Thatcher of Kesteven (born 1925) British Conservative stateswoman, Prime Minister 1979–90

Theodora (*c.* 500–48 BC) Byzantine empress, wife of Justinian

Thesiger, Wilfred (Patrick) (born 1910) English explorer

Thurmond, J. Strom (born 1902) American politician

Tiberius (full name Tiberius Julius Caesar Augustus) 42 BC–AD 37) Roman emperor AD 14–37

Historical, Political, and Military Figures *(continued)*

Trujillo, Rafael (born Rafael Leónidas Trujillo Molina; known as "Generalissimo") (1891–1961) Dominican statesman, President of the Dominican Republic 1930–38 and 1942–52

Valerian (Latin name Publius Licinius Valerianus) (died 260) Roman emperor 253–60

Van Buren, Martin (1782–1862) American Democratic statesman, 8th President of the U.S. 1837–41

Verwoerd, Hendrik (Frensch) (1901–66) South African statesman, Prime Minister 1958–66

Vespucci, Amerigo (1451–1512) Italian merchant and explorer

Victoria (1819–1901) queen of Great Britain and Ireland 1837–1901 and empress of India 1876–1901

Waldheim, Kurt (born 1918) Austrian diplomat and statesman

Weizmann, Chaim (Azriel) (1874–1952) Israeli statesman, President 1949–52

Wilhelm I (1797–1888) king of Prussia 1861–88 and emperor of Germany 1871–88

William I (known as William the Conqueror) (c. 1027–87) the first Norman king of England, reigned 1066–87

William I (known as William the Lion) (1143–1214) king of Scotland 1165–1214, grandson of David I

Williams, Roger (c. 1603–83) British-born religious leader, founder of Rhode Island

Xenophon (c. 435–c. 354 BC) Greek historian, writer, and military leader

Yamamoto, Isoroku (1884–1943) Japanese admiral

Zia ul-Haq, Muhammad (1924–88) Pakistani general and statesman, President 1978–88

9 letters

Addington, Henry, 1st Viscount Sidmouth (1757–1844) British Tory statesman, Prime Minister 1801–04

Aeschines (c. 390–c. 314 BC) Athenian statesman and orator

Akhenaten (also Akhenaton, Ikhnaton) (14th century BC) Egyptian pharaoh of the 18th dynasty, reigned 1379–1362 BC

Alexander, Harold (Rupert Leofric George), 1st Earl Alexander of Tunis (1891–1969) British Field Marshal and Conservative statesman

Alexander (known as Alexander the Great) (356–323 BC) king of Macedon 336–323

Aquitaine, Eleanor of See ELEANOR OF AQUITAINE

Aristides (known as Aristides the Just) (5th century BC) Athenian statesman and general

Athelstan (895–939) king of England 925–39

Aurangzeb (1618–1707) Mogul emperor of Hindustan 1658–1707

Bar-Cochba Jewish leader of a rebellion in AD 132

Ben-Gurion, David (1886–1973) Israeli statesman, Prime Minister 1948–53 and 1955–63

Bonaparte (Italian, Buonaparte) See NAPOLEON

Bourguiba, Habib ibn Ali (born 1903) Tunisian nationalist and statesman, President 1957–87

Buthelezi, Chief Mangosuthu (Gatsha) (born 1928) South African politician

Callaghan, (Leonard) James, Baron Callaghan of Cardiff (born 1912) British statesman, Prime Minister 1976–79

Caracalla (born Septimius Bassanius; later called Marcus

Aurelius Severus Antoninus Augustus) (188–217) Roman emperor 211–17

Caratacus (also Caractacus) (1st century AD) British chieftain, son of Cunobelinus

Ceauşescu, Nicolae (1918–89) Romanian Communist statesman, first President of the Socialist Republic of Romania 1974–89

Cetshwayo (also Cetewayo) (c. 1826–84) Zulu king

Champlain, Samuel de (1567–1635) French explorer and colonial statesman

Charles II (1630–85) king of England, Scotland, and Ireland, reigned 1660–85

Chou Enlai See ZHOU ENLAI

Christian, Fletcher (c. 1764–c. 1793) English seaman and mutineer

Churchill, Sir Winston (Leonard Spencer) (1874–1965) British Conservative statesman, Prime Minister 1940–45 and 1951–55

Clarendon, Earl of (title of Edward Hyde) (1609–74) English statesman and historian

Cleopatra (also Cleopatra VII) (69–30 BC) queen of Egypt 47–30

Cleveland, (Stephen) Grover (1837–1908) American Democratic statesman, 22nd and 24th President of the U.S. 1885–89 and 1893–97

Cymbeline (also Cunobelinus) (died c. 42 AD) British chieftain

Edinburgh, Duke of See PHILIP, PRINCE

Edward III (1312–77) king of England 1327–77, son of Edward II

Edward VII (1841–1910) king of England 1901–10, son of Queen Victoria

Elizabeth, the Queen Mother (born lady Elizabeth Angela Marguerite Bowes-Lyon) (born 1900) wife of George VI

Ellsworth, Lincoln (1880–1951) American explorer

Farrakhan, Lewis (born 1933) American Nation of Islam leader

Ferdinand (known as Ferdinand of Aragon or Ferdinand the Catholic) (1452–1516) king of Castile 1474–1516 and of Aragon 1479–1516

Forkbeard, Sweyn See SWEYN I

Fulbright, (James) William (1905–95) American senator

Galbraith, John Kenneth (born 1908) Canadian-born American economist

Garibaldi, Giuseppe (1807–82) Italian patriot and military leader

Gladstone, William Ewart (1809–98) British Liberal statesman, Prime Minister 1868–74, 1880–85, 1886, and 1892–94

Glendower, Owen (also Glyndwr) (c. 1354–c. 1417) Welsh chief

Goldwater, Barry (1909–98) American senator

Gorbachev, Mikhail (Sergeevich) (born 1931) Soviet statesman, General Secretary of the Communist Party of the U.S.S.R. 1985–91 and President 1988–91

Grenville, George (1712–70) British Whig statesman, Prime Minister 1763–65

Hammurabi (died 1750 BC) the sixth king of the first dynasty of Babylonia, reigned 1792–1750 BC

Hasdrubal (died 207 BC) Carthaginian general, son of Hamilcar

Hasdrubal (died 221 BC) Carthaginian general, son-in-law of Hamilcar

Henry VIII (1491–1547) king of England, reigned 1509–47

Ho Chi Minh (born Nguyen That Thanh) (1890–1969) Vietnamese Communist statesman, President of North Vietnam 1954–69

Ibn Batuta (c. 1304–68) Arab explorer

Isabella I (known as Isabella of Castile or Isabella the Catholic) (1451–1504) queen of Castile

Historical, Political, and Military Figures *(continued)*

1474–1504 and of Aragon 1479–1504

Isocrates (436–388 BC) Athenian orator

Jefferson, Thomas (1743–1826) American Democratic Republican statesman, 3rd President of the U.S. 1801–09

Joan of Arc, St. (known as "the Maid of Orleans") (*c.* 1412–31) French national heroine

Josephine (born Marie Josephine Rose Tascher de la Pagerie) (1763–1814) Empress of France 1796–1809

Justinian (Latin name Flavius Petrus Sabbatius Justinianus) (483–565) Byzantine emperor 627–65

Kim Il Sung (born Kim Song Ju) (1912–94) Korean Communist statesman, first Premier of North Korea 1948–72 and President 1972–94

Kissinger, Henry (Alfred) (born 1923) German-born American statesman and diplomat, Secretary of State 1973–77

Kitchener, (Horatio) Herbert, 1st Earl Kitchener of Khartoum (1850–1916) British soldier and statesman

Kosciusko, Thaddeus (or Tadeusz) (1746–1817) Polish soldier and patriot

Kropotkin, Prince Peter (1842–1921) Russian anarchist

Krushchev, Nikita (Sergeevich) (1894–1971) Soviet statesman, Premier of the U.S.S.R. 1958–64

Lafayette, Marie Joseph Paul Yves Roch Gilbert du Motier, Marquis de (also La Fayette) (1757–1834) French soldier and statesman

La Guardia, Fiorello (1882–1947) American politician, mayor of New York City

Leicester, Earl of See DUDLEY

Liverpool, 2nd Earl of (title of Robert Banks Jenkinson) (1770–1828) British Tory statesman, Prime Minister 1812–27

Louis VIII (1187–1226) king of France 1223–26

Louis XIII (1601–43) king of France 1610–43, son of Henry IV of France

Louis XVII (1785–95) titular king of France who died in prison during the Revolution, son of Louis XVI

Ludwig III (1845–1921) king of Bavaria 1913–18

Luxemburg, Rosa (1871–1919) Polish-born German revolutionary leader

MacAlpine, Kenneth See KENNETH I

MacArthur, Douglas (1880–1964) American general

MacDonald, Flor (1722–90) Scottish Jacobite heroine

MacDonald, (James) (1866–1937) British statesman, Prime Minister 1924, 1929–31, and 1931–35

MacDonald, Sir John Alexander (1815–91) Scottish-born Canadian statesman, Prime Minister 1867–73 and 1878–91

Mackenzie, Sir Alexander (1764–1820) Scottish explorer of Canada

Macmillan, (Maurice) Harold, 1st Earl of Stockton (1894–1986) British Conservative statesman, Prime Minister 1957–63

Maintenon, Marquise de (title of Françoise d'Aubigne) (1635–1719) mistress and later second wife of the French king Louis XIV

Malcolm II (*c.* 953–1034) king of Scotland 1005–34

Malcolm IV (known as Malcolm the Maiden) (1141–65) king of Scotland 1153–65, grandson of David I

Mao Zedong (also Mao Tse-tung) (1893–1976) Chinese statesman, chairman of the Communist Party of the Chinese People's Republic 1949–76 and head of state 1949–59

Marco Polo (*c.* 1254–*c.* 1324) Italian explorer

Mary Tudor See MARY I

Melbourne, William Lamb, 2nd Viscount (1779–1848) British Whig statesman, Prime Minister 1834 and 1835–41

Messalina, Valeria (also Messallina) (AD *c.* 22–48) Roman empress, third wife of Claudius

Montespan, Marquise de (title of Françoise-Athénas de Rochechouart) (1641–1707) French noblewoman

Mussolini, Benito (Amilcaro Andrea) (known as "Il Duce" = the leader) (1883–1945) Italian Fascist statesman, Prime Minister 1922–43

Mutsuhito See MEIJI TENNO

Napoleon I (known as Napoleon; full name Napoleon Bonaparte or Buonaparte) (1769–1821) Emperor of France 1804–14 and 1815

Nefertiti (also Nofretete) (*fl.* 14th century BC) Egyptian queen, wife of Akhenaten

Netanyahu, Benjamin (born 1949) Israeli Likud statesman, Prime Minister 1996–1999

Newcastle, 1st Duke of (title of Thomas Pelham-Holles) (1693–1768) British Whig statesman, Prime Minister 1754–56 and 1757–62

Nicholas I (1796–1855) czar of Russia 1825–55

Nofretete See NEFERTITI

Pankhurst, Mrs. Emmeline (1858–1928), Christabel (1880–

1958), and (Estelle) Sylvia (1882–1960) English suffragettes

Philip III (known as Philip the Bold) (1245–1285) king of France 1270–85

Philip III (1578–1621) king of Spain 1598–1621

Pinkerton, Allan (1819–84) Scottish-born American detective

Pompadour, Marquise de (title of Jeanne Antoinette Poisson; known as Madame de Pompadour) (1721–64) French noblewoman

Ramses III (12th cent. BC) Egyptian pharaoh of the 20th dynasty 1198–66 BC, son of Setnakht

Ramses VII (12th cent. BC) Egyptian pharaoh 1148–47 BC, son of Ramses VI

Rehnquist, William H. (born 1924) American jurist, chief justice of the Supreme Court

Richard II (1367–1400) king of England, reigned 1377–99

Richelieu, Armand Jean du Plessis (1585–1642) French cardinal and statesman

Roosevelt, (Anna) Eleanor (1884–1962) American humanitarian and diplomat

Roosevelt, Franklin D(elano) (known as FDR) (1882–1945) American Democratic statesman, 32nd President of the U.S. 1933–45

Roosevelt, Theodore ("Teddy") (1858–1919) American Republican statesman, 26th President of the U.S. 1901–09

Salisbury, Robert Arthur Talbot Gascoigne-Cecil, 3rd Marquess of (1830–1903) British Conservative statesman, Prime Minister 1885–86, 1886–92, and 1895–1902

San Martin, José de (1778–1850) Argentinian soldier and statesman

Schindler, Oskar (1908–74) German industrialist

Historical, Political, and Military Figures *(continued)*

Spartacus (died *c.* 71 BC) Thracian slave and gladiator

Stevenson, Adlai E. (1900–65) American politician

Suleiman I (also Soliman or Solyman) (*c.* 1494–1566) sultan of the Ottoman Empire 1520–66

Sun Yat-sen (also Sun Yixian) (1866–1925) Chinese Kuomintang statesman, provisional President of the Republic of China 1911–12 and President of the Southern Chinese Republic 1923–25

Tamerlane (also **Tamburlaine**) (born Timur Lenk, "lame Timur") (1336–1405) Mongol ruler of Samarkand 1369–1405

Theodoric (known as Theodoric the Great) (*c.* 454–526) king of the Ostrogoths 471–526

Tinbergen, Jan (1903–94) Dutch economist

Trenchard, Hugh Montague, 1st Viscount of Wolfeton (1873–1956) British marshal of the RAF

Vancouver, George (1757–98) English navigator

Vespasian (Latin name Titus Flavius Vespasianus) (AD 9–79) Roman emperor 69–79

Vitellius, Aulus (15–69) Roman emperor 69

Vladimir I (known as Vladimir the Great; canonized as St. Vladimir) (956–1015), grand prince of Kiev 980–1015

Wenceslas (also Wenceslaus) (1361–1419) king of Bohemia (as Wenceslas IV) 1378–1419

Wilhelm II (known as Kaiser Wilhelm) (1859–1941) emperor of Germany 1888–1918, grandson of Queen Victoria

William II (Rufus) (*c.* 1056–1100) king of England 1087–1100

William IV (known as the Sailor King) (1765–1837) king of England 1830–37, son of George III

Zhou Enlai (also Chou En-lai) (1898–1976) Chinese Communist statesman, Prime Minister of China 1949–76

10 letters

Alcibiades (*c.* 450–404 BC) Athenian statesman and general

Alexander I (*c.* 1077–1124) king of Scotland

Alexander I (1777–1825) czar of Russia

Amenhotep I (16th century BC) Egyptian pharaoh, reigned 1546–1526

Anne Boleyn See BOLEYN

Barbarossa (born Khair ad-Din) (*c.* 1483–1546) Barbary pirate

Barbarossa See FREDERICK I

Belshazzar (6th century BC) last king of Babylon

Bernadotte, Folke, Count (1895–1948) Swedish statesman

Bernadotte, Jean Baptiste Jules (1762–1844) French soldier, king of Sweden (as Charles XIV) 1818–44

Bloody Mary nickname of Mary I of England

Brundtland, Gro Harlem (born 1939) Norwegian stateswoman, Prime Minister 1981, 1986–89, 1990–96

Buonaparte See NAPOLEON

Charles VII (1403–61) king of France 1422–61

Charles XII (also Karl XII) (1682–1718) king of Sweden 1697–1718

Clausewitz, Karl von (1780–1831) Prussian general and military theorist

Clemenceau, Georges (Eugène Benjamin) (1841–1929) French statesman, Prime Minister 1906–69 and 1917–20

Coriolanus, Gaius (or Gnaeus) Marcius (5th century BC) Roman general

Crazy Horse (Sioux name Ta-Sunko-Witko) (c. 1849–77) Sioux chief

Cumberland, William Augustus, Duke of (1721–65) English military commander

DeMontfort, Simon See MONTFORT

Diocletian (full name Gaius Aurelius Valerius Diocletianus) (245–313) Roman emperor 284–305

Dionysius I (known as Dionysius the Elder) (c. 430–367 BC) ruler of Syracuse

Edward VIII (1894–1972) reigned in England 1936 but not crowned, son of George V

Eisenhower, Dwight David ("Ike") (1890–1969) American general and Republican statesman, 34th President of the U.S. 1953–61

Elagabalus See HELIOGABALUS

Elizabeth I (1533–1603) daughter of Henry VIII, queen of England and Ireland 1558–1603

Enver Pasha (1881–1922) Turkish political and military leader

Eric the Red (c. 940–c. 1010) Norse explorer

Franz Josef (1830–1916) emperor of Austria 1848–1916 and king of Hungary 1867–1916

Frederick I (known as Frederick Barbarossa, "Redbeard") (c. 1123–90) king of Germany and Holy Roman emperor 1152–90

Guggenheim, Meyer (1828–1905) Swiss-born American industrialist

Gulbenkian, Calouste Sarkis (1869–1955) Turkish-born British oil magnate and philanthropist, of Armenian descent

Harmsworth, Alfred Charles William See NORTHCLIFFE

Hatshepsut (died 1482 BC) Egyptian queen of the 18th dynasty, reigned c. 1503–1482

Henry Tudor See HENRY VII OF ENGLAND

Hindenburg, Paul Ludwig von Beneckendorff und von (1847–1934) German Field Marshal and statesman, President of the Weimar Republic 1925–34

Ibn Hussein, Abdullah See ABDULLAH IBN HUSSEIN

Jaruzelski, Wojciech (born 1923) Polish general and Communist statesman, Prime Minister 1981–85, head of state 1985–89, and President 1989–90

Juan Carlos (full name Juan Carlos Victor Maria de Borbon y Borbon) (born 1938) grandson of Alfonso XIII, king of Spain since 1975

Kemal Pasha See ATATÜRK

Kublai Khan (1216–94) Mongol emperor of China, grandson of Genghis Khan

Ladislaus I (canonized as St. Ladislaus) (c. 1040–94) king of Hungary 1077–95

Louis XVIII (1755–1824) king of France (1814–24, brother of Louis XVI

Ludendorff, Erich (1865–1937) German general

Maccabaeus, Judas See JUDAS MACCABAEUS

Malcolm III (known as Malcolm Canmore) (c. 1031–93) king of Scotland 1058–93, son of Duncan I

Mark Antony See ANTONY

Mary Stuart See MARY, QUEEN OF SCOTS

Maximilian (full name Ferdinand Maximilian Joseph) (1832–67) emperor of Mexico 1864–67

Meiji Tenno (born Mutshuhito) (1852–1912) emperor of Japan 1868–1912

Metternich, Klemens Wenzel Nepomuk Lothar, Prince of Metternich-Winneburg-Beilstein (1773–1859) Austrian statesman

Historical, Political, and Military Figures *(continued)*

Mihailović, Dragoljub ("Draža") (1893–1946) Yugoslav soldier

Mitterrand, François (Maurice Marie) (1916–96) French statesman, President 1981–95

Montgomery, Bernard Law, 1st Viscount Montgomery of Alamein ("Monty") (1887–1976) British Field Marshal

Napoleon II (known as the King of Rome) (1811–1832) Duke of Reichstadt

Nicholas II (1868–1918) czar of Russia 1894–1917, son of Alexander III

Old Hickory nickname of Andrew Jackson

Palmerston, Henry John Temple, 3rd Viscount (1784– 1865) British Whig statesman, Prime Minister 1855–58 and 1859–65

Pestalozzi, Johann Heinrich (1746–1827) Swiss educational reformer

Pocahontas (c. 1595–1617) American Indian princess, daughter of Powhatan (died 1618) an Algonquian chief in Virginia

Rafsanjani, Ali Akbar Hashemi (born 1934) Iranian statesman and religious leader, President since 1989

Ramses VIII (12 cent. BC) Egyptian pharaoh 1147–40 BC

Ribbentrop, Hoachim von (1893–1946) German Nazi politician

Richard III (1452–85) king of England, reigned 1483–85

Richthofen, Manfred, Freiherr von (known as "the Red Baron") (1882–1918) German fighter pilot

Rothschild, Meyer Amschel (1743–1812) German financier

Senanayake, Don Stephen (1884–1952) Sinhalese statesman, Prime Minister of Ceylon 1947–52

Shackleton, Sir Ernest Henry (1874–1922) British explorer

Talleyrand, Charles Maurice de (full surname Talleyrand-Perigord) (1754–1838) French statesman

Torquemada, Tomás de (c. 1420–98) Spanish cleric and Grand Inquisitor

Vanderbilt, Cornelius (1794–1877) American businessman and philanthropist

Wallenberg, Raoul (1912–??) Swedish diplomat

Walsingham, Sir Francis (c. 1530–90) English politician, secretary of state under Elizabeth I

Washington, Booker T (aliaferro) (1856–1915) American educator

Washington, George (1732–99) American soldier and statesman, 1st President of the U.S. 1789–97

Wellington, 1st Duke of (title of Arthur Wellesley; also known as "the Iron Duke") (1769–1852) British soldier and Tory statesman, Prime Minister 1828–30 and 1834

Wiesenthal, Simon (born 1908) Austrian Jewish investigator of Nazi war crimes

Wilhelmina (1880–1962) queen of the Netherlands 1890–1948

William III See WILLIAM OF ORANGE

11 letters

Abdul Rahman, Tunku (1903–90) Malaysian statesman, Prime Minister of Malaya 1957–63 and of Malaysia 1963–70

Albuquerque, Alfonso de (known as Albuquerque the Great) (1453– 1515) Portuguese colonial statesman

Alexander II (1198–1249) king of Scotland

Alphonso XIII (1886–1941) king of Spain 1886–1931

Artaxerxes I (died 425 BC) king of ancient Persia, reigned 464–425 BC

Baden-Powell, Robert (Stephenson Smyth), 1st Baron Baden-Powell of Gilwell (1857–1941) English soldier and founder of the Boy Scout movement

Beaverbrook, (William) Max(well) Aitken, 1st Baron (1879–1964) Canadian-born British Conservative politician and newspaper publisher

Billy the Kid See BONNEY

Black Prince (name given to Edward, Prince of Wales and Duke of Cornwall) (1330–76) eldest son of Edward III of England

Bolingbroke surname of Henry IV of England

Catherine II (known as Catherine the Great) (1729–96) empress of Russia, reigned 1762–96

Chamberlain, (Arthur) Neville (1869–1940) British Conservative statesman, Prime Minister 1937–40

Chamberlain, Joseph (1836–1914) British Liberal statesman

Charlemagne (Latin Carolus Magnus Charles the Great) (742–814) king of the Franks 768–814 and Holy Roman emperor

Chief Joseph (1840–1904) Native American chief

Cleisthenes (*c.* 570 BC–*c.* 508 BC) Athenian statesman

Constantine (known as Constantine the Great) (*c.* 274–337) Roman emperor 312–37

Cunobelinus See CYMBELINE

Demosthenes (384–322 BC) Athenian orator and statesman

Douglas-Home, Sir Alec, Baron Home of the Hirsel of Coldstream (1903–95) British Conservative statesman, Prime Minister 1963–64

Dzerzhinsky, Feliks (Edmundovich) (1877–1926) Russian Bolshevik leader, of Polish descent

Elizabeth II (born Princess Elizabeth Alexandra Mary) (born 1926) daughter of George VI, queen of the U.K. since 1952

Frederick II (known as Frederick the Great) (1712–86) king of Prussia 1740–86

Genghis Khan (1162–1227) founder of the Mongol empire

Jiang Jie Shi See CHIANG KAI-SHEK

John of Gaunt (1340–99) Duke of Lancaster

Ladislaus II (Polish name Władysław) (*c.* 1351–1434) king of Poland 1386–1434

Lloyd George, David, 1st Earl Lloyd George of Dwyfor (1863–1945) British Liberal statesman, Prime Minister 1916–22

Machiavelli, Niccolo di Bernardo del (1469–1527) Italian statesman and political philosopher

Makarios III (born Mikhail Christodolou Mouskos) (1913–77) Greek Cypriot archbishop and statesman, President of the republic of Cyprus 1960–77

Marlborough, 1st Duke of (title of John Churchill) (1650–1722) British general

Montezuma II (1466–1520) Aztec emperor 1502–20

Mountbatten, Louis (Francis Albert Victor Nicholas), 1st Earl Mountbatten of Burma (1900–79) British admiral and administrator

Muhammad Ali (1769–1849) Ottoman viceroy and pasha of Egypt 1805–49, possibly of Albanian descent

Napoleon III (known as Louis-Napoleon) (1803–73) Emperor of France 1852–70

Pisistratus (also Peisistratus) (*c.* 600–*c.* 527 BC) tyrant of Athens

Ponce de León, Juan (*c.* 1460–1521) Spanish explorer

Historical, Political, and Military Figures *(continued)*

Ranjit Singh (known as "the Lion of the Punjab") (1780–1839) Indian maharaja, founder of the Sikh state of Punjab

Robespierre, Maximilien Francois Marie Isidore de (1758–94) French revolutionary

Rockefeller, John D(avison) (1839–1937) American industrialist and philanthropist

Rockefeller, Nelson (1908–79) American politician

Schwarzkopf, H. Norman (born 1934) American military leader

Sennacherib (died 681 BC) king of Assyria 705–681

Sitting Bull (Sioux name Tatanka Iyotake) (c. 1831–90) Sioux chief

Theodosius I (known as Theodosius the Great; full name Flavius Theodosius) (c. 346–95) Roman emperor 379–95

Tutankhamen (also Tutankhamun) (died c. 1352 BC) Egyptian pharaoh of the 18th dynasty, reigned c. 1361–c. 1352 BC

Vivekananda, Swami (born Narendranath Datta) (1863–1902) Indian spiritual leader and reformer

Whittington, Sir Richard ("Dick") (died 1423) English merchant and Lord Mayor of London

Wilberforce, William (1759–1833) English politician and social reformer

12 letters

Abdul Hamid I (known as "the Great Assassin" and "the Red Sultan") (1842–1918) Sultan of the Ottoman Empire 1876–1909

Alexander III (1241–86) king of Scotland

Alexander III (1845–94) czar of Russia

Anne of Cleves (1515–57) fourth wife of Henry VIII

Antiochus III (known as Antiochus the Great) (c. 242–187 BC) Seleucid king

Ashurbanipal king of Assyria c. 668–627 BC

Bandaranaike, Sirimavo Ratwatte Dias (born 1916) Sinhalese stateswoman, Prime Minister of Sri Lanka 1960–65, 1970–77, and since 1994

Boris Godunov See GODUNOV

Bougainville, Louis Antoine de (1729–1811) French explorer

Boutros-Ghali, Boutros (born 1922) Egyptian diplomat and politician, Secretary-General of the United Nations 1992–96

Calamity Jane (born Martha Jane Cannary) (c. 1852–1903) American frontierswoman

Deng Xiaoping (also Teng Hsiao-p'ing) (1904–97) Chinese Communist statesman

Hammarskjöld, Dag (Hjalmar Agne Carl) (1906–61) Swedish diplomat and politician

Heliogabalus (also Elagabalus) (born Varius Avitus Bassianus) (AD 204–22) Roman emperor 218–22

Herod Antipas (22 BC–AD 40) tetrarch of Galilee and Peraea 4 BC–AD 40

John Sobieski See JOHN III

Julius Caesar, Gaius (100–44 BC) Roman general and statesman

Krishnamurti, Jiddu (1895–1986) Indian spiritual leader

Leif Ericsson See ERICSSON

Maria Theresa (1717–80) Archduchess of Austria, queen of Hungary and Bohemia 1740–80

Old Pretender See STUART

Park Chung Hee (1917–79) South Korean statesman, President 1963–79

Peisistratus See PISISTRATUS

Pheidippides (5th century BC)

Athenian messenger

Prince Albert See ALBERT, PRINCE

Shevardnadze, Eduard (Amvrosievich) (born 1928) Soviet statesman and head of state of Georgia from 1992

Themistocles (*c.* 528–462 BC) Athenian statesman

Tuthmosis III (died *c.* 1450 BC) Egyptian pharaoh of the 18th dynasty *c.* 1504–*c.* 1450 BC

William Rufus See WILLIAM II

13 letters

Antoninus Pius (86–161) Roman emperor 138–611

Aung San Suu Kyi (born 1945) Burmese political leader

Charles Martel (*c.* 688–741) Frankish ruler of the eastern part of the Frankish kingdom from 715 and the whole kingdom from 719

Chiang Kai-shek (also Jiang Jie Shi) (1887–1975) Chinese statesman, Prime Minister 1945–49

Haile Sclassie (born Tafari Makonnen) (1892–1975) emperor of Ethiopia 1930–74

Harun ar-Rashid (also Haroun-al-Raschid) (763–809) fifth Abbasid caliph of Baghdad 786–809

Herod Agrippa I (10 BC–AD 44) king of Judaea AD 41–44

Herod the Great (*c.* 74–4 BC) ruler of Palestine, ruled 37–34 BC

Ibarruri Gomez, Dolores (known as "La Pasionaria") (1895–1989) Spanish Communist politician

Jack the Ripper (19th century) unidentified English murderer

Kaiser Wilhelm See WILHELM II

Louis-Napoleon See NAPOLEON

Louis Philippe (1773–1850) king of France 1830–48

Maria de Medici See MARIE DE MÉDICIS

Mithridates VI (also Mithradates VI) (*c.* 132–63 BC) king of Pontus 120–63

Mujibur Rahman (known as Sheikh Mujib) (1920–75)

Bangladeshi statesman, Prime Minister 1972–75 and President 1975

Primo de Rivera, Miguel (1870–1930) Spanish general and statesman, head of state 1923–30

Prince Charles See CHARLES, PRINCE

Prince of Wales See CHARLES, PRINCE

Princess Diana See DIANA, PRINCESS

Radhakrishnan, Sir Sarvepalli (1888–1975) Indian philosopher and statesman, President 1962–67

Saddam Hussein See HUSSEIN

Teng Hsiao-p'ing See DENG XIAOPING

14 letters

Cosimo de' Medici (known as Cosimo the Elder) (1389–1464) Italian statesman and banker

Edmund Ironside nickname of Edmund II of England

Henrietta Mari (1609–69) daughter of Henry IV of France, queen consort of Charles I of England

Herod Agrippa II (AD 27–*c.* 93) king of (parts of) Palestine 50–*c.* 93

Iron Chancellor nickname of Bismark

Marcus Aurelius See AURELIUS

Marie de Médicis (Italian name Maria de' Medici) (1573–1642) queen of France

Nebuchadnezzar (*c.* 630–562 BC) king of Babylon 605–562 BC

Pérez de Cuéllar, Javier (born 1920) Peruvian diplomat

Robert the Bruce (Robert I of Scotland) (1274–1329) king of Scotland, reigned 1306–29

Shalmaneser III (died 824 BC) king of Assyria 859–824

(the) Young Pretender See STUART

15 letters

Alexander Nevsky (also Nevski) (canonized as St. Alexander Nevsky) (*c.* 1220–63) Prince of

Historical, Political, and Military Figures *(continued)*

Novgorod 1236–63 and Grand Prince of Vladimir 1252–63

Edmund the Martyr, St. (*c.* 841–70) king of East Anglia 855–70

Edward the Martyr, St. (*c.* 963–78) son of Edgar, king of England 975–78

Giscard d'Estaing, Valéry (born 1926) French statesman, President 1974–81

Haroun-al-Raschid See HARUN AR-RASHID

Hereward the Wake (11th century) semi-legendary Anglo-Saxon rebel leader

Judas Maccabaeus (died *c.* 161 BC) Jewish leader

Lorenzo de' Medici (known as Lorenzo the Magnificent) (1449–92) Italian statesman and scholar

Marie Antoinette (1755–93) French queen, wife of Louis XVI

Olaf I Tryggvason (969–1000) king of Norway, reigned 995–1000

Scipio Africanus (full name Publius Cornelius Scipio Africanus Major) (236–*c.* 184 BC) Roman general and politician

Tiglath-pileser I king of Assyria *c.* 1115–*c.* 1077 BC

William of Orange (1650–1702) joint king of Great Britain and Ireland 1689–1702

16 letters

Frederick William (known as "the Great Elector") (1620–88) Elector of Brandenburg 1640–88

Gustavus Adolphus (1594–1632) king of Sweden 1611–32

Henry Bolingbroke See HENRY IV of England

Isabella of France (1292–1358) daughter of Philip IV of France

Man in the Iron Mask a mysterious prisoner held in the Bastille and other prisons in 17th century France

Mary, Queen of Scots (known as Mary Stuart) (1542–87) queen of Scotland 1542–67

Olaf II Haraldsson (canonized as St. Olaf) (*c.* 995–1030) king of Norway 1016–30

Olaf IV Haakonsson (1370–87) king of Norway 1380–87

Scipio Aemilianus (full name Publius Cornelius Scipio Aemilianus Africanus Minor) (*c.* 185–129 BC) Roman general and politician

Tiglath-pileser II king of Assyria *c.* 964–934 BC

Victor Emmanuel II (1820–78) ruler of the kingdom of Sardinia 1849–61 and king of Italy 1861–78

17 letters

Ayatollah Khomeini See KHOMEINI

Campbell-Bannerman, Sir Henry (1836–1908) British Liberal statesman, Prime Minister 1905–08

Catherine de' Medici (1519–89) queen of France, ruled as regent (1560–74) during the minority reigns of her three sons

Catherine of Aragon (1485–1536) first wife of Henry VIII

Jiménez de Cisneros, Francisco (also Ximenes de Cisneros) (1436–1517) Spanish statesman, regent of Spain 1516–17

Olaf III Haraldsson (died 1093) king of Norway 1066–93

Philip II of Macedon (382–336 BC) king of Macedon (ancient Macedonia), father of Alexander the Great, reigned 359–336

Princes in the Tower the young sons of Edward IV, namely Edward, Prince of Wales (born 1470) and Richard, Duke of York (born 1472), supposedly murdered in the Tower of London in or shortly after 1483

Tarquinius Priscus (anglicized name Tarquin) semi-legendary Etruscan king, reigned c. 616–c. 578 BC

Tichborne claimant See ORTON

Tiglath-pileser III king of Assyria c. 745–727 BC

Valázquez de Cuéllar, Diego (c. 1465–1524) Spanish conquistador

Victor Emmanuel III (1869–1947) king of Italy 1900–46

Ximenes de Cisneros See JIMÉNEZ DE CISNEROS

18 letters

Abdullah ibn Hussein (1882–1951) king of Jordan 1946–51

Chandragupta Maurya (c. 325–297 BC) Indian emperor

Edward the Confessor, St. (c. 1003–66) son of Ethelred the Unready, king of England 1042–66

Llewelyn ap Gruffydd See LLEWELYN

Tarquinius Superbus (anglicized name Tarquin) semi-legendary Etruscan king reigned c. 534–c. 510 BC

19 letters

Bonnie Prince Charlie See STUART

Eleanor of Acquitaine (c. 1122–1204) queen of France 1137–52 and of England 1154–89

Toussaint L'Ouverture, Pierre Dominique (c. 1743–1803) Haitian revolutionary leader

William the Conqueror See WILLIAM I

21 letters

Alexander the Liberator (1818–81) czar of Russia

Pulu Tiglath-pileser III See TIGLATH-PILESER

27 letters

Home of the Hirsel of Coldstream, Baron See DOUGLAS-HOME

Religious Figures and Theologians

3 letters

Ali (c. 600–661 AD) fourth caliph of Islam (656–61 AD); considered the first caliph by the Shiites

Bab, the title of MIRZA ALI MOHAMMED

Fox, George (1624–91) English preacher and founder of the Society of Friends (Quakers)

Fry, Elizabeth (1780–1845) English Quaker prison reformer

Hus, Jan (1369–1415) Czech religious reformer

4 letters

Anne, St. traditionally the mother of the Virgin Mary

Bede, St. (known as the Venerable Bede) (c. 673–735) English monk, theologian, and historian

Caro, Joseph (ben Ephraim) (1488–1575) Jewish legal scholar and mystic

Dewi See DAVID, ST.

Eddy, Mary Baker (1821–1910) American religious leader and founder of the Christian Science movement

Huss, John (Czech name Jan Hus) (c. 1372–1415) Bohemian religious reformer

John, St. (known as St. John the Evangelist or St. John the Divine) an Apostle, son of Zebedee and

Religious Figures and Theologians *(continued)*

brother of James, and traditional author of the fourth Gospel

Jude, St. (known as Judas) an Apostle, supposed brother of James

King, Martin Luther, Jr. (1929–68) American Baptist minister and civil rights activist

Knox, John (*c.* 1505–72) Scottish Protestant reformer

Luke, St. traditional author of the third Gospel

Mark, St. an Apostle, companion of St. Peter and St. Paul, traditional author of the second Gospel

Mary (known as the [Blessed] Virgin Mary, or St. Mary, or Our Lady), mother of Jesus

Mary, St. See MARY

Moon, Sun Myung (born 1920) Korean industrialist and religious leader

More, Sir Thomas (canonized as St. Thomas More) (1478–1535) English scholar and statesman, Lord Chancellor 1529–32

Omar (*or* Umar) (died 644 AD) the second caliph of Islam (634–44)

Paul, St. (known as Paul the Apostle, or Saul of Tarsus, or "the Apostle of the Gentiles") (died *c.* 64)

Saul (also Saul of Tarsus) the original name of St. Paul

Tutu, Desmond (Mpilo) (born 1931) South African Anglican clergyman

Weil, Simone (1909–43) French mystic and philosopher

5 letters

Abduh, Muhammad (1849–1905) Egyptian Islamic scholar, jurist, and liberal reformer

Agnes, St. (4th century AD) Roman virgin martyr

Aidan, St. (died 651 AD) Irish missionary

Alban, St. (3rd century) the first British Christian martyr

Asoka (died 232 BC) Indian Buddhist emperor (?273–232 BC)

Avila, St. Teresa of (1515–82) Spanish nun and religious reformer

Baeck, Leo (1873–1956) German Jewish theologian

Barth, Karl (1886–1968) Swiss Protestant theologian

Basil, St. (known as St. Basil the Great) (*c.* 330–79) Doctor of the Church

Booth, William (1829–1912) English religious leader, founder and first general of the Salvation Army

Bride, St. See BRIDGET OF IRELAND, St.

Bruno, Giordano (1548–1600) Italian philosopher

Bruno, St. (*c.* 1032–1101) German-born French churchman

Buber, Martin (1878–1965) Israeli religious philosopher, born in Austria

Carey, George (Leonard) (born 1935) English Anglican churchman, Archbishop of Canterbury since 1991

Cyril, St. (826–69) Greek missionary, an "Apostle of the Slavs"

David, St. (also Dewi) (6th century) Welsh monk

Denis, St. (also Denys) (died *c.* 250) Italian-born French bishop, patron saint of France

Dewey, John (1859–1952) American philosopher and educator

Eddy, Mary Baker (1821–1910) American founder of Christian Science

Herzl, Theodor (1860–1904) Austrian writer, born in

Hungary; founder of the Zionist movement

Hilda, St. (614–80) English abbess

James, St. (known as St. James the Great) an Apostle, son of Zebedee and brother of John

James, St. (known as St. James the Just or "the Lord's brother") Leader of the early Christian Church at Jerusalem

James, St. (known as St. James the Less) an Apostle

James, William (1842–1910) American psychologist and philosopher

Jesus (also Jesus Christ) the central figure of the Christian religion

Judas See JUDE, ST.

Kempe, Margery (c. 1373–c. 1440) English mystic

Luria, Isaac (ben Solomon) (1534–72) Jewish mystic

Nanak (known as Guru Nanak) (1469–1539) Indian religious leader and founder of Sikhism

Oates, Titus (1649–1705) English clergyman and conspirator

Occam, William of See WILLIAM OF OCCAM

Paris, Matthew (c. 1199–1259) English chronicler and Benedictine monk

Peale, Norman Vincent (1898–1993) American religious leader

Peter, St. (born Simon) an Apostle

Renan, (Joseph) Ernest (1823–92) French historian, theologian, and philosopher

Sheen, Fulton John (born Peter Sheen) (1895–1979) American Roman Catholic priest

Simon, St. (known as Simon the Zealot) an Apostle

Smith, Joseph (1805–44) American religious leader and founder of the Church of Jesus Christ of Latter-Day Saints (the Mormons)

Titus, St. (1st century AD) Greek churchman

Truth, Sojourner (previously Isabella Van Wagener) (c. 1797–

1883) American evangelist and reformer

Varah, (Edward) Chad (1911–93) English clergyman, founder of the Samaritans

Vitus, St. (died c. 300) Christian martyr

Young, Brigham (1801–77) American Mormon leader

6 letters

Abbott, Lyman (1835–1922) American clergyman and reformer

Alcuin (or Albinus) (c. 735–804 AD) English theologian and educator

Ananda (5th century BC) the cousin, disciple, and personal attendant of the Buddha

Andrew, St. an Apostle, the brother of St. Peter

Assisi, Clare of See CLARE OF ASSISI, ST.

Assisi, Francis of See FRANCIS OF ASSISI, ST.

Becket, Thomas à See THOMAS À BECKET

Besant, Annie (1847–1933) English theosophist, writer, and political campaigner

Boehme, Jacob (1575–1624) German theosophist

Brigid, St. See BRIDGET OF IRELAND, ST.

Buddha a title given to successive teachers (past and future) of Buddhism, although it usually denotes the founder of Buddhism, Siddhartha Gautama (c. 563 BC–c. 480 BC)

Calvin, John (1509–64) French Protestant theologian and reformer

Fatima (c. 606–32 AD) youngest daughter of the prophet Muhammad and wife of the fourth caliph, Ali (died 661)

Fa Xian (or Fa-hsien; original name: Sehi) (5th century AD) Chinese Buddhist monk

Religious Figures and Theologians *(continued)*

Fisher, St. John (1469–1535) English churchman

Fuller, Thomas (1608–61) English cleric and historian

George, St. patron saint of England

Graham, William Franklin ("Billy") (born 1918) American evangelical preacher

Hilary, St. (*c.* 315–*c.* 367) French bishop

Jansen, Cornelius Otto (1585–1638) Flemish Roman Catholic theologian and founder of Jansenism

Jerome, St. (*c.* 342–420) Doctor of the Church

Joseph, St. Carpenter of Nazareth, husband of the Virgin Mary

Justin, St. (known as St. Justin the Martyr) (*c.* 100–165) Christian philosopher

Kempis, Thomas à See THOMAS À KEMPIS

Lao-Tzu (604–531 BC) Chinese founder of Taoism

Luther, Martin (1483–1546) German Protestant theologian, the principal figure of the German Reformation

Martin, St. (died 397) French bishop, a patron saint of France

Mather, Cotton (1663–1728) American Puritan and founder of Yale University

Merton, Thomas (1915–68) American Trappist monk and writer

Monica, St. (332–*c.* 387) mother of St. Augustine of Hippo

Moody, Dwight (1837–99) American evangelist

Newman, John Henry (1801–91) English prelate and theologian

Ninian, St. (*c.* 360–*c.* 432) Scottish bishop and missionary

Ockham, William of See WILLIAM OF OCCAM

Origen (*c.* 185–*c.* 254) Christian scholar and theologian, probably born in Alexandria

Pascal, Blaise (1623–62) French mathematician, physicist, and religious philosopher

Ridley, Nicholas (*c.* 1500–55) English Protestant bishop and martyr

Sunday, Billy (1862–1935) American evangelist

Suzuki, D. T. (1870–1966) Japanese Buddhist scholar

Taylor, Jeremy (1613–67) English Anglican churchman and writer

Teresa, Mother (also Theresa) (born Agnes Gonxha Bojaxhiu) (1910–97) Roman Catholic nun and missionary, born in what is now Macedonia of Albanian parentage

Teresa, St., of Avila See AVILA, ST. TERESA OF

Thomas, St. an Apostle

Tillich, Paul (1886–1965) American Protestant theologian

Uthman (died 656 AD) third caliph of Islam, who established an authoritative version of the Koran

Wesley, John (1703–91) English preacher and co-founder of Methodism

Wyclif, John (also Wycliffe) (*c.* 1330–84) English religious reformer

Xavier, St. Francis (known as "the Apostle of the Indies") (1506–52) Spanish missionary

7 *letters*

Abelard, Peter (1079–1142) French scholar, theologian, and philosopher

Abu-Bekr (also Abu-Bakr) (573–634 AD) first caliph of Islam, companion and father-in-law of Mohammed

Ambrose, St. (*c.* 339–97 AD)
Italian bishop and Doctor of the
Church

Aquinas, St. Thomas (known as
"the Angelic Doctor") (*c.*
1225–74) Italian Dominican theologian, scholastic philosopher,
and Doctor of the Church

Aylward, Gladys (May)
(1902–70) English missionary

Beecher, Henry Ward (1813–87)
American clergyman, orator, and
writer

Bernard, St. (*c.* 996–*c.* 1081)
French monk

Brendan, St. (*c.* 486–*c.* 575) Irish
abbot

Caedmon (7th century) English
monk and poet

Campion, St. Edmund
(1540–81) English Jesuit priest
and martyr

Cecilia, St. (2nd or 3rd century)
Roman martyr

Clement, St. (known as St.
Clement of Rome) (1st century
AD) Pope *c.* 88–*c.* 97

Columba, St. (*c.* 521–97) Irish
abbot and missionary

Cranmer, Thomas (1489–1556)
English churchman

Cyprian, St. (died 258)
Carthaginian bishop and martyr

Dominic, St. (Spanish name
Domingo de Guzmán) (*c.* 1170–
1221) Spanish priest and friar

Dunstan, St. (*c.* 909–88) Anglo-
Saxon prelate

Edwards, Jonathan (1703–58)
American theologian

Erasmus, Desiderius (*c.*
1466–1536) Dutch humanist
philosopher

Erastus (Swiss name Thomas
Lieber; also called Liebler or
Lüber) (1524–83) Swiss theolo-
gian and physician

Falwell, Jerry (born 1933)
American evangelist

Gautama, Siddhartha See
BUDDHA

Gregory, St. (known as St.
Gregory the Great) (*c.* 540–604)
Pope (as Gregory I) 590–604 and
Doctor of the Church

Héloise (1098–1164) French
abbess

Jackson, Jesse (born 1941)
American Baptist minister and
civil rights activist

Latimer, Hugh (*c.* 1485–1555)
English Protestant prelate and
martyr

Lydgate, John (*c.* 1370–*c.* 1450)
English poet and monk

Malthus, Thomas Robert
(1766–1834) English economist
and clergyman

Manetho (3rd century BC)
Egyptian priest

Matthew, St. an Apostle, a tax-
gatherer from Capernaum in
Galilee, traditional author of the
first Gospel

Mawlana See JALAL AD-DIN AR-
RUMI

Niebuhr, Reinhold (1892–1971)
American Protestant theologian

O'Connor, John Joseph (born
1920) American Roman Catholic
priest, U.S. Navy chaplain, and
cardinal

Patrick, St. (5th century) Apostle
and patron saint of Ireland

Paul III (born Alessandro Farnese)
(1468–1549) Italian Pope
1534–49

Pius XII (born Eugenio Pacelli)
(1876–1958) Pope 1939–58

Roberts, (Granville) Oral (born
1918) American evangelist and
founder of Oral Roberts
University

Russell, Charles T. (1852–1916)
American founder of Jehovah's
Witnesses

Sankara (8th century AD) Hindu
Vedantic philosopher

**Senussi, Sidi Mohammed ibn
Ali al** (*or* Senusi) (?1787–1859)
founder of the Muslim Senussi
sect

Religious Figures and Theologians *(continued)*

Sergius, St. (Russian name Svyatoi Sergi Radonezhsky) (1314–92) Russian monastic reformer and mystic

Steiner, Rudolf (1861–1925) Austrian founder of anthroposophy

Stephen, St. (*c.* 977–1038) king and patron saint of Hungary, reigned 1000–38

Stephen, St. (died *c.* 35) Christian martyr

Theresa, Mother See TERESA, MOTHER

Tillich, Paul (Johannes) (1886–1965) German-born American theologian and philosopher

Timothy, St. (1st century AD) convert and disciple of St. Paul

Tyndale, William (*c.* 1494–1536) English translator and Protestant martyr

Ulfilas (also Wulfila) (*c.* 311–*c.* 381) bishop and translator

Umar Tal (?1797–1864) African religious and military leader, who created a Muslim empire in West Africa

Wulfila See ULFILAS

Zwingli, Ulrich (1484–1531) Swiss Protestant reformer, the principal figure of the Swiss Reformation

8 letters

Adrian IV (born Nicholas Breakspear) (*c.* 1100–59) Pope (1154–59) the only English Pope

Averroës (1126–98) Spanish-Arabian philosopher

Barnabas, St., a Cypriot Levite and Apostle

Benedict, St. (*c.* 480–*c.* 550) Italian hermit

Berkeley, George (1685–1753) Irish philosopher and bishop

Brigitta, St. See BRIDGET OF SWEDEN, ST.

Boniface, St. (born Wynfrith; known as "the Apostle of Germany") (680–754) Anglo-Saxon missionary

Bultmann, Rudolf (Karl) (1884–1976) German Lutheran theologian

Channing, William Ellery (1780–1842) American clergyman and proponent of Unitarianism

Cuthbert, St. (died 687) English monk

Eusebius (known as Eusebius of Caesaria) (*c.* 264–*c.* 340 AD) bishop and Church historian

Flanagan, Edward Joseph (1886–1948) Irish-born American Roman Catholic priest; founder of Boys Town

Irenaeus, St. (*c.* 130–*c.* 200 AD) Greek theologian

Josephus, Flavius (born Joseph ben Matthias) (*c.* 37–*c.* 100) Jewish historian, general, and Pharisee

Khomeini, Ruholla (known as Ayatollah Khomeini) (1900–89) Iranian Shiite Muslim religious and political leader

Lawrence, St. (Latin name Laurentius) (died 258) Roman martyr and deacon of Rome

Malcolm X (born Malcolm Little) (1925–65) American Black Muslim leader and civil rights activist

Margaret, St. (*c.* 1046–93) Scottish queen, wife of Malcolm III

Matthias, St. an Apostle, chosen by lot after the Ascension to take the place left by Judas

Mohammed See MUHAMMAD

Muhammad (also Mohammed) (*c.* 570–632) Arab prophet and founder of Islam

Muhammad, Elijah (1897–1975) American leader of Black Muslims

Nicholas, St. (4th century) Christian prelate

Pelagius (*c.* 360–*c.* 420) British or Irish monk

Polycarp, St. (*c.* 69–*c.* 155) Greek bishop of Smyrna in Asia Minor

Rajneesh, Bhagwan Shree (born Chandra Mohan Jain; known as "the Bhagwan" from a Sanskrit word meaning "lord") (1931–90) Indian guru

Ramanuja (11th century AD) Indian Hindu philosopher and theologian

Ram Singh (1816–85) Indian leader of a puritanical Sikh sect

Williams, Roger (*c.* 1603–83) American clergyman

Xuan Zang (*or* Hsüan-tsang) (602–664 AD) Chinese Buddhist monk and traveler

9 *letters*

Augustine, St. (known as St. Augustine of Canterbury) (died *c.* 604) Italian churchman, the first Archbishop of Canterbury

Augustine, St. (known as St. Augustine of Hippo) (354–430) Doctor of the Church

Baha'ullah title of MIRZA HOSEIN ALI

Blavatsky, Helena (Petrovna) (known as Madame Blavatsky; née Hahn) (1831–91) Russian spiritualist, born in Ukraine

Catherine, St. (known as St. Catherine of Alexandria) (died *c.* 307) early Christian martyr

Farrakhan, Louis (born Louis Eugene Walcott) (born 1933) American Black Muslim leader

Gurdjieff, George (Ivanovich) (1877–1949) Russian spiritual leader and occultist

Gutiérrez, Gustavo (born 1928) Peruvian theologian

Joan of Arc (1412–31) French patron saint

Marquette, Jacques (1637–75) French Jesuit missionary and explorer

McPherson, Aimee Semple (1890–1944) Canadian-born American evangelist

Methodius, St. (815–85) Greek missionary, an "Apostle of the Slavs"

Nagarjuna (*c.* 150–*c.* 250 AD) Indian Buddhist monk, founder of the Madhyamika (Middle Path) school of Mahayana Buddhism

Niemöller, Martin (1892–1984) German Lutheran pastor

Robertson, Pat (born 1930) American Southern Baptist evangelist

Santayana, George (1863–1952) Spanish-born American philosopher and writer

Thaddaeus an Apostle named in St. Matthew's Gospel, traditionally identified with St. Jude

Wenceslas, St. (also Wenceslaus; known as "Good King Wenceslas") (*c.* 907–29) Duke of Bohemia and patron saint of the Czech Republic

Zoroaster (Avestan name Zarathustra) (*c.* 628–*c.* 551 BC) Persian prophet and founder of Zoroastrianism

10 *letters*

Abu Hanifah (700–67 AD) Muslim theologian and teacher of jurisprudence

Athanasius, St. (296–373 AD) Egyptian bishop of Alexandria

Bernadette, St. (born Marie Bernarde Soubirous) (1844–79) French saint

Bonhoeffer, Dietrich (1906–45) German Lutheran theologian and pastor

Breakspear, Nicholas See ADRIAN IV

Chrysostom, St. John (*c.* 347–407) Doctor of the Church, bishop of Constantinople

Religious Figures and Theologians *(continued)*

Duns Scotus, John (known as "the Subtle Doctor") (*c.* 1265–1308) Scottish theologian and scholar

Huntingdon, Selina, Countess of (title of Selina Hastings, née Shirley) (1707–91) English religious leader

ibn-al-Arabi, Muhyi-I-din (1165– 1240) Muslim mystic and poet, noted for his influence on Sufism

John Paul II (born Karol Jozef Wojtyla) (born 1920) Polish cleric, Pope since 1978

Maimonides (born Moses ben Maimon) (1135–1204) Jewish philosopher and Rabbinic scholar, born in Spain

Savonarola, Girolamo (1452–98) Italian preacher and religious leader

Schweitzer, Albert (1875–1965) German theologian, musician, and medical missionary

Stanislaus, St. (known as St. Stanislaus of Cracow; Polish name Stanisław) (1030–79) Patron saint of Poland

Swedenborg, Emanuel (1688–1772) Swedish mystic, scientist, and philosopher

Tertullian (Latin name Quintus Septimius Florens Tertullianus) (*c.* 160–*c.* 240) early Christian theologian

Virgin Mary See MARY

11 letters

Baal Shem Tov (*or* Baal Shem Tob) (original name Israel ben Eliezer) (?1700–60) Jewish religious leader; founder of modern Hasidism

Bartholomew, St. an Apostle

Bodhidharma (6th century AD) Indian Buddhist monk; considered to be the founder of Zen Buddhism

Bonaventura, St. (born Giovanni di Fidanza; known as "the Seraphic Doctor") (1221–74) Franciscan theologian

Gobind Singh, Guru (*or* Govind Singh) (1666–1708) Tenth and last Guru of the Sikhs

Judah ha-Levi (?1075–1141) Jewish poet and theological philosopher

Livingstone, David (1813–73) Scottish missionary and explorer

Melanchthon, Philipp (born Philipp Schwarzerd) (1497–1560) German Protestant reformer

Mendelssohn, Moses (1729–86) German Jewish theologian

Ramakrishna (born Gadadhar Chatterjee) (1836–86) Indian yogi and mystic

Ranjit Singh (the Lion of the Punjab) (1780–1839) founder of the Sikh kingdom in the Punjab

Vivekananda (original name Narendranath Datta) (1862–1902) Indian Hindu religious teacher

12 letters

Hasan al-Basri (died 728 AD) Muslim religious thinker

Oswald of York, St. (died 992) English prelate and Benedictine monk

Philo Judaeus (*c.* 20 BC–50 AD) Jewish theologian

13 letters

Angelic Doctor nickname of St. Thomas Aquinas

Clare of Assisi, St. (1194–1253) Italian saint and abbess

Francis Xavier, St. See XAVIER, ST. FRANCIS

Mary Magdalene, St. (in the New Testament) a woman of Magdala in Galilee

Mother Teresa See TERESA, MOTHER

Teresa of Ávila, St. See AVILA, ST. TERESA OF

Thomas à Becket (1118–70) Archbishop of Canterbury

Thomas à Kempis (born Thomas Hemerken) (c. 1380–1471) German theologian

Thomas Aquinas, St. See AQUINAS, ST. THOMAS

Usman dan Fodio (1754–1817) African mystic and revolutionary leader, who created a Muslim state in Nigeria

Vincent de Paul, St. (1581–1660) French priest

14 letters

Albertus Magnus, St. (known as "Saint Albert the Great") (c. 1200–80) German bishop, philosopher, and Doctor of the Church

Anthony of Egypt, St. (also Antony) (c. 251–356 AD) Egyptian hermit

Anthony of Padua, St. (also Antony) (1195–1231) Portuguese Franciscan friar

Francis of Sales, St. (1567–1622) French bishop

Gregory of Nyssa, St. (c. 330–c. 395) Doctor of the Eastern Church, bishop of Nyssa in Cappadocia

Gregory of Tours, St. (c. 540–94) Frankish bishop and historian

Ignatius Loyola, St. (1491–1556) Spanish theologian and founder of the Jesuits

John Chrysostom, St. See CHRYSOSTOM, ST. JOHN

John of Damascus, St. (c. 675–c. 749) Syrian theologian and Doctor of the Church

John of the Cross, St. (born Juan de Yepis y Alvarez) (1542–91) Spanish mystic and poet

John the Baptist, St. Jewish preacher and prophet, a contemporary of Jesus

Mirza Hosein Ali (1817–92) Persian religious leader; founder of Baha'ism

Peter the Hermit (c. 1050–1115) French monk

Seraphic Doctor, the nickname of St. Bonaventura

Shankaracharya (or Shankara) (9th century AD) Hindu Vedantic philosopher and teacher

Simeon Stylites, St. (c. 390–459) Syrian monk

William of Occam (also Ockham) (c. 1285–1349) English philosopher and Franciscan friar

15 letters

Bridget of Sweden, St. (also Birgitta) (c. 1303–73) Swedish nun and visionary

Francis of Assisi, St. (born Giovanni di Bernardone) (c. 1101–1226) Italian monk, founder of the Franciscan order

Judas Maccabaeus (2nd century BC) Jewish revolutionary leader

Julian of Norwich (or Juliana) (c. 1342–c. 1413) English mystic

Teresa of Lisieux, St. (also Thérèse) (born Marie-Françoise Thérèse Martin) (1873–97) French Carmelite nun

16 letters

Bridget of Ireland, St. (also Bride or Brigid) (6th century) Irish abbess

Dionysius Exiguus (died c. 556) Scythian monk and scholar

Isidore of Seville, St. (also called Isidorus Hispalensis) (c. 560–636) Spanish archbishop and Doctor of the Church

Jalal ad-Din ar-Rumi (also called Mawlana) (1207–73) Sufi mystic and poet

Mirza Ali Mohammed (1819–50) Persian religious leader; founded Babism

Thérèse of Lisieux, St. See TERESA OF LISIEUX, ST.

Religious Figures and Theologians *(continued)*

17 letters

Blessed Virgin Mary See MARY
Cyril of Alexandria, St. (died 444) Doctor of the Church and patriarch of Alexandria
John the Evangelist, St. See JOHN, ST.
Rabiah al-Adawiyyah (*or* Rabia) (*c.* 713–801 AD) Islamic saint

18 letters

Anselm of Canterbury, St. (*c.* 1033–1109) Italian theologian and philosopher, archbishop, and Doctor of the Church
Bernard of Clairvaux, St.
(1090–1153) French theologian and abbot
Gregory of Nazianzus, St. (329–89) Doctor of the Church, bishop of Constantinople

19 letters

Apollinaris Sidonius (5th century AD) Italian bishop and writer
Clement of Alexandria, St. (Latin name Titus Flavius Clemens) (*c.* 150–*c.* 215) Greek theologian

22 letters

Dionysius the Areopagite (1st century AD) Greek churchman

Scientists and Inventors

3 letters

Dee, John (1527–1608) English alchemist, mathematician, and geographer
Hoe, Richard March (1812–86) American inventor and industrialist
Ohm, Georg Simon (1789–1854) German physicist
Ray, John (1627–1705) English naturalist
Roe, Sir (Edwin) Alliott Verdon (1877–1958) English engineer and aircraft designer

4 letters

Abbe, Ernst (1840–1905) German physicist
Abel, Niels Henrik (1802–29) Norwegian mathematician
Airy, Sir George Biddell (1801–92) English astronomer and geophysicist
Auer, Carl, Baron von Welsbach (1858–1929) Austrian chemist

Baer, Karl Ernest von (1792–1876) German biologist
Bell, Alexander Graham (1847–1922) Scottish-born American scientist and inventor
Benz, Karl Friedrich (1844–1929) German engineer and motor manufacturer
Best, Charles Herbert (1899–1978) American-born Canadian physiologist
Boas, Franz (1858–1942) German-born American anthropologist
Bohr, Niels Hendrik David (1885–1962) Danish physicist and pioneer in quantum physics
Born, Max (1882–1970) German theoretical physicist and a founder of quantum mechanics
Bose, Sir Jagdis Chandra (1858–1937) Indian physicist and plant physiologist
Bose, Satyendra Nath (1894–1974) Indian physicist
Burt, Cyril Lodowic (1883–1971)

English psychologist

Bush, Vannevar (1890–1974) American electrical engineer

Cohn, Ferdinand Julius (1828–98) German botanist, a founder of bacteriology

Colt, Samuel (1814–62) American inventor

Cort, Henry (1740–1800) English ironmaster

Cray, Seymour (1925–96) American computer engineer

Dale, Sir Henry Hallett (1875–1968) English physiologist and pharmacologist

Dana, James Dwight (1813–95) American naturalist, geologist, and mineralogist

Dart, Raymond Arthur (1893–1988) Australian-born South African anthropologist and anatomist

Davy, Sir Humphry (1778–1829) English chemist, a pioneer of electrochemistry

Doll, Sir (William) Richard (Shaboc) (born 1912) English physician

Funk, Casimir (1884–1967) Polish-born American biochemist

Gray, Asa (1810–88) American botanist

Hahn, Otto (1879–1968) German chemist, co-discoverer of nuclear fission

Hale, George Ellery (1868–1938) American astronomer

Hall, Charles Martin (1863–1914) American industrial chemist

Hero (known as Hero of Alexandria) (1st century) Greek mathematician and inventor

Hess, Victor Francis (born Victor Franz Hess) (1883–1964) Austrian-born American physicist

Hill, Sir Rowland (1795–1879) British educationist, administrator, and inventor

Howe, Elias (1819–67) American inventor

Jobs, Steven (Paul) (born 1955) American computer entrepreneur

Jung, Carl (Gustav) (1875–1961) Swiss psychologist

Koch, Robert (1843–1910) German bacteriologist

Land, Edwin (1910–91) American inventor of the instant camera

Lind, James (1716–94) Scottish physician

Mach, Eernst (1838–1916) Austrian physicist and philosopher of science

Mayr, Ernst Walter (born 1904) German-born American zoologist

Mead, Margaret (1901–78) American anthropologist and social psychologist

Moog, Robert (born 1934) American inventor

Muir, John (1838–1914) Scottish-born American naturalist, a pioneer of environmental conservation

Oort, Jan Hendrik (1900–92) Dutch astronomer

Opel, Wilhelm von (1871–1948) German motor manufacturer

Otis, Elisha Graves (1811–61) American inventor and manufacturer

Otto, Nikolaus August (1832–91) German engineer

Owen, Sir Richard (1804–92) English anatomist and paleontologist

Page, Sir Frederick Handley (1885–1962) English aircraft designer

Page, Robert Morris (1903–92) American physicist

Rabi, Isidor I. (1899–1988) Austrian-born American physicist

Reed, Walter (1851–1902) American bacteriologist and pathologist

Ross, Sir Ronald (1857–1932) British physician

Ryle, Sir Martin (1918–84) English astronomer

Saha, Meghnad (1894–1956) Indian physicist

Salk, Jonas Edward (1914–95) American microbiologist

Scientists and Inventors *(continued)*

Snow, C(harles) P(ercy), 1st Baron Snow of Leicester (1905–80) English novelist and scientist

Swan, Sir Joseph Wilson (1828–1914) English physicist and chemist

Thom, Alexander (1894–1985) Scottish expert on prehistoric stone circles

Tull, Jethro (1674–1741) English agriculturalist

Urey, Harold Clayton (1893–1981) American chemist

Vine, Frederick John (born 1939) English geologist

Watt, James (1736–1819) Scottish engineer

5 letters

Adams, John Couch (1819–92) English astronomer

Adler, Alfred (1870–1937) Austrian psychologist and psychiatrist

Aiken, Howard H. (1900–73) American computer engineer

Aston, Francis William (1877–1945) English physicist

Baade, (Wilhelm Heinrich) Walter (1893–1960) German-born American astronomer

Bacon, Roger (*c.* 1214–94) English philosopher, scientist, and Franciscan monk

Baird, John Logie (1888–1946) Scottish pioneer of television

Banks, Sir Joseph (1743–1820) English botanist

Bates, Henry Walter (1825–92) English naturalist

Berry, Clifford (1918–63) American computer engineer

Binet, Alfred (1857–1911) French psychologist and pioneer of modern intelligence testing

Black, Joseph (1728–99) Scottish chemist

Boole, George (1815–64) English mathematician

Boyle, Robert (1627–91) Irish-born scientist

Bragg, Sir William Henry (1862–1942) English physicist, a founder of solid-state physics

Brahe, Tycho (1546–1601) Danish astronomer

Braun, Karl Ferdinand (1850–1918) German physicist

Braun, Wernher Magnus Maximillian von (1912–77) German-born American rocket engineer

Brown, Sir Arthur Whitten (1886–1948) Scottish aviator

Byron, Augusta Ada See LOVELACE, COUNTESS OF

Chain, Sir Ernst Boris (1906–79) German-born British biochemist

Cooke, Sir William Fothergill (1806–79) English inventor

Crick, Francis Harry Compton (born 1916) English biophysicist

Curie, Marie (1867–1934) Polish-born French physicist

Curie, Pierre (1859–1906) French physicist

Debye, Peter Joseph William (1884–1966) Dutch-born American chemical physicist

Dewar, Sir James (1842–1923) Scottish chemist and physicist

Dirac, Paul Adrian Maurice (1902–84) English theoretical physicist

Ekman, Vagn Walfrid (1874–1954) Swedish oceanographer

Ellis, (Henry) Havelock (1859–1939) English psychologist and writer

Elton, Charles Sutherland (1900–91) English zoologist

Esaki, Leo (born 1925) Japanese physicist

Euler, Leonhard (1707–83) Swiss mathematician

Euler, Ulf Svante von) (1905–83) Swedish physiologist, the son of Hans Euler-Chelpin

Evans, Sir Arthur (John) (1851–1941) English archaeologist

Fabre, Jean Henri (1823–1915) French entomologist

Fermi, Enrico (1901–54) Italian-born American atomic physicist

Frege, Gottlob (1848–1925) German philosopher and mathematician, founder of modern logic

Freud, Anna (1895–1982) Austrian-born British psychoanalyst, the youngest child of Sigmund Freud

Freud, Sigmund (1856–1939) Austrian neurologist and psychotherapist

Fuchs, (Emil) Klaus (Julius) (1911–88) German-born British physicist

Gabor, Dennis (1900–79) Hungarian-born British electrical engineer

Galen (full name Claudios Galenos; Latin name Claudius Galenus) (129–99) Greek physician

Gamow, George (1904–68) Russian-born American physicist

Gates, William (Henry) ("Bill") (born 1955) American computer entrepreneur

Gauss, Karl Friedrich (1777–1855) German mathematician, astronomer, and physicist

Geber (Latinized name of Jabir ibn Hayyan) (c. 721–c. 815) Arab chemist

Gibbs, Josiah Willard (1839–1903) American theoretical physicist

Gödel, Kurt (1906–78) Austrian-born American mathematician

Golgi, Camillo (1844–1926) Italian histologist and anatomist

Gould, Stephen Jay (born 1941) American paleontologist

Hertz, Heinrich Rudolf (1857–94) German physicist and pioneer of radio communication

Honda, Soichiro (1906–92) Japanese motor manufacturer

Hooke, Robert (1635–1703) English scientist

Hoyle, Sir Fred (born 1915) English astrophysicist, one of the proponents of the steady-state theory of cosmology

Jeans, Sir James Hopwood (1877–1946) English physicist and astronomer

Joule, James Prescott (1818–89) English physicist

Klein, Melanie (1882–1960) Austrian-born psychoanalyst

Krebs, Sir Hans Adolf (1900–81) German-born British biochemist

Lacan, Jacques (1901–81) French psychoanalyst

Laing, R(onald) D(avid) (1927–89) Scottish psychiatrist

Leary, Timothy (Francis) (1920–96) American psychologist and drug pioneer

Locke, Joseph (1805–60) English civil engineer

Loewi, Otto (1873–1961) German-born American pharmacologist and physiologist

Lyell, Sir Charles (1797–1875) Scottish geologist

Maury, Matthew Fontaine (1806–73) American oceanographer

Monod, Jacques Lucien (1910–76) French biochemist

Moore, Francis (1657–c. 1715) English physician, astrologer, and schoolmaster

Morse, Samuel F(inley) B(reese) (1791–1872) American inventor

Nervi, Pier Luigi (1891–1979) Italian engineer and architect

Nobel, Alfred Bernhard (1833–96) Swedish chemist and engineer

Noyce, Robert N. (1927–89) American computer engineer

Scientists and Inventors *(continued)*

Osler, Sir William (1849–1919) Canadian-born physician and classical scholar

Pauli, Wolfgang (1900–58) Austrian-born American physicist who worked chiefly in Switzerland

Pliny (known as Pliny the Elder; Latin name Gaius Plinius Secundus) (23–79 AD) Roman natural historian

Prout, William (1785–1850) English chemist and biochemist

Raman, Sir Chandraskekhara Venkata (1888–1970) Indian physicist

Rolls, Charles Stewart (1877–1910) English motoring and aviation pioneer

Royce, Sir (Frederick) Henry (1863–1933) English engine designer

Sabin, Albert B. (1906–93) Russian-born American physician

Sagan, Carl (Edward) (1934–96) American astronomer

Salam, Abdus (1926–96) Pakistani theoretical physicist

Sapir, Edward (1884–1939) German-born American linguistics scholar and anthropologist

Selye, Hans Hugo Bruno (1907–82) Austrian-born Canadian physician

Spock, Benjamin McLane (known as Dr. Spock) (1903–98) American pediatrician and writer

Steno, Nicolaus (Danish name Niels Steensen) (1638–86) Danish anatomist and geologist

Tesla, Nikola (1856–1943) American electrical engineer and inventor, born in what is now Croatia of Serbian descent

Volta, Alessandro Giuseppe Antonio Anastasio, Count (1745–1827) Italian physicist

Woods, Granville T. (1856–1910) American inventor

Wundt, Wilhelm (1832–1920) German psychologist

Young, Thomas (1773–1829) English physicist, physician, and Egyptologist

Zeiss, Carl (1816–88) German optical instrument-maker

6 letters

Agnesi, Maria Gaetana (1718–99) Italian mathematician and philosopher

Alcock, Sir John William (1892–1919) English aviator

Aldrin, Edwin Eugene (known as "Buzz") (born 1930) American astronaut

Alfvén, Hannes Olof Gösta (1908–95) Swedish astrophysicist

Ampère, André Marie (1775–1836) French physicist

Asimov, Isaac (1920–92) Russian-born American writer and scientist

Austin, Herbert, 1st Baron Austin of Longbridge (1866–1941) British motor manufacturer

Baeyer, Adolph Johann Friedrich Wilhelm von (1835–1917) German organic chemist

Bakker, Robert T. (born 1945) American paleontologist

Batten, Jean (1909–82) New Zealand aviator

Berger, Hans (1873–1941) German psychiatrist

Bessel, Friedrich Wilhelm (1784–1846) German astronomer and mathematician

Bordet, Jules (1870–1961) Belgian bacteriologist and immunologist

Bramah, Joseph (1748–1814) English inventor

Breuil, Henri (Édouard

Prosper) (1877–1961) French archaeologist

Briggs, Henry (1561–1630) English mathematician

Browne, Sir Thomas (1605–82) English author and physician

Brunel, Isambard Kingdom (1806–59) English engineer

Brunel, Sir Marc Isambard (1769–1849) French-born British engineer

Buffon, Georges-Louis Leclerc, Comte de (1707–88) French naturalist

Bunsen, Robert Wilhelm Eberhard (1811–99) German chemist

Burton, Sir Richard (Francis) (1821–90) English explorer, anthropologist, and translator

Calvin, Melvin (1911–97) American biochemist

Camras, Marvin (1916–95) American inventor and electrical engineer

Cannon, Annie Jump (1863–1941) American astronomer

Cantor, Georg (1845–1918) Russian-born German mathematician

Carnot, Nicolas Léonard Sadi (1796–1832) French scientist

Carrel, Alexis (1873–1944) French surgeon and biologist

Carson, Rachel (Louise) (1907–64) American marine biologist

Carver, George Washington (1864–1943) American agricultural scientist

Cauchy, Augustin Louis, Baron (1789–1857) French mathematician

Cayley, Sir George (1773–1857) British engineer, the father of British aeronautics

Chapin, Darly (1906–95) American physicist

Cuvier, Georges Léopold Chrétien Frédéric Dagobert, Baron (1769–1832) French naturalist

Dalton, John (1766–1844) English chemist, the father of modern atomic theory

Darwin, Charles (Robert) (1809–82) English natural historian and geologist, proponent of the theory of evolution by natural selection

Darwin, Erasmus (1731–1802) English physician, scientist, inventor, and poet

de Duve, Christian René (born 1917) British-born Belgian biochemist

Diesel, Rudolf (Christian Karl) (1858–1913) French-born German engineer, inventor of the diesel engine

Dunlop, John Boyd (1840–1921) Scottish inventor

Eccles, Sir John Carew (1903–97) Australian physiologist

Eckert, J. Presper, Jr. (1919–95) American computer engineer

Edison, Thomas (Alva) (1847–1931) American inventor

Eiffel, Alexandre Gustave (1832–1923) French engineer

Enders, John Franklin (1897–1985) American virologist

Euclid (*c.* 300 BC) Greek mathematician

Fermat, Pierre de (1601–65) French mathematician

Fisher, Sir Ronald Aylmer (1890–1962) English statistician and geneticist

Florey, Howard Walter, Baron (1898–1968) Australian pathologist

Fokker, Anthony Herman Gerard (1890–1939) Dutch-born American pioneer aircraft designer and pilot

Franck, James (1882–1964) German-born American physicist

Frazer, Sir James George (1854–1941) Scottish anthropologist

Frisch, Karl von (1886–1982) Austrian zoologist

Scientists and Inventors *(continued)*

Frisch, Otto Robert (1904–79)
Austrian-born British physicist

Fulton, Robert (1765–1815)
American pioneer of the steamship

Galois, Évariste (1811–32)
French mathematician

Galton, Sir Francis (1822–1911)
English scientist

Gasser, Herbert Spencer (1888–
1963) American physiologist

Geiger, Hans (Johann) Wilhelm
(1882–1945) German nuclear
physicist

Geikie, Sir Archibald
(1835–1924) Scottish geologist

Gerard, John (1545–1612)
English herbalist

Gorgas, William C. 1854–1920)
American physician, fought yellow fever in Panama Canal Zone

Graham, Thomas (1805–69)
Scottish physical chemist

Haller, Albrecht von (1708–77)
Swiss anatomist and physiologist

Halley, Edmond (1656–1742)
English astronomer and mathematician

Harvey, William (1578–1657)
English discoverer of the mecha-
nism of blood circulation and
physician to James I and Charles I

Hevesy, George Charles de
(1885–1966) Hungarian-born
radiochemist

Holmes, Arthur (1890–1965)
English geologist and geophysicist

Hooker, Sir Joseph Dalton
(1817–1911) English botanist
and pioneer in plant geography

Hubble, Edwin Powell (1889–
1953) American astronomer

Hunter, John (1728–93) Scottish
anatomist

Hutton, James (1726–97) Scottish
geologist

Huxley, Sir Andrew Fielding

(born 1917) English physiologist
and grandson of Thomas Henry
Huxley

Huxley, Sir Julian (1887–1975)
English biologist and grandson of
Thomas Henry Huxley

Huxley, Thomas Henry
(1825–95) English biologist

Jacobi, Karl Gustav Jacob (1804–
51) German mathematician

Jenner, Edward (1749–1823)
English physician, the pioneer of
vaccination

Joliot, Jean-Frédéric (1900–58)
French nuclear physicist

Kekulé, Friedrich August (full
name Friedrich August Kekulé
von Stradonitz) (1829–96)
German chemist

**Kelvin, William Thomson, 1st
Baron** (1824–1907) British
physicist, professor of natural
philosophy at Glasgow 1846–95

Kepler, Johannes (1571–1630)
German astronomer

Kinsey, Alfred Charles (1894–
1956) American zoologist and
sex researcher

Landau, Lev (Davidovich)
(1908–68) Russian-born Soviet
theoretical physicist

Leakey, Louis (Seymour Bazett)
(1903–72) Kenyan archaeologist
and anthropologist

Leakey, Mary (Douglas Nicol)
(1913–96) British-born Kenyan
archaeologist and anthropologist

Leakey, Richard (born 1944)
Kenyan paleoanthropologist

Liebig, Justus von, Baron
(1803–73) German chemist and
teacher

Lister, Joseph, 1st Baron
(1827–1912) English surgeon,
inventor of antiseptic techniques
in surgery

Lorenz, Konrad (Zacharias)
(1903–89) Austrian zoologist

Lovell, Sir (Alfred Charles) Bernard (born 1913) English astronomer and physicist, and pioneer of radio astronomy

Lowell, Percival (1855–1916) American astronomer

Manson, Sir Patrick (1844–1922) Scottish physician, pioneer of tropical medicine

Mendel, Gregor Johann (1822–84) Moravian monk, the father of genetics

Mesmer, Franz Anton (1734–1815) Austrian physician

Morgan, Thomas Hunt (1866–1945) American zoologist and geneticism

Morley, Edward Williams (1838–1923) American chemist

Muller, Hermann Joseph (1890–1967) American geneticist

Müller, Johannes Peter (1801–58) German anatomist and zoologist

Müller, Paul Hermann (1899–1965) Swiss chemist

Napier, John (1550–1617) Scottish mathematician

Nernst, Hermann Walther (1864–1941) German physical chemist

Newton, Sir Isaac (1642–1727) English mathematician and physicist

Pappus (known as Pappus of Alexandria) (*fl. c.* 300–350 AD) Greek mathematician

Pascal, Blaise (1623–62) French mathematician, physicist, and religious philosopher

Pavlov, Ivan (Petrovich) (1849–1936) Russian physiologist

Perkin, Sir William Henry (1838–1907) English chemist and pioneer of the synthetic organic chemical industry

Perrin, Jean Baptiste (1870–1942) French physical chemist

Petrie, Sir (William Matthew) Flinders (1853–1942) English archaeologist and Egyptologist

Piaget, Jean (1896–1980) Swiss psychologist

Planck, Max (Karl Ernst Ludwig) (1858–1947) German theoretical physicist, who founded the quantum theory

Proust, Joseph Louis (1754–1826) French analytical chemist

Ramsay, Sir William (1852–1916) Scottish chemist, discoverer of the noble gases

Rennie, John (1761–1821) Scottish civil engineer

Reuter, Paul Julius, Baron von (born Israel Beer Josephat) (1816–99) German pioneer of telegraphy and news reporting

Rogers, Carl (1902–87) American psychotherapist

Sanger, Frederick (born 1918) English biochemist

Savery, Thomas (known as "Captain Savery") (*c.* 1650–1715) English engineer, constructor of the first practical steam engine

Singer, Isaac Merrit (1811–75) American inventor

Sloane, Sir Hans (1660–1753) English physician and naturalist

Sperry, Roger W. (1913–94) American neurobiologist

Struve, Otto (1897–1963) Russian-born American astronomer

Talbot, (William Henry) Fox (1800–77) English pioneer of photography

Teller, Edward (born 1908) Hungarian-born American physicist

Thales (*c.* 624–*c.* 545 BC) Greek philosopher, mathematician, and astronomer

Townes, Charles Hard (born 1915) American physicist

Turing, Alan (Mathison) (1912–54) English mathematician

Wallis, Sir Barnes Neville (1887–1979) English inventor

Walton, Ernest Thomas Sinton (1903–95) Irish physicist

Watson, James Dewey (born 1928) American biologist

Scientists and Inventors *(continued)*

Watson, John Broadus
(1878–1958) American psychologist, founder of the school of behaviorism

Werner, Abraham Gottlob
(1749–1817) German geologist

Werner, Alfred (1866–1919) French-born Swiss chemist, founder of coordination chemistry

Wiener, Norbert (1894–1964) American mathematician

Wigner, Eugene (1902–95) American nuclear physicist

Wilson, Charles Thomson Rees (1869–1959) Scottish physicist

Wilson, Edward Osborne (born 1929) American social biologist

Wilson, John Tuzo (1908–93) Canadian geophysicist

Wöhler, Friedrich (1800–82) German chemist

Wright, Orville (1871–1948) and **Wilbur** (1867–1912) American aviation pioneers

Wright, Sewall (1889–1988) American geneticist

Yeager, Charles E(lwood) ("Chuck") (born 1923) American pilot

7 *letters*

Addison, Thomas (1793–1860) English physician

Agassiz, Jean Louis Rodolphe (1807–73) Swiss-born zoologist, geologist, and paleontologist

Alvarez, Luis Walter (1911–88) American physicist

Andrews, Thomas (1813–85) Irish physical chemist

Audubon, John James (1785–1851) American naturalist and artist

Babbage, Charles (1791–1871) English mathematician, inventor, and pioneer of machine computing

Babbitt, Milton (Byron) (born 1916) American composer and mathematician

Banneker, Benjamin (1731–1806) American inventor, mathematician, and astronomer

Banting, Sir Frederick Grant (1891–1941) Canadian physiologist and surgeon

Bardeen, John (1908–91) American inventor

Barnard, Christiaan Neethling (born 1922) South African surgeon

Bateson, William (1861–1926) English geneticist and coiner of the term genetics in its current sense

Behring, Emil Adolf von (1854–1917) German bacteriologist and one of the founders of immunology

Bergius, Friedrich Karl Rudolf (1884–1949) German industrial chemist

Bernard, Claude (1813–78) French physiologist

Bethune, Henry Norman (1890–1939) Canadian surgeon

Blériot, Louis (1872–1936) French aviation pioneer

Bradley, James (1693–1762) English astronomer

Brassey, Thomas (1805–70) English engineer and railroad contractor

Brattain, Walter (1902–87) American inventor

Buchner, Eduard (1860–1917) German organic chemist

Burbank, Luther (1849–1926) American naturalist and plant breeder

Cassini, Giovanni Domenico (1625–1712) Italian-born French astronomer

Celsius, Anders (1701–44) Swedish astronomer, best known for his thermometer scale

Chanute, Octave (1832–1910)
French-born American aviation
pioneer

Charcot, Jean-Martin (1825–93)
French neurologist

Cochran, Jacqueline (1910–80)
American aviator

Compton, Arthur Holly
(1892–1962) American physicist

Coulomb, Charles-Augustin de
(1736–1806) French military
engineer

Crookes, Sir William
(1832–1919) English physicist
and chemist

Curtiss, Glenn (Hammond)
(1878–1930) American air pioneer and aircraft designer

Cushing, Harvey Williams
(1969–1939) American surgeon

Daimler, Gottlieb (1834–1900)
German engineer and motor
manufacturer

Dawkins, Richard (born 1941)
English biologist

de Vries, Hugo (1848–1935)
Dutch plant physiologist and
geneticist

Doppler, Johann Christian
(1803–53) Austrian physicist

Earhart, Amelia (1898–1937)
American aviator

Eastman, George (1854–1932)
American inventor and manufacturer of photographic equipment

Ehrlich, Paul (1854–1915)
German medical scientist, one of
the founders of modern
immunology

Eijkman, Christiaan
(1858–1930) Dutch physician

Erikson, Erik (1902–94)
American psychoanalyst

Eysenck, Hans Jürgen (1916–97)
German-born British psychologist

Faraday, Michael (1791–1867)
English physicist and chemist

Fechner, Gustav Theodor
(1801–87) German physicist and
psychologist

Ferrari, Enzo (1898–1988) Italian
car designer and manufacturer

Feynman, Richard Phillips
(1918–88) American theoretical
physicist

Fischer, Emil Hermann (1852–
1919) German organic chemist

Fischer, Hans (1881–1945)
German organic chemist

Fleming, Sir Alexander (1881–
1955) Scottish bacteriologist

Fleming, Sir John Ambrose
(1849–1945) English electrical
engineer

Fourier, Jean Baptiste Joseph
(1768–1830) French mathematician

Fresnel, Augustin Jean
(1788–1827) French physicist
and civil engineer

Gagarin, Yuri (Alekseevich)
(1934–68) Russian cosmonaut

Galilei, Galileo (1564–1642)
Italian physicist

Galvani, Luigi (1737–98) Italian
anatomist

Gatling, Richard Jordan
(1818–1903) American inventor

Germain, Sophie (1776–1831)
French mathematician

Gilbert, William (1544–1603)
English physician and physicist

Glashow, Sheldon Lee (born
1932) American theoretical
physicist

Goddard, Robert Hutchings
(1882–1945) American physicist

Goodall, Jane (born 1934) English
zoologist

Gresley, Sir (Herbert) Nigel
(1876–1941) British railroad
engineer

Haeckel, Ernst Heinrich
(1834–1919) German biologist
and philosopher

**Haldane, J(ohn) B(urdon)
S(anderson)** (1892–1964)
Scottish mathematical biologist

Hawking, Stephen William (born
1942) English theoretical physicist

Scientists and Inventors *(continued)*

Haworth, Sir Walter Norman
(1883–1950) English organic
chemist

Helmont, Johannes Baptista van
(1577–1644) Belgian chemist
and physician

Hilbert, David (1862–1943)
German mathematician

Hodgkin, Sir Alan Lloyd (born
1914) English physiologist

Hodgkin, Dorothy (Crowfoot)
(1910–94) British chemist

Hopkins, Sir Frederick Gowland
(1861–1947) English biochemist,
considered the father of British
biochemistry

Huggins, Sir William
(1824–1910) British astronomer

Huygens, Christiaan (1629–95)
Dutch physicist, mathematician,
and astronomer

Hypatia (*c.* 370–415) Greek
philosopher, astronomer, and
mathematician

Johnson, Amy (1903–41) English
aviator

Jussieu, Antoine Laurent de
(1748–1836) French botanist

Kendall, Edward Calvin
(1886–1972) American bio-
chemist

Lamarck, Jean Baptiste de
(1744–1829) French naturalist,
an early proponent of organic
evolution

Langley, Samuel Pierpont
(1834–1906) American
astronomer and aviation pioneer

**Laplace, Pierre Simon, Marquis
de** (1749–1827) French applied
mathematician and theoretical
physicist

Lablanc, Nicolas (1742–1806)
French surgeon and chemist

Leibniz, Gottfried Wilhelm
(1646–1716) German rationalist
philosopher, mathematician, and
logician

Linacre, Thomas (*c.* 1460–1524)
English physician and classical
scholar

Lockyer, Sir (Joseph) Norman
(1836–1920) English astronomer

Lorentz, Hendrik Antoon (1853–
1928) Dutch theoretical physicist

Lysenko, Trofim Denisovich
(1898–1976) Soviet biologist and
geneticist

Macleod, John James Rickard
(1876–1935) Scottish physiologist

Marconi, Guglielmo (1874–1937)
Italian electrical engineer, the
father of radio

Mauchly, John W. (1908–80)
American computer engineer

Maxwell, James Clerk (1831–79)
Scottish physicist

Medawar, Sir Peter (Brian)
(1915–87) English immunologist
and author

Meitner, Lise (1878–1968)
Austrian-born Swedish physicist

Messier, Charles (1730–1817)
French astronomer

**Moissan, Ferdinand Frédéric
Henri** (1852–1907) French
chemist

Moseley, Henry Gwyn Jeffreys
(1887–1915) English physicist

Nasmyth, James (1808–90)
British engineer

Needham, Joseph (1900–95)
English scientist and historian

Neumann, John von (1903–57)
Hungarian-born American mathematician and computer pioneer

Noether, Emmy (1882–1935)
German mathematician

Oersted, Hans Christian
(1777–1851) Danish physicist,
discoverer of the magnetic effect
of an electric current

Ostwald, Friedrich Wilhelm
(1853–1932) German physical
chemist

Parsons, Sir Charles (Algernon) (1854–1931) British engineer, scientist, and manufacturer

Pasteur, Louis (1822–95) French chemist and bacteriologist

Pauling, Linus Carl (1901–94) American chemist

Pearson, Karl (1857–1936) English mathematician, the principal founder of 20th-century statistics

Perthes, Jacques Boucher de See BOUCHER DE PERTHES

Poisson, Siméon-Denis (1781–1840) French mathematical physicist

Porsche, Ferdinand (1875–1952) Austrian car designer

Prandtl, Ludwig (1875–1953) German physicist

Ptolemy (2nd century) Greek astronomer and geographer

Réaumur, René Antoine Ferchault de (1683–1757) French scientist

Renault, Louis (1877–1944) French engineer and motor manufacturer

Richter, Charles Francis (1900–85) American geologist

Riemann, (Georg Friedrich) Bernhard (1826–66) German mathematician

Röntgen, Wilhelm Conrad (1845–1923) German physicist, the discoverer of X-rays

Russell, Bertrand (Arthur William), 3rd Earl Russell (1872–1970) British philosopher, mathematician, and social reformer

Russell, Henry Norris (1877–1957) American astronomer

Scheele, Carl Wilhelm (1742–86) Swedish chemist

Schlick, Moritz (1882–1936) German philosopher and physicist

Schwann, Theodor Ambrose Hubert (1810–82) German physiologist

Seaborg, Glenn (Theodore) (born 1912) American nuclear chemist

Shannon, Claude Elwood (born 1916) American engineer

Shapley, Harlow (1885–1972) American astronomer

Siemens, Ernst Werner von (1816–92) German electrical engineer

Simpson, Sir James Young (1811–71) Scottish surgeon and obstetrician

Skinner, B(urrhus) F(rederic) (1904–90) American psychologist

Sopwith, Sir Thomas (Octave Murdoch) (1888–1989) English aircraft designer

Stanier, Sir William (Arthur) (1876–1965) English railroad engineer

Steller, Georg Wilhelm (1709–46) German naturalist and geographer

Stibitz, George R. (1904–95) American computer engineer

Szilard, Leo (1898–1964) Hungarian-born American physicist and molecular biologist

Telford, Thomas (1757–1834) Scottish civil engineer

Thomson, Sir Joseph John (1856–1940) English physicist, discoverer of the electron

Thomson, Sir William See KELVIN

Tompion, Thomas (c. 1639–1713) English clock and watchmaker

Tyndall, John (1820–93) Irish physicist

Vavilov, Nikolai (Ivanovich) (1887–c. 1943) Soviet plant geneticist

Virchow, Rudolf Karl (1821–1902) German physician and pathologist, founder of cellular pathology

Waksman, Selman Abraham (1888–1973) Russian-born American microbiologist

Scientists and Inventors (continued)

Wallace, Alfred Russel
(1823–1913) English naturalist

Warburg, Otto Heinrich
(1883–1970) German biochemist

Wegener, Alfred Lothar
(1880–1930) German meteorologist and geologist

Wheeler, John Archibald (born 1911) American theoretical physicist

Whitney, Eli (1765–1825) American inventor

Whittle, Sir Frank (1907–96) English aeronautical engineer, test pilot, and inventor of the jet aircraft engine

Wilkins, Maurice Hugh Frederick (born 1916) New Zealand-born British biochemist and molecular biologist

Windaus, Adolf (1876–1959) German organic chemist

Woolley, Sir (Charles) Leonard (1880–1960) English archaeologist

8 letters

Alembert, Jean le Rond d' (1717–83) French mathematician, physicist, and philosopher

Anderson, Carl David (1905–91) American physicist

Anderson, Elizabeth Garrett (1836–1917) English physician

Anderson, Philip Warren (1923–96) American physicist

Ångström, Anders Jonas (1814–74) Swedish physicist and astronomer

Appleton, Sir Edward Victor (1894–1965) English physicist

Avogadro, Amedeo (1776–1856) Italian chemist and physicist

Bakewell, Robert (1725–95) English pioneer in scientific methods of livestock breeding and husbandry

Barnardo, Thomas John (1845–1905) Irish-born doctor and philanthropist

Beckmann, Ernst Otto (1853–1923) German chemist

Bessemer, Sir Henry (1813–98) English engineer and inventor

Birdseye, Clarence (1886–1956) American businessman and inventor

Bjerknes, Vilhelm Frimann Koren (1862–1951) Norwegian geophysicist and meteorologist

Blackett, Patrick Maynard Stuart, Baron (1897–1974) English physicist

Brewster, Sir David (1781–1868) Scottish physicist

Bridgman, Percy Williams (1882–1961) American physicist

Brindley, James (1716–72) pioneer British canal builder

Brisbane, Sir Thomas Makdougall (1773–1860) Scottish soldier and astronomer

Buckland, William (1784–1856) English geologist

Burbidge, Margaret (born 1922) British astronomer

Candolle, Augustin Pyrame de (1778–1841) Swiss botanist

Cerenkov See CHERENKOV

Chadwick, Sir James (1891–1974) English physicist

Chauliac, Guy de (c. 1300–68) French physician

Cherwell, Frederick Lindemann, 1st Viscount (1886–1957) German-born British physicist

Clausius, Rudolf (1822–88) German physicist, one of the founders of modern thermodynamics

Cousteau, Jacques-Yves (1910–97) French oceanographer and film director

Crawford, Osbert Guy Stanhope (1886–1957) British archaeologist

Crompton, Samuel (1753–1827)
English inventor

Culpeper, Nicholas (1616–54)
English herbalist

Daguerre, Louis-Jacques-Mandé
(1789–1851) French physicist,
painter, and inventor of the first
practical photographic process

Davisson, Clinton Joseph
(1881–1958) American physicist

Dedekind, Richard (1831–1916)
German mathematician

De Forest, Lee (1873–1961)
American physicist and electrical
engineer

Durkheim, Émile (1858–1917)
French sociologist

Einstein, Albert (1879–1955)
German-born American theoretical physicist, founder of the theory of relativity, often regarded as
the greatest scientist of the 20th
century

Epicurus (341–270 BC) Greek
philosopher and scientist

Ericsson, John (1803–89) Swedish
engineer

Erlanger, Joseph (1874–1965)
American physiologist

Ferranti, Sebastian Ziani de
(1864–1930) English electrical
engineer

Foucault, Jean Bernard Léon
(1819–68) French physicist

Franklin, Benjamin (1706–90)
American statesman, inventor,
and scientist

Franklin, Rosalind Elsie
(1920–58) English physical
chemist and molecular biologist

Gassendi, Pierre (1592–1655)
French astronomer and philosopher

Gell-Mann, Murray (born 1929)
American theoretical physicist

Goethals, George W. (1858–1928)
American engineer, built Panama
Canal

Goldmark, Peter Carl (1906–77)
Hungarian-born American inventor and engineer

Goodyear, Charles (1800–60)
American inventor

Grimaldi, Francesco Maria
(1618–63) Italian Jesuit physicist
and astronomer, discoverer of the
diffraction of light

Guericke, Otto von (1602–86)
German engineer and physicist

Hamilton, Sir William Rowan
(1806–65) Irish mathematician
and theoretical physicist

Herschel, Caroline Lucretia
(1750–1848) German-born
British astronomer

**Herschel, Sir (Frederick)
William** (1738–1822) German-
born British astronomer, the
father of stellar astronomy

**Herschel, Sir John (Frederick
William)** (1792–1871) British
astronomer and physicist, son of
William Herschel

**Humboldt, Friedrich Heinrich
Alexander, Baron von**
(1769–1859) German explorer
and scientist

Ipatieff, Vladimir Nikolaievich
(1867–1952) Russian-born
American chemist

Kennelly, Arthur Edwin
(1861–1939) American electrical
engineer

Klaproth, Martin Heinrich
(1743–1817) German chemist,
one of the founders of analytical
chemistry

**Lagrange, Joseph Louis, Comte
de** (1736–1813) Italian-born
French mathematician

Langmuir, Irving (1881–1957)
American chemist and physicist

Lawrence, Ernest Orlando
(1901–58) American physicist

Linnaeus, Carolus (Latinized
name of Carl von Linné)
(1707–78) Swedish botanist,
founder of modern systematic
botany and zoology

Lippmann, Gabriel Jonas
(1845–1921) French physicist

Lovelace, Countess of (title of

Scientists and Inventors *(continued)*

Augusta Ada King *née* Byron)
(1815–52) English mathematician

Lovelock, James (Ephraim)
(born 1919) English scientist

Malpighi, Marcello (*c.* 1628–94)
Italian microscopist

Mercator, Gerardus (Latinized
name of Gerhard Kremer)
(1512–94) Flemish geographer
and cartographer, resident in
Germany from 1552

Mayerhof, Otto Fritz (1884–
1951) German-born American
biochemist

Millikan, Robert Andrews
(1868–1953) American physicist

Mitchell, R(eginald) J(oseph)
1895–1937) English aeronautical
engineer

Mosander, Carl Gustaf
(1797–1858) Swedish chemist

Newcomen, Thomas (1663–1729)
English engineer, developer of
the first practical steam engine

**Newlands, John Alexander
Reina** (1837–98) English industrial chemist

Nuffield, 1st Viscount (title of
William Richard Morris)
(1877–1963) British motor manufacturer and philanthropist

Playfair, John (1748–1819)
Scottish mathematician and geologist

Plunkett, Roy J. (1922–94)
American chemist and inventor
of Teflon (*trademark*)

Poincaré, Jules-Henri
(1854–1912) French mathematician and philosopher of science

**Rayleigh, John William Strutt,
3rd Baron** (1842–1919) English
physicist

Sakharov, Andrei (Dmitrievich)
(1921–89) Russian nuclear physicist

Sedgwick, Adam (1785–1873)
English geologist

Shockley, William (Bradford)
(1910–89) American physicist

Sikorsky, Igor (Ivanovich)
(1889–1972) Russian-born
American aircraft designer

Sinclair, Sir Clive (Marles)
(born 1940) English electronics
engineer and entrepreneur

Starling, Ernest Henry
(1866–1927) English physiologist

Stirling, James (1692–1770)
Scottish mathematician

Stirling, Robert (1790–1878)
Scottish engineer and
Presbyterian minister

Sydenham, Thomas (*c.* 1624–89)
English physician

Tombaugh, Clyde William
(1906–97) American astronomer

Van Allen, James Alfred (born
1914) American physicist

Vesalius, Andreas (1514–64)
Flemish anatomist, the founder
of modern anatomy

**von Braun, Wernher Magnus
Maximilian** See BRAUN

Weinberg, Steven (born 1933)
American theoretical physicist

**Weismann, August Friedrich
Leopold** (1834–1914) German
biologist, one of the founders of
modern genetics

Welsbach, Carl Auer, Baron von
See AUER

Woodward, Robert Burns (1917–
79) American organic chemist

**Zeppelin, Ferdinand (Adolf
August Heinrich), Count von**
(1838–1917) German aviation
pioneer

Zworykin, Vladimir (Kuzmich)
(1889–1982) Russian-born
American physicist and television
pioneer

9 letters

Anthemius (known as Anthemius
of Tralles) (6th century AD)

Greek mathematician, engineer, and artist

Arbuthnot, John (1667–1735) Scottish physician and writer

Arkwright, Sir Richard (1732–92) English inventor and industrialist

Armstrong, Edwin Howard (1890–1954) American electrical engineer

Armstrong, Neil (Alden) (born 1930) American astronaut

Arrhenius, Svante August (1859–1927) Swedish chemist

Atanasoff, John V. (1903–95) American physicist and computer engineer

Becquerel, Antoine-Henri (1852–1908) French physicist

Bernoulli, Daniel (1700–82) Swiss mathematician

Bernoulli, Jacques (1654–1705) Swiss mathematician

Bernoulli, Jean (1667–1748) Swiss mathematician

Bernoulli, Nicolas (1695–1726) Swiss mathematician

Berzelius, Jöns Jakob (1779–1848) Swedish analytical chemist

Blanchard, Jean Pierre François (1753–1809) French balloonist

Boltzmann, Ludwig (1844–1906) Austrian physicist

Bronowski, Jacob (1908–74) Polish-born British scientist, writer, and broadcaster

Carothers, Wallace Hume (1896–1937) American industrial chemist

Cavendish, Henry (1731–1810) English chemist and physicist

Cherenkov, Pavel (Alekseevich) (also Cerenkov) (1904–90) Soviet physicist

Crockcroft, Sir John Douglas (1897–1967) English physicist

Cockerell, Sir Christopher Sydney (born 1910) English engineer

Courtauld, Samuel (1876–1947) English industrialist

de Broglie, Louis-Victor, Prince (1892–1987) French physicist

de la Beche, Sir Henry Thomas (1796–1855) English geologist

Descartes, René (1596–1650) French philosopher, mathematician, and man of science, often called the father of modern philosophy

Eddington, Sir Arthur Stanley (1882–1944) English astronomer, founder of the science of astrophysics

Egas Moniz, Antonio Caetano de Abreu Freire (1874–1955) Portuguese neurologist

Einthoven, Willem (1860–1927) Dutch physiologist

Fabricius, Johann Christian (1745–1808) Danish entomologist

Fessenden, Reginald Aubrey (1866–1932) Canadian-born American physicist and radio engineer

Fibonacci, Leonardo (known as Fibonacci of Pisa) (c. 1170–c. 1250) Italian mathematician

Flamsteed, John (1646–1719) English astronomer

Gay-Lussac, Joseph Louis (1778–1850) French chemist and physicist

Heaviside, Oliver (1850–1925) English physicist and electrical engineer

Helmholtz, Hermann Ludwig Ferdinand von (1821–94) German physiologist and physicist

Heyerdahl, Thor (born 1914) Norwegian anthropologist

Hollerith, Herman (1860–1929) American engineer

Issigonis, Sir Alec (Arnold Constantine) (1906–88) Turkish-born British car designer

Kettering, Charles Franklin (1876–1958) American automobile engineer

Kirchhoff, Gustav Robert

Scientists and Inventors *(continued)*

(1824–87) German physicist, a
pioneer in spectroscopy

**Kitzinger, Sheila (Helena
Elizabeth)** (born 1929) English
childbirth educator

Lavoisier, Antoine Laurent
(1743–94) French scientist,
regarded as the father of modern
chemistry

Le Verrier, Urbain (1811–77)
French mathematician

Lindbergh, Charles (Augustus)
(1902–74) American aviator

**Lindemann, Frederick
Alexander** See CHERWELL

Mendeleev, Dmitri (Ivanovich)
(1834–1907) Russian chemist

Michelson, Albert Abraham
(1852–1931) American physicist

Minkowski, Hermann
(1864–1909) Russian-born
German mathematician

Patterson, Clair C. (1922–95)
American geochemist

Pelletier, Pierre-Joseph
(1788–1842) French chemist

Pickering, William Hayward
(born 1910) New Zealand-born
American engineer

Priestley, Joseph (1733–1804)
English scientist and theologian

**Ramanujan, Srinivasa
Aaiyangar** (1887–1920) Indian
mathematician

Shoemaker, Eugene (1928–97)
American astronomer, discovered
comets

Steinmetz, Charles P. (1865–
1923) German-born American
electrical engineer

Tinbergen, Nikolaas (1907–88)
Dutch zoologist

Verdon Roe, Sir Edwin Alliott
See ROE

Vitruvius (full name Marcus
Vitruvius Pollio) *(fl.* 1st century
BC) Roman architect and military
engineer

Whitehead, A(lfred) N(orth)
(1861–1947) English philosopher
and mathematician

Wollaston, William Hyde
(1766–1828) English chemist
and physicist

Zsigmondy, Richard Adolph
(1865–1929) Austrian-born
German chemist

10 letters

Apollonius (known as Apollonius
of Perga) *(c.* 261–*c.* 190 BC)
Greek mathematician

Archimedes *(c.* 287–*c.* 212 BC)
Greek mathematician

Aryabhata I (476–*c.* 550) Indian
astronomer and mathematician

Blumenbach, Johann Friedrich
(1752–1840) German physiologist and anatomist

Cannizzaro, Stanislao
(1826–1910) Italian chemist

Cartwright, Edmund
(1743–1823) English engineer,
inventor of the power loom

Churchward, George Jackson
(1857–1933) English railroad
engineer

Copernicus, Nicolaus (Latinized
name of Mikołaj Kopérnik)
(1473–1543) Polish astronomer

Democritus *(c.* 460–*c.* 370 BC)
Greek philosopher and scientist

Diophantus *(fl. prob. c.* 250 AD)
Greek mathematician

Du Vigneaud, Vincent (1901–78)
American biochemist

Empedocles *(c.* 493–*c.* 433 BC)
Greek philosopher, born in Sicily

Fahrenheit, Gabriel Daniel
(1686–1736) German physicist

Farnsworth, Philo T. (1906–71)
American inventor, key contribu-
tor to invention of television

FitzGerald, George Francis
(1851–1901) Irish physicist

Fraunhofer, Joseph von

(1787–1826) German optician
and pioneer in spectroscopy

Hargreaves, James (1720–78)
English inventor

Heisenberg, Werner Karl (1901–
76) German mathematical physicist and philosopher, who developed a system of quantum mechanics based on matrix algebra

Herophilus (4th–3rd centuries BC)
Greek anatomist, regarded as the
father of human anatomy

Hipparchus (*c.* 170–after 126 BC)
Greek astronomer and geographer, working in Rhodes

Ingenhousz, Jan (1730–99) Dutch
scientist

Lilienthal, Otto (1848–96)
German pioneer in the design
and flying of gliders

Malinowski, Bronisław
(1884–1942) Polish anthropologist

Mandelbrot, Benoit (born 1924)
Polish-born French mathematician

McClintock, Barbara (1902–92)
American geneticist

Paracelsus (born Theophrastus
Phillipus Aureolus Bombastus
von Hohenheim) (*c.* 1493–1541)
Swiss physician

**Rutherford, Sir Ernest, 1st
Baron Rutherford of Nelson**
(1871–1937) New Zealand
physicist

Schliemann, Heinrich (1822–90)
German archaeologist

Semmelweis, Ignaz Philipp
(born Ignác Fülöp Semmelweis)
(1818–65) Hungarian obstetrician who spent most of his working life in Vienna

Stephenson, George (1781–1848)
English engineer, the father of
railroads

Swammerdam, Jan (1637–80)
Dutch naturalist and microscopist

Swedenborg, Emanuel
(1688–1772) Swedish scientist,

philosopher, and mystic

**Tereshkova, Valentina
(Vladimirovna)** (born 1937)
Russian cosmonaut

Torricelli, Evangelista (1608–47)
Italian mathematician and physicist

Tradescant, John (1570–1638)
English botanist and horticulturalist

Tycho Brahe See BRAHE

Van de Graaf, Robert Jemison
(1901–67) American physicist

von Neumann See NEUMANN

**Watson-Watt, Sir Robert
Alexander** (1892–1973)
Scottish physicist

Wheatstone, Sir Charles (1802–
75) English physicist and inventor

11 letters

Aristarchus (known as Aristarchus
of Samos) (3rd century BC)
Greek astronomer

Bell Burnell, (Susan) Jocelyn
(born 1943) British astronomer

Bettelheim, Bruno (1903–90)
Austrian-American psychoanalyst

Chamberlain, Owen (born 1920)
American physicist

de Havilland, Sir Geoffrey
(1882–1965) English aircraft
designer and manufacturer

Goldschmidt, Victor Moritz
(1888–1947) Swiss-born
Norwegian chemist, the founder
of modern geochemistry

Handley Page, Frederick See
PAGE

Hippocrates (*c.* 460–377 BC) the
most famous of all physicians, of
whom, paradoxically, almost
nothing is known

Krafft-Ebing, Richard von
(1840–1902) German physician
and psychologist

Landsteiner, Karl (1868–1943)
Austrian-born American physician

Leeuwenhoek, Antoni van
(1632–1723) Dutch naturalist

Scientists and Inventors *(continued)*

Lévi-Strauss, Claude (born 1908) French social anthropologist

Lobachevski, Nikolai Ivanovich (1792–1856) Russian mathematician

Montgolfier, Joseph Michel (1740–1810) and **Jacques Étienne** (1745–99) French inventors

Nightingale, Florence (1820–1910) English nurse and medical reformer

Nostradamus (Latinized name of Michel de Notredame) (1503–66) French astrologer and physician

Omar Khayyám (died 1123) Persian poet, mathematician, and astronomer

Oppenheimer, Julius Robert (1904–67) American theoretical physicist

Ramón y Cajal, Santiago (1852–1934) Spanish physician and histologist

Schrödinger, Erwin (1887–1961) Austrian theoretical physicist

Sherrington, Sir Charles Scott (1857–1952) English physiologist

Spallanzani, Lazzaro (1729–99) Italian physiologist and biologist

Tsiolkovsky, Konstantin (Eduardovich) (1857–1935) Russian aeronautical engineer

Winckelmann, Johann (Joachim) (1717–68) Prussian-born German archaeologist and art historian

12 letters

Attenborough, Sir David (Frederick) (born 1926) English naturalist and broadcaster

Eratosthenes (*c.* 275–194 BC) Greek scholar, geographer, and astronomer

Euler-Chelpin, Hans Karl August Simon von (1873–1964) German-born Swedish biochemist

Szent-Györgyi, Albert von (1893–1986) Hungarian-born American biochemist

Theophrastus (*c.* 370–*c.* 287 BC) Greek philosopher and scientist

Westinghouse, George (1846–1914) American engineer

13 letters

Chandrasekhar, Subrahmanyan (1910–95) Indian-born American astronomer

Goeppert-Mayer, Maria (1906–72) German-born American physicist

Messerschmidt, Wilhelm Emil ("Willy") (1898–1978) German aircraft designer and industrialist

Regiomontanus, Johannes (born Johannes Müller) (1436–76) German astronomer and mathematician

Vening Meinesz, Felix Andries (1887–1966) Dutch geophysicist

14 letters

Evans-Pritchard, Sir Edward (Evan) (1902–73) English anthropologist

Galileo Galilei (1564–1642) Italian astronomer and physicist, one of the founder of modern science

15 letters

Kamerlingh Onnes, Heike (1853–1926) Dutch physicist, who studied cryogenic phenomena

16 letters

Boucher de Perthes, Jacques (1788–1868) French archaeologist

17 letters

Teilhard de Chardin, Pierre (1881–1955) French Jesuit philosopher and paleontologist

Artists, Cartoonists, Designers, and Architects

3 letters

Arp, Jean (also known as Hans Arp) (1887–1966) French painter, sculptor, and poet

Fry, Roger (Eliot) (1866–1934) English art critic and painter

Lee, Stan (born 1922) American comic-book artist

Lin, Maya (born 1959) American architect

Pei, I(eoh) M(ing) (born 1917) Chinese-born American architect

Ray, Man (born Emmanuel Rudnitsky) (1890–1976) American photographer, painter, and filmmaker

Rie, Dame Lucie (1902–95) Austrian-born British potter

4 letters

Adam, Robert (1728–92) Scottish architect

Arno, Peter (1904–68) American cartoonist

Bell, Vanessa (1879–1961) English painter and designer

Boyd, Arthur (Merric Bloomfield) (born 1920) Australian painter, potter, etcher, and ceramic artist

Capa, Robert (born Andrei Friedmann) (1913–54) Hungarian-born American photographer

Capp, Al (born Alfred Gerald Caplin) (1909–79) American cartoonist

Carr, Emily (1871–1945) Canadian painter and writer

Cole, Thomas (1801–48) American painter

Cram, Ralph Adams (1863–1942) American architect

Dali, Salvador (1904–89) Spanish painter

Dior, Christian (1905–57) French fashion designer

Doré, Gustave (1832–83) French illustrator

Dufy, Raoul (1877–1953) French painter and textile designer

Erté (born Romain de Tirtoff) (1892–1990) Russian-born French fashion designer and illustrator

Gabo, Naum (born Naum Neemia Pevsner) (1890–1977) Russian-born American sculptor

Gill, (Arthur) Eric (Rowton) (1882–1940) English sculptor, engraver, and typographer

Goes, Hugo van der (*fl. c.* 1467–82) Flemish painter, born in Ghent

Goya (full name Francisco José de Goya y Lucientes) (1746–1828) Spanish painter and etcher

Gray, Harold (1894–1968) American cartoonist

Gris, Juan (born José Victoriano Gonzales) (1877–1927) Spanish painter

Hals, Frans (*c.* 1580–1666) Dutch portrait and genre painter

Head, Edith (1907–81) American fashion designer

Hine, Lewis Wickes (1874–1940) American photographer

Hood, Raymond (1881–1934) American architect

Hunt, Richard Morris (1827–95) American architect

Hunt, (William) Holman (1827–1910) English painter

Ives, James Merritt (1824–95) American lithographer

Jahn, Helmut (born 1940) German-born American architect

Judd, Donald (1928–94) American sculptor

Kahn, Albert (1869–1942) German-born American architect

Kahn, Louis I. (1901–74) Estonion-born American architect

Kane, Gil (born Eli Katz) (1926–2000) Latvian-born American comic-book artist

Artists, Cartoonists, Designers, and Architects *(continued)*

Kent, William (*c.* 1685–1748) English architect and landscape gardener

Klee, Paul (1879–1940) Swiss painter, resident in Germany from 1906

Lely, Sir Peter (Dutch name Pieter van der Faes) (1618–80) Dutch portrait painter, resident in England from 1641

Miró, Joan (1893–1983) Spanish painter

Muir, Jean (Elizabeth) (1933–95) English fashion designer

Nast, Thomas (1840–1902) American political cartoonist

Phiz (pseudonym of Hablot Knight Browne) (1815–82) English illustrator

Root, John Wellborn (1850–91) American architect

Rosa, Salvator (1615–73) Italian painter and etcher

West, Benjamin (1738–1820) American painter, resident in Britain from 1763

Wood, Grant (1891–1942) American painter

Wren, Sir Christopher (1632–1723) English architect

5 letters

Aalto, (Hugo) Alvar (Henrik) (1898–1976) Finnish architect and furniture designer

Adams, Ansel (Easton) (1902–84) American photographer

Adams, Scott (born 1957) American cartoonist

Andre, Carl (born 1935) American minimalist sculptor

Appel, Karel (born 1921) Dutch painter, sculptor, and graphic artist

Arbus, Diane (1923–71) American photographer

Atget, Eugène (1856–1927) French photographer

Avery, Tex (1908–80) American cartoon animator

Bacon, Francis (1909–92) Irish painter

Bacon, Henry (1866–1924) American architect

Bakst, Léon (born Lev Samuilovich Rozenberg) (1866–1924) Russian painter and designer

Beuys, Joseph (1921–86) German artist

Blake, Peter (born 1932) English painter

Blake, William (1757–1827) English artist and poet

Blass, Bill (William Ralph) (born 1922) American fashion designer

Block, Herb (Herblock) (born 1909) American cartoonist

Bosch, Hieronymus (*c.* 1450–1516) Dutch painter

Booth, George (born 1926) American cartoonist

Brady, Mathew (1823–96) American Civil War photographer

Brown, Lancelot (known as Capability Brown) (1716–83) English landscape gardener

Burra, Edward (1905–76) English painter

Carrà, Carlo (1881–1966) Italian painter

Corot, (Jean-Baptiste) Camille (1796–1875) French landscape painter

Costa, Lúcio (1902–63) French-born Brazilian architect, town planner, and architectural historian

Crane, Roy (1901–77) American cartoonist

Crome, John (1768–1821) English painter

Curry, John Steuart (1897–1946) American painter

David, Jacques-Louis (1748–1825) French painter

Davis, Jim (born 1945) American cartoonist

Degas, (Hilaire Germain) Edgar (1834–1917) French painter and sculptor

Denis, Maurice (1870–1943) French painter, designer, and art theorist

Dürer, Albrecht (1471–1528) German painter and engraver

Ensor, James (Sydney), Baron (1860–1949) Belgian painter and engraver

Ernst, Max (1891–1976) German artist

Freud, Lucian (born 1922) German-born British painter, grandson of Sigmund Freud

Frink, Dame Elisabeth (1930–93) English sculptor and graphic artist

Gaudí, Antonio (full surname Gaudí y Cornet) (1853–1926) Spanish architect

Gehry, Frank (born 1929) American architect

Gibbs, James (1682–1754) Scottish architect

Gorky, Arshile (1904–48) Turkish-born American painter

Gould, John (1804–81) English painter, illustrator, and ornithologist

Grant, Duncan (James Corrow) (1885–1978) Scottish painter and designer

Greco, El See EL GRECO

Grosz, George (1893–1959) German painter and draftsman

Hadid, Zaha (born 1950) Iraqi architect

Hanna, Bill (born 1910) American cartoon animator; see also BARBERA

Henri, Robert (1865–1929) American painter

Hicks, Edward (1780–1849) American painter

Hoban, James (1762–1831) American architect

Homer, Winslow (1836–1910) American painter

Hooch, Pieter de See DE HOOCH

Horta, Victor (1861–1947) Belgian architect

Johns, Jasper (born 1930) American painter, sculptor, and printmaker

Jones, Chuck (born 1912) American cartoon animator

Jones, Inigo (1573–1652) English architect and stage designer

Kahlo, Frida (1907–54) Mexican painter

Karan, Donna (born 1948) American fashion designer

Keene, Charles Samuel (1823–91) English illustrator and caricaturist

Kelly, Walt (1913–73) American cartoonist

Klein, Anne (born Hannah Golofski) (1921–74) American fashion designer

Klein, Calvin (Richard) (born 1942) American fashion designer

Klimt, Gustav (1862–1918) Austrian painter and designer

Lange, Dorothea (1895–1965) American photographer

Léger, Fernand (1881–1955) French painter

Lippi, Filippino (*c.* 1457–1504) Italian painter, son of Fra Filippo Lippi

Lippi, Fra Filippo (*c.* 1406–69) Italian painter

Lotto, Lorenzo (*c.* 1480–1556) Italian painter

Louis, Morris (1912–62) American painter

Lowry, L(aurence) S(tephen) (1887–1976) English painter

Manet, Édouard (1832–83) French painter

Marin, John (1870–1953) American painter

Marsh, Reginald (1898–1954) American painter

McKim, Charles Follen (1847–1909) American architect

Artists, Cartoonists, Designers, and Architects *(continued)*

McKim, Charles M. (born 1920) American architect

Meier, Richard (born 1934) American architect

Mills, Robert (1781–1855) American architect

Monet, Claude (1840–1926) French painter

Moore, Charles Willard (1925–93) American architect

Moore, Henry (Spencer) (1898–1986) English sculptor and draftsman

Moses, Anna Mary (known as Grandma Moses) (1860–1961) American painter

Mucha, Alphonse (born Alfons Maria) (1860–1939) Czech painter and designer

Munch, Edvard (1863–1944) Norwegian painter and engraver

Myron (*fl. c.* 480–440 BC) Greek sculptor

Nolan, Sir Sidney Robert (1917–93) Australian painter

Obata, Gyo (born 1923) American architect

Peale, Charles Willson (1741–1827) American painter

Peale, Rembrandt (1778–1860) American painter

Pelli, Cesar (born 1926) Argentine-born American architect

Piper, John (1903–92) English painter and decorative designer

Pope, John Russell (1874–1937) American architect

Quant, Mary (born 1934) English fashion designer

Redon, Odilon (1840–1916) French painter and graphic artist

Riley, Bridget (born 1931) British Op art painter

Roche, Kevin (born 1922) Irish-born American architect

Rodin, Auguste (1840–1917) French sculptor

Ryder, Albert Pinkham (1847–1917) American painter

Sarto, Andrea del (born Andrea d'Agnolo) (1486–1531) Italian painter

Scott, Sir George Gilbert (1811–78) English architect

Shahn, Ben (1898–1964) American painter

Sloan, John French (1871–1951) American painter, illustrator, and etcher

Smith, David (Roland) 1906–65) American sculptor

Speer, Albert (1905–81) German architect and Nazi government official

Spode, Josiah (1755–1827) English potter

Stone, Edward Durell (1902–78) American architect

Sully, Thomas (1783–1872) English-born American painter

Tames, George (1919–94) American photographer

Tange, Kenzo (born 1913) Japanese architect

Velde, van de See VAN DE VELDE

Vinci, Leonardo da See LEONARDO DA VINCI

Watts, George Frederick (1817–1904) English painter and sculptor

White, Stanford (1853–1906) American architect

Worth, Charles Frederick (1825–95) English fashion designer, resident in France from 1845

Wyatt, James (1746–1813) English architect

Young, Chic (1901–73) American cartoonist

6 letters

Abbott, Berenice (1898–1991) American photographer

Addams, Charles (1912–88) American cartoonist

Albers, Josef (1888–1976)
German-born American artist,
designer, and teacher

Armani, Giorgio (born 1934)
Italian fashion designer

Ashley, Laura (1925–85) Welsh
fashion and textile designer

Bailey, David (born 1938) English
photographer

Beaton, Sir Cecil (Walter Hardy)
(1904–80) English photographer

Benton, Thomas Hart
(1889–1975) American painter

Bewick, Thomas (1753–1828)
English artist and wood engraver

Bodoni, Giambattista
(1740–1813) Italian printer and
type designer

**Brandt, Hermann Wilhelm
("Bill")** (1904–83) German-
born British photographer

Braque, Georges (1882–1963)
French painter

Breuer, Marcel Lajos (1902–81)
Hungarian-born American architect

Browne, Dik (1917–89) American
cartoonist

Butler, Reginald Cotterell ("Reg")
(1913–81) English sculptor

Calder, Alexander (1898–1976)
American sculptor and painter

Caniff, Milton (1907–88)
American cartoonist

Canova, Antonio (1757–1822)
Italian sculptor

Cardin, Pierre (born 1922)
French fashion designer

Caslon, William (1692–1766)
English typographer

Casson, Sir Hugh (Maxwell)
(born 1910) English architect

Catlin, George (1796–1872)
American painter

Chanel, Coco (born Gabrielle
Bonheur Chanel) (1883–1971)
French fashion designer

Chanin, Irwin (1892–1988)
American architect

Church, Frederick Edwin
(1826–1900) American painter

Clouet, Jean (c. 1485–1541)
French painter

Clouet, François (c. 1516–72)
French painter, son of Jean

Cooper, Susan Vera ("Susie")
(1902–95) English ceramic
designer and manufacturer

Copley, John Singleton
(1738–1815) American painter

Davies, Arthur Bowen
(1862–1928) American painter

Derain, André (1880–1954)
French painter

Disney, Walt (1901–66) American
cartoonist

Dobell, Sir William (1899–1970)
Australian painter

Duccio (full name Duccio di
Buoninsegna) (c. 1255–c. 1320)
Italian painter

Durand, Asher Brown (1796–
1886) American painter and
engraver

Eakins, Thomas (1844–1916)
American painter and photographer

Escher, M(aurits) C(orneille)
(1898–1972) Dutch graphic
artist

Foster, Sir Norman (Robert)
(born 1935) English architect

French, Daniel Chester
(1850–1931) American sculptor

Fuller, R(ichard) Buckminster
(1895–1983) American designer
and architect

Fuseli, Henry (born Johann
Heinrich Füssli) (1741–1825)
Swiss-born British painter and
art critic

Gilbert, Cass (1859–1934)
American architect

Giotto (full name Giotto di
Bondone) (c. 1267–1337) Italian
painter

Graham, Bruce (born 1925)
American architect

Greuze, Jean-Baptiste
(1725–1805) French painter

Guardi, Francesco (1712–93)
Italian painter

Artists, Cartoonists, Designers, and Architects *(continued)*

Hamada, Shoji (1894–1978)
Japanese potter

Hansen, Austin (1910–96)
American photographer, born in the U.S. Virgin Islands

Hassam, (Frederick) Childe (1859–1935) American painter and etcher

Hopper, Edward (1882–1967)
American realist painter

Ingres, Jean Auguste Dominique (1780–1867)
French painter

Innes, George (1825–94)
American painter

Jekyll, Gertrude (1843–1932)
English horticulturalist and garden designer

Jenney, William Le Baron (1832–1907) American architect

Kilban, B(ernard) (1935–91)
American cartoonist

Knight, Dame Laura (1877–1970) British painter

La Tour, Georges de (1593–1652)
French painter

Lauren, Ralph (born 1939)
American fashion designer

Lebrun, Charles (1619–90)
French painter, designer, and decorator

Leutze, Emanuel Gottlieb (1816–68) German-born American painter

Mabuse, Jan (Flemish name Jan Gossaert) (c. 1478–c. 1533)
Flemish painter

Man Ray See RAY

Martin, Don (1931–2000)
American cartoonist

Masson, André (1896–1987)
French painter and graphic artist

Millet, Jean (François) (1814–75) French painter

Minton, Thomas (1765–1836)
English pottery and china manufacturer

Moreau, Gustave (1826–98)
French painter

Morgan, Julia (1872–1957)
American architect

Morris, William (1834–96)
English designer, craftsman, poet, and socialist writer

Nadar See TOURNACHON

Neutra, Richard Josef (1892–1970) Austrian-born American architect

Newman, Barnett (1905–70)
American painter

Ostade, Adriaen van (1610–85)
Dutch painter and engraver

Paxton, Sir Joseph (1801–65)
English gardener and architect

Pisano, Andrea (c. 1290–c. 1348) and **Nino**, his son (died c. 1368)
Italian sculptors

Pisano, Nicola (c. 1220–c. 1278) and **Giovanni**, his son (c. 1250–c. 1314) Italian sculptors

Ramsay, Allan (1713–84) Scottish portrait painter

Renoir, (Pierre) Auguste (1841–1919) French painter

Ribera, José (*or* Jusepe) **de** (known as "Lo Spagnoletto") (c. 1591–1652) Spanish painter and etcher, resident in Italy from 1616

Rivera, Diego (1886–1957)
Mexican painter

Rogers, Sir Richard (George) (born 1933) British architect

Romney, George (1734–1802)
English portrait painter

Rothko, Mark (born Marcus Rothkovich) (1903–70) Latvian-born American painter

Rubens, Sir Peter Paul (1577–1640) Flemish painter

Ruskin, John (1819–1900) English art and social critic

Ruysch, Rachel (1664–1750)
Dutch painter

Sargent, John Singer
(1856–1925) American painter
Schulz, Charles (born 1922)
American cartoonist
Searle, Ronald (William Fordham) (born 1920) English artist
Seurat, Georges Pierre
(1859–91) French painter
Siegal, Jerry (1914–96) American cartoonist
Signac, Paul (1863–1935) French neo-impressionist painter
Sirani, Elisabetta (1638–65) Italian painter
Sisley, Alfred (1839–99) French impressionist painter, of English descent
Spence, Sir Basil (Unwin)
(1907–76) Indian-born British architect
Stella, Frank (Philip) (born 1936) American painter
Strand, Paul (1890–1976) American photographer
Stuart, Gilbert (1755–1828) American painter
Stubbs, George (1724–1806) English painter and engraver
Tanguy, Yves (1900–55) French painter
Titian (Italian name Tiziano Vecellio) (c. 1488–1576) Italian painter
Toledo, Jose Rey (1916–94) Native American painter
Turner, J(oseph) M(allord) W(illiam) (1775–1851) English painter
Upjohn, Richard (1802–78) American architect
Vasari, Giorgio (1511–74) Italian painter, architect, and biographer
Walker, (Addison) Mort(imer)
(born 1923) American cartoonist
Warhol, Andy (born Andrew Warhola) (c. 1928–87) American painter, graphic artist, and filmmaker
Weston, Edward (1886–1958) American photographer

Weyden, Rogier van der (French name Rogier de la Pasture)
(c. 1400–64) Flemish painter
Wilkie, Sir David (1785–1841) Scottish painter
Wilson, Tom (born 1931) American cartoonist
Wright, Frank Lloyd
(1869–1959) American architect
Zeuxis (fl. late 5th century BC) Greek painter, born at Heraclea in southern Italy

7 letters

Alberti, Leon Battista (1404–72) Italian architect, humanist, painter, and art critic
Allston, Washington (1779–1843) American landscape painter
Apelles (4th century BC) Greek painter
Audubon, John James
(1785–1851) American painter and ornithologist
Barbera, Joe (born 1911) American cartoon animator
Behrens, Peter (1868–1940) German architect and designer
Bellini, Gentile (c. 1429–1507) Italian artist
Bellini, Giovanni (c. 1430–1516) Italian artist
Bellini, Jacopo (c. 1400–c. 1470) Italian artist
Bellows, George Wesley
(1882–1925) American painter
Bernini, Gian Lorenzo
(1598–1680) Italian sculptor, painter, and architect
Bingham, George Caleb
(1811–79) American painter
Bonheur, Rosa (full name Maria-Rosalie Bonheur) (1822–99) French painter
Bonnard, Pierre (1867–1947) French painter and graphic artist
Borglum, Gutzon (1871–1941) American sculptor
Boucher, François (1703–70) French painter and decorative artist

Artists, Cartoonists, Designers, and Architects *(continued)*

Brouwer, Adriaen (*c.* 1605–38) Flemish painter

Bruegel, Jan (Jan Bruegel the Elder) (1568–1625) Flemish artist

Bruegel, Pieter (Bruegel the Elder) (1525–69) Flemish artist

Bruegel, Pieter (Bruegel the Younger) (?1564–?1638) Flemish artist

Burnham, Daniel Hudson (1846–1912) American architect

Cameron, Julia Margaret (1815–79) English photographer

Carrère, John Merven (1858–1911) Brazilian-born American architect

Cassatt, Mary (1844–1926) American painter

Cellini, Benvenuto (1500–71) Italian goldsmith and sculptor

Cézanne, Paul (1839–1906) French painter

Chagall, Marc (1887–1985) Russian-born French painter and graphic artist

Chirico, Giorgio de (1888–1978) Greek-born Italian painter

Courbet, Gustave (1819–77) French painter

Cranach, Lucas (known as Cranach the Elder) (1472–1553) German painter

Currier, Nathaniel (1813–88) American lithographer

Daumier, Honoré (1808–78) French painter and lithographer

da Vinci, Leonardo See LEONARDO DA VINCI

de Hooch, Pieter (also de Hoogh) (*c.* 1629–*c.* 1684) Dutch genre painter

Duchamp, Marcel (1887–1968) French-born painter, sculptor, and art theorist

El Greco (Spanish for "the Greek"; born Domenikos Theotokopoulos) (1541–1614) Cretan-born Spanish painter

Epstein, Sir Jacob (1880–1959) American-born British sculptor

Fabergé, Peter Carl (1846&1920) Russian goldsmith and jeweler, of French descent

Feiffer, Jules (born 1929) American cartoonist

Freleng, Isadore ("Fritz") (1905–95) American cartoon animator

Furness, Frank (1839–1912) American architect

Galanos, James (born 1925) American fashion designer

Gardner, Alexander (1821–82) Scottish-born American photographer

Gauguin, (Eugène Henri) Paul (1848–1903) French painter

Gibbons, Grinling (1648–1721) Dutch-born English sculptor

Gilbert, Cass (1859–1934) American architect

Goodhue, Bertram (1869–1924) American architect

Gropius, Walter (1883–1969) German-born American architect

Halprin, Lawrence (born 1916) American architect

Hamnett, Katharine (born 1952) English fashion designer

Hobbema, Meindert (1638–1709) Dutch landscape painter

Hockney, David (born 1937) English painter and draftsman

Hofmann, Hans (1880–1968) German-born American painter

Hogarth, William (1697–1764) English painter and engraver

Hokusai, Katsushika (1760–1849) Japanese painter and wood engraver

Holbein, Hans (known as Holbein the Elder) (1460–1524) German painter

Holbein, Hans (known as Holbein

the Younger) (1497–1543)
German painter

Ictinus (5th century BC) Greek
architect

Imhotep (*fl.* 27th century BC)
Egyptian architect and scholar

Jackson, William Henry
(1843–1942) American photographer

Jansens, Cornelius See JOHNSON

Johnson, Cornelius (also Jansens)
1593–*c.* 1661) English-born
Dutch portrait painter

Johnson, Philip (born 1906)
American architect

Kooning, Willem de See DE
KOONING

La Farge, John (1835–1910)
American painter

Lalique, René (1860–1945)
French jeweler

Latrobe, Benjamin Henry
(1764–1820) English-born
American architect

Le Nôtre, André (1613–1700)
French landscape gardener

Lescaze, William (1896–1969)
Swiss-born American architect

Leyster, Judith (1609–60) Dutch
painter

Lindsay, Norman Alfred William
(1879–1969) Australian artist

Lutyens, Sir Edwin (Landseer)
(1869–1944) English architect

Maillol, Aristide (1861–1944)
French sculptor

Mansart, François (1598–1666)
French architect

Martini, Simone (*c.* 1284–1344)
Italian painter

Matisse, Henri (Émile Benoît)
(1869–1954) French painter and
sculptor

Mauldin, Bill (born 1921)
American cartoonist

Maybeck, Bernard (1882–1957)
American architect

Millais, Sir John Everett
(1829–96) English painter

Montana, Bob (1920–75)
American cartoonist

Morisot, Berthe (Marie Pauline)
(1841–95) French painter

Murillo, Bartolomé Esteban (*c.*
1618–82) Spanish painter

Noguchi, Isamu (1904–88)
American sculptor

O'Keefe, Georgia (1887–1986)
American painter

Olmsted, Frederick Law
(1822–1903) American landscape architect

Orcagna (born Andrea di Cione)
(*c.* 1308–68) Italian painter,
sculptor, and architect

Palissy, Bernard (*c.* 1510–90)
French potter

Peeters, Clara (1594–*c.* 1660)
Flemish painter

Pevsner, Antoine (1886–1962)
Russian-born French sculptor
and painter

Phidias (5th century BC) Athenian
sculptor

Picasso, Pablo (1881–1973)
Spanish painter, sculptor, and
graphic artist, resident in France
from 1904)

Pollock, (Paul) Jackson
(1912–56) American painter

Poussin, Nicolas (1594–1665)
French painter

Prud'hon, Pierre-Paul
(1758–1823) French painter

Quercia, Jacopo della See DELLA
QUERCIA

Rackham, Arthur (1867–1939)
English illustrator

Raphael (Italian name Raffaello
Sanzio) (1483–1520) Italian
painter and architect

Renwick, James (1818–95)
American architect

Rouault, Georges (Henri)
(1871–1958) French painter and
engraver

Rudolph, Paul (born 1918)
American architect

Russell, Charles Marion
(1865–1926) American painter

Sargent, John Singer
(1856–1925) American painter

Artists, Cartoonists, Designers, and Architects *(continued)*

Sassoon, Vidal (born 1928) English hairstylist

Schiele, Egon (1890–1918) Austrian painter and draftsman

Sheeler, Charles (1883–1965) American painter

Shuster, Joe (1914–92) American cartoonist

Sickert, Walter Richard (1860–1942) British painter, of Danish and Anglo-Irish descent

Soutine, Chaim (1893–1943) Lithuanian-born French painter

Spencer, Sir Stanley (1891–1959) English painter

Teniers, David (known as David Teniers the Younger) (1610–90) Flemish painter

Tenniel, Sir John (1820–1914) English illustrator and cartoonist

Thomson, Tom (full name Thomas John Thomson) (1877–1917) Canadian painter

Thurber, James (1894–1961) American author and cartoonist

Tiepolo, Giovanni Battista (1696–1770) Italian painter

Tiffany, Louis Comfort (1848–1933) American glass-maker and interior decorator

Trudeau, Garry (born 1948) American cartoonist

Tussaud, Madame (neé Marie Grosholtz) (1761–1850) French founder of Madame Tussaud's waxworks, resident in Britain from 1802

Uccello, Paolo (born Paolo di Dono) (c. 1397–1475) Italian painter

Utamaro, Kitagawa (born Kitagawa Nebsuyoshi) (1753–1806) Japanese painter and print-maker

Utrillo, Maurice (1883–1955) French painter

Valadon, Suzanne (1867–1938) French painter

Van Dyck, Sir Anthony (also Vandyke) (1599–1641) Flemish painter

Van Eyck, Jan (c. 1370–1441) Flemish painter

Van Gogh, Vincent (Willem) (1853–90) Dutch painter

Venturi, Robert (Charles) (born 1925) American architect

Vermeer, Jan (1632–75) Dutch painter

Vignola, Giacomo Barozzi da (1507–73) Italian architect

Warburg, Aby (Moritz) (1866–1929) German art historian

Watteau, Jean Antoine (1684–1721) French painter, of Flemish descent

Whistler, James A. McNeill (1834–1903) American painter

Willard, Archibald MacNeal (1836–1918) American painter

Wurster, William (1895–1973) American architect

8 letters

Angelico, Fra (born Guido di Pietro, monastic name Fra Giovanni da Fiesole) (c. 1400–55) Italian painter

Annigoni, Pietro (1910–88) Italian painter

Auerbach, Frank (born 1931) German-born British painter

Beckmann, Max (1884–1950) German painter and graphic artist

Bramante, Donato (di Angelo) (1444–1514) Italian architect

Brancusi, Constantin (1876–1957) Romanian sculptor, who spent much of his working life in France

Breathed, Berkeley (born 1957) American cartoonist

Breughel See BRUEGEL

Bronzino, Agnolo (born Agnolo di

Cosimo) (1503–72) Italian
painter
Bulfinch, Charles (1763–1844)
American architect
Bunshaft, Gordon (1909–90)
American architect
Carracci, Agostino (1557–1602)
Italian painter
Carracci, Annibale (1560–1609)
Italian painter
Carracci, Ludovico (1555–1619)
Italian painter
Daubigny, Charles François
(1817–78) French landscape
painter
Delaunay, Robert (1885–1941)
French painter
del Sarto, Andrea See SARTO
Doisneau, Robert (1912–94)
French photographer
Drysdale, Sir Russell (1912–81)
British-born Australian painter
Dubuffet, Jean (1901–85) French
artist
Fabriano, Gentile da See
GENTILE DA FABRIANO
Ghiberti, Lorenzo (1378–1455)
Italian sculptor and goldsmith
Groening, Matt (born 1954)
American cartoon animator
Harrison, Peter (1716–75)
American architect
Harrison, Wallace K.
(1895–1981) American architect
Hartnell, Sir Norman (1901–79)
English fashion designer
Hastings, Thomas (1860–1929)
American architect
**Hepworth, Dame (Jocelyn)
Barbara** (1903–75) English
sculptor
Jordaens, Jacob (1593–1678)
Flemish painter
Kirchner, Ernst Ludwig
(1880–1938) German expres-
sionist painter
Kollwitz, Kathe (1867–1945)
German artist
Lachaise, Gaston (1882–1935)
American sculptor
Landseer, Sir Edwin Henry

(1802–73) English painter and
sculptor
Lawrence, Sir Thomas
(1769–1830) English painter
**Leighton, Frederic, 1st Baron
Leighton of Stretton** (1830–96)
English painter and sculptor
Lipchitz, Jacques (born Chaim
Jacob Lipchitz) (1891–1973)
Lithuanian-born French sculptor
Lorraine, Claude See CLAUDE
LORRAINE
Lysippus (4th century BC) Greek
sculptor
**Magritte, René (François
Ghislain)** (1898–1967) Belgian
painter
**Malevich, Kazimir
(Severinovich)** (1878–1935)
Russian painter and designer
Mantegna, Andrea (1431–1506)
Italian painter and engraver
Masaccio (born Tommaso
Giovanni di Simone Guidi)
(1401–28) Italian painter
Mondrian, Piet (born Pieter
Cornelis Mondriaan)
(1872–1944) Dutch painter
**Montagna, Bartolommeo
Cincani** (c. 1450–1523) Italian
painter
Niemeyer, Oscar (born 1907)
Brazilian architect
Oldfield, Bruce (born 1950)
English fashion designer
Palladio, Andrea (1508–80)
Italian architect
Paolozzi, Eduardo (Luigi) (born
1924) Scottish artist and sculp-
tor, of Italian descent
Perugino See VANNUCCI
Piranesi, Giovanni Battista
(1720–78) Italian engraver
Pissarro, Camille (1830–1903)
French painter and graphic artist
Pontormo, Jacopo da
(1494–1557) Italian painter
Reynolds, Sir Joshua (1723–92)
English painter
Robinson, Henry Peach (1830–
1901) English photographer

Artists, Cartoonists, Designers, and Architects *(continued)*

Rockwell, Norman (1894–1978) American painter and illustrator

Roebling, John Augustus (1806–69) German-born American engineer, father of Washington Augustus Roebling (1837–1926) American engineer

Rossetti, Dante Gabriel (full name Gabriel Charles Dante Rossetti) (1828–82) English painter

Rousseau, (Pierre Étienne) Théodore (1812–67) French painter

Rousseau, Henri (Julien) (known as "le Douanier," "the customs officer") (1844–1910) French painter

Ruisdael, Jacob van (also Ruysdael) (*c.* 1628–82) Dutch landscape painter

Ruysdael See RUISDAEL

Saarinen, Eero (1910–61) Finnish-born American architect

Saarinen, Eliel (1873–1950) Finnish-born American architect

Skidmore, Louis (1897–1962) American architect

Steichen, Edward Jean (born Edouard Jean Steichen) (1879–1973) Luxembourg-born American photographer

Stirling, Sir James (1926–92) English architect

Sullivan, Louis Henry (1856–1924) American architect

Trumbull, John (1756–1843) American painter

Vanbrugh, Sir John (1664–1726) English architect and dramatist

Vannucci, Pietro di Cristoforo (known as Perugino) (*c.* 1450–1523) Italian painter

Vasarely, Viktor (1908–97) Hungarian-born French painter

Veronese, Paolo (born Paolo Caliari) (*c.* 1528–88) Italian painter

Vlaminck, Maurice de (1876–1958) French painter and writer

Vuillard, (Jean) Édouard (1868–1940) French painter and graphic artist

Wedgwood, Josiah (1730–95) English potter

Whistler, James (Abbott) McNeill (1834–1903) American painter and etcher

Yamasaki, Minoru (1912–86) American architect

Zurbarán, Francisco de (1598–1664) Spanish painter

9 letters

Altdorfer, Albrecht (*c.* 1480–1538) German painter and architect

Bartholdi, Frédéric-Auguste (1834–1904) French sculptor

Beardsley, Aubrey (Vincent) (1872–98) English artist and illustrator

Belluschi, Pietro (1899–1994) Italian-born American architect

Bierstadt, Albert (1830–1902) German-born American painter

Borromini, Francesco (1599–1667) Italian architect

Caldecott, Randolph (1846–86) English graphic artist and watercolor painter

Canaletto (born Giovanni Antonio Canale) (1697–1768) Italian painter

Carpaccio, Vittore (*c.* 1455–1525) Italian painter

Claiborne, Liz (born Elisabeth Claiborne Ortenberg) Belgian-born American fashion designer

Constable, John (1776–1837) English painter

Correggio, Antonio Allegri da (born Antonio Allegri) (*c.* 1494–1534) Italian painter

Courrèges, André (born 1923)

French fashion designer

de Kooning, Willem (1904–97) Dutch-born American painter

Delacroix, (Ferdinand Victor) Eugène (1798–1863) French painter

Delaroche, (Hippolyte) Paul (1797–1856) French painter

Donatello (born Donato di Betto Bardi) (1386–1466) Italian sculptor

Du Maurier, George (Louis Palmella Busson) (1834–96) French-born British cartoonist, illustrator, and novelist

Flannagan, John Bernard (1895–1942) American sculptor

Fragonard, Jean-Honoré (1732–1806) French painter

Friedmann, Andrei See CAPA

Friedrich, Caspar David (1774–1840) German painter

Géricault, (Jean Louis André) Théodore (1791–1824) French painter

Gernreich, Rudolph ("Rudi") (1922–85) American fashion designer

Giorgione (also called Giorgio Barbarelli *or* Giorgio da Castelfranco) (*c.* 1478–1510) Italian painter

Greenaway, Catherine ("Kate") (1846–1901) English artist

Greenough, Horatio (1802–52) American sculptor

Grünewald, Mathias (born Mathis Nithardt; also called Mathis Gothardt) (*c.* 1460–1528) German painter

Guisewite, Cathy (born 1950) American cartoonist

Kandinsky, Wassily (1866–1944) Russian painter and theorist

Kauffmann, Angelica (also Kauffman) (1740–1807) Swiss painter

Leibovitz, Annie (born 1950) American photographer

McCardell, Claire (1905–58) American fashion designer

Muybridge, Eadweard (born Edward James Muggeridge) (1830–1904) English-born American photographer and motion-picture pioneer

Nicholson, Ben (1894–1982) English painter

O'Sullivan, Timothy H. (*c.* 1840–82) American photographer

Rembrandt (full name Rembrandt Harmensz van Rijn) (1606–69) Dutch painter

Remington, Frederic (1861–1901) American sculptor and painter

Sansovino, Jacopo Tatti (1486–1570) Italian sculptor and architect

Stieglitz, Alfred (1864–1946) American photographer

Vanderlyn, John (1775–1852) American painter

van Leyden, Lucas See LUCAS VAN LEYDEN

Velázquez, Diego Rodriguez de Silva y (1599–1660) Spanish painter

Vitruvius (Marcus Vitruvius Pollio) (*fl.* 1st century BC) Roman architect and military engineer

Watterson, Bill (born 1958) American cartoonist

10 letters

Anguissola, Sofonisba (*c.* 1535–1625) Italian painter

Archipenko, Aleksandr (Porfirevich) (1887–1964) Russian-born American sculptor and painter

Balenciaga, Cristóbal (1895–1972) Spanish fashion designer

Botticelli, Sandro (born Alessandro di Mariano Filipepi) (1445–1510) Italian painter

Buonarroti, Michelangelo See MICHELANGELO

Bushmiller, Ernie (1905–82) American cartoonist

Artists, Cartoonists, Designers, and Architects (continued)

Caravaggio, Michelangelo
Merisi da (c. 1571–1610) Italian
painter
Carrington, Dora (de Houghton)
(1893–1932) English painter
Cruikshank, George (1792–1878)
English painter, illustrator, and
caricaturist
Cunningham, Imogen (1883–
1976) American photographer
Giacometti, Alberto (1901–66)
Swiss sculptor and painter
Hirschfeld, Al (born 1903)
American caricaturist
Mainbocher (full name Main
Rousseau Bocher) (1891–1976)
American fashion designer
Michelozzo (full name Michelozzo
di Bartolommeo) (1396–1472)
Italian architect and sculptor
Modigliani, Amedeo (1884–
1920) Italian painter and sculp-
tor, resident in France from 1906
Moholy-Nagy, László
(1895–1946) Hungarian-born
American painter, sculptor, and
photographer
Pollaiuolo, Antonio (c. 1432–98)
and Piero (1443–96) Italian,
sculptors, painters, and engravers
Polyclitus (5th century BC) Greek
sculptor
Praxiteles (mid-4th century BC)
Athenian sculptor
Richardson, Henry Hobson
(1838–86) American architect
Rowlandson, Thomas
(1756–1827) English painter,
draftsman, and caricaturist
Sutherland, Graham (Vivian)
(1903–80) English painter
Tintoretto (born Jacopo Robusti)
(1518–94) Italian painter
Tournachon, Gaspard-Félix
(also known as Nadar)
(1820–1910) French photographer and caricaturist

van de Velde, Adriaen (1636–72)
Dutch painter
van de Velde, Esaias (c. 1591–
1630) Dutch painter
van de Velde, Henri (Clemens)
(1863–1957) Belgian architect,
designer, and teacher
van de Velde, Willem (van de
Velde the Elder) (1611–93)
Dutch painter
van de Velde, Willem (van de
Velde the Younger) (1633–1707)
Dutch painter

11 letters

Abakanowicz, Magdalena (born
1930) Polish artist and weaver
Bartolommeo, Fra (born Baccio
della Porta) (c. 1472–1517)
Italian painter
Baskerville, John (1706–75)
English printer and type designer
Bourke-White, Margaret (1906–
71) American photojournalist
Callicrates (5th century BC) Greek
architect
Chippendale, Thomas (1718–79)
English furniture maker and
designer
Della Robbia, Andrea
(1435–1525) Italian sculptor
Della Robbia, Giovanni (1469–c.
1529) Italian sculptor
Della Robbia, Girolamo
(1488–1566) Italian sculptor
Della Robbia, Luca (1400–82)
Italian sculptor
Eisenstaedt, Alfred (1898–1995)
German-born American photog-
rapher
Gentileschi, Artemisia (c. 1597–
c. 1652) Italian painter
Ghirlandaio (born Domenico di
Tommaso Bigordi) (c. 1448–94)
Italian painter
Hepplewhite, George (died 1786)
English cabinetmaker and

furniture designer

Le Corbusier (born Charles Édouard Jeanneret) (1887–1965) Swiss-born French architect and town planner

Predergast, Maurice Brazil (1859–1924) Canadian-born American painter

Thorvaldsen, Bertel (also Thorwaldsen) (c. 1770–1844) Danish neoclassical sculptor

Vigée-Lebrun, (Marie Louise) Elisabeth (1755–1842) French painter

12 letters

Brunelleschi, Filippo (born Filippo di Ser Brunellesco) (1377–1446) Italian architect

Delaunay-Terk, Sonia (1885–1979) Russian-born French painter and textile designer

della Quercia, Jacopo (c. 1374–1438) Italian sculptor

Gainsborough, Thomas (1727–88) English painter

Lichtenstein, Roy (1923–97) American painter and sculptor

Michelangelo (full name Michelangelo Buonarroti) (1475–1564) Italian sculptor, painter, architect, and poet

Parmigianino (also Parmigiano) (born Girolano Francesco Maria Mazzola) (1503–40) Italian painter

Rauschenberg, Robert (born 1925) American artist

Saint-Gaudens, Augustus (1848–1907) Irish-born American sculptor

Saint Laurent, Yves (Mathieu) (born 1936) French fashion designer

Schiaparelli, Elsa (1896–1973)

Italian-born French fashion designer

Winterhalter, Franz Xavier (1806–73) German painter

14 letters

Cartier-Bresson, Henri (born 1908) French photographer and film director

Claude Lorraine (also Lorrain) (born Claude Gellée) (1600–82) French painter

della Francesca See PIERO DELLA FRANCESCA

Gaudier-Brzeska, Henri (1891–1915) French sculptor

Lucas van Leyden (c. 1494–1533) Dutch painter and engraver

Miles van der Rohe, Ludwig (1886–1969) German-born architect and designer

15 letters

Capability Brown See BROWN, LANCELOT

Leonardo da Vinci (1452–1519) Italian painter, scientist, and engineer

Puvis de Chavannes, Pierre-Cécile (1824–98) French painter

Toulouse-Lautrec, Henri (Marie Raymond) de (1864–1901) French painter and lithographer

17 letters

Gentile de Fabriano (c. 1370–1427) Italian painter

18 letters

Jacopo della Quercia See DELLA QUERCIA

19 letters

Piero della Francesca (1416–92) Italian painter

Composers, Musicians,
Singers, and Instrument Makers

3 letters

Bax, Sir Arnold (Edward Trevor) (1833–1953) English composer

Lee, Brenda (born Brenda Mae Tarpley) (born 1944) American country singer

Ono, Yoko (born 1933) Japanese-born American musician and artist

Pop, Iggy (born James Jewell Osterberg) (born *c.* 1949) American rock musician

4 letters

Ager, Milton (1893–1979) American composer

Anka, Paul (born 1941) Canadian composer

Arne, Thomas (1710–78) English composer

Bach, Johann Sebastian (1685–1750) German composer

Baez, Joan (born 1941) American folk singer

Bart, Lionel (born 1930) English composer and lyricist

Beck (full name Beck Hansen) (born 1970) American rock musician

Berg, Alban (Maria Johannes) (1885–1935) Austrian composer

Bock, Jerry (born 1928) American composer

Bond, Carrie Jacobs (1862–1946) American composer

Bono (born Paul Hewson) (born 1960) Irish rock singer and songwriter

Brel, Jacques (1929–78) Belgian singer and composer

Byas, Don (1912–72) American jazz saxophonist

Byrd, William (1543–1623) English composer

Cage, John (Milton) (1912–92) American composer, pianist, and writer

Cahn, Sammy (1913–93) American lyricist

Cash, Johnny (born 1932) American country music singer and songwriter

Cher (born Cherilyn LaPiere Sarkisian) (born 1946) American singer and actress

Cole, Nat King (born Nathaniel Adams Coles) (1919–65) American singer and pianist

Crow, Sheryl (born 1962) American rock singer and songwriter

Dion, Celine (born 1968) Canadian pop singer

Duke, Vernon (1903–69) American composer

Ford, Tennessee Ernie (1919–91) American country singer and songwriter

Gaye, Marvin (1939–84) American soul singer and songwriter

Getz, Stan (born Stanley Gayetsky) (1927–91) American jazz saxophonist

Hart, Lorenz (1895–1943) American lyricist

Hess, Dame Myra (1890–1965) English pianist

Ives, Charles (Edward) (1874–1954) American composer

Joel, Billy (full name William Martin Joel) (born 1949) American composer and rock musician

John, Sir Elton (Hercules) (born Reginald Kenneth Dwight) (born 1947) English pop and rock singer, pianist, and composer

Kahn, Gus (1886–1941) American lyricist

Kern, Jerome (David) (1885–1945) American composer

King, B. B. (real name Riley B. King) (born 1925) American blues singer and guitarist

King, Carole (born 1942) American composer

Lind, Jenny (born Johanna Maria Lind Goldschmidt) (1820–87) Swedish soprano

Lynn, Dame Vera (born Vera Margaret Lewis) (born 1917) English singer

Monk, Thelonious (Sphere) (1917–82) American jazz pianist and composer

Orff, Carl (1895–1982) German composer

Page, Jimmy (born 1944) Irish-born English rock guitarist and songwriter

Paul, Les (born Lester Polfus) (born 1915) American guitarist and inventor of the solid-body electric guitar

Piaf, Edith (born Edith Giovanna Gassion) (1915–63) French singer

Pons, Lily (1898–1976) French operatic soprano

Prez, Josquin des See DES PREZ

Reed, Lou (full name Lewis Allan Reed) (born 1942) American rock singer, guitarist, and songwriter

Rice, Sir Tim(othy Miles Bindon) (born 1944) English lyricist and entertainer

Rich, Buddy (born Bernard Rich) (1917–87) American jazz drummer and bandleader

Rose, Fred (1898–1954) American country singer and songwriter

Ross, Diana (born 1944) American pop and soul singer

Seal (born Sealhenry Olumide Samuel) (born 1963) English pop singer and songwriter, of Brazilian and Nigerian extraction

Sims, Zoot (1925–85) American jazz saxophonist

Tate, Phyllis (1911–87) British composer

Tubb, Ernest (1914–84) American country singer and songwriter

Webb, Chick (1902–39) American bandleader

Webb, Jimmy (born 1946) American composer

Weir, Judith (born 1954) British composer

West, Dottie (1932–91) American country singer and songwriter

Wolf, Hugo (Philipp Jakob) (1860–1903) Austrian composer

Wood, Sir Henry (Joseph) (1869–1944) English conductor

5 letters

Acuff, Roy (1903–92) American country singer and songwriter

Adams, Bryan (born 1959) Canadian pop singer

Amati, Andrea (c. 1520–c. 1578) Italian violinmaker

Amati, Antonio (c. 1550–1638) Italian violinmaker

Amati, Girolamo (1551–1635) Italian violinmaker

Amati, Nicolò (1596–1684) Italian violinmaker

Arlen, Harold (1905–86) American composer

Arrau, Claudio (1903–91) Chilean pianist

Auric, Georges (1899–1983) French composer

Baker, Dame Janet (Abbott) (born 1933) English operatic mezzo-soprano

Basie, Count (born William Basie) (1904–84) American jazz pianist, organist, and bandleader

Beach, Amy (1867–1944) American composer and pianist

Berio, Luciano (born 1925) Italian composer

Berry, Chuck (born Charles Edward Berry) (born 1931) American rock singer, guitarist, and songwriter

Betts, Dickey (born Forrest Richard Betts) (born 1943) American rock guitarist

Bizet, Georges (born Alexandre César Léopold Bizet) (1838–75) French composer

Bliss, Sir Arthur (Edward Drummond) (1891–1975) English composer

Composers, Musicians, Singers, and Instrument Makers (continued)

Bloch, Ernest (1880–1959) Swiss-born American composer, of Jewish descent

Boult, Sir Adrian (Cedric) (1889–1983) English conductor

Bowie, David (born David Robert Jones) (born 1947) English rock singer, songwriter, and actor

Bream, Julian (Alexander) (born 1933) English guitarist and lute player

Brico, Antonia (1902–89) Dutch-born American conductor

Brown, James (born 1928) American soul singer and songwriter

Carey, Mariah (born 1970) American pop singer

Cline, Patsy (born Virginia Petterson Hensley) (1932–63) American country singer

Cohan, George M. (1878–1942) American composer

Cohen, Leonard (born 1934) Canadian composer

Combs, Sean ("Puffy" or "Puff Daddy") (born 1970) American hip-hop singer

Cooke, Sam (born Sam Cook) (1935–64) American rock and soul singer

David, Hal (born 1921) American composer

Davis, Miles (Dewey) (1926–91) American jazz trumpeter, composer, and bandleader

Dixon, Willy (1915–92) American blues songwriter

Dufay, Guillaume (c. 1400–74) French composer

Dukas, Paul-Abraham (1865–1935) French composer

du Pré, Jacqueline (1945–87) English cellist

Durey, Louis (1888–1979) French composer

Dylan, Bob (born Robert Allen Zimmerman) (born 1941) American singer and songwriter

Eames, Emma (1885–1952) American operatic soprano

Elgar, Sir Edward (William) (1857–1934) British composer

Evans, Gil (born Ian Ernest Gilmore Green) (1912–88) Canadian jazz pianist, composer, and arranger

Falla, Manuel de (1876–1946) Spanish composer and pianist

Fauré, Gabriel (Urbain) (1845–1924) French composer and organist

Field, John (1782–1837) Irish composer and pianist

Flatt, Lester (1914–79) American country singer

Friml, Rudolf (1879–1972) Czech-born American composer

Gigli, Beniamino (1890–1957) Italian operatic tenor

Gipps, Ruth (born 1921) British composer

Glass, Philip (born 1937) American composer

Gluck, Christoph Willibald von (1714–87) German composer

Gobbi, Tito (1915–84) Italian operatic baritone

Gordy, Berry Jr. (born 1929) American record producer

Gould, Glenn (Herbert) (1932–82) Canadian pianist and composer

Gould, Morton (1913–96) American composer

Grieg, Edvard (1843–1907) Norwegian composer, conductor, and violinist

Grofé, Ferde (born Ferdinand Rudolf von Grofé) (1892–1972) American composer

Haley, William John Clifton ("Bill") (1925–81) American rock singer

Hallé, Sir Charles (German name

Karl Halle) (1819–95) German-born pianist and conductor

Handy, W(illiam) C(hristopher) (1873–1958) American blues musician

Haydn, Franz Joseph (1732–1809) Austrian composer

Henze, Hans Werner (born 1926) German composer and conductor

Holly, Buddy (born Charles Hardin Holley) (1936–59) American rock singer, guitarist, and songwriter

Holst, Gustav (Theodore) (born Gustavus von Holst) (1874–1934) English composer of Swedish and Russian descent

James, Etta (born Jamesette Hawkins) (born 1938) American rhythm and blues singer

Jones, Tom (born Thomas Jones Woodward) (born 1940) Welsh pop singer

Joyce, Eileen (1912–91) Australian pianist

Krupa, Gene (1909–73) American drummer and bandleader

Lehár, Franz (Ferencz) (1870–1948) Hungarian composer

Lewis, Henry (1932–1996) American conductor

Lewis, Jerry Lee (born 1935) American rock singer and pianist

Liszt, Franz (1811–86) Hungarian composer and pianist

Loewe, Frederick (1901–88) American composer

Lully, Jean-Baptiste (Italian name Giovanni Battista Lulli) (1632–87) Italian-born French composer

McRae, Carmen (1920–94) American jazz singer

Melba, Dame Nellie (born Helen Porter Mitchell) (1861–1931) Australian operatic soprano

Nyman, Michael (born 1944) English composer

Ozawa, Seiji (born 1935) Japanese conductor

Parry, Sir (Charles) Hubert (Hastings) (1848–1918) English composer

Pears, Sir Peter (1910–86) English operatic tenor

Pinza, Ezio (1892–1957) Italian operatic basso

Pisan, Christine de See DE PISAN

Plant, Robert (born 1948) English rock singer and songwriter

Ravel, Maurice (Joseph) (1875–1937) French composer

Reich, Steve (born 1936) American composer

Satie, Erik (Alfred Leslie) (1866–1925) French composer

Simon, Carly (born 1945) American rock singer

Simon, Paul (born 1942) American singer and songwriter

Slick, Grace (born 1939) American rock singer

Smith, Bessie (1894–1937) American blues singer

Smyth, Dame Ethel (1858–1944) British composer

Solti, Sir Georg (1912–97) Hungarian-born British conductor

Sousa, John Philip (1854–1932) American composer and conductor

Starr, Ringo (born Richard Starkey) (born 1940) English rock and pop drummer

Styne, Jule (born Julius Kerwin Stein) (1905–94) British-born American composer

Tatum, Arthur ("Art") (1910–56) American jazz pianist

Verdi, Giuseppe (Fortunino Francesco) (1813–1901) Italian composer

Weber, Carl Maria von (1786–1826) German composer

Weill, Kurt (1900–50) German composer, resident in the US from 1935

Yanni (born Yanni Hrisomallis) (born 1954) Greek-born American composer and pianist

Young, Lester ("Pres") (1909–59) American saxophonist and composer

Young, Neil (Percival) (born

Composers, Musicians, Singers, and Instrument Makers (continued)

1945) Canadian singer, song-writer, and guitarist

Zappa, Frank (1940–93) American rock singer, musician, and songwriter

6 letters

Allman, (Howard) Duane (1946–71) American rock guitarist

Allman, Gregg (born Gregory Lenoir Allman) (born 1947) American rock singer and keyboardist

Altman, Arthur (1910–94) American composer

Arnold, Sir Malcolm (Henry) (born 1921) English composer and trumpeter

Avalon, Frankie (born Francis Thomas Avallone) (born 1940) Ameican pop singer

Barber, Samuel (1910–81) American composer

Bartók, Béla (1881–1945) Hungarian composer

Berlin, Irving (born Israel Baline) (1888–1989) Russian-born American songwriter

Blakey, Arthur ("Art") (1919–90) American jazz drummer

Bolden, Charles ("Buddy") (1868–1931) American jazz cornettist and bandleader

Boulez, Pierre (born 1925) French composer and conductor

Bowles, Paul (Frederick) (born 1910) American writer and composer

Brahms, Johannes (1833–97) German composer and pianist

Busoni, Ferruccio (Benvenuto) (1866–1924) Italian composer, conductor, and pianist

Callas, Maria (born Maria Cecilia Anna Kalageropoulos) (1923–77) American-born operatic soprano, of Greek parentage

Carter, Elliott (Cook) (born 1908) American composer

Caruso, Enrico (1873–1921) Italian operatic tenor

Casals, Pablo (also called Pau Casals) (1876–1973) Spanish cellist, conductor, and composer

Chopin, Frédéric (François) (Polish name Fryderyk Franciszek Szopen) (1810–49) Polish-born French composer

Clarke, Kenny (1914–85) American jazz drummer

Cobain, Kurt (Donald) (1967–94) American rock singer, guitarist, and songwriter

Cocker, Joe (born John Robert Cocker) (born 1944) English rock singer

Coward, Noel (1899–1973) British composer

Crooks, Richard (1900–72) American operatic tenor

Crosby, Bing (born Harry Lillis Crosby) (1904–77) American singer and actor

Czerny, Karl (1791–1857) Austrian pianist, teacher, and composer

Davies, Sir Peter Maxwell (born 1934) English composer and conductor

Delius, Frederick (1862–1934) English composer, of German and Scandinavian descent

Domino, Fats (born Antoine Domino) (born 1928) American pianist, singer, and songwriter

Dorsey, Jimmy (full name James Dorsey) (1904–57) American jazz clarinetist, saxophonist, and bandleader

Dorsey, Tommy (full name Thomas Dorsey) (1905–56) American jazz trombonist and bandleader

Dvořák, Antonín (1841–1904) Czech composer

Everly, Don (born 1937) American rock singer and guitarist, with his brother, Phil Everly (born 1939), singer and guitarist

Farrar, Geraldine (1882–1967) American operatic soprano

Fender, Leo (1907–91) American guitar maker

Foster, Stephen (Collins) (1826–64) American composer

Franck, César (Auguste) (1822–90) Belgian-born French composer

Garcia, Jerry (full name Jerome John Garcia) (1942–95) American rock singer and guitarist

Garner, Erroll (1921–77) American jazz pianist and composer

Glinka, Mikhail (Ivanovich) (1804–57) Russian composer

Gounod, Charles François (1818–93) French composer, conductor, and organist

Handel, George Frideric (or Frederick) (born Georg Friedrich Händel) (1685–1759) German-born composer, resident in England

Hanson, Howard (1896–1981) American composer

Harris, Roy Ellsworth (1898–1979) American composer

Herman, Jerry (born 1933) American composer

Herman, Woodrow ("Woody") (1913–87) American jazz bandleader

Hooker, John Lee (born 1917) American blues singer and guitarist

Jagger, Michael Philip ("Mick") (born 1943) English rock singer and songwriter

Joplin, Janis (1943–70) American rock singer

Joplin, Scott (1868–1917) American ragtime pianist and composer

Kenton, Stan (born Stanley Newcomb) (1912–79) American bandleader, composer, and arranger

Kodály, Zoltán (1882–1967) Hungarian composer

Lassus, Orlande de (Italian name Orlando di Lasso) (c. 1532–94) Flemish composer

Lennon, John (1940–80) English pop and rock singer, guitarist, and songwriter

Lerner, Alan J. (1918–86) American lyricist

Ligeti, György Sándor (born 1923) Hungarian composer

Mahler, Gustav (1860–1911) Austrian composer, conductor, and pianist

Marley, Robert Nesta ("Bob") (1945–81) Jamaican reggae singer, guitarist, and songwriter

Martin, Sir George (Leonard) (born 1926) English record producer

Menken, Alan (born 1950) American composer

Mercer, Johnny (1909–76) American lyricist

Miller, (Alton) Glenn (1904–44) American jazz trombonist and bandleader

Miller, Roger (1936–92) American country singer and songwriter

Mingus, Charles (1922–79) American jazz bassist and composer

Monroe, Bill (born William Smith Monroe) (1911–96) American bluegrass singer and songwriter

Morton, Jelly Roll (born Ferdinand Joseph La Menthe Morton) (1885–1941) American jazz pianist, composer, and bandleader

Mozart, (Johann Chrysostom) Wolfgang Amadeus (1756–91) Austrian composer

Mutter, Anne-Sophie (born 1965) German violinist

Nelson, Willie (born 1933) American country singer and songwriter

Norman, Jessye (born 1945) American operatic soprano

Composers, Musicians, Singers, and Instrument Makers (continued)

Parker, Charles Christopher ("Charlie"; known as "Bird" or "Yardbird") (1920–55) American saxophonist

Parton, Dolly (Rebecca) (born 1946) American singer and songwriter

Peerce, Jan (born Jacob Pincus) (1904–84) American operatic tenor

Porter, Cole (1892–1964) American songwriter

Previn, André (George) (born 1929) German-born American conductor, pianist, and composer

Rainey, Gertrude ("Ma") (1886–1939) American blues singer

Rameau, Jean-Philippe (1683–1764) French composer, musical theorist, and organist

Rattle, Sir Simon (Denis) (born 1955) English conductor

Ritter, Tex (born Woodward Maurice Ritter) (1907–74) American country singer and songwriter

Schütz, Heinrich (1585–1672) German composer and organist

Sedaka, Neil (born 1939) American composer

Seeger, Pete (born 1919) American folk musician and songwriter

Steber, Eleanor (1916–90) American operatic soprano

Stills, Stephen (born 1945) American rock musician

Tallis, Thomas (c. 1505–85) English composer

Tansen (c. 1500–89) Indian musician and singer

Travis, Merle (1917–83) American country singer and songwriter

Tucker, Richard (1913–75) American operatic tenor

Turner, Joe (1911–85) American blues singer

Turner, Tina (born Anna Mae Bullock) (born 1939) American rock and soul singer

Twitty, Conway (1933–93) American country singer and songwriter

Valens, Ritchie (born Richard Valenzuela) (1941–59) American rock singer of Mexican descent

Varèse, Edgar(d) (1883–1965) French-born American composer

Venuti, Joe (1904–78) American jazz violinist

Wagner, (Wilhelm) Richard (1813–83) German composer

Walker, T-Bone (born Aaron Thibeaux Walker) (1910–75) American blues guitarist

Waller, Fats (born Thomas Wright Waller) (1904–43) American jazz musician and songwriter

Walton, Sir William (Turner) (1902–83) English composer

Warren, Leonard (1911–60) American operatic baritone

Waters, Ethel (1896–1977) American jazz and blues singer

Waters, Muddy (born McKinley Morganfield) (1915–83) American blues singer and guitarist

Webern, Anton von (1883–1945) Austrian composer

Wilson, Brian (born 1942) American rock singer and songwriter

Wonder, Stevie (born Steveland Judkins Morris) (born 1950) American singer, songwriter, and musician

7 letters

Babbitt, Milton (Byron) (born 1916) American composer and mathematician

Beecham, Sir Thomas (1879–1961) English conductor and impresario

Bellini, Vincenzo (1801–35) Italian composer

Benford, Tommy (1906–94)

American jazz drummer

Berlioz, (Louis-)Hector (1803–69) French composer

Borodin, Aleksandr (Porfirevich) (1833–87) Russian composer

Britten, (Edward) Benjamin, Lord Britten of Aldeburgh (1913–76) English composer, pianist, and conductor

Brubeck, David Warren ("Dave") (born 1920) American jazz pianist, composer, and bandleader

Caballé, Montserrat (born 1933) Spanish operatic soprano

Carreño, Maria Teresa (1853–1917) Venezuelan composer and pianist

Charles, Ray (born Ray Charles Robinson) (born 1930) American pianist and singer

Checker, Chubby (born Ernest Evans Checker) (born 1941) American rock singer

Clapton, Eric (born Eric Clapp) (born 1945) English blues and rock guitarist, singer, and composer

Cochran, Eddie (born Edward Cochrane) (1938–60) American rock singer and songwriter

Coleman, Cy (born Seymour Kaufman) (born 1929) American composer

Coleman, Ornette (born 1930) American jazz saxophonist, trumpeter, violinist, and composer

Collins, Phil(ip) (born 1951) English rock singer, drummer, and songwriter

Copland, Aaron (1900–90) American composer, pianist, and conductor, of Lithuanian descent

Corelli, Arcangelo (1653–1713) Italian violinist and composer

Debussy, (Achille) Claude (1862–1918) French composer and critic

de Falla, Manuel See FALLA

Delibes, (Clément Philibert) Léo (1836–91) French composer and organist

de Pisan, Christine (also de Pizan) (c. 1364–c. 1430) Italian composer and writer, resident in France from 1369

Desmond, Paul (1924–77) American jazz alto saxophonist

des Prez, Josquin (also des Prés) (c. 1440–1521) Flemish composer

Diamond, Neil (born 1941) American singer and songwriter

Diddley, Bo (born Otha Ellas Bates McDaniels) (born 1928) American rock guitarist

Domingo, Placido (born 1941) Spanish-born tenor

Ferrier, Kathleen (1912–53) English contralto

Gabriel, Peter (born 1950) English rock musician

Gilbert, William S. (1836–1911) British lyricist

Goodman, Benjamin David ("Benny") (1909–86) American jazz clarinetist and bandleader

Górecki, Henryk (Mikotaj) (born 1933) Polish composer

Guthrie, Arlo (born 1947) American folk and rock singer and songwriter

Guthrie, Woody (born Woodrow Wilson Guthrie) (1912–67) American folk singer and songwriter

Haitink, Bernard (born 1919) Dutch conductor

Hammond, Dame Joan (1912–96) New Zealand-born Australian operatic soprano

Hawkins, Coleman Randolph (1904–69) American jazz saxophonist

Hendrix, Jimi (born Johnny Allen Hendrix; also called James Marshall Hendrix) (1942–70) American rock guitarist and singer

Herbert, Victor (1859–1924) Irish-born American composer

Heyward, DuBose (1885–1940) American lyricist

Holiday, Billie (born Eleanora Fagan) (1915–59) American jazz and blues singer

Composers, Musicians, Singers, and Instrument Makers *(continued)*

Houston, Whitney (born 1963) American pop singer

Jackson, Janet (born 1966) American pop singer

Jackson, Mahalia (1911–72) American gospel singer

Jackson, Michael (Joe) (born 1958) American singer and songwriter

Johnson, Robert (1911–38) American blues singer and guitarist

Karajan, Herbert von (1908–89) Austrian conductor

Lehmann, Lotte (1888–1929) German-born American operatic soprano

Madonna (born Madonna Louise Ciccone) (born 1958) American pop singer and actress

Mancini, Henry (1924–94) American composer

Menotti, Gian Carlo (born 1911) Italian-born American composer

Menuhin, Yehudi, Baron (born 1916) American-born British violinist

Mercury, Freddie (born Farookh Bulsara) (1946–91) Zanzibar-born British rock singer

Merrill, Bob (1921–98) American lyricist

Milhaud, Darius (1892–1974) French composer

Nielsen, Carl August (1865–1931) Danish composer

Nilsson, (Märta) Birgit (born 1918) Swedish operatic soprano

Nordica, Lillian (1857–1914) American operatic soprano

Novello, Ivor (born David Ivor Davies) (1893–1951) Welsh composer, actor, and dramatist

Poulenc, Francis (Jean Marcel) (1899–1963) French composer

Presley, Elvis (Aron) (1935–77) American rock and pop singer

Puccini, Giacomo (1858–1924) Italian composer

Purcell, Henry (1659–95) English composer

Redding, Otis (1941–67) American soul singer

Richard, Sir Cliff (born Harry Roger Webb) (born 1940) Indian-born British pop singer

Robbins, Marty (born Martin David Robinson) (1925–82) American country singer and songwriter

Robeson, Paul (1898–1976) American singer and actor

Rodgers, Jimmie (born James Charles Rodgers) (1897–1933) American country singer and songwriter

Rodgers, Richard (Charles) (1902–79) American composer

Romberg, Sigmund (1887–1951) Hungarian-born American composer

Rossini, Gioacchino Antonio (1792–1868) Italian composer

Salieri, Antonio (1750–1825) Italian composer

Sargent, Sir (Henry) Malcolm (Watts) (1895–1967) English conductor and composer

Segovia, Andrés (1893–1987) Spanish guitarist and composer

Shankar, Ravi (born 1920) Indian sitar player and composer

Sinatra, Frank (full name Francis Albert Sinatra) (1915–98) American singer and actor

Smetana, Bedrich (1824–84) Czech composer

Spector, Phil (born 1940) American record producer

Stewart, Rod(erick David) (born 1945) English rock singer and songwriter

Strauss, Johann (known as Strauss the Elder) (1804–49) Austrian composer

Strauss, Johann (known as

Strauss the Younger) (1825–99)
Austrian composer

Strauss, Richard (1864–1949)
German composer

Strouse, Charles (born 1928)
American composer

Tibbett, Lawrence (1896–1960)
American operatic baritone

Vaughan, Sarah (Lois) (1924–90)
American jazz singer and pianist

Vivaldi, Antonio (Lucio) (1678–1741) Italian composer and violinist

Webster, Paul Francis (1907–84)
American lyricist

Wynette, Tammy (born Tammy Wynette Pugh) (1942–98)
American country singer

Xenakis, Iannis (born 1922)
French composer and architect, of Greek descent

8 letters

Albinoni, Tomaso (1671–1751)
Italian composer

Anderson, Marian (1902–93)
American operatic contralto

Bacewicz, Grazyna (1909–69)
Polish composer and violinist

Berkeley, Sir Lennox (Randall Francis) (1903–89) English composer

Bruckner, Anton (1824–96)
Austrian composer and organist

Calloway, Cab(ell) (1907–94)
American jazz singer and bandleader

Carreras, José (born 1946)
Spanish operatic tenor

Cheatham, Doc (born Adolphus Anthony Cheatham) (1905–97)
American jazz trumpeter

Coltrane, John (William) (1926–67) American jazz tenor saxophonist and composer

Costello, Elvis (born Declan MacManus) (born 1955) English rock and jazz musician

Couperin, François (1668–1733)
French composer, organist, and harpsichordist

Dalcroze See JAQUES-DALCROZE

Franklin, Aretha (born 1942)
American soul and gospel singer

Gershwin, George (born Jacob Gershovitz) (1898–1937)
American composer and pianist, of Russian Jewish parentage, brother of Ira Gershwin

Gershwin, Ira (born Israel Gershovitz) (1896–1983) American lyricist, of Russian Jewish parentage, brother of George Gershwin

Glazunov, Aleksandr (Konstantinovich) (1865–1936) Russian composer

Grainger, (George) Percy (Aldridge) (1882–1961)
Australian-born American composer and pianist

Guarneri, Giuseppe ("del Gesù") (1687–1744) Italian violinmaker

Hamlisch, Marvin (born 1944)
American composer

Harrison, George (born 1943)
English rock and pop guitarist

Honegger, Arthur (1892–1955)
French composer, of Swiss descent

Horowitz, Vladimir (1904–89)
Russian pianist

Hovaness See HOVHANESS

Iglesias, Julio (born 1943)
Spanish singer

Kreisler, Fritz (1875–1962)
Austrian-born American violinist and composer

Liberace (full name Wladziu Valentino Liberace) (1919–87)
American pianist and entertainer

Marsalis, Wynton (born 1962)
American jazz and classical trumpet player

Mascagni, Pietro (1863–1945)
Italian composer and conductor

Messiaen, Olivier (Eugène Prosper Charles) (1908–92)
French composer

Mitchell, Joni (born Roberta Joan Anderson) (born 1943)
Canadian singer and songwriter

Composers, Musicians,
Singers, and Instrument Makers *(continued)*

Morrison, James Douglas ("Jim")
(1943–71) American rock singer

Morrison, Van (full name George
Ivan Morrison) (born 1945)
Northern Irish singer, song-
writer, and musician

Mulligan, Gerry (1927–96) American jazz saxophonist and songwriter

Musgrave, Thea (born 1928)
Scottish composer

Norworth, Jack (1879–1959)
American lyricist

Paganini, Niccolò (1782–1840)
Italian violinist and composer

Peterson, Oscar (Emmanuel)
(born 1925) Canadian jazz
pianist and composer

Ponselle, Rosa (1897–1981)
American operatic soprano

Respighi, Ottorino (1879–1936)
Italian composer

Richards, Keith (born 1943)
English rock guitarist

Robinson, Smokey (born William
Robinson) (born 1940) American
singer and songwriter

Schubert, Franz (1797–1828)
Austrian composer

Schumann, Clara (1819–96)
German pianist and composer

Schumann, Robert (Alexander)
(1810–56) German composer

Scriabin, Aleksandr (Nikolaevich)
(also Skryabin) (1872–1915)
Russian composer and pianist

Sibelius, Jean (born Johan Julius
Christian Sibelius) (1865–1957)
Finnish composer

Skryabin See SCRIABIN

Sondheim, Stephen (Joshua)
(born 1930) American composer
and lyricist

Stanford, Sir Charles (Villiers)
(1852–1924) Irish-born British
composer

Steinway, Henry (Engelhard)
(born Heinrich Engelhard
Steinweg) (1797–1871) German
piano builder, resident in the US
from 1849

Sullivan, Sir Arthur (Seymour)
(1842–1900) English composer

Te Kanawa, Dame Kiri (Janette)
(born 1944) New Zealand operatic soprano, resident in Britain
since 1966

Telemann, Georg Philipp
(1681–1767) German composer
and organist

Van Halen, Eddie (born 1955)
Dutch-born American rock guitarist

Victoria, Tomás Luis de
(1548–1611) Spanish composer

Whiteman, Paul (1890–1967)
American jazz bandleader

Williams, Hank, Sr. (born Hiram
King Williams) (1923–53) American country singer and songwriter

Williams, John (born 1932)
American composer

Williams, John (Christopher)
(born 1941) Australian guitarist
and composer

9 letters

Armstrong, (Daniel) Louis
(known as "Satchmo") (1900–
71) American jazz trumpeter and
singer

**Ashkenazy, Vladimir
(Davidovich)** (born 1937) Russian-born pianist and conductor

Bacharach, Burt (born 1929)
American writer of popular songs

Barenboim, Daniel (born 1942)
Argentine-born Israeli pianist
and conductor

**Bechstein, Friedrich Wilhelm
Carl** (1826–1900) German
piano builder

Beethoven, Ludwig van
(1770–1827) German composer

Bernstein, Leonard (1918–90) American composer, conductor, and pianist

Boulanger, Nadia Juliette (1887–1979) French composer and conductor

Buxtehude, Dietrich (c. 1637–1707) Danish organist and composer

Chaliapin, Fyodor (Ivanovich) (1873–1938) Russian operatic bass

Chaminade, Cécile Louise (1857–1944) French composer

Cleveland, James (1931–91) American composer and singer

Donaldson, Walter (1893–1947) American composer

Donizetti, Gaetano (1797–1848) Italian composer

Dunstable, John (c. 1390–1453) English composer

Ellington, Duke (born Edward Kennedy Ellington) (1899–1974) American jazz pianist, composer, and bandleader

Gillespie, Dizzy (born John Birks Gillespie) (1917–93) American jazz trumpet player, composer, and bandleader

Grappelli, Stephane (1908–97) French jazz violinist

Hovhaness (also Hovaness), Alan (born 1911) American composer, of Armenian and Scottish descent

Hindemith, Paul (1895–1963) German composer

Jefferson, Blind Lemon (1897–1930) American blues singer

Klemperer, Otto (1885–1973) German-born conductor and composer

Ledbetter, Huddle (called "Leadbelly") (1888–1949) American blues singer

McCartney, Sir (James) Paul (born 1942) English pop and rock singer, songwriter, and bass guitarist

Meyerbeer, Giacomo (born Jakob Liebmann Beer) (1791–1864) German composer

Offenbach, Jacques (born Jacob Offenbach) (1819–80) German composer, resident in France from 1833

Pachelbel, Johann (1653–1706) German composer and organist

Pavarotti, Luciano (born 1935) Italian operatic tenor

Reinhardt, Django (born Jean Baptiste Reinhardt) (1910–53) Belgian jazz guitarist

Scarlatti, (Pietro) Alessandro (Gaspare) (1660–1725) Italian composer

Scarlatti, (Giuseppe) Domenico (1685–1757) Italian composer

Stokowski, Leopold (1882–1977) British-born American conductor, of Polish descent

Streisand, Barbra (Joan) (born 1942) American singer, actress, and film director

Tortelier, Paul (1914–90) French cellist

Toscanini, Arturo (1867–1957) Italian conductor

10 letters

Boccherini, Luigi (1743–1805) Italian composer and cellist

Carmichael, Hoagy (born Howard Hoagland Carmichael) (1899–1981) American jazz pianist, composer, and singer

Fitzgerald, Ella (1917–96) American jazz singer

Monteverdi, Claudio (1567–1643) Italian composer

Mussorgsky, Modest (Petrovich) (also Moussorgsky) (1839–81) Russian composer

Paderewski, Ignacy Jan (1860–1941) Polish pianist, composer, and statesman (prime minister 1919)

Palestrina, Giovanni Pierluigi da (c. 1525–94) Italian composer

Penderecki, Krzysztof (born 1933) Polish composer

Rubinstein, Anton (Grigorevich)

Composers, Musicians, Singers, and Instrument Makers *(continued)*

(1829–94) Russian composer and pianist

Rubinstein, Artur (1888–1982) Polish-born American pianist

Saint-Saëns, (Charles) Camille (1835–1921) French composer, pianist, and organist

Schoenberg, Arnold (1874–1951) Austrian-born American composer

Stradivari, Antonio (*c.* 1644–1737) Italian violinmaker

Stravinsky, Igor (Fyodorovich) (1882–1971) Russian-born American composer

Sutherland, Dame Joan (born 1926) Australian operatic soprano

Villa-Lobos, Heitor (1887–1959) Brazilian composer

11 letters

Beiderbecke, Bix (born Leon Bismarck Beiderbecke) (1903–31) American jazz musician and composer

Furtwängler, Wilhelm (1886–1954) German conductor

Hammerstein, Oscar (full name Oscar Hammerstein II) (1895–1960) American librettist

Humperdinck, Engelbert (1854–1921) German composer

Leoncavallo, Ruggero (1858–1919) Italian composer

Lloyd Webber, Andrew, Baron (born 1948) English composer of musicals

Lutosławski, Witold (1913–94) Polish composer

Mendelssohn, Felix (full name Jakob Ludwig Felix Mendelssohn-Bartholdy) (1809–47) German composer and pianist

Moussorgsky See MUSSORGSKY

Rachmaninov, Sergei (Vasilevich) (1873–1943) Russian composer and pianist, resident in the US from 1917

Schwarzkopf, Dame (Olga Maria) Elisabeth (Friederike) (born 1915) German-born British soprano

Springsteen, Bruce (born 1949) American rock singer, songwriter, and guitarist

Stockhausen, Karlheinz (born 1928) German composer

Tailleferre, Germaine (1892–1983) French composer and pianist

Tchaikovsky, Pyotr (Ilich) (1840–93) Russian composer

Theodorakis, Mikis (born 1925) Greek composer

12 letters

Dallapiccola, Luigi (1904–75) Italian composer

Khachaturian, Aram (Ilich) (1903–78) Georgian-born Soviet composer

Shostakovich, Dmitri (Dmitrievich) (1906–75) Russian composer

14 letters

Fischer-Dieskau, Dietrich (born 1925) German baritone

Glanville-Hicks, Peggy (1912–90) American composer

Jaques-Dalcroze, Émile (1865–1950) Austrian-born Swiss music teacher and composer

Josquin des Prez See DES PREZ

15 letters

Vaughan Williams, Ralph (1872–1958) English composer

17 letters

Hildegard of Bingen, St. (1098–1179) German abbess, scholar, composer, and mystic

Salerno-Sonnenberg, Najda (born 1961) American violinist

People Involved in Movies, Theater, and Dance

2 letters

Ho, Don (born 1930) American
actor

3 letters

Bow, Clara (1905–65) American
actress

Cox, Wally (1924–73) American
actor

Day, Doris (born Doris
Kappelhoff) (born 1924)
American actress and singer

Dee, Ruby (born Ruby Ann
Wallace) (born 1923) American
actress

Dee, Sandra (born Alexandra
Zuck) (born 1942) American
actress

Dru, Joanne (1923–96) American
actress

Fox, Michael J. (born 1961)
Canadian actor

Foy, Eddie (1857–1928) American
actor and dancer

Lee, Bruce (born Lee Yuen Kam)
(1941–73) American actor

**Lee, Christopher (Frank
Carandini)** (born 1922) English
actor

Lee, Gypsy Rose (born Rose
Louise Hovick) (1914–70)
American striptease artist

Lee, Spike (born Shelton Jackson
Lee) (born 1957) American
movie director and actor

Lom, Herbert (born 1917)
Czech-born American actor

Loy, Myrna (born Myrna
Williams) (1905–93) American
actress

May, Elaine (born 1932)
American actress and comedian

Mix, Tom (1880–1940) American
actor

Ray, Aldo (1926–91) American
actor

Ray, Satyajit (1921–92) Indian
movie director

4 letters

Alda, Alan (born Alphonso
d'Abruzzo) (born 1936)
American actor

Alda, Robert (1914–86) American
actor

Ball, Lucille (1911–89) American
comedian

Bara, Theda (born Theodosia
Goodman) (1890–1955)
American actress

Burr, Raymond (1917–93)
American actor

Caan, James (born 1939)
American actor

Cobb, Lee J. (born Leo Jacoby)
(1911–76) American actor

Coca, Imogene (born 1908)
American actress and comedian

Cody, William Frederick See
BUFFALO BILL

Cook, Peter (Edward) (1937–94)
English comedian and actor

Culp, Robert (born 1930)
American actor

Dahl, Arlene (born 1928) American actress

Daly, Tyne (born 1947) American
actress

Dean, James (born James Byron)
(1931–55) American actor

Dern, Bruce (born 1967)
American actor

Duke, Patty (born 1946)
American actress

Duse, Eleonora (1858–1924)
Italian actress

Eden, Barbara (born Barbara
Huffman) (born 1934) American
actress

Falk, Peter (born 1927) American
actor

Ford, Glenn (born 1916)
Canadian-born American actor

Ford, Harrison (born 1942)
American actor

Ford, John (born Sean Aloysius
O'Feeney) (1895–1973)

People Involved in Movies, Theater, and Dance *(continued)*

American movie director

Foxx, Redd (born John Sanford) (1922–91) American actor and comedian

Garr, Teri (born 1945) American actress

Gere, Richard (born 1949) American actor

Gish, Lillian (1896–1993) American actress

Gray, Spaulding (born 1941) American actor

Grey, Joel (born Joe Katz) (born 1932) American actor

Hall, Arsenio (born 1955) American actor and talk show host

Hart, William S. (1870–1946) American actor

Hawn, Goldie (born 1945) American actress

Head, Edith (1907–81) American costume designer

Hill, Benny (born Alfred Hawthorne) (1925–92) English comedian

Holm, Celeste (born 1919) American actress

Hope, Bob (born Leslie Townes Hope) (born 1903) British-born American comedian

Hurt, William (born 1950) American actor

Kahn, Madeline (1943–99) American actress

Kaye, Danny (born David Daniel Kaminski) (1913–87) American actor and comedian

Kean, Edmund (1787–1833) English actor

Ladd, Alan (1913–64) American actor

Ladd, Cheryl (born Cheryl Stoppelmoore) (born 1951) American actress

Lahr, Bert (1895–1967) American actor

Lake, Veronica (born Constance Ockleman) (1919–73) American actress

Lang, Fritz (1890–1976) Austrian-born movie director

Lean, Sir David (1908–91) English movie director

Lear, Norman (born 1922) American television producer

Leno, Jay (born 1950) American television personality

Lowe, Rob (born 1964) American actor

Lunt, Alfred (1893–1977) American actor; husband of Lynn Fontanne

Marx, Chico (Leonard) (1886–1961) American comic actor

Marx, Groucho (Julius Henry) (1890–1977) American comic actor

Marx, Gummo (Milton) (1893–1977)

Marx, Harpo (Adolph) (1888–1964) American comic actor

Marx, Zeppo (Herbert) (1901–1979) American comic actor

Mull, Martin (born 1943) American actor and comedian

Neal, Patricia (born 1926) American actress

Paar, Jack (born 1918) American television personality

Peck, (Eldred) Gregory (born 1916) American actor

Penn, Arthur (born 1922) American movie director

Penn, Sean (born 1960) American actor

Pitt, Brad (born 1964) American actor

Raft, George (1895–1980) American actor

Reed, Donna (born Donna Belle Mullenger) (1921–86) American actress

Rose, Billy (1899–1966) American theater promoter and producer

Ryan, Meg (born Margaret Hyra) (born 1961) American actress

Ryan, Robert (1909–73) American actor

Shaw, Robert (1927–78) American actor

Swit, Loretta (born 1937) American actress

Tati, Jacques (born Jacques Tatischeff) (1908–82) French movie director and actor

Todd, Michael (1909–58) American movie producer

Torn, Rip (born Elmore Rual Torn, Jr.) (born 1931) American actor

Webb, Jack (1920–82) American actor

Weir, Peter (born 1944) Australian movie director

Weld, Tuesday (born 1943) American actress

West, Mae (1892–1980) American actress and dramatist

Wood, Natalie (born Natasha Gurdin) (1938–81) American actress

Wray, Fay (born 1907) Canadian-born American actress

Wynn, Ed (1886–1966) American actor; father of Keenan Wynn (1916–86)

5 letters

Ailey, Alvin (1931–89) American dancer and choreographer

Allen, Gracie (1906–64) American actress and comedian

Allen, Woody (born Allen Stewart Konigsberg) (born 1935) American movie director, writer, and actor

Alley, Kirstie (born 1951) American actress

Arden, Eve (born Eunice Quedens) (1908–90) American actress

Arkin, Alan (born 1934) American actor

Autry, Gene (1907–98) American actor, singer, and sports executive

Ayres, Lew (1908–96) American actor,

Bacon, Kevin (born 1958) American actor

Baker, Josephine (1906–75) American dancer

Beery, Wallace (1889–1949) American actor

Benny, Jack (born Benjamin Kubelsky) (1894–1974) American comedian and actor

Berle, Milton (born 1908) American comedian and actor

Berry, Halle (born 1968) American actress

Booth, Edwin (1833–93) American actor

Booth, John Wilkes (1838–65) American actor, assassin of President Lincoln

Booth, Junius Brutus (1796–1852) American actor; father of Edwin Booth and John Wilkes Booth

Boyer, Charles (1897–1977) French-born American actor

Boyle, Peter (born 1933) American actor

Brice, Fanny (born Fanny Borach) (1891–1951) American actress and comedian

Brook, Peter (Stephen Paul) (born 1925) English theater director

Bruce, Lenny (born Leonard Alfred Schneider) (1925–66) American comedian

Burns, George (born Nathan Birnbaum) (1896–1996) American comedian

Caine, Sir Michael (born Maurice Micklewhite) (born 1933) English movie actor

Capra, Frank (1897–1991) Italian-born American movie director

Chase, Chevy (born 1943) American actor and comedian

Clair, René (born Rene Lucien Chomette) (1898–1981) French movie director

People Involved in Movies, Theater, and Dance *(continued)*

Clift, (Edward) Montgomery (1920–66) American actor

Close, Glenn (born 1947) American actress

Cohan, George M. (1878–1942) American actor and theatrical producer

Cosby, Bill (born 1937) American comedian and actor

Dafoe, Willem (born 1955) American actor

Davis, Bette (born Ruth Elizabeth Davis) (1908–89) American actress

Davis, Ossie (born 1917) American actor

Dench, Dame Judi(th Olivia) (born 1934) English actress

Derek, Bo (born Mary Cathleen Collins) (born 1956) American actress

Dolin, Sir Anton (born Sydney Francis Patrick Chippendall Healey-Kay) (1904–83) English dancer and choreographer

Ebsen, Buddy (born 1908) American actor

Evans, Dale (born Frances Smith) (born 1912) American actress and singer

Evans, Dame Edith (Mary) (1888–1976) English actress

Flynn, Errol (born Leslie Thomas Flynn) (1909–59) Australian-born American actor

Fonda, Henry (1905–82) American actor

Fonda, Jane (born 1937) American actress

Fonda, Peter (born 1939) American actor

Fosse, Bob (1927–87) American dancer and choreographer

Gable, (William) Clark (1901–60) American actor

Gabor, Eva (1920–95) Hungarian-born American actress

Gabor, Zsa Zsa (born 1917) Hungarian-born American actress

Gance, Abel (1889–1991) French movie director

Garbo, Greta (born Greta Gustafsson) (1905–90) Swedish-born American actress

Grant, Cary (born Alexander Archibald Leach) (1904–86) British-born American actor

Gwynn, Eleanor ("Nell") (1650–87) English actress

Hagen, Uta (born 1919) German-born American actress

Hanks, Tom (Thomas J.) (born 1956) American movie actor

Hardy, Oliver See LAUREL AND HARDY

Havoc, June (born 1916) American actress

Hawks, Howard (1896–1977) American movie director, producer, and screenwriter

Hawks, Howard (1896–1977) American movie director

Hayes, Helen (born Helen Brown) (1900–93) American actress

Ivory, James (born 1928) American movie director

Jones, James Earl (born 1931) American actor

Jones, Tommy Lee (born 1946) American actor

Julia, Raul (1940–94) Puerto Rican actor

Kazan, Elia (born Elia Kazanjoglous) (born 1909) Turkish-born American movie and theater director

Keach, Stacy (born 1943) American actor

Kelly, Gene (born Eugene Curran Kelly) (1912–96) American dancer and choreographer

Kelly, Grace (Patricia) (also called (from 1956) Princess Grace of Monaco) (1928–82)

American movie actress

Lange, Jessica (born 1949) American actress

Leigh, Janet (born Jeannette Morrison) (born 1927) American actress

Leigh, Vivien (born Vivian Mary Hartley) (1913–67) British actress, born in India

Lewis, Jerry (born Joseph Levitch) (born 1926) American comedian and actor

Limón, José (1908–72) Mexican-born American dancer and choreographer

Lloyd, Harold (Clayton) (1893–1971) American movie comedian

Loren, Sophia (born Sophia Scicolone) (born 1934) Italian actress

Lorre, Peter (born Laszlo Lowenstein) (1904–64) Hungarian-born American actor

Lucas, George (born 1944) American movie director, producer, and screenwriter

Lucci, Susan (born 1948) American actress

Lynch, David (born 1946) American movie director

Malle, Louis (1932–95) French movie director

Marin, Cheech (born 1946) American actor and comedian

Mason, James (Neville) (1909–84) English actor

Mayer, Louis B(urt) (born Eliezer Mayer) (1885–1957) Russian-born American movie executive

Meara, Anne (born 1929) American comedian

Mills, Sir John (Lewis Ernest Watts) (born 1908) English actor

Mineo, Sal (1939–76) American actor

Moore, Demi (born Demetria Guynes) (born 1962) American actress

Moore, Dudley (Stuart John)

(born 1935) English actor, comedian, and musician

Moore, Mary Tyler (born 1936) American actress

Myers, Mike (born 1963) Canadian actor and comedian

Neill, Sam (born Nigel John Dermot) (born 1947) New Zealand actor

Nimoy, Leonard (born 1931) American actor

Nolte, Nick (born 1940) American actor

Novak, Kim (born 1933) American actress

O'Hara, Maureen (Maureen Fitzsimons) (born 1920) Irish-born American actress

O'Neal, Ryan (born 1941) American actor; father of Tatum O'Neal (born 1963) actress

Olmos, Edward James (born 1947) American actor

Papas, Irene (born 1926) Greek actress

Pathé, Charles (1863–1957) French movie pioneer

Pesci, Joe (born 1943) American actor

Pitts, Zasu (1898–1963) American actress

Price, Vincent (1911–93) American stage and movie actor

Pryor, Richard (born 1940) American comedian and actor

Quaid, Randy (born 1950) American actor; brother of Dennis Quaid (born 1954) actor

Quinn, Anthony (born 1915) Mexican-born American actor

Rains, Claude (1890–1967) English-born American actor

Reeve, Christopher (born 1952) American actor

Ryder, Winona (born Winona Horowitz) (born 1971) American actress

Saint, Eva Marie (born 1924) American actress

Scott, George C. (1927–99) American actor

People Involved in Movies, Theater, and Dance *(continued)*

Scott, Ridley (born 1939) English movie director

Shawn, Ted (1891–1972) American dancer, choreographer, teacher, and promoter

Sheen, Martin (born Ramon Estevez) (born 1940) American actor; father of actors Emilio Estevez (born 1962) and Charlie Sheen (born Carlos Irwin Estevez) (born 1965)

Stack, Robert (born Robert Modini) (born 1919) American actor

Stone, Oliver (born 1946) American movie director, screen-writer, and producer

Stone, Sharon (born 1958) American actress

Tandy, Jessica (1909–94) English-born American actress

Terry, Dame (Alice) Ellen (1847–1928) English actress

Tracy, Spencer (1900–67) American actor

Tyson, Cicely (born 1933) American actress

Vidor, King (1896–1982) American movie director

Wajda, Andrzej (born 1929) Polish movie director

Wayne, John (born Marion Michael Morrison; known as "the Duke") (1907–79) American actor

Welch, Raquel (born Raquel Tejada) (born 1940) American actress

Wyman, Jane (born Sarah Jane Fulks) (born 1914) American actress

Zukor, Adolph (1873–1976) American movie producer

6 letters

Abbott, Bud (1895–1974) American actor

Aiello, Danny (born 1933) American actor

Altman, Robert (born 1925) American movie director

Altman, Robert (born 1925) American movie director and producer

Ameche, Don (1908–93) American actor

Artaud, Antonin (1896–1948) French actor, director, and poet

Ashton, Sir Frederick (William Mallandaine) (1904–88) British ballet-dancer and choreographer

Bacall, Lauren (born 1924) American actress

Bardot, Brigitte (born Camille Javal) (born 1934) French actress

Barnum, P(hineas) T(aylor) (1810–91) American showman

Beatty, Clyde (1904–65) American circus performer

Beatty, Warren (born 1937) American actor; brother of Shirley MacLaine

Beatty, Warren (born Henry Warren Beaty) (born 1937) American actor, movie director, and screenwriter

Bejart, Maurice (born Maurice Jean Berger) (born 1927) French choreographer

Blades, Ruben (born 1948) Panamanian actor and singer

Blasis, Carlo (1803–78) Italian dancer, choreographer, and teacher

Bogart, Humphrey (DeForest) (1899–1957) American actor

Branagh, Kenneth (Charles) (born 1960) English actor, producer, and director

Brando, Marlon (born 1924) American actor

Brooks, Mel (born Melvin Kaminsky) (born 1927)

American movie director and actor

Buñuel, Luis (1900–83) Spanish movie director

Burton, Richard (born Richard Jenkins) (1925–84) Welsh actor

Caesar, Sid (born 1922) American comedian and actor

Cagney, James (1899–1986) American actor

Carney, Art (born 1918) American actor

Carrey, Jim (born 1962) Canadian actor

Carson, John William ("Johnny") (born 1925) American television personality

Carvey, Dana (born 1955) American actor and comedian

Chaney, Lon (full name Alonso Chaney) (1883–1930) American actor

Cibber, Colley (1671–1757) English actor, theater manager, and dramatist

Cleese, John (Marwood) (born 1939) English comic actor and writer

Coburn, James (born 1928) American actor

Coogan, Jackie (1914–84) American actor

Cooper, Gary (born Frank James Cooper) (1901–61) American actor

Coward, Sir Noel (Pierce) (1899–1973) English dramatist, actor, and composer

Crabbe, Buster (1908–93) American actor

Cronyn, Hume (born 1911) Canadian-born American actor

Cruise, Tom (born Thomas Mapother IV) (born 1962) American actor

Curtis, Tony (born Bernard Schwartz) (born 1925) American actor

Danson, Ted (born 1947) American actor

Davies, Marion (1897–1961) American actress

De Niro, Robert (born 1943) American actor

De Sica, Vittorio (1901–74) Italian movie director and actor

De Vito, Danny (born Daniel Michaeli) (born 1944) American actor

Disney, Walter Elias ("Walt") (1901–66) American animator and movie producer

Duncan, Isadora (1878–1927) American dancer and teacher

Duvall, Robert (born 1931) American actor

Farrow, Mia (born 1945) American actress

Ferrer, José (1912–92) American actor

Fields, Dame Gracie (born Grace Stansfield) (1898–1979) English singer and comedienne

Fields, W.C. (born William Claude Dukinfield) (1880–1946) American movie actor

Finney, Albert (born 1936) English actor

Fokine, Michel (born Mikhail Mikhailovich Fokin) (1880–1942) Russian-born American dancer and choreographer

Forman, Milos (born 1932) Czech-born American movie director

Foster, Jodie (born Alicia Christian Foster) (born 1962) American movie actress

Garner, James (born James Bumgarner) (born 1928) American actor

Garson, Greer (1904–96) American actress

Gibson, Mel (Columcille Gerard) (born 1956) American-born Australian actor and director

Godard, Jean-Luc (born 1930) French movie director

Gordon, Ruth (1896–1985) American actress

Graham, Martha (1893–1991)

People Involved in Movies, Theater, and Dance *(continued)*

American dancer, teacher, and choreographer

Hagman, Larry (born 1931) American actor

Harlow, Jean (born Harlean Carpenter) (1911–37) American movie actress

Harris, Julie (born 1925) American actress

Hayden, Melissa (born Mildred Herman) (born 1923) Canadian dancer

Herzog, Werner (born Werner Stipetic) (born 1942) German movie director

Heston, Charlton (born John Charlton Carter) (born 1924) American actor

Hopper, Dennis (born 1936) American actor

Howard, Leslie (born Leslie Howard Stainer) (1893–1943) English actor

Howard, Trevor (Wallace) (1916–88) English actor

Hudson, Rock (born Roy Scherer, Jr.) (1925–85) American actor

Hughes, Howard (Robard) (1905–76) American industrialist, movie producer, and aviator

Huston, Anjelica (born 1951) Ameerican actress

Huston, John (1906–87) American-born movie director

Jessel, George (1898–1981) American entertainer

Jolson, Al (born Asa Yoelson) (1886–1950) Russian-born American singer, movie actor, and comedian

Keaton, Buster (born Joseph Francis Keaton) (1895–1966) American actor and director

Keaton, Diane (born Diane Hall) (born 1946) American actress

Keitel, Harvey (born 1939) American actor

Kelley, Emmet (1898–1977) American circus performer

Kemble, Frances Anne ("Fanny") (1809–93) English actress

Kidman, Nicole (born 1967) American actress

Kovacs, Ernie (1919–62) American actor and comedian

Lamarr, Hedy (born Hedwig Kiesler) (1913–2000) Austrian-born American actress

Landon, Michael (born Eugene Orowitz) (1936–91) American actor

Lauder, Sir Harry (born Hugh MacLennan Lauder) (1870–1950) Scottish music-hall performer

Lemmon, Jack (born John Uhler) (born 1925) American actor

Lugosi, Bela (born Béla Ferenc Blasko) (1884–1956) Hungarian-born American actor

Malden, Karl (born Mladen Sekulovich) (born 1913) American actor

Martin, Dean (born Dino Paul Crocetti) (1917–95) American singer and actor

Martin, Mary (1913–90) American actress

Martin, Steve (born 1945) American actor and comedian

Marvin, Lee (1924–87) American actor

Merman, Ethel (born Ethel Zimmerman) (1908–84) American actress and singer

Midler, Bette (born 1945) American actress and comedian

Mifune, Toshiro (1920–97) Japanese actor

Monroe, Marilyn (born Norma Jean Mortenson, later Baker) (1926–62) American actress

Montez, Lola (born Marie

Dolores Eliza Rosanna Gilbert)
(1818–61) Irish dancer

Moreau, Jeanne (born 1928)
French actress

Moreau, Jeanne (born 1928)
French actress

Mostel, Zero (1915–77) American
actor

Murnau, Friedrich W. (1889–
1931) German movie director

Murphy, Audie (1924–71)
American war hero and actor

Murphy, Eddie (born 1961)
American comedian and actor

Murray, Bill (born 1950)
American actor and comedian

Nelson, Ozzie (1906–75)
American actor; husband of
Harriet (Hilliard) Nelson
(1914–94) and father of Ricky
Nelson (1940–85)

Newman, Paul (born 1925)
American actor and movie direc-
tor; husband of Joanne
Woodward

Norris, Chuck (born Carlos Ray)
(born 1940) American actor

O'Toole, (Seamus) Peter (born
1932) Irish-born British actor

Oakley, Annie (1860–1926)
American entertainer and sharp-
shooter

Pacino, Al(fred) (born 1940)
American movie actor

Petipa, Marius (Ivanovich)
(1818–1910) French ballet-
dancer and choreographer, resident in Russia from 1847

Primus, Pearl (1919–95)
Trinidadian-born American
dancer and choreographer

Reagan, Ronald (born 1911)
American actor and politician

Reeves, Keanu (born 1964)
Lebanese-born American actor

Reiner, Carl (born 1922)
American actor and comedian

Reiner, Rob (born 1945)
American actor; son of Carl
Reiner

Renoir, Jean (1894–1979) French

movie director, son of Auguste

Rogers, Fred "Mister" (born
1928) American television personality

Rogers, Ginger (born Virginia
Katherine McMath) (1911–95)
American actress and dancer

Rogers, Roy (born Leonard
Franklin Slye) (1911–98)
American singer and actor

Rooney, Mickey (born Joseph Yule
Jr.) (born 1920) American actor

Sayles, John (born 1950)
American movie director

Seberg, Jean (1938–79) American
actress

Sharif, Omar (born Michael
Shalhoub) (born 1932)
Egyptian-born actor

Spacek, Sissy (born 1949)
American actress

Streep, Meryl (born Mary Louise
Streep) (born 1949) American
actress

Taylor, Elizabeth (born 1932)
American actress, born in
England

Temple, Shirley (later Shirley
Temple Black) (born 1928)
American child star

Thomas, Danny (born Muzyad
Yakhoob) (1912–91) American
actor

Tomlin, Lily (born 1939) American comedian and actress

Tucker, Sophie (born Sophia
Kalish) (1884–1966) Russian-
born American singer and entertainer

Valois, Dame Ninette de See DE
VALOIS

Vereen, Ben (born 1946)
American actor

Walken, Christopher (born 1943)
American actor

Waters, John (born 1946)
American movie director

Welles, (George) Orson
(1915–85) American movie
director and actor

Wilder, Billy (born Samuel

People Involved in Movies, Theater, and Dance *(continued)*

Wilder) (born 1906) American movie director and screenwriter, born in Austria

Willis, Bruce (born 1955) American actor

Zanuck, Darryl F(rancis) (1902–79) American movie producer

7 *letters*

Abraham, F. Murray (born 1939) American actor

Andress, Ursula (born 1936) Swiss-born actress

Andrews, Julie (born Julia Elizabeth Wells) (born 1935) English actress and singer

Astaire, Fred (born Frederick Austerlitz) (1899–1987) American dancer, singer, and actor

Aykroyd, Dan (born 1952) Canadian actor and comedian

Belushi, John (1949–82) American actor and comedian

Bergman, (Ernst) Ingmar (born 1918) Swedish movie and theater director

Bergman, Ingrid (1915–82) Swedish actress

Blondin, Charles (born Jean-Francois Gravelet) (1824–97) French acrobat

Bogarde, Sir Dirk (born Derek Niven van den Bogaerde) (1921–99) British actor and writer, of Dutch descent

Bresson, Robert (born 1907) French movie director

Bridges, Lloyd (1913–98) American actor; father of actors Beau Bridges (born 1941) and Jeff Bridges (born 1949)

Bronson, Charles (born Charles Buchinski) (born 1922) American actor

Brynner, Yul (born Taidje Khan) (1915–85) Russian-born

American actor

Burbage, Richard (c. 1567–1619) English actor

Campion, Jane (born 1954) New Zealand movie director and screenwriter

Carlyle, Robert (born 1962) Scottish actor

Chabrol, Claude (born 1930) French movie director

Chaplin, Sir Charles Spencer ("Charlie") (1889–1977) English movie actor and director

Colbert, Claudette (born Lily Chauchoin) (1903–96) French actress

Collins, Joan (Henrietta) (born 1933) English actress

Connery, Sean (born Thomas Connery) (born 1930) Scottish actor

Coppola, Francis Ford (born 1939) American movie director, writer, and producer

De Mille, Agnes (1909–93) American choreographer

de Mille, Cecil B(lount) (1881–1959) American movie producer and director

Deneuve, Catherine (born Catherine Dorléac) (born 1943) French actress

Douglas, Kirk (born Issur Danielovitch Demsky) (born 1916) American actor; father of actor Michael Douglas (born 1944)

Douglas, Melvyn (born Melvyn Hesselberg) (1901–81) American actor

Dukakis, Olympia (born 1931) American actress

Dunaway, Faye (born 1941) American actress

Durante, Jimmy (1893–1980) American entertainer

Estevez, Emilio (born 1962)

American actor; son of Martin Sheen

Estevez see SHEEN, Martin

Fellini, Federico (1920–93) Italian movie director

Fetchit, Stepin (born Lincoln Perry) (1898–1985) American actor

Fonteyn, Dame Margot (born Margaret Hookham) (1919–91) English ballet-dancer

Freeman, Morgan (born 1937) American actor

Gardner, Ava (Lavinia) (1922–90) American actress

Garland, Judy (born Frances Gumm) (1922–69) American singer and actress

Garrick, David (1717–79) English actor, manager, and dramatist

Gielgud, Sir John (born 1904) English actor

Gleason, Jackie (1916–87) American actor and entertainer

Goddard, Paulette (1905–90) American actress

Godfrey, Arthur (1903–83) American television personality

Goldwyn, Samuel (born Schmuel Gelbfisz; changed to Goldfish then Goldwyn) (1882–1974) Polish-born American movie producer

Gregory, Dick (born 1932) American comedian and social activist

Hackman, Gene (born 1930) American actor

Hepburn, Audrey (1929–93) British actress, born in Belgium

Hepburn, Katharine (born 1909) American actress

Hoffman, Dustin (Lee) (born 1937) American actor

Hopkins, Sir Anthony (Philip) (born 1937) Welsh actor

Houdini, Harry (born Erik Weisz) (1874–1926) Hungarian-born American magician and escape artist

Jackson, Glenda (born 1936) English actress and politician

Jewison, Norman (born 1926) Canadian movie director and producer

Joffrey, Robert (1930–88) American choreographer and ballet organizer

Karloff, Boris (born William Henry Pratt) (1887–1969) British-born American actor

Kubrick, Stanley (1928–1999) American movie director, producer, and writer

Langtry, Lillie (born Emilie Charlotte le Breton) (1853–1929) British actress

Lombard, Carole (1908–42) American actress

Lumière, Auguste Marie Louis Nicholas (1862–1954) and **Louis Jean** (1864–1948) French inventors and pioneers of cinema

Madonna (Ciccone) (born 1958) American singer and actress

Marceau, Marcel (born 1923) French mime artist

Markova, Dame Alicia (born Lilian Alicia Marks) (born 1910) English ballet-dancer

Massine, Léonide Fëdorovich (born Leonid Fedorovich Myassin) (1895–1979) Russian-born choreographer and ballet-dancer

McQueen, Steve (1930–80) American actor

Mitchum, Robert (1917–97) American actor

Montand, Yves (1921–91) Italian-born French actor

Newhart, Bob (born 1929) American actor and comedian

Nichols, Mike (born Michael Igor Peschkowsky) (born 1931) German-born American comedian and director

Nureyev, Rudolf (1939–93) Russian-born ballet-dancer and choreographer

O'Connor, Carroll (born 1924) American actor

People Involved in Movies, Theater, and Dance *(continued)*

Olivier, Laurence (Kerr), Baron Olivier of Brighton (1907–89) English actor and director

Palance, Jack (born Walter Palanuik) (born 1920) American actor

Paltrow, Gwyneth (born 1973) American actress

Parson, Estelle (born 1927) American actress and drama teacher

Pavlova, Anna (Pavlovna) (1881–1931) Russian dancer, resident in Britain from 1912

Perkins, Anthony (1932–92) American actor

Phoenix, River (1970–93) American actor

Poitier, Sidney (born 1924) American actor and movie director

Rambert, Dame Marie (born Cyvia Rambam) (1888–1982) British ballet-dancer, teacher and director, born in Poland

Randall, Tony (born Leonard Rosenberg) (born 1920) American actor

Redford, (Charles) Robert (born 1936) American movie actor

Resnais, Alain (born 1922) French movie director

Robards, Jason (born 1922) American actor

Roberts, Julia (born 1967) American actress

Robeson, Paul (1898–1976) American actor, singer, and social activist

Roscius (full name Quintus Roscius Gallus) (died 62 BC) Roman actor

Russell, Jane (born 1921) American actress

Russell, Ken (born Henry Kenneth Alfred Russell) (born 1927) English movie director

Russell, Lillian (1861–1922) American actress

Sandler, Adam (born 1956) American comedian and actor

Savalas, Telly (1924–94) American actor

Sellers, Peter (1925–80) English comic actor

Sennett, Mack (born Mickall Sinnott) (1884–1960) Canadian-born American movie director

Serling, Rod (1924–75) American movie director

Seymour, Lynn (born 1939) Canadian ballet-dancer

Shankar, Uday (1900–77) Indian dancer

Shatner, William (born 1931) Canadian actor

Shearer, Moira (full name Moira Shearer King) (born 1926) Scottish ballet-dancer and actress

Shepard, Sam (born 1943) American actor and dramatist

Shields, Brooke (born 1965) American actress

Siddons, Mrs. Sarah (*née* Kemble) (1755–1831) English actress

Silvers, Phil (born Philip Silversmith) (1912–85) American actor and comedian

Skelton, Red (1913–97) American comedian

St. Denis, Ruth see SAINT DENIS

Steiger, Rod (born 1925) American actor

Stewart, James (Maitland) (1908–97) American actor

Swanson, Gloria (born Gloria May Josephine Svensson) (1899–1983) American actress

Thurman, Uma (born 1970) American actress

Ulanova, Galina (Sergeevna) (1910–98) Russian ballet-dancer

Ullmann, Liv (born 1939)

Swedish actress

Ustinov, Sir Peter (Alexander) (born 1921) British actor, director, and dramatist, of Russian descent

Van Dyke, Dick (born 1925) American actor

Wallach, Eli (born 1915) American actor

Winkler, Henry ("the Fonz") (born 1945) American actor

Winters, Shelley (born 1922) American actress

Wiseman, Frederick (born 1930) American documentary moviemaker

Woolley, Monty (1888–1963) American actor and entertainer

8 letters

Anderson, Lindsay (Gordon) (1923–94) English movie director

Arbuckle, Roscoe "Fatty" (1887–1933) American actor

Ashcroft, Dame Peggy (Edith Margaret Emily) (1907–91) English actress

Bancroft, Anne (born Anna Maria Italiano) (born 1931) American actress

Banderas, Antonio (born 1960) Spanish actor

Bankhead, Tallulah (1903–68) American actress

Barrault, Jean-Louis (1910–94) French actor and director

Basinger, Kim (born 1953) American actress

Belmondo, Jean-Paul (born 1933) French actor

Berkeley, Busby (born William Berkeley Enos) (1895–1976) American choreographer and movie director

Borgnine, Ernest (born 1917) American actor

Champion, Gower (1921–80) American dancer and choreographer; husband of Marge Champion (born 1923) dancer and choreographer

Channing, Carol (born 1923) American actress

Costello, Lou (1906–59) American actor and comedian

Crawford, Joan (born Lucille le Sueur) (1908–77) American actress

Danilova, Alexandra (1903–97) Russian dancer and ballet teacher

de Valois, Dame Ninette (born Edris Stannus) (born 1898) Irish choreographer, ballet-dancer, and teacher

Dewhurst, Colleen (1924–91) Canadian-born actress

DiCaprio, Leonardo (born 1974) American actor

Dietrich, Marlene (born Maria Magdelene von Losch) (1902–92) German-born American actress and singer

Eastwood, Clint (born 1930) American movie actor and director

Fontaine, Joan (born Joan de Havilland) (born 1917) American actress; sister of Olivia de Havilland

Fontanne, Lynn (1887–1983) English-born American actress; wife of Alfred Lunt

Goldberg, Whoopi (born Caryn Johnson) (born 1949) American comedian and actress

Grierson, John (1898–1972) Scottish movie director and producer

Griffith, D(avid) W(ark) (1875–1948) American movie director

Guinness, Sir Alec (born 1914) English actor

Harrison, Sir Rex (born Reginald Carey Harrison) (1908–90) English actor

Hayworth, Rita (born Margarita Carmen Cansino) (1918–87) American actress and dancer

Houseman, John (1902–88)

People Involved in Movies, Theater, and Dance *(continued)*

Romanian-born American actor

Humphrey, Doris (1895–1958)
American dancer, choreographer, and teacher

Jannings, Emil (1886–1950)
Swiss-born German actor

Kirstein, Lincoln (1907–96)
American dance producer and organizer

Kurosawa, Akira (1910–98)
Japanese movie director

Laughton, Charles (1899–1962)
British-born American actor

Lawrence, Gertrude (born Gertrude Klasen) (1898–1952)
English-born American actress

MacLaine, Shirley (born Shirley Beaty) (born 1934) American actress; sister of Warren Beatty

Marshall, E.G. (1910–98)
American actor

McGregor, Ewan (born 1971)
Scottish actor

Merchant, Ismail (born 1936)
Indian movie producer

Mercouri, Melina (born Anna Amalia Mercouri) (1925–94)
Greek actress and politician

Meredith, Burgess (1909–97)
American actor

Milligan, Spike (born Terence Alan Milligan) (born 1918)
British comedian and writer, born in India

Minnelli, Liza (born 1946)
American singer and actress; daughter of singer Judy Garland (1922–69) and director Vincente Minnelli (1910–86)

Nijinsky, Vaslav (Fomich) (1890–1950) Russian ballet-dancer and choreographer

Nikolais, Alwin (1910–93)
American choreographer

O'Donnell, Rosie (born 1962)
American comedian and actress

Pickford, Mary (born Gladys Mary Smith) (1893–1979)
Canadian-born American actress

Polanski, Roman (born 1933)
French movie director of Polish descent

Rathbone, Basil (1892–1967)
English actor

Redgrave, Corin (born 1939)
English actor

Redgrave, Lynn (born 1943)
English actress

Redgrave, Sir Michael (1908–85)
English actor

Redgrave, Vanessa (born 1937)
English actress

Reynolds, Burt (born 1936)
American actor

Reynolds, Debbie (born 1932)
American actress

Robinson, Bill "Bojangles" (1878–1949) American tap dancer and actor

Sarandon, Susan (born Susan Tomaling) (born 1946)
American actress

Scorsese, Martin (born 1942)
American movie director

Seinfeld, Jerry (born 1954)
American comedian and actor

Selznick, David O(liver) (1902–65) American movie producer

Signoret, Simone (1921–85)
French actress

Smothers, Dick (born 1939)
American comedian and singer; brother of Tommy Smothers

Smothers, Tommy (born 1937)
American comedian and singer; brother of Dick Smothers

Stallone, Sylvester "Sly" (born 1946) American actor

Sullivan, Ed (1902–74) American television personality

Thompson, Emma (born 1959)
English actress and screenwriter

Truffaut, François (1932–84)
French movie director

Visconti, Luchino (full name Don Luchino Visconti, Conte di Modrone) (1906–76) Italian movie and theater director

von Sydow, Max (born 1929) Swedish actor

Wallenda, Karl (1905–78) American circus performer; patriarch of Wallenda circus family

Williams, Bert (1877–1922) Bahamian-born American comedian, actor, and singer

Williams, Robin (born 1952) American comedian and actor

Woodward, Joanne (born 1930) American actress; wife of Paul Newman

Ziegfeld, Florenz (1869–1932) American theater manager

9 letters

Almodóvar, Pedro (born 1949) Spanish movie director

Antonioni, Michelangelo (born 1912) Italian movie director

Barrymore, Drew (born 1975) American actress

Barrymore, Ethel (1879–1959) American actress

Barrymore, John (1882–1942) American actor

Barrymore, Lionel (1878–1954) American actor

Bel Geddes, Barbara (born 1922) American actress

Bernhardt, Sarah (born Henriette Rosine Bernard) (1844–1923) French actress

Bojangles see ROBINSON, Bill

Chevalier, Maurice (1888–1972) French singer and actor

Dandridge, Dorothy (1923–65) American actress

Depardieu, Gérard (born 1948) French actor

Diaghilev, Sergei (Pavlovich) (1872–1929) Russian ballet impresario

Dickinson, Angie (born Angelina Brown) (born 1931)

American actress

Fairbanks, Douglas (Elton) (born Julius Ullman) (1883–1939) American actor

Fishburne, Lawrence (born 1961) American actor

Funicello, Annette (born 1942) American actress

Harrelson, Woody (born 1961) American actor

Hitchcock, Alfred (1899–1980) British movie director

Lancaster, Burt(on Stephen) (1913–94) American movie actor

Letterman, David (born 1947) American television personality

Mansfield, Jayne (1932–67) American actress

Montalban, Ricardo (born 1920) Mexican actor

Morecambe, Eric (born John Eric Bartholomew) (1926–84) English comedian

Nicholson, Jack (born 1937) American actor and director

O'Sullivan, Maureen (1911–98) American actress

Preminger, Otto (Ludwig) (1906–86) Austrian-born American movie director

Reinhardt, Max (born Max Goldmann) (1873–1943) Austrian theater director and impresario

Spielberg, Steven (born 1947) American movie director and producer

Stapleton, Maureen (born 1925) American actress

Strasberg, Lee (born Israel Strassberg) (1901–82) American actor, director, and drama teacher, born in Austria

Streisand, Barbra (born 1942) American singer and actress

Tallchief, Maria (born 1925) American dancer

Tarantino, Quentin (Jerome) (born 1963) American movie director, screenwriter, and actor

People Involved in Movies, Theater, and Dance (continued)

Thorndike, Dame (Agnes) Sybil (1882–1976) English actress

Valentino, Rudolph (born Rudolfo Guglielmi di Valentina d'Antonguolla) (1895–1926) Italian-born American actor

Zimbalist, Efrem, Jr. (born 1923) American actor

Zinnemann, Fred (1907–97) Austrian-born American movie director

10 letters

Balanchine, George (born Georgi Melitonovich Balanchivadze) (1904–83) Russian-born American ballet-dancer and choreographer

Bertolucci, Bernardo (born 1940) Italian movie director

Cassavetes, John (1929–89) American movie director and screenwriter

Cunningham, Merce (born 1919) American dancer and choreographer

D'Oyly Carte, Richard (1844–1901) English impresario and producer

Eisenstein, Sergei (Mikhailovich) (1898–1948) Soviet movie director, born in Latvia

Fassbinder, Rainer Werner (1946–82) German movie director

Littlewood, (Maud) Joan (1914–91) English theater director

Richardson, Sir Ralph (David) (1902–83) English actor

Rossellini, Roberto (1906–77) Italian movie director

Rutherford, Dame Margaret (1892–1972) English actress

Saint Denis, Ruth (born Ruth Dennis) (1877–1968) American dancer and dance teacher

Zeffirelli, Franco (born Gianfranco Corsi) (born 1923) Italian movie and theater director

11 letters

Baryshnikov, Mikhail (Nikolaevich) (born 1948) American ballet-dancer, born in Latvia of Russian parents

Buffalo Bill (born William Frederick Cody) (1846–1917) American showman

de Havilland, Olivia (born 1916) American actress

Mastroianni, Marcello (1924–96) Italian actor

Riefenstahl, Leni (full name Bertha Helene Amalie Riefenstahl) (born 1902) German movie-maker, photographer, and Nazi propagandist

Roddenberry, Gene (full name Eugene Wesley Roddenberry) (1921–91) American television producer and scriptwriter

von Stroheim, Erich (1885–1957) German actor

Weissmuller, John Peter ("Johnny") (1904–84) American swimmer and actor

12 letters

Attenborough, Richard (Samuel) (born 1923) English movie actor, producer, and director

von Sternberg, Josef (1894–1969) Austrian-born American movie director

14 letters

Laurel and Hardy, Stan Laurel (born Arthur Stanley Jefferson) (1890–1965) and **Oliver Hardy** (1892–1957) American comedy duo

Schwarzenegger, Arnold (born 1947) Austrian-born American movie actor

15 letters

Granville-Barker, Harley (1877–1946) English dramatist,

critic, theater director, and actor

Ozzie and Harriet see NELSON, Ozzie

17 letters

Abbott and Costello see ABBOTT, Bud, and COSTELLO, Lou

Writers, Philosophers, and Scholars

2 letters

AE, pseudonym of George William Russell

Fo, Dario (born 1926) Italian dramatist

H.D., pseudonym of Hilda DOOLITTLE

Oe, Kenzaburo (born 1935) Japanese novelist

3 letters

Bly, Robert (born 1926) American poet

Boz pseudonym used by Charles DICKENS in his *The Pickwick Papers* and contributions to the Morning Chronicle

Eco, Umberto (born 1932) Italian novelist and semiotician

Fry, Christopher (Harris) (born (1907) English dramatist

Gay, John (1685–1732) English poet and dramatist

Kyd, Thomas (1558–94) English dramatist

Lee, (Nelle) Harper (born 1926) American novelist

Lee, Laurie (1914–97) English writer

Nin, Anas (1930–77) American writer

Paz, Octavio (1914–98) Mexican poet and essayist

Poe, Edgar Allan (1809–49) American short-story writer, poet, and critic

Pym, Barbara (Mary Crampton) (1913–80) English

novelist

Tan, Amy (born 1952) American novelist

4 letters

Agee, James (Rufus) (1909–55) American novelist, poet, and movie critic

Amis, Martin (Louis) (born 1949) English novelist, son of Kingsley Amis

Amis, Sir Kingsley (1922–95) English novelist and poet

Asch, Sholem (1880–1957) Polish-born American novelist and Yiddish playwright

Ayer, Sir A(lfred) J(ules) (1910–89) English philosopher

Baum, Lyman Frank (1856–1919) American childrens' author and dramatist

Behn, Aphra (1640–89) English novelist and dramatist

Bell, Currer, Ellis, and **Acton** pseudonyms used by Charlotte, Emily and Anne BRONTË

Bell, Gertrude (1868–1926) English archaeologist and writer

Böll, Heinrich (Theodor) (1917–85) German novelist and short-story writer

Bolt, Robert (Oxton) 1924–95) English dramatist and screenwriter

Bond, Edward (born 1934) English dramatist

Buck, Pearl S(ydenstricker) (1892–1973) American writer

Writers, Philosophers, and Scholars *(continued)*

Cain, James M(allahan) (1892–1977) American novelist and journalist

Carr, Emily (1871–1945) Canadian writer and painter

Cary, (Arthur) Joyce (Lunel) (1888–1957) English novelist

Dahl, Roald (1916–90) British writer, of Norwegian descent

Dana, Richard Henry (1815–82) American adventurer, lawyer, and writer

Du Fu See Tu Fu

Edel, (Joseph) Leon (born 1907) American literary scholar and biographer

Elia pseudonym adopted by Charles Lamb in his *Essays of Elia* (1823) and *Last Essays of Elia* (1833)

Fast, Howard (born 1914) American novelist and memoirist

Ford, Ford Madox (born Ford Hermann Hueffer) (1873–1939) English novelist and editor

Ford, John (1586–c. 1639) English dramatist

Foxe, John (1516–87) English religious writer

Frye, (Herman) Northrop (1912– 91) Canadian literary critic

Gide, André (Paul Guillaume) (1849–1951) French novelist, essayist, and critic

Gray, Thomas (1716–71) English poet

Grey, Zane (1872–1939) American novelist

Gunn, Thom (full name Thomson William Gunn) (born 1929) English poet

Hall, Donald (born 1928) American poet

Hite, Shere (born 1942) American feminist

Hogg, James (1770–1835) Scottish poet and novelist

Hood, Thomas (1799–1845) English poet and humorist

Howe, Irving (1920–93) American literary and social critic

Hugo, Richard (1923–82) American poet

Hugo, Victor(-Marie) (1802–85) French poet, novelist, and dramatist

Hume, David (1711–76) Scottish philosopher, economist, and historian

Inge, William (1913–73) American playwright

Jong, Erica (Mann) (born 1942) American poet and novelist

Kant, Immanuel (1724–1804) German philosopher

King, Stephen (born 1947) American novelist and short-story writer

Knox, Ronald Arbuthnott (1888–1957) English theologian and writer

Koch, Kenneth (born 1925) American poet

Lamb, Charles (1775–1834) English essayist and critic

Lear, Edward (1812–88) English humorist and illustrator

Levi, Primo (1919–87) Italian novelist and poet

Li Bo See Li Po

Li Po (also Li Bo, Li T'ai Po) (AD 701–62) Chinese poet

Livy (Latin name Titus Livius) (59 BC– AD 17) Roman historian

Loos, Anita (1893–1981) American novelist and playwright

Loti, Pierre (pseudonym of Louis Marie Julien Viaud) (1850–1923) French novelist

Lyly, John (c. 1554–1606) English prose writer and dramatist

Mann, Horace (1796–1859) American educational theorist

Mann, Thomas (1875–1955) German novelist and essayist

Mare, Walter, de al See DE LA MARE

Marx, Karl (Heinrich) (1818–83) German political philosopher and economist, resident in England from 1849

Mead, Margaret (1901–79) American anthropologist

Mill, John Stuart (1806–73) English philosopher and economist

More, Sir Thomas (canonized as St. Thomas More) (1478–1535) English scholar and statesman, Lord Chancellor 1529–32

Moss, Howard (1922–87) American poet

Muir, Edwin (1887–1959) Scottish poet and translator

Muir, John (1838–1914) American writer on nature

Nash, (Frederic) Ogden (1902–71) American poet

Ovid (full name Publius Ovidius Naso) (43 BC–AD *c.* 17) Roman poet

Owen, Wilfred (1893–1918) English poet

Pope, Alexander (1688–1744) English poet

Rand, Ayn (born Alissa Rosenbaum) (1905–82) American writer and philosopher, born in Russia

Reed, Ishmael (born 1938) American novelist and poet

Rhys, Jean (pseudonym of Ella Gwendolen Rees Williams) (1890–1979) British novelist and short-story writer, born in Dominica

Rice, Anne (born 1941) American novelist

Rich, Adrienne (born 1929) American poet

Roth, Henry (1906–99) American novelist

Roth, Philip (Milton) (born 1933) American novelist and short-story writer

Rowe, Nicholas (1674–1718) English dramatist

Ryle, Gilbert (1900–76) English philosopher

Sade, Donatien Alphonse François, Comte de (known as the Marquis de Sade) (1740–1814) French writer and soldier

Sadi (also Saadi) (born Sheikh Muslih Addin) (*c.*1213–*c.* 1291) Persian poet

Said, Edward W(adi) (born 1935) American critic and writer, born in Palestine

Saki (pseudonym of Hector Hugh Munro) (1870–1916) British short-story writer, born in Burma

Sand, George (pseudonym of Amandin-aurore Lucille Dupin, Baronne Dudevant) (1804–76) French novelist

Shaw, George Bernard (1856–1950) Irish dramatist and writer

Shaw, Irwin (1913–84) American playwright and novelist

Snow, C(harles) P(ercy), 1st Baron Snow of Leicester (1905–80) English novelist and scientist

Tate, Nahum (1652–1715) Irish dramatist and poet, resident in London from the 1670's

Tu Fu (AD 712–70) Chinese poet

Uris, Leon (born 1924) American novelist

Vega, Lope de (full name Lope Felix de Vega Carpio) (1562–1635) Spanish dramatist and poet

Vico, Giambattista (1668–1744) Italian philosopher

Vine, Barbara (pseudonym used by Ruth Rendell)

Wain, John (Barrington) (1925–94) English writer

Ward, Mrs. Humphry (*née* Mary Augusta Arnold) (1851–1920) English writer and anti-suffrage campaigner

Writers, Philosophers, and Scholars *(continued)*

Webb, (Gladys) Mary
(1881–1927) English novelist

Weil, Simone (1909–43) French
essayist, philosopher, and mystic

West, Dame Rebecca (born
Cicily Isabel Fairfield)
(1892–1983) British writer and
feminist, born in Ireland

West, Nathanael (born Nathan
Wallenstein Weinstein)
(1903–40) American novelist and
satirist

Wood, Mrs. Henry (*née* Ellen
Price) (1814–87) English
novelist

Wouk, Herman (born 1915)
American novelist

Wren, P(ercival) C(hristopher)
(1885–1941) English novelist

Zeno (known as Zeno of Citium)
(*c.* 335–*c.* 263 BC) Greek
philosopher, founder of Stoicism

Zeno (known as Zeno of Elea) (*fl.*
5th century BC) Greek philosopher

**Zola, Émile (Édouard Charles
Antoine)** (1840–1902), French
novelist and critic

5 letters

Adams, Henry (1838–1918)
American historian and autobi-
ographer

Aesop (6th century BC) Greek sto-
ryteller

Aiken, Conrad (1889–1973)
American poet and novelist

Albee, Edward Franklin (born
1928) American dramatist

Alger, Horatio (1832–99)
American author of inspirational
boys' stories

Auden, W(ysten) H(ugh)
(1907–73) British-born poet

**Awdry, Reverend W(ilbert)
V(ere)** (born 1911) English
writer of children's stories

Baker, Russell (born 1925)
American journalist and autobi-
ographer

Banks, Russell (born 1940)
American novelist

Barth, John (Simmons) (born
1930) American novelist and
short-story writer

Bates, H(erbert) E(rnest)
(1905–74) English novelist and
short-story writer

Beard, Charles A[ustin]
(1874–1948) American historian

Behan, Brendan (Francis)
(1923–64) Irish dramatist and
poet

Benét, Stephen Vincent
(1889–1943) American poet

Berry, Wendell (born 1934)
American poet and essayist

Betti, Ugo (1892–1953) Italian
dramatist, poet, and short-story
writer

Blake, William (1757–1827)
English poet and artist

**Bowen, Elizabeth (Dorothea
Cole)** (1899–1973) British novelist and short-story writer, born
in Ireland

Boyle, Kay (1903–94) American
novelist and short-story writer

Brink, André (born 1935) South
African novelist, short-story
writer, and dramatist

Broun, Heywood (1888–1939)
American journalist and critic

Brown, Rita Mae (born 1944)
American novelist

Bruno, Giordano (1548–1600)
Italian philosopher

Buber, Martin (1878–1965)
Israeli religious philosopher,
born in Austria

Burke, Edmund (1729–97) Irish
politician, philosopher, and
writer

Burke, John (1787–1848) Irish
genealogical and heraldic
writer

Burns, Robert (1759–96) Scottish poet

Byatt, A(ntonia) S(usan) (born 1936) English novelist and literary critic

Byron, George Gordon, 6th Baron (1788–1824) English poet

Cable, George Washington (1844–1925) American novelist and short-story writer

Camus, Albert (1913–60) French novelist, dramatist, and essayist

Čapek, Karel (1890–1938) Czech novelist and dramatist

Clare, John (1793-1864) English poet

Comte, Auguste (1709–1857) French philosopher, one of the founders of sociology

Corso, Gregory (born 1930) American poet

Crane, (Harold) Hart (1899-1932) American poet

Crane, Stephen (1871–1900) American writer

Croce, Benedetto (1866–1952) Italian philosopher

Dante (full name Dante Alighieri) (1265–1321) Italian poet

David, Elizabeth (1913–92) British cookery writer

Defoe, Daniel (1660–1731) English novelist and journalist

Dewey, John (1859–1952) American philosopher and social critic

Donne, John (1572–1631) English poet and preacher

Doyle, Sir Arthur Conan (1859–1930) Scottish novelist

Draco (7th century BC) Athenian legislator

Dumas, Alexandre (known as Dumas père) (1802–70) French novelist and dramatist

Dunne, John William (1875–1949) English philosopher

Duras, Marguerite (pseudonym of Marguerite Donnadieu) (1914–96) French novelist,

movie director, and dramatist

Eliot, George (pseudonym of Mary Ann Evans) (1819–80) English novelist

Eliot, T(homas) S(tearns) (1888–1965) American-born British poet, critic, and dramatist

Elkin, Stanley (born 1930) American novelist

Field, Eugene (1850–95) American poet and journalist

Frame, Janet (Paterson) (born 1924) New Zealand novelist

Frege, Gottlob (1848–1925) German philosopher and mathematician, founder of modern logic

Frost, Robert (Lee) (1874–1963) American poet

Genet, Jean (1910–86) French novelilst, poet, and dramatist

Gogol, Nikolai (Vasilevich) (1809–52) Russian novelist, dramatist, and short-story writer, born in Ukraine

Gorky, Maxim (pseudonym of Aleksei Maksimovich Peshkov) (1868–1936) Russian writer and revolutionary

Grass, Günter (Wilhelm) (born 1927) German novelist, poet, and dramatist

Greer, Germaine (born 1939) Australian feminist and writer

Grimm, Jacob (Ludwig Carl) (1785–1863) and **Wilhelm (Carl)** (1786–1859) German philologists and folklorists

Ha ek, Jaroslav (1883–1923) Czech novelist and short-story writer

Haley, Alex (1921–92) American journalist and novelist

Hardy, Thomas (1840–1928) English novelist and poet

Harte, (Francis) Bret (1836–1902) American short-story writer and poet

Hearn, Lafcadio (1850–1904) Grecian-born American journalist and novelist

Writers, Philosophers, and Scholars *(continued)*

Hecht, Ben (1894–1964)
American journalist, novelist,
and short-story writer

Hegel, Georg Wilhelm Friedrich
(1770–1831) German philosopher

**Heine, (Christian Johann)
Heinrich** (1797–1856) German
poet

Henry, O. (pseudonym of William
Sidney Porter) (1862–1910)
American short-story writer

Herzl, Theodor (1860–1904)
Hungarian-born journalist,
dramatist, and Zionist leader

Hesse, Hermann (1877–1962)
German-born Swiss novelist and
poet

Heyer, Georgette (1902–74)
English novelist

Hicks, Granville (1901–82)
American critic and novelist

Homer (8th century BC) Greek
epic poet

Ibsen, Henrik (1828–1906)
Norwegian dramatist

Iqbal, Sir Muhammad
(1875–1938) Indian poet and
philosopher, generally regarded
as the father of Pakistan

James, C(yril) L(ionel) R(obert)
(1901–89) Trinidadian historian,
journalist, political theorist, and
novelist

James, Clive (Vivian Leopold)
(born 1939) Australian television
personality, writer, and critic

James, Henry (1843–1916)
American-born British novelist
and critic

**James, P(hyllis) D(orothy).
Baroness** (born 1920) English
writer of detective fiction

James, William (1842–1910)
American philosopher and psy-
chologist, brother of Henry
James

Jarry, Alfred (1873–1907) French
dramatist

Jones, Daniel (1881–1967) British
linguist and phonetician

Jones, James (1921–77) American
novelist

Jones, Leroi (after 1965 called
Imamu Amiri Baraka) (born
1934) American poet and playwright

**Joyce, James (Augustine
Aloysius)** (1882–1941) Irish
writer

Kafka, Franz (1883–1924) Czech
novelist, who wrote in German

Kazin, Alfred (born 1915)
American literary critic

Keats, John (1795–1821) English
poet

Kesey, Ken (Elton) (born 1935)
American novelist

Kumin, Maxine (born 1925)
American poet

Lacan, Jacques (1901–81) French
psychoanalyst and writer

Lewis, C(live) S(taples)
(1898–1963) British novelist,
religious writer, and literary
scholar

Lewis, (Harry) Sinclair
(1885–1951) American novelist

Lewis, (Percy) Wyndham
(1882–1957) British novelist,
critic, and painter, born in
Canada

Lewis, Cecil Day See DAY LEWIS

Llosa, Mario Vargas See VARGAS
LLOSA

Locke, John (1632–1704) English
philosopher, a founder of empiri-
cism and political liberalism

Lodge, David (John) (born 1935)
English novelist and academic

Lorca, Federico Garciá
(1898–1936) Spanish poet and
dramatist

Lorde, Audre (1934–92)
American poet

Lowry, (Clarence) Malcolm

(1909–57) English novelist

Lucan (Latin name Marcus Annaeus Lucanus) (AD 39–65) Roman poet, born in Spain

Lurie, Alison (born 1926) American novelist

Mamet, David (born 1947) American playwright

Marsh, Dame Ngaio (Edith) (1899–1982) New Zealand writer of detective fiction

Mason, A(lfred) E(dward) W(oodley) (1865–1948) English novelist

McKay, Claude (1890–1948) Jamaican-born American poet and novelist

Milne, A(lan) A(lexander) (1882–1956) English writer of stories and poems for children

Moody, William Vaughn (1869–1910) American playwright and poet

Moore, G(eorge) E(dward) (1873–1958) English philosopher

Moore, George (Augustus) (1852–1933) Irish novelist

Moore, Marianne (1887–1972) American poet

Moore, Thomas (1779–1852) Irish poet and musician

Munro, Alice (born 1931) Canadian novelist

Munro, H(ector) H(ugh) See SAKI

Musil, Robert (1880–1942) Austrian novelist

Nader, Ralph (born 1934) American lawyer and reformer

Nashe, Thomas (1567–1601) English writer

Neill, A(lexander) S(utherland) (1883–1973) Scottish teacher and educationist

Newby, (George) Eric (born 1919) English travel writer

O'Hara, Frank (1926–66) American poet

O'Hara, John (1905–70) American novelist and short-story writer

Oates, Joyce Carol (born 1938) American novelist and short-story writer

Occam, William of See WILLIAM OF OCCAM

Odets, Clifford (1906–63) American dramatist

Olson, Charles (1910–70) American poet

Orczy, Baroness Emmusca (1865–1947) Hungarian-born British novelist

Orton, Joe (born John Kingsley Orton) (1933–67) English dramatist

Otway, Thomas (1652–85) English dramatist

Ouida (pseudonym of Marie Louise de la Ramée) (1839–1908) English novelist

Ozick, Cynthia (born 1928) American novelist and critic

Paine, Thomas (1737–1809) English political writer

Paley, Grace (born 1922) American short-story writer

Paris, Matthew (*c.* 1199–1259) English chronicler and Benedictine monk

Pater, Walter (Horatio) (1839–94) English essayist and critic

Paton, Alan (Stewart) (1903–88)

Peake, Mervyn (Laurence) (1911–68) British novelist, poet, and artist, born in China

Pepys, Samuel (1633–1703) English diarist and naval administrator

Percy, Walker (1916–90) American novelist and essayist

Philo Judaeus (also known as Philo of Alexandria) (*c.* 15 BC–AD *c.* 50)

Pindar (*c.* 518–*c.* 438 BC) Greek lyric poet

Plath, Sylvia (1932–63) American poet

Plato (*c.* 429–*c.* 347 BC) Greek philosopher

Pliny (known as Pliny the Younger;

Writers, Philosophers, and Scholars *(continued)*

Latin name Gaius Plinius Caecilius Secundus) (*c.* 61–*c.* 112) Roman senator and writer

Ponte, Lorenzo Da See DA PONTE

Pound, Ezra (Weston Loomis) (1885–1972) American poet and critic

Queen, Ellery (pseudonym of **Frederic Dannay** (1905–82) and **Manfred Lee** (1905–71) American writers of detective fiction

Quine, Willard Van Orman (born 1908) American philosopher and logician

Rawls, John (born 1921) American philosopher

Reade, Charles (1814–84) English novelist and dramatist

Rechy, John (born 1934) American novelist

Renan, (Joseph) Ernest (1823–92) French historian, theologian, and philosopher

Riley, James Whitcomb (1849–1916) American poet

Rilke, Rainer Maria (pseudonym of René Karl Wilhelm Josef Maria Rilke) (1875–1926) Austrian poet, born in Bohemia

Roget, Peter Mark (1779–1869) English scholar

Saadi See SADI

Sachs, Hans (1494–1576) German poet and dramatist

Sagan, Françoise (pseudonym of Francoise Quoirez) (born 1935) French novelist, dramatist, and short-story writer

Scott, Sir Walter (1771–1832) Scottish novelist and poet

Seuss, Doctor (pseudonym of Theodore Seuss Geisel) (1904–91), author of children's books

Shute, Nevil (pseudonym of Nevil Shute Norway) (1899–1960)

English novelist

Simon, (Marvin) Neil (born 1927) American dramatist

Smith, Adam (1723–90) Scottish economist and philosopher

Smith, Stevie (pseudonym of Florence Margaret Smith) (1902–71) English poet and novelist

Smith, Sydney (1771–1845) English Anglican churchman, essayist and wit

Spark, Dame Muriel (born 1918) Scottish novelist

Staël, Mme. de See DE STAËL

Steel, Danielle (born 1947) American novelist

Stein, Gertrude (1874–1946) American writer

Stone, Irving (1903–89) American writer of fictionalized biography

Stone, Robert (born 1937) American novelist

Stout, Rex (1886–1975) American detective novelist

Stowe, Harriet (Elizabeth) Beecher (1811–96) American novelist

Suyin, Han (pseudonym of Elizabeth Comber) (born 1917) Chinese-born British writer and doctor

Swift, Jonathan (known as Dean Swift) (1667–1745) Irish satirist, poet, and Anglican cleric

Synge, (Edmund) J(ohn) M(illington) (1871–1909) Irish dramatist

Twain, Mark (pseudonym of Samuel Langhorne Clemens) (1835–1910) American novelist and humorist

Tyler, Anne (born 1941) American novelist

Tzara, Tristan (born Samuel Rosenstock) (1896–1963) Romanian-born French poet

Varro, Marcus Terentius (116–27

BC) Roman scholar and satirist

Verne, Jules (1828–1905) French novelist

Vigny, Alfred Victor, Comte de (1797–1863) French poet, novelist, and dramatist

Watts, Alan (1915–73) English-born American writer on religion

Watts, Isaac (1674–1748) English hymn-writer and poet

Waugh, Evelyn (Arthur St. John) (1903–66) English novelist

Weber, Wilhelm Eduard (1804–91) German physicist

Wells, H(erbert) G(eorge) (1866–1946) English novelist

Welty, Eudora (born 1909) American novelist, short-story writer, and critic

White, E(lwyn) B(rooks) (1899–1985) American humorist, essayist, and writer for children

White, Patrick (Victor Martindale) (1912–90) Australian novelist, born in Britain

White, T(erence) H(anbury) (1906–64) British novelist, born in India

White, Theodore H(arold) (1915–86) American journalist

White, William Allen (1868–1944) American journalist, essayist, and novelist

Wilde, Oscar (Fingal O'Flahertie Wills) (1854–1900) Irish dramatist, novelist poet, and wit

Wolfe, Thomas (Clayton) (1900–38) American novelist

Wolfe, Tom (full name Thomas Kennerley Wolfe Jr.) (born 1931) American writer

Woolf, (Adeline) Virginia (*née* Stephen) (1882–1941) English novelist, essayist, and critic

Wyatt, Sir Thomas (1503–42) English poet

Wylie, Eleanor (1885–1928) American poet

Yeats, W(illiam) B(utler) (1865–1939) Irish poet and dramatist

Yerby, Frank (1916–91) American novelist

6 *letters*

Achebe, Chinua (born Albert Chinualumgu) (born 1930) Nigerian novelist, poet, short-story writer, and essayist

Addams, Jane (1860–1935) American social reformer and theorist

Adorno, Theodor Wiesengrund (born Theodor Wiesengrund) (1903–69) German philosopher, sociologist, and musicologist

Agnesi, Maria Gaetana (1718–99) Italian philosopher and mathematician

Alcott, Louisa May (1832 88) American novelist

Aldiss, Brian W(ilson) (born 1925) English novelist and critic

Algren, Nelson (Abraham) (1909–81) American novelist

Andrić, Ivo (1892–1975) Serbian writer

Arendt, Hannah (1906–75) German-born American philosopher and political theorist

Arnold, Matthew (1822–88) English poet, essayist, and social critic

Ascham, Roger (1515–68) English scholar and writer

Asimov, Isaac (1920–92) Russian-born American writer and scientist

Atwood, Margaret (Eleanor) (born 1939) Canadian novelist, poet, critic, and short-story writer

Aubrey, John (1626–97) English antiquarian and author

Austen, Jane (1775–1817) English novelist

Austin, John Langshaw (1911–60) English philosopher

Austin, John (1790–1859) English jurist

Writers, Philosophers, and Scholars *(continued)*

Balzac, Honoré de (1799–1850) French novelist

Baraka, Amiri see JONES, Leroi

Barker, George (Granville) (1913–91) English poet

Barnes, Djuna (1892–1982) American novelist and playwright

Barrie, Sir J(ames) M(atthew) (1860–1937) Scottish dramatist and novelist

Barzun, Jacques (born 1907) French-born American social critic and scholar

Baxter, James K(eir) (1926–72) New Zealand poet, dramatist, and critic

Beeton, Mrs. Isabella Mary (1836– 65) English writer on cookery

Belloc, (Joseph) Hilaire (Pierre René) (1870–1953) French-born British writer, historian, and poet, of French-British descent

Bellow, Saul (born 1915) Canadian-born American novelist, of Russian Jewish descent

Berlin, Sir Isaiah (1909–97) Latvian-born British philosopher

Besant, Annie (1847–1933) English writer, theosophist, and political campaigner

Bierce, Ambrose (Gwinnett) (1842–c. 1914) American writer

Bishop, Elizabeth (1911–79) American poet

Blixen, Karen (Christentze), Baroness Blixen-Finecke (*née* Dinesen; also known by the pseudonym of Isak Dinesen) (1885– 1962) Danish novelist and short-story writer

Blyton, Enid (1897–1968) English writer of children's fiction

Borges, Jorge Luis (1899–1986) Argentinian poet, short-story writer, and essayist

Borrow, George (Henry) (1803–81) English writer

Bowles, Paul (Frederick) (born 1910) American writer and composer

Braine, John (Gerard) (1922–86) English novelist

Brecht, (Eugen) Bertolt (Friedrich) (1898–1956) German dramatist, producer, and poet

Breton, André (1896–1966) French poet, essayist, and critic

Brontë, Charlotte (1816–55), **Emily** (1818–48), and **Anne** (1820–49), English novelists

Brooke, Rupert (Chawner) (1887–1915) English poet

Brooks, Cleanth (1906–94) American teacher and critic

Brooks, Gwendolyn (born 1917) American poet

Brooks, Van Wyck (1886–1963) American literary historian and critic

Bryant, William Cullen (1794–1878) American poet

Buchan, John, 1st Baron Tweedsmuir (1875–1940) Scottish novelist and statesman

Bunyan, John (1628–88) English writer

Burney, Frances ("Fanny") (1752–1840) English novelist

Burton, Sir Richard (Francis) (1821–90) English explorer, anthropologist, and translator

Butler, Samuel ("Hudibras") (1612–80) English poet

Butler, Samuel (1835–1902) English novelist

Céline, Louis-Ferdinand (pseudonym of Louis-Ferdinand Destouches) (1894–1961) French novelist

Cabell, James Branch (1879–1958) American novelist and short-story writer

Camoes, Luis (Vaz) de (also

Camoëns) (c. 1524–80)
Portuguese poet

Capote, Truman (born Truman
Streckfus Persons) (1924–84)
American writer

Carnap, Rudolf (1891–1970)
German-born American philosopher

Carson, Rachel (1907–64)
American nature writer and
social critic

Carter, Angela (1940–92) English
novelist and short-story writer

Carver, Raymond (1939–89)
American novelist and short-story writer

Cather, Willa (Sibert)
(1876–1974) American novelist
and short-story writer

Cavafy, Constantine (Peter)
(born Konstantinos Petrou
Kavafis) (1863–1933) Greek poet

Chopin, Kate (O'Flaherty)
(1851–1904) American novelist
and short-story wrtier

Ciardi, John (1916–85) American
poet

Cicero, Marcus Tullius (106–43
BC) Roman statesman, orator,
and writer

**Clarke, Marcus (Andrew
Hislop)** (1846–81) British-born
Australian writer

Clarke, Sir Arthur C(harles)
(born 1917) English writer of
science fiction

Clough, Arthur Hugh (1819–61)
English poet

Conrad, Joseph (born Józef
Teodor Konrad Korzeniowski)
(1857–1924) Polish-born British
novelist

Cooper, James Fenimore
(1789–1851) American novelist

Coward, Sir Noel (Pierce)
(1899–1973) English dramatist,
actor, and composer

Cowley, Malcolm (1898–1989)
American poet and critic

Cowper, William (1731–1800)
English poet

Crabbe, George (1754–1832)
English poet

Cronin, A(rchibald) J(oseph)
(1896–1981) Scottish novelist

Cullen, Countee (1903–46)
American poet

Daudet, Alphonse (1840–97)
French novelist and dramatist

Davies, (William) Robertson
(1913–95) Canadian novelist,
dramatist, and journalist

Davies, W(illiam) H(enry)
(1871–1940) English poet

de Sade, Marquis See SADE

De Voto, Bernard (1897–1955)
American historian, teacher, and
critic

Dekker, Thomas (c. 1570–1632)
English dramatist and novelist

Dickey, James (1923–97)
American poet and novelist

Didion, Joan (born 1934)
American novelist

Dowson, Ernest (Christopher)
(1867–1900) English poet

Dryden, John (1631–1700)
English poet, dramatist and
critic

**Du Bois, W(illiam) E(dward)
B(urghardt)** (1868–1963)
American writer and political
activist

Dunbar, Paul Laurence
(1872–1906) American poet

Dunbar, William (c. 1456–c.
1513) Scottish poet

Éluard, Paul (pseudonym of
Eugène Grindel) (1895–1952)
French poet

Empson, Sir William (1906–84)
English poet and literary critic

Engels, Friedrich (1820–95)
German socialist and political
philosopher, resident chiefly in
England from 1842

Ennius, Quintus (239–169 BC)
Roman poet and dramatist

Evelyn, John (1620–1706) English
diarist and writer

Ferber, Edna (1887–1968)
American novelist and playwright

Writers, Philosophers, and Scholars *(continued)*

Fichte, Johann Gottlieb (1762–1814) German philosopher

Fowles, John (Robert) (born 1926) English novelist

France, Anatole (pseudonym of Jacques-Anatole-François Thibault) (1844–1924) French writer

Fugard, Athol (born 1932) South African dramatist

Gaddis, William (born 1922) American novelist

George, Henry (1839–97) American social critic

Gibbon, Edward (1737–94) English historian

Gibbon, Lewis Grassic (pseudonym of James Leslie Mitchell) (1901–35) Scottish writer

Gibran, Khalil (also Jubran) (1883–1931) Lebanese-born American writer and artist

Godwin, William (1756–1836) English social philosopher and novelist

Goethe, Johann Wolfgang von (1749–1832) German poet, dramatist, and scholar

Graves, Robert (Ranke) (1895–1985) English poet, novelist, and critic

Greene, (Henry) Graham (1904–91) English novelist

Hamsun, Knut (pseudonym of Knut Pedersen) (1859-1952) Norwegian novelist

Harris, Frank (1856–1931) Irish-born American journalist, biographer, and essayist

Harris, Frank (born James Thomas Harris) (1856–1931) Irish writer

Harris, Joel Chandler (1848–1908) American folklorist and novelist

Hawkes, John (1925–98) American novelist

Heaney, Seamus (Justin) (born 1939) Irish poet

Heller, Joseph (1923–99) American novelist

Hersey, John (1914–93) American novelist and journalist

Hesiod (*c.* 700 BC) Greek poet

Hobes, Thomas (1588–1679) English philosopher

Holmes, Oliver Wendell (1809–94) American physician and writer

Holmes, Oliver Wendell (1809–94) American poet, essayist, and lecturer

Horace (full name Quintus Horatius Flaccus) (65–8 BC) Roman poet of the Augustan period

Horgan, Paul (1903–95) American historian, novelist, and travel writer

Hughes, (James Mercer) Langston (1902–67) American writer

Hughes, Ted (1930–1999) English poet

Huxley, Aldous (Leonard) (1894–1963) English novelist and essayist

Illich, Ivan (born 1926) Austrian-born American educationist and writer

Irving, John (born 1942) American novelist

Irving, Washington (1783–1859) American writer

Jacobs, William Wymark (1863–1943) English short-story writer

Jerome, Jerome K(lapka) (1859–1927) English novelist and dramatist

Jewett, Sarah Orne (1849–1909) American short-story writer

Jonson, Benjamin ("Ben") (1572–1637) English dramatist and poet

Jubran, Khalil See GIBRAN

Kaiser, Georg (1878–1945)
German dramatist

Kantor, MacKinlay (1904–77)
American novelist

Keller, Helen (Adams)
(1880–1968) American writer,
social reformer, and academic

Kennan, George F(rost) (born
1904) American diplomat, historian, and memoirist

Kilmer, (Alfred) Joyce
(1886–1918) American poet

Krantz, Judith (born 1928)
American novelist

Kunitz, Stanley (Jasspon) (born
1905) American poet and editor

L'Amour, Louis (1910?–88)
American novelist

**Laclos, Pierre (-Ambroise-
François) Choderlos de**
(1741–1803) French novelist

Landor, Walter Savage
(1775–1864) English poet and
essayist

Lanier, Sidney (1842–81)
American poet

Larkin, Philip (Arthur)
(1922–85) English poet

Le Fanu, (Joseph) Sheridan
(1814–73) Irish novelist

Le Guin, Ursula K. (born 1929)
American science fiction writer
and novelist

Lerner, Alan J(ay) (1918–86)
American lyricist and dramatist

Lesage, Alain-René (1668–1747)
French novelist and dramatist

Levine, Philip (born 1928)
American poet

Littré, Émile (1801–81) French
lexicographer and philosopher

London, Jack (pseudonym of John
Griffith Chaney) (1876–1916)
American novelist

Lowell, Amy (Lawrence)
(1874–1925) American poet

Lowell, James Russell (1819–91)
American poet and critic

Lowell, Robert (Traill Spence)
(1917–77) American poet

Ludlum, Robert (born 1927)
American novelist

Lukács, György (1885–1971)
Hungarian philosopher, literary
critic, and politician

Lytton, 1st Baron (born Edward
George Earle Bulwer-Lytton)
(1803–73) British novelist,
dramatist and statesman

Mailer, Norman (born 1923)
American novelist and essayist

Malory, Sir Thomas (c.
1400–1471) English writer

Mather, Cotton (1663–1728)
American theologian and contro-
versialist

McKuen, Rod (born 1933)
American poet and songwriter

McPhee, John (born 1931)
American journalist and writer
on nature

Mengzi See MENCIUS

Merton, Thomas (1915–69)
American religious writer

Merwin, W(illiam) S(tanley)
(born 1927) American poet

Millay, Edna St. Vincent
(1892–1950) American poet

Miller, Arthur (born 1915)
American dramatist

Miller, Henry (Valentine)
(1891–1980) American novelist

Miller, Perry (1905–63) American
literary scholar

Milosz, Czeslaw (born 1911)
Lithuanian-born American poet
and essayist

Milton, John (1608–74) English
poet

**Murray, (George) Gilbert
(Aimé)** (1866–1957) Australian-
born British classical scholar

Neruda, Pablo (born Ricardo
Eliezer Neftalí Reyes) (1904–73)
Chilean poet and diplomat

Nesbit, E(dith) (1858–1924)
English novelist

Norris, Frank (1870–1902)
American novelist

Norton, Charles Eliot
(1827–1908) American scholar

Writers, Philosophers, and Scholars *(continued)*

O'Brien, Edna (born 1932) Irish novelist and short-story writer

O'Brien, Flann (pseudonym of Brian O'Nolan) (1911–66) Irish novelist and journalist

O'Casey, Sean (1880–1964) Irish dramatist

O'Neill, Eugene (Gladstone) (1888–1953) American dramatist

Ockham, William of See WILLIAM OF OCCAM

Orwell, George (pseudonym of Eric Arthur Blair) (1903–50) British novelist and essayist

Paglia, Camille (Anna) (born 1947) American cultural critic

Pagnol, Marcel (1895–1974) French dramatist, movie director, and writer

Panini (lived sometime between 7th and 4th centuries BC) Indian grammarian

Parker, Dorothy (Rothschild) (1893–1967) American humorist, literary critic, short-story writer, and poet

Pascal, Blaise (1623–62) French mathematician, physicist, and religious philosopher

Passos, John Dos See DOS PASSOS

Pavese, Cesare (1908–50) Italian novelist, poet, and translator

Peirce, Charles Sanders (1839–1914) American philosopher and logician

Pinero, Sir Arthur Wing (1855–1934) English dramatist and actor

Pinter, Harold (born 1930) English dramatist, actor, and director

Popper, Sir Karl Raimund (1902–94) Austrian-born British philosopher

Porter, Katherine Anne (1890–1980) American short-story writer and novelist

Porter, Peter (Neville Frederick) (born 1929) Australian poet, resident chiefly in England since 1951

Potter, (Helen) Beatrix (1866–1943) English writer of children's stories

Potter, Dennis (Christopher George) (1935–94) English television dramatist

Powell, Anthony (Dymoke) (born 1905) English novelist

Proulx, E. Annie (born 1935) American novelist

Proust, Marcel (1871–1922) French novelist, essayist, and critic

Pyrrho (*c.* 365–*c.* 270 BC) Greek philosopher

Racine, Jean (1639–99) French dramatist

Ransom, John Crowe (1888–1974) American poet and critic

Rosten, Leo (1908–97) American humorist and scholar

Runyon, (Alfred) Damon (1884–1946) American author and journalist

Sandoz, Mari (1896–1966) American novelist

Sappho (early 7th century BC) Greek lyric poet

Sarton, May (1912–95) Belgian-born American poet and memoirist

Sartre, Jean-Paul (1905–80) French philosopher, novelist, dramatist and critic

Sayers, Dorothy L(eigh) (1893–1957) English novelist and dramatist

Seldes, Gilbert (1893–1970) American journalist and critic

Sendak, Maurice (born 1928) American illustrator and author of children's books

Seneca, Lucius Annaeus (known as Seneca the Younger) (*c.* 4 BC–AD 65) Roman statesman, philosopher, and dramatist

Sexton, Anne (1928–74)
American poet

Shange, Ntozake (born Paulette Williams) (born 1948) American playwright and novelist

Sidney, Sir Philip (1554–86)
English poet and soldier

Singer, Isaac Bashevis (1904–91)
Polish-born American novelist and short-story writer

Snyder, Gary (born 1930)
American poet

Sontag, Susan (born 1933)
American writer and critic

Steele, Sir Richard (1672–1729)
Irish essayist and dramatist

Sterne, Laurence (1713–68) Irish novelist

Stoker, Abraham ("Bram") (1847–1912) Irish novelist and theater manager

Strabo (c. 63 BC–AD c. 23) historian and geographer of Greek descent

Strand, Mark (born 1934)
Canadian-born American poet

Styron, William (born 1925)
American novelist and essayist

Sumner, William Graham (1840–1910) American social scientist and economist

Swados, Harvey (1920–72)
American novelist and short-story writer

Symons, Julian (Gustave) (1912–94) English writer of detective fiction

Tagore, Rabindranath (1861–1941) Indian writer and philosopher

Taylor, Bayard (1825–78)
American poet and journalist

Terkel, Studs (born 1912)
American biographer and oral historian

Thomas, (Philip) Edward (1878–1917) English poet

Thomas, Dylan (Marlais) (1914–53) Welsh poet

Thomas, R(onald) S(tuart) (born 1913) Welsh poet and clergyman

Thrale, Mrs. Hester Lynch (later Hester Lynch Piozzi) (1741–1821) English writer

Timrod, Henry (1828–67)
American poet

Toomer, Jean (1894–1967)
American poet and dramatist

Trevor, William (pseudonym of William Trevor Cox) (born 1928) Irish novelist and short-story writer

Troyes, Chrétien de See CHRÉTIEN DE TROYES

Trumbo, Dalton (1905–76)
American novelist and scriptwriter

Ulpian (Latin name Domitius Ulpianus) (died c. 228), Roman jurist, born in Phoenicia

Updike, John (Hoyer) (born 1932) American novelist, poet, and short-story writer

Uttley, Alison (1884–1976)
English writer

Valéry, (Ambroise) Paul (Toussaint Jules) (1871–1945) French poet, essayist, and critic

Veblen, Thorstein (Bunde) (1857–1929) American economist and social scientist

Vergil See VIRGIL

Villon, François (born François de Montcorbier of François des Loges) (1431–?1463) French poet

Virgil (also Vergil) (Latin name Publius Vergilius Maro) (70–19 BC) Roman poet

Walker, Alice (Malsenior) (born 1944) American writer and poet

Walker, Alice (born 1944)
American novelist and poet

Walker, Margaret (1915–99)
American poet and novelist

Walton, Izaak (1593–1683)
English writer

Warren, Robert Penn (1905–89)
American poet, novelist, and critic

Writers, Philosophers, and Scholars *(continued)*

Wesker, Arnold (born 1932)
English dramatist

Wiesel, Elie (full name Eliezer
Wiesel) (born 1928) Romanian-
born American human-rights
campaigner, novelist, and academic

Wilbur, Richard (born 1921)
American poet

Wilcox, Ella Wheeler
(1850–1919) American poet,
novelist, and short-story writer

Wilder, Laura Ingalls
(1867–1957) American writer of
children's stories

Wilder, Thornton (Niven)
(1897–1975) American novelist
and dramatist

Wilson, August (born 1945)
American playwright

Wilson, Edmund (1895–1972)
American critic, essayist, and
short-story writer

Wilson, Lanford (born 1937)
American playwright

**Wilson, Sir Angus (Frank
Johnstone)** (1913–91) English
novelist and short-story writer

Wister, Owen (1860–1938) American novelist and short-story writer

Wright, James (1927–80)
American poet

Wright, Richard (1908–60)
American novelist and essayist

7 letters

Abelard, Peter (1079–1142)
French scholar, theologian, and
philosopher

Addison, Joseph (1672–1719)
English poet, dramatist, essayist,
and Whig politician

Aelfric (*c.* 955–*c.* 1020) Anglo-
Saxon writer

Alarcón, Pedro Antonio de
(1833–91) Spanish novelist

Alcaeus (6th century BC) Greek
lyric poet

Angelou, Maya (born 1928)
American novelist and poet

Anouilh, Jean (1910–87) French
dramatist

Ariosto, Ludovico (1474–1533)
Italian poet

Ashbery, John (born 1927)
American poet

Bagehot, Walter (1826–77)
English economist and journalist

Baldwin, James (Arthur)
(1924–87) American novelist

Ballard, J(ames) G(raham)
(born 1930) British novelist and
short-story writer, born in
China

Barbour, John (*c.* 1320–95)
Scottish poet and prelate

Barrett, Elizabeth See BROWNING

Barthes, Roland (1915–80)
French writer and critic

Beckett, Samuel (Barclay)
(1906–89) Irish dramatist, novelist, and poet

Bellamy, Edward (1850–98)
American novelist and social
reformer

Bennett, (Enoch) Arnold
(1867–1931) English novelist,
dramatist, and critic

Bennett, Alan (born 1934)
English dramatist and actor

Bentham, Jeremy (1748–1832)
English philosopher and jurist

Bentley, Edmund Clerihew
(1875–1956) English journalist
and novelist

Bergson, Henri (Louis)
(1859–1941) French philosopher

Blunden, Edmund (Charles)
(1896–1974) English poet and
critic

Boileau, Nicholas (full surname
Boileau-Despréaux) (1636–
1711) French critic and poet

Boswell, James (1740–95)
Scottish author and biographer

Braille, Louis (1809–52) French educationist

Bridges, Robert (Seymour) (1844–1930) English poet and literary critic

Brodsky, Joseph (born Iosif Aleksandrovich Brodsky) (1940–96) Russian-born American poet

Buckley, William F(rank) (born 1925) American political writer and novelist

Burgess, Anthony (pseudonym of John Anthony Burgess Wilson) (1917–93) English novelist and critic

Burnett, Frances (Eliza) Hodgson (1849–1924) British-born American novelist

Caedmon (7th century) English poet and monk

Calvino, Italo (1923–87) Italian novelist and short-story writer, born in Cuba

Campbell, (Ignatius) Roy(ston Dunnachie) (1901–57) South African poet

Campbell, Thomas (1777–1844) Scottish poet

Canetti, Elias (1905–94) Bulgarian-born British writer

Carlyle, Thomas (1795–1881) Scottish historian and political philosopher

Carroll, Lewis (pseudonym of Charles Lutwidge Dodgson) (1832–98) English writer

Chapman, George (c. 1560–1634) English poet and dramatist

Chaucer, Geoffrey (c. 1342–1400) English poet

Cheever, John (1912–82) American short-story writer and novelist

Chekhov, Anton (Pavlovich) (1860–1904) Russian dramatist and short-story writer

Chomsky, (Avram) Noam (born 1928) American theoretical linguist and political activist

Clemens, Samuel Langhorne See TWAIN

Cobbett, William (1763–1835) English writer and political reformer

Cocteau, Jean (1889–1963) French dramatist, novelist, and movie director

Coetzee, J(ohn M(axwell) (born 1940) South African novelist

Colette (born Sidonie Gabrielle Claudine) (1873–1954) French novelist

Collins, (William) Wilkie (1824–89) English novelist

Cookson, Dame Catherine (Anne) (1906–98) English writer

Corelli, Marie (pseudonym of Mary Mackay) (1855–1924) English writer of romantic fiction

Creeley, Robert (born 1926) American poet

Cudlipp, Hugh, Baron Cudlipp of Aldingbourne (1913–98) British newspaper editor

Da Ponte, Lorenzo (born Emmanuele Conegliano) (1749–1838) Italian poet and librettist

De Lillo, Don (born 1936) American novelist

de Pisan, Christine (also de Pizan) (c. 1364–c. 1430) Italian writer, resident in France from 1369

de Staël, Mme. (née Anne-Louise Germaine Necker) (1766–1817) French novelist and critic

Derrida, Jacques (born 1930) French philosopher

Dickens, Charles (John Huffam) (1812–70) English novelist

Diderot, Denis (1713–84) French philosopher, writer, and critic

Dillard, Annie (born 1945) American writer on nature

Dinesen, Isak See BLIXEN

Dodgson, Charles Lutwidge See CARROLL

Writers, Philosophers, and Scholars *(continued)*

Donatus, Aelius (4th century) Roman grammarian

Douglas, Lord Alfred (Bruce) (1870–1945) English poet

Drabble, Margaret (born 1939) English novelist

Dreiser, Theodore (Herman Albert) (1871–1945) American novelist

Durrell, Gerald (Malcolm) (1925–95) English zoologist and writer, brother of Lawrence Durrell

Durrell, Lawrence (George) (1912–90) English novelist, poet, and travel writer

Eastman, Max (1883–1969) American social critic

Ellison, Ralph (Waldo) (1914–94) American novelist and essayist

Emerson, Ralph Waldo (1803–82) American philosopher and poet

Erasmus, Desiderius (Dutch name Gerhard Gerhards) (*c.* 1469–1536) Dutch humanist and scholar

Erastus (Swiss name Thomas Lieber; also called Liebler or Lüber) (1524–83) Swiss theologian and physician

Erdrich, Louise (born 1954) American novelist

Everson, William (1912–94) American poet

Farrell, J(ames) G(ordon) (1935–79) English novelist

Farrell, J(ames) T(homas) (1904–79) American novelist

Feydeau, Georges (1862–1921) French dramatist

Flecker, James (Herman) Elroy (1884–1915) English poet

Fleming, Ian (Lancaster) (1908–64) English novelist

Forster, E(dward) M(organ) (1879–1970) English novelist

and literary critic

Forsyth, Frederick (born 1938) English novelist

Francis, Richard Stanley ("Dick") (born 1920) English jockey and writer

Freneau, Philip (1752–1832) American poet

Friedan, Betty (born 1921) American feminist and writer

Fuentes, Carlos (born 1928) Mexican novelist and writer

Gardner, Erle Stanley (1899–1970) American novelist and short-story writer

Garland, Hamlin (1860–1940), American novelist and short-story writer

Gaskell, Mrs. Elizabeth (Cleghorn) (1810–65) English novelist

Gilbert, Sir W(illiam) S(chwenck) (1836–1911) English dramatist and librettist

Gissing, George (Robert) (1857–1903) English novelist

Glasgow, Ellen (1874–1945) American novelist

Golding, Sir William (Gerald) (1911–93) English novelist

Goodman, Paul (1911–72) American social critic

Grafton, Sue (born 1940) American novelist

Gramsci, Antonio (1891–1937) Italian political theorist and activist

Greeley, Horace (1811–72) American journalist and political leader

Grisham, John (born 1955) American novelist

Grotius, Hugo (Latinized name of Huig de Groot) (1583–1645) Dutch jurist and diplomat

Haeckel, Ernst Heinrich (1834–1919) German biologist and philosopher

Haggard, Sir Henry Rider
(1856–1925) English novelist

Hakluyt, Richard (*c.* 1552–1616)
English geographer and historian

Hammett, (Samuel) Dashiell
(1894–1961) American novelist

Hartley, L(eslie) P(oles)
(1895–1972) English novelist

Hazlitt, William (1778–1830)
English essayist and critic

Hellman, Lillian (Florence)
(1907–84) American dramatist

Herbert, George (1593–1633)
English metaphysical poet

Herbert, Sir A(lan) P(atrick)
(1890–1970) English writer and
politician

Herrick, Robert (1591–1674)
English poet

Herriot, James (pseudonym of
James Alrfred Wight) (1916–95)
English short-story writer and
veterinary surgeon

Heyward, DuBose (1885–1940)
American novelist

Hopkins, Gerard Manley
(1844–89) English poet

Hornung, Ernest William
(1866–1921) English novelist

Housman, A(lfred) E(dward)
(1859–1936) English poet and
classical scholar

Howells, Willam Dean
(1837–1920) American novelist,
short-story writer, and journalist

Hurston, Zora Neale (1901–60)
American novelist

**Husserl, Edmund (Gustav
Albrecht)** (1859–1938) German
philosopher

Hypatia (*c.* 370–415) Greek
philosopher, astronomer, and
mathematician

Ionesco, Eugène (1912–94)
Romanian-born French dramatist

Jarrell, Randall (1914–65)
American poet

Jeffers, Robinson (1887–1962)
American poet

Johnson, James Weldon
(1871–1938) American poet,
novelist, and essayist

Johnson, Samuel (known as Dr.
Johnson) (1709–84)

Juvenal (Latin name Decimus
Junius Juvenalis) (*c.* 60–*c.* 140)
Roman satirist

Kennedy, William (born 1928)
American novelist

Kerouac, Jack (born Jean-Louis
Lebris de Kérouac) (1922–69)
American novelist and poet, of
French-Canadian descent

Kinnell, Galway (born 1927)
American poet

Kipling, (Joseph) Rudyard
(1865–1936) English novelist,
short-story writer, and poet

Knowles, John (born 1926)
American novelist

Kundera, Milan (born 1929)
Czech novelist

La Barca, Pedro Calderón de
See CALDERÓN DE LA BARCA

Lardner, Ring[gold] (1885–1933)
American sports writer and
satirist

Layamon (late 12th century)
English poet and priest

Lazarus, Emma (1849–87)
American poet

Le Carré, John (pseudonym of
David John Moore Cornwell)
(born 1931) English novelist

Leibniz, Gottfried Wilhelm
(1646–1716) German rationalist
philosopher, mathematician, and
logician

Leonard, Elmore (John) (born
1925) American writer of
thrillers

Leopold, Aldo (1887–1948)
American writer on nature

Lessing, Doris (May) (born
1919) British novelist and short-
story writer, brought up in
Rhodesia

Li T'ai Po See LI PO

Lindsay, Vachel (1879–1931)
American poet

Writers, Philosophers, and Scholars *(continued)*

Lydgate, John (*c.* 1370–*c.* 1450)
English poet and monk

Lyotard, Jean-Francois
(1924–98) French philosopher
and literary critic

Márquez, Gabriel Garcia See
GARCÍA MÁRQUEZ

Maclean, Alistair (1922–87)
Scottish novelist

Mahfouz, Naguib (born 1911)
Egyptian novelist and short-story
writer

Malamud, Bernard (1914–86)
American novelist and short-
story writer

Malamud, Bernard (1914–86)
American novelist and short-
story writer

Malraux, André (1901–76)
French novelist, politician and
art critic

Manning, Olivia (Mary)
(1908–80) English novelist

Manzoni, Alessandro
(1785–1873) Italian novelist,
dramatist, and poet

Marcuse, Herbert (1898–1979)
German-born American philosopher

Marlowe, Christopher (1564–93)
English dramatist and poet

Marquis, Don (1878–1937)
American journalist and
humorist

Marryat, Frederick (known as
Captain Marryat) (1792–1848)
English novelist

Martial (Latin name Marcus
Valerius Martialis) (AD *c.* 40–*c.*
104) Roman epigrammatist,
born in Spain

Marvell, Andrew (1621–78)
English poet

Masters, Edgar Lee
(1868?–1950) American poet
and biographer

Maugham, (William) Somerset
(1874–1965) British novelist,

short-story writer, and dramatist

Mauriac, François (1885–1970)
French novelist, dramatist, and
critic

Mawlana See JALAL AD-DIN AR-
RUMI

McLuhan, (Herbert) Marshall
(1911–80) Canadian writer and
thinker

Mencius (Latinized name of
Meng-tzu or Mengzi, "Meng the
Master") (*c.* 371–*c.* 289 BC)
Chinese philosopher

Mencken, H(enry) L(ouis)
(1880–1956) American journalist
and literary critic

Meng-tzu See MENCIUS

Merrill, James (1926–95)
American poet

Millett, Katherine ("Kate")
(born 1934) American feminist

Mishima, Yukio (pseudonym of
Hiraoka Kimitake) (1925–70)
Japanese writer

Mitford, Nancy (Freeman)
(1904–73) and her sister **Jessica
(Lucy)** (1917–96) English writers

Molière (pseudonym of Jean-
Baptiste Poquelin) (1622–73)
French dramatist

Mumford, Lewis (1895–1990)
American social critic

Murdoch, Dame (Jean) Iris
(1919–1999) British novelist and
philosopher, born in Ireland

**Nabokov, Vladimir
(Vladimorovich)** (1899–1977)
Russian-born American novelist
and poet

**Naipaul, V(idiadhar) S(ura-
jprasad)** (born 1932)
Trinidadian novelist and travel
writer of Indian descent, resident
in Britain since 1950

**Narayan, R(asipuram) K(rish-
naswamy)** (born 1906) Indian
novelist and short-story writer

Nemerov, Howard (Stanley)
(1920–91) American poet and
novelist
Nennius (*fl. c.* 800) Welsh chronicler
O'Connor, (Mary) Flannery
(1925–64) American novelist and
short-story writer
Osborne, John (James)
(1929–94) English dramatist
Parkman, Francis (1823–93)
American historian
Patchen, Kenneth (1911–72)
American poet
**Patmore, Coventry (Kersey
Dighton)** (1823–96) English
poet
Peacock, Thomas Love
(1785–1866) English novelist
and poet
Plautus, Titus Maccius (*c.*
250–184 BC) Roman comic
dramatist
Pynchon, Thomas (Ruggles)
(born 1937) American novelist
Quincey, Thomas De See DE
QUINCEY
Rölvaag, O(le) E(dvart)
(1876–1931) Norwegian-born
American novelist, who wrote in
Norwegian
Ransome, Arthur (Michell)
(1884–1967) English novelist
Renault, Mary (pseudonym of
Mary Challans) (1905–83)
British novelist, resident in South
Africa from 1948
**Rendell, Ruth (Barbara),
Baroness** (born 1930) English
writer of detective fiction and
thrillers
Richler, Mordecai (born 1931)
Canadian novelist
Richter, Conrad (1890–1968)
American novelist and essayist
**Rimbaud, (Jean Nicholas)
Arthur** (1854–91) French poet
Robbins, Tom (born 1936)
American novelist
Roethke, Theodore (1908–63)
American poet
Rolland, Romain (1866–1944)
French novelist, dramatist, and
essayist
Rostand, Edmond (1868–1918)
French dramatist and poet
Rukeyser, Muriel (1913–80)
American poet
Rushdie, (Ahmed) Salman (born
1947) Indian-born British novel-
ist
**Russell, Bertrand (Arthur
William), 3rd Earl Russell**
(1872–1970) British philosopher,
mathematician, and social
reformer
Russell, George William (known
as AE) (1867–1935) Irish poet
and writer
Sallust (Latin name Gaius
Sallustius Crispus) (86–35 BC)
Roman historian and politician
Saroyan, William (1908–81)
American short-story writer
Sassoon, Siegfried (Lorraine)
(1886–1967) English poet and
writer
Shapiro, Karl (born 1913)
American poet and author
Shelley, Mary (Wollstonecraft)
(1797–1851) English writer, wife
of Percy Bysshe Shelley
Shelley, Percy Bysshe
(1792–1822) English poet
Shepard, Sam (born Samuel
Shepard Rogers) (born 1943)
American playwright and actor
**Simenon, Georges (Joseph
Christian)** (1903–89) Belgian-
born French novelist
Simpson, Louis (born 1923)
Jamaican-born American poet
Sitwell, Dame Edith (Louisa)
(1887–1964) English poet
Skelton, John (*c.* 1460–1529)
English poet
Southey, Robert (1774–1843)
English poet and writer
Soyinka, Wole (born 1934) Niger-
ian dramatist, novelist, and critic
Spencer, Herbert (1820–1903)
English philosopher and sociolo-
gist

Writers, Philosophers, and Scholars *(continued)*

Spender, Sir Stephen (1909–95)
English poet and critic

Spenser, Edmund (*c.* 1552–99)
English poet

Spinoza, Baruch de (or Benedict)
(1632–77) Dutch philosopher, of
Portuguese Jewish descent

Statius, Publius Papinius (AD *c.*
45–96) Roman poet

Stegner, Wallace (1909–93)
American novelist and essayist

Steinem, Gloria (born 1934)
American social critic and essayist

Steiner, Rudolf (1861–1925)
Austrian philosopher, founder of
anthroposophy

Stevens, Wallace (1879–1955)
American poet

Surtees, Robert Smith
(1805–64) English journalist and
novelist

Swenson, May (1927–89)
American poet

Tacitus (full name Publius, or
Gaius, Cornelius Tacitus) (AD *c.*
56–*c.* 120) Roman historian

Taggard, Genevieve (1894–1948)
American poet

Terence (Latin name Publius
Terentius Afer) (*c.* 190–159 BC)
Roman comic dramatist

Theroux, Paul (born 1941)
American novelist, travel writer,
and essayist

Thespis (6th century BC) Greek
dramatic poet

Thomson, James (1700–48)
Scottish poet

Thoreau, Henry David (1817–
62) American essayist and poet

Thurber, James (Grover)
(1894–1961) American humorist
and cartoonist

Tillich, Paul (Johannes) (1886–
1965) German-born American
theologian and philosopher

Tolkien, J(ohn) R(onald) R(euel)

(1892–1973) British novelist and
academic, born in South Africa

Tolstoy, Leo (Russian name Count
Lev Nikolaevich Tolstoi)
(1828–1910) Russian writer

Toynbee, Arnold (Joseph)
(1889–1975) English historian

Trillin, Calvin (born 1935)
American journalist, humorist,
and essayist

Tuchman, Barbara (1912–89)
American historian

Vaughan, Henry (1621–95) Welsh
poet

Vicente, Gil (*c.* 1465–*c.* 1536)
Portuguese dramatist and poet

**Wallace, (Richard Horatio)
Edgar** (1875–1932) English
novelist, short-story writer, and
journalist

Wallace, Lew[is] (1827–1905)
American soldier, government
official, and novelist

Walpole, Sir Hugh (Seymour)
(1884–1941) British novelist

Webster, John (*c.* 1580–*c.* 1625)
English dramatist

Webster, Noah (1758–1843)
American lexicographer and
philologist

Wescott, Glenway (1901–87)
American novelist and essayist

Wharton, Edith (Newbold)
(1862–1937) American novelist
and short-story writer, resident
in France from 1907

Whitman, Walt (1819–92)
American poet

Wideman, John Edgar (born
1941) American novelist and
memoirist

William of Occam (also Ockham)
(*c.* 1285–1349) English philosopher and Franciscan friar

Winters, Yvor (1900–68)
American poet and critic

Wyndham, John (pseudonym of
John Wyndham Parkes Lucas

Beynon Harris) (1903–69)
English writer of science fiction

8 letters

Albertus Magnus, St. (known as
Saint Albert the Great) (*c.*
1200–80) German bishop,
philosopher, and Doctor of the
Church

Andersen, Hans Christian
(1805–75) Danish writer

Anderson, Maxwell (1888–1959)
American novelist and playwright

Anderson, Sherwood
(1876–1941) American novelist
and short-story writer

Apuleius (2nd century AD) Roman
writer and rhetorician

Asturias, Miguel Ángel (1899–
1974) Guatemalan novelist

Averroës (1126–98) Spanish-
Arabian philosopher

Avicenna (Arabic name ibn-Sina)
(980–1037) Persian-born Islamic
philosopher and physician

Beaumont, Francis (1584–1616)
English dramatist

Beauvoir, Simone de See DE
BEAUVOIR

Beckford, William (1759–1844)
English writer and collector

**Beerbohm, Sir Henry
Maximilian ("Max")**
(1872–1956) English lexicographer, writer, critic and conversa-
tionalist

Benchley, Robert (1889–1945)
American humorist and critic

Berenson, Bernard (1865–1959)
American art historian and critic

Bergerac See CYRANO DE
BERGERAC

Berkeley, George (1685–1753)
Irish philosopher and bishop

Betjeman, Sir John (1906–84)
English poet

Bradbury Ray (Douglas) (born
1920) American writer of science
fiction

Bradbury, Malcolm (Stanley)
(born 1932) English novelist,

critic, and academic

Brookner, Anita (born 1928)
English novelist and art historian

Browning, Elizabeth Barrett
(1806–61) English poet

Browning, Robert (1812–89)
English poet

Bukowski, Charles (1920–94)
American poet

Caldwell, Erskine (Preston)
(1903–87) American novelist and
short-story writer

Campbell, Joseph (1904–87)
American scholar on myth

**Cartland, Dame (Mary)
Barbara (Hamilton)** (born
1901) English writer

Catullus, Gaius Valerius (*c.* 84–*c.*
54 BC) Roman poet

Chandler, Raymond (Thornton)
(1888 1959) American novelist

Chandler, Raymond (1888–1959)
American detective novelist

Channing, William Ellery
(1780–1842) American Uni-
tarian writer; uncle of William
Ellery Channing (1818–1901),
poet and biographer

Congreve, William (1670–1729)
English dramatist

Connolly, Cyril (Vernon)
(1903–74) English writer

Crompton, Richmal (pseudonym
of Richmal Crompton Lamburn)
(1890–1969) English writer

cummings, e(dward e(stlin)
(1894–1962) American poet and
novelist

Cynewulf (late 8th–9th centuries)
Anglo-Saxon poet

Day Lewis, C(ecil) (1904–72)
English poet and critic

de la Mare, Walter (John) (1873–
1956) English poet and novelist

de Troyes, Chrétien See
CHRÉTIEN DE TROYES

**Deighton, Leonard Cyril
("Len")** (born 1929) English
novelist

Diogenes (*c.* 400–*c.* 325 BC)
Greek philosopher

Writers, Philosophers, and Scholars *(continued)*

Doctorow, E[dgar] L[awrence] (born 1931) American novelist

Eberhart, Richard (born 1904) American poet

Farquhar, George(1678–1707) Irish dramatist

Faulkner, William (1897–1962) American novelist

Fielding, Henry (1707–54) English novelist

Flaubert, Gustave (1821–80) French novelist and short-story writer

Fletcher, John (1579–1625) English dramatist

Forester, C(ecil) S(cott) (pseudonym of Cecil Lewis Troughton Smith) (1899–1966) English novelist

Foucault, Michel (1926–84) French philosopher

Franklin, (Stella Maria Sarah) Miles (1879–1954) Australian novelist

Garrison, William Lloyd (1805–79) American journalist and social reformer

Gassendi, Pierre (1592–1655) French philosopher and astronomer

Ginsberg, Allen (1926–97) American poet

Gobineau, Joseph Arthur, Comte de (1816–82) French writer and anthropologist

Goncourt, Edmond de (1822–96) and **Jules de** (1830–70) French novelists and critics

Gordimer, Nadine (born 1923) South African novelist and short-story writer

Habermas, Jürgen (born 1929) German social philosopher

Han Suyin See SUYIN

Heat-Moon, William Least (born 1939) American memoirist and travel writer

Heinlein, Robert A[nson] (1907–88) American science-fiction writer

Hijuelos, Oscar (born 1952) American novelist

Hoffmann, E(rnst) T(heodor) A(madeus) (1776–1822) German novelist, short-story writer, and music critic

Ishiguro, Kazuo (born 1954) Japanese-born British novelist

Jean Paul (pseudonym of Johann Paul Friedrich Richter) (1763–1825) German novelist

Kalidasa (5th century AD) Indian poet and dramatist

Karadžić, Vuk Stefanović (1787–1864) Serbian writer grammarian, lexicographer, and folklorist

Kawabata, Yasunari (1899–1972) Japanese novelist

Keneally, Thomas (Michael) (born 1935) Australian novelist

Kingsley, Charles (1819–75) English novelist and clergyman

Koestler, Arthur (1905–83) Hungarian-born British novelist and essayist

Kosinski, Jerzy (1933–91) Polish-born American novelist

Kotzebue, August von (1761–1819) German dramatist

Lagerlöf, Selma (Ottiliana Lovisa) (1858–1940) Swedish novelist

Langland, William (*c.* 1330–*c.* 1400) English poet

Laurence, (Jean) Margaret (1926–87) Canadian novelist

Lawrence D(avid) H(erbert) (1885–1930) English novelist, poet, and essayist

Lawrence, T(homas) E(dward) (known as Lawrence of Arabia) (1888–1935) British soldier and writer

Levertov, Denise (born 1923)

English-born American poet

Longinus (*fl.* 1st century AD) Greek scholar

Lovelace, Richard (1618–57) English poet

Lycurgus (9th century BC) Spartan lawgiver

Macaulay, Dame (Emilie) Rose (1881–1958) English novelist and essayist

Macaulay, Thomas Babington, 1st Baron (1800–59) English historian, essayist, and philanthropist

MacLeish, Archibald (1892–1982) American poet and essayist

MacNeice, (Frederick) Louis (1907–63) Northern Irish poet

Malherbe, François de (1555–1628) French poet

Marquand, J[ohn] P[hilip] (1893–1960) American novelist

McCarthy, Mary (Therese) (1912–89) American novelist and critic

McMurtry, Larry (born 1936) American novelist

Meleager (*fl.* 1st century BC) Greek poet

Melville, Herman (1819–91) American novelist and short-story writer

Menander (*c.* 342–292 BC) Greek dramatist

Meredith, George (1828–1909) English novelist and poet

Michener, James A[lbert] (1907–97) American novelist

Mitchell, Margaret (1900–49) American novelist

Mitchell, Margaret (1900–49) American novelist

Morrison, Toni (full name Chloe Anthony Morrison) (born 1931) American novelist

Ondaatje, (Philip) Michael (born 1943) Canadian writer, born in Sri Lanka

Overbury, Sir Thomas (1581–1613) English writer and

courtier

Palgrave, Francis Turner (1824–97) English critic and poet

Pasolini, Pier Paolo (1922–75) Italian movie director, poet, and novelist

Perelman, S(idney) J(oseph) (1904–79) American humorist and writer

Perelman, S[idney] J[oseph] (1904–79) American humorist and playwright

Perrault, Charles (1628–1703) French writer

Petrarch (Italian name Francesco Petrarca) (1304–74) Italian poet

Phillips, David Graham (1867–1911) American journalist and novelist

Plotinus (*c.* 205–70) Philosopher, probably of Roman descent, the founder and leading exponent of Neoplatonism

Plutarch (Latin name Lucius Mestrius Plutarchus) (*c.* 46–*c.* 120) Greek biographer and philosopher

Polybius (*c.* 200–*c.* 118 BC) Greek historian

Porphyry (born Malchus) (*c.* 232–303) Syrian-born neoplatonist philosopher

Priscian (full name Priscianus Caesariensis) (6th century AD) Byzantine grammarian

Proudhon, Pierre Joseph (1809–65) French social philosopher and journalist

Rabelais, François (*c.* 1494–1553) French satirist

Rattigan, Sir Terence (Mervyn) (1911–77) English dramatist

Rawlings, Marjorie Kinnan (1896–1953) American novelist

Remarque, Erich Maria (1898–1970) German-born American novelist

Richards, I(vor) A(rmstrong) (1893–1979) English literary critic and poet

Writers, Philosophers, and Scholars *(continued)*

Robinson, Edwin Arlington (1869–1935) American poet

Rossetti, Christina (Georgina) (1830–94) English poet

Rossetti, Dante Gabriel (full name Gabriel Charles Dante Rossetti) (1828–82) English painter and poet

Rousseau, Jean-Jacques (1712–78) French philosopher and writer, born in Switzerland

Salinger, J(erome) D(avid) (born 1919) American novelist and short-story writer

Sandburg, Carl (1878–1967) American poet, folklorist, and journalist

Scaliger, Joseph Justus (1540–1609) French scholar

Scaliger, Julius Caesar (1484–1558) Italian-born French classical scholar

Schiller (Johann Christoph) Friedrich (von) (1759–1805) German dramatist, poet, and writer

Schlegel, August Wilhelm von (1767–1845) German poet, critic, and translator

Schwartz, Delmore (1913–66) American poet and critic

Sheridan, Richard Brinsley (1751–1816) Irish dramatist and Whig politician

Sherwood, Robert (1896–1955) American playwright

Sillitoe, Alan (born 1928) English writer

Sinclair, Upton (Beall) (1878–1968) American novelist and social reformer

Smollett, Tobias (George) (1721–71) Scottish novelist

Socrates (469–399 BC) Greek philosopher

Spengler, Oswald (1880–1936) German philosopher

Spillane, Mickey (pseudonym of Frank Morrison Spillane) (born 1918) American writer

Stafford, Jean (1915–79) American novelist

Steffens, Lincoln (1866–1936) American journalist and social critic

Stendhal (pseudonym of Marie Henri Beyle) (1783–1842) French novelist

Stoppard, Sir Tom (born Thomas Straussler) (born 1937) British dramatist, born in Czechoslovakia

Strachey, (Giles) Lytton (1880–1932) English biographer

Suckling, Sir John (1609–42) English poet, dramatist, and Royalist leader

Tennyson, Alfred, 1st Baron Tennyson of Aldworth and Freshwater (1809–92) English poet

Thompson, Flora (Jane) (1876–1947) English writer

Thompson, Francis (1859–1907) English poet

Thompson, Hunter S. (born 1939) American journalist and writer

Tibullus, Albius (*c.* 50–29 BC) Roman elegiac poet

Traherne, Thomas (1637–74) English prose writer and poet

Trilling, Lionel (1905–75) American literary and cultural critic

Trollope, Anthony (1815–82) English novelist

Trollope, Frances (1780–1863) English social critic, novelist, and travel writer in the United States

Trumbull, John (1750–1831) American essayist and satirist

Tulsidas (*c.* 1543–1623) Indian poet

Turgenev, Ivan (Sergeevich) (1818–83) Russian novelist

Van Doren, Carl (1885–1950)

American literary historian and biographer; brother of Mark Van Doren (1894–1972), literary critic, biographer, and novelist

Vanbrugh, Sir John (1664–1726) English architect and dramatist

Verlaine, Paul (1844–96) French poet

Voltaire (pseudonym of François-Marie Arouet) (1694–1778) French writer, dramatist, and poet

Vonnegut, Kurt (born 1922) American novelist and short-story writer

Wedekind, Frank (1864–1918) German dramatist

Wheatley, Phillis (1753?–84) African-born American poet

Whittier, John Greenleaf (1807–92) American poet and abolitionist

Williams, Tennessee (born Thomas Lanier Williams) (1911–83) American dramatist

Williams, William Carlos (1883–1963) American poet, essayist, and novelist

Woodward, C[omer] Vann (born 1908) American historian and essayist

Xenophon (*c.* 435–*c.* 354 BC) Greek historian, writer, and military leader

Zukofsky, Louis (1904–78) American poet

9 letters

Akhmatova, Anna (pseudonym of Anna Andreevna Gorenko) (1889–1966) Russian poet

Althusser, Louis (1918–90) French philosopher

Aristotle (384–322 BC) Greek philosopher and scientist

Ayckbourn, Sir Alan (born 1939) English dramatist

Barthelme, Donald (1931–89) American novelist

Bertillon, Alphonse (1853–1914) French criminologist

Blackmore, R(ichard) D(oddridge) (1825–1900) English novelist and poet

Blackwood, Algernon (Henry) (1869–1951) English writer

Boccaccio, Giovanni (1313–75) Italian writer, poet, and humanist

Bodenheim, Maxwell (1893–1954) American poet and novelist

Brautigan, Richard (1935–84) American novelist and short-story writer

Burroughs, Edgar Rice (1875–1950) American novelist and writer of science fiction

Burroughs, John (1837–1921) American writer and conservationist

Burroughs, William S(eward) (1914–97) American novelist

Callaghan, Morley (1903–90) Canadian novelist

Cervantes, Miguel de (full surname Cervantes Saavedra) (1547–1616) Spanish novelist and dramatist

Churchill, Caryl (born 1938) English dramatist

Churchill, Winston (1871–1947) American novelist

Coleridge, Samuel Taylor (1772–1834) English poet, critic, and philosopher

Confucius (Latinized name of K'ung Fu-tzu = "Kong the master") (551–479 BC) Chinese philosopher

Corneille, Pierre (1606–84) French dramatist

d'Annunzio, Gabriele (1863–1938) Italian novelist, dramatist, and poet

de la Roche, Mazo (1879–1961) Canadian novelist

de Spinoza, Baruch See SPINOZA

Descartes, René (1596–1650) French philosopher, mathematician, and man of science, often called the father of modern philosophy

Writers, Philosophers, and Scholars *(continued)*

Dickinson, Emily (Elizabeth)
(1830–86) American poet

Dos Passos, John (Roderigo)
(1896– 1970) American novelist

Du Maurier, Dame Daphne
(1907–89) English novelist

Edgeworth, Maria (1767–1849)
Irish novelist, born in England

Ehrenburg, Ilya (Grigorevich)
(1891–1967) Russian novelist
and journalist

Epictetus (*c.* 55–*c.* 135 AD) Greek
philosopher

Euripides (480–*c.* 406 BC) Greek
dramatist

Feuerbach, Ludwig (Andreas)
(1804–72) German materialist
philosopher

Goldsmith, Oliver (1728–74)
Irish novelist, poet, essayist, and
dramatist

Goncharov, Ivan (1812–91)
Russian novelist

**Hölderlin, (Johann Christian)
Friedrich** (1770–1843) German
poet

Hauptmann, Gerhart (1862–
1946) German dramatist

Hawthorne, Nathaniel (1804–64)
American novelist and short-
story writer

Heidegger, Martin (1889–1976)
German philosopher

Hemingway, Ernest (Miller)
(1899–1961) American writer

Herodotus (known as "the Father
of History") (5th century BC)
Greek historian

Highsmith, Patricia (born
Patricia Plangman) (1921–95)
American writer of detective fic-
tion

Holinshed, Raphael (died *c.*
1580) English chronicler

Hopkinson, Francis (1737–91)
American essayist

**Isherwood, Christopher
(William Bradshaw)**

(1904–86) British-born poet,
dramatist, and critic

Lindbergh, Anne Morrow (born
1906) American essayist, memoirist, and poet

Lucretius (full name Titus
Lucretius Carus) (*c.* 94–*c.* 55
BC) Roman poet and philosopher

Macdonald, Dwight (1906–82)
American literary and social
critic

Mansfield, Katherine (pseudo-
nym of Kathleen Mansfield
Beauchamp) (1888–1923) New
Zealand short-story writer

Martineau, Harriet (1802–76)
English writer

Masefield, John (Edward)
(1878–1967) English poet and
novelist

Massinger, Philip (1583–1640)
English dramatist

McCullers, (Lula) Carson
(1917–67) American writer

Middleton, Thomas (*c.* 1570–
1627) English dramatist

Podhoretz, Norman (born 1930)
American literary and social
critic

Santayana, George (1863–1952)
Spanish-born American philosopher, essayist, and novelist

Schulberg, Budd (born 1914)
American novelist and screenwriter

Steinbeck, John (1902–68)
American novelist

Whitehead, Alfred North
(1861–1947) English philosopher
and mathematician

**Wodehouse, Sir P(elham)
G(renville)** (1881–1975)
British-born writer

Woollcott, Alexander (1887–
1943) American literary and dramatic critic

Wycherley, William (*c.* 1640–
1716) English dramatist

Yezierska, Anzia (1885–1970)
Russian-born American novelist
and short-story writer

Yourcenar, Marguerite (pseudonym of Marguerite de
Crayencoeur) (1903–87) French
writer

10 letters

Anaxagoras (*c.* 500–428 BC)
Greek philosopher

Anaximander (*c.* 610–*c.* 546 BC)
Greek philosopher

Apollonius (known as Apollonius
of Rhodes) (3rd century BC)
Greek poet

Aristippus (known as Aristippus
the Elder) (late 5th century BC)
Greek philosopher

Ballantyne, R(obert) M(ichael)
(1825–94) Scottish writer

Baudelaire, Charles (Pierre)
(1821–67) French poet and critic

Blackstone, Sir William
(1723–80) English jurist

Bloomfield, Leonard
(1887–1949) American linguist

Bradstreet, Anne (*c.* 1612–72)
English-born American poet

Chatterton, Thomas (1752–70)
English poet

Chesterton, G(ilbert) K(eith)
(1874–1936) English essayist,
novelist, and critic

Conan Doyle See DOYLE

Conegliano, Emmanuele See DA
PONTE

**Cr&egr;vecoeur, J. Hector St.
John de** (1735–1813) French-
born American essayist

de Beauvoir, Simone (1908–86)
French existentialist philosopher,
novelist, and feminist

**Dostoevsky, Fyodor
Mikhailovich** (also
Dostoyevsky) (1821–81) Russian
novelist

Fitzgerald, Edward (1809–83)
English scholar and poet

**Fitzgerald, F(rancis) Scott
(Key)** (1896–1940) American
novelist

Heraclitus (*c.* 500 BC) Greek
philosopher

La Fontaine, Jean de (1621–95)
French poet

Longfellow, Henry Wadsworth
(1807–82) American poet

MacDiarmid, Hugh (pseudonym
of Christopher Murray Grieve)
(1892–1978) Scottish poet and
nationalist

Maimonides (born Moses ben
Maimon) (1135–1204) Jewish
philosopher and Rabbinic scholar, born in Spain

Mandelstam, Osip (Emilevich)
(also Mandelshtam)
(1891–1938) Russian poet

**Maupassant, (Henri René
Albert) Guy de** (1850–93)
French novelist and short-story
writer

**Mayakovsky, Vladimir
(Vladimirovich)** (1893–1930)
Soviet poet and dramatist, born
in Georgia

McGonagall, William
(1830–1902) Scottish poet

Montessori, Maria (1870–1952)
Italian educationist

Montgomery, Lucy Maud
(1874–1942) Canadian novelist

Parmenides (*fl.* 5th century BC)
Greek philosopher

Propertius, Sextus (*c.* 50–*c.* 16
BC) Roman poet

Pythagoras (known as Pythagoras
of Samos) (*c.* 580–500 BC)
Greek philosopher

Quintilian (Latin name Marcus
Fabius Quintilianus) (AD *c.* 35–*c.*
96) Roman rhetorician

Richardson, Samuel
(1689–1761) English novelist

**Saint-Simon, Claude-Henri de
Rouvroy, Comte de**
(1760–1825) French social
reformer and philosopher

**Saint-Simon, Louis de Rouvroy,
Duc de** (1675–1755) French
writer

Writers, Philosophers, and Scholars *(continued)*

Sorrentino, Gilbert (born 1929) American novelist and poet

Strindberg, (Johan) August (1849–1912) Swedish dramatist and novelist

Swedenborg, Emanuel (1688–1772) Swedish scientist, philosopher, and mystic

Tannhäuser (*c.* 1200–*c.* 1270) German poet

Tarkington, Booth (1869–1946) American novelist and writer for youth

Theocritus (*c.* 310–*c.* 250 BC) Greek poet, born in Sicily

Thucydides (*c.* 455–*c.* 400 BC) Greek historian

Untermeyer, Louis (1885–1977) American poet

Van Vechten, Carl (1880–1964) American critic and essayist

Vargas Llosa, (Jorge) Mario (Pedro) (born 1936) Peruvian novelist, dramatist, and essayist

Washington, Booker T[aliaferro] (1856–1915) American educator and social critic

Williamson, Henry (1895–1977) English novelist and wildlife writer

Wordsworth, Dorothy (1771–1855) English diarist, sister of William Wordsworth

Wordsworth, William (1770–1850) English poet

Xenophanes (*c.* 435–*c.* 480 BC) Greek philosopher

11 letters

Apollinaire, Guillaume (pseudonym of Wilhelm Apollinaris de Kostrowitzki) (1880–1918) French poet

Archilochus (8th or 7th century BC) Greek poet

Aristarchus (known as Aristarchus of Samothrace) (*c.* 217–145 BC) Greek critic and grammarian

Auchincloss, Louis (born 1917) American novelist

Baudrillard, Jean (born 1929) French sociologist and cultural critic

Callimachus (*c.* 305–*c.* 240 BC) Greek poet and scholar

Champollion, Jean-François (1790–1832) French Egyptologist

Garcia Lorca See LORCA

Grosseteste, Robert (*c.* 1175–1253) English churchman, philosopher, and scholar

Kierkegaard, Søren (1813–55) Danish philosopher

Liddell Hart, Sir Basil Henry (1895–1970) British military historian and theorist

Maeterlinck, Count Maurice (1862–1949) Belgian poet, dramatist, and essayist

Matthiessen, F[rancis] O[tto] (1902–50) American literary scholar

Matthiessen, Peter (born 1927) American novelist and travel writer

Montesquieu, Baron de La Brède et de (title of Charles Louis de Secondat) (1689–1755) French political philosopher

Omar Khayyám (died 1123) Persian poet, mathematician, and astronomer

Sainte-Beuve, Charles Augustin (1804–69) French critic and writer

Shakespeare, William (also known as "the Bard (of Avon)") (1564–1616) English dramatist

Tocqueville, Alexis, Comte de (1805–59) French social critic and essayist

Yevtushenko, Yevgeni (Aleksandrovich) (born 1933) Russian poet

12 letters

Aristophanes (*c.* 450–*c.* 385 BC) Greek comic dramatist

Beaumarchais, Pierre Augustin Caron de (1732–99) French dramatist

Bulwer-Lytton See LYTTON

de Maupassant, Guy See MAUPASSANT

Ferlinghetti, Lawrence (Monsanto) (born Lawrence Ferling) (born 1919) American poet and publisher

Hofmannsthal, Hugo von (1874–1929) Austrian poet and dramatist

Matthew Paris See PARIS, MATTHEW

Robbe-Grillet, Alain (born 1922) French novelist

Saint-Exupéry, Antoine (Marie Roger de) (1900–44) French writer and aviator

Schopenhauer, Arthur (1788–1860) German philosopher

Solzhenitsyn, Alexander (Russian name Aleksandr Isaevich Solzhenitsyn) (born 1918) Russian novelist

Wittgenstein, Ludwig (Josef Johann) (1889–1951) Austrian-born philosopher

13 letters

Aldus Manutius (Latinized name of Teobaldo Manucci; also known as Aldo Manuzio) (1450–1515) Italian scholar, printer, and publisher

Chateaubriand, François-René, Vicomte de (1768–1848) French writer and diplomat

García Márquez, Gabriel (born 1928) Colombian novelist

Ortega y Gasset, José (1883–1955) Spanish philosopher

Sackville-West, Vita (full name Victoria Mary Sackville-West) (1892–1962) English novelist and poet

14 letters

Compton-Burnett, Dame Ivy (1884–1969) English novelist

Leconte de Lisle, Charles Marie René (1818–94) French poet

Prévost d'Exiles, Antoine-François (known as Abbé Prévost) (1696–1763) French novelist

Sholom Aleichem (pseudonym of Solomon Rabinowitz) (1859–1916) Ukrainian-born American journalist and fiction writer in Yiddish

Wollstonecraft, Mary (1759–97) English writer and feminist, of Irish descent

15 letters

Alarcón y Mendoza, Juan Ruiz de (1581–1639) Spanish dramatist

La Rochefoucauld, François de Marsillac, Duc de (1613–80) French writer and moralist

16 letters

Cyrano de Bergerac, Savinien (1619–55) French soldier, duelist, and writer

Jalal ad-Din ar-Rumi (also called Mawlana) (1207–73) Persian poet and Sufi mystic

17 letters

Calderón de la Barca, Pedro (1600–81) Spanish dramatist and poet

18 letters

Anselm of Canterbury St. (*c.* 1033–1109) Italian theologian and philosopher, archbishop, and Doctor of the Church

Geoffrey of Monmouth (*c.* 1100–*c.* 1154) Welsh chronicler

Velleius Paterculus (*c.* 19 BC–AD *c.* 30) Roman historian and soldier

Writers, Philosophers, and Scholars *(continued)*

21 letters
Ruiz de Alarcón y Mendoza, Juan (1580–1639) Spanish dramatist, born in Mexico City

24 letters
Dionysius of Halicarnassus (1st century BC) Greek historian, literary critic, and rhetorician

Sports Figures

2 letters
Oh, Sadaharu (born 1940) Japanese baseball player

3 letters
Ali, Muhammad (born Cassius Marcellus Clay) (born 1942) American boxer

Coe, Sebastian (born 1956) British middle-distance runner and Conservative politician

Dr. J see ERVING, Julius

Fox, Nellie (1927–75) American baseball player

Moe, Tommy (born 1970) American skier

Orr, Bobby (born 1948) Canadian hockey player

Ott, Mel (1909–58) American baseball player

Pep, Willie (born 1922) American boxer

Pre see PREFONTAINE, Steve

Roy, Patrick (born 1965) Canadian hockey player

Yaz see YASTRZEMSKI, Carl

4 letters
Ashe, Arthur (Robert) (1943–93) American tennis player

Bell, James ("Cool Papa") (1903–91) American baseball player

Berg, Patty (born 1918) American golfer

Best, George (born 1946) Northern Irish footballer

Bird, Larry (born 1956) American basketball player

Borg, Björn (Rune) (born 1956) Swedish tennis player

Camp, Walter (1859–1925) American football coach; considered the "father of American football"

Clay, Cassius See ALI, MUHAMMAD

Cobb, Ty[rus Raymond] (1886–1961) American baseball player

Daly, John (born 1966) American golfer

Dean, Dizzy (1911–74) American baseball player

Doby, Larry (born 1924) American baseball player

Fisk, Carlton (born 1947) American baseball player

Fixx, Jim (1932–84) American runner and author

Ford, Whitey (born 1928) American baseball player

Foxx, Jimmie ("Double X") (1907–67) American baseball player

Foyt, A. J. (born 1935) American race driver

Gipp, George ("the Gipper") (1895–1920) American football player

Graf, Stephanie ("Steffi") (born 1969) German tennis player

Hamm, Mia (born 1972) American soccer player

Hill, (Norman) Graham (1929–75) English motor-racing driver

Hill, Grant (born 1974) American basketball player

Hoad, Lewis Alan (1934–94) Australian tennis player

Howe, Gordie (born 1928) Canadian hockey player

Huff, Sam (born 1934) American football player

Hull, Bobby (born 1939) Canadian hockey player; father of hockey player Brett Hull (born 1964)

Hunt, James (1947–93) British motor-racing driver

Jagr, Jaromir (born 1972) Czech hockey player

Kidd, Billy (born 1943) American skier

King, Billie Jean (born 1943) American tennis player

King, Don (born 1931) American boxing promoter

Kite, Tom (born 1949) American golfer

Kwan, Michelle (born 1980) American figure skater

Lyle, Sandy (born 1958) British golfer

Mack, Connie (Cornelius MacGillicuddy) (1862–1956) American baseball executive and manager

Mays, Willie ("Say Hey") (born 1931) American baseball player

Milo (late 6th century BC) Greek wrestler of legendary strength

Moss, Stirling (born 1929) English motor-racing driver

Page, Alan (born 1945) American football player and jurist

Pelé (born Edson Arantes do Nascimento) (born 1940) Brazilian footballer

Reed, Willis (born 1942) American basketball player

Rice, Jerry (born 1962) American football player

Rose, Pete (born 1941) American baseball player

Rupp, Adolph (1901–77) American basketball coach

Ruth, Babe (born George Herman Ruth) (1895–1948) American baseball player

Ryan, Nolan (born 1947) American baseball player

Sosa, Sammy (born 1968) Dominican baseball player

Wade, (Sarah) Virginia (born 1945) English tennis player

West, Jerry (born 1938) American basketball player

5 letters

Nurmi, Paavo Johannes (1897–1973) Finnish middle-distance runner

Aaron, Henry ("Hammerin' Hank" or "the Hammer") (born 1934) American baseball player

Baiul, Oksana (born 1977) Ukrainian figure skater

Banks, Ernie (born 1931) American baseball player

Banks, Gordon (born 1937) English soccer player

Baugh, Sammy (born 1914) American football player

Bench, Johnny (born 1947) American baseball player

Berra, Yogi (born Lawrence Peter Berra) (born 1925) American baseball player

Blair, Bonnie (born 1964) American speed skater

Boggs, Wade (born 1958) American baseball player

Bonds, Barry (born 1964) American baseball player; son of Bobby Bonds, baseball player (born 1946)

Bossy, Mike (born 1957) Canadian hockey player

Brett, George (born 1953) American baseball player

Brock, Lou (born 1939) American baseball player

Brown, Jim (born 1936) American football player and actor

Bruno, Frank(lin Ray) (born 1961) English boxer

Bubka, Sergey (born 1963)

Sports Figures *(continued)*

Ukrainian pole-vaulter

Budge, John Donald ("Don") (1915–2000) American tennis player

Bueno, Maria (Esther) (born 1939) Brazilian tennis player

Carew, Rod (born 1945) Panamanian-born American baseball player

Cousy, Bob (born 1928) American basketball player

Ditka, Mike (born 1939) American football player

Elway, John (born 1960) American football player

Evert, Christine Marie ("Chris") American tennis player

Ewing, Patrick (born 1962) Jamaican-born American basketball player

Faldo, Nicholas Alexander ("Nick") (born 1957) English golfer

Gomez, Lefty (1908–89) American baseball player

Grace, W(illiam) G(ilbert) (1848–1915) English cricketer

Grove, Lefty (1900–75) American baseball player

Hagen, Walter Charles (1892–1969) U.S. professional golfer

Halas, George ("Papa Bear") (1895–1983) American football player and coach

Hasek, Dominik (born 1965) Czech hockey player

Hayes, Bob (born 1942) American Olympic runner and football player

Hayes, Elvin ("the Big E") (born 1945) American basketball player

Henie, Sonja (1912–69) Norwegian figure skater

Hogan, Ben (1912–97) U.S. professional golfer

Hoppe, Willie (1887–1959) American billiards player

Hyman, Flo[rence] (1954–86)

American volleyball player

Jones, Robert Tyre ("Bobby") (1902–71) American golfer

Killy, Jean-Claude (born 1943) French skier

Kiner, Ralph (born 1922) American baseball player

Krone, Julie (born 1963) American jockey

Lauda, Nikolaus Andreas ("Niki") (born 1949) Austrian motor-racing driver

Laver, Rodney George ("Rod") (born 1938) Australian tennis player

Lendl, Ivan (born 1960) Czech-born tennis player

Lewis, Frederick Carleton ("Carl") (born 1961) American athlete

Lopez, Nancy (born 1957) American golfer

Louis, Joe (born Joseph Louis Barrow) (1914–81) American boxer

Maris, Roger (1934–85) American baseball player

Mikan, George (born 1924) American basketball player

Moore, Archie (born Archibald Lee Wright) (1913–99) American boxer

Moore, Robert Frederick ("Bobby") (1941–93) English soccer player

Moses, Ed(win Corley) (born 1955) American athlete

O'Neal, Shaquille ("the Shaq") (born 1972) American basketball player

Owens, Jesse (born James Cleveland Owens) (1913–80) American athlete

Paige, Leroy "Satchel" (1906–82) American baseball player

Perry, Frederick John ("Fred") (1909–95) British-born American tennis player

Petty, Richard (born 1937) American race (stock car) driver

Prost, Alain (born 1955) French motor-racing driver

Reese, Harold "Pee Wee" (1919–99) American baseball player

Riggs, Bobby (1918–95) American tennis player

Seles, Monica (born 1973) American tennis player, born in Yugoslavia

Senna, Ayrton (1960–94) Brazilian motor-racing driver

Shore, Eddie (1902–85) Canadian hockey player

Shula, Don (born 1930) American football coach

Smith, Emmitt (born 1969) American football player

Snead, Sam (born 1912) American golfer

Spahn, Warren (born 1921) American baseball player

Spitz, Mark (Andrew) (born 1950) American swimmer

Spitz, Mark (born 1950) American swimmer

Stagg, Amos Alonzo (1862–1965) American football coach

Starr, Bart (born 1934) American football player

Tomba, Alberto (born 1966) Italian skier

Tyson, Michael Gerald ("Mike") (born 1966) American boxer

Unser, Al (born 1939) American race driver; brother of Bobby Unser, race driver (born 1934); father of Al Unser, Jr., race driver (born 1962)

Veeck, Bill (1914–86) American baseball executive

Viren, Lasse Artturi (born 1949) Finnish middle-distance runner

Waitz, Grete (born 1953) Norwegian distance runner

White, Byron "Whizzer" (born 1917) American football player and Supreme Court justice

White, Reggie (born 1961) American football player

Wills (Moody), Helen (also Helen W. Roark) (1905–98) U.S. tennis player

Woods, Tiger (born Eldrick Woods) (born 1975) U.S. golfer

Young, (Denton True) "Cy" (1867–1955) American baseball player

6 letters

Agassi, André (born 1970) American tennis player

Aikman, Troy (born 1966) American football player

Aouita, Sad (born 1960) Moroccan runner

Arcaro, Eddie (1916–97) American jockey

Austin, Tracy (born 1962) American tennis player

Baylor, Elgin (born 1934) American basketball player

Beamon, Robert ("Bob") (born 1946) American athlete

Becker, Boris (born 1967) German tennis player

Biondi, Matt (born 1965) American swimmer

Blanda, George (born 1927) American football player

Bryant, Paul "Bear" (1913–83) American football coach

Butkus, Dick (born 1942) American football player

Button, Dick (born 1929) American figure skater

Carter, Don (born 1926) American bowler

Carter, Rubin "Hurricane" (born 1937) American boxer

Casper, Billy (born 1931) American golfer

Cosell, Howard (born Howard Cohen) (1920–95) American sports announcer and commentator

Crabbe, Buster (1910–83) American swimmer and actor

Cruyff, Johan (born 1947) Dutch soccer player and football manager

Sports Figures *(continued)*

Dancer, Stanley (born 1927)
American harness racing driver

Dionne, Marcel (born 1951)
Canadian hockey player

Edberg, Stefan (born 1966)
Swedish tennis player

Ederle, Gertrude (born 1906)
American swimmer

Erving, Julius ("Doctor J")
(born 1950) American basketball
player

Fangio, Juan Manuel (1911–95)
Argentinian motor-racing driver

Feller, Bob (born 1918)
American baseball player

Fleming, Peggy (born 1948)
American figure skater

Flutie, Doug (born 1962)
American football player

Fraser, Dawn (born 1937)
Australian swimmer

Gehrig, Henry Louis ("Lou")
(1903–41) American baseball
player

Gervin, George ("the Ice Man")
(born 1952) American basketball
player

Gibson, Althea (born 1927)
American tennis player

Gibson, Bob (born 1935)
American baseball player

Gibson, Josh (1911–47) American
baseball player

Gordon, Jeff (born 1971)
American racing driver

Graham, Otto (born 1921)
American football player

**Grange, Red ("the Galloping
Ghost")** (1903–91) American
football player

Greene, "Mean" Joe (born 1946)
American football player

Gwynn, Tony (born 1960)
American baseball player

Harris, Franco (born 1950)
American football player

Hingis, Martina (born 1980)
Swiss-born tennis player

Holmes, Larry (born 1949)
American boxer

Hunter, (Jim) Catfish (1946–99)
American baseball player

Jordan, Michael (Jeffrey) (born
1963) American basketball player

Kaline, Al (born 1934) American
baseball player

Karpov, Anatoli (born 1951)
Russian chess player

Knight, Bobby (born 1940)
American basketball coach

Korbut, Olga (born 1955) Soviet
gymnast, born in Belarus

Koufax, Sandy (Sanford) (born
1935) American baseball player

Lajoie, Napoleon ("Nap")
(1874–1959) American baseball
player

Landis, Kenesaw Mountain
(1866–1944) American jurist and
commissioner of baseball

Lasker, Emanuel (1868–1941)
German chess player

LeMond, Greg (born 1961)
American bicycle racer

Liston, Sonny (born Charles
Liston) (1932–70) American
boxer

Maddux, Greg (born 1966)
American baseball player

Malone, Karl (born 1963)
American basketball player

Mantle, Mickey (1931–95)
American baseball player

Marino, Dan (born 1961)
American football player

McGraw, John (1873–1934)
American baseball manager

Merckx, Eddy (born 1945)
Belgian racing cyclist

Mikita, Stan (born 1940)
Canadian hockey player

Morphy, Paul Charles (1837–84)
U.S. chess player

Musial , Stan ("the Man") (born
1920) American baseball player

Namath, Joe (born 1943)

American football player

Nelson, Byron (born 1912) American golfer

Norman, Gregory John ("Greg") (born 1955) Australian golfer

Oerter, Al (born 1936) American discus thrower

Palmer, Arnold (Daniel) (born 1929) American golfer

Palmer, Jim (born 1945) American baseball player

Payton, Walter (1954–99) American football player

Payton, Walter (born 1954) American football player

Pettit, Bob (born 1932) American basketball player

Pincay, Laffit, Jr. (born 1946) Panamanian jockey

Plante, Jacques (1929–86) Canadian hockey player

Player, Gary (born 1936) South African golfer

Ramsey, Sir Alf(red Ernest) (born 1920) English soccer player and manager

Rickey, Branch (1881–1965) American baseball executive

Ripken, Cal, Jr. (born 1960) American baseball player

Rockne, Knute (1888–1931) Norwegian-born American football coach

Rodman, Dennis (born 1961) American basketball player

Sayers, Gale (born 1943) American football player

Seaver, Tom ("Tom Terrific") (born 1944) American baseball player

Sisler, George (1893–1973) American baseball player

Snider, Duke (born 1926) American baseball player

Sobers, Sir Garfield St. Aubrun ("Gary") (born 1936) West Indian cricketer

Street, Picabo (born 1971) American skier

Sutton, Don (born 1945) American baseball player

Taylor, Lawrence (born 1959) American football player

Thorpe, Jim (1888–1953) American football and baseball player and Olympic athlete

Tilden, Bill ("Big Bill") (1893–1953) American tennis player

Tittle, Y[elverton] A[braham] (born 1926) American football player

Tunney, Gene (1897–1978) U.S. boxer

Turner, Ted (born 1938) American yacht racer and baseball and television executive

Unitas, Johnny (born 1933) American football player

Wagner, Honus (1874–1955) American baseball player

Walker, Herschel (born 1962) American football player

Walker, John (born 1952) New Zealand athlete

Warner, Glenn ("Pop") (1871–1954) American football coach

Watson, Tom (born 1949) American golfer

Weaver, Earl (born 1930) American baseball manager

Wilson, Hack (1900–48) American baseball player

Wooden, John (born 1910) American basketball coach

7 *letters*

Allison, Bobby (born 1937) American auto racer; father of auto racer Davey Allison (1961–93)

Anthony, Earl (born 1938) American bowler

Barkley, ("Sir") Charles (born 1963) American basketball player

Boycott, Geoffrey (born 1940) English cricketer

Brabham, Sir John Arthur ("Jack") (born 1926) Australian motor-racing driving

Bradley, Bill (born 1943)

Sports Figures *(continued)*

American basketball player and politician

Bradman, Sir Donald George ("Don") (born 1908) Australian cricketer

Burrell, Leroy (born 1967) American runner

Butcher, Susan (born 1956) American dog sled racer

Capriati, Jennifer (born 1976) American tennis player

Carlton, Steve ("Lefty") (born 1944) American baseball player

Carnera, Primo (1906–67) Italian boxer

Clemens, Roger ("the Rocket") (born 1962) American baseball player

Collins, Eddie (1887–1951) American baseball player

Connors, James Scott ("Jimmy") (born 1952) American tennis player

Connors, Jimmy (born 1952) American tennis player

Corbett, James J. (1866–1933) American boxer

Cordero, Angel, Jr. (born 1942) Puerto Rican jockey

Dempsey, Jack ("the Manassa Mauler") (born William Harrison Dempsy) (1895–1983) American boxer

Doctor J see ERVING, Julius

Dorsett, Tony (born 1954) American football player

Emerson, Roy (born 1936) Australian tennis player

Eusebio (full name Ferraira da Silva Eusebio) (born 1942) Mozambican-born Portuguese soccer player

Fischer, Robert James ("Bobby") (born 1943) American chess player

Foreman, George (born 1948) American boxer

Fosbury, Richard (born 1947) American high jumper

Frazier, Joseph ("Joe") (born 1944) American boxer

Frazier, Walt ("Clyde") (born 1945) American basketball player

Gretzky, Wayne (born 1961) Canadian ice-hockey player

Griffey, Ken, Jr. (born 1969) American baseball player; son of Ken Griffey, Sr. (born 1950), baseball player

Harding, Tonya (born 1970) American figure skater

Hartack, Bill (born 1932) American jockey

Heisman, John (1869–1936) American football coach

Hillary, Sir Edmund (born 1919) New Zealand mountaineer, first to reach summit of Everest

Hinault, Bernard (born 1954) French racing cyclist

Hornsby, Roger ("the Rajah") (1896–1963) American baseball player

Hornung, Paul (born 1935) American football player

Hubbell, Carl ("the Meal Ticket") (1903–88) American baseball player

Jackson, "Shoeless" Joe (1889–1951) American baseball player

Jackson, Bo (born 1962) American football and baseball player

Jackson, Reggie (born 1946) American baseball player

Johnson, Earvin (known as "Magic Johnson") (born 1959) American basketball player

Johnson, Jack (1878–1946) American boxer

Johnson, Michael (born 1967) American track athlete

Johnson, Walter ("Big Train") (1887–1946) American baseball player

Lemieux, Mario (born 1965)
Canadian hockey player
Lenglen, Suzanne (1899–1938)
French tennis player
Leonard, Sugar Ray (real name
Ray Charles Leonard) (born
1956) American boxer
Mansell, Nigel (born 1954)
English motor-racing driver
Mathews, Eddie (born 1931)
American baseball player
Mathias, Bob (born 1930)
American Olympic decathlon
champion
McCovey, Willie (born 1938)
American baseball player
McEnroe, John (Patrick) (born
1959) American tennis player
McGwire, Mark (born 1963)
American baseball player
Messier, Mark (born 1961)
Canadian hockey player
Montana, Joe (born 1956)
American football player
Mosconi, Willie (1913–93)
American billiards player
Nastase, Ilie (born 1946)
Romanian tennis player
Paterno, Joe (born 1926)
American football coach
Piggott, Lester (Keith) (born
1935) English jockey
Puckett, Kirby (born 1961)
American baseball player
**Richard, Maurice ("the
Rocket")** (born 1921) Canadian
hockey player
Rizzuto, Phil ("Scooter") (born
1918) American baseball player
and broadcaster
Robeson, Paul (1898–1976)
American athlete, singer, actor,
and political activist
Rozelle, Pete (1926–96) American
football executive
Rudolph, Wilma (1940–94)
American runner
Russell, Bill (born 1934)
American basketball player
Sampras, Pete (born 1971) U.S.
tennis player

Sanders, Deion ("Neon Deion")
(born 1967) American baseball
and football player
Sarazen, Gene (1902–99)
American golfer
Schmidt, Mike (born 1949)
American baseball player
Simmons, Al (1902–56) American
baseball player
Simpson, O(renthal) J(ames)
(born 1947) American football
player, actor, and celebrity
Spassky, Boris (Vasilyevich)
(born 1937) Russian chess player
Speaker, Tris (1885–1958)
American baseball player
**Stengel, Casey ("the Old
Perfesser")** (1890–1975)
American baseball player and
manager
Stewart, Jackie (born John Young
Stewart) (born 1939) British
motor-racing driver
Surtees, John (born 1934) British
racing motorcyclist
Trevino, Lee (Buck) (known as
"Supermex") (born 1939)
American golfer
Walcott, Jersey Joe (1914–94)
American boxer
Williams, Venus (born 1980)
American tennis player; sister of
Serena Williams (born 1981)
tennis player
Zamboni, Frank (1901–88)
American inventor of ice resur-
facing machine
Zatopek, Emil (born 1922) Czech
long-distance runner

8 letters

Alekhine, Alexander (born
Aleksandr Aleksandrovich
Alyokhin) (1892–1946) Russian-
born French chess player
Andretti, Mario (Gabriele)
(born 1940) Italian-born
American motor-racing driver
Auerbach, Red (Arnold) (born
1917) American basketball coach
and executive

Sports Figures *(continued)*

Beliveau, Jean (born 1931)
Canadian hockey player

Bradshaw, Terry (born 1948)
American football player

Campbell, Donald (Malcolm)
(1921–67) English motor-racing
driver and holder of world speed
records, son of Sir Malcolm
Campbell

Campbell, Earl (born 1955)
American football player

Campbell, Sir Malcolm
(1885–1948) English motor-racing driver and holder of world
speed records

Charlton, John ("Jack") (born
1935) English soccer player and
manager, brother of Bobby
Charlton

Charlton, Sir Robert ("Bobby")
(born 1937) English soccer player, brother of Jack Charlton

Christie, Linford (born 1960)
Jamaican-born British sprinter

Clemente, Roberto (1934–72)
Puerto Rican baseball player

Comaneci, Nadia (born 1961)
Romanian-born American
gymnast

Connolly, Maureen Catherine
(known as "Little Mo") (1934–
69) American tennis player

DiMaggio, Joseph Paul ("Joe")
(1914–99) American baseball
player

Drysdale, Don (1936–93)
American baseball player

Durocher, Leo ("the Lip")
(1905–91) American baseball
manager

Esposito, Phil (born 1942)
Canadian hockey player

Gonzales, (Richard) Pancho
(1928–95) American tennis
player

Graziano, Rocky (1922–90)
American boxer

Hamilton, Scott (born 1958)
American figure skater

Havlicek, John ("Hondo") (born
1940) American basketball player

Indurain, Miguel (born 1964)
Spanish cyclist

Joselito (José Gómez)
(1895–1920) Spanish matador

Kasparov, Gary (born Gary
Weinstein) (born 1963)
Azerbaijani chess player, of
Armenian Jewish descent

Kerrigan, Nancy (born 1969)
American figure skater

Korchnoi, Viktor (Lvovich) (born
1931) Russian chess player

Lipinski, Tara (born 1982)
American figure skater

Lombardi, Vince (1913–70)
American football coach

Louganis, Greg (born 1960)
American diver

Maradona, Diego (Armando)
(born 1960) Argentinian footballer

Maravich, Pete ("Pistol Pete")
(1948–88) American basketball
player

Marciano, Rocky (born Rocco
Francis Marchegiano) (1923–69)
American boxer

Matthews, Sir Stanley (born
1915) English soccer player

Nagurski, Bronko (1908–90)
Canadian-born American football player

Naismith, James (1861–1939)
Canadian inventor of basketball

Newcombe, John (born 1944)
Australian tennis player

Nicklaus, Jack (William) (born
1940) American golfer

Olajuwon, Hakeem (born 1963)
Nigerian-born American basketball player

Robinson, Brooks (born 1937)
American baseball player

Robinson, Frank (born 1935)
American baseball player and

manager

Robinson, Jackie (Jack Roosevelt) (1919–72) American baseball player

Robinson, Sugar Ray (born Walker Smith) (1920–89) American boxer

Rosewall, Ken (born 1934) Australian tennis player

Staubach, Roger (born 1942) American football player

Stockton, John (born 1962) American basketball player

Sullivan, John L. (1858–1918) American boxer

Thompson, Daley (born 1958) English athlete

Williams, Ted (born 1918) American baseball player

Zaharias, Babe Didrikson (1914–56) American Olympic athlete and golfer

9 letters

Alexander, Grover Cleveland ("Pete") (1887–1950) American baseball player

Armstrong, Henry (1912–88) American boxer

Armstrong, Lance (born 1971) American bicycle racer

Bannister, Sir Roger (Gilbert) (born 1929) British middle-distance runner and neurologist

Davenport, Lindsay (born 1976) American tennis player

Didrikson see ZAHARIAS, Babe Didrikson

Earnhardt, Dale (born 1951) American auto (stock car) racer

Geoffrion, Bernie ("Boom Boom") (born 1931) Canadian hockey player

Goolagong, Evonne (later Cawley) (born 1951) Australian tennis player

Greenberg, Hank (1911–86) American baseball player

Henderson, Rickey (born 1958) American baseball player

Holyfield, Evander (born 1962)

American boxer

Killebrew, Harmon (born 1936) American baseball player

Mathewson, Christy (1880–1925) American baseball player

Patterson, Floyd (born 1935) American boxer

Robertson, Oscar ("the Big O") (born 1938) American basketball player

Samuelson, Joan Benoit (born 1957) American distance runner

Schmeling, Max (born 1905) German boxer

Shoemaker, Willie (born 1931) American jockey

Tarkenton, Fran (born 1940) American football player

10 letters

Campanella, Roy (1921–93) American baseball player

Capablanca, José Raúl (1888–1942) Cuban chess player

Carpentier, Georges (1894–1975) French boxer

Chichester, Sir Francis (Charles) (1901–72) English yachtsman

Culbertson, Ely (1891–1955) American bridge player

Fittipaldi, Emerson (born 1946) Brazilian motor-racing driver

Kahanamoku, Duke (1890–1968) American swimmer and surfer

11 letters

Abdul-Jabbar, Kareem (born Lew Alcindor) (born 1947) American basketball player

Ballesteros, Severiano ("Sevvy") (born 1957) Spanish golfer

Beckenbauer, Franz (born 1945) German soccer player and manager

Chamberlain, Wilt ("the Stilt") (1936–99) American basketball player

Fitzsimmons, Bob (1862–1917) New Zealand boxer

Sports Figures *(continued)*

Navratilova, Martina (born 1956) Czech-born American tennis player
Prefontaine, Steve ("Pre") (1951–75) American distance runner
Weissmuller, John Peter ("Johnny") (1904–84) American swimmer and actor
Yastrzemski, Carl ("Yaz") (born 1939) American baseball player

12 letters
Steinbrenner, George (born 1930) American baseball executive

13 letters
Tenzing Norgay (*c.* 1914–86) Sherpa mountaineer

14 letters
Griffith Joyner, Florence (1959–98) American runner
Sanchez-Vicario, Arantxa (born 1971) Spanish tennis player
Torvill and Dean Jayne Torvill (born 1957) and **Christopher (Colin) Dean** (born 1958) English ice skaters

Tribes of the U.S. and Canada

(whether the name applies to a language or a culture is indicated in parentheses)

3 letters
Fox
Kaw
Oto(e)
Sac
Ute

4 letters
Cree
Crow
Dene
Erie
Eyak
Gila
Hare
Hopi
Hupa
Iowa
Kere
Mono
Pima
Pomo
Sauk
Tewa
Tiwa
Waco
Yahi
Yana
Yuma
Zuñi

5 letters
Adena (culture)
Aleut
Blood
Caddo
Comox
Creek
Haida
Hokan (language)
Houma
Huron

Inuit
Kansa
Karok
Kaska
Kiowa
Kutin
Lummi
Métis (mixed-race
 group)
Maidu
Makah
Miami
Mingo
Miwok
Modoc
Omaha
Osage
Ponca
Sarci (or Sarcee)
Sioux
Slave(y)
Snake
Teton
Washo(e)
Wiyot
Yokut
Yuchi
Yukon
Yuman (language)
Yurok

6 letters
Abnaki
Apache
Atsina
Beaver
Biloxi
Calusa
Cayuga
Cayuse
Clovis (culture)
Cocopa

Dakota
Digger
Dogrib
Eskimo
Kichai
Lakota
Lenape
Lumbee
Mandan
Micmac (or Mi'kmaq)
Mohawk
Mojave (or Mohave)
Munsee
Nadene (or Na-Dene;
 language)
Nauset
Navajo (or Navaho)
Nootka
Oglala (or Oglalla)
Ojibwa
Oneida
Ottawa
Paiute
Papago
Pawnee
Peoria
Pequot
Piegan
Plains (culture)
Pueblo
Quapaw
Salish
Sandia (culture)
Santee
Sarcee (or Sarci)
Seneca
Shasta
Siouan (language)
Spokan
Tanana
Tunica
Umpqua

Tribes of the U.S. and Canada (continued)

Wintun
Yakima

7 letters

Abenaki (or Wabanaki)
Alabama
Anasazi (culture)
Arapaho
Arikara
Atakapa
Bannock
Beothuk
Carrier
Catawba
Chinook
Choctaw
Chumash
Clallam
Cochise (culture)
Croatan
Gosiute (or Goshute)
Hidatsa
Hohokam (culture)
Ingalik
Inupiat
Keresan (language)
Klamath
Kutchin
Kutenai (or Kootenai
  or Kootenay)
Mashpee
Mission
Mogollon (culture)
Mohegan
Mohican (or Mahican)
Naskapi
Natchez
Neutral
Niantic
Nipmuck
Oglalla (or Oglala)
Palouse
Pamlico
Plateau (culture)
Praying
Raritan
Shawnee
Shuswap

Siuslaw
Siwanoy
Tahltan
Tlingit
Tobacco
Tonkawa
Walapai
Wichita
Wyandot
Yamasee
Yavapai

8 letters

Algonkin
Anadarko
Cahuilla
Canarsee (or Canarsie)
Cherokee
Cheyenne
Chippewa
Colville
Comanche
Cowichan
Delaware
Flathead
Hitchiti
Hopewell (culture)
Hualapai
Illinois
Iroquois (Confederacy)
Kalispel
Kickapoo
Kootenai (or Kutenai
  or Kootenay)
Kwakiutl
Loucheux
Malecite (or Maliseet)
Maricopa
Meherrin
Mimbreno
Missouri
Nez Percé
Nottaway
Onondaga
Pamunkey
Panamint
Paviotso
Penutian (language)

Pit River
Powhatan
  (Confederacy)
Puyallup
Quinault
Sahaptin
Salishan (language)
Seminole
Shoshone (or
  Shoshoni)
Tawaconi
Tuskegee
Umatilla
Wabanaki (or Abenaki)
Wakashan (language)

9 letters

Algonquin
Apalachee
Blackfoot (or
  Blackfeet)
Bois Brûlé (mixed-race
  group)
Chilcotin
Chipewyan
Costanoan (language)
Coushatta
Havasupai
Iroquoian (language)
Jicarilla
Kaskaskia
Manhattan
Mattaponi
Menominee
Mescalero
Montagnais
Muskogean (language)
Nanticoke
Nipissing
Nisqually
Paugusset
Pennacook
Penobscot
Sac and Fox
Tillamook
Tsimshian
Tuscarora
Wampanoag

Wappinger
Winnebago
Yanktonai

10 letters
Algonquian (language)
Athabascan (or
  Athapaskan, lan-
  guage)
Bella Bella
Bella Coola
Chemehuevi
Chiricahua
Chitimacha
Gabrielino
Gros Ventre
Miccosukee
Piankashaw
Potawatomi (or
  Pottawatomi)
Sheepeater
Six Nations

Tiononanti
Walla Walla

11 letters
Assiniboine
Aztec-Tanoan (lan-
  guage)
Chickamauga
Coeur d'Alene
Five Nations
Hokan-Siouan (lan-
  guage)
Lenni Lenape
Minniconjou
Monongahela
Muckleshoot
Pend Oreille
Pottawatomi (or
  Potawatomi)

12 letters
Chickahominy

Cliff Dweller (culture)
Massachusett
Mound Builder (cul-
  ture)
Narragansett
Tohono o'Odham

13 letters
Passamaquoddy
Red Paint People (cul-
  ture)
Susquehannock

15 letters
Eastern Woodland
  (culture)

19 letters
Five Civilized Tribes
White Mountain
  Apache

Empires

4 letters
Evil
Inca
Mali

5 letters
Aztec
Khmer
Mayan
Mogul
Roman

6 letters
Asokan
French
Fulani
German
Inland
Median
Mongol

7 letters
British

Hittite
Islamic
Ottoman
Russian
Songhai
Spanish

8 letters
Assyrian
Athenian
Austrian
Frankish
Parthian
Venetian

9 letters
Almoravid
Byzantine
Holy Roman

10 letters
Babylonian
Macedonian

Phoenician
Portuguese

12 letters
Carthaginian

13 letters
Eastern (Roman)
  Empire
Western (Roman)
  Empire

14 letters
Central African

15 letters
Austro-Hungarian
Spanish American

Chinese Dynasties

3 letters

Han	206 BC–AD 220
Jin	AD 295–420; same as Chin or Tsin
Qin	221–206 BC; same as Ch'in
Sui	AD 581–618
Yin	1523–1027 BC; same as Shang

4 letters

Chin	AD 265–420; same as Tsin
Ch'in	See QIN
Chou (or Zhou)	1027–256 BC
Hsia	1994–1523 BC
Liao	AD 947–1125
Ming	AD 1368–1644
Qing	AD 1644–1912; same as Ch'ing or Manchu
Sung (or Song)	AD 960–1279
T'ang	AD 618–c. 906

Tsin	See CHIN
Yuan (or Yüan)	AD 1259–1368

5 letters

Ch'ing	See QING
Shang	See YIN

6 letters

Manchu	See QING

11 letters

Ten Kingdoms	See FIVE DYNASTIES AND TEN KINGDOMS

13 letters

Five Dynasties	See FIVE DYNASTIES AND TEN KINGDOMS
Three Kingdoms	AD 220–265

27 letters

Five Dynasties and Ten Kingdoms	AD 907–960

Political Philosophies and Systems

6 letters

Maoism
Nazism (also Naziism)

7 letters

fascism
leftism
Marxism
Naziism (also Nazism)
New Deal
Titoism

8 letters

centrism
Leninism
populism
rightism

9 letters

anarchism
democracy
dogoodism
pluralism
socialism
Sovietism
Stalinism
theocracy
timocracy
tribalism

10 letters

absolutism
aristocracy
chauvinism
federalism
liberalism
monarchism

plutocracy
radicalism
Trotskyism
Utopianism

11 letters

Americanism
imperialism
McCarthyism
meritocracy
nationalism
New Frontier
syndicalism
technocracy
Thatcherism

12 letters

collectivism
conservatism

situationism
laissez-faire

13 letters
communism
ethnocentrism
Eurocommunism
individualism
neoliberalism
progressivism

14 letters
egalitarianism
know-nothingism
libertarianism
utilitarianism

15 letters
neoconservatism
totalitarianism

16 letters
authoritarianism

18 letters
anarcho-syndicalism

Wars and Battles

4 letters

Iuka, Battle of	1862
Jena, Battle of	1806
Nile, Battle of the	1798

5 letters

Alamo, Battle (Siege) of the	1836
Boyne, Battle of the	1690
Bulge, Battle of the	1944–45
Issus, Battle of	333 BC
Marne, Battle of	1914
Somme, Battle of the	1916
Ypres, Battle of	1914, 1915, 1917

6 letters

Actium, Battle of	31 BC
Arbela, Battle of	331 BC
Midway, Battle of	1942
Shiloh, Battle of	1862
Verdun, Battle of	1916
Xuzhou, Battle of	1949

7 letters

Atlanta, Battle of	1864
Boer War	1880–81
Britain, Battle of	1940
Bull Run, Battle of	1861, 1862
Cambrai, Battle of	1917
Cold War	1945–89
Concord, Battle of	1775
Erzurum, Battle of	1877, 1916
Gulf War	1991
Iwo Jima, Battle of	1945

Jutland, Battle of	1916
Megiddo, Battle of	1469 BC, 1918
Salamis, Battle of	480 BC
Samnite Wars	343–341 BC, 316–314 BC, 298–290 BC
Trenton, Battle of	1776

8 letters

Antietam, Battle of	1862
Atlantic, Battle of the	1940–43
Ayacucho, Battle of	1824
Civil War, U.S.	1861–65
Coral Sea, Battle of the	1942
Culloden, Battle of	1746
Hastings, Battle	1066
Manassas, Battle of	1861, 1862
Marathon, Battle of	490 BC
Omdurman, Battle of	1898
Pea Ridge, Battle of	1862
Waterloo, Battle of	1815
Yorktown, Battle of	1781, 1862

9 letters

Agincourt, Battle of	1415
Balaclava, Battle of	1854
El Alamein, Battle of	1942
El Mansûra, Battle of	1250
Korean War	1950–53
Lexington, Battle of	1775
Leyte Gulf, Battle of	1944
Manila Bay, Battle of	1898
Opium Wars	1839–42, 1856–60

Wars and Battles *(continued)*

Pequot War	1637
Pharsalus, Battle of	48 BC
Princeton, Battle of	1777
Punic Wars	264–241 BC, 218–201 BC, 149–146 BC
Six Day War	1967
Trafalgar, Battle of	1805
Vicksburg, Siege of	1863
War of 1812	1812–14
World War I	1914–18

10 letters

Balkan Wars	1912–13
Ball's Bluff, Battle of	1861
Bunker Hill, Battle of	1775
Cerro Gordo, Battle of	1847
Cold Harbor, Battle of	1864
Corregidor, Battle of	1942
Crimean War	1853–56
Gallic Wars	58–51 BC
Gettysburg, Battle of	1863
Lundy's Lane, Battle of	1814
Mexican War	1846–48
New Orleans, Battle of	1814
River Plate, Battle of the	1939
Stalingrad, Battle of	1942–43
Tannenberg, Battle of	1914
Vietnam War	1954–75
World War II	1939–45

11 letters

Belleau Wood, Battle of	1918
Chapultepec, Battle of	1847
Chickamauga, Battle of	1863
Dien Bien Phu, Battle of	1954
Guadalcanal, Battle of	1942–43
Iran-Iraq War	1980–88
Persian Wars	5th century BC
San Juan Hill, Battle of	1898
Thermopylae, Battle of	480 BC

Ticonderoga, Battle of	1759
Wounded Knee, Massacre at	1890

12 letters

Falklands War	1982
Monte Cassino, Battle of	1944
Tet Offensive	1968
Yom Kippur War	1973

13 letters

Kasserine Pass, Battle of the	1943
Little Bighorn, Battle of the	1876
Peninsular War	1808–14
Seven Years War	1756–63
The Wilderness, Battle of	1864

14 letters

Château-Thierry, Battle of	1918
Fredericksburg, Battle of	1862
King Philip's War	1675–76
Macedonian Wars	214–205 BC, 200–196 BC, 171–168 BC, 149–148 BC
Napoleonic Wars	1805–15
Plains of Abraham, Battle of the	1759
Thirty Years War	1618–48
Wars of the Roses	1455–85

15 letters

Bosnian Civil War	1992–95
English Civil War	1642–49
Hundred Years War	1337–1453
Lookout Mountain, Battle of	1863
Missionary Ridge, Battle of	1863
Russian Civil War	1918–21
Spanish Civil War	1936–39

16 letters

American Civil War	1861–65
Chancellorsville, Battle of	1863
Great Northern War	1700–21
Kennesaw Mountain, Battle of	1864
Russo-Japanese War	1904–05
Sino-Japanese Wars	1894–95, 1937–45

17 letters

French Indochina War	1946–54
Peloponnesian Wars	431–404 BC
Seven Days' Campaign	1862
War of the Secession	1861–65

18 letters

Franco-Prussian War	1870–71

French and Indian War	1754–63
Peninsular Campaign	1862
Spanish-American War	1898

19 letters

War between the States	1861–65

20 letters

Battle above the Clouds	1863
French Wars of Religion	1562–98

25 letters

War of American Independence	1775–83
War of the Spanish Succession	1701–14
War of the Austrian Succession	1740–48

Seven Wonders of the Ancient World

6 letters
Pharos (of Alexandria)

8 letters
Colossus (of Rhodes)
Pyramids (of Egypt)

9 letters
Mausoleum (of Halicarnassus)

12 letters
Statue of Zeus (at Olympia)

15 letters
Temple of Artemis (at Ephesus)

22 letters
Lighthouse of Alexandria

23 letters
Hanging Gardens of Babylon

British Ranks of Hereditary Peerage

4 letters	**7 letters**	**8 letters**	**11 letters**
Duke	Duchess	Baroness	Marchioness
Earl		Countess	Viscountess
		Marquess	
5 letters		Viscount	
Baron			

Military Ranks

British Military Ranks

ARMY

5 letters

Major

7 letters

Captain
Colonel
General

9 letters

Brigadier

10 letters

Lieutenant

12 letters

Field Marshal
Major General

16 letters

Second
Lieutenant

17 letters

Lieutenant
Colonel
Lieutenant
General

ROYAL NAVY

7 letters

Admiral
Captain

9 letters

Commander
Commodore

10 letters

Lieutenant
Midshipman

11 letters

Rear Admiral
Vice Admiral

13 letters

Sub Lieutenant

17 letters

Admiral of the
Fleet

19 letters

Lieutenant
Commander

ROYAL AIR FORCE

10 letters

Air Marshal

12 letters

Air Commodore
Group Captain
Pilot Officer

13 letters

Flying Officer
Wing
Commander

14 letters

Air Vice-
Marshal
Squadron
Leader

15 letters

Air Chief
Marshal

16 letters

Flight
Lieutenant

25 letters

Marshal of the
Royal Air
Force

U.S. Military Ranks

ARMY AND AIR FORCE

5 letters

Major

7 letters

Captain
Colonel
General

12 letters

Chief of Staff
Major General

15 letters

First Lieutenant

16 letters

Brigadier
General

Second
Lieutenant
General of the
Army

17 letters

Lieutenant
Colonel
Lieutenant
General

NAVY

2 letters

j.g. (Lieutenant
junior grade)

6 letters

Ensign

7 letters

Admiral
Captain

9 letters

Commander

10 letters

Lieutenant
Midshipman

11 letters

Rear Admiral
Vice Admiral

12 letters

Fleet Admiral

19 letters

Lieutenant
Commander

20 letters

Lieutenant jun-
ior grade (j.g.)

22 letters

Chief of Naval
Operations

ALL FORCES

16 letters

Commander in
Chief

30 letters

Chairman of the
Joint Chiefs of
Staff

Weapons

2 letters
M-1
V-1
V-2

3 letters
ABM
axe
BAR
bow
gat
gun
M-16
Ram
RDX (Research
  Department
  Explosive)
Rod
SAM
TNT (trinitro-
  toluene)
Uzi

4 letters
AK-47
bill
bola
bolt
cane
club
Colt (*trademark*)
cosh
dart
dirk
épée
fist
flak
foil
ICBM
IRBM
iron
kris
mace
mine
MIRV (multiple
  independently-
  targeted re-
  entry vehicle)

pike
shiv
whip

5 letters
A-bomb
arrow
BB gun
billy
blade
flail
flare
fusil
Glock
  (*trademark*)
grape
H-bomb
knife
kukri
lance
lathi
Luger
  (*trademark*)
panga
piece
razor
rifle
Ruger
  (*trademark*)
saber
shell
sling
spear
staff
stave
stick
sword

6 letters
ack-ack
airgun
atlatl
bullet
cannon
cudgel
dagger
Exocet
  (*trademark*)

Garand (rifle)
  (*trademark*)
hanger
heater
mortar
musket
napalm
parang
pellet
petard
pistol
pom-pom
rapier
rocket
Semtex
  (*trademark*)
subgun
swivel
toledo
tracer
zipgun

7 letters
assegai
bayonet
bazooka
blowgun
Bren gun
burp gun
carbine
car bomb
chopper
cordite
cutlass
garrote
gisarme
grenade
hackbut
halberd
handgun
harpoon
hatchet
longbow
lyddite
machete
Patriot
  (*trademark*)
Polaris

poleaxe
shotgun
sidearm
Sten gun
torpedo
trident
woomera

8 letters
arbalest
arquebus
atom-bomb
ballista
birdshot
blowpipe
bludgeon
buckshot
buzz bomb
canister
catapult
claymore
crossbow
death ray
dynamite
falchion
falconet
field gun
firebomb
gas shell
heavy gun
howitzer
kamikaze
landmine
mangonel
Maxim gun
nerve gas
partisan
pistolet
repeater
revolver
scimitar
shrapnel
siege gun
skean-dhu
stiletto
time bomb
tomahawk
tommy-gun

whiz-bang
yataghan

9 letters

automatic
battleaxe
Big Bertha
billy club
blackjack
Bofors gun
bombshell
booby trap
boomerang
box cutter
Brown Bess
chain shot
derringer
doodle bug
fléchette
flintlock
forty-five (.45)
gelignite
grape shot
grease gun
gun cotton
gunpowder
Lewis gun
matchlock
Mills bomb
Minuteman
plastique
Remington
  (*trademark*)
slingshot
smart bomb
smoke bomb
star shell
trebuchet
truck bomb
truncheon
twenty-two
  (.22)

10 letters

assault gun
banderilla

bowie knife
broadsword
clasp knife
flick knife
flying bomb
Gatling gun
knobkerrie
letter bomb
limpet mine
machine gun
Mannlicher
  (*trademark*)
nightstick
petrol bomb
shillelagh
sidewinder
six-shooter
smoothbore
swordstick
throw-stick
Winchester
  (*trademark*)

11 letters

Agent Orange
blockbuster
blunderbuss
brass cannon
cannon royal
cluster bomb
depth charge
eighty-eight
elephant gun
Garand rifle
hand grenade
kalashnikov
mine-thrower
neutron bomb
nuclear bomb
Scud
  (*trademark*)
  missile
Smith & Wesson
  (*trademark*)
Springfield
  (*trademark*)

switchblade
thirty-eight
  (.38)
water cannon

12 letters

acoustic mine
battering ram
breech-loader
cavalry sword
Enfield rifle
flame thrower
fowling piece
hydrogen bomb
magnetic mine
muzzle-loader
potato masher
quarterstaff
thirty-thirty

13 letters

brass knuckles
cat o' nine tails
cruise missile
guided missile
knuckleduster
machine pistol
magazine rifle
semi-automatic
streetsweeper
submachine gun

14 letters

anti-tank
  weapon
duelling pistol
incendiary
  bomb
nitroglycerine
repeating rifle

15 letters

air-to-air missile
anti-aircraft gun
Molotov cock-
  tail

sawed-off shot-
  gun
trinitrotoluene
  (TNT)

16 letters

ballistic missile
plastic explosive

17 letters

concussion
  grenade
fragmentation
  bomb

18 letters

anti-missile
  missile
Molotov bread-
  basket
particle beam
  weapon

19 letters

surface-to-air
  missile

20 letters

anti-ballistic-
  missile
Saturday night
  special

23 letters

surface-to-sur-
  face missile

27 letters

Research
  Department
  Explosive
  (RDX)

32 letters

intercontinental
  ballistic missile

— RELIGION AND MYTHOLOGY —

Religions and Major Denominations

3 letters
Zen

4 letters
Jodo

5 letters
Amish
Druse (*or Druze*)
Islam
Norse
Wicca
Zande

6 letters
Babism
Satmar (Hasidism)
Shiism
Sufism
Taoism
Voodoo
Yogism

7 letters
Amidism
animism
Bahaism
Baptism
Gideons
Jainism
Judaism
Lamaism
Orphism
Quakers
Sabaism
Saktism
Sikhism
Sivaism
Zionism

8 letters
Buddhism
Caodaism
Druidism
Hasidism
Hinduism

Humanism
Mazdaism
Nichiren (Buddhism)
Paganism
Pure Land
  (Buddhism)
Shaktism
Tantrism
Totemism
Wahabism

9 letters
Adventism
cabbalism
cargo cult
Jansenism
Lubavitch (Hasidism)
Methodism
Mithraism
Mormonism
Pantheism
Parseeism
Rabbinism
Shamanism
Shia Islam
Shintoism
Vedantism
Vishnuism
Waldenses

10 letters
Anabaptism
Brahmanism
Evangelism
Hare Krishna
Millerites
Pharisaism
Puritanism
Sunni Islam

11 letters
Anglicanism
Catholicism
Hanafi Islam
Lutheranism
Moravianism

Scientology (*trademark*)
Zen Buddhism

12 letters
Aum Shinrikyu
Christianity
Confucianism
Ismaili Islam
Salvationism
Spiritualism
Unitarianism
Universalism

13 letters
Eleusinianism
Nation of Islam
Protestantism
Reform Judaism

14 letters
Orthodox Church
Rastafarianism
Zoroastrianism

15 letters
ancestor-worship
Episcopalianism
Latter-Day Saints,
  Church of Jesus
  Christ of
Orthodox Judaism
Presbyterianism

16 letters
Christian Science
Eastern Orthodoxy
Mahayana Buddhism
Messianic Judaism
Plymouth Brethren
Roman Catholicism

17 letters
Congregationalism
Jehovah's Witnesses
Reconstructionism
Theravada Buddhism

Religions and Major Denominations *(continued)*

19 letters

Conservative Judaism
Dutch Reformed
  Church
Seventh Day
  Adventism

20 letters

Native American
  Church

21 letters

Unitarian Universalism

United Methodist
  Church

31 letters

African Methodist
  Episcopal Church

Religious Festivals and Dates

(with religion and date)

4 letters

Holi	Hindu	Feb., Mar.
Lent	Christian	Feb., Mar., Apr.

5 letters

Purim	Jewish	Feb., Mar.
Vesak	Buddhist	Apr., May

6 letters

Advent	Christian	Nov., Dec.
Diwali	Hindu, Sikh	Oct., Nov.
Easter	Christian	Mar., Apr.
Imbolc	Pagan	Jan.
Kwanza	African-American (cultural)	Dec., Jan.
Lammas	Pagan	Aug.
Pesach	Jewish	See PASSOVER

7 letters

Beltane	Pagan	Apr.
New Year	Chinese traditional religions	Jan., Feb.
Samhain	Pagan	Oct.
Succoth (also Sukkot)	Jewish	Sept., Oct.

8 letters

Baisakhi	Sikh	Apr.
Bodhi Day	Buddhist	Nov.
Dusshera	Hindu	Oct.
Epiphany	Christian	Jan.
Hanukkah (also Chanukah)	Jewish	Dec.
Passover	Jewish	Mar., Apr.
Shavuoth (also Shavuot)	Jewish	May, June

9 letters

Ching Ming	Chinese traditional religions	Mar., Apr.
Christmas	Christian	Dec.

Eid ul-Adha (also Id al-Adha)	Islamic	July
Eid ul-Fitr (also Id al-Fitr)	Islamic	May, June
Pentecost	Christian	Apr., May
Rama Naumi	Hindu	Mar., Apr.
Yom Kippur	Jewish	Sept., Oct.

10 letters

Palm Sunday	Christian	Mar., Apr.

11 letters

All Soul's Day	Christian	Nov.
Dhammacakka	Buddhist	July
Holi Mohalla	Sikh	Mar., Apr.
Janmashtami	Hindu	Aug., Sept.
Rosh Hashana	Jewish	Sept., Oct.

12 letters

All Saint's Day	Christian	Nov.
Ash Wednesday	Christian	Feb., Mar.
Lailat ul-Qadr	Islamic	May, June
Moon Festival	Chinese traditional religions	Sept.

13 letters

Corpus Christi	Christian	May, June
Lailat ul-Bara'h	Islamic	Apr., May
Raksha Bandhan	Hindu	Aug.
Shrove Tuesday	Christian	Feb., Mar.
Three Kings' Day	Hispanic name for Epiphany	Jan.

14 letters

Mahashivaratri	Hindu	Feb., Mar.
Summer Solstice	Pagan	June
Winter Festival	Chinese traditional religious	Dec.
Winter Solstice	Pagan	Dec.

18 letters

Dragon Boat Festival	Chinese traditional religions	June
Guru Nanak's Birthday	Sikh	Nov.

20 letters

Lailat ul-Isra wal Mi'raj	Islamic	Apr., May
Martyrdom of Guru Arjan	Sikh	May, June

25 letters

Birthday of Guru Gobind Singh	Sikh	Dec., Jan.

26 letters

Martyrdom of Guru Tegh Bahadur	Sikh	Dec., Jan.

Christian Saints

(with feast dates)

4 letters

Anne	July 26
Bede	May 27
Jude	Oct. 28
Leo I	Feb. 18 *E. Ch.*, Apr. 11 *W. Ch.*
Lucy	Dec. 13
Luke	Oct. 18
Mark	Apr. 25
Mary	Jan. 1 *R.C. Ch.*, Mar. 25, Aug. 15, Sept. 8
Paul	June 29

5 letters

Aidan	Aug. 31
Alban	June 22
Basil	Jan. 2, June 14
Bruno	Oct. 6
Cyril	Feb. 14
David	Mar. 1
Denis	Oct. 9
Giles	Sept. 1
Louis	Aug. 25
Peter	June 29
Simon	Oct. 28
Titus	Aug. 23 *E. Ch.*, Feb. 6 *W. Ch.*
Vitus	June 15

6 letters

Andrew	Nov. 30
Anselm	Apr. 21
Edmund	Nov. 16
George	Apr. 23
Helena	May 21 *E. Ch.*, Aug. 18 *W. Ch.*
Hilary	Jan. 13, Jan. 14 *R.C. Ch.*
Jerome	Sept. 30
Joseph	Mar. 19
Justin	June 1
Martha	July 29
Martin	Nov. 11
Monica	Aug. 27
Olaf II	July 29
Philip	June 6

Thomas	Dec. 21
Ursula	Oct. 21

7 letters

Ambrose	Dec. 7
Anthony	Jan. 17
Bernard	Aug. 20
Campion	Dec. 1
Cecilia	Nov. 22
Clement (of Rome)	Nov. 23
Columba	June 9
Crispin	Oct. 25
Cyprian	Sept. 16, 26
Dominic	Aug. 8
Dunstan	May 19
Matthew	Sept. 21
Michael	Sept. 29
Patrick	Mar. 17
Sergius	Sept. 25
Stephen	Dec. 26 *W. Ch.*, Dec. 27 *E. Ch.*
Swithin	July 15
Thérèse	Oct. 3
Timothy	Jan. 26, Jan. 22
Wilfrid	Oct. 12

8 letters

Aloysius	June 21
Barnabas	June 11
Benedict	July 11
Birgitta	Oct. 8
Boniface	June 5
Cuthbert	Mar. 20
Irenaeus	Aug. 23 *E. Ch.*, June 28 *W. Ch.*
Lawrence	Aug. 10
Margaret	Nov. 16
Matthias	May 14 *W. Ch.*, Aug. 9 *E. Ch.*
Nicholas	Dec. 6
Polycarp	Feb. 23

9 letters

Augustine (of Canterbury)	May 26
Augustine (of Hippo)	Aug. 28
Catherine (of Alexandria)	Nov. 25
Elizabeth	Nov. 5

Geneviève	Jan. 3
Joan of Arc	May 30
Sebastian	Jan. 20
Valentine	Feb. 14
Vladimir I	July 15
Wenceslas	Sept. 28

10 letters

Athanasius	May 2
John Fisher	June 22
Ladislaus I	June 27
Stanislaus	Apr. 11
Thomas More	June 22

11 letters

Agnes of Rome	Jan. 21
Bartholomew	Aug. 24
Bonaventura	July 15
Mother Seton	Jan. 4

12 letters

James the Just	May 1
James the Less	Oct. 9 E. Ch., May 1 W. Ch.
Oswald of York	Feb. 28

13 letters

Clare of Assisi	Aug. 11
Francis Xavier	Dec. 3
James the Great	July 25
Mary Magdalene	July 22
Oliver Plunket	July 11
Teresa of Ávila	Oct. 15
Thomas à Becket	Dec. 29
Thomas Aquinas	Jan. 28
Vincent de Paul	July 22

14 letters

Agnes of Bohemia	Mar. 2
Albertus Magnus	Nov. 15
Anthony of Padua	June 13

John Chrysostom	Jan. 27
Francis of Sales	Jan. 24
Gregory of Nyssa	Mar. 9
Gregory of Tours	Nov. 17
Ignatius Loyola	July 31
John of Damascus	Dec. 4
John of the Cross	Dec. 14
John the Baptist	June 24
Simeon Stylites	Jan. 5

15 letters

Alexander Nevsky	Aug. 30, Nov. 23
Bridget of Sweden	Feb. 1
Edward the Martyr	Nov. 20
Francis of Assisi	Oct. 4
Gregory the Great	Mar. 12

16 letters

Bridget of Ireland	July 23
Catherine of Siena	Apr. 29
Edmund the Martyr	Nov. 20
Isidore of Seville	Apr. 4
Stephen of Hungary	Sept. 2

17 letters

Cyril of Alexandria	Feb. 9
Elizabeth Ann Seton (Mother Seton)	Jan. 4
John the Evangelist	Dec. 27
Joseph of Arimathea	Mar. 17

18 letters

| Edward the Confessor | Oct. 13 |
| Gregory of Nazianzus | Jan. 25 and 30 E. Ch., Jan. 2 W. Ch. |

19 letters

| Bernadette of Lourdes | Feb. 18 |
| Clement of Alexandria | Dec. 5 |

The Twelve Tribes of Israel

3 letters
Dan
Gad

4 letters
Levi

5 letters
Asher
Judah

6 letters
Reuben
Simeon

7 letters
Zebulun

8 letters
Benjamin
Issachar
Manasseh
Naphtali

Orders of Angels

6 letters
angels
powers

7 letters
thrones
virtues

8 letters
cherubim
seraphim

9 letters
archangels

11 letters
dominations

14 letters
principalities

Biblical Characters

(indicates the twelve apostles; OT indicates Old Testament;
NT indicates New Testament)*

3 letters
Eve (OT)
Ham (OT)
Job (OT)
Lot (OT)

4 letters
Abel (OT)
Adam (OT)
Baal (OT)
Cain (OT)
Esau (OT)
Jael (OT)
*John (NT)
*Jude (NT)
*Levi (NT)
Luke (NT)
Mark (NT)
Mary (NT)
Noah (OT)
Onan (OT)
Paul (Saul) (NT)
Ruth (OT)
Saul (Paul) (NT)
Saul (OT)
Shem (OT)

5 letters
Aaron (OT)
David (OT)
Enoch (OT)
Isaac (OT)
Jacob (OT)
James (NT)
Jesus (NT)
Jonah (OT)
Judah (OT)
Laban (OT)
Moses (OT)
Naomi (OT)
*(Simon) Peter (NT)
Sarah (OT)
Simon (NT)
Titus (NT)
Uriah (OT)

6 letters
*Andrew (NT)
Daniel (OT)
Elijah (OT)
Elisha (OT)
Esther (OT)
Gideon (OT)
Isaiah (OT)

Israel (OT)
Joseph (NT)
Joseph (OT)
Joshua (OT)
Martha (NT)
Miriam (OT)
Nathan (OT)
*Philip (NT)
Rachel (OT)
Salome (NT)
Samson (OT)
Samuel (OT)
Sisera (OT)
*Thomas (NT)

7 letters
Abishag (OT)
Abraham (OT)
Absalom (OT)
Barabas (NT)
Delilah (OT)
Ephraim (OT)
Ezekiel (OT)
Gabriel (NT)
Goliath (OT)
Ishmael (OT)
Japheth (OT)

Jezebel (OT)
Lazarus (NT)
*Matthew (NT)
Meshach (OT)
Michael (NT)
Rebekah (OT)
Solomon (OT)
Stephen (NT)
Timothy (NT)

8 letters

Abednego (OT)
Barabbas (NT)
Benjamin (OT)
Benjamin (OT)
Caiaphas (NT)
Habakkuk (OT)
Hezekiah (OT)
Jeremiah (OT)
Jeroboam (OT)
Jonathan (OT)
Matthias (NT)
Mordecai (OT)
Rehoboam (OT)

Shadrach (OT)
*Thaddeus (NT)

9 letters

Abimelech (OT)
Ahasuerus (OT)
Bathsheba (OT)
*Nathaniel (NT)
Nicodemus (NT)

10 letters

Belshazzar (OT)
Methuselah (OT)
Simon Peter (NT)
Zerubbabel (OT)

11 letters

*Bartholomew (NT)

12 letters

Herod Agrippa (NT)
Herod Antipas (NT)
*James the Less (NT)

13 letters

Herod the Great (NT)
*Judas Iscariot (NT)
Mary Magdalene (NT)
Pontius Pilate (NT)
Simon of Cyrene (NT)

14 letters

Herod Agrippa II (NT)
John the Baptist (NT)

15 letters

*James the Greater (NT)

17 letters

Joseph of Arimathea (NT)
Mary the Holy Mother (NT)
*Simon the Canaanite (NT)

Books of the Bible

Old Testament

3 letters

Job

4 letters

Amos
Ezra
Joel
Ruth

5 letters

Hosea
Jonah
Micah
Nahum

6 letters

Daniel
Esther
Exodus
Haggai
Isaiah
Joshua
Judges
Kings I
Psalms

7 letters

Ezekiel
Genesis
Kings II
Malachi

Numbers
Obadiah
Samuel I

8 letters

Habakkuk
Jeremiah
Nehemiah
Proverbs
Samuel II

9 letters

Leviticus
Zephaniah
Zechariah

11 letters

Chronicles I
Deuteronomy

12 letters

Chronicles II
Ecclesiastes
Lamentations

13 letters

Song of
    Solomon

Books of the Bible

New Testament

4 letters
Acts
John
Jude
Luke
Mark

5 letters
James
John I
Titus

6 letters
John II
Peter I
Romans

7 letters
Hebrews
John III
Matthew
Peter II

8 letters
Philemon
Timothy I

9 letters
Ephesians
Galatians
Timothy II

10 letters
Colossians
Revelation

11 letters
Philippians

12 letters
Corinthians I

13 letters
Corinthians II

14 letters
Thessalonians I

15 letters
Thessalonians II

Apocrypha

5 letters
Tobit

6 letters
Baruch
Judith

7 letters
Esdras I
Susanna

8 letters
Esdras II

10 letters
Maccabees I

11 letters
Maccabees II

14 letters
Ecclesiasticus

15 letters
Bel and the
   Dragon
Wisdom of
   Solomon

16 letters
Letter of
   Jeremiah
Prayer of
   Manasses

26 letters
Additions to the
   Book of Esther
Song of the
   Three Holy
   Children

Monastic Orders

6 letters
Minims

7 letters
Culdees
Jesuits
Marists

8 letters
Blue Nuns
Gray Nuns
Jacobins
Paulines
Piarists

Servites
Studites

9 letters
Antonians
Bonhommes
Capuchins
Minorites
Salesians
Somascans
Theatines
Trappists
Ursulines

10 letters
Barnabites
Black Monks
Carmelites
Dominicans
Gray Friars
Marianists
Oratorians
Poor Clares

11 letters
Bernardines
Black Friars
Brigittines

Carthusians
Cistercians
Conventuals
Franciscans
Friars Minor
Gilbertines
Norbertines
Passionists
White Friars

12 letters
Austin Friars
Benedictines
Camaldolites

Hieronymites
Hospitallers
Ignorantines
Sylvestrines
Trinitarians
Visitandines

13 letters

Canons Regular
Doctrinarians

14 letters

Conceptionists

Knights
  Templar

15 letters

Friars Preachers

16 letters

Sisters of
  Charity

17 letters

Christian
  Brothers

18 letters

Augustinian
  Hermits

19 letters

Praemonstraten
sians

20 letters

Brothers
  Hospitallers

21 letters

Sisters of the
  Love of God

23 letters

Brethren of the
  Common
  Life
Poor Soldiers of
  the Temple
Sisters of the
  Sacred Cross

Christian Ecclesiastical Officers

4 letters

dean
pope

5 letters

canon
elder
pastor
vicar

6 letters

beadle
bishop
cantor
cleric
curate

deacon
father
parson
priest
rector
sexton
verger

7 letters

acolyte
almoner
apostle
pontiff
prelate
primate

8 letters

cardinal
chaplain
minister
thurifer

9 letters

confessor
counselor
deaconess
Monsignor
patriarch
precentor
president
succentor
suffragan

10 letters

archbishop

12 letters

churchwarden
metropolitan

14 letters

stake president

17 letters

clerk in holy
  orders

Names of God

(in the Judaeo-Christian-Islamic traditions)

3 letters
Jah

4 letters
Lord, the

5 letters
Allah (Islam)
Deity, the
Maker, the

6 letters
Divine Being
Father, the
Yahweh
   (Judaism)

7 letters
Creator, the
Eternal, the
Godhead, the
Holy One, the
Jehovah
Trinity, the

8 letters
Almighty, the
Our Maker

9 letters
God the Son
Holy Ghost, the
Our Father

10 letters
First Cause
Holy Spirit
Prime Mover,
   the

11 letters
Almighty God
God Almighty
Holy Trinity, the
King of Kings
Lord of Lords
Spirit of God

12 letters
God the Father

primum mobile
Supreme Being,
   the

13 letters
Alpha and
   Omega

17 letters
Everlasting
   Father

21 letters
Father, Son, and
   Holy Ghost

Names for the Devil

(in Christianity)

4 letters
deil

5 letters
Deuce
Satan

6 letters
Belial
Moloch
Old One

7 letters
Abbadon

dickens
Evil One, the
Lucifer
Old Nick
Scratch
Tempter, the

8 letters
Mephisto
Old Harry

9 letters
Arch-fiend, the
Auld Thief

Beelzebub
Foul Fiend
Old Hornie
Wicked One

10 letters
Old Cootie

11 letters
Old Scratchy

12 letters
old gentleman
   (in black)

14 letters
Lord of the
   Flies
Mephistopheles

16 letters
Prince of
   Darkness

17 letters
His Satanic
   Majesty

Seven Virtues

4 letters
hope
love (charity)

5 letters
faith

7 letters
charity (love)
justice

8 letters
prudence

9 letters
fortitude

10 letters
temperance

Seven Deadly Sins

4 letters
envy
lust

5 letters
anger
pride
sloth

8 letters
gluttony

12 letters
covetousness

Parts of a Church

4 letters
apse
dome
font
nave

5 letters
aisle
choir
conch
crypt
spire

6 letters
chevet
flèche
vestry

7 letters
chancel
galilee
narthex
steeple

8 letters
buttress
crossing
sacristy
transept
vaulting
westwork

9 letters
triforium

10 letters
ambulatory
baptistery
blind-story
clerestory
clearstory
rood-screen

14 letters
flying buttress
tribune gallery

Greek Gods and Goddesses

(with Roman equivalent)

3 letters

Eos	
Pan	
Dis (Hades)	Aurora
	Faunus
	Pluto

Zeus — Jupiter

5 letters

Hades (Dis) — Pluto

4 letters

Ares	Mars
Eros	Cupid
Gaia	Ge
Hebe	Juventas
Hera	Juno
Iris	
Nike	Victoria
Rhea	Cybele

6 letters

Apollo	
Athene	Minerva
Cronos	Saturn
Furies (Eumenides)	
Graces (Charites)	Aglaia, Euphrosyne, Thalia
Hecate	
Helios	Sol

Greek Gods and Goddesses *(continued)*

Hermes	Mercury	Dionysus	Bacchus
Hestia	Vesta	Poseidon	Neptune
Hypnos	Somnus	Thanatos	Mors
Selene	Luna		

7 letters

9 letters

Artemis	Diana	Aphrodite	Venus
Demeter	Ceres	Asclepius	Aesculapius
Nemesis		Eumenides	
Ouranos	Uranus		

8 letters

10 letters

		Hephaestus	Vulcan
Charites (Graces)	Aglaia,	Persephone	Proserpine
	Euphrosyne, Thalia		

Roman Gods and Goddesses

(with Greek equivalent)

2 letters

Ge	Gaia

3 letters

Sol	Helios

4 letters

Juno	Hera
Luna	Selene
Mars	Ares
Mors	Thanatos

5 letters

Ceres	Demeter
Cupid	Eros
Diana	Artemis
Janus	
Pluto	Hades
Venus	Aphrodite
Vesta	Hestia

6 letters

Apollo	
Aurora	Eos
Cybele	Rhea
Faunus	Pan
Graces	Charites

Hecate	Hecate
Saturn	Cronos
Somnus	Hypnos
Uranus	Ouranos
Vulcan	Hephaestus

7 letters

Bacchus	Dionysus
Fortuna	Tuche
Jupiter	Zeus
Mercury	Hermes
Minerva	Athene
Neptune	Poseidon

8 letters

Juventas	Hebe
Victoria	Nike

10 letters

Proserpine	Persephone

11 letters

Aesculapius	Asclepius

15 letters

Lares and Penates	

The Three Fates

6 letters
Clotho   (spins the thread of life)

7 letters
Atropos   (cuts the thread of life)

8 letters
Lachesis   (assigns a person's destiny)

The Nine Muses

4 letters
Clio   (history)

5 letters
Erato   (lyric and love poetry)

6 letters
Thalia   (comic and pastoral poetry)
Urania   (astronomy)

7 letters
Euterpe   (music)

8 letters
Calliope   (eloquence, epic poetry)

9 letters
Melpomene   (tragedy)

10 letters
Polyhymnia   (singing, rhetoric)

11 letters
Terpsichore   (dancing)

Characters from Greek and Roman Mythology

2 letters
Io

3 letters
Ino

4 letters
Ajax
Ceyx
Dido
Hero
Leda

5 letters
Atlas
Chloe
Circe

Creon
Damon
Horae (Hours)
Hydra
Ixion
Jason
Lamia
Medea
Midas
Niobe
Orion
Priam
Remus
Satyr
Sibyl
Siren

6 letters
Adonis
Aeneas
Aeolus
Amazon
Atreus
Boreas
Castor
Charon
Chiron
Dryads
Europa
Hector
Hecuba
Icarus
Medusa
 (Gorgon)

Mentor
Naiads
Nestor
Nymphs
Oreads
Pollux
Scylla
Stheno
 (Gorgon)
Thetis
Thisbe

7 letters
Actaeon
Admetus
Arachne
Ariadne

Characters from
Greek and Roman Mythology *(continued)*

Calypso
Cepheus
Chimera
Cyclops
Daphnis
Electra
Euryale
  (Gorgon)
Gorgons
  (Euryale,
  Medusa,
  Stheno)
Harpies
Jocasta
Lapiths
Leander
Maenads
Oedipus
Olympus
Orestes
Orpheus
Pandora
Pegasus
Perseus

Pyramus
Pythian
Romulus
Theseus
Ulysses

8 letters
Achilles
Alcestis
Antigone
Atalanta
Centaurs
Cerberus
Daedalus
Diomedes
Endymion
Eteocles
Eurydice
Ganymede
Heracles
  (Hercules)
Iphicles
Meleager
Menelaus

Minotaur
Nausicaa
Odysseus
Pasiphae
Penelope
Phaethon
Sisyphus
Tantalus
Thyestes

9 letters
Aegisthus
Agamemnon
Andromeda
Charybdis
Iphigenia
Narcissus
Palinurus
Patroclus
Polynices

10 letters
Andromache
Cassiopeia

Hamadryads
Iphigeneia
Philoctetes
Polyphemus
Prometheus
Rhea Silvia
Telemachus

11 letters
Bellerophon
Helen of Troy
Philoctetes

12 letters
Clytemnestra

13 letters
Ajax the Lesser

14 letters
Hermaphroditus
Telamonian
  Ajax

The Labors of Hercules

10 letters
(The) Cretan
  bull
(The) Nemean
  lion

13 letters
(The) Augean
  stables
(The) Ceryneian
  hind

(The) Lernaean
  hydra

14 letters
(The) cattle of
  Geryon

15 letters
(The) mares of
  Diomedes

16 letters
(The)
  Stymphalian
  birds

17 letters
(The) capture of
  Cerberus
(The) girdle of
  Hippolyte

20 letters
(The) wild
  boar of
  Erymanthus

27 letters
(The) golden
  apples of the
  Hesperides

Rivers of Hades

4 letters	5 letters	7 letters	10 letters
Styx	Lethe	Acheron	Phlegethon

Egyptian Gods and Goddesses

2 letters
Ra

3 letters
Bes
Geb
Min
Mut
Nun
Nut
Set (Seth)
Shu

4 letters
Aten
Atum
Bast
Buto
Hapi

Isis
Maat
Mont
Ptah
Sati
Seth (Set)
Shai

5 letters
Ament
Ammon
Anhur
Heket
Horus
Khnum
Neheh
Sebek
Seker
Thoth

6 letters
Amon-Ra
Anquet
Anubis
Hathor
Khensu
Osiris
Renpet
Selket
Tefnut
Upuaut

7 letters
Behdety
Imhotep
Khepera
Renenet
Sekhmet

Sesheta
Taueret

8 letters
Haroeris
Meskhent
Nefertum
Nekhebit
Nephthys

9 letters
Harakhtes
Harmakhis
Harsaphes
Harsiesis
Mertseger

Hindu Gods and Goddesses

3 letters
Uma

4 letters
Agni
Devi
Kali
Kama
Mara
Rama
Siva (Shiva)
Sita
Soma
Vata
Yama

5 letters
Aditi
Durga
Indra
Kurma
Mitra
Radha
Rudra
Sakti (Shakti)
Shiva (Siva)
Surya
Ushas

6 letters
Brahma
Matsya

Puchan
Ravana
Shakti (Sakti)
Skanda
Vamana
Varaha
Varuna
Vishnu

7 letters
Ganesha
Hanuman
Krishna
Lakshmi
Parvati
Savitar

8 letters
Bhairavi
Tvashtar

9 letters
Kartikeya
Narasinha
Prajapati
Sarasvati

10 letters
Jagannatha
   (Juggernaut)

Celtic Gods, Goddesses, and Heroes

3 letters
Anu (Dana *or* Danu)
Ket
Lêr
Roc

4 letters
Bran
Dana (Danu *or* Anu)
Emer
Goll (MacMorna)
Laeg
Ludd (Nudd)
Lugh
Maev
Niam
Ogma
Ross (the Red)
Usna

5 letters
Boann
Conan
Conor
Dagda, the
Etain

Epona
Macha
Midir (the Proud)
Murna (of the White
  Neck)
Naisi
Nuada
Oisin
Pwyll
Sidhe, the

6 letters
Boanna, the
Brigit
Conall
Cormac
Dermot (O'Dyna)
Fergus
Fianna, the
Fomors
Gobniu
Ossian
Skatha

7 letters
Branwen

Deirdre
Firbolgs, the
Sualtam

8 letters
Etain Olg
Fuamnach
MacMorna (Goll)
Manannan (Mananan)
Rhiannon
Taliesin

9 letters
Cernunnos
Cuchulain(n)
Dian Cecht
Red Branch, the

11 letters
Finn MacCool (Finn
  Mac Cumhal)

14 letters
Tuatha Dé Dannan

Norse Gods, Goddesses, and Other Mythological Figures

3 letters
Ask	first man
Hel	goddess of death
Sif	wife of Thor
Tyr	god of war

4 letters
Buri	grandfather of Odin
Gerd	wife of Freyr
Loki	trickster god
Odin (Wotan)	chief god
Surt	lord of Muspelheim
Thor	god of thunder
Urth (Norn)	Fates

Ymir	giant from whose body the world was created

5 letters
Aesir	tribe of the gods
Embla	first woman
Freyr	protector of living things
Hoder	blind god
Njord	leader of the Vanir
Norns (Urth, Verthandi, Skuld)	Fates
Skuld (Norn)	Fates

Vanir	gods of fertility	Niflheim	home of the dead
Vidar	son of Odin	Ragnarok	final battle between gods and giants
Wotan (Odin)	chief god	Sleipnir	Odin's eight-legged horse

6 letters

Asgard	home of the gods	Valhalla	hall of the gods in Asgard
Balder	god of the sun		
Fenrir	wolf		
Freyja	goddess of love	**9 letters**	
Frigga	wife of Odin	Aurgelmir	primeval giant
Kvasir	god whose death created poetry	Mannaheim (Midgard)	world of men
Njorth	leader of the Vanir	Valkyries	nine warrior goddesses

7 letters

		Verthandi (Norn)	Fates
Alfheim	region of Asgard	Yggdrasil	the Cosmic Tree
Audumla	primeval cow		
Bifrost	rainbow bridge	**10 letters**	
Gungnir	Odin's spear	Jörmungand	serpent
Heimdal	guardian of Bifrost	Muspelheim	realm of fire
Midgard	(Mannaheim) world of men		

11 letters

| | | Skidbladnir | magic ship |

8 letters

Brynhild	leader of the Valkyries	**12 letters**	
		Wayland Smith	lord of the elves
Draupnir	Odin's magic ring		
Mjollnir	Thor's hammer		

Arthurian Legend

3 letters

Kay	Arthur's foster brother	**7 letters**	
		Camelot	capital of Arthur's kingdom
Lot	father of Gawain	Galahad	knight
		Mordred	son of Morgan Le Fay

6 letters

Arthur	legendary British king	**8 letters**	
Avalon	paradise	Lancelot (Launcelot)	knight
Elaine	mother of Galahad	Percival (Perceval)	knight
Gawain	knight	Tristram	knight
Iseult	lover of Tristram		
Merlin	magician	**9 letters**	
Modred	son of Morgan Le Fay	Excalibur	Arthur's sword
Nineve	Lady of the Lake		

Arthurian Legend *(continiued)*

Guinevere — Arthur's wife
Holy Grail — used by Christ at the Last Supper
Launcelot (Lancelot) — knight

10 letters
Fisher King — custodian of the Holy Grail

11 letters
Morgan Le Fay — magician; Arthur's sister

14 letters
Uther Pendragon — Arthur's father

Monsters and Demons

3 letters
orc

4 letters
ogre
yeti

5 letters
afanc
bogey
ghoul
gnome
golem
harpy
hodag
Hydra
lamia
mormo
troll

6 letters
afreet
bunyip
caddie (Cad-borosaurus)
dragon

goblin
Gorgon
kraken
Lilith
Medusa
Nessie
Ravana
Scylla
sphinx
wyvern
zombie

7 letters
bigfoot
bugbear
Caliban
centaur
chimera
Grendal
griffin
incubus
ngarara
Ogopogo
sciapod
taniwha
tao-tieh

Tityrus
vampire
windigo

8 letters
basilisk
behemoth
Cerberus
Godzilla
King Kong
Minotaur
succubus
werewolf

9 letters
Charybdis
fire-drake
hobgoblin
leviathan
manticore
sasquatch

10 letters
cockatrice
hippogriff

11 letters
hippocampus

13 letters
Cadborosaurus (caddie)

15 letters
Loch Ness Monster (Nessie)

16 letters
Headless Horseman, the

17 letters
abominable snowman

20 letters
Frankenstein's monster

Countries of the World

(with capital cities)

4 letters

Chad	N'Djamena
Fiji	Suva
Iran	Tehran
Iraq	Baghdad
Laos	Vientiane
Mali	Bamako
Oman	Muscat
Peru	Lima
Togo	Lomé

5 letters

Aruba	Oranjestad
Benin	Porto Novo
Burma	See MYANMAR
Chile	Santiago
China	Beijing *or* Peking
Congo,	Brazzaville
Congo,	Kinshasa
Democratic Republic of (formerly Zaire)	
Egypt	Cairo
Gabon	Libreville
Ghana	Accra
Haiti	Port-au-Prince
India	New Delhi
Italy	Rome
Japan	Tokyo
Kenya	Nairobi
Libya	Tripoli
Malta	Valletta
Nauru	
Nepal	Kathmandu
Niger	Niamey
Palau	Koror
Qatar	Doha
Samoa (formerly Western Samoa)	Apia
Spain	Madrid
Sudan	Khartoum
Syria	Damascus
Tonga	Nuku'alofa
Yemen	Sana'a
Zare	See CONGO, DEMOCRATIC REPUBLIC OF

6 letters

Angola	Luanda
Belize	Belmopan
Bhutan	Thimphu
Brazil	Brasilia
Brunei	Bandar Seri Begawan
Canada	Ottawa
Cyprus	Nicosia
France	Paris
Gambia, The	Banjul
Greece	Athens
Guinea	Conakry
Guyana	Georgetown
Israel	Jerusalem (*de facto*)
Jordan	Amman
Kuwait	Kuwait City
Latvia	Riga
Malawi	Lilongwe
Mexico	Mexico City
Monaco	
Norway	Oslo
Panama	Panama City
Poland	Warsaw
Russia	Moscow
Rwanda	Kigali
Serbia	Belgrade
Sweden	Stockholm
Taiwan	Taipei
Turkey	Ankara
Tuvalu	Funafuti
Uganda	Kampala
Zambia	Lusaka

7 letters

Albania	Tirana
Algeria	Algiers
Andorra	Andorra la Vella
Armenia	Yerevan
Austria	Vienna
Bahamas, The	Nassau
Bahrain	Manama
Belarus	Minsk
Belgium	Brussels
Bolivia	La Paz
Burundi	Bujumbura

Countries of the World *(continued)*

Comoros	Moroni
Croatia	Zagreb
Denmark	Copenhagen
Ecuador	Quito
Eritrea	Asmara
Estonia	Tallinn
Finland	Helsinki
Georgia	Tbilisi
Germany	Berlin
Grenada	St. George's
Hungary	Budapest
Iceland	Reykjavik
Ireland, Republic of	Dublin
Jamaica	Kingston
Lebanon	Beirut
Lesotho	Maseru
Liberia	Monrovia
Moldova	Chişinău
Morocco	Rabat
Myanmar	(formerly Burma)
	Rangoon *or* Yangon
Namibia	Windhoek
Nigeria	Abuja
Romania	Bucharest
St. Lucia	Castries
Senegal	Dakar
Somalia	Mogadishu
Tunisia	Tunis
Ukraine	Kiev
Uruguay	Montevideo
Vanuatu	Vila
Vietnam	Hanoi

8 letters

Barbados	Bridgetown
Botswana	Gaborone
Bulgaria	Sofia
Cambodia	Phnom Penh
Cameroon	Yaoundé
Colombia	Bogota
Djibouti	Djibouti
Dominica	Roseau
Ethiopia	Addis Ababa
Honduras	Tegucigalpa
Kiribati	Bairiki
Malaysia	Kuala Lumpur
Maldives	Male
Mongolia	Ulan Bator

Pakistan	Islamabad
Paraguay	Asunción
Portugal	Lisbon
Slovakia	Bratislava
Slovenia	Ljubljana
Sri Lanka	Colombo
Suriname	Paramaribo
Tanzania	Dodoma
Thailand	Bangkok
Zimbabwe	Harare

9 letters

Argentina	Buenos Aires
Australia	Canberra
Costa Rica	San José
Guatemala	Guatemala City
Indonesia	Djakarta
Lithuania	Vilnius
Macedonia (Former	
Yugoslav Republic of)	Skopje
Mauritius	Port Louis
Nicaragua	Managua
San Marino	San Marino
Singapore	Singapore
Swaziland	Mbabane
Venezuela	Caracas

10 letters

Azerbaijan	Baku
Bangladesh	Dhaka
El Salvador	San Salvador
Ivory Coast	Yamoussoukro
Kazakhstan	Akmola
Kyrgyzstan	Bishkek
Luxembourg	Luxembourg
Madagascar	Antananarivo
Mauritania	Nouakchott
Micronesia	Kolonia
Montenegro	Podgorica
Mozambique	Maputo
New Zealand	Wellington
North Korea	Pyongyang
Seychelles, The	Victoria
South Korea	Seoul
Tajikistan	Dushanbe
Uzbekistan	Tashkent
Yugoslavia	See SERBIA, MONTENEGRO, etc.

11 letters

Afghanistan	Kabul
Burkina Faso	Ouagadougou
Netherlands, The	Amsterdam
Philippines	Manila
Saudi Arabia	Riyadh
Sierra Leone	Freetown
South Africa	Pretoria
Switzerland	Berne
Vatican City	

12 letters

Guinea-Bissau	Bissau
Turkmenistan	Ashgabat

13 letters

Czech Republic	Prague
Liechtenstein	Vaduz

14 letters

Papua New Guinea	Port Moresby
St. Kitts and Nevis	Basseterre
Solomon Islands	Honiara

15 letters

Marshall Islands	Majuro

16 letters

Cape Verde Islands	Praia
Equatorial Guinea	Malabo
Trinidad and Tobago	Port of Spain

17 letters

Antigua and Barbuda	St. John's
Bosnia-Herzegovina	Sarajevo
Dominican Republic	Santo Domingo

18 letters

São Tomé and Principe	São Tomé
United Arab Emirates	Abu Dhabi

22 letters

Central African Republic	Bangui

25 letters

St. Vincent and the Grenadines	Kingstown

Capital Cities

(with countries)

4 letters

Apia	Samoa (formerly Western Samoa)
Baku	Azerbaijan
Doha	Qatar
Kiev	Ukraine
Lima	Peru
Lomé	Togo
Male	Maldives
Oslo	Norway
Riga	Latvia
Rome	Italy
Suva	Fiji
Vila	Vanuatu

5 letters

Abuja	Nigeria
Accra	Ghana
Amman	Jordan
Berne	Switzerland

Cairo	Egypt
Dakar	Senegal
Dhaka	Bangladesh
Hanoi	Vietnam
Kabul	Afghanistan
Koror	Palau
La Paz	Bolivia
Minsk	Belarus
Paris	France
Praia	Cape Verde Islands
Quito	Ecuador
Rabat	Morocco
Sana'a	Yemen
Seoul	Korea, South
Sofia	Bulgaria
Tokyo	Japan
Tunis	Tunisia
Vaduz	Liechtenstein

Capital Cities *(continued)*

6 letters

Akmola	Kazakhstan
Ankara	Turkey
Asmara	Eritrea
Athens	Greece
Bamako	Mali
Bangui	Central African Republic
Banjul	Gambia, The
Beirut	Lebanon
Berlin	Germany
Bissau	Guinea-Bissau
Bogota	Colombia
Dodoma	Tanzania
Dublin	Ireland, Republic of
Harare	Zimbabwe
Havana	Cuba
Kigali	Rwanda
Lisbon	Portugal
London	U.K.
Luanda	Angola
Lusaka	Zambia
Madrid	Spain
Majuro	Marshall Islands
Malabo	Equatorial Guinea
Manama	Bahrain
Manila	Philippines
Maputo	Mozambique
Maseru	Lesotho
Moroni	Comoros
Moscow	Russia
Muscat	Oman
Nassau	Bahamas, The
Niamey	Niger
Ottawa	Canada
Peking	China
Prague	Czech Republic
Riyadh	Saudi Arabia
Roseau	Dominica
Skopje	Macedonia (Former Yugoslav Republic of)
Taipei	Taiwan
Tehran	Iran
Tirana	Albania
Vienna	Austria
Warsaw	Poland
Yangon	Myanmar (formerly Burma)
Zagreb	Croatia

7 letters

Algiers	Algeria
Baghdad	Iraq
Bairiki	Kiribati
Bangkok	Thailand
Beijing	China
Bishkek	Kyrgyzstan
Caracas	Venezuela
Colombo	Sri Lanka
Conakry	Guinea
Honiara	Solomon Islands
Kampala	Uganda
Kingston	Jamaica
Kolonia	Micronesia
Managua	Nicaragua
Mbabane	Swaziland
Nairobi	Kenya
Nicosia	Cyprus
Rangoon	Myanmar (formerly Burma)
San José	Costa Rica
São Tomé	São Tomé and Principe
St. John's	Antigua and Barbuda
Tallinn	Estonia
Tbilisi	Georgia
Thimphu	Bhutan
Tripoli	Libya
Vilnius	Lithuania
Yaoundé	Cameroon
Yerevan	Armenia

8 letters

Abu Dhabi	United Arab Emirates
Ashgabat	Turkmenistan
Asunción	Paraguay
Belgrade	Serbia
Belmopan	Belize
Brasilia	Brazil
Brussels	Belgium
Budapest	Hungary
Canberra	Australia
Castries	St. Lucia
Chişinău	Moldova
Damascus	Syria
Djakarta	Indonesia
Djibouti	Djibouti
Dushanbe	Tajikistan

Freetown	Sierra Leone
Funafuti	Tuvalu
Gaborone	Botswana
Helsinki	Finland
Khartoum	Sudan
Kinshasa	Congo, Democratic Republic of (formerly Zare)
Lilongwe	Malawi
Monrovia	Liberia
N'Djamena	Chad
New Delhi	India
Pretoria	South Africa
Santiago	Chile
Sarajevo	Bosnia-Herzegovina
Tashkent	Uzbekistan
Valletta	Malta
Victoria	Seychelles, The
Windhoek	Namibia

9 letters

Bucharest	Romania
Bujumbura	Burundi
Islamabad	Pakistan
Jerusalem (de facto)	Israel
Kathmandu	Nepal
Kingstown	St. Vincent and the Grenadines
Ljubljana	Slovenia
Mogadishu	Somalia
Nuku'alofa	Tonga
Phnom Penh	Cambodia
Podgorica	Montenegro
Port Louis	Mauritius
Porto Novo	Benin
Pyongyang	Korea, North
Reykjavik	Iceland
San Marino	San Marino
Singapore	Singapore
St. George's	Grenada
Stockholm	Sweden
Ulan Bator	Mongolia
Vientiane	Laos

10 letters

Addis Ababa	Ethiopia
Amsterdam	Netherlands, The

Basseterre	St. Kitts and Nevis
Bratislava	Slovakia
Bridgetown	Barbados
Copenhagen	Denmark
Georgetown	Guyana
Kuwait City	Kuwait
Libreville	Gabon
Luxembourg	Luxembourg
Mexico City	Mexico
Montevideo	Uruguay
Nouakchott	Mauritania
Oranjestad	Aruba
Panama City	Panama
Paramaribo	Suriname
Washington, DC	U.S.
Wellington	New Zealand

11 letters

Brazzaville	Congo
Buenos Aires	Argentina
Kuala Lumpur	Malaysia
Ouagadougou	Burkina Faso
Port Moresby	Papua New Guinea
Port of Spain	Trinidad and Tobago
San Salvador	El Salvador
Tegucigalpa	Honduras

12 letters

Antananarivo	Madagascar
Port-au-Prince	Haiti
Santo Domingo	Dominican Republic
Yamoussoukro	Ivory Coast

13 letters

Guatemala City	Guatemala

14 letters

Andorra la Vella	Andorra

17 letters

Bandar Seri Begawan	Brunei

U.S. States

(with abbreviations and capitals)

4 letters

Guam (territory)	GU	Agaña
Iowa	IA *or* Ia.	Des Moines
Ohio	OH *or* Oh.	Columbus
Utah	UT *or* Ut.	Salt Lake City

5 letters

Idaho	ID *or* Ida.	Boise
Maine	ME *or* Me.	Augusta
Texas	TX *or* Tex.	Austin

6 letters

Alaska	AK *or* Alas.	Juneau
Hawaii	HI	Honolulu
Kansas	KS *or* Kan.	Topeka
Nevada	NV *or* Nev.	Carson City
Oregon	OR *or* Oreg.	Salem

7 letters

Alabama	AL *or* Ala.	Montgomery
Arizona	AZ *or* Ariz.	Phoenix
Florida	FL *or* Fla.	Tallahassee
Georgia	GA *or* Ga.	Atlanta
Indiana	IN *or* Ind.	Indianapolis
Montana	MT *or* Mont.	Helena
New York	NY *or* N.Y.	Albany
Vermont	VT *or* Vt.	Montpelier
Wyoming	WY *or* Wyo.	Cheyenne

8 letters

Arkansas	AR *or* Ark.	Little Rock
Colorado	CO *or* Colo.	Denver
Delaware	DE *or* Del.	Dover
Illinois	IL *or* Ill.	Springfield
Kentucky	KY *or* Ken.	Frankfort
Maryland	MD *or* Md.	Annapolis
Michigan	MI *or* Mich.	Lansing
Missouri	MO *or* Mo.	Jefferson City
Nebraska	NE *or* Nebr.	Lincoln
Oklahoma	OK *or* Okla.	Oklahoma City
Virginia	VA *or* Va.	Richmond

9 letters

Louisiana	LA *or* La.	Baton Rouge
Minnesota	MN *or* Minn	St. Paul
New Jersey	NJ *or* N.J.	Trenton
New Mexico	NM *or* N.M.	Santa Fe

Tennessee	TN or Tenn.	Nashville
Wisconsin	WI or Wisc.	Madison

10 letters

California	CA or Cal. or Calif.	Sacramento
Puerto Rico (commonwealth)	PR or P.R.	San Juan
Washington	WA or Wash.	Olympia

11 letters

Connecticut	CT or Conn. or Ct.	Hartford
Mississippi	MS or Miss.	Jackson
North Dakota	ND or N. Dak. or N.D.	Bismarck
Rhode Island	RI or R.I.	Providence
South Dakota	SD or S. Dak. or S.D.	Pierre

12 letters

New Hampshire	NH or N.H.	Concord
Pennsylvania	PA or Pa. or Penn. or Penna.	Harrisburg
West Virginia	WV or W. Va.	Charleston

13 letters

Massachusetts	MA or Mass.	Boston
North Carolina	NC or N.C.	Raleigh
South Carolina	SC or S.C.	Columbia
Virgin Islands (territory)	VI or V.I.	Charlotte Amalie

18 letters

District of Columbia	DC or D.C.	Washington

U.S. Capitals

(with states)

5 letters

Agaña	Guam
Boise	Idaho
Dover	Delaware
Salem	Oregon

6 letters

Albany	New York
Austin	Texas
Boston	Massachusetts
Denver	Colorado
Helena	Montana
Juneau	Alaska
Pierre	South Dakota

Topeka	Kansas

7 letters

Atlanta	Georgia
Augusta	Maine
Concord	New Hampshire
Jackson	Mississippi
Lansing	Michigan
Lincoln	Nebraska
Madison	Wisconsin
Olympia	Washington
Phoenix	Arizona
Raleigh	North Carolina
San Juan	Puero Rico

U.S. Capitals *(continued)*

Sante Fe	New Mexico	Little Rock	Arkansas
Trenton	New Jersey	Montgomery	Alabama
		Montpelier	Vermont
8 letters		Providence	Rhode Island
Bismarck	North Dakota	Sacramento	California
Cheyenne	Wyoming		
Columbia	South Carolina	*11 letters*	
Columbus	Ohio	Springfield	Illinois
Hartford	Connecticut	Tallahassee	Florida
Honolulu	Hawaii		
Richmond	Virginia	*12 letters*	
		Indianapolis	Indiana
9 letters		Oklahoma City	Oklahoma
Annapolis	Maryland	Salt Lake City	Utah
Des Moines	Iowa	Washington, D.C.	United States
Frankfort	Kentucky		
Nashville	Tennessee	*13 letters*	
Saint Paul	Minnesota	Jefferson City	Missouri
10 letters		*15 letters*	
Carson City	Nevada	Charlotte Amalie	U.S. Virgin
Charleston	West Virginia		Islands
Harrisburg	Pennsylvania		

States and Territories of Australia

(with capitals)

8 letters		*16 letters*	
Tasmania	Hobart	Western Australia	Perth
Victoria	Melbourne	*17 letters*	
10 letters		Northern Territory	Darwin
Queensland	Brisbane	*26 letters*	
13 letters		Australian Capital	Canberra
New South Wales	Sydney	Territory	(federal capital)
14 letters			
South Australia	Adelaide		

Provinces and Territories of Canada

(with postal designations and capitals)

6 letters		Saskatchewan (SK)	Regina
Quebec (PQ)	Quebec	**14 letters**	
7 letters		Yukon Territory (YT)	Whitehorse
Alberta (AB)	Edmonton	**15 letters**	
Nunavut (NT)	Iqaluit	British Columbia (BC)	Victoria
Ontario (ON)	Toronto	**18 letters**	
8 letters		Prince Edward	
Manitoba (MB)	Winnipeg	Island (PE)	Charlottetown
10 letters		**20 letters**	
Nova Scotia (NS)	Halifax	Northwest	
12 letters		Territories (NT)	Yellowknife
New Brunswick (NB)	Fredericton	**23 letters**	
Noufoundland	See	Newfoundland and	
	NEWFOUNDLAND	Labrador (NF)	St. John's
	AND LABRADOR		

Canadian Capitals

(with provinces)

6 letters		**10 letters**	
Ottawa	Canada	Saint Johns	Newfoundland
Quebec (City)	Quebec	Whitehorse	Yukon Territory
7 letters		**11 letters**	
Halifax	Nova Scotia	Fredericton	New Brunswick
Iqaluit	Nunavut	Yellowknife	Northwest
Toronto	Ontario		Territories
8 letters		**13 letters**	
Edmonton	Alberta	Charlottetown	Prince Edward
Victoria	British Columbia	Island	
Winnipeg	Manitoba		

Mexican States

(with capitals)

6 letters		Michoacán	Morelia
Colima	Colima	Nuevo León	Monterrey
México	Toluca	Querétaro	Querétaro
Oaxaca	Oaxaca	Zacatecas	Zacatecas
Puebla	Puebla		
Sonora	Hermosillo	*10 letters*	
		Guanajuato	Guanajuato
7 letters		Tamaulipas	Ciudad Victoria
Chiapas	Tuxtla Gutiérrez		
Durango	Durango	*11 letters*	
Hidalgo	Pachuca	Quintana Roo	Chetumal
Jalisco	Guadalajara		
Morelos	Cuernavaca	*13 letters*	
Nayarit	Tepic	San Luis Potosí	San Luis Potosí
Sinaloa	Culiacán		
Tabasco	Villahermosa	*14 letters*	
Yucatán	Mérida	Aguascalientes	Aguascalientes
8 letters		*15 letters*	
Campeche	Campeche	DistritoFederal	Ciudad de
Coahuila	Saltillo		México (Mexico City)
Guerrero	Chilpancingo		
Tlaxcala	Tlaxcala	*17 letters*	
Veracruz	Jalapa	Baja California Sur	La Paz
9 letters		*19 letters*	
Chihuahua	Chihuahua	Baja California Norte	Mexicali

Provinces of New Zealand

NORTH ISLAND	*10 letters*	**SOUTH ISLAND**	*10 letters*
7 letters	Wellington	*5 letters*	Canterbury
Waikato	*11 letters*	Otago	*11 letters*
8 letters	Bay of Plenty	*6 letters*	Marlborough
Auckland	*16 letters*	Nelson	**ISLANDS**
Gisborne	Manawatu-	Tasman	
Taranaki	Wanganui		*14 letters*
9 letters		*9 letters*	Chatham
Hawkes Bay		Southland	Islands
Northland		West Coast	Stewart Islands

Provinces of South Africa

(with capitals)

7 letters	**9 letters**	**11 letters**
Gauteng (formerly Pretoria—Witwatersrand-Vereeniging [PWV]) Johannesburg	North-West Mafikeng Free State (formerly Orange Free State) Bloemfontein	Eastern Cape Bisho Western Cape Cape Town
8 letters	**10 letters**	**12 letters** KwaZulu/Natal Ulundi Northern Cape Kimberley
Northern (formerly Northern Transvaal) Pietersburg	Mpumalanga (formerly Eastern Transvaal) Nelspruit	

Cities, Towns, and Villages

2 letters	**4 letters**		
Ur	Agra	Cana	Graz
	Aiea	Cary	Győr
3 letters	Ajax	Cebu	Ha'il
Aba	Aksu	Cheb	Hami
Abo	Albi	Cody	Hamm
Ada	Alma	Cork	Hays
Ayr	Alta	Dali	Hebi
Dan	Alva	Deva	Hell
Ede	Ames	Doha	Heze
Ely	Amol	Durg	Hilo
Hof	Amoy	Edam	Hino
Hué	Anda	Eden	Hope
Ife	Arad	Eger	Hove
Iwo	Arak	Elda	Hull
Jos	Arta	Elea	Ilam
Lee	Avon	Elis	Iola
Moe	Ayer	Elis	Ipoh
Oka	Bath	Elko	Iuka
Ome	Bell	Enid	Jena
Osh	Bend	Erie	Ji'an
Ota	Bole	Faro	Jixi
Pau	Bonn	Fier	Kano
Peć	Bose	Galt	Katy
Qum	Bray	Gary	Kofu
Roy	Brno	Gath	Kota
Rye	Bude	Gaya	Kure
Spa	Bury	Genk	Laie
Ulm	Caen	Gera	Laon
Vác	Cali	Gifu	Lehi
		Gort	Lens

Cities, Towns, and Villages *(continued)*

León	Seto	Aksum	Bodie
Lima	Sion	Alcoy	Bogor
Linz	Soka	Alice	Boise
Lodi	Stow	Allen	Boone
Łodz	Suhl	Alloa	Bosra
Loja	Sumy	Alost	Botou
Lugo	Susa	Altay	Bowie
Lund	Ta'iz	Alton	Braga
Lyme	Taos	Alton	Breda
Lynn	Taza	Alwar	Brest
Mari	Thun	Amana	Bryan
Maun	Trim	Amman	Brzeg
Mayo	Troy	Aného	Bugis
Melk	Tula	Anoka	Butte
Meru	Tver	Aosta	Buzau
Mesa	Vail	Aqtau	Bytom
Metz	Waco	Argos	Cadiz
Moab	Wall	Arles	Cairo
Mold	Wawa	Arrah	Calvi
Naas	Wels	Aspen	Capua
Napa	Wick	Assen	Capua
Nice	Wise	Aswan	Cayce
Noda	Wuxi	Asyut	Celje
Nome	Yazd	Azusa	Cheju
Novi	York	Babel	Chiba
Ojai	Yuci	Babol	Chico
Olds	Yuma	Bacau	Chili
Omsk	Yuxi	Baden	Chino
Oral	Zion	Baeza	Chita
Orem	Zlin	Baker	Cluny
Orsk	Zoar	Balkh	Clyde
Palu		Balkh	Cocoa
Pécs	**5 letters**	Banff	Colón
Pegu	Aalen	Baoji	Comox
Perm	Aalst	Barre	Copán
Peru	Abuja	Basle	Corby
Pisa	Accra	Batna	Cowes
Pula	Adams	Baurú	Crécy
Puno	Adana	Bei'an	Crewe
Puri	Adoni	Belém	Cuneo
Qena	Adria	Benha	Cuzco
Qufu	Afyon	Benxi	Damas
Reno	Ahlen	Berea	Dania
Reus	Aiken	Berne	Davao
Rome	Ajmer	Berry	David
Rowe	Akita	Bhamo	Davie
Saco	Akkad	Blida	Davis
Sarh	Akron	Blois	Delft

Delhi	Guise	Kursk	Mitla
Delta	Haeju	Kyoto	Monza
Derby	Hagen	Lacey	Mopti
Dhaka	Hapur	Lagos	Moshi
Dhule	Havre	Lagos	Mosul
Digby	Hechi	Lahti	Mozir
Dijon	Hemet	Laiwu	Murom
Dixon	Herat	Lamar	Nampa
Douai	Herne	Largo	Navan
Dover	Hobbs	Larne	Ndola
Downe	Holne	Lassa	Neath
Dubbo	Homer	Latur	Nerja
Dukou	Hondo	Laval	Neuss
Duras	Hoorn	Lecce	Niles
Düren	Hotan	Leduc	Nîmes
Duyun	Houma	Leeds	Nitra
Eagan	Hubli	Lenox	Nokia
Edina	Huron	Lewes	Nyack
Eilat	Hurst	Lille	Ocala
El Kef	Idlib	Limbe	Ocoee
Elche	Ikeda	Linhe	Ogaki
Elgin	Ikeja	Linyi	Ogden
Elgin	Ilion	Lisle	Okara
Elvas	Indio	Logan	Olean
Ennis	Ionia	Lorca	Olmos
Enshi	Irbid	Loudi	Olney
Enugu	Iruma	Lubec	Omagh
Epsom	Islip	Lucca	Omaha
Erode	Itami	Luohe	Omiya
Espoo	Iwaki	Luton	Omuta
Essen	Izmit	Macon	Opole
Essex	Iznik	Mafra	Orapa
Évora	Jalna	Magog	Orion
Ezhou	Jambi	Mainz	Orono
Fargo	Jinja	Malö	Oruro
Flint	Jujuy	Manta	Ostia
Flint	Kaili	Marfa	Otaru
Forlì	Kansk	Marib	Oujda
Fürth	Kanye	Massa	Paarl
Gadag	Karaj	Mbeya	Pagan
Gafsa	Kasur	Mdina	Pakse
Galax	Kazan	Medan	Pampa
Gaspé	Keene	Media	Paoli
Gates	Kelso	Melun	Paris
Ghent	Khiva	Mende	Parma
Gijón	Kiryu	Miami	Pasay
Gimli	Kitwe	Miass	Pasco
Globe	Kochi	Milan	Pasig
Gotha	Konin	Minoo	Patan
Gouda	Korla	Minot	Pavia
Greer	Kranj	Minsk	Pecos

Cities, Towns, and Villages (continued)

Pekin	Tanis	Yuyao	Aqmola
Pella	Tanta	Zadar	Aqtöbe
Penza	Taree	Zaria	Aquila
Petra	Tartu	Zunyi	Ararat
Pharr	Telde		Arcata
Pinsk	Tempe	**6 letters**	Arezzo
Piqua	Terni	Aachen	Armagh
Plano	Thane	Aarhus	Arusha
Ponce	Tiefa	Abadan	Arvada
Poole	Tikal	Abéché	Assisi
Prato	Tokaj	Abomey	Astana
Prome	Tomsk	Abydos	Athens
Provo	Tours	Abydos	Attica
Pskov	Tracy	Adrian	Auburn
Radom	Trail	Agadez	Aurora
Rasht	Traun	Agadir	Austin
Raton	Troon	Aihole	Avignon
Rauma	Truro	Aintab	Avlona
Ripon	Tulsa	Akashi	Baabda
Rolla	Tumen	Albany	Baguio
Ronda	Tunxi	Albany	Baiyin
Rugby	Tuzla	Albena	Balboa
Rydal	Tychy	Albion	Bangor
Sagar	Tyler	Albury	Bangor
Sakai	Udine	Aleppo	Baotou
Salem	Ukiah	Alfred	Barrie
Sandy	Union	Almaty	Barrow
Sanya	Utica	Almelo	Bartow
Scone	Varna	Alpena	Bat Yam
Sedan	Venlo	Alpine	Batala
Selby	Vichy	Amalfi	Batman
Selma	Vidin	Ambala	Battle
Sétif	Viseu	Ambato	Bayamo
Siena	Vista	Amberg	Bayeux
Sitka	Wahoo	Amenia	Beacon
Sneek	Wasco	Amroha	Beaune
Sohag	Wayne	Angers	Béchar
Solon	Wells	Angola	Beihai
Sorel	Wigan	Ankara	Beirut
Soria	Worms	Ankeny	Bejaa
Steyr	Wuhai	Annaba	Bel Air
Stowe	Xenia	Anqing	Beloit
Suita	Xinyu	Anshan	Belovo
Taber	Yanji	Anshun	Belsen
Tábor	Yibin	Antony	Belton
Taegu	Yreka	Anvers	Beltsy
Tai'an	Yukon	Anyang	Bengbu
Tampa	Yulin	Apopka	Benoni

Benton	Carson	Denton	Évreux
Bergen	Cashel	Denver	Faenza
Berlin	Casper	Dessau	Fallon
Berwyn	Cawdor	Deyang	Fátima
Bethel	Celaya	Dezhou	Flores
Bhopal	Celina	Dieppe	Foggia
Bilbao	Cesena	Dinant	Folsom
Biloxi	Chaohu	Dinard	Fresno
Binche	Chaska	Dinuba	Fuling
Bisbee	Cheraw	Donora	Fulton
Biskra	Chieti	Dorval	Galena
Bisley	Chinon	Dothan	Gallup
Blaine	Cicero	Douala	Gander
Bochum	Clovis	Downey	Ganvie
Bodmin	Coburg	Dracut	Garoua
Bodrum	Cognac	Dryden	Geddes
Bodrum	Cohoes	Duffel	Gerona
Bofors	Colton	Duluth	Getafe
Bogotá	Conroe	Dum Dum	Ghazni
Bolton	Conway	Duncan	Gilroy
Bombay	Corbin	Dundas	Girard
Bongor	Corona	Dundee	Gitega
Bonham	Cortez	Dunhua	Glamis
Borger	Cos Cob	Dunmow	Glynde
Boston	Covina	Durban	Golden
Boston	Cracow	Durham	Gondar
Bouaké	Creede	Durham	Gondia
Braila	Cudahy	Easton	Gorgan
Brasov	Cuenca	Eccles	Gorham
Bratsk	Cuiabá	Ecorse	Goshen
Brazil	Curicó	Edmond	Gotham
Bremen	Da Nang	El Djem	Graham
Brewer	Dachau	Elmont	Gramsh
Bruges	Dakhla	El Paso	Granby
Bukavu	Dallas	El Reno	Grants
Burgas	Dalton	Elstow	Grasse
Burgos	Daqing	El Toro	Gretna
Butler	Darien	Elkins	Groton
Buxton	Dawson	Elkton	Guarda
Byblos	Daxian	Elmira	Gubbio
Caguas	Dayton	Elyria	Guelph
Cahaba	De Kalb	Emmaus	Guelph
Cairns	De Land	Epping	Guéret
Calama	De Pere	Erfurt	Gujrat
Camden	De Smet	Esopus	Guntur
Campos	De Soto	Etawah	Gwymon
Canaan	Dedham	Euclid	Hadano
Candia	Del Mar	Eugene	Haddam
Canton	Del Rio	Euless	Hadley
Carmel	Delano	Eunice	Hailar
Carnac	Dennis	Eureka	Hailey

Cities, Towns, and Villages *(continued)*

Hakone	Kaluga	Lawton	Meerut
Halden	Kalyan	Laxton	Mégara
Hamden	Kampen	Layton	Meknès
Hamlet	Kanata	Leiria	Melton
Handan	Kankan	Le Mans	Mendon
Harlow	Kariba	Le Mars	Mentor
Havant	Kariya	Lenexa	Merced
Hawick	Karnak	Lenoir	Mérida
Hearst	Karnal	Leoben	Milton
Hegang	Karshi	Leshan	Minden
Heihei	Kashan	Lidice	Mitaka
Helena	Kassel	Likasi	Mobile
Helwan	Kaunas	Limoux	Modena
Heshan	Kearny	Linden	Mohács
Hikone	Kediri	Linfen	Moline
Himeji	Kendal	Linhai	Monroe
Hospet	Kenner	Linxia	Monywa
Huambo	Kenora	Lishui	Moscow
Hudson	Keokuk	Lompoc	Mostar
Humble	Kerava	London	Motala
Hwange	Kerman	Lorain	Multan
Ibadan	Khulna	Loreto	Muncie
Ilesha	Kielce	Lowell	Murray
Ilkley	Kilifi	Luanda	Mutare
Ilorin	Kilkís	Lublin	Mwanza
Imatra	Kirkuk	Ludlow	Mystic
Indore	Kiruna	Lugano	Nabeul
Insein	Kitami	Lusaka	Nablus
Inuvik	Kladno	Luzhou	Nadiad
Iringa	Kodiak	Macapá	Nagoya
Irvine	Kohima	Macomb	Nagpur
Irving	Kokomo	Madera	Nahant
Ithaca	Komaki	Madrid	Nakuru
Jarrow	Kosice	Mahwah	Nanded
Jasper	Kourou	Maikop	Nantes
Jerash	Kovrov	Malden	Naples
Jhansi	Krosno	Manaus	Naseby
Jijiga	Kumasi	Mandan	Nashik
Jinhua	Kurgan	Mandya	Nashua
Jining	Kurume	Mantua	Natick
Jinshi	Kuytun	Maradi	Nauvoo
Jishou	La Baie	Marion	Nelson
Joliet	La Mesa	Maroua	Neosho
Joplin	Lander	Masaya	Nepean
Juárez	Lanham	Matera	New Ulm
Kaduna	Laredo	Matsue	Newark
Kailua	Latina	McLean	Newton
Kalisz	Laurel	Medina	Nicaea

Nimrud	Qazvin	Sharon	Tooele
Normal	Quebec	Shashi	Topeka
Norman	Queluz	Shelby	Toyota
Novara	Quincy	Shiloh	Tralee
Novato	Quogue	Shiraz	Tromsø
Numazu	Quzhou	Shiyan	Tucson
Nutley	Rabaul	Sidney	Tulare
Oak Bay	Racine	Siegen	Tumkur
Oaxaca	Rahway	Simcoe	Tupelo
Odessa	Raipur	Sintra	Turpan
Olathe	Rajkot	Siping	Tustin
Oldham	Rampur	Skokie	Tyumen
Olinda	Ramsey	Sliema	Ujjain
Oneida	Ratlam	Slough	Ulundi
Orange	Redcar	Slupsk	Upland
Örebro	Regina	Smyrna	Urbana
Orange	Rennes	Sonoma	Urbino
Orlova	Renton	Sonora	Uvalde
Osasco	Resita	Sopron	Valdez
Öskmen	Reston	Sparks	Val d'Or
Oshawa	Revere	Storrs	Valera
Osijek	Rialto	Stroud	Vanier
Osorno	Rivera	Struga	Vantaa
Oswego	Rizhao	Stuart	Varese
Ottawa	Roslyn	Suihua	Vaslui
Owosso	Rosyth	Summit	Venice
Oxford	Rudnyy	Sumter	Verdun
Oxnard	Ruston	Surgut	Vernon
Pailin	Ryazan	Surrey	Verona
Palmer	Saigon	Suzuka	Vestal
Paphos	Sakura	Sydney	Viborg
Passau	Salina	Syzran	Viedma
Pelham	Samara	Tacoma	Wabash
Peoria	Sanger	Tahoua	Walnut
Pernik	Sangli	Tainan	Warren
Pesaro	Santee	Taipei	Warsaw
Pierre	Santos	Tamale	Waupur
Plauen	Sardis	Tambov	Wausau
Pleven	Sarnia	Tarija	Weihai
Pomona	Sasebo	Tarnów	Weimar
Potosí	Saugus	Tarsus	Weinan
Prague	Saumur	Taylor	Welkom
Preyov	Savona	Temple	Weston
Privas	Sayama	Temuco	Whitby
P'ohang	Sedona	Tetovo	Widnes
Puebla	Seguin	The Pas	Wilson
Pueblo	Seixal	Tiffin	Wilton
Purnia	Sendai	Tigard	Winona
Putian	Serowe	Tivoli	Witten
Putney	Seward	Toccoa	Woburn
Puyang	Shaowu	Toledo	Woking

Cities, Towns, and Villages *(continued)*

Wonsan
Wuzhou
Xánthi
Xigaze
Xintai
Yakima
Yamato
Yambol
Yelets
Yeovil
Yining
Yiyang
Zabrze
Zamora
Zanjan
Zhuhai
Zigong
Zinder
Zwolle

7 letters

Aalborg
Abidjan
Abilene
Achinsk
Addison
Airdrie
Akjoujt
Alameda
Algiers
Aligarh
Alkmaar
Alloway
Almadén
Alnwick
Altoona
Amherst
Anaheim
Andijon
Andover
Andújar
Angarsk
Ansbach
Ansonia
Antakya
Antalya
Antioch
Aracajú

Arcadia
Ardabil
Ardmore
Arecibo
Argolis
Armavir
Artesia
Artigas
Arundel
Arzamas
Asansol
Ashford
Ashland
Assyria
Astoria
Athínai
Athlone
Atlanta
Augusta
Augusta
Avebury
Baalbek
Babylon
Bacolod
Badulla
Baghdad
Bahamas
Baldwin
Ballina
Ballwin
Bamberg
Bamenda
Banbury
Bandung
Bangkok
Baniyas
Banning
Banqiao
Baoding
Baoshan
Baraboo
Barinas
Barstow
Barysaw
Bastrop
Batalha
Bayamón
Bay City

Bayonne
Baytown
Beckley
Bedford
Beipiao
Belfast
Belfort
Belgaum
Bellary
Belmont
Belzoni
Bemidji
Bendigo
Benicia
Bergama
Bergamo
Bethany
Beverly
Bhiwani
Bijapur
Bikaner
Billund
Binzhou
Bishkek
Blarney
Blue Ash
Bohemia
Bolivar
Bologna
Boonton
Borstal
Bothell
Bottrop
Boulder
Bozeman
Braemar
Bramber
Brandon
Branson
Brawley
Brenham
Brescia
Brevard
Bristol
Brixham
Bryansk
Bucyrus
Buffalo

Bukhara
Burbank
Burnaby
Burnley
Bushehr
Cabimas
Cabinda
Cáceres
Cahokia
Caledon
Calgary
Calvary
Camrose
Caracas
Caracol
Caribou
Carrara
Cassino
Castine
Catania
Cetinje
Chablis
Chadron
Chang'an
Changde
Changji
Chanute
Chärjew
Chatham
Chawton
Cheddar
Chelles
Chelmno
Chelsea
Chengde
Chengdu
Chesham
Chester
Chicago
Chifeng
Chillán
Cholula
Chorley
Chorzów
Chuzhou
Clemson
Clifden
Clifton

Clinton	Donetsk	Gharyan	Hopkins
Clonmel	Douglas	Glasgow	Hoquiam
Cloquet	Downend	Glencoe	Hornell
Colditz	Dresden	Godhavn	Houlton
Colonie	Dubuque	Gorazde	Houston
Coblenz	Dundalk	Gordium	Huaibei
Coimbra	Dunedin	Görlitz	Huaihua
Cologne	Dunwich	Gosport	Huainan
Colombo	Durango	Gourock	Huaiyin
Colonia	Edenton	Grafton	Huánuco
Comilla	Edmonds	Granada	Huizhou
Compton	El Cajon	Greeley	Ibaraki
Concord	Elbasan	Gresham	Imperia
Coos Bay	Elkhart	Grevená	Indiana
Copiapó	El Minya	Groznyy	Inkster
Coppell	Emporia	Gruyère	Ipswich
Córdoba	Enfield	Guaymas	Iqaluit
Cordova	Entebbe	Guthrie	Ironton
Corinth	Épernay	Gwalior	Isesaki
Corning	Ephesus	Haining	Ivanovo
Corozal	Ephrata	Halabja	Iwakuni
Corydon	Epworth	Halifax	Jackson
Cosenza	Estevan	Hamadan	Jalgaon
Cotonou	Estoril	Hamburg	Jericho
Cottbus	Etruria	Hamhung	Jessore
Cowpens	Eveleth	Hammond	Jiamusi
Craiova	Everett	Hampden	Jiaozou
Crawley	Evesham	Hampton	Jiaxing
Cremona	Exmouth	Hanahan	Jihlava
Crowley	Fairfax	Hanover	Jingmen
Crystal	Falaise	Harappa	Jinzhou
Cullman	Falkirk	Hardwar	Jiuquan
Cut Bank	Farndon	Harlech	Joensuu
Cypress	Farnham	Harmony	Jundiaí
Danbury	Fayette	Harvard	Juneau
Danvers	Ferrara	Hasselt	Jupiter
Darkhan	Eufaula	Hayward	Kaesong
Dauphin	Findlay	Heerlen	Kahului
Decatur	Flodden	Heinola	Kaifeng
Decorah	Fontana	Hengelo	Kaiyuan
Del City	Fremont	Hitchin	Kajaani
Denbigh	Fridley	Herning	Kamsack
Denison	Gabrovo	Hershey	Kaneohe
Deolali	Gadsden	Hialeah	Karamay
Derbent	Gaffney	Hibbing	Karbala
Detroit	Gaillac	Hickory	Karviná
Dhahran	Gardena	Hitachi	Kashiwa
Dhanbad	Gardner	Hoboken	Kasugai
Dharwar	Garland	Holguin	Katihar
Dispura	Gautier	Holland	Katonah
Dobrich	Geneseo	Holyoke	Katsuta

Cities, Towns, and Villages *(continued)*

Kavieng	Leticia	Massena	Nanyang
Kawagoe	Leyland	Mathura	Nashua
Kayenta	Liberal	Matlock	Natchez
Kelowna	Liberec	Matmata	Needham
Kenosha	Liberty	Matsqui	Nellore
Keswick	Lifford	Mattoon	Neptune
Ketchum	Limoges	Maumee	Neuguén
Kewanee	Linares	Mayapan	New Bern
Key West	Lincoln	Maywood	New City
Khandwa	Linqing	McAllen	New Hope
Kilgore	Lipizza	Medford	New York
Killeen	Lisburn	Meissen	Newberg
Kingman	Lismore	Mei Xian	Newbury
Kinross	Live Oak	Melrose	Newport
Kinston	Livonia	Memphis	Newquay
Kittery	Lobatse	Menasha	Newtown
Knossos	Logroño	Mendoza	Nikopol
Kodaira	Lombard	Meriden	Nineveh
Koganei	Longmen	Merrick	Nogales
Kolomna	Longyan	Methuen	Noginsk
Komatsu	Lourdes	Midland	Norfolk
Korhogo	Lubango	Milagro	Norilsk
Kouvola	Lubbock	Mildura	Norwalk
Krefeld	Lucknow	Miletus	Norwich
Kunming	Lushnjë	Milford	Norwood
Kutaisi	Lynwood	Mirabel	Novi Sad
Kyongju	Machala	Miramar	O'Fallon
Lachine	Macheng	Mishima	Oak Lawn
Laconia	Machias	Miskolc	Oak Park
La Habra	Machida	Mission	Oakdale
Lahaina	Madison	Moberly	Oakland
La Jolla	Madurai	Modesto	Oberlin
La Junta	Magenta	Mödling	Obihiro
Langley	Mahabad	Mombasa	Odawara
Lansing	Malmédy	Moncton	Odienné
Laramie	Malvern	Moraine	Oil City
La Oroya	Manassa	Morelia	Okayama
La Porte	Mankato	Morpeth	Okazaki
Larkana	Manlius	Morwell	Old Lyme
Larnaca	Manteca	Moulins	Olomouc
La Salle	Manzini	Moundou	Olsztyn
Latrobe	Maoming	Münster	Olympia
La Verne	Maramba	Mycenae	Oneonta
Lebanon	Marengo	Nagaoka	Onitsha
Ledyard	Margate	Nalchik	Ontario
Legnica	Marsala	Nampula	Oologah (*or*
Leipzig	Mascara	Nanaimo	Oolagah)
Le Sueur	Mashpee	Nanping	Opelika

Orillia	Reading	Shawnee	Thorold
Orizaba	Red Bank	Shelton	Tieling
Orlando	Red Deer	Sherman	Tighina
Orvieto	Redding	Shihezi	Tijuana
Oshkosh	Redmond	Shimizu	Tilburg
Oshogbo	Reigate	Shimoga	Timmins
Ostrava	Roanoke	Shirley	Tindouf
Otavalo	Romulus	Shishou	Tisbury
Paducah	Roselle	Sialkot	Tlemcen
Paisley	Rosetta	Sikasso	Tonghua
Palatka	Rotorua	Sinuiju	Topsham
Palm Bay	Roubaix	Skagway	Toronto
Palmyra	Roxbury	Slidell	Torquay
Panipat	Runcorn	Socorro	Torreón
Parsons	Rustavi	Sondrio	Travnik
Passaic	Rutland	Sozopol	Trenton
Patiala	Rybinsk	Spencer	Trieste
Pattaya	Saanich	Spokane	Turlock
Peabody	Safford	Spoleto	Uberaba
Penn Yan	Saginaw	Staines	Udaipur
Pereira	Saidpur	Stanton	Ulanhot
Perugia	St. Louis	Stendal	Ulan Ude
Phoenix	Salavat	Sterling	Uruapán
Pitesti	Salford	Stilton	Utrecht
Plassey	Salinas	Sturgis	Valdese
Podolsk	Samaria	Suceava	Vallejo
Poltava	Samarra	Sudbury	Vellore
Pontiac	Sambhal	Suffern	Ventura
Popayán	Sanford	Suffolk	Vicenza
Portage	San Jose	Suizhou	Vidalia
Posadas	San Juan	Sulphur	Villach
Potenza	San Luis	Sun City	Visalia
Potsdam	Sanming	Sunbury	Viterbo
Preston	Santa Fe	Sunrise	Vologda
Préveza	Sapporo	Swansea	Vorkuta
Prizren	Sapulpa	Swindon	Wailuku
Pulaski	Sarapul	Syosset	Walpole
Pullman	Saratov	Szolnok	Walsall
Qinzhou	Scranton	Taiping	Waltham
Qitaihe	Seaford	Taiyuan	Wantage
Quesnel	Seaside	Takaoka	Wantagh
Quilpué	Seattle	Tamarac	Wanxian
Radford	Sebring	Tampico	Wareham
Raichur	Sedalia	Tangail	Warnham
Raleigh	Seekonk	Tarboro	Warwick
Randers	Segovia	Taunton	Watauga
Rangpur	Selkirk	Teaneck	Watford
Rantoul	Seraing	Tel Aviv	Waverly
Ravenna	Sewanee	Telford	Weirton
Rawlins	Seymour	Tenafly	Welland
Raytown	Shakhty	Thimphu	Wenzhou

Cities, Towns, and Villages *(continued)*

Weslaco	Agrinion	Beaulieu	Carefree
Wheaton	Albacete	Bedworth	Carlisle
Whiting	Alcobaça	Belgorod	Carlsbad
Whyalla	Alhambra	Bellagio	Carniola
Wichita	Altamira	Bellevue	Carolina
Willmar	Altamura	Berenice	Carthage
Windham	Amarillo	Berkeley	Catskill
Windsor	Amersham	Bhatpara	Certaldo
Wisbech	Amesbury	Bhiwandi	Cessnock
Wolcott	Amravati	Bhusawal	Chambéry
Wooster	Amritsar	Bicester	Chamonix
Worksop	Anaconda	Bideford	Chan Chan
Wrexham	Anadarko	Bilaspur	Chandler
Wuzhong	Anápolis	Billings	Changshu
Xiaogan	Anderson	Blantyre	Changzhi
Xichang	Ann Arbor	Blenheim	Chaoyang
Xingtai	Anniston	Blumenau	Charikar
Xinyang	Anniston	Boa Vista	Chartres
Xinzhou	Appleton	Bodhgaya	Chemnitz
Xuchang	Aranjuez	Bogazköy	Chiclayo
Yakeshi	Arequipa	Bolsover	Chicopee
Yankton	Armidale	Bonampak	Chuziong
Yaphank	Arnsberg	Bordeaux	Clovelly
Yichang	Ashgabat	Borodino	Coalport
Yingtan	Asunción	Borujerd	Colossae
Yonkers	Auckland	Botosani	Columbia
Youghal	Augsburg	Boys Town	Columbus
Yucaipa	Aviemore	Bradford	Cooktown
Zagazig	Ayacucho	Braganza	Cornwall
Zahedan	Ayia Napa	Brampton	Coventry
Zhambyl	Babahoyo	Bridgend	Cuddapah
Zhangye	Baccarat	Brighton	Culloden
Zhdanov	Bahraich	Brisbane	Curepipe
Zhoukou	Baicheng	Brockton	Curitiba
Zhuzhou	Baikonur	Bromberg	Dalkeith
Zwickau	Bakewell	Browning	Damanhur
	Balakovo	Brussels	Damascus
8 letters	Bamburgh	Budapest	Dangriga
Aalsmeer	Barbizon	Bulawayo	Danville
Aberdare	Barcelos	Bundoran	Darmstad
Aberdeen	Bareilly	Cagliari	Dartford
Abergele	Bar-le-Duc	Calcutta	Dearborn
Abingdon	Barnsley	Caloocan	Debrecen
Abu Dhabi	Basildon	Camagüey	Dehiwala
Acapulco	Bastille	Camborne	Dehra Dun
Adelaide	Bathurst	Campinas	Deventer
Adiyaman	Bayreuth	Cangzhou	Dewsbury
Ado-Ekiti	Bearsden	Cardigan	Diekirch

Dinajpur	Hengshui	Kostroma	Naga City
Dindigul	Hengyang	Koszalin	Nagasaki
Dingwall	Hereford	Kraljevo	Namangan
Diredawa	Hesperia	Krusevac	Nanchong
Dongying	Hillerod	Kumagaya	Narbonne
Dornbirn	Hirakata	Kusadasi	Nazareth
Dortmund	Hirosaki	La Ciotat	Nijmegen
Dumfries	Huancayo	Lakeland	North Bay
Dunhuang	Huangshi	Lakewood	Novgorod
Durgapur	Hunjiang	La Laguna	Nuneaton
Dushanbe	Ichihara	Landshut	Oak Ridge
Earlston	Ichikawa	Langfang	Oakville
Eastwood	Igualada	Laohekou	Omdurman
Ebbw Vale	Ioánnina	La Serena	Onomichi
Ech Chief	Iowa City	Las Vegas	Orenburg
Eidsvoll	Irapuato	Lausanne	Oristano
Eisenach	Istanbul	Lawrence	Paignton
El Centro	Itanagar	Le Cannet	Palenque
El Jadida	Iwatsuki	Lefkosia	Palmdale
Enschede	Jabalpur	Leonding	Palo Alto
Ensenada	Jaboatão	Liaoyang	Pamplona
Erlangen	Jamnagar	Liaoyuan	Panihati
Eversley	Jedburgh	Limassol	Parbhani
Faizabad	Jiangmen	Llanelli	Paterson
Falmouth	Jinchang	Londrina	Pavlodar
Flin Flon	Jincheng	Longmont	Penzance
Frascati	Jipijapa	Longview	Peterlee
Freiberg	Jiujiang	Ludhiana	Piltdown
Fujisawa	Joliette	Lüderitz	Ploiesti
Gaborone	Kairouan	Ma'anshan	Plymouth
Gastonia	Kakogawa	Macerata	Poitiers
Ghardaa	Kamakura	Machakos	Prïytina
Glace Bay	Kanazawa	Mahilyou	Pucallpa
Glendale	Kaposvar	Maitland	Quanzhou
Gneizeno	Karaklis	Malegaon	Ramsgate
Gomorrah	Karlovac	Mandurah	Rancagua
Gorlovka	Karlstad	Marbella	Ratisbon
Grantham	Kastoriá	Masvingo	Redditch
Grasmere	Kasukabe	Maynooth	Redlands
Gulbarga	Kateríni	Medellín	Richland
Habikino	Katowice	Mianyang	Richmond
Hachioji	Kawasaki	Milpitas	Ringsted
Haicheng	Kemerovo	Mirzapur	Riobamba
Hamilton	Kerkrade	Mmabatho	Río Tinto
Hammamet	Kineshma	Monastir	Rochdale
Hancheng	Kingston	Monclova	Rockford
Hanzhong	Kirkenes	Monterey	Rothesay
Hastings	Kirkwall	Montreux	Rottweil
Hatfield	Kisarazu	Moose Jaw	Royal Oak
Hattusas	Kolhapur	Morogoro	Sabadell
Helpston	Koriyama	Mount Isa	St. Albans

Cities, Towns, and Villages *(continued)*

St. Helens	Teresina	Yuncheng	Aylesbury
St. Helier	Tewantin	Zaanstad	Aylesford
St. Joseph	Thetford	Zalantun	Ayutthaya
Salvador	Tianshui	Zhaodong	Badminton
Sanandaj	Tiberias	Zhaotong	Bafoussam
San Diego	Timimoun	Zlatoust	Balaclava
San Mateo	Tintagel	Zouerate	Ballymote
Santa Ana	Tiraspol		Baltimore
Santarém	Tiruppur	**9 letters**	Bangalore
Sarajevo	Tongliao	Äänekoski	Banja Luka
Sarasota	Tongling	Abbeville	Baracaldo
Sargodha	Torrance	Aberfoyle	Barcelona
Satu Mare	Toulouse	Abu Simbel	Bardolino
Savannah	Tremadoc	Adapazari	Beaumaris
Schwerin	Tübingen	Agincourt	Beaverton
Scranton	Valencia	Ahmadabad	Bebington
Selborne	Varadero	Albufeira	Beckenham
Semarang	Varaždin	Aldeburgh	Beenleigh
Shangqiu	Vercelli	Aldershot	Beersheba
Shangrao	Verviers	Aldwinkle	Berezniki
Shaoguan	Veszprém	Aleksinac	Bethlehem
Shaoshan	Victoria	Algeciras	Bhagalpur
Shaoxing	Vineland	Allahabad	Bharatpur
Shaoyang	Voronezh	Allentown	Bialystok
Shenzhen	Votkinsk	Almoravid	Bielefeld
Shymkent	Waitangi	Altenburg	Blackburn
Siauliai	Wallasey	Altötting	Blackfoot
Silistra	Wallsend	Amagasaki	Boca Raton
Simbirsk	Warangal	Amaravati	Bolan Pass
Skegness	Waterloo	Ambleside	Bracknell
Smolensk	Waterloo	Amsterdam	Braintree
Solihull	Waukegan	Amstetten	Brantford
Solingen	Waukesha	Anantapur	Brentwood
Sorocaba	Weymouth	Anchorage	Brighouse
Sorrento	Whittier	Angostura	Brookline
Stafford	Winnetka	Antequera	Brunswick
Stamford	Worthing	Antsirabe	Bucharest
Stockton	Würzburg	Apeldoorn	Buena Park
Strabane	Xiangfan	Apollonia	Bujumbura
Strumica	Xiangtan	Arlington	Bundaberg
Subotica	Xianning	Asahikawa	Byzantium
Sukhotal	Xianyang	Asheville	Cajamarca
Syracuse	Xilinhot	Ashington	Callanish
Taichung	Xinxiang	Ashquelon	Camarillo
Takasaki	Yamagata	Astrakhan	Camberley
Tamworth	Yangquan	Attleboro	Cambridge
Tangshan	Yongzhou	Avranches	Cambridge
Tauranga	Yorktown	Axminster	Camembert

Cape Coral	East Coker	Hyderabad	Llandudno
Capernaum	Eau Claire	Innsbruck	Lockerbie
Cariacica	Ekibastuz	Inverness	Long Beach
Castlebar	El Mansura	Jacobabad	Long Eaton
Catanzaro	Elizabeth	Jalalabad	Los Alamos
Cerignola	Encinitas	Järvenpää	Los Mochis
Chalcedon	Epidaurus	Jiaojiang	Lowestoft
Changchun	Escondido	Jiayuguan	Lynchburg
Changzhou	Escuintla	Joinville	Magdeburg
Chantilly	Essaouira	Jonquière	Mahalapye
Charleroi	Esslingen	Kagoshima	Maidstone
Charlotte	Esztergom	Kalamazoo	Maiduguri
Cheapside	Fairbanks	Kalulushi	Manizales
Cherkassy	Fairfiled	Karakorum	Manzhouli
Chernigov	Fall River	Kardhítsa	Matamoros
Chernobyl	Famagusta	Karlsruhe	Matsubara
Chiangmai	Faridabad	Kashihara	Matsumoto
Chigasaki	Feldkirch	Kawanishi	Matsuyama
Chihuahua	Firozabad	Kecskemét	Mayerling
Chinatown	Flagstaff	Kettering	Mejicanos
Chongqing	Fort Smith	Kharagpur	Melbourne
Churchill	Fort Wayne	Khaylitsa	Melitopol
Cîmpulung	Fort Worth	Khouribga	Monterrey
Cleveland	Fullerton	Killarney	Moradabad
Cloncurry	Gällivare	Kimberley	Morecambe
Coleraine	Galveston	King's Lynn	Mullingar
Colwyn Bay	Gateshead	Kirkcaldy	Mykolayiv
Comayagua	Gattinara	Kirovohad	Nagercoil
Constanza	Germiston	Kisangani	Nawabganj
Cookstown	Ghaziabad	Kitchener	Nawabshah
Costa Mesa	Godalming	Kitty Hawk	Newmarket
Cox's Bazar	Godoy Cruz	Knoxville	Neyshabur
Craigavon	Gorakhpur	Kokubunji	Nicomedia
Cristobál	Göttingen	Koshigaya	Nicopolis
Ctesiphon	Gravesend	Koudougou	Nizamabad
Darbhanga	Guayaquil	Kurashiki	Oceanside
Dartmouth	Guildford	Ladysmith	Ogbomosho
Dashhowuz	Guimarães	Lafayette	Oldenburg
Davangere	Hachinohe	Lancaster	Osnabrück
Davenport	Halesowen	Las Cruces	Paderborn
Deauville	Hallstatt	Latacunga	Palembang
Des Moines	Hamamatsu	Le Creusot	Palm Beach
Dettingen	Haverhill	Leicester	Panmunjom
Dodge City	Hawthorne	Les Abymes	Pavlograd
Doncaster	Heilbronn	Levittown	Pawtucket
Dongchuan	Henderson	Lexington	Perpignan
Dongguang	Hervey Bay	Liaocheng	Pforzheim
Dongsheng	High Point	Lichfield	Pine Bluff
Dordrecht	Hilversum	Linköping	Pingxiang
Droitwich	Hiratsuka	Livermore	Pirmasens
Dubrovnik	Huangshan	Liverpool	Pompadour

Cities, Towns, and Villages *(continued)*

		10 letters	Canterbury
Pontypool	Soyapango	Abbottabad	Carchemish
Porbandar	Stakhanov	Addis Ababa	Casablanca
Princeton	Stavanger	Ahmadnagar	Cerne Abbas
Ramillies	Stevenage	Albarracin	Chandigarh
Rapid City	Steventon	Alcobendas	Charleston
Remscheid	Stockport	Alexandria	Chelmsford
Rio Branco	Stornoway	Almetyevsk	Chernivtsi
Rio Cuarto	Stralsund	Altrincham	Chesapeake
Riverside	Stretford	Amersfoort	Chichester
Rochester	Stuttgart	Amityville	Chicoutimi
Rochester	Sundsvall	Antigonish	Choibalsan
Rosenheim	Szekszárd	Asamankese	Chula Vista
Rotherham	Takatsuki	Aurangabad	Cienfuegos
Rotterdam	Tapachula	Baden-Baden	Cincinnati
Rovaniemi	Taroudant	Baharampur	Clearwater
Rubtsovsk	Tatabánya	Bahawalpur	Clonakilty
St. Andrews	Tolpuddle	Balashikha	Clouds Hill
St. Charles	Tombstone	Balbriggan	Cluj-Napoca
Sainte-Foy	Tongchuan	Ballymahon	Coatbridge
St. Émilion	Tourcoing	Ballymena	Cober Pedy
Saint John	Traralgon	Barnstaple	Cochabamba
St.-Nazaire	Tuticorin	Baton Rouge	Coimbatore
St.-Quentin	Uddevalla	Battambang	Colchester
Salamanca	Uffington	Battenberg	Concepción
Salisbury	Vacaville	Batticaloa	Coon Rapids
Sambalpur	Vancouver	Bedlington	Cranbourne
San Angelo	Vicksburg	Belize City	Cuernavaca
San Miguel	Vila Velha	Belleville	Darlington
San Simeon	Vitsyebsk	Bellflower	Daugavpils
Santa Rosa	Volgograd	Bellingham	Dharamsala
Saskatoon	Volzhskiy	Bernkastel	Down Ampney
Sausalito	Wadi Halfa	Bhadravati	Düsseldorf
Schwabach	Wakefield	Binghamton	Dzerzhinsk
Seinäjoki	Waterbury	Birkenhead	Eastbourne
Sevenoaks	Westerham	Birmingham	East Orange
Sheerness	Wokingham	Bjorneborg	El Escorial
Sheffield	Wolfsberg	Bournville	Esquipulas
Sincelejo	Wolfsburg	Bratislava	Evansville
Sioux City	Woodstock	Bridgeport	Faisalabad
Skara Brae	Worcester	Bridgwater	Forest Lawn
Slavyansk	Wuppertal	Broken Hill	Frauenfeld
Smederovo	Yamaguchi	Bromsgrove	Galashiels
Solferino	Yattenden	Buchenwald	Ganganagar
Solikamsk	Yokkaichi	Buckingham	Gettysburg
Sonsonate	Zhangzhou	Burlington	Gillingham
Sosnowiec	Zhumadian	Burnsville	Glenrothes
South Bend	Zrenjanin	Caerphilly	Gloucester
Southport		Camperdown	

Gorgonzola
Great Falls
Greensboro
Greenville
Greifswald
Haddington
Hartlepool
Heidelberg
Hildesheim
Huntingdon
Huntington
Huntsville
Ichinomiya
Imperatriz
Ingolstadt
Interlaken
Janesville
Jersey City
João Pessoa
Kalgoorlie
Kapfenberg
Karaikkudi
Kaufbeuren
Kenilworth
Kilmarnock
Kirriemuir
Kislovodsk
Kitakyushu
Klagenfurt
Klerksdorp
Kragujevac
Kralendijk
Kramatorsk
Kyustendil
Lambersart
Launceston
Le Lamentin
Les Mureaux
Letchworth
Lethbridge
Leverkusen
Linlithgow
Llangollen
Los Angeles
Louisville
Lubumbashi
Maidenhead
Malmesbury
Malplaquet
Miami Beach
Michurinsk

Minatitlán
Miyakonojo
Molepolole
Montélimar
Montebello
Morristown
Mudanjiang
Naperville
New Britain
New Orleans
Ngaoundéré
Nieuwegein
Nkongsamba
Norrköping
Nottingham
Nova Iguaçu
Oberhausen
Orange Walk
Paris-Plage
Pazardzhik
Peenemunde
Persepolis
Petrópolis
Pico Rivera
Piracicaba
Pittsburgh
Plantation
Pleasanton
Ponferrada
Pontefract
Pontypridd
Port Arthur
Port Talbot
Portalegre
Portoviejo
Portsmouth
Puente Alto
Punta Gorda
Pyatigorsk
Qaraghandy
Quatre Bras
Quezon City
Rawalpindi
Richardson
Ringkøbing
Rocamadour
Rockingham
Sagamihara
Saharanpur
Salzgitter
San Antonio

Santa Clara
Santa Maria
São Goncalo
Scunthorpe
Shepparton
Sherbrooke
Shizuishan
Shreveport
Shrewsbury
Silchester
Silver City
Simferopol
Simi Valley
Sioux Falls
Skellefteå
Sunderland
Swakopmund
Terre Haute
The Dalles
Thionville
Thunder Bay
Trowbridge
Tskhinvali
Tuscaloosa
Uberlândia
Ulhasnagar
Utsunomiya
Valledupar
Vénissieux
Versailles
Viña del Mar
Volgodonsk
Walsingham
Wangaratta
Warrington
Washington
West Covina
West Orange
Westward Ho
Winchester
Winterthur
Wittenberg
Xochimilco
Yoshkar-Ola
Zoetermeer

11 letters

Aberystwyth
Adrianopole
Aix-les-Bains
Albertville

Albuquerque
Aldermaston
Alessandria
Alfortville
Aphrodisias
Armentiéres
Arthur's Seat
Bajram Curri
Bakersfield
Balquhidder
Bannockburn
Battle Creek
Berkhamsted
Bingerville
Birchington
Biscayne Bay
Blagoevgrad
Bloomington
Bognor Regis
Bossier City
Bournemouth
Brazzaville
Bridlington
Broken Arrow
Brownsville
Bucaramanga
Buenos Aires
Bukittinggi
Canandaigua
Capo di Monte
Carcassonne
Caxias do Sul
Cedar Rapids
Charlestown
Chattanooga
Chelyabinsk
Cherepovets
Cirencester
Clarksville
Cleethorpes
Cockermouth
Constantine
Cootamundra
Crosthwaite
Czestochowa
Danjiangkou
Dawson Creek
Delmenhorst
Dien Bien Phu
Divinópolis
Downpatrick

Cities, Towns, and Villages *(continued)*

Dunfermline
East Dereham
East Lansing
Ecclefechan
Elektrostal
Farnborough
Farrukhabad
Fort Collins
Fort Raleigh
Fort William
Francistown
Frankenthal
Gainesville
Gandhinagar
Garden Grove
Glastonbury
Grand Rapids
Grangemouth
Gretna Green
Helensburgh
Herculaneum
High Wycombe
John o' Groats
Khorramabad
King's Cliffe
Kinnesswood
Krugersdorp
Laguna Beach
Lake Charles
Lengshuitan
Mazatenango
Medicine Hat
Midwest City
Minneapolis
Mississauga
Mohenjo-Daro
Monbazillac
Montbéliard
Montpellier
Mount Vernon
New Plymouth
New Rochelle
Newport News
Newton Abbot
Nishinomiya
Northampton
Novosibirsk
Nuevo Laredo

Nyiregyháza
Ouagadougou
Oystermouth
Pervouralsk
Point-à-Pitre
Polonnaruwa
Port Dickson
Portmeirion
Puerto Plata
Port St. Lucie
Prestonpans
Prokopyevsk
Rajahmundry
Rajapalayam
Rambouillet
Saint-Hubert
St. Peter Port
San Bernardo
Sankt Pölten
Savannakhet
Scarborough
Schenectady
Schweinfurt
Sharpeville
Shibin el Kom
Southampton
Spanish Town
Staryy Oskal
Sterlitamak
Tegucigalpa
Ticonderoga
Tordesillas
Vereeniging
Vila do Conde
Vladikavkaz
Walnut Creek
Warrnambool
West Malvern
Zielona Gora

12 letters

Aigues-Mortes
Antananarivo
Anuradhapura
Aschersleben
Atlantic City
Auchterarder
Bakhchisarai

Baranavichiy
Barquisimeto
Batangas City
Beaconsfield
Beverly Hills
Bowling Green
Brooklyn Park
Cagayan de Oro
Caltanisetta
Chalatenango
Charlesbourg
Chesterfield
Christchurch
Ciudad Madero
Coff's Harbour
Coral Springs
Dalandzadgad
Daytona Beach
Dun Laoghaire
East Bergholt
East Budleigh
East Kilbride
Fayetteville
Fianarantsoa
Fotheringhay
Gamlakarleby
Gómez Palacio
Grand Prairie
Great Malvern
Grootfontein
Harpers Ferry
Higher Walton
Hillsborough
Huancavelica
Huddersfield
Independence
Invercargill
Johannesburg
Kafr el Dauwar
Kafr el Sheikh
Kakamigahara
Keetmanshoop
Lisdoonvarna
Loughborough
Macclesfield
Maroochydore
Mazar-e-Sharif
Milton Keynes

Mission Viejo
Monterey Park
Montes Claros
Moulay Idriss
Mount Gambier
Mountain View
Muzzaffarpur
National City
Newport Beach
Newtownabbey
North Shields
Novokuznetsk
Novomoskovsk
Oberammergau
Örnsköldsvik
Ottery St. Mary
Overland Park
Petaling Jaya
Peterborough
Philadelphia
Pingdingshan
Pompano Beach
Port Sunlight
Prince George
Redondo Beach
Richmond Hill
St. Catherines
Saint-Laurent
St. Petersburg
Salt Lake City
San Francisco
San Sebastian
Santa Barbara
Selebi-Phikwe
Severodvinsk
Shuangyashan
Sidi-bel-Abbès
Skelmersdale
South Shields
Stellenbosch
Tennant Creek
Thousand Oaks
Valenciennes
West Bromwich
Wethersfield
Wichita Falls
Williamsburg
Zalaegerszeg

Zelazowa Wola

13 letters

Aix-en-Provence
Aschaffenburg
Bandar Lampung
Belaya Tserkov
Belo Horizonte
Bishopsbourne
Bobo-Dioulasso
Campina Grande
Champs Elysées
Ciudad Bolivar
Ciudad Guayana
Ciudad Obregón
Cockburnspath
Council Bluffs
Duque de Caxias
Florianópolis
Guatemala City
Ho Chi Minh City
Hollywood Bowl
Kawachinagano
Lengshuijiang
Mogi das Cruzes
Passchendaele
Pembroke Pines
San Bernardino
Severodonetsk
Villavicencio
Virginia Beach
West Palm Beach

14 letters

Abbot's Langley
Aix-la-Chapelle
Almirante Brown
Annapolis Royal
Ashby-de-la-Zouch
Aubervilliers
Auchtermuchty
Ayot St. Lawrence
Berchtesgaden
Bourg-en-Bresse
Bury St. Edmunds
Campagna di Roma
Château-Thierry
Chaudière Falls
Ciudad Victoria
College Station
Constantinople

Dolores Hidalgo
Esch-sur-Alzette
Feira de Santana
Fort Lauderdale
Fountain Valley
Fredericksburg
Great Yarmouth
Haarlemmermeer
Hradec Králové
Huntington Park
Kidderminster
Kirkcudbright
Klosterneuburg
La Roche-sur-Yon
Lons-le-Saunier
Melton Mowbray
Merthyr Tydfil
Middlesbrough
Mount Prospect
Muzzaffarnagar
Neubrandenburg
Newton Aycliffe
Nizhnevartovsk
Northallerton
Port el Kantaoui
Port Macquarie
Sensuntepeque
Sergiyev Posad
Slavonsky Brod
Stockton-on-Tees
Udhagamandalam
Vanderbijlpark
Veliko Turnovo
Wiener Neustadt

15 letters

Alcalá de Henares
Alexandroupolis
Beaumes de Venise
Blagoveshchensk
Bokaro Steel City
Burton upon Trent
České Budějovice
Chavín de Huántar
Clermont-Ferrand
Colorado Springs
Forster-Tuncurry
Higashimura-yama
Huntington Beach
Mönchengladbach
Nizhniy Novgorod

North Little Rock
Palmerston North
Saratoga Springs
Sutton Courtenay

16 letters

Alcalá de Guadaira
Alphen aan den Rijn
Anzhero-Sudzhensk
Arlington Heights
Bergisch Gladbach
Berwick-upon-Tweed
Brive-la-Gaillarde
Caesarea Philippi
Cleveland Heights
Greenwich Village
Lytham Saint Anne's
Newton St. Boswells
Pietermaritzburg
Welwyn Garden City

17 letters

Newcastle upon Tyne
Santiago del Estero

18 letters

Castellón de la Plana
Newcastle under Lyme
Vitoria Da Conquista
Widecombe-in-the-
  Moor

19 letters

Caprese Michelangelo
Roquefort-sur-Soulzon

25 letters

Aleksandrovsk-
  Sakhalinskiy

58 letters

Llanfairpwllgwyngyllg-
  ogerychwyrndrobwll-
  llantysiliogogogoch

Oceans and Seas

(element "sea" or "ocean" NOT included in letter count)

3 letters
Red Sea

4 letters
Aral Sea
Azov, Sea of
Dead Sea
Java (Jawa) Sea
Kara Sea
Ross Sea
Savu (Sawu) Sea
Sulu Sea

5 letters
Banda Sea
Black Sea
Bohol Sea
China Sea
Coral Sea
Irish Sea
Japan, Sea of
North Sea
South Sea
South Seas
White Sea

6 letters
Aegean Sea

Arctic Ocean
Baltic Sea
Bering Sea
Flores Sea
Indian Ocean
Inland Sea
Ionian Sea
Laptev Sea
Salton Sea
Scotia Sea
Tasman Sea
Tethys Sea (former)
Yellow Sea

7 letters
Andaman Sea
Arabian Sea
Arafura Sea
Barents Sea
Caspian Sea
Celebes Sea
Chukchi Sea
Galilee, Sea of
Lincoln Sea
Marmara, Sea of
Molucca Sea
Okhotsk, Sea of
Pacific Ocean

Sibuyan Sea
Visayan Sea
Weddell Sea

8 letters
Adriatic Sea
Atlantic Ocean
Beaufort Sea
Labrador Sea
Ligurian Sea
Sargasso Sea
Southern Ocean

9 letters
Antarctic Ocean
Caribbean Sea
East China Sea
Greenland Sea

10 letters
Philippine Sea
South China Sea
Tyrrhenian Sea

13 letters
Mediterranean Sea

Lakes and Reservoirs: U.S. and Canada

(With locations. The elements "lake," "lakes," "reservoir," "pond," etc., are listed below but are NOT included in the letter count. A reservoir that is called "Lake" has (res) following its name. (Glacial) indicates a former lake that has left remnants.)

3 letters

Red Lake	MN

4 letters

Char, Lake	MA
Erie, Lake	MI/OH/ON/PA/NY
Four Lakes	WI
Mead, Lake (res)	NV/AZ
Mono Lake	CA
Oahe, Lake (res)	SD
Seul, Lac	ON
Tule Lake	CA
Utah Lake	UT

5 letters

Arrow Lakes	BC
Baker Lake	NT (Nunavut)
Caddo Lake	TX
Cedar Lake (res)	MB
Clark, Lake	AK
Clear Lake	CA
Eagle Lake	CA
Goose Lake	CA/OR
Great Lakes	U.S./Can
Huron, Lake	MI/ON
Keuka Lake	NY
Leech Lake	MN
Meech Lake	PQ
Moses Lake	WA
Owens Lake	CA
Pepin, Lake	WI/MN
Rainy Lake	MN/ON
Squam Lake	NH
("Golden Pond")	
Storm Lake	IA
Tahoe, Lake	CA/NV
Woods, Lake of the	MN/ON
(full name 14 letters)	

6 letters

Babine Lake	BC
Borgne, Lake	LA
Cayuga, Lake	NY

Chelan, Lake	WA
Crater Lake	OR
Croton Reservoir	NY
Devils Lake	ND
Donner Lake	CA
Falcon Reservoir	TX/Mex
Finger Lakes	NY
Folsom Lake (res)	CA
Geneva, Lake	WI
George, Lake	NY
Havasu, Lake	AZ/CA
Hayden Lake	ID
Itasca, Lake	MN
Louise, Lake	AB
Marion, Lake (res)	SC
Monona, Lake	WI
Norris Lake (res)	TN
Oneida Lake	NY
Otsego Lake	NY (also called Glimmerglass)
Owasco Lake	NY
Ozarks, Lake of the (res)	MO
(full form 15 letters)	
Placid, Lake	NY
Powell, Lake (res)	UT
Priest Lake	ID
Rideau Lakes	ON
Sabine Lake	TX/LA
Salton Sea	CA
Scugog, Lake	ON
Sebago Lake	ME
Seneca Lake	NY
Shasta, Lake (res)	CA
Simcoe, Lake	ON
Spirit Lake	IA
Teslin, Lake	YT
Texoma, Lake (res)	TX/OK
Tulare Lake	CA
Tupper Lake	NY
Walden Pond	MA
Walker Lake	NV
Walled Lake	MI
Wilson, Lake (res)	AL
Winona Lake	IN

Lakes and Reservoirs: U.S. and Canada *(continued)*

7 letters

Abitibi, Lake	PQ/ON
Agassiz, Lake (glacial)	U.S./Can
Almanor, Lake (res)	CA
Amistad Reservoir	TX/Mex
Ashokan Reservoir	NY
Big Bear Lake (res)	CA
Bras d'Or, Lake	
(ocean inlet)	NS
Iliamna, Lake	AK
Jackson Lake (res)	WY
Kegonsa, Lake	WI
Kensico Reservoir	NY
Klamath Lakes	OR/CA
Mendota, Lake	WI
Merritt, Lake	CA
Muskoka Lakes	ON
Nipigon, Lake	ON
Ontario, Lake	ON/NY
Ossipee, Lake	NH
Pompton Lakes	NJ
Pyramid Lake	NV
Quabbin Reservoir	MA
Saranac Lakes	NY
Seminoe Reservoir	WY
Success, Lake	NY
Sunapee, lake	NH
Tellico Lake (res)	TN
Trinity Lake (res)	CA
Umbagog Lake	NH
Wanaque Reservoir	NJ
Watauga Lake (res)	TN
Wheeler Lake (res)	AL
Whitney, Lake (res)	TX
Wissota, Lake	WI

8 letters

Belgrade Lakes	ME
Bomoseen, Lake	VT
Buchanan, Lake (res)	TX
Chippewa, Lake	WI
Cowichan Lake	BC
Dworshak Reservoir	ID
Elsinore, Lake	CA
Flathead Lake	MT
Fort Peck Lake (res)	MT
Garrison Reservoir	ND
(now L. Sakakawea)	

Harrison Lake	BC
Highland Lakes	TX
Houghton Lake	MI
Kawartha Lakes	ON
Kentucky Lake (res)	KY/TN
Kirkland Lake	ON
Kootenay Lake	BC
Lahontan, Lake (glacial)	NV/CA
Manitoba, Lake	MB
Maurepas, Lake	LA
Meredith, Lake (res)	TX
Michigan, Lake	MI/IL/IN
New Found Lake	NH
Okanagan, Lake	BC
Onondaga Lake	NY
Pepacton Reservoir	NY
Rangeley Lakes	ME
Raquette Lake	NY
Raystown Lake (res)	PA
Reelfoot Lake	TN
Reindeer Lake	SK/MB
Superior, Lake	MI/WI/MN/ON
Temagami, Lake	ON
Waterton Lakes	AB
Watts Bar Lake (res)	TN
Williston Lake (res)	BC
Winnipeg, Lake	MB

9 letters

Allatoona, Lake (res)	GA
Ampersand Lake	NY
Arrowhead Lake	TX
Berryessa, Lake (res)	CA
Champlain, Lake	NY/VT/PQ
Cherokees,	
Lake o' the (res)	OK
(full form 17 letters)	
Clear Lake Reservoir	CA
Great Bear Lake	NT
Great Salt Lake	UT
Greenwood Lake	NY/NJ
Hopatcong, Lake	NJ
Iowa Great Lakes	IA
Koocanusa, Lake (res)	MT/BC
Mille Lacs Lake	MN
Moosehead Lake	ME
Nipissing, Lake	ON
Quidi Vidi Lake	NF

Saint-Jean, Lac	PQ
Sakakawea, Lake (res)	ND
Schoharie Reservoir	NY
Smallwood Reservoir	NF (Lab)
White Bear Lake	MN
Winnebago, Lake	WI

10 letters

Candlewood Lake (res)	CT
Chautauqua Lake	NY
Chesuncook Lake	ME
Clair Engle Lake (res)	CA
Cochituate, Lake	MA
Dale Hollow Lake (res)	TN/KY
Great Slave Lake	NT
Meddybemps Lake	ME
Minnetonka, Lake	MN
Nettilling, Lake	NT (Nunavut)
Okeechobee, Lake	FL
Pathfinder Reservoir	WY
Pymatuning Reservoir	OH
Ronkonkoma, Lake	NY
Sabbathday Lake	ME
Saint Clair, Lake	MI/ON
Toledo Bend Reservoir	TX/LA
Washington, Lake	WA

11 letters

Chickamauga Lake (res)	TN
Choke Canyon Reservoir	TX
Coeur d'Alene Lake	ID
Connecticut Lakes	NH
Fort Loudoun Lake (res)	TN
Grand Coulee (res)	WA
Hetch Hetchy Reservoir	CA
Lesser Slave Lake	AB
Manicouagan Reservoir	PQ
Pend Oreille, Lake	OR
Skaneateles Lake	NY
Yellowstone Lake	WY

12 letters

| Belle Fourche Reservoir | SD |

Blue Mountain Lake	NY
Flaming Gorge Reservoir	WY/UT
Lower Klamath Lake	CA
Memphremagog, Lake	PQ/VT
Quinsigamond, Lake	MA
Upper Klamath Lake	OR
Winnipegosis, Lake	MB

13 letters

Pontchartrain, Lake	LA
Possum Kingdom Lake (res)	TX
Wallenpaupack, Lake	PA
Winnipesaukee, Lake	NH

14 letters

Chiputneticook Lakes	ME
Great Sacandaga Lake (res)	NY
Winnibigoshish, Lake	MN

15 letters

| Tear of the Clouds, Lake | NY |

17 letters

Chaubunagungamaug, Lake	MA
(also called Char, Webster)	
Mooselookmeguntic, Lake	ME
Theodore Roosevelt	
Lake (res)	AZ

18 letters

| Franklin D. | |
| Roosevelt Lake (res) | WA |

19 letters

| Tikchik and Wood | |
| River Lakes | AK |

44 letters

Chargoggagoggman-	
chaugagoggchau-	
bunagungamaugg, Lake	MA

Lakes, Lochs, and Loughs:
Outside of the U.S. and Canada

(with location)

(Note: "res" indicates reservoir)

3 letters

Awe	Scotland
Ree	Republic of Ireland
Tay	Scotland
Van	Turkey

4 letters

Bala	Wales
Biwa	Japan
Chad	Chad, Niger, Nigeria, Cameroon
Como	Italy
Derg	Republic of Ireland
Erne	Northern Ireland
Eyre	Australia
Kivu	Democratic Republic of Congo, Rwanda
Mask	Republic of Ireland
Nemi	Italy
Ness	Scotland
Tana	Ethiopia

5 letters

Celyn	Wales
Foyle	Ireland
Garda	Italy
Kyoga (Kioga)	Uganda
Léman	Switzerland, France
Leven	Scotland
Lochy	Scotland
Maree	Scotland
Neagh	Northern Ireland
Nyasa (Nyassa)	Malawi, Tanzania, Mozambique
Onega	Russia
Taupo	New Zealand
Tegid	Wales
Tsana	Ethiopia
Urmia	Iran
Volta	Ghana

6 letters

Albert	Uganda, Democratic Republic of Congo
Baikal	Russia

Corrib	Republic of Ireland
Edward	Uganda, Democratic Republic of Congo
Ericht	Scotland
Geneva	Switzerland, France
Kariba (res)	Zambia, Zimbabwe
Ladoga	Russia
Lomond	Scotland
Lop Nur (Lop Nor)	China
Malawi	Malawi, Tanzania, Mozambique
Mobutu	Uganda, Democratic Republic of Congo
Nasser (res)	Egypt
Natron	Tanzania
Nyassa (Nyasa)	Malawi, Tanzania, Mozambique
Padarn	Wales
Peipus	Russia, Estonia
Poyang (P'o-yang)	China
Rudolf	Kenya, Ethiopia
Saimaa	Finland
Vänern	Sweden
Vyrnwy	Wales

7 letters

Aral Sea	Kazakhstan, Uzbekistan
Balaton	Hungary
Belfast	Northern Ireland
Breydon	England
Chapala	Mexico
Cwellyn	Wales
Katrine	Scotland
Koko Nor	China
Nu Jiang	China, Myanmar (formerly Burma)
Rannoch	Scotland
Red Tarn	England
Rutland	England
Texcoco	Australia
Torrens	Australia
Turkana	Kenya, Ethiopia

8 letters

Balkhash	Kazakhstan

Chiemsee	Germany	**10 letters**	
Clywedog	Wales	Buttermere	England
Coniston	England	Caspian Sea	Iran, Russia,
Dongting	China		Azerbaijan,
Grasmere	England		Kazakhstan
Issyk-kul	Kyrgyzstan	Hawes Water	England
Maggiore	Italy, Switzerland	Ijsselmeer	
Menindee	Australia	(Ysselmeer)	The Netherlands
Neusiedl	Austria, Hungary	Rydal Water	England
Titicaca	Peru, Bolivia	Serpentine,	
Tonle Sap	Cambodia	The (artificial)	England
Tungting	China	Strangford	Northern Ireland
Tung-t'ing	China	Tanganyika	Democratic
Victoria	Uganda,		Republic of Congo,
	Tanzania, Kenya	Burundi, Tanzania, Zambia	
		Windermere	England
9 letters		Xochimilco	Mexico
Bangweulu	Zambia		
Constance	Germany	**11 letters**	
Ennerdale	England	Oulton Broad	England
Esthwaite	England		
Maracaibo	Venezuela	**12 letters**	
Nicaragua	Nicaragua	Derwent Water	England
Patzcuaro	Mexico	Kara-Bogaz-Gol	Turkmenistan
Qinghai Hu	China		
Thirlmere	England	**13 letters**	
Trasimeno	Italy	Bassenthwaite	England
Ullswater	England	Hickling Broad	England
Wast Water	England		
Ysselmeer		**18 letters**	
(Ijsselmeer)	The Netherlands	Vierwaldstättersee	Switzerland

Rivers: U.S. and Canada

(elements "river," "creek," etc., not included in letter count unless noted)

3 letters		Duck	TN
Bow	AB	East (tidal)	NY
Dan	VA/NC	Gila	NM/AZ
Don	ON	Iowa	IA
Fox	WI/IL	Kern	CA
Haw	NC	Loup	NE
Hay	NT	Milk	MT/AB
Kaw (or Kansas)	KS	Napa	CA
Mad	VT	Ohio	PA/WV/OH/
Red	TX/OK/AR/LA		KY/IN/IL
Tar	NC	Rock (Creek)	MD/DC
		Rock	WI/IL
4 letters		Saco	NH/ME
Bear	UT/WY/ID	Wind	WY

Rivers: U.S. and Canada *(continued)*

Wolf	WI
York	VA
Yuba	CA

5 letters

Black	MO/AR
Broad	NC/SC
Bronx	NY
Cedar	MN/IA
Coosa	GA/AL
Flint	GA
Grand	(various)
Green	KY, WY/CO/UT
Hayes	MB
James (also Dakota)	ND/SD
James	VA
Kings	CA
Larch	PQ
Miami	OH
Mouse	See SOURIS
Neuse	NC
Obion	TN
Osage	MO
Owens	CA
Peace	BC/AB
Pearl	MS/LA
Pecos	NM/TX
Rainy	MN/ON
Rogue	OR
Rouge	MI
Skunk	IA
Slave	AB/NT
Snake	WY/ID/OR/WA
Spoon	IL
Teton	WY
White	AR/MO, IN, NE/SD, VT
Yazoo	MS
Yukon	YT/AK

6 letters

Albany	ON
Ashley	SC
Beaver (or North Canadian)	NM/TX/OK
Brazos	TX
Cahaba	AL
Carson	NV/CA
Cherry (Creek)	CO

Clinch	VA/TN
Cooper	SC
Croton	NY
Fraser	BC
Harlem (tidal)	NY
Hoosic	MA/VT/NY
Hudson	NY/NJ
Humber	NF
Indian (lagoon)	FL
Kansas (or Kaw)	KS
Kinzua (Creek)	PA
Lehigh	PA
Marias	MT
Maumee	OH/IN
Merced	CA
Mobile	AL
Mohawk	NY
Mystic	MA
Neches	TX
Nelson	MB
Nemaha	NE
Neosho	OK/KS/MO
Nueces	TX
Oconee	GA
Ottawa	PQ/ON
Owyhee	NV/ID/OR
Pee Dee	NC/SC
Platte	NE
Powder	WY/MT
Raisin	MI
Ramapo	NY/NJ
Rideau	ON
Sabine	TX/LA
Saline	AR, KS
Salmon	ID
Saluda	SC
Santee	SC
Scioto	OH
Sevier	UT
Skagit	BC/WA
Skeena	BC
Souris (Mouse)	SK/ND/MB
Swanee	See SUWANEE
Teslin	YT
Thames	CT, ON
Thelon	NT (Nunavut)
Tongue	WY/MT
Tygart	WV

Umpqua	OR
Wabash	OH/IN/IL
Walker	NV
Yadkin	NC
Yakima	WA

7 letters

Alabama	AL
Au Sable (or Ausable)	MI, NY
Big Blue	MO, NE/KS
Big Hole	MT
Bighorn	WY/MT
Bonanza (Creek)	YT
Buffalo	AR
Bull Run	VA
Calumet	IL/IN
Catawba	NC/SC
Chagrin	OH
Charles	MA
Chicago	IL
Concord	MA
Conecuh	AL/FL
Cripple (Creek)	CO
Detroit	MI/ON
Elkhorn	NE
Feather	CA
Genesee	NY
Hatchie	MS/TN
Hocking	OH
Holston	TN
John Day	OR
Juniata	PA
Kanawha	WV
Klamath	OR/CA
Koksoak	PQ
Licking	KY
Madison	MT
Malheur	OR
Mullica	NJ
Nechako	BC
Niagara	NY/ON
Nodaway	IA/MO
Pamlico	NC
Passaic	NJ
Peconic	NY
Pembina	AB, MB/ND
Perdido	AL/FL
Potomac	WV/MD/VA/DC
Raccoon	IA
Rapidan	VA
Raritan	NJ

Red Deer	AB
Red Rock	MT
Rosebud (Creek)	MT
Russian	CA
Stikine	BC
Suwanee (or Swanee)	GA/FL
Trinity	CA, TX
Truckee	NV
Washita	TX/OK
Watauga	NC/TN
Wateree	SC
Wichita	TX

8 letters

Allagash	ME
Altamaha	GA
American	CA
Arkansas	CO/KS/OK/AR
Big Black	MS
Big Muddy (also nickname for Missouri R.)	IL
Big Sioux	SD/IA
Canadian (also called South Canadian)	NM/TX/OK
Cape Fear	NC
Chenango	NY
Cheyenne	WY/SD
Chippewa	MN
Choptank	DE/MD
Cimarron	NM/OK/CO/KS
Colorado	CO/UT/AZ/ NM/CA/Mex
Columbia	BC/WA/OR
Colville	AK
Congaree	SC
Cuyahoga	OH
Delaware	NY/PA/NJ/DE
Eastmain	PQ
Exploits	NF
Flathead	BC/MT
Gatineau	PQ
Gunnison	CO
Hamilton (now Churchill)	NF(Lab)
Humboldt	NV
Iditarod	AK
Illinois	IL
Kankakee	IN/IL
Kennebec	ME

Rivers: U.S. and Canada *(continued)*

Kentucky	KY
Keya Paha	SD/NE
Kiamichi	OK
Klondike	YT
Kootenai	BC/MT/ID
La Grande	PQ
Mahoning	OH/PA
Missouri	U.S.
Monocacy	PA/MD
Niobrara	NE/WY
Nottoway	VA
Ocmulgee	GA
Ogeechee	GA
Ouachita (or Washita)	AR/LA
Pamunkey	VA
Patapsco	MD
Patuxent	MD
Pocomoke	DE/MD
Quinault	WA
Raquette	NY
Roanoake	VA/NC
Saguenay	PQ
Salt Fork	
(of the Arkansas)	KS/OK
Sandusky	OH
Sangamon	IL
Savannah	GA/SC
Sheyenne	ND
Sing Sing (Kill)	NY
(full name 12 letters)	
Tallulah	GA
Tuolumne	CA
Umatilla	OR
Waccamaw	NC/SC
Winnipeg	ON/MB
Winooski	VT

9 letters

Allegheny	NY/PA
Anacostia	DC
Annapolis	NS
Athabasca	AB
Big Nemaha	NE
Calcasieu	LA
Caney Fork	TN
Chattooga	NC/GA/SC
Chaudière	PQ
Christina	PA/MD/DE

Churchill	NF (Lab), SK/MB
Clark Fork	MT/ID
Conemaugh	PA
Conestoga (Creek)	PA
Des Moines	IA
Deschutes	OR
Gasconade	MO
Jefferson	MT
Kaskaskia	IL
Kissimmee	FL
Klickitat	WA
Kuskokwim	AK
Lodgepole (Creek)	WY/NE/CO
Mackenzie	NT
Madawaska	ME/NB
Maquoketa	IA
Mattaponi	VA
Menominee	MI/WI
Merrimack	NH/MA
Milwaukee	WI
Minnesota	MN
Miramichi	NB
Mokelumne	CA
Muskingum	OH
Nanticoke	DE/MD
Naugatuck	CT
North Anna	VA
Pawcatuck	CT/RI
Penobscot	ME
Peribonca	PQ
Porcupine	YT/AK
Qu'Appelle	SK/MB
Richelieu	PQ
Saint John	ME/NB
Saugatuck	CT
Schoharie	NY
Smoky Hill	CO/KS
Sunflower (or Big	
Sunflower)	MS
Tennessee	TN/AL/MS/KY
Tombigbee	MS/AL
Verdigris	KS/OK
Vermilion	IL
Wenatchee	WA
Wisconsin	WI
Yalobusha	MS

10 letters

Appomattox	VA
Batten Kill	VT/NY
Bayou Teche (the Teche)	LA
(second element 5 letters)	
Bitterroot	MT
Blackstone	MA/RI
Brandywine (Creek)	PA/DE
Cannonball	ND
Clearwater	ID
Coppermine	NT
Cumberland	KY/TN
Des Plaines	IL
Great Miami	OH
Hackensack	NY/NJ
Housatonic	MA/CT
Hutchinson	NY
Nolichucky	NC/TN
Pascagoula	MS
Pedernales	TX
Piscataqua	ME/NH
Providence	RI
Purgatoire	CO
Quinnipiac	CT
Republican	CO/NE/KS
Sacramento	CA
Saint Clair	MI
Saint Croix	ME/NB, MN/WI
Saint Johns	FL
Saint Marys	GA/FL, ON/MI
Saint Regis	NY
San Jacinto	TX
Schuylkill	PA
Shenandoah	VA/WV
Snoqualmie	WA
Tallapoosa	GA/AL
Tippecanoe	IN
Tuscarawas	OH
Two-Hearted	MI
Vermillion	SD
Walhonding	OH
Willamette	OR

11 letters

Assiniboine	SK/MB
Atchafalaya	LA
Caniapiscau	PQ
Chickamauga (Creek)	GA/TN
Coeur D'Alene	ID
Connecticut	NH/VT/MA/CT
French Broad	NC/TN

Kaaterskill (Creek)	NY
Kill van Kull (tidal)	NY/NJ
Lac Qui Parle	SD/MN
Manicouagan	PQ
Mississippi	U.S., ON (two)
Monongahela	WV/PA
Musselshell	MT
North Platte	CO/WY/NE
Pend Oreille	ID
Restigouche	NB
Roaring Fork	CO
South Platte	CO/NE
Susquehanna	NY/PA/MD
Yellowstone	WY/MT/ND

12 letters

Androscoggin	NH/ME
Apalachicola	FL
Belle Fourche	WY/SD
Big Sunflower	See SUNFLOWER
Black Warrior	AL
Chickahominy	VA
Little Nemaha	NE
Pottawatomie (Creek)	KS
Rappahannock	VA
Saint Francis	MO/AR
Saint-Maurice	PQ
Saskatchewan	SK/MB
Tallahatchie	MS
Wapsipinicon	IA
Youghiogheny	WV/MD/PA

13 letters

Big Two-Hearted	See TWO HEARTED
Chattahoochee	GA
Little Bighorn	WY/MT
North Canadian (or Beaver)	NM/TX/OK
Saint Lawrence	ON/NY/PQ

14 letters

Bayou Lafourche	LA
(second element 9 letters)	
Great Egg Harbor	NJ
Little Colorado	AZ
Little Missouri	AR,WY/MT/ SD/ND

15 letters

Little Tennessee	GA/NC/TN

Rivers: U.S. and Canada *(continued)*

Marais des Cygnes	KS/MO	**17 letters**
Ogallala Aquifer	SD/NE/KS	North Saskatchewan	AB/SK
(underground	CO/WY/OK	South Saskatchewan	AB/SK
resource)	TX		

Rivers: Ouside of the U.S. and Canada

(with location)

2 letters		
Ob	Russia	
Po	Italy	

3 letters		
Ain	France	
Aln	England	
Bug	Ukraine, Poland, Germany	
Dee	Scotland; Wales, England	
Don	Russia, Scotland, England, France, Australia	
Ems	Germany, The Netherlands	
Esk	Australia	
Exe	England	
Fal	England	
Fly	Papua New Guinea	
Han	China	
Kwa	Democratic Republic of Congo	
Lea	England	
Lee	Republic of Ireland	
Lot	France	
Rur	Germany	
Rye	England	
Tay	Scotland	
Ure	England	
Usk	Wales, England	
Wey	England	
Wye	Wales, England	
Yeo	England	

4 letters		
Adda	Italy	
Adur	England	
Aire	England; France	
Amur	Mongolia, Russia, China	
Arno	Italy	
Arun	Nepal	

Aube	France
Avon	England
Bann	Northern Ireland
Beas	India
Bure	England
Cher	France
Coln	England
Dart	England
Doon	Scotland
Dove	England
Ebro	Spain
Eden	England, Scotland
Elbe	Germany, Czech Republic
Emba	Kazakhstan
Isis	England
Juba	Ethiopia, Somalia
Kama	Russia
Kura	Turkey, Georgia, Azerbaijan
Lahn	Germany
Lech	Germany, Austria
Lena	Russia
Lune	England
Lüne	Germany
Maas	Netherlands
Main	Germany
Miño	Spain
Mole	England
Nile	Sudan, Egypt
Oder	Germany, Czech Republic, Poland
Oise	France
Ouse	England
Oxus	Turkmenistan, Uzbekistan
Peel	Australia
Ravi	India, Pakistan
Rede	England
Ruhr	Germany

Saar	Germany, France	Marne	France
Spey	Scotland	Maros	Indonesia
Taff	Wales	Meuse	France, Belgium
Tajo	Spain	Minho	Spain, Portugal
Tarn	France	Mureş	Romania, Hungary
Tawe	Wales	Negro	Spain; Brazil, Argentina,
Tawi	India		Bolivia, Paraguay,
Tees	England		Uruguay, Venezuela
Tejo	Brazil	Neman	Belarus, Lithuania
Test	England	Niger	Nigeria, Mali, Guinea
Tyne	Scotland, England	Otter	England
Ural	Russia, Kazakhstan	Pearl	China
Vaal	South Africa	Piave	Italy
Wear	England	Purus	Brazil
Yare	England	Rance	France
		Rhine	Switzerland, Germany,

5 letters

			The Netherlands
Adige	Italy	Saale	Germany
Aisne	France	Saône	France
Allan	Scotland; Syria	Seine	France
Aller	Spain; Germany	Somme	France
Annan	Scotland	Stour	England
Benue	Nigeria	Swale	England
Brent	England	Tagus	Portugal, Spain
Camel	England	Tamar	England
Chari	Cameroon, Chad	Tiber	Italy
Clyde	Scotland	Trent	England
Colne	England	Tweed	England, Scotland
Congo	Congo, Democratic	Volga	Russia
	Republic of Congo	Volta	Ghana
Dnepr	Russia, Belarus, Ukraine	Weser	Germany
Doubs	France, Switzerland	Xingu	Brazil
Douro	Spain, Portugal		
Dovey	Wales	**6 letters**	
Drava	Italy, Austria,	Allier	France
	Yugoslavia, Hungary	Amazon	Peru, Brazil
Duero	Spain	Angara	Russia
Dvina	Russia	Bío-Bío	Chile
Forth	Scotland	Chenab	Pakistan
Frome	Australia	Clutha	New Zealand
Indus	India, Pakistan, China	Cooper	Australia
James	Australia	Coquet	England
Jumna	India	Crouch	England
Juruá	Brazil	Danube	Germany, Austria,
Kafue	Zambia		Romania, Hungary,
Kasai	Angola, Democratic		Slovakia, Bulgaria
	Republic of Congo	Dnestr	Ukraine, Moldova
Kuban	Russia	Escaut	Belgium, France
Lagan	Northern Ireland	Gambia	Gambia, Senegal
Lippe	Germany	Ganges	India
Loire	France	Glomma	Norway

Rivers: Ouside of the U.S. and Canada *(continued)*

Hunter	Australia
Irtysh	China, Kazakhstan, Russia
Itchen	England
Japurá	Brazil
Jordan	Israel, Jordan
Kolyma	Russia
Liffey	Republic of Ireland
Lodden	Australia, England
Mamoré	Brazil, Bolivia
Medway	England
Mekong	Laos, China
Mersey	England
Monnow	England, Wales
Murray	Australia
Neckar	Germany
Neisse	Poland, Germany
Ogooué	Gabon
Orange	South Africa
Orwell	England
Paraná	Brazil
Ribble	England
Salado	Agentina, Cuba, Mexico
Severn	England
St. John	Liberia
Sutlej	Pakistan, India, China
Thames	England
Ticino	Italy, Switzerland
Tigris	Iraq, Turkey
Tugela	South Africa
Ussuri	China, Russia
Vienne	France
Vltava	Czech Republic
Weaver	England
Yellow	China, Papua New Guinea

7 letters

Bermejo	Argentina
Cauvery	India
Damodar	India
Darling	Australia
Derwent	England
Durance	France
Garonne	France
Gironde	France
Helmand	Afghanistan
Hooghly	India

Huang Ho	China
Lachlan	Australia
Limpopo	South Africa, Zimbabwe, Mozambique
Lualaba	Democratic Republic of Congo
Madeira	Brazil
Marañón	Brazil, Peru
Maritsa	Bulgaria
Möselle	Germany
Orontes	Syria
Pechora	Russia
Salween	Myanmar (formerly Burma), China
Scheldt	Belgium
Senegal	Senegal
Shannon	Republic of Ireland
Songhua	Vietnam, China
Sungari	China
Uruguay	Uruguay, Brazil
Vistula	Poland
Waikato	New Zealand
Xi Jiang	China
Yangtze	China
Yenisei	Russia
Zambezi	Zambia, Angola, Zimbabwe, Mozambique

8 letters

Amu Darya	Turkmenistan, Uzbekistan
Araguaia	Brazil
Charente	France
Cherwell	England
Demerara	Guyana
Dordogne	France
Godavari	India
Manawatu	New Zealand
Menderes	Turkey
Paraguay	Paraguay
Putumayo	Ecuador
Río Bravo	Mexico
Syr Darya	Uzbekistan, Kazakhstan
Torridge	England
Tunguska	Russia

Volturno	Italy
Wansbeck	England
Windrush	England

9 letters

Essequibo	Guyana
Euphrates	Iraq
Great Ouse	England
Hsi Chiang	China
Irrawaddy	Myanmar (formerly Burma)
Mackenzie	Australia
Magdalena	Colombia
Rio Grande	Jamaica

10 letters

Chang Jiang	China
Chao Phraya	Thailand
Coppermine	Canada
Hawkesbury	Australia

11 letters

Brahmaputra	Tibet, India
Shatt al-Arab	Iran, Iraq

12 letters

Guadalquivir	Spain
Murrumbidgee	Australia
Río de la Plata	Argentina, Uruguay

Waterfalls

(with location)

3 letters

Jog	India

5 letters

Akaka	Hawaii
Angel	Venezuela
Della	British Columbia
Glass	Brazil
Kegon	Japan

6 letters

Iguaçu	Argentina/Brazil
Tugela	South Africa

7 letters

Cauvery	India
Kalambo	Tanzania/Zambia
Niagara	New York/Ontario
Passaic, Great Falls of the	New Jersey
Ruacana	Angola

8 letters

American	New York/Ontario
Candelas	Colombia
Cuquenán	Venezuela
Gavarnie	Austria
Kabalega	Uganda

Shoshone	Idaho
Takakkaw	British Columbia
Victoria	Zimbabwe/Zambia
Wallaman	Australia
Yosemite	California

9 letters

Augrabies	South Africa
Horseshoe	New York/Ontario
Kapachira	Malawi
Minnehaha	Minnesota
Multnomah	Oregon

10 letters

Bridalveil	California
Sutherland	New Zealand

11 letters

Cumberland	Kentucky
Montmorency	Quebec
Reichenbach	Switzerland
Trummelbach	Switzerland
Yellowstone	Wyoming

13 letters

Grande Cascade	France
Mardalsfossen	Norway

Mountains
(with location)

2 letters

K2	India

3 letters

Jay (Peak)	Vermont
Red	Alabama
Tom	Massachusetts
Ute	Colorado

4 letters

Bear	New York
Blue	Pennsylvania, etc.
Etna	Italy
Gore	New York
Hawk	Pennsylvania
Hood	Oregon
Jaya	Indonesia
Kitt (Peak)	Arizona
Lowe	California
Muir	California
Nebo	Arkansas, Utah
Sand	Tennessee/ Georgia/ Alabama
Toro (Peak)	California

5 letters

Adams	New Hampshire, Washington
Aneto, Pico de	Spain
Blanc, Mont	Italy/France
Droop	West Virginia
Evans	Colorado
Kenya	Kenya
Kineo	Maine
Kings	North Carolina
Locke	Texas
Logan	Yukon Territory
Marcy	New York
Okemo	Vermont
Pikes (Peak)	Colorado
Pilot	Noth Carolina
Royal	Quebec
Scott (Peak)	Idaho
Shade	Pennsylvania
Shasta	California
Slide	New York

South	Pennsylvania/ Maryland/Virginia
Split	California
Squaw	Maine
Stone	Georgia
Yucca	Nevada

6 letters

Ararat	Turkey
Bonete	Argentina
Cannon	New Hampshire
Clinch	Virginia/Tennessee
Denali	See McKinley (Alaska)
Elbert	Colorado
Elbrus	Russia
Harney (Peak)	South Dakota
Katmai	Alaska
Ktaadn	See Katahdin (Maine)
Lassen (Peak)	California
Muztag	China
Pisgah	North Carolina, etc. (and biblical)
Pissis	Argentina
Pobedy, Pik	Kyrgyzstan
Riding	Manitoba
Rogers	Virginia
Sandia (Peak)	New Mexico
Seward	New York
Steens	Oregon
Taylor	New Mexico
Walden (Ridge)	Tennessee

7 letters

Alberta	Alberta
Dykh-Tau	Russia
Equinox	Vermont
Everest	Nepal/Tibet
Gannett (Peak)	Massachusetts
Holyoke	Massachusetts
Langley	California
Lookout	Tennessee
Madison	New Hampshire
Makalu I	Nepal/Tibet
Massive	Colorado
Nittany	Pennsylvania

Orizaba (*or* Citlaltépetl)	Mexico
Palomar	California
Pembina	Manitoba
Rainier	Washington
Redoubt (Volcano)	Alaska
Shuksan	Washington
Snowdon	Wales
Springer	Georgia
Stratton	Vermont
Wheeler (Peak)	New Mexico
Whitney	California
Wildcat	New Hampshire

8 letters

Ben Nevis	Scotland
Cadillac	Maine
Cheyenne	Colorado
Chocorua	New Hampshire
Columbia	Alberta
Cotopaxi	Ecuador
Damavand	Iran
Fujiyama	Japan
Greylock	Massachusetts
Katahdin	Maine
Kennesaw (or Kenesaw)	Georgia
Kinabalu	Malaysia
Mauna Kea	Hawaii
Mauna Loa	Hawaii
McKinley	Alaska
Megantic	Quebec
Mitchell	North Carolina
Old Baldy	See MT. SAN ANTONIO (California); also many other peaks
Rushmore	South Dakota
Skylight	New York
Taum Sauk	Missouri

9 letters

Aconcagua	Argentina
Annapurna	Nepal
Camelback	Arizona
Communism (Peak)	Tajikistan
Garibaldi	British Columbia
Holy Cross, Mount of the	Colorado
Huascarán	Peru
Jefferson	New Hampshire
Kearsarge	New Hampshire
Lafayette	New Hampshire
Mansfield	Vermont

Monadnock or Great Monadnock)	New Hampshire
Novarupta (Volcano)	Alaska
Pohatcong	New Jersey
Rabun Bald	Georgia
Ras Dashen	Ethiopia
Roman Nose	Montana
Sassafras	South Carolina
Scapegoat	Montana
Storm King	New York
Sugarloaf	Brazil, etc.
Sugarloaf	Maine
Tamalpais	California
Telescope (Peak)	California
Tirich Mir	Pakistan
Tremblant	Quebec
Tupungato	Argentina/Chile
Wachusett	Massachusetts
Weisshorn	Switzerland
Whiteside	North Carolina
Zugspitze	Germany

10 letters

Chimborazo	Ecuador
Heliograph (Peak)	Arizona
Killington (Peak)	Vermont
Kittatinny	New Jersey/ Pennsylvania
Margherita	Democratic Republic of Congo, Rwanda
Matterhorn	Switzerland, Italy
Saddleback	Maine
Saint Elias	Yukon Territory/Alaska
San Antonio	California
Shenandoah	Virginia/ West Virginia
Shishaldin (Volcano)	Alaska
Sir Douglas	Alberta
Spruce Knob	West Virginia
Veniaminof	Alaska
Waddington	British Columbia
Washington	New Hampshire

11 letters

Assiniboine	Alberta/British Columbia
Edith Cavell	Alberta
Fairweather	British Columbia

Mountains (continued)

Golden Hinde	British Columbia
Kilimanjaro	Tanzania
Maroon Bells (paired)	Colorado
Massanutten	Virginia
Nanga Parbat	Pakistan
Saint Helena	California
Saint Helens	Washington
San Gorgonio	California
Scafell Pike	England
Sir Sandford	British Columbia
Uncompahgre (Peak)	Colorado

12 letters

Citlaltépetl (or Orizaba)	Mexico
Dufourspitze	Switzerland
Godwin-Austen	India

Ixtaccihuatl (or Iztaccihuatl)	Mexico
Kanchenjunga	Nepal/India
Passaconaway	New Hampshire
Popocatépetl	Mexico
Slieve Donard	Northern Ireland

13 letters

Carrantuohill	Republic of Ireland
Grossglockner	Austria
Ojos del Salado	Argentina/Chile
Sleeping Giant	Connecticut

16 letters

Sir Wilfrid Laurier	British Columbia

Mountain Ranges

(with location)

(With location. Assume element "mountains" is part of name, unless otherwise indicated. Many ranges rendered here in singular are also encountered as plural, e.g., "the Little Belts" for the Little Belt Mountains; coversely, a plural, e.g. "Himalayas," may be encountered in the singular, as "Himalaya Mts.")

3 letters

Wet	Colorado

4 letters

Alps	Europe
Bald	North Carolina/ Tennessee
Blue (Hills)	Massachusetts
Blue	Australia
Egan (Range)	Nevada
Gila	Arizona
Gore (Range)	Colorado
Harz	Germany
Inyo	California
Kofa	Arizona
Moon, Mts. of the (Ruwenzori)	Uganda/Dem. Rep. of the Congo
Park (Range)	Colorado

Ruby	Nevada
Ural	Russia
Zuñi	New Mexico

5 letters

Altai	Kazakhstan/ China/Mongolia
Andes	South America
Atlas	Morocco/Algeria/ Tunisia
Black (Hills)	South Dakota/Wyoming
Black Wales,	North Carolina
Coast (Mountains)	western Canada/U.S.
Coast (Ranges)	western Canada/U.S.
Davis	Texas
Ghats	India

Glass	Texas
Green	Vermont
Gunks, the	See SHAWANGUNK MTS., New York
Hueco	Texas/New Mexico
Jemez	New Mexico
Juras (Jura Alps)	France/Switzerland
Kenai	Alaska
La Sal	Utah
Organ	New Mexico
Ozark	Arkansas/Oklahoma/ Missouri/Kansas
Pamir	Tajikistan/China/ Afghanistan
Pelly	Yukon Territory
Pinal	Arizona
Rocky	U.S./Canada
Sayan	Russia
Sheep (Range)	Utah
Smoky	eastern U.S.
Snake (Range)	Nevada
Snowy	Australia
South	Arizona
Teton (Range)	Wyoming
Unaka (Range)	North Carolina/ Tennessee
Uinta	Utah
White	Arizona, California, New Hampshire

6 letters

Alaska (Range)	Alaska
Chisos	Texas
Chuska	Arizona/New Mexico
Diablo	California
Hoggar	Algeria
Hoosac (Range)	Massachusetts
Koolau (Range)	Hawaii
Ladakh	India/Pakistan/ China
Laguna	California
Marble	California
Mesabi (Range)	Minnesota
Mourne	Northern Ireland
Ochoco	Oregon
Pindus	Tyrkey
Pocono	Pennsylvania
Ramapo	New York/ New Jersey
Ritter (Range)	California

Salmon	California
Sandia	New Mexico
Selwyn	Yukon Terr./ Northwest Terrs.
Spring	Nevada
Tatras (Tatra Mts.)	Poland/Slovakia
Taurus	Turkey
Turtle	North Dakota/ Manitoba
Tushar	Utah
Unicoi	North Carolina/ Tennessee
Warner	California
Zagros	Iran

7 letters

Avawatz	California
Balkans (Balkan Mts.)	Bulgaria
Bear Paw	Montana
Bighorn	Montana/Wyoming
British	Yukon Terr./Alaska
Cabinet	Montana/Idaho
Caribou	British Columbia
Cascade (Range)	Oregon/ Washington
Cassiar	British Columbia
Chinati	Texas
Chugach	Alaska
Dragoon	Arizona
Gabilan (Range)	California
Gogebic (Range)	Michigan
Klamath	California/Oregon
Laramie	Wyoming
Lebanon	Lebanon
Manzano	New Mexico
Mimbres	New Mexico
Ogilvie	Yukon Territory
Olympic	Washington
Pahvant (Range)	Utah
Palomar (Range)	California
Phoenix	Arizona
Picacho	Arizona
Purcell	British Columbia
Pyramid	New Mexico
Quitman	Texas
Rockies (Rocky Mts.)	U.S. and Canada
San Juan	Colorado/New Mexico
Sawatch (Range)	Colorado
Smokies (Smoky, or Great Smoky, Mts.)	eastern U.S.

Mountain Ranges *(continued)*

Taconic	New York/
	Connecticut/Vermont
Temblor (Range)	California
Toiyabe	Nevada
Torngat	Quebec/Labrador
Trinity	California
Truchas (Peaks)	New Mexico
Van Horn	Texas
Verdugo	California
Waianae	Hawaii
Wallowa	Oregon
Wasatch (Range)	Idaho/Utah
Wichita	Oklahoma
Willapa (Hills)	Washington

Pennines (or,	England
Pennine Chain)	
Pinaleno	Arizona
Pyrenees	France/Spain
Santa Ana	California
Sawtooth (Range)	Idaho
Shoshone	Nevada
Siskiyou	California/Oregon
Snowbird	North Carolina
Tien Shan	Kyrgyzstan/China/
	Mongolia
Uwharrie	North Carolina
Watchung	New Jersey
Wrangell	Alaska

8 letters

Absaroka	Wyoming/Montana
Aleutian (Range)	Alaska
Amargosa (Range)	
	California/Nevada
Apennine (Hills, or	Italy
Apennines)	
Arbuckle	Oklahoma
Cévennes	France
Cambrian	Wales
Catoctin	Maryland
Caucasus	Russia/Georgia/
	Azerbaijan/Armenia
Cobequid	Nova Scotia
Cumbrian	England
Delaware	Texas
Endicott	Alaska
Flathead	Montana
Flinders (Range)	Australia
Franklin	Northwest Territories
Grampian	Scotland
Harcuvar	Arizona
Hualapai	Arizona
Kaikoura (Ranges)	New Zealand
Mahoosuc (Range)	Maine
Mazatzal	Arizona
McDowell	Arizona
Mogollon	New Mexico
Monashee	British Columbia
Musgrave (Ranges)	Australia
Ouachita	Arkansas/
	Oklahoma
Panamint (Range)	California

9 letters

Allegheny	eastern U.S.
Beartooth (Range)	Montana/
	Wyoming
Berkshire (Hills)	Massachusetts
Blue Ridge	eastern U.S.
Chic-Chocs	Quebec
(Shickshocks)	
Chocolate	California
Deep Creek (Range)	Utah
Dolomites	Italy
(or, Dolomite Alps)	
Franconia	New Hampshire
Guadalupe	New Mexico/Texas
Hamersley (Range)	Australia
Himalayas	China/India/
	Pakistan/Nepal/Bhutan
Hindu Kush	Afghanistan/Pakistan
Jicarilla	New Mexico
Karakoram	Afghanistan/Pakistan/
	China/India
Kuskokwim	Alaska
Long Range	Newfoundland
(Mountains)	
Mackenzie	Yukon Terr./
	Northwest Terrs.
Nantahala	North Carolina/
	Georgia
Notre Dame	Quebec
Palisades (Peaks)	California
Ruwenzori (Mountains	
of the Moon)	Uganda/Dem.
	Rep. of the Congo

San Andres	New Mexico
San Rafael	California
Santa Cruz	California
Santa Rita	Arizona
Santa Rosa	California
Santa Ynez	California
Talkeetna	Alaska
Tehachapi	California
Texas Alps	Texas
Tuscarora	Nevada
Wenatchee	Washington
White Tank	Arizona
Wind River (Range)	Wyoming

10 letters

Adirondacks	New York
Bitterroot (Range)	Idaho/Montana
Cairngorms	Scotland
Cantabrian	Czech Rep./Slovakia/Poland/Romania/Ukraine
Chiricahua	Arizona
Chuckwalla	California
Front Range (of the Rockies)	Wyoming/Colorado/New Mexico
Grand Teton	Wyoming
Great Smoky	eastern U.S.
Kunlun Shan	China
Laurentian	Quebec
Little Belt	Montana
Longfellow	Maine
Los Angeles (Ranges)	California
MacDonnell	Australia
Middleback	Australia
New England	Australia
Peninsular (Ranges)	California/Mexico
Promontory	Utah
Richardson	Yukon Terr./Northwest Terrs.
Sacramento	New Mexico
Saint Elias	Alaska/Yukon Terr.
San Gabriel	California
San Jacinto	California
Santa Lucia (Range)	California
Shawangunk	New York
Shickshock (or, Chic-Chocs)	Quebec
Transverse (Ranges)	California
Yolla Bolly	California

11 letters

Anti-Lebanon	Lebanon/Syria
Baboquivari	Arizona
Bernese Alps (Bernese Oberland)	Switzerland
Carpathians	Czech Rep./Slovakia/Poland/Romania
Drakensberg	South Africa/Lesotho
Horse Heaven (Hills)	Washington
Medicine Bow	Wyoming
Monteregian (Hills)	Quebec
Santa Monica	California
Santa Susana	California
Seven Devils	Idaho
Sierra Madre (Mountains),	California/Wyoming
Sierra Madre	Mexico
Sierra Morena	Spain
Sierra Nevada	California/Nevada

12 letters

12 Appalachians	eastern U.S./Canada
Golan Heights	Syria/Israel
Peaks of Otter	Virginia
Presidential (Range)	New Hampshire
San Francisco (Peaks)	Arizona
Sierra Blanca	New Mexico
Sierra Diablo	Texas
Superstition	Arizona

13 letters

Brecon Beacons	Wales
San Bernardino	California
Sangre de Cristo	Colorado/New Mexico
Santa Catalina	California
Sierra Maestra	Cuba
Stinking Water	Oregon

15 letters

| Sierra del Carmen | Texas/Mexico |

17 letters

| Cordillera Central | Puerto Rico, etc. |

19 letters

| Macgillicuddy's Reeks | Ireland |

Volcanoes

(with location)

3 letters

Aso	Japan
Awu	Indonesia

4 letters

Atka	Alaska
Etna	Sicily
Fogo	Cape Verde
Fuji (Fujiyama)	Japan
Gede	Indonesia
Kaba	Indonesia
Laki	Iceland
Nila	Indonesia
Poas	Costa Rica
Siau	Indonesia
Taal	Philippines

5 letters

Agung	Indonesia
Asama	Japan
Askja	Iceland
Dempo	Indonesia
Fuego	Guatemala
Hekla	Iceland
Katla	Iceland
Kelud	Indonesia
Kiska	Alaska
Manam	Papua New Guinea
Mayon	Philippines
Noyoe	Iceland
Okmok	Alaska
Paloe	Indonesia
Pelée	Martinique
Spurr	Alaska

6 letters

Alcedo	Galapagos Islands (Ecuador)
Ambrim	Vanuatu
Buleng	Indonesia
Colima	Mexico
Dukono	Indonesia
Erebus	Antarctica
Izalco	El Salvador
Katmai	Alaska
Lascar	Chile
Lassen	California

Llaima	Chile
Lopevi	Vanuatu
Marapi	Indonesia
Meakan	Japan
Merapi	Indonesia
Mihara	Japan
O'shima	Japan
Osorno	Chile
Pacaya	Guatemala
Pavlof	Alaska
Puracé	Colombia
Sangay	Ecuador
Semeru	Indonesia
Slamat	Indonesia
Tacana	Guatemala
Unauna	Indonesia

7 letters

Atitlan	Guatemala
Bárcena	Mexico
Bulusan	Philippines
Didicas	Philippines
El Misti	Peru
Galeras	Colombia
Iliamna	Alaska
Jorullo	Mexico
Kilauea	Hawaii
Ometepe	Nicaragua
Orizaba (Citlaltépetl)	Mexico
Puyehue	Chile
Redoubt	Alaska
Ruapehu	New Zealand
Sabrina	Azores
Soputan	Indonesia
Surtsey	Iceland
Tambora	Indonesia
Ternate	Indonesia
Tjareme	Indonesia
Tokachi	Japan
Vulcano	Italy

8 letters

Bogoslof	Alaska
Cameroon	Cameroon
Cotopaxi	Ecuador
Demavend	Iran
Fonualei	Tongas

Fujiyama	Japan
Hualalai	Hawaii
Kerintji	Indonesia
Krakatau	Indonesia
Krakatoa	Indonesia
Mauna Kea	Hawaii
Mauna Loa	Hawaii
Niuafo'ou	Tonga
Pinatubo	Indonesia
Rindjani	Indonesia
Sangeang	Indonesia
Tarawera	New Zealand
Vesuvius	Italy
Wrangell	Alaska
Yakedake	Japan

Cerro Negro	Nicaragua
Chimborazo	Ecuador
Guallatiri	Chile
Hibok Hibok	Philippines
Long Island	Papua New Guinea
Miyakejima	Japan
Nyamiagira	Democratic Republic of Congo
Nyiragongo	Democratic Republic of Congo
Santa Maria	Guatemala
Shishaldin	Alaska
Tungurahua	Ecuador
Veniaminof	Alaska
Villarrica	Chile

9 letters

Amburombu	Indonesia
Bandai-san	Japan
Cleveland	Alaska
Coseguina	Nicaragua
Cotacachi	Ecuador
El Chichon	Mexico
Gamkonora	Indonesia
Grimsvötn	Iceland
Momotombo	Nicaragua
Myozin-syo	Japan
Ngauruhoe	New Zealand
Novarupta	Alaska
Paricutín	Mexico
Rininahue	Chile
Santorini	Greece
Stromboli	Italy
Tongariro	New Zealand

10 letters

| Acatenango | Guatemala |
| Capelinhos | Azores |

11 letters

Chances Peak	Montserrat
Great Sitkin	U.S.
Kilimanjaro	Tanzania
La Soufrière	Montserrat
Saint Helens, Mt.	Washington
Tupungatito	Chile
White Island	New Zealand

12 letters

Huainaputina	Peru
Ixtaccihuatl (or Iztaccihuatl)	Mexico
Popocatépetl	Mexico

13 letters

| Nevado del Ruiz | Colombia |

16 letters

| Mount Saint Helens | Washington |

Major Deserts

3 letters

Lut	Iran

4 letters

Gila	Arizona
	(part of Sonoran)
Gobi	Mongolia/China
Thar	India/Pakistan
Yuma	Arizona
	(part of Sonoran)

5 letters

Nafud	Saudi Arabia
Namib	Namibia
Negev	Israel
Sturt	Australia

6 letters

Gibson	Australia
Libyan	Libya
Mojave (or Mohave)	California
Nubian	Sudan
Sahara	North Africa
Syrian	Syria/Iraq/Jordan/
	Saudi/Arabia

7 letters

Arabian	Egypt
Atacama	Chile
Eastern	Egypt

Kara Kum	Turkmenistan
Painted	Arizona
Simpson	Australia
Sonoran	U.S., Mexico
Western	Egypt

8 letters

Colorado	California
Kalahari	South Africa/Namibia/
	Botswana
Kyzyl Kum	Kazakhstan/
	Uzbekistan

9 letters

Black Rock	Nevada

10 letters

Chihuahuan	U.S./Mexico
Great Basin	U.S.
Great Sandy	Australia
Patagonian	Argentina
Rub' al Khali	SaudiArabia/
	Oman/Yemen/United
	Arab Emirates
Taklimakan	China

13 letters

Great Salt Lake	Utah
Great Victoria	Australia

Major Earthquakes

(with location and dates)

4 letters

Iran		1978
Iran		1997
Kobe	Japan	1995

5 letters

Chile		1960
Gansu	China	1920,
		1932
India		1993

6 letters

Alaska	U.S.	1964, 1965
Oaxaca	Mexico	1999
Taiwan		1999

7 letters

Antioch	Syria	AD 526
Armenia		1988
Managua	Nicaragua	1972
Messina	Italy	1908
Shaanxi	China	1556

8 letters

Hokkaido	Japan	1730
Calcutta	India	1737
Yokohama	Japan	1923
Chimbote	Peru	1970
Tangshan	China	1976

9 letters

New Madrid	Missouri	1811

10 letters

Charleston	South Carolina	1886
Mexico City	Mexico	1985

Los Angeles	(Northridge) California	1994

11 letters

Afghanistan	1997,1998

12 letters

San Francisco	California	1906,1989

13 letters

Guatemala City	Guatemala	1976

Bridges

(with location)

3 letters

Bay (San Francisco-Oakland Bay)	California
Key	Maryland

5 letters

Cairo	Illinois/Kentucky
Chain	District of Columbia/Virginia
Forth	Scotland
Peace	New York/Ontario
Sighs, Bridge of	Italy
Tobin	Massachusetts

6 letters

Bourne (Sagamore)	Massachusetts
Humber	England
Pinang	Malaysia
Quebec	Quebec
Rialto	Italy
Severn	England

7 letters

Avignon	France
Bayonne	New York/New Jersey
Bendorf	Germany
Huang Ho	China
Rainbow	New York
Remagen	Germany

8 letters

Bosporus	Turkey
Brooklyn	New York
Goethals	New York/New Jersey
Hell Gate (rail)	New York
Mackinac (Straits)	Michigan
Pont-Neuf	France
Sagamore	Massachusetts
Transbay	California

9 letters

Angostura (Suspension)	Venezuela
Tappan Zee	New York

10 letters

Ambassador	Michigan/Ontario
Arthur Kill	New York/New Jersey
Golden Gate	California
Kosciusko	New York
Queensboro (59th Street)	New York
Rio-Niteroi	Brazil
Royal Gorge	Colorado
Storebaelt (East Bridge)	Denmark
Tagus River	Portugal
Throgs Neck	New York
Triborough	New York

Bridges *(continued)*

11 letters

Gladesville	Australia
Menai Straits	Wales
Oland Island	Sweden
Walt Whitman	Pennsylvania/ New Jersey

12 letters

Akashi Kaikyo	Japan
Bear Mountain	New York
Hooghly River	India
Lacey V. Murrow (Floating)	Washington
Seaway Skyway	New York
Williamsburg	New York

13 letters

Chesapeake Bay (Bridge-Tunnel)	Virginia
Confederation	Prince Edward Island/ New Brunswick
New River Gorge	West Virginia
Pierre Laporte	Quebec
Pulaski Skyway	New Jersey
Second Narrows	British Columbia
Tacoma-Narrows	Washington

14 letters

Jacques Cartier	Quebec
Sunshine Skyway	Florida

15 letters

Bronx-Whitestone (Whitestone)	New York
Galloping Gertie	Washington (former Tacoma Narrows Bridge, destroyed 1940)
Overseas Highway	Florida
Pont des Artistes	France

16 letters

Benjamin Franklin (Ben Franklin)	Pennsylvania/ New Jersey
Delaware Memorial	New Jersey/ Delaware
George Washington	New York/ New Jersey
Starrucca Viaduct (rail)	Pennsylvania
Verrazano-Narrows	New York
Zarate-Brazo Largo	Argentina

17 letters

Lake Pontchartrain (Causeway)	Louisiana

19 letters

Outerbridge Crossing	New York/ New Jersey

22 letters

San Francisco-Oakland Bay	California

Dams

(with location)

4 letters

Guri	Venezuela
Mica	Canada
Oahe	South Dakota

5 letters

Davis	Nevada/Arizona
Iguri	Georgia
Nurek	Tajikistan
Rogun	Tajikistan

6 letters

Chivor	Colombia
Croton	New York
Folsom	California
Hoover (Boulder)	Nevada
Itaipú	Paraguay
Kariba	Zambia, Zimbabwe
Mangla	Pakistan
Manic 2	Quebec
Manic 5 (Barrage Daniel-Johnson)	
Quebec	
McNary	Washington/Oregon
Parker	California/Arizona
Supung	Korea
Vaiont	Italy

7 letters

Atatürk	Turkey
Boulder (Hoover)	Nevada
El Cajón	Honduras
Fengman	China

John Day	Oregon/Washington
Tarbela	Pakistan
Turcuruí	Brazil

8 letters

Akosombo	Ghana
Fort Peck	Montana
Garrison	North Dakota
Oroville	California

9 letters

Chicoasén	Mexico
Mauvoisin	Switzerland

10 letters

Bonneville	Oregon
Glen Canyon	Arizona
Three Gorges	China
W.A.C. Bennett	British Columbia

11 letters

Chief Joseph	Washington
Grand Coulee	Washington

12 letters

Aswan High Dam	Egypt
Grand Dixence	Switzerland

19 letters

New Cornelia Tailings	Arizona

Canals

(With location. Element "canal" is not included in letter count.)

4 letters

Erie (Canal)	New York
Kiel	Germany
Love (Canal)	New York
Suez (Canal)	Egypt
Thal (Canal)	Pakistan

5 letters

Grand (Canal)	China, Italy
Trent (Canal; or Trent-Severn Waterway)	Ontario

6 letters

Gezira (Canals)	Sudan
Moscow (Canal)	Russia
Panama (Canal)	Panama
Rideau (Canal)	Ontario

7 letters

Cape Cod (Canal)	Massachusetts
Corinth (Canal)	Greece
Lachine (Canal)	Quebec

8 letters

Volga-Don (Canal)	Russia

10 letters

Grand Union (Canal)	England

11 letters

All-American (Canal)	Arizona/California

12 letters

Miami and Erie (Canal)	Ohio

13 letters

Western Yamuna (Canal)	India

16 letters

Baltimore and Ohio (Canal)	Maryland/District of Columbia/West Virginia
Illinois Waterway	Illinois

17 letters

Delaware and Hudson (Canal)	New York
New York State Barge (Canal)	New York

18 letters

Cauvery Delta System	India
Delaware and Raritan (Canal)	New Jersey
Houston Ship Channel	Texas

19 letters

Manchester Ship (Canal)	England
Saint Lawrence Seaway	New York/Ontario/Quebec

22 letters

Chicago Sanitary and Ship (Canal)	Illinois

24 letters

Gulf Intracoastal Waterway	U.S.

28 letters

Atlantic Intracoastal Waterway	U.S.

TRANSPORT

Motor Vehicles

2 letters
RV

3 letters
bus
cab
car
4X4
ATV
SUV
van

4 letters
duck
DUKW
4-by-4
Jeep (*trademark*)
kart
limo
Mini
  (*trademark*)
semi
tank
taxi
tram

5 letters
coach
coupé
crate
float
sedan
truck
wagon
wreck

6 letters
camper
digger
estate
go-kart
grader
hearse
hot rod
humvee

jitney
midget (racer)
saloon
short
tanker
tourer
wheels

7 letters
backhoe
chopper
cruiser
flivver
hard top
Indy car
omnibus
open top
race car
soft top
tour bus
tractor
trailer

8 letters
carryall
dragster
golf cart
gypsy cab
low-rider
rally car
roadster
runabout
snowplow
stock car

9 letters
ambulance
automatic
bubble car
bulldozer
cabriolet
charabanc
dump truck
dune buggy
18-wheeler

half-track
hatchback
Land Rover
  (*trademark*)
limousine
off-roader
patrol car
racing car
sports car
sprint car
streetcar

10 letters
armored car
automobile
beach buggy
bookmobile
crash wagon
fire engine
hackney cab
juggernaut
light truck
mobile home
motorcycle
paddy wagon
removal van
snowmobile
tracklayer
trolleybus

11 letters
bloodmobile
Caterpillar
  (*trademark*)
convertible
electric car
people mover
semitrailer
steamroller
stretch limo
transporter

12 letters
garbage truck
monster truck

motor caravan
station wagon

13 letters
delivery truck
forklift truck
people carrier
tandem trailer

14 letters
articulated bus
car transporter
crawler tractor
Stanley Steamer
tractor-trailer

15 letters
double-decker
  bus
refrigerated van

16 letters
combine
  harvester
stretch
  limousine

17 letters
all-terrain
  vehicle
four-wheel-drive
  car

19 letters
recreational
  vehicle

20 letters
public service
  vehicle
sports utility
  vehicle

Motorless Vehicles

3 letters
cab
fly
gig
rig

4 letters
cart
drag
dray
trap
wain

5 letters
brake
break
buggy
coach
sulky
wagon

6 letters
calash
chaise

fiacre
gharry
hansom
herdic
landau
oxcart
surrey

7 letters
bicycle
britzka
chariot
dog cart
droshky
hackney
hay-cart
haywain
phaeton
tilbury
travois
trishaw
tumbrel (or
  tumbril)
vis-à-vis

8 letters
barouche
brougham
Cape cart
carriage
carriole
carry-all
clarence
curricle
equipage
rickshaw
rockaway
tricycle
Victoria

9 letters
buckboard
jinriksha (or jin-
  rikisha)
tarantass
wagonette

10 letters
four-in-hand

jinrikisha (or jin-
  riksha)
post-chaise
stagecoach

11 letters
jaunting car
wheelbarrow

12 letters
coach-and-four
covered wagon
soapbox racer

13 letters
spider phaeton

14 letters
Conestoga
  wagon

15 letters
prairie schooner

Vehicle Parts

3 letters
ABS
cam

4 letters
axle
boot
cowl
dash
gate
gear
hood
horn
seal
wing

5 letters
brake

choke
crank
gauge
reach
rotor
shaft
shift
sprag
stick
strut
trunk
valve

6 letters
air bag
bonnet
bumper
clutch

fender
grille
hubcap
lug nut
oil pan
piston
points
tow bar
winker

7 letters
blinker
bushing
chassis
fan belt
flasher
gas tank
gearbox

low gear
magneto
muffler
reverse
roll bar
starter
tailfin
top gear

8 letters
bodywork
camshaft
cylinder
flywheel
fuel line
fuel pump
ignition
manifold

odometer
oil gauge
radiator
roof rack
seat belt
silencer
solenoid
tailpipe
track rod

9 letters

bench seat
brake drum
crankcase
dashboard
disc brake
drum brake
filler cap
freewheel
gear lever
generator
headlight
indicator
monocoque
overrider
radius rod
reflector
sidelight
spark plug
stop light

tail wheel
universal
water pump

10 letters

alternator
brake light
bucket seat
carburetor
drive train
fluid drive
hypoid gear
idiot light
radial tire
rumble seat
stick shift
suspension
tachograph
turn signal
windshield

11 letters

accelerator
backup light
distributor
hazard light
ignition key
number plate
power brakes
rocker panel

speedometer
splashboard

12 letters

cylinder head
differential
driving wheel
hood ornament
license plate
overrun brake
parking light
rotary engine
running board
starter motor
steering gear
transmission
trip odometer

13 letters

anti-lock brake
connecting rod
cruise control
pneumatic tire
power steering
rack-and-pinion
shock absorber
steering wheel

14 letters

automatic choke

emergency
  brake
four-wheel drive
hydraulic brake
propeller shaft
sideview mirror
steering column

15 letters

shoulder harness
universal joint
windshield
  wiper

16 letters

differential gear

18 letters

catalytic
  converter

19 letters

hydraulic
  suspension

21 letters

antilock braking
  system
automatic
  transmission

Famous Locomotives and Types of Locomotive

3 letters
TGV

5 letters
Chief
Mogul
Old 97

6 letters
Big Boy
Mikado
Rocket
Super C
Zephyr

7 letters
Blücher
Mistral
Novelty
Pioneer

8 letters
Canadian
Capitole
Colonial
Diplomat
Fast Mail
Night Owl

9 letters
Aerotrain
El Capitan
Le Shuttle
New Castle
South Wind

10 letters
Cannonball
Dixie Flyer
Fuel Foiler
Le Lyonnais
Locomotion
Metroliner
Sans Pareil

Super Chief

11 letters
Bullet train
Royal George

12 letters
Beyer-Garrett
Cuban Special
Puffing Billy

13 letters
Catch-Me-
  Who-Can
Coast Daylight

Famous Locomotives
and Types of Locomotive *(continued)*

Consolidation
Coyote Special
DeWitt Clinton
Empire Builder
Intercolonial
Orient Express
Overland Flyer
Pioneer Zephyr
Powhatan Arrow
Sunset Limited

14 letters
Capitol Limited
Federal Express
Flying
  Dutchman
Flying
  Scotsman
General
  Sherman
Pacific Express
Shasta Daylight

15 letters
Atlantic Express
Exposition Flyer
Midnight
  Special
National
  Limited
Overland
  Limited

16 letters
American
  Standard
Bar Harbor
  Express
California
  Zephyr
City of New
  Orleans
Columbian
  Express
Merchants
  Limited
New England

States
Super-
  Continental

17 letters
California
  Limited
North Coast
  Limited
North Shore
  Limited
San Francisco
  Chief

18 letters
Broadway
  Limited
Empire State
  Express
Fast Western
  Express
Sacramento
  Daylight

19 letters
Chicago Night
  Express
Pacific Fruit
  Express
Pennsylvania
  Limited
Southwestern
  Limited
Train à Grande
  Vitesse

22 letters
Best Friend of
  Charleston
Canadian
  Pacific Limited

23 letters
Twentieth
  Century
  Limited

Railroads, U.S. and Canada

*(Includes well-known abbreviations and acronyms. Words "railroad'"or "railway"
not included in number count. Ampersand [&] is counted as "and" = three letters.)*

3 letters
CSX
MKT
RFP
Via (Rail Canada)

4 letters
ATSF
Erie
Katy
LIRR

5 letters
B&O

C&O
D&H

6 letters
Amtrak
Frisco
Harlem
Pennsy
Wabash

7 letters
Chessie
Conrail
Georgia

Pacific
Reading
Santa Fe
Soo Line

8 letters
New Haven
Red River
Seaboard
Southern

9 letters
Fitchburg
Old Colony

Rio Grande
West Shore
Yellow Dog

10 letters

Burlington
Grand Trunk
Lackawanna
Long Island
Metro North
Nova Scotia
Petersburg
Rock Island

11 letters

Family Lines System
Granger Road
Hudson River
Penn Central
Sunset Route
Susquehanna

12 letters

Great Western
Iron Mountain
Maine Central
Pennsylvania
Union Pacific

13 letters

Denver Pacific
Great Northern
Jersey Central
Kansas Pacific
Lehigh Valley
Milwaukee Road
Mobile & Ohio
North Carolina

14 letters

Boston & Maine
Cairo & Fulton
Camden & Amboy
Central Pacific
Central Vermont
Erie, Lackawanna
Morris & Essex
New York Central
Red River Valley
Shore Line Route
Western Pacific

15 letters

Boston & Albany
Boston & Lowell
Canadian Pacific
Chicago & Alton
Illinois Central
Kentucky Central
Lehigh & Hudson
Michigan Central
Mohawk & Hudson
Nickel Plate Road
Norfolk Southern
Northern Central
Northern Pacific
Oregon Short Line
Seaboard Air Line
Southern Pacific
Texas & Pacific
Virginia Central
Water Level Route
Western Maryland

16 letters

Allegheny Portage
Baltimore & Ohio
Canadian National
Canadian Northern
Cumberland Valley
Florida East Coast
Michigan Southern
New York & Harlem
Shenandoah Valley
Wisconsin Central

17 letters

Atchison & Topeka
Atlantic Coast Line
California Western
Camden & Atlantic
Central
  New England
Chesapeake & Ohio
Delaware & Hudson
Durham & Southern
Georgia & Florida
Grand Trunk Pacific
Gulf, Mobile & Ohio
Indiana & Madison
Norfolk & Western
Seaboard Coastline

18 letters

Atlantic & Pacific
Bangor & Aroostook
Boston & Worcester
Burlington Northern
Central of New Jersey
Cleveland & Toledo
Kansas City Southern
Montreal & Lachine
Seaboard & Roanoke
Western & Atlantic

19 letters

Atlanta & West Point
Boston & Providence
Colorado & Southern
Minnesota & Pacific
Oregon & California
Richmond & Danville
Rio Grande & Western
Saint Paul & Pacific
Utica & Schenectady

20 letters

Albany & Susquehanna
Charleston & Hamburg
Chicago & Rock Island
Portsmouth & Roanoke
Richmond &
  Allegheny
Saint Andres & Quebec
Wilmington & Raleigh

21 letters

Cincinnati & Lake Erie
Galena & Chicago
  Union
Marietta & Cincinnati
Richmond &
  Petersburg

22 letters

Buffalo & Niagara Falls
Hannibal & Saint
  Joseph
Louisville & Nashville
Mississippi & Missouri
Missouri, Kansas &
  Texas
Montgomery & West
  Point

Railroads, U.S. and Canada *(continued)*

Philadelphia &
  Reading
Providence &
  Worcester
Toledo, Peoria &
  Western

23 letters

Carolina &
  Northwestern
Detroit Toledo &
  Ironton
Houston, East & West
  Texas
Nashville &
  Chattanooga

24 letters

Atchison, Topeka &
  Santa Fe
Duluth Winnipeg &
  Pacific
New York, Ontario &
  Western
Rio Grande-Missouri
  Pacific
Saint Lawrence &
  Atlantic

25 letters

Burlington Northern
  Santa Fe
Champlain & Saint
  Lawrence
Chicago & Eastern
  Illinois
Denver, South Park &
  Pacific
Middle Tennessee &
  Alabama
Pittsburgh & West
  Virginia
Spokane Portland &
  Seattle
Yazoo and Mississippi
  Valley

26 letters

Atlantic, Mississippi &
  Ohio
Chicago, Burlington &
  Quincy
New York, New Haven
  & Hartford
New York, West Shore
  & Buffalo
Ogdensburg & Lake
  Champlain
Pittsburgh &
  Connellsville

27 letters

Chicago, Rock Island
  & Pacific
Lake Shore &
  Michigan Central
Missouri & Northern
  Arkansas
New York, Chicago &
  Saint Louis
New York, Westchester
  & Boston

28 letters

Chicago, Saint Paul &
  Fond du Lac
Delaware, Lackawanna
  & Western
Galveston Houston &
  Henderson
Lake Shore &
  Michigan Southern
Saint Paul & Sault
  Sainte Marie

29 letters

Chicago, South Shore
  & South Bend
Kansas City, Fort
  Scott & Memphis
Pittsburgh, Fort Wayne
  & Chicago
Toledo, Walhonding
  Valley & Ohio

30 letters

Charleston, Cincinnati
  & Chicago
Columbus, Hocking
  Valley & Toledo

31 letters

East Tennessee,
  Virginia & Georgia
National
  Transcontinental
  Railway
Saint Louis Kansas
  City & Northern
Saint Paul,
  Minneapolis &
  Manitoba

32 letters

Richmond,
  Fredericksburg &
  Potomac
Staten Island &
  Chicago South Shore
Wilmington Baltimore
  & Washington

33 letters

Saint Louis, Iron
  Mountain &
  Southern

34 letters

Georgetown,
  Breckenridge &
  Leadville
Michigan Southern &
  Northern Indiana

35 letters

Chicago, Milwaukee,
  Saint Paul & Pacific

Ships and Boats

3 letters
gig
tug

4 letters
dory
duck
DUKW
punt
raft
scow

5 letters
barge
botel
canoe
E-boat
ferry
kayak
laker
liner
Q-ship
  (or Q-boat)
shell
tramp
umiak

6 letters
argosy
bireme
bottom
dinghy
dugout
galley
launch
packet
randan
sampan
tanker

tender
whaler
wherry

7 letters
bumboat
charter
coaster
collier
coracle
crabber
cruiser
dredger
drifter
gondola
iceboat
jetboat
lighter
pinnace
pirogue
pontoon
rowboat
sculler
trawler
trireme
tugboat

8 letters
car ferry
coal ship
fireboat
flagship
flat boat
Indiaman
Ironclad
keelboat
lifeboat
longboat
long ship

mailboat
outboard
showboat
surfboat
York boat

9 letters
cable ship
canal boat
cargo ship
ferryboat
freighter
houseboat
hydrofoil
motorboat
oil tanker
outrigger
party boat
pilot boat
powerboat
ship's boat
speedboat
steamboat
steamship
water taxi
whaleboat

10 letters
battleship
cruise ship
dragon boat
hovercraft
hydroplane
icebreaker
monkey-boat
narrow boat
ocean liner
paddle boat
school ship

Viking ship (or
  long ship)

11 letters
bulk carrier
factory ship
sailing ship
side-wheeler
supertanker
torpedo boat

12 letters
cabin cruiser
hospital ship
mosquito boat
sternwheeler
tramp steamer
troop carrier

13 letters
canot du maître
cigarette boat
container ship
paddle steamer
paddlewheeler
passenger ship
revenue cutter
roll-on roll-off

14 letters
blockade runner
sportfisherman

16 letters
inflatable dinghy

22 letters
amphibious
  landing craft

Naval Vessels

3 letters

DDE	destroyer escort
LCA	landing craft assault
LCM	landing craft mechanized
LCT	landing craft tank
LSD	landing ship dock
LSI	landing ship infantry
LSM	landing ship medium
LST	landing ship tank
MTB	motor torpedo boat
ram	
sub	

4 letters

LCIL	landing craft infantry large
LCVP	landing craft vehicle personnel
LSMR	landing ship medium rocket

5 letters

e-boat
sloop
U-boat

6 letters

cutter
picket (boat)

PT	boat patrol torpedo

tanker
tender
tin can

7 letters

carrier
collier
cruiser
flattop
frigate
monitor

8 letters

corvette
flagship

9 letters

destroyer
mine layer
sub chaser
sub tender
submarine

10 letters

battleship
patrol boat
repair ship

11 letters

battlewagon
capital ship
dreadnought
Higgins boat
landing ship
Liberty Ship
minesweeper
missile ship
torpedo boat

12 letters

Aegis cruiser
floating dock
  (or floating drydock)

heavy cruiser
landing craft
light cruiser

13 letters

battle cruiser
ship of the line

14 letters

Aegis destroyer
ammunition ship
missile frigate
seaplane tender

15 letters

aircraft carrier
destroyer escort
submarine chaser
submarine tender

16 letters

missile submarine
motor torpedo boat
pocket battleship
Polaris submarine

17 letters

replenishment ship

19 letters

fast attack submarine

21 letters

fast combat support
  ship

Sailing Ships and Boats

4 letters
dhow
junk
pink
proa
scow
yawl

5 letters
ketch
razee
sabot
skiff
sloop
smack
xebec
yacht

6 letters
barque
caique
cutter
dinghy
galley

hooker
lateen
lugger
nuggar
rigger
tartan

7 letters
caravel
carrack
catboat
clipper
dromond
felucca
frigate
galleon
galliot
lighter
pinnace
polacre
shallop
snekkja
12-meter

8 letters
fireship
galleass
in-rigger
longboat
longship
man-of-war
monohull
schooner
skipjack
tall ship
trimaran

9 letters
catamaran
jolly boat
multihull
one-design
outrigger
turnabout

10 letters
barkentine (or
  barquentine)

brigantine
dragon boat
full-rigger
gaff cutter
sloop of war
windjammer

11 letters
barquentine
  (or barkentine)
merchantman
twelve-meter

12 letters
merchant ship
square-rigger

17 letters
hermaphrodite
  brig

Nautical Terms

3 letters
aft
bow
fid
gam
jib
lee
log
rig
way

4 letters
ahoy
alee
alow
beam
bitt
boom

bo's'n
bunt
clew
fore
frap
gaff
hold
hull
jibe
keel
knot
line
main
mate
poop
port
prow
reef

spar
stem
swab
vang
veer
wake
warp

5 letters
aback
abaft
abeam
aloft
apeak
aport
atrip
avast
awash

belay
berth
bilge
bosun
bouse
cable
caulk
cleat
Genoa
hatch
hawse
hitch
jenny
kedge
orlop
screw
stern
truck

Nautical Terms (*continued*)

vigia
watch
weigh

6 letters

astern
aweigh
becket
bridge
bunker
burgee
burton
drogue
fathom
fo'c'sle
galley
hawser
kelson
  (*or* keelson)
league
lubber
mizzen
poppet
purser
shroud
splice
stoker
tackle
yawing

7 letters

admiral
ballast
boomkin

boxhaul
bulwark
easting
euphroe
futtock
gangway
grapnel
gunwale
keelson
  (*or* kelson)
killick
lanyard
outhaul
pontoon
quarter
scupper
scuttle
sea mile
tonnage
transom
yardarm

8 letters

aweather
binnacle
boltrope
bowsprit
bulkhead
coxswain
crowfoot
dog watch
downhaul
garboard
halyards

keelhaul
larboard
moorings
pitching
ratlines
scuppers
taffrail
windlass
windward

9 letters

about ship
amidships
broadside
companion
crosstree
crow's nest
freeboard
spinnaker
starboard
sundowner
waterline

10 letters

batten down
deadlights
deadweight
first watch
fore and aft
forecastle
landlubber
supercargo

11 letters

belaying pin
Flinders bar
lubber's hole
middle watch
quarterdeck
wing and wing

12 letters

athwartships
companionway
flying bridge
marlinespike
nautical mile
plimsoll line

13 letters

Admiralty mile
quartermaster

14 letters

Bristol fashion
dolphin striker
horse latitudes
Roaring Forties
superstructure

15 letters

companion
  ladder
Davy Jones'
  locker

Ports

3 letters

Bar
Fao
Gao
Hué
Lae
Lax
Vác

4 letters

Acre
Aden
Apra
Baku
Bari
Bata
Bodø

Boma
Bône
Cebu
Cóbh
Díli
Erie
Faro
Gary

Hilo
Hull
Ifni
Irún
Kemi
Kiel
Kiev
Kobe

Lomé
Naha
Nuuk
Oban
Omsk
Oran
Ordu
Oulu
Pegu
Pori
Pula
Riga
Rota
Ruse
Safi
Sète
Suez
Suva
Tema
Tver
Tyre
Umeå
Wuhu

5 letters

Adria
Akita
Ambon
Anzio
Aqaba
Arica
Assab
Banff
Basra
Beira
Belém
Benin
Bonny
Brega
Brest
Cadiz
Cairo
Calvi
Canea
Colón
Dakar
Davao
Digby
Dover
Dubai
Eilat

Fargo
Fiume
Gabès
Galle
Gävle
Genoa
Ghent
Gijón
Haeju
Haifa
Hanau
Handa
Hanko
Horta
Hydra
Ibiza
Izmir
Izmit
Jaffa
Jilin
Kazan
Kerch
Kochi
Kotka
Lagos
La Paz
Larne
Lewes
Liège
Limón
Luleå
Lyons
Macao
Magwe
Mahón
Malmö
Masan
Mbini
Miami
Mocha
Mokpo
Murom
Nampo
Natal
Newry
Osaka
Ostia
Otaru
Pemba
Perth
Plock

Ponce
Poole
Praia
Prome
Pusan
Rabat
Rivne
Rouen
Salem
Ségou
Semey
Seria
Sidon
Sines
Sinop
Skien
Sligo
Sochi
Surat
Tampa
Tanga
Tokyo
Tomsk
Toruń
Tulsa
Tunis
Turku
Ulsan
Vaasa
Varna
Vidin
Volos
Wuhan
Yalta
Zadar

6 letters

Abadan
Agadir
Akashi
Albany
Amalfi
Ancona
Annaba
Aomori
Arklow
Ashdod
Aveiro
Avilés
Bamberg
Bangor

Banten
Bastia
Batumi
Beihai
Bejaa
Bergen
Bilbao
Biloxi
Bissau
Bombay
Bootle
Boston
Bremen
Burgas
Burnie
Calais
Callao
Camden
Chukot
Cochin
Dalian
Da Nang
Danzig
Dieppe
Dinard
Dingle
Douala
Dublin
Duluth
Dundee
Durban
Durrës
Elblag
Fécamp
Galatz
Galway
Garoua
Gdańsk
Gdynia
Gomera
Haikou
Halden
Hamina
Havana
Hobart
Hrodna
Huelva
Inchon
Jaffna
Jarrow
Jeddah

Ports *(continued)*

Juneau	Owendo	Yambol	Dhahran
Kaluga	Padang	Yantai	Drammen
Kampot	Panaji		Dubuque
Kankan	Paraná	*7 letters*	Dunedin
Kaunas	Patras	Aalborg	Esjberg
Kelang	Peoria	Abidjan	Everett
Keokuk	Pesaro	Ajaccio	Exmouth
Kigoma	Phuket	Akranes	Fukuoka
Laredo	Pyrgos	Algiers	Funchal
Larvik	Quebec	Almeria	Geelong
Lobito	Quilon	Antalya	Giurgiu
London	Quincy	Antibes	Gourock
Lorain	Rabaul	Antwerp	Grimsby
Luanda	Racine	Aracajú	Guaymas
Lübeck	Rashid	Arecibo	Halifax
Lüshun	Rawson	Arendal	Hamburg
Maceió	Recife	Astoria	Harwich
Madras	Rhodes	Ballina	Hodeida
Malabo	Rijeka	Bangkok	Honiara
Málaga	Ryazan	Barisal	Horsens
Manado	Samara	Bassein	Hsinchu
Manama	Samsun	Bay City	Imabari
Manaus	Santos	Bayonne	Ipswich
Mersin	Sarnia	Belfast	Iquique
Mobile	Sasebo	Berbera	Iquitos
Mohács	Sittwe	Bharuch	Karachi
Muscat	Skikda	Bizerta	Kaválla
Mystic	Sousse	Bristol	Keelung
Nacala	St.-Malo	Buffalo	Kenitra
Nagoya	Sydney	Bunbury	Kenosha
Namibe	Szeged	Bushehr	Key West
Nantes	Tacoma	Calabar	Kherson
Napier	Thurso	Catania	Kismayu
Naples	Timaru	Catoosa	Kuching
Narvik	Tobruk	Cayenne	Kushiro
Nassau	Toledo	Chicago	Kyrenia
Nelson	Tonkin	Chilung	La Ceiba
Newark	Toulon	Cirebon	La Plata
Niamey	Tralee	Cologne	Larache
Ningbo	Tromsø	Colombo	Latakia
Nyborg	Ugarit	Conakry	Leghorn
Odense	Valdez	Coos Bay	Lerwick
Odessa	Vyatka	Cordova	Leticia
Oporto	Weihai	Corinto	Liepaja
Orange	Whitby	Corunna	Lorient
Osijek	Wismar	Cuttack	Malindi
Ostend	Wonsan	Dandong	Manzini
Ouidah	Xiamen	Detroit	Marsala

Massawa
Memphis
Messina
Mombasa
Mukalla
Münster
Mykonos
Nanaimo
Nauplia
Negombo
Nellore
Newport
New York
Niigata
Niihama
Niterói
Nobeoka
Norfolk
Oakland
Olympia
Paducah
Palermo
Pelotas
Piraeus
Qiqihar
Randers
Rangoon
Rosario
Roscoff
Rostock
Rybinsk
St. Louis
Salerno
San Juan
Santa Fe
São Luis
Sarapul
Seattle
Setúbal
Seville
Shantou
Sharjah
Šibenik
Shimizu
Sinuiju
Skagway
Stanley
Swansea
Szolnok
Tallinn
Tampico

Tangier
Tel Aviv
Tianjin
Tilbury
Toronto
Tottori
Trabzon
Trapani
Trieste
Tripoli
Ushuaia
Vallejo
Vitória
Wenzhou
Windsor
Wroclaw
Yakutsk
Yingkou

8 letters

Aabenraa
Aalesund
Abu Dhabi
Acapulco
Adelaide
Akrotiri
Akureyri
Alicante
Alleppey
Arbroath
Arrecife
Asunción
Babruysk
Balkhash
Barahona
Barletta
Beaumont
Belgrade
Belle-Ile
Benguela
Berenice
Biarritz
Bideford
Bismarck
Bordeaux
Boulogne
Brindisi
Brisbane
Buchanan
Caesarea
Cagliari

Calamata
Camagüey
Campeche
Castries
Changsha
Chetumal
Chimbote
Cooktown
Coquimbo
Damietta
Darmstad
Djibouti
Dortmund
Drogheda
Drouzhba
Falmouth
Flushing
Freeport
Fujairah
Fukuyama
Gisborne
Gonaves
Greenock
Haiphong
Hakodate
Halmstad
Hamilton
Helsinki
Holyhead
Honolulu
Istanbul
Jamnagar
Jayapura
Kamyshin
Keflavik
Kimchaek
Kineshma
Kingston
Kirkwall
Klaipeda
Kusadasi
La Spezia
Limassol
Mandalay
Mannheim
Mariupol
Matanzas
Mazatlán
Mbandaka
Mexicali
Miyazaki

Monastir
Montreal
Moulmein
Murmansk
Mytilene
Naestved
Nagasaki
Nakhodka
Narbonne
N'Djamena
Neijiang
Newhaven
Nykøbing
Nykøping
Pago Pago
Panchevo
Paysandú
Pembroke
Piacenza
Port Bell
Portland
Port Said
Pucallpa
Rajshahi
Ramsgate
Richmond
Roskilde
Rosslare
Salvador
Sandakan
San Diego
Santarém
Savannah
Semarang
Shanghai
Shizuoka
Silistra
Smolensk
Stockton
St. Tropez
Syracuse
Szczecin
Taganrog
Taichung
Tauranga
Tekirdag
Ullapool
Valencia
Valletta
Västerås
Veracruz

Ports *(continued)*

Victoria
Wanganui
Yokohama
Yokosuka

9 letters

Adamstown
Algeciras
Angoulême
Archangel
Ardrossan
Astrakhan
Baltimore
Barcelona
Berdyansk
Bhavnagar
Bundaberg
Bydgoszcz
Cartagena
Cherkassy
Chernigov
Cleveland
Concordia
Constanza
Cox's Bazar
Cuddalore
Dartmouth
Djajapura
Dordrecht
Dubrovnik
Elizabeth
Essaouira
Esztergom
Fall River
Famagusta
Flensburg
Fortaleza
Frankfurt
Fremantle
Galveston
Geraldton
Gladstone
Guayaquil
Hachinohe
Härnösand
Heilbronn
Heraklion
Immingham

Inhambane
Jakobstad
Jamestown
Jiaojiang
Jyväskylä
Kagoshima
Kaohsiung
Karlsruhe
Kimberley
King's Lynn
Kirkcaldy
Knoxville
Krasnodar
Kurashiki
Las Palmas
Liverpool
Lowestoft
Magdeburg
Mahajanga
Maldonado
Mangalore
Maracaibo
Mariehamn
Matamoros
Matsuyama
Milwaukee
Mogadishu
Morecambe
Mossel Bay
Nashville
Návpaktos
Newcastle
Oldenburg
Palembang
Pekanbaru
Pensacola
Peterhead
Phnom Penh
Pontianak
Porbandar
Port Blair
Port Louis
Porto Novo
Port Pirie
Port Sudan
Rethymnon
Reykjavik
Rio Grande

Rochester
Rotterdam
Saint John
St.-Nazaire
Santander
Sheerness
Smederovo
Stavanger
St. George's
Stockholm
Stranraer
Stuttgart
Sundsvall
Takamatsu
Tarragona
Toamasina
Togliatti
Tokushima
Tomakomai
Trondheim
Tuticorin
Uddevalla
Vancouver
Vicksburg
Vientiane
Volgograd
Walvis Bay
Whangarei
Yaroslavl
Yokkaichi
Zamboanga
Zeebrugge
Zhanjiang
Zonguldak
Zrenjanin

10 letters

Alexandria
Balikpapan
Basse-Terre
Belize City
Birkenhead
Bluefields
Bratislava
Bridgeport
Bridgetown
Cap Hatien
Casablanca

Cheboksary
Chittagong
Cienfuegos
Concepción
Copenhagen
Corrientes
East London
Esmeraldas
Felixstowe
Folkestone
Fray Bentos
Fredericia
Georgetown
George Town
Gothenburg
Greenville
Hammerfest
Hartlepool
Iskenderun
Karlskrona
Kitakyushu
Kompong Som
Kuwait City
La Rochelle
Leeuwarden
Libreville
Marseilles
Montego Bay
Montevideo
Mostaganem
Mymensingh
New Bedford
New Orleans
Norrköping
Nouadhibou
Nouakchott
Oranjestad
Paramaribo
Pontevedra
Port Arthur
Port-Gentil
Port Kelang
Port Rashid
Portsmouth
Puntarenas
Rockingham
Saint-Denis
San Nicolas

Sebastapol
Strasbourg
Sunderland
Swakopmund
Talcahuano
Thunder Bay
Townsville
Wellington
Wilmington
Wollongong
Workington
Ziguinchor

11 letters

Antofagasta
Antseranana
Arkhangelsk
Bahía Blanca
Bandar Abbas
Banjarmasin
Brazzaville
Bremerhaven
Bridlington
Brownsville
Charlestown
Dar es Salaam
Encarnación
Fredrikstad
Grangemouth
Helsingborg
Kaliningrad
Kompong Cham
Londonderry
Makhachkala
Mar del Plata
Maryborough
Minneapolis
Nakhon Sawan
Narayanganj
New Plymouth
Newport News
Pietarsaari

Port Augusta
Port Hedland
Pôrto Alegre
Puerto Montt
Rio Gallegos
Rockhampton
Rostov-on-Don
Southampton
Sterlitamak
Willemstadt

12 letters

Aigues-Mortes
Alexandretta
Barranquilla
Buenaventura
Cagnes-sur-Mer
Frederiksted
Grevenmacher
Jacksonville
Khorramshahr
Kota Kinabalu
Kristiansand
Kristiansund
Ludwigshafen
Milford Haven
New Caledonia
New Hampshire
Novorossiysk
Petrozavodsk
Philadelphia
Ponta Delgada
Port-au-Prince
Prince Rupert
Puerto Cortés
San Sebastian
Santo Domingo
South Shields
St. Petersburg
Thessaloníki
Ujung Pandang
Villahermosa

13 letters

Aschaffenburg
Bandar
  Lampung
Carrickfergus
Châtellerault
Christiansted
Ciudad Bolivar
Civitavecchia
Coatzacoalcos
Corpus Christi
Dahlak Islands
Ellesmere Port
Great Yarmouth
Ho Chi Minh
  City
Hook of Holland
Machilipatnam
Middlesbrough
New Providence
Petropavlovsk
Port Elizabeth
Puerto Barrios
Torre del Greco
Trois-Rivières
Visakhapatnam

14 letters

Châlon-sur-
  Saône
Dniepropetrovsk
Loyalty Islands
Port
  Sweetenham
Santiago de
  Cuba
Viana do Castelo

15 letters

Alexandroupolis
Angra do
  Heroismo

Barrancabermeja
Barrow-in-
  Furness
Charlotte Amalie
Nizhniy
  Novgorod
Rochefort-sur-
  Mer

16 letters

Dniprodzerzhinsk

17 letters

Comodoro
  Rivadavia

18 letters

Castellón de la
  Plana
Gorzów
  Wiclkopolski
Jervis Bay
  Territory

19 letters

Linea de la
  Concepción
Santa Cruz de
  Tenerife

21 letters

Queen
  Charlotte
  Islands

25 letters

Aleksandrovsk-
  Sakhalinskiy

Aircraft

5 letters
drone

6 letters
Airbus
  (*trademark*)
bomber
canard
glider
pusher

7 letters
biplane

fighter
jump jet

8 letters
aerodyne
airliner
autogiro
Concorde
jet plane
jumbo jet
seaplane
triplane
turbofan

turbojet

9 letters
amphibian
freighter
swing-wing
taxiplane
turboprop

10 letters
dive bomber
flying boat
gyrocopter

helicopter
microlight
multiplane

11 letters
interceptor

12 letters
night fighter

13 letters
convertiplane
fighter-bomber

Military Aircraft

(Includes types, in lower-case, and make/model names in upper case. Individual aircraft name in italics.)

3 letters
MiG
PBY
Yak

4 letters
Avro
Bear
Hawk
Skua
Spad
Zero

5 letters
AWACS
Bison
Camel
chase
Cobra
drone
Orion

6 letters
Fokker
glider
Macchi

Meteor
patrol
tanker
Voodoo

7 letters
Avenger
Bearcat
Bristol
Buffalo
Corsair
Dornier
Firefly
Halifax
Heinkel
Hellcat
Junkers
Mustang
Neptune
pursuit
Sopwith
Stealth
Tempest
trainer
Tupolev
Typhoon

Vickers
Warhawk
Wildcat

8 letters
Blenheim
Catalina
Enola Gay
Fortress
Ilyushin
Intruder
kamikaze
Marauder
Mosquito
Nieuport
Sikorsky
Spitfire
Tigercat
Tomahawk
Yakovlev
Zeppelin

9 letters
Barracuda
Blackhawk
Focke-Wulf

Gladiator
Hurricane
Lancaster
Liberator
Lightning
Super Fort
Swordfish
transport

10 letters
Black Widow
dive bomber
flying boat
Mitsubishi
Sunderland

11 letters
interceptor
Thunderbolt

12 letters
flying boxcar
night fighter
patrol bomber
Shooting Star

13 letters
fighter-bomber
Messerschmitt
stealth bomber
torpedo bomber

14 letters
Flying Fortress
reconnaissance
stealth fighter

17 letters
helicopter
gunship

Major Airports

(with cities or areas served)

3 letters
BWI	Baltimore-Washington Intl.
DFW	Dallas-Fort Worth Intl.
JFK	See JOHN F. KENNEDY
LAX	Los Angeles Intl.

4 letters
Love (Field)	Dallas
Orly	Paris

5 letters
Hobby (Field)	Houston
Kimpo	Seoul
Logan	Boston
O'Hare	Chicago
Tegel	Berlin

6 letters
Changi	Singapore
Dorval	Montreal
Dulles	Washington
Findel	Luxembourg
Juarez	Mexico City
Linate	Milan
Midway	Chicago
Narita	Tokyo
Okecie	Warsaw
Subang	Kuala Lumpur

7 letters
Arlanda	Stockholm
Ataturk	Istanbul
Barajas	Madrid
Bradley	Hartford
Burbank	Los Angeles
Douglas	Charlotte
Fornebu	Oslo
Gatwick	London
Hopkins	Cleveland
Lambert	St. Louis
Meacham (Field)	Fort Worth
Mirabel	Montreal
Pearson	Toronto
Stewart	Newburgh, N.Y.
T. F. Green	Providence

8 letters
Cointrin	Geneva
Heathrow	London
Hongqiao	Shanghai
McCarran	Las Vegas
National	Washington
Schiphol	Amsterdam
Stansted	London

9 letters
Fiumicino (Leonardo da Vinci)	Rome
John Wayne	Lost Angeles
La Guardia	New York
Lindbergh (Field)	San Diego
MacArthur	Long Island, N.Y.
Sky Harbor	Phoenix
Stapleton (closed)	Denver

10 letters
Hartsfield	Atlanta
King Khaled	Riyadh
Will Rogers	Oklahoma City

11 letters
John F. Kennedy	New York
Ninoy Aquino	Manila
Tullamarine	Melbourne
Wayne County	Detroit

12 letters
Echterdingen	Stuttgart

Major Airports *(continued)*

Benito Juarez	Mexico City	**14 letters**	
Mid-Continent	Wichita	Helsinki-Vantaa	Helsinki
Sheremetyevo	Moscow	Kingsford Smith	Sydney
		Luis Muñoz Marin	San Juan

13 letters

Chiang Kai-Shek	Taipei	**15 letters**	
Seattle-Tacoma (SeaTac)	Seattle,	Charles De Gaulle	Paris
	Tacoma	Dallas-Fort Worth	Dallas
Soekarno Hatta	Jakarta	Leonardo da Vinci	Rome
		(Fiumicino)	

— SCIENCE AND TECHNOLOGY —

Units of Measurement

2 letters

em
en

3 letters

amu
are
bel
bit
cup
day
erg
gal
kip
lea
lux
mho
mil
nit
ohm
rad
rod
tog
ton
var

4 letters

acre
baud
butt
byte
cord
dyne
foot
gill
gram
gray
hank
hour
inch
knot
last
line
link
mile
mole

nail
octa
okta
peck
phon
phot
pica
pint
pipe
pole
rood
slug
span
torr
volt
watt
week
yard
year

5 letters

cable
carat
chain
curie
cusec
cycle
daraf
darcy
epoch
farad
fermi
gamma
gauss
grade
grain
henry
hertz
joule
liter
lumen
meter
minim
month
neper
ounce

perch
point
poise
pound
quart
sabin
stilb
stone
tesla
therm
tonne
weber
x-unit

6 letters

ampere
barrel
bushel
candle
cental
dalton
degree
denier
fathom
firkin
gallon
jansky
kelvin
league
micron
minute
morgan
newton
noggin
parsec
pascal
radian
second
stokes

7 letters

air mile
calorie
candela
centner
chronon

coulomb
decibel
diopter
faraday
fresnel
furlong
gilbert
kiloton
maxwell
megaton
oersted
poundal
quarter
quintal
röntgen
scruple
siemens
sievert

8 letters

angstrom
centiarc
hogshead
kilogram
magneton
millibar
puncheon
quartern
roentgen

9 letters

becquerel
degree-day
kilderkin
kilocycle
kilometer
light year
steradian
troy ounce

10 letters

atmosphere
barleycorn
Hoppus foot
horsepower
Mach number

Units of Measurement *(continued)*

micrometer
rutherford

11 letters
circular mil
millimicron

12 letters
electronvolt

kilowatt-hour
nautical mile

13 letters
hundredweight

14 letters
atomic mass
  unit

16 letters
astronomical
  unit
Board of Trade
  Unit
gram-atomic
  weight

18 letters
British thermal
  unit

19 letters
gram-molecular
  weight

Elementary Particles

4 letters
kaon
muon
pion

5 letters
boson
gluon
meson
quark

6 letters
baryon
hadron
lepton
photon
proton

7 letters
fermion
neutron
nucleon

8 letters
electron
neutrino
positron

9 letters
antiquark

10 letters
antiproton

11 letters
antineutrino
psi particle
tau particle

12 letters
antielectron

14 letters
lambda particle

Chemical Elements

(with symbols)

3 letters
tin   Sn

4 letters
gold   Au
iron   Fe
lead   Pb
neon   Ne
zinc   Zn

5 letters
argon   Ar
boron   B
radon   Rn
xenon   Xe

6 letters
barium   Ba
carbon   C
cerium   Ce
cobalt   Co
copper   Cu
curium   Cm
erbium   Er
helium   He
indium   In
iodine   I
nickel   Ni
osmium   Os
oxygen   O
radium   Ra

silver   Ag
sodium   Na

7 letters
arsenic   As
bismuth   Bi
bohrium   Bh
bromine   Br
cadmium   Cd
caesium   Cs
calcium   Ca
dubnium   Db
fermium   Fm
gallium   Ga
hafnium   Hf

hahnium	Ha	lutetium	Lu	ruthenium	Ru
hassium	Hs	nitrogen	N	strontium	Sr
holmium	Ho	nobelium	Nb	tellurium	Te
iridium	Ir	platinum	Pt	ytterbium	Yb
krypton	Kr	polonium	Po	zirconium	Zr
lithium	Li	rubidium	Rb		
mercury	Hg	samarium	Sm	**10 letters**	
niobium	Nb	scandium	Sc	dysprosium	Dy
rhenium	Re	selenium	Se	gadolinium	Gd
rhodium	Rh	tantalum	Ta	lawrencium	Lr
silicon	Si	thallium	Tl	meitnerium	Mt
sulphur	S	titanium	Ti	molybdenum	Mo
terbium	Tb	tungsten (wolfram)	W	phosphorus	P
thorium	Th	vanadium	V	promethium	Pm
thulium	Tm			seaborgium	Sg
uranium	U	**9 letters**		technetium	Tc
wolfram (tungsten)	W	aluminum	Al		
yttrium	Y	americium	Am	**11 letters**	
		berkelium	Bk	californium	Cf
8 letters		beryllium	Be	einsteinium	Es
actinium	Ac	germanium	Ge	mendelevium	Md
antimony	Sb	lanthanum	La		
astatine	At	magnesium	Mg	**12 letters**	
chlorine	Cl	manganese	Mn	praseodymium	Pr
chromium	Cr	neodymium	Nd	protactinium	Pa
europium	Eu	neptunium	Np		
fluorine	F	palladium	Pd	**13 letters**	
francium	Fr	plutonium	Pu	rutherfordium	Rf
hydrogen	H	potassium	K		

Mathematical Terms

3 letters
set
sum

4 letters
base
cube
mean
node
ring
root
sine
surd

5 letters
array

digit
field
group
limit
locus
power
proof
ratio
unity

6 letters
cosine
factor
googol
matrix
median

origin
scalar
secant
series
square
subset
tensor
vector

7 letters
algebra
divisor
formula
fractal
integer
inverse

Mathematical Terms (continued)

modulus
product
tangent
unknown

8 letters

abscissa
addition
analysis
binomial
calculus
cosecant
cube root
division
equation
exponent
fraction
function
fuzzy set
gradient
identity
Julia set
Lie group
multiple
operator
quotient
solution
sub-group
variable

9 letters

algorithm
asymptote
Cantor set
conjugate
cotangent
expansion
factorial
integrand
intercept
iteration
logarithm
numerator
parameter
recursion
remainder
set theory
transform

10 letters

derivative
difference
eigenvalue
fractal set
game theory
googolplex
inequality
multiplier
percentile
polynomial
quaternion
real number
reciprocal
square root

11 letters

aliquot part
Banach space
chaos theory
coefficient
denominator
determinant
eigenvector
Galois group
group theory
integration
Klein bottle
magic square
Markov chain
Möbius strip
permutation
power series
prime number
subtraction
Venn diagram
whole number

12 letters

Bayes' theorem
decimal point
Eratosthenes, sieve of
Gödel numbers
Hilbert space
long division
multiplicand
Newton method
number theory

Simpson's rule
square number
substitution
Taylor series

13 letters

antilogarithm
Argand diagram
complex number
eigenfunction
Euclid's axioms
Euler's formula
extrapolation
Fourier series
Gauss's theorem
geometric mean
Green's theorem
interpolation
L'Hôpital's rule
Mandelbrot set
ordinal number
perfect number
perfect square
proper fraction
queuing theory
Stokes' theorem

14 letters

arithmetic mean
associative law
Boolean algebra
cardinal number
Cauchy sequence
commutative law
Euler's constant
hyperbolic sine
linear equation
multiplication
natural numbers
null hypothesis
rational number
root-mean-square
vulgar fraction

15 letters

Bessel functions
binomial theorem
differentiation

Dirichlet series
distributive law
Fourier analysis
Hermitian matrix
imaginary number
Laplace operator
Leibniz's theorem
Maclaurin series
Mersenne numbers
midpoint theorem
Pascal's triangle
Russell's paradox
stationary point

16 letters

Bernoulli numbers
definite integral
de Moivre's formula
Fibonacci numbers
four-color theorem
Hilbert's problems
hyperbolic cosine
improper fraction
integral calculus
irrational number
Lagrange's theorem
Monte Carlo method
natural logarithm
polar coordinates

recurring decimal
remainder theorem
repeating decimal

17 letters

Apollonius' theorem
catastrophe theory
common denominator
Euclidean geometry
hyperbolic tangent
partial derivative
point of inflection
Pythagoras' theorem
significant figure
transfinite number

18 letters

coordinate geometry
Fermat's last theorem
indefinite integral
least squares method
Napierian logarithm
Riemannian geometry

19 letters

Briggsian logarithms
Diophantine equation
exponential function
harmonic progression

highest common factor
Legendre polynomials
Poisson distribution

20 letters

Cartesian coordinates
differential calculus
differential equation
Gaussian distribution
geometric progression
lowerst common
  multiple

21 letters

arithmetic progression
infinitesimal calculus
Lobachevskian
  geometry
simultaneous equations
trigonometric function

22 letters

Stirling's approximation
transcendental function

23 letters

Chinese remainder
  theorem
lowerst common
  denominator

Branches of Engineering

10 letters
ergonomics
hydraulics

11 letters
electronics

12 letters
aerodynamics
astronautics
cosmonautics

13 letters
fluid dynamics

16 letters
civil engineering
naval engineering

17 letters
mining engineering

18 letters
nuclear engineering

19 letters
chemical engineering

20 letters
aerospace engineering

21 letters
automotive engineer-
  ing
electrical engineering
mechanical engineering
production engineering

23 letters
aeronautical engineer-
  ing
agricultural engineering

24 letters
environmental engi-
  neering

Computer Programming Languages

1 letter
B
C

3 letters
Ada
APL
C++
CPL
PL/I
POP

4 letters
BCPL
JAVA
Lisp
Logo

5 letters
Algol
Basic
Cobol
COMAL

CORAL
Forth

6 letters
JOVIAL
Modula
Pascal
Prolog
SIMULA
SNOBOL

7 letters
Fortran

9 letters
Smalltalk

11 letters
Visual Basic

Computer Parts and Peripherals

3 letters
ALU (arithmetic and logic unit)
bus
CPU (central processing unit)
MTU (magnetic-tape unit)
RAM (random access memory)
ROM (read only memory)
VDU (visual display unit)

4 letters
disk
DRAM (dynamic RAM)
port
SRAM (static RAM)
wand

5 letters
CD-ROM
EPROM (erasable programmable
    read-only memory)
modem
mouse

6 letters
buffer
memory

7 letters
console
monitor
plotter

printer
scanner
zip disk

8 letters
cassette
diskette
fax modem
firmware
hard disk
hardware
joystick
keyboard
light-pen
minidisk
register
software
terminal
zip drive

9 letters
cartridge
digitizer
fixed disk
processor
sound card
static RAM (SRAM)
video card

10 letters
dynamic RAM (DRAM)

floppy disk
main memory

11 letters

cache memory
control unit
drum scanner
flash memory
microfloppy
motherboard
optical disk
trackerball

12 letters

minidiskette
tape streamer

13 letters

bar-code reader
dynamic memory
primary memory
removable disk

14 letters

flat-bed plotter
flat-bed scanner
microprocessor
read only memory (ROM)
Winchester disk

15 letters

acoustic coupler
input-output port
secondary memory

16 letters

magnetic-tape unit (MTU)
maths coprocessor
solid-state memory
voice synthesizer

17 letters

input-output device
non-volatile memory
visual display unit (VDU)

18 letters

random access memory (RAM)

19 letters

semiconductor memory

21 letters

central processing unit (CPU)

22 letters

arithmetic and logic unit (ALU)

34 letters

erasable programmable read-only
memory (EPROM)

Rocks and Minerals

Sedimentary Rocks

3 letters
rag

4 letters
coal
marl

5 letters
chalk
chert
flint
shale

6 letters

oolite
rudite

7 letters
arenite
breccia
tillite

8 letters
dolomite
mudstone

9 letters
argillite

claystone
ironstone
limestone
sandstone
siltstone

11 letters
radiolarite

12 letters
conglomerate

17 letters
diatomaceous earth

Rocks and Minerals (continued)

Metamorphic Rocks

5 letters
slate

6 letters
gneiss
marble
schist

7 letters
verdite

8 letters
eclogite
hornfels
phyllite
psammite

9 letters
epidosite
granulite
quartzite

10 letters
epidiorite
pyroxenite

11 letters
amphibolite

Igneous Rocks

4 letters
lava
trap
tuff

6 letters
aplite
basalt
dunite
gabbro
pumice

7 letters
diorite
felsite

granite
picrite
syenite

8 letters
andesite
dolerite
obsidian
prophyry
rhyolite
tephrite
tonalite
trachyte

9 letters
monzonite
pegmatite
phonolite
variolite

10 letters
amygdaloid
kimberlite
peridotite
vitrophyre

11 letters
anorthosite
lamprophyre

Minerals

4 letters
mica
opal
talc

5 letters
beryl
borax
emery
topaz

6 letters
augite
galena
garnet
gypsum

halite
illite
pyrite
quartz
rutile
zircon

7 letters
apatite
biotite
diamond
mullite
pyrites
realgar
thorite
zeolite

zincite

8 letters
asbestos
cinnabar
corundum
dolomite
euxenite
feldspar
hyacinth
ilmenite
massicot
saponite
siderite
sodalite
stannite

9 letters
anhydrite
blackjack
fluorspar
fool's gold
fulgurite
haematite
harmotome
kaolinite
malachite
marcasite
periclase
scolecite
tungstite
turquoise

10 letters
hornblende
meerschaum
oligoclase
orthoclase
polybasite
sapphirine
serpentine
sphalerite
tourmaline
wolframite

11 letters
cassiterite
chrysoberyl

lapis lazuli
molybdenite
pitchblende
plagioclase
vesuvianite

12 letters
anorthoclase
chalcopyrite

13 letters
water sapphire

14 letters
Chile saltpeter

Metal Ores

6 letters
galena

7 letters
bauxite
zincite

8 letters
chromite
cinnabar
hematite

limonite
litharge
siderite
stibnite
tinstone

9 letters
anglesite
argentite
carnotite
cerrusite

haematite
ironstone
lodestone
magnetite
mispickel

10 letters
chalcocite
zinc blende

11 letters
cassiterite
pitchblende
smithsonite

12 letters
arsenopyrite
chalcopyrite

13 letters
copper pyrites

Geological Ages, Eras, Periods, and Epochs

6 letters
Eocene (epoch)
Recent (epoch)

7 letters
Miocene (epoch)
Permian (period)

8 letters
Cambrian (period)
Cenozoic (era)
Devonian (period)
Holocene (epoch)

Jurassic (period)
Mesozoic (era)
Pliocene (epoch)
Silurian (period)
Tertiary (period)
Triassic (period)

9 letters
Oligocene (epoch)
Paleocene (epoch)
Paleozoic (era)

10 letters
Cretaceous (period)

Ordovician (period)
Quaternary (period)

11 letters
Phanerozoic (era)
Pleistocene (epoch)
Precambrian (era)

13 letters
Carboniferous (period)
Mississippian (period)
Pennsylvanian (period)

Galaxies

11 letters
Helix Galaxy

13 letters
Spindle Galaxy

14 letters
Black-eye Galaxy
Nubecular Major (Large
  Magellanic Cloud)
Milky Way Galaxy
Pinwheel Galaxy
Nubecular Minor (Small
  Magellanic Cloud)
Sombrero Galaxy

15 letters
Andromeda Galaxy
Cartwheel Galaxy
Sunflower Galaxy
Whirlpool Galaxy

16 letters
Triangulum Galaxy

20 letters
Large Magellanic Cloud
  (Nubecular Major)
Small Magellanic Cloud
  (Nubecular Minor)

Constellations

(with common names)

3 letters
Ara	Altar
Leo	Lion

4 letters
Apus	Bird of Paradise
Crux (Australis)	Southern Cross
Grus	Crane
Lynx	
Lyra	Lyre
Pavo	Peacock
Vela	Sails

5 letters
Aries	Ram
Cetus	Whale
Draco	Dragon
Hydra	Sea Serpent
Indus	Indian
Lepus	Hare
Libra	Balance or Scales
Lupus	Wolf
Mensa	Table
Musca	Fly
Norma	Level or Rule
Orion	Hunter

Pyxis	Compass Box
Virgo	Virgin

6 letters
Antlia	Air Pump
Aquila	Eagle
Auriga	Charioteer
Boötes	Herdsman or Bear Driver
Caelum	Chisel
Cancer	Crab
Carina	Keel
Corvus	Crow
Crater	Cup
Cygnus	Swan
Dorado	Swordfish or Goldfish
Fornax	Furnace
Gemini	Twins
Hydrus	Water Snake
Octans	Octant
Pictor	Painter's Easel
Pisces	Fishes
Puppis	Stern or Poop
Scutum	Shield
Taurus	Bull
Tucana	Toucan
Volans	Flying Fish

7 letters

Cepheus	
Columba	Dove
Lacerta	Lizard
Pegasus	
Perseus	
Phoenix	
Sagitta	Arrow
Serpens	Serpent
Sextans	Sextant

8 letters

Aquarius	Water Bearer
Circinus	Compasses
Equuleus	Little Horse *or* Foal
Eridanus	River
Hercules	
Leo Minor	Little Lion
Scorpius	Scorpion
Sculptor	

9 letters

Andromeda	
Australis (Crux)	Southern Cross
Centaurus	Centaur
Delphinus	Dolphin
Monoceros	Unicorn
Ophiuchus	Serpent Bearer
Reticulum	Net
Ursa Major	Great Bear
Ursa Minor	Little Bear
Vulpecula	Fox

10 letters

Canis Major	Great Dog
Canis Minor	Little Dog
Cassiopeia	
Chamaeleon	Chameleon
Horologium	Clock
Triangulum	Triangle

11 letters

Capricornus	Goat *or* Sea Goat
Sagittarius	Archer
Telescopium	Telescope

12 letters

Microscopium	Microscope

13 letters

Canes Venatici	Hunting Dogs
Coma Berenices	Berenice's Hair

14 letters

Camelopardalis	Giraffe
Corona Borealis	Northern Crown

15 letters

Corona Australis	Southern Crown
Piscis Austrinus	Southern Fish

18 letters

Triangulum Australe	Southern Triangle

Planets

4 letters

Mars

5 letters

Earth
Venus
Pluto

6 letters

Saturn
Uranus

7 letters

Jupiter
Mercury
Neptune

Satellites of the Planets

EARTH

4 letters
Moon

JUPITER

2 letters
Io

4 letters
Leda

5 letters
Metis
Thebe
Elara
Carme

6 letters
Europa
Ananke
Sinope

7 letters
Himalia

8 letters
Adrastea
Amalthea
Ganymede
Callisto

Lysithea
Pasiphae

MARS

6 letters
Deimos
Phobos

NEPTUNE

5 letters
Naiad

6 letters
Nereid
Triton

7 letters
Despina
Galatea
Larissa
Proteus

8 letters
Thalassa

PLUTO

6 letters
Charon

SATURN

3 letters
Pan

4 letters
Rhea

5 letters
Atlas
Dione
Janus
Mimas
Titan

6 letters
Helene
Phoebe
Tethys

7 letters
Calypso
Iapetus
Pandora
Telesto

8 letters
Hyperion

9 letters
Enceladus

10 letters
Epimetheus
Prometheus

URANUS

4 letters
Puck

5 letters
Ariel

6 letters
Bianca
Juliet
Oberon
Portia

7 letters
Belinda
Miranda
Ophelia
Titania
Umbriel

8 letters
Cordelia
Cressida
Rosalind

9 letters
Desdemona

Comets

4 letters
Faye
West

5 letters
Biela
Encke
Kopff

6 letters
Halley
Lexell
Olbers
Tuttle

7 letters
Bennett
Whipple

8 letters
Borrelly
Hale-Bopp
Kohoutek
Westphal

9 letters
Comas Solá
Crommelin

10 letters
Pons-Brooks
Schaumasse

11 letters
Arend-Roland

12 letters
Pons-Winnecke

13 letters	14 letters	15 letters
Daylight Comet	Bronsen-	Giacobini-
Shoemaker-	Metcalf	Zinner
Levy		Grigg-Skiellerup
Stephan-		
Oterma		

Winds

(with locations)

4 letters		
bise	Central Europe
bora	Central Europe
Föhn (Foehn)	Central Europe

5 letters	
buran	Central Asia
Foehn (Föhn)	Central Europe
gibli (ghibli)	N Africa

6 letters	
ghibli (gibli)	N Africa
samiel (simoom)	N Africa
simoom (samiel)	N Africa

7 letters	
chinook	Rocky Mountains, U.S.
etesian	E Mediterranean
khamsin	Egypt
meltemi	E Mediterranean
mistral	Mediterranean
monsoon	S Asia
norther	Texas, Oklahoma

sirocco	N Africa

8 letters	
levanter	W Mediterranean
Santa Ana	California
williwaw	U.S., Canada

9 letters	
harmattan	W Africa
nor'wester	New Zealand
sou'wester	Eastern U.S.

10 letters	
Cape doctor	South Africa
tramontana	W Mediterranean
wet chinook	NW U.S.

14 letters	
Alberta clipper	Central U.S.
smoky sou'wester	Eastern U.S.

15 letters	
southerly buster	SE Australia

Clouds

6 letters	9 letters	12 letters	15 letters
cirrus	rain cloud	cirrocumulus	lenticular cloud
nimbus		cirrostratus	
	10 letters	cumulonimbus	16 letters
7 letters	anvil cloud	nimbostratus	noctilucent
cumulus	storm cloud	thundercloud	cloud
stratus			
	11 letters	13 letters	
	altocumulus	cumulostratus	
	altostratus	stratocumulus	

MEDICINE AND
THE HUMAN BODY

Human Bones

3 letters
rib

4 letters
ulna

5 letters
anvil
costa
femur
hyoid
ilium
incus
pubis
skull
spine
talus
tibia
vomer

6 letters
carpal
cuboid
fibula
hallux

hammer
pelvis
rachis
radius
sacrum
stapes
tarsal

7 letters
cranium
ethmoid
humerus
ischium
jawbone
kneecap
malleus
maxilla
patella
phalanx
scapula
sternum
stirrup

8 letters
backbone

clavicle
heel bone
mandible
scaphoid
shin bone
sphenoid
vertebra

9 letters
ankle bone
calcaneus
cheekbone
funny bone
nasal bone
thigh bone
wrist bone

10 letters
astragalus
breastbone
collarbone
lunate bone
metacarpal
metatarsal

11 letters
floating rib
frontal bone

12 letters
parietal bone
pisiform bone
sesamoid bone
spinal column
temporal bone

13 letters
navicular bone
occipital bone
shoulder blade
zygomatic bone

14 letters
innominate
  bone

15 letters
vertebral col-
  umn

Parts of the Human Ear

5 letters
anvil (incus)
incus (anvil)
pinna (auricle)

6 letters
hammer (malleus)
stapes (stirrup)

7 letters
auricle (pinna)
cochlea
eardrum (tympanic

  membrane)
malleus (hammer)
saccule
stirrup (stapes)
utricle

8 letters
hair cell
inner ear
outer ear

9 letters
endolymph

middle ear
perilymph
vestibule

12 letters
organ of Corti

13 letters
auditory canal
auditory nerve

14 letters
Eustachian tube

15 letters
basilar membrane

16 letters
tympanic membrane
  (eardrum)

17 letters
semicircular canal
tectorial membrane

Human Glands

Endocrine Glands

5 letters
ovary

6 letters
testis

11 letters
pineal gland

12 letters
adrenal gland
corpus luteum
thyroid gland

14 letters
pituitary gland

16 letters
parathyroid gland

18 letters
islets of Langerhans

Exocrine Glands

5 letters
liver

6 letters
breast

8 letters
pancreas

10 letters
sweat gland

11 letters
buccal gland
tarsal gland
  (meibomian gland)

12 letters
Cowper's gland (bulbo-
  urethral gland)
gastric gland
mammary gland
parotid gland

13 letters
Brunner's gland
lacrimal gland
prostate gland
salivary gland

14 letters
meibomian gland
  (tarsal gland)
preputial gland
sebaceous gland

15 letters
Bartholin's gland
sublingual gland

16 letters
Lieberkühn's gland

17 letters
submaxillary gland
  (submandibular
  gland)

18 letters
bulbo-urethal gland
  (Cowper's gland)
submandibular gland
  (submaxillary gland)

Parts of the Human Eye

3 letters
rod

4 letters
cone
iris
lens

5 letters
fovea
orbit

6 letters
cornea
cilium (eyelash)
eyelid (blepharon or
  palpebra)
limbus
retina
sclera
stroma

7 letters
choroid
eyeball
eyelash (cilium)

8 letters
palpebra (eyelid or
  blepharon)

9 letters
blepharon (eyelid or
  palpebra)
blind spot

10 letters
optic nerve
tear glands (lacrimal
  glands)

11 letters
ciliary body

conjunctiva
tarsal plate

12 letters
optic foramen

13 letters
aqueous humour

14 letters
lacrimal glands (tear
  glands)
vitreous humour

15 letters
extrinsic muscle

18 letters
suspensory ligament

Human Muscles

5 letters
psoas

6 letters
biceps
soleus

7 letters
deltoid
gluteus
triceps

8 letters
scalenus
splenius

9 letters
sartorius
trapezius

10 letters
quadriceps

11 letters
rhomboideus

13 letters
gastrocnemius

14 letters
pectoral muscle
peroneal muscle

16 letters
abdominal muscles

Medical Specialties

7 letters
otology
surgery
urology

8 letters
nosology
oncolgoy
osteology
podiatry
serology

9 letters
chiropody
dentistry
neurology
pathology
radiology

10 letters
cardiology
exodontics
geriatrics
gynecology
hematology
immunology
nephrology
obstetrics
pediatrics
teratology

11 letters
anesthetics
dermatology
diagnostics
endodontics
ENT medicine
(car, nose, &
throat)

gerontology
orthopedics
pedodontics
venereology

12 letters
brain surgery
chiropractic
epidemiology
heart surgery
neurosurgery
orthodontics
periodontics
radiotherapy
rheumatology

13 letters
endocrinology
ophthalmology

14 letters
otolaryngology
plastic surgery
prosthodontics

16 letters
gastroenterology

17 letters
forensic pathol-
ogy

19 letters
otorhinolaryn-
gology

Types of Medication and Drug

5 letters
tonic

6 letters
emetic

7 letters
antacid
steroid

8 letters
antidote
diuretic
laxative
sedative

9 letters
analgesic
fungicide
stimulant

10 letters
antibiotic
antiemetic
antifungal
antiseptic
depressant

11 letters
anesthetic
antipyretic
antitussive
beta blocker
expectorant
vasodilator

12 letters
anthelmintic
decongestant
tranquilizer

13 letters
antibacterial

anticoagulant
antiepileptic
antihistamine
antipsychotic

14 letters
anticonvulsant
antidepressant
bronchodilator
muscle relaxant

15 letters
vasoconstrictor

16 letters
anti-inflammatory

17 letters
immunosuppressive

19 letters
appetite suppressant

Diseases and Medical Conditions

2 letters

ME (myalgic encephalitis)
MS (multiple sclerosis)

3 letters

ADD (attention deficit disorder)
ALS (amyotrophic lateral sclerosis)
BPH (bening prostatic hyperplasia)

4 letters

AIDS
gout
yaws

5 letters

lupus
mumps

6 letters

anemia
angina
asthma
autism
cancer
dengue
eczema
goiter
herpes
plague
rabies
scurvy
typhus

7 letters

cholera
colitis
ileitis
leprosy
malaria
measles
rickets
rubella (German measles)
tetanus

8 letters

beriberi
cyanosis
cystitis
diabetes
dysentery
epilepsy
glaucoma
impetigo
jaundice
kala-azar
leukemia
pellagra
pruritis
ringworm
shingles
smallpox
syphilis
tinnitus
trachoma

9 letters

arthritis
bilharzia
brown lung
cirrhosis
dhobi itch
emphysema
gonorrhea
hepatitis
influenza
nephritis
pneumonia
porphyria
psoriasis
psychosis
silicosis
sinusitis

10 letters

acromegaly
asbestosis
bronchitis
chickenpox
common cold
dermatitis
diphtheria
Ebola fever

hemophilia
laryngitis
Lassa fever
meningitis
narcolepsy
salmonella

11 letters

brucellosis
candidiasis
kwashiorkor
listeriosis
Lyme disease
peritonitis
psittacosis
spina bifida
thalassemia
tonsillitis
yellow fever

12 letters

appendicitis
avitaminosis
encephalitis
osteoporosis
scarlet fever
tuberculosis
typhoid fever
Weil's disease

13 letters

actinomycosis
celiac disease
Chagas' disease
Crohn's disease
elephantiasis
food poisoning
German measles (rubella)
Graves' disease
leptospirosis
Paget's disease
poliomyelitis
St. Vitus's dance
schizophrenia
toxoplasmosis
whooping cough

14 letters

Bright's disease
bulimia nervosa
cystic fibrosis
glandular fever
Kaposi's sarcoma
pneumoconiosis
rheumatic fever
sleepy sickness

15 letters

Addison's disease
anorexia nervosa
Cushing's disease
gastroenteritis
Hodgkin's disease
hyperthyroidism
Kawasaki disease
Ménière's disease
phenylketonuria
Raynaud's disease
Sydenham's chorea
venereal disease

16 letters

myasthenia gravis
sickle cell anemia
sleeping sickness
sweating sickness

17 letters

Alzheimer's disease
Asperger's syndrome
Huntington's chorea
Lou Gehrig's Disease
multiple sclerosis
(MS)
muscular dystrophy
Parkinson's disease
Tourette's syndrome

18 letters

clinical depression
toxic shock syndrome

19 letters

legionnaires' disease

motor neurone disease
myalgic encephalitis
(ME)
rheumatoid arthritis

20 letters

coronary heart disease
Münchhausen's syn-
drome (by proxy)

24 letters

attention deficit
disorder (ADD)

26 letters

bening prostatic hyper-
plasia (BPH)

27 letters

amyotrophic lateral
sclerosis (ALS)

Surgical Operations

(with description)

7 letters

myotomy	incision of muscle

8 letters

lobotomy	incision of nerve fibers from frontal lobe of brain
tenotomy	incision of tendon
vagotomy	incision of vagus nerve

9 letters

colectomy	removal of colon
colostomy	opening of colon
cystotomy	incision of bladder
lithotomy	removal of kidney stone
lobectomy	removal of lobe of an organ
neurotomy	incision of nerve
ostectomy	removal of bone
osteotomy	incision of bone
valvotomy	incision of heart valve

vasectomy	removal of all or part of vas deferens

10 letters

craniotomy	incision of skull
cystectomy	removal of bladded
cystostomy	opening of bladder
enterotomy	incision of intestine
episiotomy	incision of vaginal opening
gastrotomy	incision of stomach
laparotomy	incision of abdomen
lumpectomy	removal of breast tumor
mastectomy	removal of breast
nephrotomy	incision of kidney
neurectomy	removal of nerve
ovariotomy	incision of ovary
phlebotomy	incision of vein
pleurotomy	incision of pleural membrane

Surgical Operations *(continued)*

thymectomy	removal of thymus gland
varicotomy	excision of varicose vein

11 letters

angioplasty	repair of blood vessel
arteriotomy	incision of artery
cystoplasty	repair of bladder
embolectomy	removal of blood clot
enterostomy	opening of small intestine
gastrectomy	removal of whole or part of stomach
gastrostomy	opening of stomach
glossectomy	removal of all or part of tongue
hepatectomy	removal of all or part of liver
hysterotomy	incision of womb
laryngotomy	incision of larynx
mammaplasty	reshaping of breast
nephrectomy	removal of kidney
nephrostomy	opening of kidney
orchidotomy	incision of testis
ovariectomy	removal of ovary
polypectomy	removal of polyp
rhinoplasty	repair of nose
splenectomy	removal of spleen
thoracotomy	incision of chest cavity
tracheotomy	incision of windpipe
ureterotomy	incision of ureter
urethrotomy	incision of urethra

12 letters

appendectomy (appendicectomy)	removal of appendix
cheiloplasty	repair of lips
gastroplasty	repair of stomach
hysterectomy	removal of womb
laryngectomy	removal of larynx
oophorectomy	removal of ovary
orchidectomy	removal of testis
palatoplasty	repair of cleft palate
phalloplasty	repair of penis
thrombectomy	removal of blood clot
tonsillotomy	incision of tonsil
tracheostomy	opening of windpipe
ureterectomy	removal of ureter
ureterostomy	opening of ureter

13 letters

adenoidectomy	removal of adenoids
dermatoplasty	repair of skin
esophagectomy	opening of esophagus
hepaticostomy	opening of bile duct
perineoplasty	repair of vaginal opening
pharyngectomy	removal of pharynx
pneumonectomy	removal of lung
prostatectomy	removal of prostate gland
salpingectomy	removal of fallopian tube
salpingostomy	opening of fallopian tube
thoracoplasty	repair of thorax
thyroidectomy	removal of all or part of thyroid gland
tonsillectomy	removal of tonsils
urethroplasty	repair of urethra

14 letters

appendicectomy (appendectomy)	removal of appendix
cholecystotomy	incision of gall bladder
pancreatectomy	removal of pancreas
pericardectomy (pericardiectomy)	removal of all or part of membrane around heart
pericardiotomy	incision of membrane around heart

15 letters

cholecystectomy — removal of gall bladder

pericardiectomy (pericardectomy) — removal of all or part of membrane around heart

16 letters

hemorrhoidectomy — removal of hemorrhoids

Therapies

7 letters
shiatsu

10 letters
art therapy
Gerson cure
homeopathy
osteopathy
sex therapy

11 letters
acupuncture
naturopathy
play therapy
reflexology

12 letters
aromatherapy
chiropractic
color therapy
drama therapy
group therapy
hydrotherapy
hypnotherapy
music therapy

narcotherapy
shock therapy
sleep therapy
sound therapy

13 letters
balneotherapy
family therapy
primal therapy
psychotherapy

14 letters
crystal therapy
electrotherapy
Gestalt therapy
mechanotherapy
release therapy

15 letters
aversion therapy
behavior therapy
Rogerian therapy

16 letters
cognitive therapy

17 letters
humanistic therapy
regression therapy
relaxation therapy

18 letters
megavitamin therapy

19 letters
electroshock therapy
insulin shock therapy
occupational therapy
recreational therapy

20 letters
confrontation therapy
metrazol shock therapy

22 letters
rational-emotive therapy

24 letters
electroconvulsive therapy

Branches of Psychology

8 letters
ethology

11 letters
behaviorism
Freudianism
psychometry

12 letters
psychography

13 letters
psychobiology
structuralism

14 letters
associationism
metapsychology
parapsychology
psychoanalysis
psychodynamics
psychogenetics

15 letters
apperceptionism
child psychology
group psychology
neuropsychology
psychobiography
psychopathology

16 letters
animal psychology
configurationism
psychophysiology
social psychology

17 letters
applied psychology
Gestalt psychology
Jungian psychology
psycholinguistics

18 letters
abnormal psychology
Adlerian psychology
clinical psychology
Horneyan psychology
Lacanian psychology
psychobiochemistry
psychopharmacology
Reichian psychology

19 letters
cognitive psychology
Pavlovian psychology
Watsonian psychology

20 letters
analytical psychology
humanistic psychology

Skinnerian psychology

21 letters
comparative
  psychology
educational
  psychology

22 letters
experimental
  psychology
occupational
  psychology

23 letters
developmental
  psychology
introspection
  psychology
physiological
  psychology

37 letters
industrial and
  organizational
  psychology

Phobias

9 letters

apiphobia	bees
atephobia	ruin
neophobia	new things
zoophobia	animals

10 letters

acrophobia	high places, sharpness
aerophobia	air travel
algophobia	pain
aurophobia	gold
autophobia	loneliness
batophobia	high buildings
cibophobia	food
cryophobia	ice
cymophobia	waves
cynophobia	dogs
demophobia	crowds
dikephobia	justice
doraphobia	fur
eosophobia	dawn
ergophobia	work
gynophobia	women
hadephobia	hell
hemophobia	blood
homophobia	homosexuals
hodophobia	travel
ideophobia	ideas
kenophobia	voids
kopophobia	fatigue
lalophobia	speech
logophobia	words
maniphobia	insanity
musophobia	mice
mysophobia	dirt
nosophobia	disease, illness
ochophobia	vehicles
oikophobia	home
osmophobia	smell
panophobia	everything
papaphobia	The Pope
pedophobia	children
potophobia	drink
pyrophobia	fire
sciophobia	shadows
Sinophobia	Chinese people and things
sitophobia	food

theophobia	God
tocophobia	childbirth
topophobia	places
toxiphobia	poison
xenophobia	foreigners

11 letters

acarophobia	itching, mites
acerophobia	sourness
agoraphobia	open places
androphobia	men
anemophobia	wind
Anglophobia	English people and things
anthophobia	flowers
antlophobia	floods
atelophobia	imperfection
bathophobia	depth
clinophobia	bed
cnidophobia	insect stings
coitophobia	coitus
coprophobia	feces
crysophobia	gold
emetophobia	vomiting
enetophobia	pins
erotophobia	sex
febriphobia	fever
Gallophobia	French people and things
hagiophobia	saints
haptophobia	touch
heliophobia	sun
hierophobia	priests
hippophobia	horses
hormephobia	shock
hydrophobia	water
hygrophobia	dampness
hypnophobia	sleep
hypsophobia	high places
iconophobia	religious works of art
Italophobia	Italian people and things
koniophobia	dust
leprophobia	leprosy
limnophobia	lakes
lyssophobia	insanity
microphobia	small things
necrophobia	corpses

Phobias *(continued)*

Negrophobia	Black people and things	kinetophobia	motion
nephophobia	clouds	kleptophobia	stealing
nyctophobia	night	linonophobia	string
ochlophobia	crowds, mobs	musicophobia	music
pantophobia	everything	odontophobia	teeth
pathophobia	disease	ommetaphobia	eyes
peniaphobia	poverty	phasmophobia	ghosts
phagophobia	swallowing	pinaciphobia	lists
phobophobia	fear	pogonophobia	beards
phonophobia	speech	potamophobia	rivers
photophobia	light	rhabdophobia	magic
poinephobia	punishment	Satanophobia	Satan
Russophobia	Russian people and things	scabiophobia	scabies
		siderophobia	stars
Scotophobia	Scottish people and things	spermophobia	germs
		stygiophobia	hell
scotophobia	darkness	technophobia	technology
stasophobia	standing	teratophobia	giving birth to monsters
tachophobia	speed		
Teutophobia	German people and things	thassophobia	idleness
		thermophobia	heat
uranophobia	heaven	trichophobia	hair

13 letters

		Americophobia	American people and things
		arachnophobia	spiders
ailurophobia	cats	asthenophobia	weakness
anginophobia	narrowness	astrapophobia	lightning
apeirophobia	infinity	bacillophobia	microbes
belonephobia	needles	carcinophobia	cancer
blennophobia	slime	electrophobia	electricity
brontophobia	thunder	erythrophobia	blushing
cardiophobia	heart disease	ornithophobia	birds
cheimaphobia	cold	gephyrophobia	bridges
chionophobia	snow	Germanophobia	German people and things
chromophobia	color		
chronophobia	time	geumatophobia	taste
cometophobia	comets	hamartophobia	sin
cremnophobia	precipices	harpaxophobia	robbers
entomophobia	insects	hypegiaphobia	responsibility
ermitophobia	loneliness	ichthyophobia	fish
Francophobia	French people and things	keraunophobia	thunder
		mastigophobia	beating
gametophobia	marriage	mechanophobia	machinery
glossophobia	speech	metallophobia	metal
graphophobia	writing	olfactophobia	smell
hedonophobia	pleasure	onomatophobia	names
Judaeophobia	Jewish people and things		

12 letters

ophidiophobia	snakes	phronemophobia	thinking
patroiophobia	heredity	phthisiophobia	tuberculosis
philosophobia	philosophy	politicophobia	politics
pteronophobia	feathers	symmetrophobia	symmetry
syphilophobia	venereal disease	thalassophobia	sea
teratrophobia	monsters	traumatophobia	injury
thanatophobia	death	zelotypophobia	jealousy
tonitrophobia	thunder		
trypanophobia	inoculation		
tyrannophobia	tyrants		
vaccinophobia	inoculation		

14 letters

15 letters

anthropophobia	people
bacteriophobia	bacteria, germs
ballistophobia	bullets
batrachophobia	reptiles
chrematophobia	money
claustrophobia	enclosed places
ecclesiophobia	church
eisoptrophobia	mirrors
epistolophobia	correspondence
homichlophobia	fog
katagelophobia	ridicule
microbiophobia	microbes
parasitophobia	parasites
pediculophobia	lice
pharmacophobia	drugs

acousticophobia	sound
eleutherophobia	freedom
helminthophobia	worms
telephonophobia	telephone

16 letters

bromidrosiphobia	body odor
coprostasophobia	constipation
dermatosiophobia	skin disease
hydrophobophobia	rabies
katastichophobia	lists

17 letters

siderodromophobia	rail travel
triskaidekaphobia	thirteen

18 letters

dermatopathophobia	skin disease
kakorrhaphiaphobia	failure

ANITALS, PLANTS, AND AGRICULTURE

Collective Names for Animals and Birds

3 letters

cry	hounds
gam	whales
mob	kangaroos
pod	seals

4 letters

army	caterpillars
bale	turtles
band	gorillas
bask	crocodiles
bevy	roe deer, quails, larks, pheasants
bury	rabbits
cete	badgers
dout	wild cats
down	hares
erst	bees
gang	elk
herd	cattle, elephants
hive	bees
knot	toads
leap (lepe)	leopards
mute	hares
pace	asses
pack	hounds, grouse
safe	ducks
sawt	lions
span	mules
stud	mares
trip	goats
turn	turtles
yoke	oxen
zeal	zebras

5 letters

bloat	hippopotami

brood	chickens
charm	finches
cloud	gnats
covey	partridges
crash	rhinoceros
drift	swine
drove	horses, bullocks
flock	sheep
hover	trout
labor	moles
pride	lions
siege	herons
shoal	fish
skein	geese in flight
skulk	foxes
sloth	bears
smack	jellyfish
stare	owls
swarm	flies, bees
troop	baboons
watch	nightingales

6 letters

desert	lapwings
gaggle	geese on land
kennel	dogs
kindle	kittens
litter	kittens, pigs
murder	crows
muster	peacocks, penguins
parade	elephants
parcel	penguins
rafter	turkeys
school	dolphins, porpoises, whales
spring	teal
string	horses
tiding	magpies

7 letters

clowder	cats
descent	woodpeckers
fluther	jellyfish
rookery	rooks
turmoil	porpoises

8 letters

busyness	ferrets
paddling	ducks on water

9 letters

bellowing	bullfinshes
obstinacy	buffalo

10 letters

chattering	choughs
exaltation	larks
parliament	owls
shrewdness	apes
unkindness	ravens

11 letters

murmuration	starlings
pandemonium	parrots

12 letters

congregation	plovers

Many of these are fanciful or humorous terms that probably never had any real currency. They were taken up by Joseph Sturt in Sports & Pastimes of England (1801) and by other antiquarian writers.

Adjectives Relating to Animals and Birds

5 letters

apian	bee
avian	bird
ovine	sheep

6 letters

bovine	cow
canine	dog
cervid	deer
equine	horse
feline	cat
lupine	wolf
murine	mouse, rat
oscine	songbird
otarid	seal, sea lion
simian	monkey
ursine	bear

7 letters

anguine	snake
asinine	donkey
caprine	goat
cervine	deer
corvine	crow
hircine	goat
leonine	lion
phocine	seal
piscine	fish
porcine	pig
saurian	lizard
taurine	bull
turdine	thrush
vulpine	fox

8 letters

anserine	goose
aquiline	eagle
cetacean	dolphin, porpoise, whale
leporine	hare
ophidian	snake
sciurine	chipmunk, marmot, squirrel
viperine	viper
viperous	viper

9 letters

arachnoid	spider
cetaceous	dolphin, porpoise, whale
chelonian	terrapin, tortoise, turtle

colubrine	snake
columbine	dove
hirundine	swallow
musteline	ferret, skunk, weasel
passerine	sparrow
vermiform	worm
viverrine	civet, mongoose

10 letters

batrachian	frog, toad
crustacean	crab, lobster, shrimp
psittacine	parrot
serpentine	snake

11 letters

crustaceous	crab, lobster, shrimp
elephantine	elephant

12 letters

anguilliform	eel
gallinaceous	fowl

Names for Male and Female Animals

Male

3 letters

cob	swan
dog	coyote, dog, wolf
fox	fox
ram	impala, sheep
tom	bobcat, cat, cougar

4 letters

boar	badger, bear, pig, weasel
buck	antelope, hare, jackrabbit, kangaroo
bull	buffalo, camel, cattle, elephant, giraffe, hartebeest, moose, rhinoceros, seal, whale
cock	chicken, fish, lobster, pheasant
jack	ferret
lion	lion
stag	caribou, deer

5 letters

drake	duck
tiger	tiger

Names for Male and Female Animals *(continued)*

6 letters	
gander	goose

7 letters	
bullock	ox
jackass	donkey
leopard	leopard

peacock	peacock

8 letters	
stallion	horse, zebra

9 letters	
billygoat	goat

Female

3 letters	
cow	buffalo, camel, cattle, elephant, giraffe, hartebeest, moose, ox, rhinoceros, seal, weasel, whale
doe	antelope, caribou, deer, hare, jackrabbit, kangaroo impala, sheep
ewe	impala, sheep
hen	chicken, fish, lobster, pheasant
pen	swan
sow	badger, bear, pig

4 letters	
duck	duck
jill	ferret
mare	horse, zebra

5 letters	
bitch	coyote, dog, wolf
queen	cat
vixen	fox
goose	goose

6 letters	
peahen	peacock

7 letters	
lioness	bobcat, cougar, lion
tigress	tiger

8 letters	
jennyass	donkey

9 letters	
nannygoat	goat

10 letters	
leopardess	leopard

Young of Animals

3 letters	
cub	badger, bear, fox, leopard, lion, tiger, walrus, wolf
fry	fish
kid	antelope, goat, roe deer
kit	beaver, fox, weasel

4 letters	
calf	buffalo, camel, cattle, elephant, elk, giraffe, hartebeest, rhinoceros, seal, whale
colt	horse
eyas	hawk
fawn	caribou, deer
foal	horse, zebra
joey	kangaroo
lamb	sheep

5 letters	
chick	chicken, hawk, pheasant

elver	eel
filly	horse
puppy	coyote, dog
squab	pigeon
whelp	dog, wolf

6 letters

cygnet	swan
eaglet	eagle
kitten	bobcat, cat, cougar, jackrabbit, skunk

| piglet | pig |

7 letters

cheeper	grouse, partridge, quail
gosling	goose
leveret	hare
tadpole	frog, toad

8 letters

| duckling | duck |

Mammals

2 letters

ai
ox

3 letters

ape
ass
bat
cat
cow
dog
elk
fox
gnu
hog
kob
pig
rat
yak

4 letters

anoa
bear
boar
cavy
cony
deer
eyra
gaur
goat
hare
ibex
kudu
lion

lynx
mara
mink
mole
mule
oryx
paca
pika
puma
saki
seal
sika
tahr
titi
unau
urus
vole
wolf
zebu

5 letters

bison
bongo
camel
chiru
civet
coati
coypu
dhole
dingo
drill
eland
fossa
gayal

genet
goral
hinny
hippo
horse
hutia
hyena
hyrax
indri
kiang
lemur
liger
llama
loris
moose
mouse
nyala
okapi
oribi
otter
ounce
panda
potto
ratel
rhino
sable
saiga
serow
sheep
shrew
skunk
sloth
stoat
swine

takin
tapir
tayra
tiger
tigon
whale
zebra

6 letters

agouti
alpaca
aoudad
aye-aye
baboon
badger
beaver
bobcat
cattle
chital
colugo
cougar
coyote
desman
dik-dik
donkey
dugong
duiker
ermine
fennec
ferret
fisher
galago
gelada
gerbil

Mammals *(continued)*

gibbon
gopher
grison
guenon
impala
jackal
jaguar
jerboa
kit fox
langur
margay
marmot
marten
monkey
musk ox
nilgai
ocelot
olingo
onager
rabbit
racoon (raccoon)
red fox
sambar
sea cow
serval
sifaka
suslik
tenrec
vervet
vicuña
walrus
wapiti
weasel
wisent

7 letters

ant bear
aurochs
banteng
bettong
bighorn
blue fox
buffalo
cane rat
caracal
caribou
chamois
cheetah

colobus
dolphin
foumart
gazelle
gemsbok
gerenuk
giraffe
glutton
gorilla
grampus
guanaco
gymnure
hamster
lemming
leopard
linsang
macaque
manatee
markhor
meerkat
mole rat
moon rat
mouflon
muntjac
muskrat
narwhal
noctule
pack rat
panther
peccary
polecat
raccoon
  (racoon)
red deer
roe deer
rorqual
sea lion
siamang
souslik
sun bear
tamarin
tamarou
tarsier
warthog
wildcat
wild dog
wood rat
zorilla

8 letters

aardvark
aardwolf
anteater
antelope
axis deer
babirusa
bushbaby
bushbuck
cachalot
capybara
chipmunk
dormouse
elephant
entellus
fruit bat
grey wolf
hedgehog
kinkajou
mandrill
mangabey
marmoset
mongoose
mule deer
musk deer
musquash
pangolin
porpoise
reedbuck
reindeer
sea otter
sei whale
squirrel
steinbok
talapoin
tamandua
viscacha
water rat
wild boar

9 letters

Arctic fox
armadillo
binturong
black bear
blackbuck
blue whale
brown bear

catamount
chickaree
deer mouse
desert rat
dromedary
dziggetai
flying fox
golden cat
groundhog
guinea pig
hamadryas
honey bear
mouse deer
orangutan
palm civet
pampas cat
polar bear
porcupine
pronghorn
silver fox
sitatunga
sloth bear
solenodon
springbok
tree shrew
waterbuck
water vole
wolverine
woodchuck

10 letters

angwantibo
Arctic hare
bottlenose
cacomistle
chevrotain
chimpanzee
chinchilla
coatimundi
cottontail
fallow deer
fieldmouse
golden mole
harbor seal
hartebeest
hooded seal
jackrabbit
jaguarundi

Kodiak bear
mona monkey
otter shrew
Pallas's cat
pilot whale
pine marten
pouched rat
prairie dog
raccoon dog
rhinoceros
right whale
sperm whale
springhaas
timber wolf
vampire bat
water shrew
white whale
wildebeest

11 letters
barbastelle
barking deer
Cape buffalo
douroucouli
flying lemur
grass monkey
grizzly bear
honey badger
kangaroo rat
killer whale
leopard seal

mountain cat
patas monkey
pipistrelle
pocket mouse
prairie wolf
red squirrel
sea elephant
serotine bat
snow leopard
stone marten

12 letters
cinnamon bear
elephant seal
goat antelope
grey squirrel
harvest mouse
hippopotamus
horseshoe bat
howler monkey
jumping mouse
klipspringer
mountain goat
mountain lion
pocket gopher
rhesus monkey
roan antelope
snowshoe hare
spider monkey
Virginia deer
water buffalo

woolly monkey

13 letters
Bactrian camel
crabeater seal
European bison
hairy hedgehog
humpback
  whale
mountain sheep
royal antelope
sable antelope
scaly anteater
spiny dormouse

14 letters
capuchin
  monkey
clouded leopard
flying squirrel
ground squirrel
Indian elephant
mountain
  beaver
New World
  monkey
Old World
  monkey
Père David's
  deer
spectacled bear

squirrel monkey
tailless tenrec

15 letters
proboscis
  monkey
white rhinoceros

16 letters
Chinese water
  deer
woolly
  rhinoceros

17 letters
pygmy hip-
  popotamus
Rocky
  Mountain goat
saber-toothed
  tiger

18 letters
woolly spider
  monkey

19 letters
scaly-tailed
  squirrel

Marsupials

5 letters
bilby
yapok

6 letters
cuscus
numbat
quokka
wombat

7 letters
dalgyte
dasyure

opossum
wallaby

8 letters
kangaroo

9 letters
bandicoot
koala bear
pademelon
phalanger
planigale
thylacine

10 letters
honey mouse
rat opossum

11 letters
hare wallaby
rat kangaroo
rock wallaby

12 letters
marsupial rat
mouse opossum
tree kangaroo

13 letters
marsupial mole
Tasmanian wolf

14 letters
marsupial
  mouse
Tasmanian devil

15 letters
flying phalanger
rabbit bandicoot

Birds

3 letters
auk
emu
hen
jay
kea
owl
tui

4 letters
chat
coly
coot
crow
dove
duck
erne
gull
hawk
huia
ibis
kagu
kite
kiwi
knot
lark
lory
nene
rail
rhea
rook
ruff
shag
skua
smew
swan
teal
tern
wren

5 letters
booby
crake
crane
diver
eagle
egret
finch

goose
grebe
heron
hobby
junco
macaw
noddy
ouzel
pipit
raven
robin
scaup
serin
snipe
stork
twite

6 letters
auklet
avocet
barbet
bulbul
canary
chough
condor
cuckoo
curlew
darter
dipper
dunlin
falcon
fulmar
gannet
godwit
grouse
hoopoe
jabiru
jacana
kakapo
lanner
linnet
magpie
martin
merlin
motmot
oriole
osprey
parrot

peewee
peewit
petrel
phoebe
pigeon
plover
puffin
pukeko
roller
shrike
siskin
takahe
thrush
toucan
towhee
trogon
turkey
whydah
willet

7 letters
anhinga
antbird
babbler
barn owl
bittern
blue tit
bunting
bush tit
bustard
buzzard
catbird
chicken
coal tit
cowbird
dunnock
emu-wren
fantail
finfoot
fish owl
flicker
gadwall
goshawk
grackle
harrier
hawk owl
hoot owl
jacamar

jackdaw
kestrel
kinglet
lapwing
mallard
manakin
minivet
moorhen
oilbird
ortolan
ostrich
peacock
peafowl
pelican
penguin
pintail
pochard
quetzal
redhead
redpoll
redwing
rosella
seagull
seriema
skimmer
skylark
sparrow
sunbird
swallow
tanager
tinamou
titlark
touraco
vulture
wagtail
warbler
waxbill
waxwing
wrybill
wryneck

8 letters
amadavat
bee-eater
bellbird
blackcap
bluebill
bluebird

boatbill
bobolink
bobwhite
bush wren
caracara
cardinal
cockatoo
curassow
dabchick
eagle owl
fernbird
flamingo
garganey
great tit
grosbeak
hawfinch
hornbill
killdeer
kingbird
laverock *Scot.*
lorikeet
lovebird
lyrebird
megapode
mute swan
nightjar
notornis
nuthatch
ovenbird
oxpecker
parakeet
pheasant
redshank
redstart
reedbird
reedling
ricebird
ringdove
rock dove
scops owl
screamer
shelduck
shoebill
snowy owl
starling
swiftlet
tawny owl
thrasher
titmouse
tragopan
wheatear

whimbrel
whinchat
whip bird
whistler
woodchat
woodcock
wood duck

9 letters

albatross
bald eagle
blackbird
black swan
bowerbird
brambling
broadbill
bullfinch
cassowary
chaffinch
chickadee
cockatiel
cormorant
corncrake
crossbill
eider duck
fieldfare
firecrest
francolin
friarbird
frogmouth
gallinule
goldcrest
goldeneye
goldfinch
goosander
guillemot
gyrfalcon
horned owl
kittiwake
little owl
merganser
mousebird
mynah bird
nighthawk
partridge
phalarope
pilot bird
ptarmigan
razorbill
rifle bird
ring ouzel

ruddy duck
sandpiper
sapsucker
snake bird
snow goose
spoonbill
stonechat
thickhead
thornbill
turnstone

10 letters

Arctic tern
brent goose
budgerigar
canvasback
chiffchaff
crested tit
flycatcher
gooney bird
grassfinch
greenfinch
greenshank
hammerhead
harpy eagle
honeyeater
honeyguide
hooded crow
kingfisher
kookaburra
meadowlark
muttonbird
night heron
nutcracker
pigeon hawk
roadrunner
saddleback
sanderling
sand martin
screech owl
shearwater
sheathbill
song thrush
sun bittern
tailorbird
tropicbird
turtle dove
wattlebird
weaver bird
woodpecker
yellowhead

11 letters

brush turkey
butcherbird
Canada goose
carrion crow
diamond-bird
frigate bird
gnatcatcher
golden eagle
herring gull
house martin
hummingbird
lammergeier
laughing owl
lily-trotter
mockingbird
Muscovy duck
nightingale
reed warbler
scrub turkey
snow bunting
sparrowhawk
stone curlew
storm petrel
treecreeper
wallcreeper
weaver finch
whitethroat
woodcreeper

12 letters

adjutant bird
burrowing owl
cuckoo shrike
fairy penguin
flowerpecker
greylag goose
hedge sparrow
honeycreeper
house sparrow
mandarin duck
marabou stork
marsh harrier
mistle thrush
mourning dove
shoveler duck
umbrella bird
whippoorwill
yellowhammer

Birds (continued)

13 letters
barnacle goose
bateleur eagle
crocodile bird
harlequin duck
Hawaiian goose
long-tailed tit
oystercatcher
pipiwharauroa
secretary bird
turkey vulture
whooping crane
willow warbler

14 letters
bird of paradise
emperor penguin
griffon vulture
owlet-frogmouth
plains-wanderer
rhinoceros bird

15 letters
Baltimore oriole
chipping sparrow
demoiselle crane
laughing jackass

Montagu's harrier
peregrine falcon

16 letters
tyrant flycatcher

18 letters
ring-necked pheasant

19 letters
Mother Carey's chicken

Reptiles

3 letters
asp

5 letters
adder
agama
anole
cobra
gecko
krait
mamba
racer
skink
snake
tokay
viper

6 letters
ameira
caiman
  (cayman)
cooter
goanna
iguana
lizard
moloch
mugger
python
slider

taipan
turtle

7 letters
gharial
tuatara

8 letters
anaconda
basilisk
matamata
moccasin
pit viper
rat snake
rinkhals
sea snake
slow-worm
terrapin
tortoise

9 letters
alligator
blindworm
boomslang
box turtle
bull snake
chameleon
corn snake
crocodile

king cobra
king snake
milk snake
puff adder
scalyfoot
tree snake
vine snake
wart snake
whip snake

10 letters
bandy-bandy
black snake
blind snake
brown snake
bushmaster
chuckwalla
copperhead
coral snake
death adder
fer-de-lance
glass snake
grass snake
horned toad
pond turtle
rainbow boa
rock python
sand lizard
sidewinder

tiger snake
wall lizard
water snake
worm lizard

11 letters

amphisbaena
bloodsucker
cottonmouth
fence lizard
flying snake
Gaboon viper
garter snake
Gila monster
glass lizard
gopher snake
green turtle
horned viper
Indigo snake
leatherback
rattlesnake
ribbon snake
royal python
smooth snake

12 letters

carpet python
flying lizard
hognose snake
Indian python
jungle runner
Komodo dragon
legless skink

13 letters

bearded dragon
frilled lizard
giant tortoise
legless lizard
mangrove snake
monitor lizard
Nile crocodile
Russell's viper
spitting cobra
water moccasin

14 letters

boa constrictor
egg-eating snake

harlequin snake
snapping turtle

15 letters

alligator lizard
hawksbill turtle

16 letters

loggerhead turtle
viviparous lizard

17 letters

reticulated python
soft-shelled turtle

19 letters

diamondback terrapin

22 letters

diamondback rat-
  tlesnake
Galapagos giant tor-
  toise

Amphibians

3 letters

olm

4 letters

frog
newt
toad

5 letters

siren

7 letters

axolotl

8 letters

bullfrog
Congo eel
mud puppy

platanna
tree frog

9 letters

caecilian
giant toad
hairy frog

10 letters

clawed toad
hellbender
horned toad
salamander
smooth newt

11 letters

crested newt
Goliath frog

midwife toad

12 letters

Suriname toad

13 letters

spadefoot toad

14 letters

fire salamander
natterjack toad

15 letters

fire-bellied newt
fire-bellied toad
poison-arrow frog
Tiger Salamander

Fish

3 letters
bib
cod
dab
eel
ide
ray

4 letters
bass
carp
char
chub
cusk
dace
dory
drum
goby
hake
jack
ling
mako
opah
orfe
pike
pope
pout
rudd
scad
scat
scup
shad
sole
tope
tuna

5 letters
bleak
bream
brill
cisco
cobia
danio
fluke
grunt
guppy
loach
manta

molly
perch
porgy
powan
roach
ruffe
saury
shark
skate
smelt
snook
sprat
tench
tetra
trout
wahoo

6 letters
barbel
beluga
bichir
blenny
bonito
bowfin
burbot
darter
discus
dorado
groper
gunnel
madtom
marlin
minnow
mullet
plaice
pollan
redfin
remora
roughy
saithe
salmon
sauger
shanny
sucker
tarpon
tautog
tomcod
turbot

weever
wirrah
wrasse
zander

7 letters
alewife
anchovy
batfish
boxfish
bummalo
candiru
capelin
catfish
cichlid
crappie
croaker
dogfish
eelpout
garfish
garpike
gourami
grunion
gudgeon
gurnard
gwyniad
haddock
hagfish
halibut
herring
hogfish
houting
ice fish
jewfish
koi carp
lamprey
mudfish
oarfish
oilfish
old wife
piranha
pollack
pomfret
pompano
ratfish
redfish
sand eel
sardine

sawfish
sculpin
sea bass
skipper
snapper
sterlet
sunfish
vendace
walleye
whiting

8 letters
albacore
arapaima
bandfish
billfish
blowfish
bluefish
boarfish
bonefish
brisling
bullhead
cavefish
characin
chimaera
coalfish
dealfish
devil ray
dragonet
eagle ray
filefish
firefish
flatfish
flathead
flounder
frogfish
goatfish
goldfish
grayling
halfbeak
John Dory
kingfish
kingklip
lungfish
mackerel
menhaden
monkfish
moonfish

moray eel
pickerel
pilchard
pipefish
rockling
sailfish
sandfish
sea bream
sea horse
sea perch
searobin
sea trout
sparling
stingray
sturgeon
toadfish
trevally
weakfish
wolffish
X-ray fish

9 letters

allis shad
amberjack
angelfish
argentine
barracuda
blackfish
blindfish
blue shark
clingfish
conger eel
glassfish
globefish
goosefish
grenadier
gulper eel
killifish
knifefish
lake trout
lemon sole
mudminnow
mummichog

Murray cod
pearlfish
pikeperch
pilot fish
porbeagle
sheatfish
shubunkin
snipe fish
spadefish
spearfish
stargazer
stone bass
stonefish
swordfish
swordtail
thornback
threadfin
tigerfish
tommy ruff
toothcarp
topminnow
trunkfish
viperfish
whitebait
whitefish
zebra fish

10 letters

angel shark
angler fish
archer fish
barramundi
bitterling
Bombay duck
bonnethead
butterfish
candlefish
chum salmon
coelacanth
cornetfish
damselfish
dragonfish
flying fish

guitarfish
lancetfish
livebearer
lizardfish
lumpsucker
midshipman
mudskipper
needlefish
nurse shark
paddlefish
parrotfish
puffer fish
rabbitfish
ribbonfish
sheepshead
shovelhead
shovelnose
silverside
tiger shark
torpedo ray
twaite shad
whale shark
white shark
yellow jack
yellowtail

11 letters

anemone fish
bonnetmouth
buffalo fish
carpet shark
crucian carp
cutlass fish
dolphinfish
electric eel
electric ray
hatchetfish
lantern fish
Moorish idol
muskellunge
pumpkinseed
sharksucker
smooth hound

stickleback
surgeon fish
triggerfish
weatherfish

12 letters

butterfly ray
fighting fish
four-eyed fish
miller's thumb
mosquitofish
rainbow trout
requiem shark
scorpion fish
sergeant fish
skipjack tuna

13 letters

butterfly fish
climbing perch
flying gurnard
horse mackerel
labyrinth fish
leatherjacket
porcupine fish
sargassum fish
snake mackerel
sockeye salmon
thresher shark

14 letters

humpback
  salmon

15 letters

hammerhead
  shark

17 letters

elephant-snout
  fish

Insects and Arachnids

3 letters
ant
bee
bug
fly
ked

4 letters
flea
mite
moth
tick
wasp

5 letters
aphid
borer
louse
midge

6 letters
bedbug
bee fly
beetle
bot fly
chafer
cicada
earwig
gadfly
hornet
katipo
locust
May bug
mayfly
mygale
red ant
red bug
sawfly
scarab
spider
thrips
weevil

7 letters
ant lion
army ant
blowfly
chigger

corn borer
cricket
cutworm
deer fly
fire ant
firefly
June bug
katydid
redback
sandfly
stylops
termite

8 letters
alder fly
army worm
blackfly
bookworm
crane fly
firebrat
fruit fly
gall wasp
glowworm
greenfly
honey ant
honey bee
horntail
horsefly
housefly
hoverfly
itch mite
lacewing
ladybird
mason bee
mealworm
mealy bug
mosquito
plant bug
scorpion
sheep ked
snakefly
stink bug
stonefly
water bug
white ant
whitefly
wireworm
wood tick

woodwasp
woodworm

9 letters
amazon ant
bloodworm
body louse
booklouse
bumblebee
butterfly
caddis fly
capsid bug
chinch bug
cockroach
crab louse
croton bug
damselfly
dobsonfly
dor beetle
dragonfly
driver ant
gall midge
ground bug
head louse
ichneumon
lac insect
oil beetle
orb weaver
robber fly
screwworm
sheep tick
shield bug
squash bug
sun spider
tarantula
tsetse fly
warble fly
whirligig
wood borer

10 letters
bark beetle
black widow
bluebottle
boll weevil
cockchafer
digger wasp
drosophila

dung beetle
flea beetle
froghopper
harvestman
kissing bug
lantern fly
leaf beetle
leafhopper
leaf insect
phylloxera
pond skater
potter wasp
raft spider
rove beetle
silverfish
Spanish fly
spider mite
spider wasp
spittlebug
springtail
stag beetle
tree hopper
webspinner
wolf spider

11 letters
assassin bug
backswimmer
black beetle
bristletail
buffalo gnat
bush cricket
camel spider
click beetle
grain weevil
grasshopper
greenbottle
harvest mite
mole cricket
money spider
plant hopper
scale insect
scorpion fly
stick insect
tiger beetle
water beetle
water spider

12 letters
brown recluse
carpenter bee
carpet beetle
diadem spider
diving beetle
ground beetle
harlequin bug
jockey spider
potato beetle
sexton beetle
violin spider
water boatman
water strider
whip scorpion
wind scorpion

13 letters
blister beetle

burying beetle
cotton stainer
daddy longlegs
elm bark beetle
false scorpion
giant water bug
Goliath beetle
hunting spider
leafcutter ant
leafcutter bee
leatherjacket
praying mantis
red spider mite
retiary spider
soldier beetle
water scorpion

14 letters
ambrosia beetle

cabbage root fly
cardinal spider
darkling beetle
Hercules beetle
huntsman spider
scorpion spider
slave-making ant
tortoise beetle
trapdoor spider

15 letters
funnel-web
  spider

16 letters
bird-eating
  spider
bombardier
  beetle

cuckoo-spit
  insect
deathwatch
  beetle
devil's coach-
  horse
rhinoceros
  beetle

17 letters
white-tailed
  spider

20 letters
Colorado potato
  beetle

Butterflies and Moths

3 letters
pug

4 letters
blue

5 letters
argus
brown
comma
eggar
heath

6 letters
apollo
burnet
copper
dagger
ermine
io moth
lackey
lappet
morpho
tineid

7 letters
drinker
emerald
monarch
noctuid
pyralid
ringlet
satyrid
silver Y
skipper
sulphur
tortrix
wax moth

8 letters
birdwing
goat moth
grayling
hawkmoth
luna moth
milkweed
oak eggar
puss moth
silk moth
vapourer

9 letters
atlas moth
fruit moth
geometrid
gypsy moth
large blue
nymphalid
orange tip
owlet moth
plume moth
prominent
swift moth
tiger moth
underwing
wall brown

10 letters
Adonis blue
fritillary
gatekeeper
hairstreak
magpie moth
papilionid
red admiral
winter moth

yellow-tail

11 letters
angle shades
bagworm moth
clothes moth
codling moth
emperor moth
leopard moth
lobster moth
meadow brown
painted lady
tussock moth

12 letters
cabbage white
cecropia moth
cinnabar moth
marbled white
peppered moth
silkworm moth
speckled wood
white admiral

Butterflies and Moths *(continued)*

13 letters
clearwing moth
clouded yellow
Mother Shipton
mourning cloak
purple emperor
tortoiseshell

14 letters
burnished brass

15 letters
merveille du jour

16 letters
Camberwell Beauty
peacock butterfly

18 letters
brimstone butterfly
death's head hawk-
  moth

20 letters
swallowtail butterfly

Invertebrates

4 letters
clam
slug

5 letters
conch
fluke
leech
murex
snail
squid
whelk

6 letters
chiton
cockle
cowrie
limpet
mussel
oyster
quahog
teredo
volute
winkle

7 letters
abalone
Cestoda
eelworm
eyeworm
fanworm
filaria
geoduck
lugworm

octopus
piddock
pinworm
ragworm
scallop
sea hare
sea slug
tubifex

8 letters
argonaut
ark shell
cone worm
flatworm
hairworm
hookworm
lungworm
nautilus
nematode
sea lemon
sea mouse
shipworm
tapeworm
top shell
whipworm

9 letters
arrow worm
beard worm
cone shell
earthworm
giant clam
hard-shell
heartworm

planarian
roundworm
scaleworm
slit shell
tusk shell
venus clam
worm shell

10 letters
auger shell
bamboo worm
blood fluke
cuttlefish
guinea worm
kidney worm
liver fluke
miter shell
nudibranch
olive shell
paddleworm
palolo worm
peanut worm
periwinkle
razor shell
ribbonworm
threadworm
tooth shell
wentletrap

11 letters
annelid worm
bristle worm
helmet shell
money cowrie

peacock worm
schistosome
spider conch
tiger cowrie
triton shell

12 letters
bootlace worm
pogonophoran
sea butterfly
slipper shell

13 letters
feather duster
horsehair worm
keyhole limpet
paper nautilus
parchment
  worm
platyhelminth
proboscis worm
soft-shell clam

14 letters
pearly nautilus

15 letters
coat-of-mail
  shell

18 letters
elephant's-tusk
  shell

Seashells

3 letters

tun

4 letters

clam
cone
harp
lima

5 letters

auger
chank
conch
drill
drupe
gaper
miter
murex
olive
ormer
venus
whelk

6 letters

bonnet
cockle
cowrie
helmet
limpet
lucine
mussel
nerite
oyster
quahog
tellin
triton
turban
volute

winkle

7 letters

abalone
junonia
piddock
scallop
sundial

8 letters

ark shell
dog whelk
ear shell
fig shell
hard clam
jewel box
lion's paw
nautilus
Noah's ark
nut shell
pen shell
sea snail
top shell

9 letters

angel wing
cask shell
dove shell
file shell
frog shell
giant clam
hoof shell
horn shell
moon shell
rock shell
slit shell
tusk shell
vase shell

Venus clam
worm shell

10 letters

canoe shell
coat-of-mail
date mussel
marginella
otter shell
periwinkle
razor shell
slit limpet
spire shell
tooth shell
tower shell
tulip shell
turkey wing
wedge shell
wentletrap
wing oyster

11 letters

basket shell
bubble shell
carpet shell
furrow shell
heart cockle
horse mussel
jingle shell
money cowrie
nutmeg shell
oyster drill
spider conch
sunset shell
tiger cowrie
trough shell
turret shell
zebra mussel

12 letters

carrier shell
cup-and-saucer
pelican's foot
pyramid shell
queen scallop
saddle oyster
spindle shell
thorny oyster
trumpet shell

13 letters

fighting conch
keyhole limpet
necklace shell
pheasant shell
slipper limpet
umbrella shell

14 letters

flamingo tongue
partridge shell
pearly nautilus
staircase shell
triton's trumpet
violet sea snail

15 letters

cock's-comb
  oyster

17 letters

chambered
  nautilus

Trees and Shrubs

3 letters
ash
box
elm
fir
koa
may
oak
yew

4 letters
dhak
lime
mako
maté
nipa
palm
pine
shea
sorb
tawa
teak

5 letters
alder
apple
aspen
balsa
beech
belah
birch
cacao
cedar
ebony
elder
hazel
holly
iroko
karri
kauri
kiaat
larch
lilac
maple
matai
ngaio
osier
plane

rowan
savin
sumac (sumach)
thuja
wilga
yucca

6 letters
acacia
almond
banyan
baobab
bo tree
cassia
cornel
deodar
Gaboon
gidgee
ginkgo
gomuti
jarrah
jojoba
kalmia
kamala
kowhai
laurel
linden
mimosa
myrtle
peepul
poplar
privet
redbud
sapele
spruce
styrax
sumach (sumac)
totara
tupelo
walnut
wandoo
wattle
willow
yarran
yaupon

7 letters
arbutus

assegai
banksia
bay tree
bebeeru
champac
cypress
dogwood
guayule
gum tree
hickory
juniper
lantana
logwood
madroño
palmyra
quassia
redwood
robinia
sequoia
seringa
spindle
tea tree

8 letters
calabash
chestnut
coolabah
corkwood
divi-divi
guaiacum
hawthron
hornbeam
ironwood
jelutong
kawakawa
kingwood
magnolia
mahogany
mangrove
manna ash
mesquite
mulberry
ocotillo
oleander
pyinkado
rain tree
rewarewa
rosewood

sandarac
shagbark
soapbark
sourwood
sycamore
tamarack
tamarind
tamarisk
wine palm

9 letters
araucaria
buckthorn
coco-de-mer
coral tree
eaglewood
fever tree
firethorn
flame tree
ivorywood
jacaranda
Judas tree
kahikatea
kurrajong
lemonwood
nux vomica
paulownia
quebracho
saskatoon
sassafras
simarouba
stinkwood
terebinth
thorn tree
whitebeam
zebrawood

10 letters
blackthorn
bottle tree
coffee tree
dragon tree
eucalyptus
frangipani
fringe tree
Joshua tree
kaffirboom
lilly-pilly

macrocarpa
mock orange
pagoda tree
pepper tree
pohutukawa
pyracantha
ribbonwood
sandalwood
sappanwood
sneezewood
sorrel tree

tallow tree
tallow wood
witch hazel
ylang-ylang

11 letters
bottlebrush
camphor tree
lacquer tree
rubber plant
sandbox tree

service tree
varnish tree

12 letters
monkey puzzle
rhododendron
snowball tree
traveler's joy
umbrella tree
wellingtonia

13 letters
toothache tree
wayfaring tree

14 letters
maidenhair tree
silk-cotton tree
strawberry tree
turpentine tree

Flowers

3 letters
hop
rue

4 letters
dock
flax
iris
lily
mint
pink
rose
sage

5 letters
aster
avens
broom
bugle
daisy
furze (gorse)
gorse (furze)
lotus
lupin
oxlip
pansy
peony
phlox
poppy
stock
tansy
thyme
tulip
vetch

yucca

6 letters
azalea
balsam
borage
bryony
burnet
cactus
catnip
clover
cowpea
crocus
dahlia
mallow
nettle
orchid
salvia
sorrel
spurge
sundew
teasel
violet
yarrow
zinnia

7 letters
aconite
aklanet
alyssum
anemone
begonia
bramble
bugloss

burdock
campion
catmint
comfrey
cowslip
figwort
freesia
fuchsia
gentian
heather
hemlock
henbane
hogweed
honesty
jasmine
jonquil
kingcup
lobelia
mayweed
mullein
petunia
primula
ragwort
rosebay
thistle
trefoil
verbena
vervain

8 letters
acanthus
agrimony
arum lily
asphodel

bedstraw
bindweed
bluebell
buddleia
camellia
camomile
catchfly
clematis
crowfoot
cyclamen
daffodil
dropwort
duckweed
fleabane
foxglove
gardenia
geranium
harebell
hawkweed
hibiscus
hyacinth
japonica
knapweed
laburnum
larkspur
lavender
marigold
mayapple
milkwort
plantain
primrose
rock rose
samphire
scabious

Flowers (continued)

shamrock
snowdrop
soapwort
sweet pea
toadflax
valerian
veronica
wisteria
wolfbane
wormwood

9 letters

amaryllis
arrowroot
aubrietia
buttercup
candytuft
carnation
celandine
chickweed
clovepink
coltsfoot
columbine
dandelion
edelweiss
eglantine
eyebright
forsythia
gladiolus
golden rod
goosefoot
groundsel
hellebore
herb Paris
hollyhock
houseleek
hydrangea
knotgrass

lemon balm
mayflower
mistletoe
monkshood
narcissus
pimpernel
saxifrage
snakeroot
speedwell
spikenard
stonecrop
sunflower
tiger lily
twayblade
water lily
witchweed
woundwort

10 letters

aspidistra
belladonna
bellflower
busy Lizzie
butterwort
cinquefoil
coneflower
cornflower
cow parsley
cransebill
cuckoo pint
dead nettle
delphinium
fritillary
herb Gerard
herb Robert
lady's smock
mignonette
montbretia

moonflower
motherwort
nasturtium
nightshade
pennyroyal
peppermint
poinsettia
polyanthus
snapdragon
stitchwort
thorn apple
touch-me-not
wallflower
willowherb
wood sorrel

11 letters

acidanthera
bittersweet
bladderwort
cheese plant
convolvulus
cotoneaster
forget-me-not
gillyflower
helleborine
honeysuckle
lady's finger
loosestrife
meadowsweet
ragged robin
St. John's wort
slipperwort
spider plant
wintergreen

12 letters

globe thistle

lady's slipper
lady's tresses
morning glory
pasque flower
pitcher plant
rhododendron
Solomon's seal
sweet william
tradescantia
Venus flytrap

13 letters

African violet
bleeding heart
carrion flower
chrysanthemum
meadow saffron
passion flower

14 letters

black-eyed
   Susan
cardinal flower
Chinese lantern
lords and ladies
moccasin flower

15 letters

evening prim-
   rose
herb
   Christopher
lily of the valley
yellow archangel

16 letters

deadly night-
   shade

Parts of a Flower

3 letters
lip

4 letters
cyme
spur

5 letters
bract
calyx
glume
lemma
ovary
ovule
palea
petal
sepal

spike
style
tepal
umbel

6 letters
anther
carpel
catkin
corymb
floret
pollen
raceme
spadix
spathe
stamen
stigma

7 letters
corolla
nectary
panicle
pedicel
rhachis

8 letters
bractede
cyathium
filament
ladicule
nucellus
peduncle
placenta
spikelet

9 letters
capitulum
gynoecium
involucel
involucre
pollinium

10 letters
androecium
carpophore
hypanthium
receptacle

11 letters
monochasium
pollen grain

Fruits and Nuts

3 letters
fig

4 letters
bael
date
kaki
lime
nipa
pear
plum
sloe

5 letters
acorn
apple
carob
gourd
grape
guava
lemon
mango
melon
olive
peach

pecan

6 letters
almond
ananas
babaco
banana
cashew
cherry
citron
cobnut
conker
damson
durian
feijoa
gum nut
hognut
jujube
longan
loquat
lychee
medlar
mombin
muscat
orange

pawpaw
peanut
pignut
pippin
pomelo
quince
sal nut
tomato
walnut

7 letters
apricot
avocado
bullace
coconut
 (cocoanut)
cola nut
costard
currant
filbert
geebung
genipap
kumquat
palm nut
pine nut

satsuma
soursop
tangelo

8 letters
areca nut
barberry
bayberry
beechnut
bergamot
betel nut
bilberry
breadnut
coc-de-mer
cocoanut
 (coconut)
dewberry
earthnut
hazelnut
ivory nut
mandarin
minneola
mulberry
persimmon
plantain

Fruits and Nuts (continued)

quandong
rambutan
sour plum
sweetsop
tamarind
tayberry

9 letters

bakeapple
bearberry
bitternut
blueberry
Brazil nut
butternut
candlenut
carambola
cherimoya
chestnut
chincapin
coffee nut
crab apple
cranberry
crowberry
greengage
groundnut

grugru nut
hackberry
jackfruit
kiwi fruit
litchi nut
mockernut
monkey nut
musk melon
myrobalan
nectarine
pineapple
pistachio
raspberry
sapodilla
sour gourd
star apple
star fruit
tamarillo
tangerine
Ugli fruit
  (trademark)

10 letters

blackberry
breadfruit

chinaberry
chokeberry
clementine
elderberry
gooseberry
granadilla
grapefruit
hickory nut
jaboticaba
loganberry
mangosteen
manzanilla
redcurrant
saouari nut
sour cherry
sour orange
spiceberry
strawberry
tree tomato
watermelon
youngberry

11 letters

boysenberry
coquilla nut

huckleberry
lingonberry
pomegranate
prickly pear
salmonberry
sharon fruit
white walnut

12 letters

blackcurrant
burrawang nut
macadamia nut
passion fruit
serviceberry
white currant
whortleberry
winter cherry

13 letters

alligator pear
dwarf chestnut
horse chestnut
Queensland nut
sweet chestnut
water chestnut

Vegetables

3 letters

yam

4 letters

bean
beet
kale
leek
okra
taro

5 letters

chard
cress
gourd
gumbo
onion

savoy
swede

6 letters

carrot
celery
endive
fennel
lentil
manioc
marrow
orache
pepper
potato
radish
squash
tomato

turnip

7 letters

cabbage
cardoon
cassava
chayote
chervil
chicory
gherkin
lettuce
mustard
pak choi
parsnip
pumpkin
salsify
sea kale

shallot
spinach
succory

8 letters

beetroot
broccoli
capsicum
celeriac
cucumber
eggplant
kohlrabi
pimiento
rutabaga
scallion
zucchini

9 letters

artichoke
asparagus
aubergine
calabrese
courgette
curly kale
mangetout
sweet corn

10 letters

breadfruit
scorzonera
watercress

11 letters

avocado pear
cauliflower
oyster plant
spinach beet

sweet potato

12 letters

bamboo shoots
corn on the cob
marrow squash

13 letters

Chinese leaves
water chestnut

14 letters

Brussels sprout
Chinese
  cabbage
dishcloth gourd

18 letters

Jerusalem
  artichoke

Grasses, Sedges, and Rushes

3 letters

fog
oat
rye
tef

4 letters

bent
corn
reed
rice
rush

5 letters

brome
durra
maize
paddy
panic
sedge
spelt
wheat

6 letters

bamboo
barley
darnel
fescue
fiorin

melick
millet
quitch
redtop
zoysia

7 letters

bulrush
esparto
foxtail
papyrus
sorghum
wild oat

8 letters

cutgrass
dogstail
oat grass
reed mace
ryegrass
spartina
spinifex
teosinte
wild rice
woodrush

9 letters

bluegrass
broomcorn

cocksfoot
cordgrass
crabgrass
gama grass
hair grass
lyme grass
reed grass
star grass
sugar cane
wire grass

10 letters

beach grass
beard grass
bunch grass
China grass
couch grass
herd's-grass
Indian corn
Indian rice
lemon grass
quack grass
spear grass
sword grass

11 letters

canary grass
cotton grass
finger grass

marram grass
meadow grass
pampas grass
switch grass
twitch grass
vernal grass

12 letters

Bermuda grass
bristle grass
buffalo grass
feather grass
orchard grass
quaking grass
timothy grass
tussock grass
Yorkshire fog

13 letters

elephant grass

17 letters

Kentucky
  bluegrass
squirreltail grass

Fungi and Algae

3 letters
cep

4 letters
kelp

5 letters
dulse
ergot
fucus
laver
morel
wrack

6 letters
agaric
blewit
bolete
bonnet
bulgar
desmid
diatom
elf cup
fucoid
ink cap
miller
nostoc
prince
wax cap

7 letters
amanita
blusher
boletus
euglena
jew's ear
lorchel
milk cap
oarweed
redware
russula
sea lace
seaware
truffle

8 letters
anabaena
anise cap

bull kelp
club foot
conferva
death cap
deceiver
earth fan
grisette
gulfweed
milk drop
penny bun
polypore
puffball
rockweed
sea wrack
sickener
spike cap
tuckahoe

9 letters
bay bolete
butter cap
carrageen
chlorella
coral spot
ear fungus
earth ball
earthstar
fairy club
fly agaric
funnel cap
laminaria
nullipore
poison pie
sac fungus
sargassum
sea tangle
spirogyra
stinkhorn
stonewort
toadstool
velvet cap
wood witch

10 letters
cage fungus
Ceylon moss
champignon
club fungus

cramp balls
fairy cakes
false morel
fire fungus
liberty cap
panther cap
sea lettuce
tough shank
velvet foot
wood blewit

11 letters
black bulgar
brain fungus
chanterelle
coral fungus
earth tongue
fairy button
flame fungus
ghost fungus
honey fungus
jelly babies
jelly fungus
jelly tongue
russet shank
scarlet hood
sulphur tuft
velvet shank

12 letters
bladderwrack
devil's bolete
dog stinkhorn
dryad's saddle
horn of plenty
peacock's tail
shaggy inkcap
slippery jack
weeping widow
wood hedgehog
wood mush-
  room

13 letters
artist's fungus
bracket fungus
clouded agaric
ear pick fungus

false death cap
field mushroom
giant puffball
horse mushroom
scarlet elf cup
shaggy parasol
spring amanita
sulphur fungus
tawny grisette
witches' butter
yellow stainer
  (yellow-stain-
  ing mushroom)

14 letters
bootlace fungus
dinoflagellate
hedgehog fun-
  gus (hedgehog
  mushroom)
meadow
  mushroom
oyster
  mushroom
saffron milkcap
wood woollyfoot

15 letters
beefsteak fungus
bird's-nest
  fungus
blushing bracket
Caesar's
  mushroom
cowpat toadstool
dead man's
  fingers
destroying angel
parasol
  mushroom
parrot toadstool
plums and
  custard
porcelain fungus
stag's-horn
  fungus
stinking parasol

16 letters
amethyst deceiver
false chanterelle
hedgehog mushroom (hedgehog fungus)
King Alfred's cakes
old man of the woods
orange peel fungus

poached egg fungus

17 letters
candle snuff fungus
caterpillar fungus
cauliflower fungus
chicken of the woods

fairy-ring mushroom
herald of the winter
horsehair mushroom (horsehair toadstool)
St. George's mushroom
yellow brain fungus

18 letters
horsehair toadstool (horsehair mushroom)
lawyer's wig mushroom

22 letters
yellow-staining mushroom (yellow stainer)

Types of Farming

8 letters
forestry

9 letters
husbandry

11 letters
fish farming
hydroponics
viticulture

12 letters
dairy farming
floriculture
horticulture
mixed farming
share farming
silviculture

13 letters
arboriculture
arable farming
sharecropping

14 letters
factory farming
organic farming

15 letters
market gardening

16 letters
extensive farming

intensive farming
livestock farming

18 letters
subsistence farming

Breeds of Horse and Pony

4 letters
Arab
Barb
Russ

5 letters
Fjord
Huçul
Konik
Lokai
Pinto
Timor

6 letters
Breton

brumby
Hunter
Kazakh
Morgan
Nonius
Pottok
Tarpan
Viatka

7 letters
Bashkir
Budenny
Caspian
Comtois
criollo

Gotland
Hackney
Jutland
Landais
Murgese
mustang
Noriker
Salerno
trotter

8 letters
Ariègois
Camargue
Fell pony
Friesian

Galiceño
Galloway
Kabardin
Karabakh
Palomino
Paso Fino
polo pony
Welsh cob

9 letters
Anglo-Arab
Appaloosa
Conestoga
Dales pony
Falabella

Breeds of Horse and Pony *(continued)*

Haflinger
Percheron
Pinzgauer
Schleswig
Trakehner

10 letters

Andalusian
Bardigiano
Basuto pony
Clydesdale
Dutch draft
Exmoor pony
Hanoverian
Holsteiner
Irish draft
Kathiawari
Lippizaner
Mangalarga
Mérens pony
Saddlebred
Shire horse
Tartar pony

11 letters

Iceland pony

Irish hunter
Lundy Island
Manipur pony
Oldenburger
Rhinelander
Sable Island
Shales horse

12 letters

Cleveland Bay
Dartmoor pony
Gelderlander
Highland pony
Orlov trotter
Peruvian Paso
Quarter Horse
Shetland pony
Standardbred
Suffolk Punch

13 letters

Connemara
  pony
New Forest pony
Württemberger

14 letters

Colorado
  Ranger
Dutch warm-
  blood
Indian Half-bred
Plateau Persian
Waler warm-
  blood

15 letters

Danish warm-
  blood

16 letters

Asiatic Wild
  Horse
Russian warm-
  blood
Swedish warm-
  blood

17 letters

miniature
  Shetland
  pony of the

Americas
Russian heavy
  draft
Tersk
  thoroughbred
Welsh Mountain
  pony

19 letters

Yorkshire coach
  horse

21 letters

Tennessee
  walking horse

22 letters

Norwegian
  racing trotter

24 letters

Czechoslovakian
  warmblood
Missouri fox-
  trotting horse

Points of a Horse

4 letters

dock
frog
heel
hock
hoof
knee
loin
mane
poll
ribs
tail

5 letters

cheek
chest

crest
croup
elbow
ergot
flank
shank

6 letters

gaskin
gullet
sheath
stifle
tendon

7 letters

coronet
fetlock
forearm
pastern
withers

8 letters

chestnut
feathers
forelcok
shoulder
windpipe

9 letters

pedal bone

10 letters

cannon bone
chin groove
coffin bone
point of hip
splint bone

12 letters

fetlock joint
hind quarters

13 letters

navicular bone

15 letters

point of shoul-
  der

Breeds of Cattle

5 letters
Devon
Kerry
Kyloe
Luing
N'Dama

6 letters
Bangus
Dexter
Durham
Jersey
Sussex

7 letters
Barrosã
Beefalo
Brahman
Miranda
Red Poll

8 letters
Ayrshire
Chianina
Friesian
Galloway

Guernsey
Hereford
Highland
Limousin
Longhorn
Shetland

9 letters
Charolais
Danish Red
Mongolian
Pinzgauer
Romagnola
Shorthorn
Simmental
White Park

10 letters
Africander
Andalusian
Brown Swiss
Lincoln Red
Maine Anjou
Murray Grey
South Devon
Welsh Black

11 letters
Belgian Blue
Belted Welsh
Irish Moiled
Jamaica Hope

12 letters
British White
German Yellow
Red Ruby
  Devon
West Highland

13 letters
Aberdeen Angus
Beef Shorthorn
Droughtmaster
Galician Blond
Texas Longhorn
White Galloway

14 letters
Belted Galloway
Polled Hereford
Santa Gertrudis

16 letters
Blonde
  d'Aquitaine
Holstein-
  Friesian
Meuse-Rhine-
  Ijssel
Polled Welsh
  Black

18 letters
Swedish Red-
  and-White

19 letters
Red-and-White
  Friesian

28 letters
Australian
  Illawarra
  Shorthorn

Breeds of Sheep

3 letters
Mug

4 letters
Kent
Lonk
Soay

5 letters
Altai
Chios
Jacob
Lacho
Lamon
Lleyn

Masai
Texel

6 letters
Awassi
Berber
Biella
Dorper
Galway
Manech
Merino
Orkney
Panama
Radnor
Tsigai

7 letters
Bergamo
Cheviot
Colbred
Karakul
Lacaune
Lourdes
Précoce
Romanov
Ryeland
Suffolk
Targhee
Tibetan

8 letters
Askanian

Columbia
Cotswold
Dartmoor
Herdwick
Kivircik
Polwarth
Portland
Rhiw Hill
Shetland
Sicilian
Talavera

9 letters
Blackface
Caucasian
Dales-Bred

Breeds of Sheep (continued)

Dubrovnik
Hebridean
Icelandic
Kerry Hill
Leicester
Llanwenog
Mongolian
Romeldale
Rough Fell
Sardinian
Southdown
Swaledale
Teeswater

10 letters

Abyssinian
Africander
Clun Forest
Corriedale
Dorset Down
Dorset Horn
Exmoor Horn
Hill Radnor
Karakachan
Oxford Down
Poll Dorset
Red Karaman
Shropshire

South Devon

11 letters

Greek Zackel
Ile-de-France
Manx Loghtan
Norfolk Horn
Rambouillet
Romney Marsh
Wensleydale

12 letters

Cannock Chase
Old Norwegian

13 letters

Devon
 Longwool
Hampshire
 Down
Spanish Merino
Tyrol Mountain
Welsh Mountain
Wiltshire Horn

14 letters

Devon
 Closewool

Island Pramenka
North Ronaldsay

15 letters

Border Leicester
Bosnian
 Mountain
English
 Longwool
Lincoln
 Longwool
Wicklow
 Mountain

16 letters

Australian
 Merino
Blackhead
 Persian
Campanian
 Barbary
Castlemilk
 Moorit
Swiss White
 Alpine

17 letters

Brazilian
 Woolless

French
 Blackheaded
Scottish
 Blackface
Whiteface
 Dartmoor

18 letters

Beulah Speckled
 Face
Black Welsh
 Mountain
Bluefaced
 Leicester
South Wales
 Mountain
Swiss White
 Mountain
Whiteface
 Woodlands

19 letters

Derbyshire
 Gritstone
North Country
 Cheviot

Wild Sheep

5 letters
urial

6 letters
aoudad
argali
bharal

7 letters
bighorn
mouflon

9 letters
blue sheep
dall sheep

10 letters
white sheep

12 letters
barbary sheep

13 letters
mountain sheep

Breeds of Fowl

BANTAM

6 letters
Booted
Nankin

8 letters
Frizzles
Rosecomb
Rumpless
Sebright

14 letters
Old English
  Game

CHICKEN

5 letters
Malay

6 letters
Ancona
Brahma
Bresse
Cochin
Houdan
Marans
Orloff
Poland
Redcap
Silkie
Sultan
Sussex

7 letters
Campine
Dorking
Ixworth
Leghorn
Malines
Phoenix
Spanish

8 letters
Hamburgh
La Fleche
Yokohama

9 letters
Crèvecour
Faverolle
Orpington
Scots Grey
Welsummer
Wyandotte

10 letters
Andalusian
Australorp
Indian Game
Marsh Daisy
Modern Game
Scots Dumpy

11 letters
Jersey Giant
Lakenfelder
Norfolk Grey
Sumatra Game

12 letters
Plymouth Rock

13 letters
Croad Langshan

14 letters
Modern
  Langshan
Rhode Island
  Red

15 letters
New Hampshire
  Red

16 letters
North Holland
  Blue

17 letters
Jubilee Indian
  Game
Sicilian
  Buttercup

22 letters
Old English
  Pheasant Fowl
Transylvanian
  Naked Neck

DUCK

5 letters
Rouen

6 letters
Cayuga
Magpie

7 letters
Crested
Muscovy

9 letters
Aylesbury
Orpington

10 letters
Whalesbury

12 letters
Indian Runner

13 letters
Khaki Campbell

14 letters
Welsh
  Harlequin

15 letters
Black East
  Indian

GOOSE

5 letters
Roman

6 letters
Embden

7 letters
Chinese
Pilgrim

8 letters
Toulouse

10 letters
Brecon Buff
Sebastopol

GUINEA FOWL

5 letters
White

8 letters
Lavender

9 letters
Pearl Grey

TURKEY

8 letters
Nicholas

10 letters
Bourbon Red

12 letters
Black Norfolk
Narragansett
White Holland

13 letters
Mammoth
  Bronze
White Austrian

15 letters
Cambridge
  Bronze

18 letters
Broad-Breasted
  White

19 letters
Broad-Breasted
  Bronze

Breeds of Dog

3 letters
pug

4 letters
chow
puli
tosa

5 letters
akita
boxer
corgi
husky
laika
spitz

6 letters
Afghan
beagle
borzoi
Briard
collie
kelpie
Kuvasz
poodle
saluki
setter
vizsla

7 letters
basenji
bulldog
griffon
harrier
Ivicene
mastiff
pointer
Samoyed
shih-tzu
spaniel
terrier
whippet

8 letters
Alsatian
elkhound
Eurasier
foxhound

Hovawart
keeshond
Komondor
Malamute
papillon
Pekinese

9 letters
chihuahua
coonhound
dachshund
Dalmatian
deerhound
Great Dane
greyhound
Lhasa apso
retriever
St. Bernard
schnauzer
staghound

10 letters
bloodhound
fox terrier
Leonberger
otter hound
Pomeranian
Rottweiler
schipperke
Weimaraner
Welsh corgi
Welsh hound

11 letters
basset hound
Bichon Frise
bullmastiff
bull terrier
Groenendael
Ibizan hound
Irish setter
Skye terrier

12 letters
Border collie
cairn terrier
field spaniel
Finnish spitz

Gordon setter
Irish terrier
Newfoundland
Pharaoh hound
Welsh terrier

13 letters
affenpinscher
Bearded Collie
Boston terrier
cocker spaniel
English setter
Great Pyrenees
Siberian husky

14 letters
Clumber spaniel
Giant
  Schnauzer
Ibicencan hound
Irish wolfhound
Istrian pointer
Maltese terrier
Norfolk terrier
Norwich terrier
pit bull terrier

15 letters
Aberdeen terrier
Airedale terrier
Alaskan mala-
  mute
Belgian malinois
Blenheim
  spaniel
Brussels griffon
golden retriever
Lakeland terrier
Mexican hairless
Scottish terrier
Sealyham terrier
springer spaniel

16 letters
Kerry blue
  terrier
Pyrenean sheep-
  dog

Shetland
  sheepdog
Yorkshire terrier

17 letters
Australian
  terrier
Bedlington
  terrier
Dobermann
  pinscher
Labrador
  retriever
Manchester
  terrier
Norwegian
  elkhound
Pyrenean
  wolfhound
Scottish
  deerhound

18 letters
Bernese
  mountain dog
Bouvier des
  Flandres
Jack Russell
  terrier
King Charles
  spaniel
Old English
  sheepdog
Rhodesian
  ridgeback

19 letters
Pyrenean
  mountain dog
West Highland
  terrier

20 letters
Black and Tan
  Coonhound
Dandie Dinmont
  terrier
wirehaired fox
  terrier

22 letters
Tervuren
  Tibetan
  Terrier

24 letters
Staffordshire
  bull terrier

26 letters
Cavalier King
  Charles
  spaniel

Breeds of Cat

3 letters
Rex

4 letters
Manx

5 letters
Cameo
Cream
Korat
Smoke
Tabby

6 letters
Birman
Bombay
Cymric
Havana
Ocicat
Somali
Sphynx

7 letters
Burmese
Kashmir
Malayan
Persian

Siamese
Tiffany

8 letters
Balinese
Devon Rex
Javanese
Snowshoe

9 letters
Himalayan
Singapura
Tonkinese

10 letters
Abyssinian
Chartreuse
Chinchilla
Cornish Rex
red-pointed
Turkish Van

11 letters
Blue Burmese
blue-pointed
British Blue
Egyptian Mau

Russian Blue
seal-pointed

12 letters
lilac-pointed
Maine Coon
  Cat
Scottish Fold
tabby-pointed

13 letters
domestic tabby
Tortoiseshell
Turkish Angora

14 letters
British Spotted

15 letters
Exotic Shorthair
Japanese Bobtail

16 letters
American
  Wirehair
chocolate-
  pointed

domestic long-
  hair

17 letters
American
  Shorthair
European
  Shorthair
Oriental
  Shorthair

18 letters
Norwegian
  Forest Cat

19 letters
Colorpoint
  Shorthair

20 letters
tortoiseshell-
  pointed

LITERATURE AND LANGUAGE

Literary Terms

4 letters
epic
foot
iamb
myth
plot

5 letters
elegy
fable
genre
ictus
irony
lyric
meter
motif
rhyme
scene
style
theme

6 letters
ballad
bathos
cliché
dactyl
hubris
lament
monody
parody
pathos
satire
simile
sonnet
stanza
stress

7 letters
acmeism
caesura
conceit
couplet
Dadaism
diction

eclogue
elision
epigram
epistle
epitaph
euphony
fabliau
imagery
imagism
kenning
nemesis
paradox
Pléiade, la
prosody
realism
spondee
subplot
tragedy
trochee
ubi sunt
verismo

8 letters
allegory
anapaest
Augustan
episodic
euphuism
exemplum
eye rhyme
futurism
limerick
metaphor
metonymy
Movement, the
oxymoron
quatrain
rhetoric
scansion
syllable
trimeter

9 letters
absurdism

ambiguity
assonance
burlesque
catharsis
euphemism
free verse
Gongorism
Gothicism
half rhyme
hexameter
hypoerbole
hypotaxis
Lake poets
leitmotif (leitmotiv)
mannerism
modernism
monometer
octameter
pararhyme
parataxis
sibilance
symbolism
vorticism

10 letters
blank verse
caricature
classicism
denouement
epic simile
heptameter
minimalism
mock heroic
naturalism
neorealism
pentameter
picaresque
Spoonerism
surrealism
tetrameter

11 letters
anachronism
courtly love

didacticism
end stopping
enjambement
Gothic novel
hermeticism
Horatian ode
malapropism
medievalism
objectivity
pastoralism
primitivism
prosopopeia
  (prosopopoeia)
Romanticism
synechdoche
tragicomedy

12 letters
aestheticism
alliteration
doppelgänger
epithalamium
  (epithalamion)
magic realism
onomatopoeia
prosopopoeia
  (prosopopoeia)
subjectivity

13 letters
expressionism
Georgian poets
heroic couplet
internal rhyme
neoclassicism
postmodernism
social realism
structuralism
Sturm und Drang

14 letters
beat generation
deconstruction
existentialism
feminine ending
Liverpool poets
Miltonic sonnet
pre-Romanticism
reported speech
sentimentality

15 letters
Bloomsbury group
epistolary novel
masculine ending
pathetic fallacy
personification
pre-Raphaelitism

16 letters
anthropomorphism
Petrarchan sonnet
Russian formalism
socialist realism

17 letters
alliterative verse
free indirect style
Harlem Renaissance
interior monologue
metaphysical poets
post-structuralism
transcendentalism

18 letters
negative capability
omniscient narrator

19 letters
Renaissance humanism

20 letters
first person narrative
objective correlative
third person narrative

21 letters
stream of consciousness

Meters and Metrical Feet

4 letters
iamb

5 letters
ionic
paeon

6 letters
choree
cretic
dactyl
dipody

7 letters
dimeter
distich
pyrrhic
spondee
trochee

8 letters
anapaest
choriamb
tribrach
trimeter

9 letters
hexameter
octameter

10 letters
amphibrach
amphimacer
duple meter
heptameter
pentameter
tetrameter

11 letters
alexandrine

13 letters
heroic couplet

14 letters
elegiac couplet
elegiac distich

16 letters
iambic
  pentameter

Characters from Well-Known Works of Fiction

(with titles and authors)

3 letters

HCE (Humphrey Chimpden Earwicker) (*Finnegans Wake*, James Joyce)

Kim (*Kim*, Rudyard Kipling)

Owl (*Winnie the Pooh*, A. A. Milne)

Pen (Arthur Pendennis) (*Pendennis*, William Makepeace Thackeray)

Roo (*Winnie the Pooh*, A. A. Milne)

Tom (*The Water-Babies*, Charles Kingsley)

4 letters

Abel (*Middlemarch*, George Eliot)

East (*Tom Brown's Schooldays*, Thomas Hughes)

Judy (*Wee Willie Winkie*, Rudyard Kipling)

O-Lan (*The Good Earth*, Pearl S. Buck)

Puck (Robin Goodfellow) (*Puck of Pook's Hill*, Rudyard Kipling)

Rama (Tiger Tiger) (*The Jungle Book*, Rudyard Kipling)

5 letters

Akela (*The Jungle Book*, Rudyard Kipling)

Aslan (*The Lion, the Witch, and the Wardrobe*, C. S. Lewis)

Athos (*The Three Musketeers*, Alexandre Dumas)

Baloo (*The Jungle Book*, Rudyard Kipling)

Becky (Rebecca Sharp) (*Vanity Fair*, William Makepeace Thackeray)

Bruff (*The Moonstone*, Wilkie Collins)

Kanga (*Winnie the Pooh*, A. A. Milne)

Mercy (*The Pilgrim's Progress*, John Bunyan)

Piggy (*Lord of the Flies*, William Golding)

Porgy (*Porgy*, Du Bose Heywood)

Punch (*Wee Willie Winkie*, Rudyard Kipling)

Ralph (*Lord of the Flies*, William Golding)

Ratty (Water Rat) (*The Wind in the Willows*, Kenneth Grahame)

Sambo (*Just-So Stories*, Rudyard Kipling)

Sandi (Sanders) (*Sanders of the River*, Edgar Wallace)

Sloth (*The Pilgrim's Progress*, John Bunyan)

Tarka (*Tarka the Otter*, Henry Williamson)

Topsy (*Uncle Tom's Cabin*, Harriet Beecher Stowe)

Uncas (*The Last of the Mohicans*, James Fenimore Cooper)

6 letters

Aitken (*Prester John*, John Buchan)

Aramis (*The Three Musketeers*, Alexandre Dumas)

Ayesha (*She*, Henry Rider Haggard)

Bessie (*Jane Eyre*, Charlotte Brontë)

Cackle (*Vanity Fair*, William Makepeace Thackeray)

Eeyore (*Winnie the Pooh*, A. A. Milne)

Friday (*Robinson Crusoe*, Daniel Defoe)

George (*Three Men in a Boat*, Jerome K. Jerome)

Grimes (*The Water-Babies*, Charles Kingsley)

Jeeves (*Thank you, Jeeves*, P. G. Wodehouse)

Laurie (*Little Women*, Louisa May Alcott)

Lungri (*The Jungle Book*, Rudyard Kipling)

Mowgli (*The Jungle Book*, Rudyard Kipling)

Mr. Mole (*The Wind in the Willows*, Kenneth Grahame)

Mr. Toad (*The Wind in the Willows*, Kenneth Grahame)

Pinkie (*Brighton Rock*, Graham Greene)

Rabbit (*Winnie the Pooh*, A. A. Milne)

Roxana (*Roxana*, Daniel Defoe)

Square (*Tom Jones*, Henry Fielding)

Tarzan (*Tarzan of the Apes*, Edgar Rice Burroughs)

Umpopa (*King Solomon's Mines*, Henry Rider Haggard)

7 letters

Antonia (*My Antonia*, Willa Cather)

Babbitt (*Babbitt*, Sinclair Lewis)

Bagster (*Middlemarch*, George Eliot)

Beesley (*Lucky Jim*, Kingsley Amis)

Beloved (*Beloved*, Toni Morrison)

Ben Gunn (*Treasure Island*, Robert Louis Stevenson)

Brer Fox (*Uncle Remus*, Joel Chandler Harris)

Dorothy (*The Wizard of Oz*, Frank L. Baum)

Hawkeye (*The Last of the Mohicans*, James Fenimore Cooper)

Ishmael (*Moby Dick*, Herman Melville)

Jo March (*Little Women*, etc., Louisa May Alcott)

Lawless (*The Black Arrow*, Robert Louis Stevenson)

Lord Jim (*Lord Jim*, Joseph Conrad)

Messala (*Ben Hur*, Lew Wallace)

Mr. Otter (*The Wind in the Willows*, Kenneth Grahame)

Porthos (*The Three Musketeers*, Alexandre Dumas)

Rebecca (*Rebecca*, Daphne du Maurier)

Rebecca (*Rebecca of Sunnybrook Farm*, Kate D. Wiggin)

Red King (*Through the Looking-Glass*, Lewis Carroll)

Reed, Mrs. (*Jane Eyre*, Charlotte Brontë)

Sanders (Sandi) (*Sanders of the River*, Edgar Wallace)

Spenser (*Early Autumn*, etc., Robert B. Parker)

Tom Joad (*The Grapes of Wrath*, John Steinbeck)

William (*Just William*, Richmal Crompton)

8 letters

Adam Bede (*Adam Bede*, George Eliot)

Amy March (*Little Women*, etc., Louisa May Alcott)

Angelica (*The Rose and the Ring*, William Makepeace Thackeray)

Apollyon (*The Pilgrim's Progress*, John Bunyan)

Bagheera (*The Jungle Book*, Rudyard Kipling)

Basil Seal (*Put Out More Flags*, Evelyn Waugh)

Beau Nash (Richard) (*Monsieur Beaucaire*, Booth Tarkington)

Black Dog (*Treasure Island*, Robert Louis Stevenson)

"Brer" Wolf (*Uncle Remus*, Joel Chandler Harris)

Dr. Moreau (*The Island of Dr. Moreau*, H. G. Wells)

Flashman (*Tom Brown's Schooldays*, Thomas Hughes)

Jack Ryan (*Patriot Games*, etc., Tom Clancy)

Jane Eyre (*Jane Eyre*, Charlotte Brontë)

John Easy (*Mr. Midshipman Easy*, Captain Marryat)

John Ridd (*Lorna Doone*, R. D. Blackmore)

Judah Hur (*Ben Hur*, Lew Wallace)

Lockwood (*Wuthering Heights*, Emily Brontë)

Meg March (*Little Women*, etc., Louisa May Alcott)

Michael K (*Life and Times of Michael K*, J. M. Coetzee)

Mr. Ramsay (*To the Lighthouse*, Virginia Woolf)

Mrs. Moore (*A Passage to India*, E. M. Forster)

Characters from Well-Known
Works of Fiction *(continued)*

Napoleon (*Animal Farm*, George Orwell)

Red Queen (*Through the Looking-Glass*, Lewis Carroll)

Sam Spade (*The Maltese Falcon*, Dashiell Hammett)

Svengali (*Trilby*, George du Maurier)

Thwackum (*Tom Jones*, Henry Fielding)

Tom Alibi (*Waverley*, Walter Scott)

Tom Jones (*Tom Jones*, Henry Fielding)

Tom Thumb (*The Tale of Two Bad Mice*, Beatrix Potter)

"Uncle" Tom (*Uncle Tom's Cabin*, Harriet Beecher Stowe)

Wang Lung (*The Good Earth*, Pearl S. Buck)

Water Rat (Ratty) (*The Wind in the Willows*, Kenneth Grahame)

Whiteoak (family) (*The Whiteoak Chronicles*, Mazo de la Roche)

White-Tip (*Tarka the Otter*, Henry Williamson)

9 letters

A. J. Raffles (*Raffles* series, E. W. Hornung)

Barrymore (*The Hound of the Baskervilles*, Arthur Conan Doyle)

Beau Geste (*Beau Geste*, P. C. Wren)

Beth March (*Little women*, etc., Louisa May Alcott)

Chainmail (*Crotchet Castle*, Thomas Love Peacock)

Christian (*The Pilgrim's Progress*, John Bunyan)

D'Artagnan (*The Three Musketeers*, Alexandre Dumas)

Dr. Proudie (*Framley Parsonage* and other "Barsetshire" novels, Anthony Trollope)

Ellen Dean (*Wuthering Heights*, Emily Brontë)

Eppie Cass (*Silas Marner*, George Eliot)

Huw Morgan (*How Green Was My Valley*, Richard Llewellyn)

Indian Joe (*The Adventures of Tom Sawyer*, Mark Twain)

James Bond (*Dr. No, Thunderball*, etc., Ian Fleming)

Jay Gatsby (*The Great Gatsby*, F. Scott Fitzgerald)

Jim Turner (Captain Flint) (*Swallows and Amazons*, Arthur Ransome)

Joe Harman (*A Town like Alice*, Nevil Shute)

Little Eva (Evangeline St. Clare) (*Uncle Tom's Cabin*, Harriet Beecher Stowe)

Lucy Snowe (*Villette*, Charlotte Brontë)

March Hare (*Alice in Wonderland*, Lewis Carroll)

Mr. Cypress (*Nightmare Abbey*, Thomas Love Peacock)

Mrs. Ramsay (*To the Lighthouse*, Virginia Woolf)

Mrs. Weston (*Emma*, Jane Austen)

Nero Wolfe (*Fer-de-Lance*, etc., Rex Stout)

Paul Morel (*Sons and Lovers*, D. H. Lawrence)

Red Knight (*Through the Looking-Glass*, Lewis Carroll)

Shere Khan (Lungri) (*The Jungle Book*, Rudyard Kipling)

Tiger Lily (*Peter Pan*, J. M. Barrie)

Tom Sawyer (*The Adventures of Tom Sawyer*, Mark Twain)

Yossarian (*Catch-22*, Joseph Heller)

10 letters

Allan-a-Dale (*Ivanhoe*, Walter Scott)

Amy Robsart (*Kenilworth*, Walter Scott)

Angel Clare (*Tess of the D'Urbervilles*, Thomas Hardy)

Arrowpoint (*Daniel Deronda*, George Eliot)

Belladonna (*Vanity Fair*, William Makepeace Thackeray)

"Brer" Rabbit (*Uncle Remus*, Joel Chandler Harris)

Dorian Gray (*The Picture of Dorian Gray*, Oscar Wilde)

Edward Bear (Winnie-the-Pooh) (*Winnie-the-Pooh*, A. A. Milne)

Edward Hyde (*Dr. Jekyll and Mr. Hyde*, Robert Louis Stevenson)

Effie Deans (*The Heart of Midlothian*, Walter Scott)

Emma Bovary (*Madame Bovary*, Gustave Flaubert)

Grace Poole (*Jane Eyre*, Charlotte Brontë)

Heathcliff (*Wuthering Heights*, Emily Brontë)

Hunca Munca (*The Tale of Two Bad Mice*, Beatrix Potter)

Irene Adler (*The Adventures of Sherlock Holmes*, Arthur Conan Doyle)

Jackanapes (*Jackanapes*, Juliana H. Ewing)

Jake Barnes (*The Sun Also Rises*, Ernest Hemingway)

James Dixon (*Lucky Jim*, Kingsley Amis)

Jane Bennet (*Pride and Prejudice*, Jane Austen)

Jane Marple (*A Pocket Full of Rye*, Agatha Christie)

Jim Hawkins (*Treasure Island*, Robert Louis Stevenson)

Joe Lampton (*Room at the Top*, John Braine)

John Walker (*Swallows and Amazons*, Arthur Ransome)

Jon Forsyte (*The Forsyte Saga*, John Galsworthy)

Kit Sorrell (*Sorrell and Son*, Warwick Deeping)

Lorelei Lee (*Gentlemen Prefer Blondes*, Anita Loos)

Lorna Doone (*Lorna Doone*, R. D. Blackmore)

Major Major (*Catch-22*, Joseph Heller)

Mary Bennet (*Pride and Prejudice*, Jane Austen)

Mercy Chant (*Tess of the D'Urbervilles*, Thomas Hardy)

Mike Hammer (*I, the Jury*, etc., Mickey Spillane)

Miss Temple (*Jane Eyre*, Charlotte Brontë)

Mock Turtle (*Alice's Adventures in Wonderland*, Lewis Carroll)

Molly Bloom (*Ulysses*, James Joyce)

Mrs. Danvers (*Rebecca*, Daphne du Maurier)

Mrs. Fairfax (*Jane Eyre*, Charlotte Brontë)

Mrs. Proudie (*Framley Parsonage* and other "Barsetshire" novels, Anthony Trollope)

Mrs. Western (*Tom Jones*, Henry Fielding)

Rev. Jim Casy (*The Grapes of Wrath*, John Steinbeck)

Thady Quirk (*Castle Rackrent*, Maria Edgeworth)

Tiger Tiger (Rama) (*The Jungle Book*, Rudyard Kipling)

Tinker Bell (*Peter Pan*, J. M. Barrie)

Tom Tiddler (*Adam's Opera*, Clemence Dane)

Tweedledee (*Through the Looking-Glass*, Lewis Carroll)

Tweedledum (*Through the Looking-Glass*, Lewis Carroll)

Uncle Remus (*Uncle Remus* series, Joel Chandler Harris)

11 letters

Alfred Polly (*The History of Mr. Polly*, H. G. Wells)

Arthur Kipps (*Kipps*, H. G. Wells)

Bennet Hatch (*The Black Arrow*, Robert Louis Stevenson)

Captain Ahab (*Moby Dick*, Herman Melville)

Don (Vito) Corleone (*The Godfather*, Mario Puzo)

Characters from Well-Known
Works of Fiction (continued)

Edgar Linton (*Wuthering Heights*, Emily Brontë)

Harriet Vane (*Strong Poison*, Dorothy L. Sayers)

Henry Jekyll (*Dr. Jekyll and Mr. Hyde*, Robert Louis Stevenson)

Henry Tilney (*Northanger Abbey*, Jane Austen)

Hetty Sorrel (*Adam Bede*, George Eliot)

India Wilkes (*Gone with the Wind*, Margaret Mitchell)

Israel Hands (*Treasure Island*, Robert Louis Stevenson)

Jabberwocky (*Alice Through the Looking-Glass*, Lewis Carroll)

Jane Fairfax (*Emma*, Jane Austen)

Jeanie Deans (*The Heart of Midlothian*, Walter Scott)

Leonard Lamb (*Middlemarch*, George Eliot)

Lydia Bennet (*Pride and Prejudice*, Jane Austen)

Minna Harker (*Dracula*, Bram Stoker)

Montmorency (the dog) (*Three Men in a Boat*, Jerome K. Jerome)

Natty Bumppo (*The Last of the Mohicans*, James Fenimore Cooper)

Phineas Finn (*Phineas Finn*, Anthony Trollope)

Prince Bulbo (*The Rose and the Ring*, William Makepeace Thackeray)

Rhett Butler (*Gone with the Wind*, Margaret Mitchell)

Richard Nash (Beau) (*Monsieur Beaucaire*, Booth Tarkington)

Roger Walker (*Swallows and Amazons*, Arthur Ransome)

Sal Paradise (*On The Road*, Jack Kerouac)

Silas Marner (*Silas Marner*, George Eliot)

Simon Legree (*Uncle Tom's Cabin*, Harriet Beecher Stowe)

Susan Walker (*Swallows and Amazons*, Arthur Ransome)

Titty Walker (*Swallows and Amazons*, Arthur Ransome)

Tom Tulliver (*The Mill on the Floss*, George Eliot)

Vicky Walker (*Swallows and Amazons*, Arthur Ransome)

Walter Mitty (*The Secret Life of Walter Mitty*, James Thurber)

White Rabbit (*Alice's Adventures in Wonderland*, Lewis Carroll)

12 letters

Alice Aisgill (*Room at the Top*, John Braine)

Ashley Wilkes (*Gone with the Wind*, Margaret Mitchell

Benjy Compson (*The Sound and the Fury*, William Faulkner)

Brocklehurst (*Jane Eyre*, Charlotte Brontë)

Captain Flint (Jim Turner) (*Swallows and Amazons*, Arthur Ransome)

Charles Ryder (*Brideshead Revisited*, Evelyn Waugh)

Chingachgook (*The Last of the Mohicans*, James Fenimore Cooper)

Count Dracula (*Dracula*, Bram Stoker)

Dean Moriarty (*On the Road*, Jack Kerouac)

Duke of Omnium (Family name Palliser) (The "Palliser" series, Anthony Trollope, the "Barsetshire" series, Angela Thirkell)

Fleur Forsyte (*The Forsyte Saga*, John Galsworthy)

Giant Despair (*The Pilgrim's Progress*, John Bunyan)

Hester Prynne (*The Scarlet Letter*, Nathaniel Hawthorne)

Humpty-Dumpty (*Through the Looking-Glass*, Lewis Carroll)

Irene Forsyte (*The Forsyte Sage*, John Galsworthy)

Isabel Archer (*The Portrait of a Lady*, Henry James)

Judith Hearne (*The Lonely Passion of Judith Hearne*, Brian Moore)

Kimball O'Hara (*Kim*, Rudyard Kipling)

Leopold Bloom (*Ulysses*, James Joyce)

Meg Merrilies (*Guy Mannering*, Walter Scott)

Moll Flanders (*Moll Flanders*, Daniel Defoe)

Nick Carraway (*The Great Gatsby*, F. Scott Fitzgerald)

Rebecca Sharp (Becky) (*Vanity Fair*, William Makepeace Thackeray)

Sergeant Cuff (*The Moonstone*, Wilkie Collins)

Simon Dedalus (*A Portrait of the Artist as a Young Man*, *Ulysses*, James Joyce)

Sister Carrie (*Sister Carrie*, Theodore Dreiser)

Squire Gordon (*Black Beauty*, Anna Sewell)

St. John Rivers (*Jane Eyre*, Charlotte Brontë)

(The) Virginian (*The Virginian*, Owen Wister)

Will Ladislaw (*Middlemarch*, George Eliot)

Winston Smith (*Nineteen Eighty-Four*, George Orwell)

13 letters

Archie Goodwin (*Fer-de-Lance*, etc., Rex Stout)

Becky Thatcher (*The Adventures of Tom Sawyer*, Mark Twain)

Bertie Wooster (*Thank You, Jeeves*, etc., P. G. Wodehouse)

Blanche DuBois (*A Streetcar Named Desire*, Tennessee Williams)

Continental Op (*Red Harvest*, etc., Dashiell Hammett)

Darsie Latimer (*Redgauntlet*, Walter Scott)

David Crawfurd (*Prester John*, John Buchan)

Drusilla Clack (*The Moonstone*, Wilkie Collins)

Emma Woodhouse (*Emma*, Jane Austen)

Franklin Blake (*The Moonstone*, Wilkie Collins)

Gabriel Conroy ("The Dead," *Dubliners*, James Joyce)

Harry Angstrom (*Rabbit, Run*, John Updike)

Henry Dashwood (*Sense and Sensibility*, Jane Austen)

Hercule Poirot (*The Mysterious Affair at Styles*, etc., Agatha Christie)

Hilda Lessways (*The Clayhanger Trilogy*, Arnold Bennett)

Jacob Armitage (*The Children of the New Forest*, Captain Marryat)

Jolyon Forsyte (*The Forsyte Sage*, John Galsworthy)

Joseph Andrews (*Joseph Andrews*, Henry Fielding)

Martin Rattler (*Martin Rattler*, R. M. Ballantyne)

Mother Shipton (*The Luck of Roaring Camp*, Bret Harte)

Mycroft Holmes (*The Return of Sherlock Holmes*, Arthur Conan Doyle)

Nigel Olifaunt (*The Fortunes of Nigel*, Walter Scott)

Philip Marlowe (*The Big Sleep*, Raymond Chandler)

Richard Hannay (*The Thirty-Nine Steps*, John Buchan)

Scarlett O'Hara (*Gone with the Wind*, Margaret Mitchell)

Soames Forsyte (*The Forsyte Sage*, John Galsworthy)

Sophia Western (*Tom Jones*, Henry Fielding)

Squire Western (*Tom Jones*, Henry Fielding)

Winnie-the-Pooh (Edward Bear) (*Winnie-the-Pooh*, A. A. Milne)

14 letters

Angharad Morgan (*How Green Was My Valley*, Richard Llewellyn)

Characters from Well-Known
Works of Fiction *(continued)*

Captain Smollet (*Treasure Island*, Robert Louis Stevenson)

Charles Bingley (*Pride and Prejudice*, Jane Austen)

Colonel Brandon (*Sense and Sensibility*, Jane Austen)

Dorothea Brooke (*Middlemarch*, George Eliot)

Dr. Andrew Manson (*The Citadel*, A. J. Cronin)

Dr. Thomas Thorne (*Doctor Thorne*, Anthony Trollope)

Duke of St. Bungay (*Phineas Finn*, Anthony Trollope)

Edward Waverley (*Waverley*, Walter Scott)

Frank Churchill (*Emma*, Jane Austen)

George Knightly (*Emma*, Jane Austen)

Gilbert Markham (*The Tenant of Wildfell Hall*, Anne Brontë)

Gudrun Brangwen (*The Rainbow, Women in Love*, D. H. Lawrence)

Holly Golightly (*Breakfast at Tiffany's*, Truman Capote)

Isabella Thorpe (*Northanger Abbey*, Jane Austen)

John Willoughby (*Sense and Sensibility*, Jane Austen)

Jonathan Harker (*Dracula*, Bram Stoker)

Lady Isabel Vane (*East Lynne*, Mrs. Henry Wood)

Lemuel Gulliver (*Gulliver's Travels*, Jonathan Swift)

Long John Silver (*Treasure Island*, Robert Louis Stevenson)

Lord Mauleverer (*Cranford*, Mrs. Gaskell)

Maggie Tulliver (*The Mill on the Floss*, George Eliot)

Major Jay Gatsby (*The Great Gatsby*, F. Scott Fitzgerald)

Masterman Ready (*Masterman Ready*, Captain Marryat)

Mrs. Tiggy-Winkle (*The Tale of Mrs. Tiggy-Winkle*, Beatrix Potter)

Rebecca Randall (*Rebecca of Sunnybrook Farm*, Kate D. Wiggin)

Richard Shelton (*The Black Arrow*, Robert Louis Stevenson)

Rikki-Tikki-Tavi (*The Jungle Book*, Rudyard Kipling)

Robin Macgregor (*Rob Roy*, Walter Scott)

Robinson Crusoe (*Robinson Crusoe*, Daniel Defoe)

Sherlock Holmes (*The Adventures of Sherlock Holmes, The Hound of the Baskervilles*, etc., Arthur Conan Doyle)

Shirley Keeldar (*Shirley*, Charlotte Brontë)

Sir Thomas Booby (*Joseph Andrews*, Henry Fielding)

Squirrel Nutkin (*The Tale of Squirrel Nutkin*, Beatrix Potter)

Stella Kowalski (*A Streetcar Named Desire*, Tennessee Williams)

Stephen Dedalus (*A Portrait of the Artist as a Young Man, Ulysses*, James Joyce)

Tertius Lydgate (*Middlemarch*, George Eliot)

Trilby O'Ferrall (*Trilby*, George du Maurier)

Tristram Shandy (*Tristram Shandy*, Laurence Sterne)

Ursula Brangwen (*The Rainbow, Women in Love*, D. H. Lawrence)

Worldly-Wiseman (*The Pilgrim's Progress*, John Bunyan)

15 letters

Allan Quatermain (*King Solomon's Mines*, Henry Rider Haggard)

Arthur Pendennis (Pen) (*Pendennis*, William Makepeace Thackeray)

Bertha Rochester (*Jane Eyre*, Charlotte Brontë)

Catherine Bennet (*Pride and Prejudice*, Jane Austen)

Catherine Glover (*The Fair Maid of Perth*, Walter Scott)

Earl of Leicester (*Kenilworth*, Walter Scott)

Earl of Southdown (*Vanity Fair*, William Makepeace Thackeray)

Elizabeth Bennet (*Pride and Prejudice*, Jane Austen)

Holden Caulfield (*The Catcher in the Rye*, J. D. Salinger)

Horace Abbeville (*Cannery Row*, John Steinbeck)

Huckleberry Finn (*The Adventures of Huckleberry Finn, The Adventures of Tom Sawyer*, Mark Twain)

Lady Trumpington (*The Virginians*, William Makepeace Thackeray)

Melanie Hamilton (*Gone with the Wind*, Margaret Mitchell)

Penrod Schofield (*Penrod and Sam*, Booth Tarkington)

Peregrine Pickle (*Peregrine Pickle*, Tobias Smollett)

Rev. Obadiah Slope (*Barchester Towers*, Anthony Trollope)

Robin Goodfellow (Puck) (*Puck of Pook's Hill*, Rudyard Kipling)

Robin Goodfellow (*St. Ronan's Well*, Walter Scott)

Rupert of Hentzau (*The Prisoner of Zenda*, Anthony Hope)

Squire Allworthy (*Tom Jones*, Henry Fielding)

Squire Trelawney (*Treasure Island*, Robert Louis Stevenson)

Stanley Kowalski (*A Streetcar Named Desire*, Tennessee Williams)

Teresa Marchmain (*Brideshead Revisited*, Evelyn Waugh)

Tess Durbeyfield (*Tess of the D'Urbervilles*, Thomas Hardy)

Valiant-for-Truth (*The Pilgrim's Progress*, John Bunyan)

Violet Elizabeth (*Just William*, Richmal Crompton)

16 letters

Arthur Dimmesdale (*The Scarlet Letter*, Nathaniel Hawthorne)

Catherine Morland (*Northanger Abbey*, Jane Austen)

Clarissa Dalloway (*Mrs. Dalloway*, Virginia Woolf)

Fitzwilliam Darcy (*Pride and Prejudice*, Jane Austen)

Frederick Fairlie (*The Woman in White*, Wilkie Collins)

Godfrey Ablewhite (*The Moonstone*, Wilkie Collins)

Judith Starkadder (*Cold Comfort Farm*, Stella Gibbons)

Lord Frederic Fawn (*Phineas Finn*, Anthony Trollope)

Mrs. Daisy Quantock (*Queen Lucia*, E. F. Benson)

Old Mrs. Starkadder (*Cold Comfort Farm*, Stella Gibbons)

Paul Pennyfeather (*Decline and Fall*, Evelyn Waugh)

Rev. Cuthbert Eager (*A Room with a View*, E. M. Forster)

Rudolf Rassendyll (*The Prisoner of Zenda*, Anthony Hope)

Theodore Laurence (*Little Women*, Louisa May Alcott)

17 letters

Bathsheba Everdene (*Far from the Madding Crowd*, Thomas Hardy)

Captain Billy Bones (*Treasure Island*, Robert Louis Stevenson)

Catherine Earnshaw (*Wuthering Heights*, Emily Brontë)

Evangeline St. Clare (Little Eva) (*Uncle Tom's Cabin*, Harriet Beecher Stowe)

Henry Pootel Piglet (*Winnie the Pooh*, A. A. Milne)

Horatio Hornblower (The *Hornblower* series, C. S. Forester)

Isabella Woodhouse (*Emma*, Jane Austen)

Lady Grizzel Binkie (*Vanity Fair*, William Makepeace Thackeray)

Lady Julia Verinder (*The Moonstone*, Wilkie Collins)

Nicholas Bulstrode (*Middlemarch*, George Eliot)

Pollyanna Whittier (*Pollyanna*, Eleanor H. Porter)

Rev. Edward Casaubon (*Middlemarch*, George Eliot)

Characters from Well-Known
Works of Fiction *(continued)*

Rev. William Collins (*Pride and Prejudice*, Jane Austen)

Sir Andrew Ffoulkes (*The Scarlet Pimpernel*, Baroness Orczy)

William Crimsworth (*The Professor*, Charlotte Brontë)

18 letters

Bennett Addenbrooke (*Raffles*, E. W. Hornung)

Lady Julia Marchmain (*Brideshead Revisited*, Evelyn Waugh)

Maximilian De Winter (*Rebecca*, Daphne du Maurier)

Victor Frankenstein (*Frankenstein*, Mary Wollstonecraft Shelley)

19 letters

Mrs. Tabitha Twitchett (*The Tale of Tom Kitten*, Beatrix Potter)

Plantagenet Palliser (*Phineas Finn*, Anthony Trollope)

Professor Challenger (*The Lost World*, Arthur Conan Doyle)

Sergeant Francis Troy (*Far from the Madding Crowd*, Thomas Hardy)

20 letters

Captain John Yossarian (*Catch-22*, Joseph Heller)

Captain Sir Amyas Leigh (*Westward Ho!*, Charles Kingsley)

Lady Glencora Palliser (*Phineas Finn*, Anthony Trollope)

Little Lord Fauntleroy (*Little Lord Fauntleroy*, Frances Hodgson Burnett)

21 letters

Lady Catherine De Bourgh (*Pride and Prejudice*, Jane Austen)

Lady Cordelia Marchmain (*Brideshead Revisited*, Evelyn Waugh)

Michael, Duke of Strelsau (*The Prisoner of Zenda*, Anthony Hope)

22 letters

Edward Fairfax Rochester (*Jane Eyre*, Charlotte Brontë)

Lestrade of Scotland Yard (*A Study in Scarlet*, Arthur Conan Doyle)

Lord Sebastian Marchmain (*Brideshead Revisited*, Evelyn Waugh)

Professor James Moriarty (*Memoirs of Sherlock Holmes*, Arthur Conan Doyle)

Wilfred, Knight of Ivanhoe (*Ivanhoe*, Walter Scott)

23 letters

Mrs. Thomasina Tittlemouse (*The Tale of Mrs. Tittlemouse*, Beatrix Potter)

Percival William Williams (*Wee Willie Winkie*, Rudyard Kipling)

25 letters

Bishop of Barchester Grantly (*The Warden*, *Barchester Towers*, Anthony Trollope)

Earl of Brideshead Marchmain (*Brideshead Revisited*, Evelyn Waugh)

Humphrey Chimpden Earwicker (HCE) (*Finnegans Wake*, James Joyce)

Lord Cedric Errol Fauntleroy (*Little Lord Fauntleroy*, Frances Hodgson Burnett)

26 letters

Lord Peter Death Bredon Wimsey (*Whose Body?*, Dorothy L. Sayers)

Sir Arthur Darsie Redgauntlet (*Redgauntlet*, Walter Scott)

Characters from the Novels of Charles Dickens

(with novels)

2 letters
Jo (Bleak House)

3 letters
Cly (A Tale of Two Cities)
Joe (The Pickwick Papers)

4 letters
Anne (Dombey and Son)
Baps (Dombey and Son)
Fogg (The Pickwick Papers)
Grip (Barnaby Rudge)
Hugh (Barnaby Rudge)
Kags (Oliver Twist)
Mary (The Pickwick Papers)
Omer (David Copperfield)
Peak (Barnaby Rudge)
Riah (Our Mutual Friend)

5 letters
Betsy (The Pickwick Papers)
Clark (Dombey and Son)
Clive (Little Dorrit)
Crowl (Nicholas Nickleby)
David (Nicholas Nickleby)
Fagin (Oliver Twist)
Janet (David Copperfield)
Krook (Bleak House)
Mealy (David Copperfield)
Minus (Sketches by Boz)
Molly (Great Expectations)
Mould (Martin Chuzzlewit)
Nancy (Oliver Twist)
Perch (Dombey and Son)
Quale (Bleak House)
Sharp (David Copperfield)
Slurk (The Pickwick Papers)
Smike (Nicholas Nickleby)
Stagg (Barnaby Rudge)
Trabb (Great Expectations)
Watty (The Pickwick Papers)

6 letters
Barkis (David Copperfield)
Barney (Oliver Twist)
Bitzer (Hard Times)
Bonney (Nicholas Nickleby)
Briggs (Dombey and Son)
Bumble (Oliver Twist)
Calton (Sketches by Boz)
Clarke (The Pickwick Papers)
Curdle (Nicholas Nickleby)
Dadson (Sketches by Boz)
Dodson (The Pickwick Papers)
Dorker (Nicholas Nickleby)
Feeder (Dombey and Son)
Feenix (Dombey and Son)
Foliar (Nicholas Nickleby)
George (The Pickwick Papers)
George (The Old Curiosity Shop)
Gunter (The Pickwick Papers)
Marton (The Old Curiosity Shop)
Mivins (The Pickwick Papers)
Morfin (Dombey and Son)
Mr. Fips (Martin Chuzzlewit)
Pancks (Little Dorrit)
Perker (The Pickwick Papers)
Phunky (The Pickwick Papers)
Scaley (Nicholas Nickleby)
Sloppy (Our Mutual Friend)
Sownds (Dombey and Son)
Tacker (Martin Chuzzlewit)
Toodle (Dombey and Son)
Tupple (Sketches by Boz)
Vholes (Bleak House)
Vuffin (The Old Curiosity Shop)
Wopsle (Great Expectations)

7 letters
Barbara (The Old Curiosity Shop)
Blotton (The Pickwick Papers)
Brogley (Dombey and Son)
Brooker (Nicholas Nickleby)
Bullamy (Martin Chuzzlewit)
Charley (David Copperfield)
Chuffey (Martin Chuzzlewit)
Creakle (David Copperfield)
Crookey (The Pickwick Papers)
Dolloby (David Copperfield)
Dubbley (The Pickwick Papers)
Estella (Great Expectations)
Gaspard (A Tale of Two Cities)
Gridley (Bleak House)
Grimwig (Oliver Twist)

Characters from the
Novels of Charles Dickens *(continued)*

Jaggers (Great Expectations)
Jinkins (Martin Chuzzlewit)
Jorkins (David Copperfield)
Lewsome (Martin Chuzzlewit)
Mallard (The Pickwick Papers)
Mat Jowl (The Old Curiosity Shop)
Meagles (Little Dorrit)
Minerva (The Pickwick Papers)
Miss Tox (Dombey and Son)
Mr. Hardy (Sketches by Boz)
Mrs. Mann (Oliver Twist)
Mrs. Miff (Dombey and Son)
Mr. Venus (Our Mutual Friend)
Nadgett (Martin Chuzzlewit)
O'Bleary (Sketches by Boz)
Quinion (David Copperfield)
Snagsby (Bleak House)
Snawley (Nicholas Nickleby)
Startop (Great Expectations)
Trundle (The Pickwick Papers)
Watkins (Nicholas Nickleby)
Wemmick (Great Expectations)
Withers (Dombey and Son)

8 letters

Ada Clare (Bleak House)
Betsy Bet (Oliver Twist)
Bullseye (Oliver Twist)
Cluppins (The Pickwick Papers)
D'Aulnais (A Tale of Two Cities)
Dr. Lumley (Nicholas Nickleby)
Dr. Strong (David Copperfield)
Gashford (Barnaby Rudge)
Hon. Snobb (Nicholas Nickleby)
Hortense (Bleak House)
Langdale (Barnaby Rudge)
Lenville (Nicholas Nickleby)
Littimer (David Copperfield)
Losberne (Oliver Twist)
Mary Anne (David Copperfield)
Matthews (Nicholas Nickleby)
Miss Knag (Nicholas Nickleby)
Miss Wade (Little Dorrit)
Mr. Cutler (Nicholas Nickleby)
Mr. George (Bleak House)
Mr. Merdle (Little Dorrit)
Mr. P. Toots (Dombey and Son)

Mrs. Brown (Dombey and Son)
Mrs. Crupp (David Copperfield)
Mrs. Donny (Bleak House)
Mrs. Lupin (Martin Chuzzlewit)
Mrs. Tibbs (Sketches by Boz)
Mr. Wardle (The Pickwick Papers)
"Old" Lobbs (The Pickwick Papers)
Potatoes (David Copperfield)
Stiggins (The Pickwick Papers)
Tom Green (Barnaby Rudge)
Tom Pinch (Martin Chuzzlewit)
Tom Scott (The Old Curiosity Shop)

9 letters

Amy Dorrit (Little Dorrit)
Berinthia (Dombey and Son)
Bill Sikes (Oliver Twist)
Bob Sawyer (The Pickwick Papers)
Chuckster (The Old Curiosity Shop)
C. J. Stryver (A Tale of Two Cities)
Compeyson (Great Expectations)
Dr. Blimber (Dombey and Son)
Dr. Chillip (David Copperfield)
Dr. Haggage (Little Dorrit)
Dr. Manette (A Tale of Two Cities)
Dr. Pilkins (Dombey and Son)
Dr. Slammer (The Pickwick Papers)
Gregsbury (Nicholas Nickleby)
Isaac List (The Old Curiosity Shop)
Jack Adams (Dombey and Son)
Joe Willet (Barnaby Rudge)
John Chick (Dombey and Son)
Lillyvick (Nicholas Nickleby)
Mary Dawes (Dombey and Son)
Mary Jones (Barnaby Rudge)
Mary Rudge (Barnaby Rudge)
Miss Flite (Bleak House)
Miss Miggs (Barnaby Rudge)
Miss Pross (A Tale of Two Cities)
Mr. Bobster (Nicholas Nickleby)
Mr. Garland (The Old Curiosity Shop)
Mr. Johnson (Nicholas Nickleby)

Mr. Larkins (David Copperfield)
Mr. Podsnap (Our Mutual Friend)
Mrs. Barton (Sketches by Boz)
Mrs. Bedwin (Oliver Twist)
Mrs. Codger (Martin Chuzzlewit)
Mrs. Cooper (Sketches by Boz)
Mrs. Corney (Oliver Twist)
Mrs. Cutler (Nicholas Nickleby)
Mrs. Dibabs (Nicholas Nickleby)
Mrs. Harris (Martin Chuzzlewit)
Mrs. Jarley (The Old Curiosity Shop)
Mr. Skylark (David Copperfield)
Mrs. Maylie (Oliver Twist)
Mrs. Raddle (The Pickwick Papers)
Mrs. Tisher (Edwin Drood)
Mr. Trimmer (Sketches by Boz)
Ned Dennis (Barnaby Rudge)
Old Barley (Great Expectations)
Phil Squod (Bleak House)
Priscilla (Bleak House)
Ruth Pinch (Martin Chuzzlewit)
Sam Weller (The Pickwick Papers)
Silas Wegg (Our Mutual Friend)
Uriah Heep (David Copperfield)
Walter Gay (Dombey and Son)

10 letters

Alice Brown (Dombey and Son)
B. B. Barnwell (Martin Chuzzlewit)
Chevy Slyme (Martin Chuzzlewit)
Edwin Drood (Edwin Drood)
Harry Gowan (Little Dorrit)
Jack Bamber (The Pickwick Papers)
Jack Malden (David Copperfield)
Jane Betsey (Dombey and Son)
Jesse Hexam (Our Mutual Friend)
Job Trotter (The Pickwick Papers)
Joe Gargery (Great Expectations)
John Carker (Dombey and Son)
John Harmon (Our Mutual Friend)
John Willet (Barnaby Rudge)
Julia Mills (David Copperfield)
Lady Tippin (Our Mutual Friend)
Maria Lobbs (The Pickwick Papers)
Mark Tapley (Martin Chuzzlewit)
Mary Graham (Martin Chuzzlewit)

Mick Walker (David Copperfield)
M. P. Dingwall (Sketches by Boz)
Mr. Brownlow (Oliver Twist)
Mr. Cripples (Little Dorrit)
Mr. Flamwell (Sketches by Boz)
Mrs. Bangham (Little Dorrit)
Mrs. Crewler (David Copperfield)
Mrs. Garland (The Old Curiosity Shop)
Mrs. General (Little Dorrit)
Mrs. Grudden (Nicholas Nickleby)
Mrs. Jellyby (Bleak House)
Mrs. Pipchin (Dombey and Son)
Mrs. Sparsit (Hard Times)
Mrs. Taunton (Sketches by Boz)
Mrs. Todgers (Martin Chuzzlewit)
Mrs. Wickham (Dombey and Son)
Paul Dombey (Dombey and Son)
Phil Barker (Oliver Twist)
Pip Gargery (Great Expectations)
Rev. M. Howler (Dombey and Son)
Rosa Dartle (David Copperfield)
Rose Maylie (Oliver Twist)
Sally Brass (The Old Curiosity Shop)
Simon Tuggs (Sketches by Boz)
Sowerberry (Oliver Twist)
Tattycoram (Little Dorrit)
Tilda Price (Nicholas Nickleby)
Tom Neckett (Bleak House)
Tony Weller (The Pickwick Papers)
Walter Bray (Nicholas Nickleby)
Waterbrook (David Copperfield)

11 letters

Abel Garland (The Old Curiosity Shop)
Alick Cheggs (The Old Curiosity Shop)
Arthur Gride (Nicholas Nickleby)
Bella Wilfer (Our Mutual Friend)
Betty Higden (Our Mutual Friend)
Bob Cratchit (A Christmas Carol)
Cecilia Jupe (Hard Times)
Charles Mell (David Copperfield)
Clara Barley (Great Expectations)
Daniel Doyce (Little Dorrit)
Daniel Quilp (The Old Curiosity Shop)
"Dismal Jimmy" (The Pickwick Papers)

Characters from the
Novels of Charles Dickens *(continued)*

Dolly Varden (Barnaby Rudge)
Dora Spenlow (David Copperfield)
Emily Wardle (The Pickwick Papers)
Emma Neckett (Bleak House)
Fanny Dombey (Dombey and Son)
Fanny Dorrit (Little Dorrit)
"Game Chicken" (Dombey and Son)
Ham Peggotty (David Copperfield)
Jack Dawkins (Oliver Twist)
Jacob Barton (Sketches by Boz)
Jacob Marley (A Christmas Carol)
James Carker (Dombey and Son)
Jane Wackles (The Old Curiosity Shop)
Jarvis Lorry (A Tale of Two Cities)
Jemima Evans (Sketches by Boz)
John Browdie (Nicholas Nickleby)
John Chivery (Little Dorrit)
John Edmunds (The Pickwick Papers)
John Evenson (Sketches by Boz)
Joseph Tuggs (Sketches by Boz)
Laura Badger (Bleak House)
Lizzie Hexam (Our Mutual Friend)
Louisa Chick (Dombey and Son)
Major Hominy (Martin Chuzzlewit)
Malta Badger (Bleak House)
Mark Gilbert (Barnaby Rudge)
Miss Barbary (Bleak House)
Miss Gazingi (Nicholas Nickleby)
Miss Mowcher (David Copperfield)
Miss Tamaroo (Martin Chuzzlewit)
Mr. Malderton (Sketches by Boz)
Mr. Mantalini (Nicholas Nickleby)
Mrs. Craddock (The Pickwick Papers)
Mr. Wickfield (David Copperfield)
Mr. Witherden (The Old Curiosity Shop)
Nellie Trent (The Old Curiosity Shop)
Newman Noggs (Nicholas Nickleby)

O. A. Pardiggle (Bleak House)
Old Fledgeby (Our Mutual Friend)
Oliver Twist (Oliver Twist)
Percy Noakes (Sketches by Boz)
Peter Magnus (The Pickwick Papers)
Pumblechook (Great Expectations)
Sarah Pocket (Great Expectations)
Solomon Pell (The Pickwick Papers)
Susan Nipper (Dombey and Son)
Toby Crackit (Oliver Twist)
Tom Traddles (David Copperfield)
Tony Jobling (Bleak House)
Tracy Tupman (The Pickwick Papers)
Tulkinghorn (Bleak House)

12 letters

Abel Magwitch (Great Expectations)
Agnes Fleming (Oliver Twist)
Alfred Jingle (The Pickwick Papers)
Alfred Lammle (Our Mutual Friend)
Amelia Budden (Sketches by Boz)
Barnaby Rudge (Barnaby Rudge)
Biddy Gargery (Great Expectations)
Caddy Jellyby (Bleak House)
Charley Bates (Oliver Twist)
Charlie Hexam (Our Mutual Friend)
Colonel Diver (Martin Chuzzlewit)
David Crimple (Martin Chuzzlewit)
Dr. Parker Peps (Dombey and Son)
Edith Granger (Dombey and Son)
Edward Dorrit (Little Dorrit)
Elijah Pogram (Martin Chuzzlewit)
Emma Haredale (Barnaby Rudge)
Fanny Cleaver (Our Mutual Friend)
Fanny Squeers (Nicholas Nickleby)
Harrie Maylie (Oliver Twist)
John Jarndyce (Bleak House)

John Westlock (Martin Chuzzlewit)
Kate Nickleby (Nicholas Nickleby)
Lady Scadgers (Hard Times)
Lord Mutanhed (The Pickwick
Papers)
Louisa Dombey (Dombey and Son)
Lucie Manette (A Tale of Two Cities)
Madeline Bray (Nicholas Nickleby)
Major Pawkins (Martin
Chuzzlewit)
Minverva Pott (The Pickwick
Papers)
Miss Bravassa (Nicholas Nickleby)
Miss Havisham (Great Expectations)
Miss La Creevy (Nicholas
Nickleby)
Miss Skiffins (Great Expectations)
Montague Tigg (Martin
Chuzzlewit)
Mr. Ayresleigh (The Pickwick
Papers
Mrs. Fibbitson (David Copperfield)
Mrs. Sarah Gamp (Martin
Chuzzlewit)
Ned Cheeryble (Nicholas
Nickleby)
Noah Claypole (Oliver Twist)
Peepy Jellyby (Bleak House)
Rachel Wardle (The Pickwick
Papers)
Quebec Badger (Bleak House)
Sampson Brass (The Old
Curiosity Shop)
"Shiny William" (The Pickwick
Papers)
Solomon Daisy (Barnaby Rudge)
Solomon Gills (Dombey and Son)
Solomon Lucas (The Pickwick
Papers)
Solomon Pross (A Tale of Two
Cities)
Sophy Crewler (David Copperfield)
Sweet William (The Old Curiosity
Shop)
Sydney Carton (A Tale of Two
Cities)
T. Balderstone (Sketches by Boz)
Thomas Codlin (The Old
Curiosity Shop)
Tommy Bardell (The Pickwick
Papers)
William Guppy (Bleak House)

13 letters

Anastasia Rugg (Little Dorrit)
Arabella Allen (The Pickwick
Papers)
Arthur Clennam (Little Dorrit)
Beadle Simmons (Sketches by Boz)
Benjamin Allen (The Pickwick
Papers)
Captain Bailey (David
Copperfield)
Captain Bunsby (Dombey and
Son)
Captain Dowler (The Pickwick
Papers)
Captain Hawdon (Bleak House)
Charles Darnay (A Tale of Two
Cities)
Clara Peggotty (David Copperfield)
Dr. John Jobling (Martin
Chuzzlewit)
Edward Chester (Barnaby Rudge)
Edward Leeford (Oliver Twist)
Gabriel Varden (Barnaby Rudge)
General Conway (Barnaby Rudge)
George Heyling (The Pickwick
Papers)
George Nupkins (The Pickwick
Papers)
George Sampson (Our Mutual
Friend)
Harriet Carker (Dombey and Son)
Herbert Pocket (Great
Expectations)
Hon. Mr. Crushton (The Pickwick
Papers)
Hon. Mrs. Skewton (Dombey and
Son)
Horatio Fizkin (The Pickwick
Papers)
Jane Murdstone (David
Copperfield)
Jerry Cruncher (A Tale of Two
Cities)
Judy Smallweed (Bleak House)
Kitty Skimpole (Bleak House)
Laura Skimpole (Bleak House)
Lavinia Wilfer (Our Mutual Friend)
Madame Defarge (A Tale of Two
Cities)
Major Bagstock (Dombey and
Son)

Characters from the
Novels of Charles Dickens *(continued)*

Master Belling (Nicholas Nickleby)

Matthew Badger (Bleak House)

Matthew Pocket (Great Expectations)

Miss Belvawney (Nicholas Nickleby)

Mrs. Macstinger (Dombey and Son)

Mrs. Ridger Begs (David Copperfield)

Mrs. Rouncewell (Bleak House)

Ralph Nickleby (Nicholas Nickleby)

Sergeant Buzuz (The Pickwick Papers)

Seth Pecksniff (Martin Chuzzlewit)

Sophie Wackles (The Old Curiosity Shop)

Watkins Tottle (Sketches by Boz)

William Dorrit (Little Dorrit)

Young Fledgeby (Our Mutual Friend)

14 letters

Agnes Wickfield (David Copperfield)

Alexander Trott (Sketches by Boz)

Allan Woodcourt (Bleak House)

Augustus Cooper (Sketches by Boz)

Augustus Moddle (Martin Chuzzlewit)

Benjamin Bailey (Martin Chuzzlewit)

Bentley Drummle (Great Expectations)

Betsey Trotwood (David Copperfield)

Captain Boldwig (The Pickwick Papers)

Captain Kedgick (Martin Chuzzlewit)

Cecilia Bobster (Nicholas Nickleby)

Charlotte Tuggs (Sketches by Boz)

Count Smorltork (The Pickwick Papers)

Daniel Peggotty (David Copperfield)

Dr. Bayham Badger (Bleak House)

Edmund Sparkler (Little Dorrit)

Eugene Wrayburn (Our Mutual Friend)

Florence Dombey (Dombey and Son)

Frank Cheeryble (Nicholas Nickleby)

Frederick Trent (The Old Curiosity Shop)

Gabriel Baillie (The Pickwick Papers)

Gabriel Parsons (Sketches by Boz)

Harold Skimpole (Bleak House)

Isabella Wardle (The Pickwick Papers)

James Harthouse (Hard Times)

Jefferson Brick (Martin Chuzzlewit)

Joseph Smiggers (The Pickwick Papers)

(The) Marchioness (The Old Curiosity Shop)

Melissa Wackles (The Old Curiosity Shop)

Mercy Pecksniff (Martin Chuzzlewit)

Miss Snevellici (Nicholas Nickleby)

Monsieur Rigaud (Little Dorrit)

Mrs. Spottletoes (Martin Chuzzlewit)

Mr. Tite-Barnacle (Little Dorrit)

Nicodemus Dumps (Sketches by Boz, The Pickwick Papers)

Octavius Budden (Sketches by Boz)

Professor Dingo (Bleak House)

Reginald Wilfer (Our Mutual Friend)

Reuben Haredale (Barnaby Rudge)

Rev. Frank Milvey (Our Mutual Friend)

Roger Riderhood (Our Mutual Friend)
Samuel Pickwick (The Pickwick Papers)
Simon Tappertit (Barnaby Rudge)
Sir John Chester (Barnaby Rudge)
Thomas Plornish (Little Dorrit)
Toby Chuzzlewit (Martin Chuzzlewit)
William Simmons (Martin Chuzzlewit)
Woolwich Badger (Bleak House)
Young Mr. Crawley (The Pickwick Papers)

15 letters

Belinda Cratchit (A Christmas Carol)
Conkey Chickweed (Oliver Twist)
Ebenezer Scrooge (A Christmas Carol)
Edward Murdstone (David Copperfield)
Esther Summerson (Bleak House)
Frederick Dorrit (Little Dorrit)
Godfrey Nickleby (Nicholas Nickleby)
Hannibal Chollop (Martin Chuzzlewit)
Henrietta Boffin (Our Mutual Friend)
James Steerforth (David Copperfield)
John Edward Nandy (Little Dorrit)
Jonas Chuzzlewit (Martin Chuzzlewit)
Josephine Sleary (Hard Times)
Joshua Smallweed (Bleak House)
Josiah Bounderby (Hard Times)
Julia Wititterly (Nicholas Nickleby)
La Fayette Kettle (Martin Chuzzlewit)
Louisa Gradgrind (Hard Times)
Morleena Kenwigs (Nicholas Nickleby)
Nathaniel Pipkin (The Pickwick Papers)
Nathaniel Winkle (The Pickwick Papers)
Nicodemus Boffin (Our Mutual Friend)

Ninetta Crummles (Nicholas Nickleby)
Paul Sweedlepipe (Martin Chuzzlewit)
Professor Mullet (Martin Chuzzlewit)
Sergeant Snubbin (The Pickwick Papers)
Sir Mulberry Hawk (Nicholas Nickleby)
Thomas Gradgrind (Hard Times)
Tiny Tim Cratchet (A Christmas Carol)
Vincent Crummles (Nicholas Nickleby)
Volumnia Dedlock (Bleak House)
Von Koeldwethout (Nicholas Nickleby)
Wackford Squeers (Nicholas Nickleby)
Wilkins Micawber (David Copperfield)

16 letters

Affery Flintwinch (Little Dorrit)
Arethusa Skimpole (Bleak House)
Bradley Headstone (Our Mutual Friend)
Captain Ned Cuttle (Dombey and Son)
Charity Pecksniff (Martin Chuzzlewit)
Charles Cheeryble (Nicholas Nickleby)
Charlotte Neckett (Bleak House)
Christopher Casby (Little Dorrit)
Clara Copperfield (David Copperfield)
David Copperfield (David Copperfield)
Francis Pardiggle (Bleak House)
Geoffrey Haredale (Barnaby Rudge)
George Chuzzlewit (Martin Chuzzlewit)
Georgiana Podsnap (Our Mutual Friend)
Hon. Samuel Slumkey (The Pickwick Papers)
Jeremiah Cruncher (A Tale of Two Cities)
Lawrence Boythorn (Bleak House)

Characters from the
Novels of Charles Dickens *(continued)*

Lord George Gordon (Barnaby Rudge)

Martin Chuzzlewit (Martin Chuzzlewit)

Mrs. Flora Finching (Little Dorrit)

Mrs. Martha Bardell (The Pickwick Papers)

Mrs. Ned Chuzzlewit (Martin Chuzzlewit)

Nicholas Nickleby (Nicholas Nickleby)

Prince Turveydrop (Bleak House)

Rev. Horace Crewler (David Copperfield)

Richard Swiveller (The Old Curiosity Shop)

Sir Thomas Clubber (The Pickwick Papers)

Stephen Blackpool (Hard Times)

Theophile Gabelle (A Tale of Two Cities)

Zephaniah Scadder (Martin Chuzzlewit)

17 letters

Angelo Cyrus Bantam (The Pickwick Papers)

Anthony Chuzzlewit (Martin Chuzzlewit)

Augustus Snodgrass (The Pickwick Papers)

Charles Kitterbell (Sketches by Boz)

Diggory Chuzzlewit (Martin Chuzzlewit)

Ephraim Flintwinch (Little Dorrit)

Hamilton Veneering (Our Mutual Friend)

"Honest" James Groves (The Old Curiosity Shop)

Justice Stareleigh (The Pickwick Papers)

Miss Maria Crumpton (Sketches by Boz)

Mortimer Lightwood (Our Mutual Friend)

Pleasant Riderhood (Our Mutual Friend)

Sir Barnet Skittles (Dombey and Son)

Sophronia Akershem (Our Mutual Friend)

18 letters

Anastasia Veneering (Our Mutual Friend)

Christopher Nubbles (The Old Curiosity Shop)

Jeremiah Flintwinch (Little Dorrit)

Junior Tite-Barnacle (Little Dorrit)

Little Em'ly Peggotty (David Copperfield)

Miss Amelia Crumpton (Sketches by Boz)

19 letters

Sir Leicester Dedlock (Bleak House)

20 letters

Bartholomew Smallweed (Bleak House)

Clarence Tite-Barnacle (Little Dorrit)

Marquis de St. Evremonde (A Tale of Two Cities)

21 letters

Alexander August Budden (Sketches by Boz)

Ferdinand Tite-Barnacle (Little Dorrit)

Marquise de St. Evremonde (A Tale of Two Cities)

22 letters

Lord Frederick Verisopht (Nicholas Nickleby)

23 letters

Lord Decimus Tite-Barnacle (Little Dorrit)

Characters from the Plays of William Shakespeare

(with plays)

3 letters

Hal [Henry V] (1 Henry IV)
Nym (Henry V, The Merry Wives of Windsor)

4 letters

Adam (As You Like It)
Ajax (Troilus and Cressida)
Anne (Richard III)
Eros (Antony and Cleopatra)
Grey (Henry V)
Hero (Much Ado About Nothing)
Iago (Othello)
Iras (Antony and Cleopatra)
Lear (King Lear)
Peto (2 Henry IV)
Puck (A Midsummer Night's Dream)
Snug (A Midsummer Night's Dream)

5 letters

Aaron (Titus Andronicus)
Ariel (The Tempest)
Blunt (2 Henry IV)
Celia (As You Like It)
Cleon (Pericles)
Corin (As You Like It)
Diana (All's Well That Ends Well)
Edgar (King Lear)
Elbow (Measure for Measure)
Feste (Twelfth Night)
Flute (A Midsummer Night's Dream)
Froth (Measure for Measure)
Lafew (All's Well That Ends Well)
Maria (Love's Labour's Lost, Twelfth Night)
Osric (Hamlet)
Paris (Troilus and Cressida)
Percy (1 Henry IV)
Phebe (As You Like It)
Pinch (The Comedy of Errors)
Poins (1 Henry IV, 2 Henry IV)
Priam (Troilus and Cressida)
Regan (King Lear)
Romeo (Romeo and Juliet)

Snout (A Midsummer Night's Dream)
Titus (Titus Andronicus)
Viola (Twelfth Night)

6 letters

Aegeon (The Comedy of Errors)
Alonso (The Tempest)
Angelo (Measure for Measure)
Antony (Julius Caesar, Antony and Cleopatra)
Armado (Love's Labour's Lost)
Audrey (As You Like It)
Banquo (Macbeth)
Bianca (The Taming of the Shrew, Othello)
Bottom (A Midsummer Night's Dream)
Brutus (Julius Caesar, Coriolanu)
Cassio (Othello)
Chiron (Titus Andronicus)
Cloten (Cymbeline)
Dennis (As You Like It)
Dromio (The Comedy of Errors)
Dumain (Love's Labour's Lost)
Duncan (Macbeth)
Edmund (King Lear)
Emilia (Othello)
Fabian (Twelfth Night)
Fulvia (Antony and Cleopatra)
Hamlet (Hamlet)
Hecate (Macbeth)
Hector (Troilus and Cressida)
Helena A Midsummer Night's Dream, All's Well That Ends Well)
Henry V (1 Henry IV, 2 Henry IV, Henry V)
Hermia (A Midsummer Night's Dream)
Imogen (Cymbeline)
Juliet (Romeo and Juliet, Measure for Measure)
Lucius (Titus Andronicus)
Marina (Pericles)
Mutius (Titus Andronicus)
Oberon (A Midsummer Night's Dream)

Characters from the Plays of
William Shakespeare (continued)

Oliver (As You Like It)
Olivia (Twelfth Night)
Orsino (Twelfth Night)
Oswald (King Lear)
Pistol (2 Henry IV, Henry V, The Merry Wives of Windsor)
Pompey (Measure for Measure, Antony and Cleopatra)
Portia (The Merchant of Venice)
Quince (A Midsummer Night's Dream)
Rumour (2 Henry IV)
Scroop (Henry IV)
Tamora (Titus Andronicus)
Thasia (Pericles)
Tybalt (Romeo and Juliet)
Verges (Much Ado About Nothing)

7 letters

Adriana (The Comedy of Errors)
Aemilia (The Comedy of Errors)
Agrippa (Julius Caesar, Antony and Cleopatra)
Alarbus (Titus Andronicus)
Antonio (The Merchant of Venice, The Tempest)
Berowne (Love's Labour's Lost)
Bertram (All's Well That Ends Well)
Calchas (Troilus and Cressida)
Caliban (The Tempest)
Capulet (Romeo and Juliet)
Cesario (Twelfth Night)
Caludio (Much Ado About Nothing, Measure for Measure)
Costard (Love's Labour's Lost)
Dionyza (Pericles)
Douglas (1 Henry IV)
Escalus (Measure for Measure)
Fleance (Macbeth)
Goneril (King Lear)
Gonzalo (The Tempest)
Helenus (Troilus and Cressida)
Henry IV (Richard II, 1 Henry IV, 2 Henry IV)
Henry VI (1 Henry VI, 2 Henry VI, 3 Henry VI)

Horatio (Hamlet)
Hotspur (1 Henry IV)
Iachimo (Cymbeline)
Jacques (As You Like It)
Jessica (The Merchant of Venice)
Laertes (Hamlet)
Lavinia (Titus Andronicus)
Leontes (The Winter's Tale)
Lepidus (Julius Caesar, Antony and Cleopatra)
Lorenzo (The Merchant of Venice)
Luciana (The Comedy of Errors)
Macbeth (Macbeth)
Macduff (Macbeth)
Malcolm (Macbeth)
Mariana (Measure for Measure, All's Well That Ends Well)
Martius (Titus Andronicus)
Miranda (The Tempest)
Nerissa (The Merchant of Venice)
Octavia (Antony and Cleopatra)
Ophelia (Hamlet)
Orlando (As You Like It)
Othello (Othello)
Paulina (The Winter's Tale)
Perdita (The Winter's Tale)
Pisanio (Cymbeline)
Proteus (The Two Gentlemen of Verona)
Quintus (Titus Andronicus)
Shylock (The Merchant of Venice)
Silence (2 Henry IV)
Silvius (As You Like It)
Slender (The Merry Wives of Windsor)
Solinus (The Comedy of Errors)
Theseus (A Midsummer Night's Dream)
Titania (A Midsummer Night's Dream)
Troilus (Troilus and Cressida)
Ulysses (Troilus and Cressida)
William (As You Like It)

8 letters

Achilles (Troilus and Cressida)
Aufidius (Coriolanus)

Baptista (The Taming of the Shrew)
Bardolph (1 Henry IV, 2 Henry IV, Henry V, The Merry Wives of Windsor)
Bassanio (The Merchant of Venice)
Beatrice (Much Ado About Nothing)
Belarius (Cymbeline)
Benedick (Much Ado About Nothing)
Benvolio (Romeo and Juliet)
Bernardo (Hamlet)
Charmian (Antony and Cleopatra)
Claudius (Hamlet)
Cominius (Coriolanus)
Cordelia (King Lear)
Cressida (Troilus and Cressida)
Diomedes (Antony and Celopatra, Troilus and Cressida)
Dogberry (Much Ado About Nothing)
Don Pedro (Much Ado About Nothing)
Edward IV (2 Henry VI, 3 Henry VI)
Falstaff (1 Henry IV, 2 Henry IV, The Merry Wives of Windsor)
Florizel (The Winter's Tale)
Gertrude (Hamlet)
Gratiano (The Merchant of Venice, Othello)
Hermione (The Winter's Tale)
Isabella (Measure for Measure)
Lucentio (The Taming of the Shrew)
Lysander (A Midsummer Night's Dream)
Malvolio (Twelfth Night)
Margaret (2 Henry VI, 3 Henry VI, Richard III)
Menenius (Coriolanus)
Mercutio (Romeo and Juliet)
Montague (Romeo and Juliet)
Mortimer (1 Henry IV)
Pandarus (Troilus and Cressida)
Parolles (All's Well That Ends Well)
Pericles (Pericles)
Philoten (Pericles)
Polonius (Hamlet)

Prospero (The Tempest)
Roderigo (Othello)
Rosalind (As You Like It)
Rosaline (Love's Labour's Lost)
Sicinius (Coriolanus)
Stephano (The Tempest)
Trinculo (The Tempest)
Violenta (All's Well That Ends Well)
Volumnia (Coriolanus)

9 letters

Agamemnon (Troilus and Cressida)
Antiochus (Pericles)
Arviragus (Cymbeline)
Bassianus (Titus Andronicus)
Brabantio (Othello)
Cambridge (Henry V)
Cleopatra (Antony and Cleopatra)
Cornelius (Hamlet)
Cymbeline (Cymbeline)
Demetrius (Titus Andronicus, A Midsummer Night's Dream, Antony and Cleopatra)
Desdemona (Othello)
Donalbain (Macbeth)
Elizabeth (Henry VI, Richard III)
Enobarbus (Antony and Cleopatra)
Ferdinand (Love's Labour's Lost, The Tempest)
Frederick (As You Like It)
Guiderius (Cymbeline)
Helicanus (Pericles)
Henry VIII (Henry VIII)
Hippolyta (A Midsummer Night's Dream)
Hortensio (The Taming of the Shrew)
Katherina (The Taming of the Shrew)
Katherine (Henry V, Love's Labour's Lost)
Mamillius (The Winter's Tale)
Marcellus (Hamlet)
Patroclus (Troilus and Cressida)
Petruchio (The Taming of the Shrew)
Polixenes (The Winter's Tale)
Posthumus (Cymbeline)
Richard II (Richard II)

Characters from the Plays of
William Shakespeare (continued)

Sebastian (The Tempest, Twelfth Night)
Vincentio (Measure for Measure, The Taming of the Shrew)
Voltimand (Hamlet)

10 letters

Antipholus (The Comedy of Errors)
Coriolanus (Coriolanus)
Fortinbras (Hamlet)
Jaquenetta (Love's Labour's Lost)
Longaville (Love's Labour's Lost)
Lysimachus (Pericles)
Mark Antony (Julius Caesar, Antony and Cleopatra)
Richard III (2 Henry VI, 3 Henry VI, Richard III)
Saturninus (Titus Andronicus)
Touchstone (As You Like It)

11 letters

Lady Macbeth (Macbeth)
Lady Macduff (Macbeth)
Rosencrantz (Hamlet)

12 letters

Duke of Albany (King Lear)
Guildenstern (Hamlet)
Julius Caesar (Julius Caesar)
Sir Toby Belch (Twelfth Night)

13 letters

Doll Tearsheet (2 Henry IV)
Friar Laurence (Romeo and Juliet)
Owen Glendower (1 Henry IV)

14 letters

Caesar Octavius (Julius Caesar, Antony and Cleopatra)
Christopher Sly (The Taming of the Shrew)
Duke of Cornwall (King Lear)
Justice Shallow (2 Henry IV, The Merry Wives of Windsor)

15 letters

Mistress Quickly (1 Henry IV, 2 Henry IV, The Merry Wives of Windsor)

16 letters

Earl of Gloucester (King Lear)
Henry Bolingbroke [Henry IV] (Richard III)

18 letters

Sir Andrew Aguecheek (Twelfth Night)

19 letters

Henry, Earl of Richmond [Henry VII] (Richard III)

20 letters

George, Duke of Clarence (Henry VI, Richard III)

23 letters

Richard, Duke of Gloucester [Richard III] (2 Henry VI, 3 Henry VI, Richard III)

Rhetorical Devices

5 letters
trope

6 letters
aporia
simile

7 letters
diacope
litotes

8 letters
anaphora

chiasmus
enallage
epiphora
isocolon
metaphor
symploce

9 letters
assonance
epizeuxis
hendiadys
dypallage
hyperbole

10 letters
anastrophe
antithesis
epistrophe
hyperbaton
palindrome
paralipsis
polyptoton

11 letters
anacoluthon
anadiplosis
antiphrasis

antistrophe
catechresis
epanalepsis
periphrasis

12 letters
alliteration
epanorthosis
prosopopoeia

16 letters
hysteron pro-
teron

Theatrical Terms

2 letters
LX
SM (stage
  manager)

3 letters
act
ASM (assistant
  stage manager)
cue
gel
ham
leg
pit
rep
run
set

4 letters
blue
book
boom
busk
call
drop
exit
flat
gaff
GOBO

gods
grid
iris
leko
mask
mime
olio
pipe
prop
rake
rose
sock
tabs
tail
trap

5 letters
above
actor
ad lib
agent
apron
arena
aside
below
cloth
enter
flies
float

foyer
gauze
glory
gypsy
halls
heavy
hoist
house
inset
manet
odeum
perch
revue
scene
scrim
skene
slips
slote
stage
truck
visor
wings

6 letters
barrel
batten
boards
border
box set

bridge
buskin
cellar
chorus
circle
critic
dimmer
encore
flyman
makeup
masque
mummer
old man
puppet
return
runway
scruto
sea row
stalls
teaser
toggle
walk-on

7 letters
act drop
actress
balcony
benefit
call boy

Theatrical Terms (continued)

catwalk
circuit
curtain
diorama
diseuse
flipper
gallery
jornada
manager
matinée
on stage
pinspot
rain box
resting
rostrum
scenery
sky dome
spot bar
tableau
top drop
tumbler
unities
upstage
utility
valance

8 letters

arc light
audition
blackout
blocking
book flat
book wing
business
call door
clouding
crush bar
cut-cloth
designer
director
dumb show
elevator
epilogue
fox wedge
juvenile
lashline
libretto
lighting

off stage
old woman
panorama
paradiso
parallel
pass door
platform
playbill
producer
prologue
prompter
property
set piece
sill iron
sky cloth
star trap
traveler
vamp trap
wardrobe

9 letters

backcloth
backstage
boat truck
box office
call board
carpet cut
cothurnus
cyclorama
downstage
fan effect
footlight
grave trap
green room
ground row
hand-props
light pipe
limelight
noises off
open stage
orchestra
periaktoi
plot sheet
projector
promenade
reflector
rehearsal
repertory

rod-puppet
rope house
sand-cloth
scene dock
set waters
sightline
sky border
slapstick
slip stage
soubrette
spotlight
stage crew
stage door
stage rake
throwline
thyristor
tormentor
trickwork
water rows

10 letters

anti-masque
auditorium
built stuff
color wheel
corner trap
coryphaeus
curtain set
double take
drag artist
floodlight
follow spot
frontcloth
ghost glide
house light
impresario
inner stage
in the round
knockabout
lycopodium
marionette
pipe batten
prompt book
prompt side
saddle-iron
sciopticon
show portal
stage brace

stage cloth
strip light
thunder run
tree border
understudy
wagon stage

11 letters

backing flat
book ceiling
border light
bristle trap
catastrophe
center stage
curtain call
dress circle
falling flap
formal stage
fresnel spot
light batten
low comedian
mise en scéne
off-broadway
profile spot
protagonist
rise-and-sink
roll ceiling
spieltreppe
strobe light
summer stock
switchboard
tritagonist
upper circle
wind machine

12 letters

actor-manager
amphitheater
author's night
cauldron trap
ceiling-cloth
corsican trap
dressing room
flying effect
front of house
light console
lobsterscope
masking piece

orchestra pit
pepper's ghost
profile board
rundhorizont
scissor cross
sound effects
stage manager
  (SM)
stage setting
stereopticon
stichomythia
stock company
thundersheet
transparency

13 letters

curtain-raiser
detail scenery
deus ex machina
deuteragonist
grooves system
improvisation
platform stage
portal opening
safety curtain
stage lighting
supernumerary
word rehearsal

14 letters

drapery setting
dress rehearsal
footlights trap
general utility
jackknife stage
kuppelhorizont
lanterna magica
mezzanine floor
off-off-broadway
pageant lantern
proscenium arch
revolving stage
stage direction
touring company

15 letters

barn door
  shutter
carpenter's
  scene
flexible staging
hand worked
  house
incidental music
multiple setting
proscenium
  doors
quick-change
  room

stage-door
  keeper
traverse curtain

16 letters

alienation effect
asphaleian
  system
composite
  setting
dramatis
  personae
proscenium
  border

18 letters

bespeak per-
  formance
collective cre-
  ation
command per-
  formance
drum-and-shaft
  system
female imper-
  sonator
linsenscheinwer-
  fer
technical
  rehearsal

19 letters

counterweight
  system
promenade pro-
  duction
simultaneous
  setting
transformation
  scene

20 letters

advertisement
  curtain
chariot-and-pole
  system

21 letters

assistant stage
  manager
  (ASM)

22 letters

carriage-and-
  frame system
synchronous
  winch system

26 letters

silicon con-
  trolled rectifier

Languages

2 letters

Ga
Ho
Wa

3 letters

Edo
Ewe
Fan
Fon
Fox
Ibo
Ido
Ijo
Ila

Kru
Lai
Lao (Laotian)
Laz
Luo
Mam
Mon
Oto
Rai
San
Suk
Tiv
Twi
Ute
Vai

Yao
Zia

4 letters

Ainu
Akan
Avar
Beja
Chin
Chol
Coos
Cree
Crow
Dani
Dyak

Efik
Eyak
Garo
Ge'ez
Gond
Hano
Hopi
Igbo
Iowa
Kawi
Komi
Kond
Kono
Krio
Kuki

Languages *(continued)*

Lapp (Lappish)
Loma
Lozi
Luba
Manx
Maya
Miao
Mixe
Mono
Motu
Naga
Nama
Norn
Nuba
Nuer
Nupe
Pali
Pano
Pima
Pomo
Riff
Sauk
Seri
Shan
Sulu
Susu
Taos
Teso
Tewa
Thai
Tiwa
Toda
Tulu
Tupi
Tuva
Uduk
Urdu
Veps
Yuki
Yuma
Zulu
Zuni

5 letters
Acoma
Aleut
Aztec
Bajau

Batak
Bemba
Bugis
Caddo
Czech
Dinka
Duala
Dusun
Dutch
Dyula
Fante
Farsi
Fulah
Galla
Greek
Haida
Hausa
Hindi
Hmong
Irish
Jemez
Kamba
Karen
Karok
Khasi
Khmer
Kiowa
Kissi
Kongo
Korwa
Kumyk
Lamba
Lamut
Latin
Limbu
Lunda
Maidu
Malay
Maori
Masai
Mende
Modoc
Mossi
Nambe
Nguni
Nogay
Norse
Nyasa

Nyoro
Omaha
Oraon
Oriya
Osage
Otomi
Ponca
Punic
Ronga
Sakai
Samal
Sango
Sarsi
Sasak
Sebei
Senoi
Sepik
Shina
Sotho
Swazi
Taino
Taita
Tajik
Tamil
Tatar
Temne
Tigré
Tolai
Tonga
Uigur
Uzbek
Venda
Vogul
Warao
Washo
Welsh
Wiyot
Wolof
Xhosa
Yakut
Yaqui
Yuchi
Yupik
Yurok
Zande
Zoque

6 letters
Abnaki
Apache
Arabic
Aranda
Arawak
Aymara
Basque
Bihari
Bokmål
Brahui
Breton
Buryat (Buriat)
Cahita
Cayuga
Chagga
Coptic
Creole
Dakota
Danish
Divehi
Fijian
French
Fulani
Gaelic
Galibi
German
Gothic
Gurung
Hebrew
Herero
Ibanag
Ibibio
Ingush
Isleta
Jivaro
Kachin
Kalmyk
  (Kalmuck)
Kazakh
Kikuyu
Kolami
Korean
Koryak
Kuchin
Kurukh
Kyrgyz
  (Kirghiz)

Ladino
Laguna
Lahnda
Lepcha
Lushai
Lycian
Magyar
Manchu
Mandan
Micmac
Mixtec
Mohave
Mohawk
Mongol
  (Mongolian)
Mysian
Navajo
  (Navaho)
Nenets
Nepali
Newari
Niuean
Nootka
Nyanja
Ojibwa
Oneida
Ostyak
Ottawa
Ovambo
Pahari
Paiute
Papago
Pashto
Pawnee
Peguan
Polish
Quiché
Rawang
Rejang
Romaic
Romany
Rwanda
Samoan
Sandia
Seneca
Shasta
Shelta
Shilha
Sidamo
Sindhi
Slovak

Somali
Sukuma
Syriac
Taensa
Tamang
Telugu
Ticuna
Tongan
Trique
Tsonga
Tswana
Tungus
Udmurt
Wintun
Yokuts
Yoruba
Zyrian

7 letters

Amharic
Andaman
Aramaic
Arapaho
Baluchi
Barotse
Bashkir
Bengali
Burmese
Catalan
Catawba
Chaldee
  (Chaldean)
Chechen
Chinese
Chinook
Choctaw
Chontal
Chukchi
Chumash
Chuvash
Cochiti
Cornish
Danakil
Elamite
English
Finnish
Flemish
Frisian
Gaulish
Guarani
Hidatsa

Hittite
Huastec
Italian
Kalmuck
  (Kalmyk)
Kannada
Khalkha
Kikongo
Kirghiz
  (Kyrgyz)
Kirundi
Klamath
Konkani
Koranko
Kurdish
Kutenai
Laotian (Lao)
Lappish (Lapp)
Latvian
Lingala
Luganda
Lugbara
Malinke
Maltese
Marathi
Mazatec
Mordvin
Nahuatl
Natchez
Ndebele
Ngbandi
Occitan
Osmanli
Pahlavi
Palauan
Palaung
Panjabi
  (Punjabi)
Persian
Pictish
Picuris
Pintupi
Prakrit
Quechua
Quechua
Quileut
Riksmål
Romanes
Russian
Sabaean
Saharan

Salinan
Samburu
Sandawe
Santali
Serbian
Sesotho
Shawnee
Sherbro
Shilluk
Siamese
Slovene
Sogdian
Songhai
Sorbian
Spanish
Swahili
Swedish
Tagalog
Tesuque
Tibetan
Tlingit
Tonkawa
Totonac
Tumbuka
Turkish
Turkmen
Tzeltal
Tzotzil
Venetic
Volapük
Walapai
Wendish
Wichita
Wishram
Yavapai
Yenisei
Yiddish
Yucatec

8 letters

Achinese
Achumawi
Akkadian
Albanian
Aleutian
Annamese
Armenian
Assamese
Assyrian
Balinese
Botocudo

Languages *(continued)*

Caingang
Chagatai
Chaldean
  (Chaldee)
Cherokee
Cheyenne
Chichewa
Comanche
Croatian
Cuicatec
Delaware
Dzongkha
Egyptian
Estonian
Etruscan
Faeroese
Formosan
Fulfulde
Galician
Georgian
Guaycuru
Gujarati
Gurkhali
Hawaiian
Iroquois
Japanese
Javanese
Kalispel
Kanarese
Karelian
Kashmiri
Kickapoo
Kingwana
Kwakiutl
Lacandón
Lesghian
Livonian
Lusatian
Madurese
Malagasy
Malecite

Mandarin
Manganja
Manipuri
Menomini
Messapic
Misquito
Missouri
Nyamwezi
Onondaga
Ossetian
Paviotso
Phrygian
Pojoaque
Popoloca
Prussian
Rhaetian
Romanian
Scythian
Sehaptin
Seminole
Setswana
Shoshoni
Sumerian
Tahitian
Tamashek
Tarascan
Sanskrit
Thracian
Tigrinya
Tomansch
Tshiluba
Ugaritic
Warlpiri
Yaghnobi

9 letters

Abkhazian
Afrikaans
Algonquin
Bulgarian
Cantonese

Cheremiss
Chiapanec
Chickasaw
Chinantec
Chipewyan
Congolese
Havasupai
Hottentot
Hungarian
Icelandic
Inuktitut
Kabardian
Karankawa
Kashubian
Kiswahili
langue d'oc
Lycaonian
Malayalam
Marquesan
Mongolian
  (Mongol)
Norwegian
Pampangan
Penobscot
Provençal
Rajmahali
Ruthenian
Sahaptian
Sardinian
Sindebele
Sinhalese
Sundanese
Tehuelche
Tocharian
Tsimshian
Tuscarora
Ukrainian
Wapishana
Winnebago

10 letters

Anglo-Saxon
Assiniboin
Babylonian
Beach-la-mar
Blackfoot
Circassian
Gilbertese
Himyaritic
Hindustani
Kara-Kalpak
Karamojong
langue d'ol
Lithuanian
Macedonian
Mingrelian
Nicobarese
Pangasinan
Phoenician
Police Motu
Portuguese
Potawatomi
Rajasthani
Rarotongan
Serbo-Croat
Tarahumara
Vietnamese

11 letters

Azerbaijani
Belorussian
Coeur-d'Alene
Langobardic
Marshallese

13 letters

Chinook Jargon

15 letters

Bahasa
  Indonesia

Accents and Diacritical Marks

5 letters
acute
breve
grave
hacek
hamza
tilde

6 letters
macron
umlaut

7 letters
cedilla

9 letters
diaeresis

10 letters
circumflex

Phonetic Alphabet

4 letters
Echo
Golf
Kilo
Lima
Mike
Papa
X-ray
Zulu

5 letters
Alpha
Bravo
Delta
Hotel
India
Oscar
Romeo
Tango

6 letters
Juliet
Quebec
Sierra
Victor
Whisky
Yankee

7 letters
Charlie
Foxtrot
Uniform

8 letters
November

Puntuation Marks

4 letters
dash
mark
rule
stop

5 letters
brace
caret
colon
comma
point

6 letters
accent
dagger
em dash (rule)
en dash (rule)
hyphen

obelus
period
stroke

7 letters
bracket
solidus
virgule

8 letters
asterisk
asterism
ellipsis
full stop

9 letters
semicolon
swung dash

10 letters
apostrophe

11 letters
parenthesis

12 letters
omission mark
printer's mark
question mark

13 letters
inverted comma
quotation mark
square bracket

15 letters
diacritical mark
exclamation mark

Grammatical Terms

4 letters

case
dual
mood
noun
verb

5 letters

affix
infix
tense
voice

6 letters

adverb
aorist
aspect
clause
copula
dative
deixis
gender
gerund
govern
neuter
number
object
person
phrase
plural
prefix
sandhi
suffix
tmesis

7 letters

adjunct
binding
cognate
deictic
inflect
jussive
pronoun
subject

8 letters

ablative
anaphora
conjunct
deponent
disjunct
enclitic
ergative
feminine
genitive
locative
mass noun
modifier
negative
optative
particle
sentence
singular
subjunct
vocative
weak verb

9 letters

adjective
causative
countable
gerundive
imperfect
iterative
masculine
modal verb
parataxis
partitive
past tense
predicate
preterite
proclitic
reflexive

10 letters

accusative
antecedent
complement
declension

determiner
diminutive
finite verb
government
imperative
indicative
infinitive
inflection
main clause
nominative
paratactic
participle
perfective
pluperfect
possessive
proper noun
reciprocal
strong verb

11 letters

active voice
comparative
conditional
conjugation
conjunction
final clause
future tense
intensifier
middle voice
oblique case
phrasal verb
preposition
subjunctive
substantive
superlative

12 letters

direct object
distributive
imperfective
indeclinable
instrumental
interjection
passive voice

perfect tense
periphrastic
postpositive
present tense

13 letters

auxiliary verb
defective verb
demonstrative
frequentative
future perfect
interrogative
irregular verb
objective case
predeterminer

14 letters

collective noun
impersonal verb
indirect object
relative clause
subjective case
transitive verb

15 letters

definite article
personal pro-
  noun
relative pronoun
uncountable
  noun

16 letters

ablative absolute
intransitive verb

17 letters

indefinite article

Branches of Philosophy

5 letters
logic

6 letters
ethics

8 letters
axiology
ideology
ontology

9 letters
bioethics
cosmology
teleology

10 letters
aesthetics
deontology
gnosiology
metaethics
modal logic

11 letters
formal logic
legal ethics
metaphysics
metempirics

12 letters
epistemology

13 letters
phenomenology

15 letters
moral philosophy
philosophy of law

16 letters
philosophy of mind

19 letters
philosophy of science
political philosophy

20 letters
analytical philosophy
linguistic philosophy
philosophy of language
philosophy of religion

22 letters
mathematical
    philosophy
philosophy of
    psychology

23 letters
philosophy of
    mathematics

Sports and Sporting Activities

4 letters

beam
crew
golf
judo
luge
pato
polo
pool

5 letters

bandy
darts
kendo
rings
rodeo
track
vault

6 letters

aikido
boules (boccie)
boxing
caving
discus
diving
hammer
hiking
hockey
karate
kenipo
kiting
kung fu
pelota (jai alai)
rowing
running
shinty
skiing
slalom
soccer
sprint
squash
super-G
tai chi
tennis

7 letters

angling
archery
bowling
cricket
croquet
curling
cycling
extreme
fencing
fishing
gliding
haphido
high bar (horizontal bar)
hurdles
hurling
jai alai (pelota)
javelin
jujitsu
kabaddi
karting
netball
shot put
snooker
surfing
walking

8 letters

baseball
beagling
biathlon
canoeing
climbing
coursing
dressage
falconry
football
freefall
gridiron
gymkhana
handball
high jump
kayaking
korfball

lacrosse
langlauf
long jump
marathon
petanque
ping-pong (table tennis)
rambling
rounders
sculling
shooting
skittles
softball
speedway
swimming
trotting
tug of war
tumbling

9 letters

air racing
autocross
badminton
billiards
canoe polo
decathlon
ferreting
ice hockey
ice skating
jet skiing
motocross
pole vault
potholing
puissance
skydiving
speedball
stoolball
tae kwon do
tang soo do
triathlon
water polo
wrestling

10 letters

aerobatics

auto racing
ballooning
basketball
bouldering
drag racing
flat racing
fly-fishing
fox hunting
gymnastics
heptathlon
ice dancing
kick boxing
lawn tennis
rally cross
rugby fives
rugby union
scrambling
sea fishing
ski jumping
snorkeling
spelunking
Thai boxing
triple jump
volleyball

11 letters

bear baiting
blood sports
cycle racing
fell running
field events
field hockey
game fishing
giant slalom
hang gliding
hillwalking
horseracing
ice climbing
martial arts
mink hunting
parachuting
paragliding
pommel horse
racquetball
relay racing
roller derby
rugby league
sailplaning
scuba diving
sepak takrow
short tennis

showjumping
table tennis (ping-pong)
tobogganing
track events
water sports
wildfowling
windsurfing
yacht racing

12 letters

Alpine skiing
bullfighting
bunji jumping
caber tossing
canoe sailing
cock fighting
darts cricket
deerstalking
field archery
laser sailing
matchfishing
Nordic skiing
orienteering
otter hunting
parallel bars
parascending
pigeon racing
point-to-point
rock climbing
roller hockey
roller skiing
skibob racing
snowboarding
speed skating
steeplechase
team handball
trampolining
trapshooting
winter sports

13 letters

coarse fishing
court handball
darts football
equestrianism
figure skating
French cricket
horizontal bar (high bar)
rifle shooting
roller skating

rough shooting
sharpshooting
sidecar racing
skateboarding
skeet shooting
sled-dog racing
squash rackets
target archery
tenpin bowling
three-day event
track and field
weightlifting

14 letters

airgun shooting
Alpine climbing
asymmetric bars
big-game fishing
carom billiards
downhill racing
flat-green bowls
floor exercises
Gaelic football
grouse shooting
mountain biking
mountaineering
off-piste skiing
pigeon shooting
pistol shooting
sports aerobics
stock-car racing

15 letters

bobsleigh racing
cross bow archery
crown-green bowls
freestyle skiing
greyhound racing
mountain running
powerboat racing
wild water racing

16 letters

automobile racing
modern pentathlon
motorcycle racing
pheasant shooting
underwater diving

17 letters

canoe slalom racing

Sports and Sporting Activities *(continued)*

canoe sprint racing
horseshoe pitching
short board sailing
ski mountaineering
whitewater rafting

18 letters

clay pigeon shooting
crosscountry skiing (Nordic skiing)
free pistol shooting
harness horseracing
rhythmic gymnastics

19 letters

Alpine combined event
association football (soccer)
Canadian canoe racing
down-the-line shooting
long-distance running
Nordic combined event
offshore yacht racing

20 letters

synchronized swimming

21 letters

middle-distance running
Olympic French shooting

22 letters

Canadian five-pin bowling
short-track speed skating

23 letters

Australian rules football
rapid-fire pistol shooting

25 letters

running game target shooting

Sports Terms

2 letters

DH (designated hitter)
DL (disabled list)
k.o. (knockout)
o.g. (own goal)

3 letters

ace
box
bye
cox
cue
end
ERA (earned run average)
key
lap
let
lob

MVP (most valuable player)
out
par
pot
RBI (runs batted in)
try

4 letters

away
base
bell
bunt
curl
dive
down
draw
dunk
épée

foil
foul
goal
heat
home
hook
hoop
mitt
pass
post
puck
punt
push
putt
race
rank
ruck
save
seed
spar
tuck

wing
zone

5 letters

alley
arena
belay
bench
blade
blitz
block
bogey
coach
count
court
crawl
curve
deuce
drive
dummy
eagle

fault
feint
final
flick
frame
glove
links
mound
pacer (pacemaker)
paint
parry
piste
piton
pivot
plate
put-in
rally
saber
scoop
scrum
scull
serve
slide
split
steal
swing

6 letters

abseil
assist
basket
batter
birdie
bowler
bunker
by-ball
by-line
cannon
corner
course
fumble
inning
miscue
onside
pocket
racket
rappel
replay
rookie
runner

slalom
slider
sprint
stance
streak
strike
stroke
tackle
tee off
volley

7 letters

batsman
bullpen
catcher
chicane
defense
doubles
dribble
end zone
fairway
fielder
foul out
free hit
home leg
home run
infield
kickoff
line-out
offense
offside
own goal (o.g.)
peel off
penalty
pitcher
pit lane
pit stop
playoff
qualify
quarter
racquet
rain out
ranking
rebound
referee
regatta
shutout
shuttle
(shuttlecock)
sky hook
striker

sweeper
throw-in
time-out
toe-poke

8 letters

backhand
back heel
back pass
bully off
cross bar
dead ball
dead heat
division
drop ball
drop goal
drop kick
drop shot
en rappel
fast ball
forehand
foul line
free ball
free kick
fullback
full time
goal kick
goal line
goal post
halfback
halftime
handball
handicap
hat trick
high feet
home goal
jump ball
jump shot
kiss shot
knockout (k.o.)
left back
left half
left hook
left wing
linesman
midfield
outfield
rain date
receiver
reserves
rotation

sixth man
slam dunk
spit ball
split end
tailback
tight end
uppercut
wildcard
wing back

9 letters

advantage
albatross
arabesque
back crawl
box scores
butterfly
cartwheel
extra time
field goal
freestyle
free throw
give and go
gold medal
infielder
karabiner
nose guard
pacemaker (pacer)
place kick
promotion
prusiking
right back
right half
right hook
right wing
scrimmage
scrum half
scrummage
shortstop
stanchion
strike out
touchdown
touchline

10 letters

backstroke
bush league
center back
center half
conversion

Sports Terms *(continued)*

cover point
extra cover
false start
front crawl
goal attack
goalkeeper
half volley
high tackle
injury time
inside left
linebacker
on the ropes
outfielder
possession
post season
relegation
return game
sidestroke
somersault
speech play
substitute
wing attack

11 letters

base on balls
bronze medal

flanker back
forward pass
Fosbury flop
goal defense
goal shooter
inside right
knuckle ball
left fielder
left forward
obstruction
offside trap
outside left
penalty kick
penalty spot
perfect game
photo finish
quarterback
running back
short corner
shuttlecock
  (shuttle)
silver medal
springboard
squeeze play
sudden death
through-ball

wing defense
wing forward
zone defense

12 letters

breaststroke
disabled list
home straight
left wing-back
outside right
overhead kick
penalty flick
personal foul
pole position
quarterfinal
right fielder
right forward
scissors kick
stand-off half
stoppage time
three quarter
touching ball
wide receiver
zonal defense

13 letters

center fielder
center forward
checkered flag
follow-through
nominated ball
penalty corner
right wing-back
slip-streaming

14 letters

goal difference
left center-back
left defenseman
starting blocks
starting pistol

15 letters

man-to-man
  defense
penalty shoot-
  out
right center-
  back
right defenseman

Gymnastic Events

4 letters

beam

5 letters

rings

7 letters

high bar

8 letters

tumbling

10 letters

horse vault

11 letters

pommel horse

12 letters

parallel bars
trampolining

14 letters

asymmetric bars
floor exercises
side horse vault
sports aerobics

18 letters

rhythmic gymnastics

Trophies, Awards, and Events

(with sport)

3 letters
MVP (Most Valuable Player)   football, basketball, baseball

4 letters
Oaks   horseracing

5 letters
Ashes   cricket
Derby   horseracing

6 letters
Le Mans   automobile racing
U.S. Open   golf, tennis

7 letters
St. Leger   horseracing
Sun Bowl   football
Uber Cup   badminton
Masters   golf

8 letters
Boat Race   rowing
Classics   horseracing
Davis Cup   tennis
Iditarod   sled dog racing
Marathon   track and field
Milk Race   cycling
Rose Bowl   football
Ryder Cup   golf
Super Cup   handball
World Cup   soccer

9 letters
Gator Bowl   football
Grand Prix   automobile racing
Grand Slam   tennis
Preakness   horseracing
Sugar Bowl   football
Superbowl   football
Walker Cup   golf
Wimbledon   tennis
World Bowl   football

10 letters
Cotton Bowl   football
Daytona 500   NASCAR racing
Fiesta Bowl   football

Trophies, Awards, and Events *(continued)*

French Open	tennis
Haarlem Cup	soccer
Orange Bowl	football
Stanley Cup	ice hockey
Test Series	cricket, rugby
Winston Cup	NASCAR racing

11 letters

Admiral's Cup	sailing
America's Cup	sailing
Breeders' Cup	horseracing
Gillette Cup	cricket
Icy Smith Cup	ice hockey
Iroquois Cup	lacrosse
Isle of Man TT	motorcycle racing
Kinnaird Cup	fives
Sudirman Cup	badminton
Triple Crown	horseracing, rugby
Wightman Cup	sailing
World Series	baseball

12 letters

Cornhill Test	cricket
Cy Young Award	baseball
Golden Gloves	boxing
Hambletonian	harness racing
Lombard Rally	automobile racing
Lonsdale Belt	boxing
Olympic Games	
Outland Award	football
Royal Hunt Cup	horseracing
Tour de France	cycling
Yellow Jersey	cycling

13 letters

Belmont Stakes	horseracing
Federation Cup	tennis
Grand National	greyhound racing
Heisman Trophy	football
Highland Games	
Kentucky Derby	horseracing
Man of the Match	cricket, soccer
Strathcona Cup	curling
Swaythling Cup	table tennis

14 letters

Australian Open	tennis
Guinness Trophy	tiddlywinks

15 letters

Golden Boot Award	soccer
Indy Five Hundred (Indianapolis Five Hundred)	automobile racing
Middlesex Sevens	rugby
Monte Carlo Rally	automobile racing
Wingfield Skulls	rowing

16 letters

European Super Cup	soccer
Harmsworth Trophy	powerboat racing
John R. Wooden Award	basketball
Jules Rimet Trophy	soccer
RAC Tourist Trophy	automobile racing
PGA Championships [Professional Golf Association]	golf

17 letters

African Nations Cup	soccer
Cheltenham Gold Cup	horseracing
Coca Cola (League) Cup	soccer
Commonwealth Games	track and field
Football League Cup	soccer
World Championship	snooker

18 letters

Daytona Five Hundred	automobile racing
Henley Royal Regatta	rowing
King George V Gold Cup	equestrian
Most Valuable Player (MVP)	football, basketball
One Thousand Guineas	horseracing
Prudential World Cup	cricket
Two Thousand Guineas	horseracing

19 letters

Alpine Championships	skiing
Nordic Championships	skiing
Queen Elizabeth II Cup	equestrian

20 letters

Air Canada Silver Broom	curling
Badminton Horse Trials	equestrian
European Champions' Cup	soccer, basketball

21 letters

English Greyhound Derby	greyhound racing
European Championships	soccer
European Cup-Winner's Cup	soccer
World Club Championship	soccer

Trophies, Awards, and Events *(continued)*

22 letters
All-Ireland Championship	Gaelic football, hurling

23 letters
All-England Championships (Wimbledon)	tennis
British Open Championship	golf, snooker
Five Nations' Championship	rugby
Indianapolis Five Hundred	automobile racing
Open Croquet Championship	croquet
Rugby League Challenge Cup	rugby

24 letters
Gorden International Medal	curling

25 letters
Grand National Steeplechase	horseracing
International Championship	bowling
Premier League Championship	soccer
South American Championship	soccer
World Masters Championships	darts

26 letters
Football League Championship	soccer
National Coarse Championship	angling

29 letters
National Westminster Bank Trophy	cricket

30 letters
National Hunt Jockey Championship	horseracing

31 letters
Macrobertson International Shield	croquet

32 letters
Camanachd Association Challenge Cup	shinty
Uniroyal World Junior Championships	curling

34 letters
Formula One Drivers' World Championship	automobile racing

37 letters
International Cross-country Championship	track and field

39 letters
International Inter-city Industrial Fairs Cup	soccer

Stadiums and Venues

(with main sport)

5 letters

Ascot	horseracing
Forum, The, Los Angeles	basketball
Ibrox, Glasgow	soccer

6 letters

Belfry, The	golf
Lahore	cricket
Summit, The, Houston	basketball

7 letters

Aintree	horseracing
Anfield, Liverpool	soccer
Nou Camp, Barcelona	soccer
San Siro, Milan	soccer
Sky Dome, Toronto	basketball

8 letters

Highbury, London	soccer
Kay Arena, Seattle	basketball
Kingdome, Seattle	football
Moor Park, Rickmansworth	golf
Newlands, Cape Town	cricket, rugby

9 letters

Alamodome, San Antonio	basketball
Astrodome, Houston	baseball
Edgbaston	cricket
Gund Arena, Cleveland	basketball
Metrodome, Minneapolis	football
Newmarket	horseracing
Superdome, Louisiana	most sports
Villa Park, Birmingham	soccer
White City	greyhound racing
Wimbledon	tennis

10 letters

Brooklands	automobile racing
Celtic Park, Glasgow	soccer
Epsom Downs	horseracing
Headingley	cricket
Meadowbank	track and field
Twickenham	rugby

11 letters

Belmont Park, Long Island	horseracing
Brands Hatch	automobile racing

Stadiums and Venues *(continued)*

Delta Center, Salt Lake City	basketball
Eden Gardens, Calcutta	cricket
Hampden Park, Glasgow	soccer
Murrayfield	rugby
Old Trafford, Manchester	cricket, soccer
Silverstone	automobile racing
Windsor Park, Belfast	soccer

12 letters

Goodison Park, Liverpool	soccer
Hillsborough, Sheffield	soccer
Lenin Stadium, Moscow	soccer
Oakland Arena, Oakland	basketball
Odsal Stadium, Bradford	rugby
Reunion Arena, Dallas	basketball
Target Center, Minneapolis	basketball
Texas Stadium	most sports

13 letters

Azteca Stadium, Mexico City	Olympics, soccer
Boston Gardens, Boston	basketball
Bradley Center, Milwaukee	basketball
Caesar's Palace, Las Vegas	boxing
Crystal Palace	track and field
Francorchamps, Belgium	automobile racing
Heysel Stadium, Brussels	soccer
Stahov Stadium, Prague	gymnastics
White Hart Lane, London	soccer

14 letters

Anaheim Stadium, California	baseball
Central Stadium, Kiev	soccer
Landsdowne Road, Dublin	rugby
McNichols Arena, Denver	basketball
Olympic Stadium, Berlin	track and field, soccer
Wembley Stadium	soccer, rugby

15 letters

Bernabau Stadium, Madrid	soccer
Cardiff Arms Park	rugby
Maracana Stadium, Brazil	soccer
Shanghai Stadium	gymnastics

16 letters

Memorial Coliseum, Los Angeles	most sports

18 letters

Big Four Curling Rink	curling

Corporation Stadium, Calicur	cricket
Lords Cricket Ground	cricket
Senayan Main Stadium, Jakarta	cricket

19 letters

Madison Square Garden, New York City	basketball

20 letters

Munich Olympic Stadium	track and field, soccer

23 letters

Wembley Conference Centre	darts

25 letters

Cleveland Municipal Stadium	baseball

28 letters

Daytona International Speedway	automobile racing, motorcycling

34 letters

Royal and Ancient Golf Club of St. Andrews	golf

Baseball Stadiums

National League

9 letters

(The) Astrodome	Houston Astros

10 letters

Coors Field	Colorado Rockies

11 letters

Shea Stadium	New York Mets
Turner Field	Atlanta Braves

12 letters

Busch Stadium	St. Louis Cardinals
Cinergy Field	Cincinnati Reds
Wrigley Field	Chicago Cubs

13 letters

Dodger Stadium	Los Angeles Dodgers

14 letters

Olympic Stadium	Montreal Expos

15 letters

Bank One Ballpark	Arizona Diamondbacks
Qualcomm Stadium	San Diego Padres
Veterans Stadium	Philadelphia Phillies

16 letters

Pro Player Stadium	Florida Marlins

18 letters

Three Rivers Stadium	Pittsburgh Pirates

26 letters

3 Com Park at Candlestick Point	San Francisco Giants

Baseball Stadiums *(continued)*

American League

7 letters

SkyDome   Toronto Blue Jays

9 letters

(Hubert H. Humphrey)
  Metrodome   Minnesota Twins

10 letters

Fenway Park   Boston Red Sox

11 letters

Edison Field   Anaheim Angels
Jacobs Field   Cleveland Indians
  ('The Jake')
Safeco Field   Seattle Mariners

12 letters

Comiskey Park   Chicago White Sox
Tiger Stadium   Detroit Tigers

13 letters

Yankee Stadium   New York Yankees

14 letters

Tropicana Field   Tampa Bay Devil
                                             Rays

15 letters

Kauffman Stadium   Kansas City
                                             Royals
Oakland Coliseum   Oakland A's

22 letters

(The) Ballpark in   Texas Rangers
  Arlington
Milwaukee County
  Stadium   Milwaukee Brewers

23 letters

Oriole Park at   Baltimore Orioles
  Camden Yards

NFL Stadiums

7 letters

RCA Dome (Indianapolis)   Colts

8 letters

Kingdome (Seattle)   Seahawks
3 Com Park   49ers
  (San Francisco)

9 letters

Metrodome   Vikings
  (Minneapolis)

11 letters

Georgia Dome (Atlanta)   Falcons
Rich Stadium (Buffalo)   Bills

12 letters

Cinergy Field   Bengals
  (Cincinnati)

Lambeau Field   Packers
  (Green Bay)
Soldier Field (Chicago)   Bears

13 letters

ALLTEL Stadium   Jaguars
  (Jacksonville)
Giants Stadium   Giants, Jets
  (E. Rutherford)

14 letters

Foxboro Stadium   Patriots
  (Massachusetts)
Trans World Dome   Rams
  (St. Louis)

15 letters

Ericsson Stadium   Panthers
  (Charlotte)

Memorial Stadium (Baltimore)	Ravens	**18 letters**	
Qualcomm Stadium (San Diego)	Chargers	Louisiana Superdome (New Orleans)	Saints
Sun Devil Stadium (Tempe)	Cardinals	Three Rivers Stadium (Pittsburgh)	Steelers
Veterans Stadium (Philadelphia)	Eagles	**20 letters**	
		Jack Kent Cooke Stadium (Maryland)	Redskins
16 letters			
Arrowhead Stadium (Kansas City)	Chiefs	**21 letters**	
Houlihan's Stadium (Tampa)	Buccaneers	Denver Mile High Stadium (Colorado)	Broncos
Pro Player Stadium (Miami)	Dolphins	**26 letters**	
		Liberty Bowl Memorial Stadium (Memphis)	Oilers
17 letters			
Pontiac Silverdome (Michigan)	Lions	**28 letters**	
		Oakland-Alameda County Coliseum (California)	Raiders

Football Teams

11 letters

New York Jets

12 letters

Buffalo Bills
Chicago Bears
Detroit Lions

13 letters

Dallas Cowboys
Denver Broncos
Houston Oilers
Miami Dolphins
New York Giants

14 letters

Atlanta Falcons
Los Angeles Rams

15 letters

Cleveland Browns
Green Bay Packers
Seattle Seahawks

16 letters

Kansas City Chiefs
Minnesota Vikings
New Orleans Saints
Phoenix Cardinals
San Diego Chargers

17 letters

Indianapolis Colts
Los Angeles Raiders

18 letters

New England Patriots
Philadelphia Eagles
Pittsburgh Steelers
Tampa Bay Buccaneers
Washington Redskins

23 letters

San Francisco Forty-Niners

Baseball Teams

11 letters
Chicago Cubs
New York Mets

12 letters
Boston Red Sox
Texas Rangers

13 letters
Atlanta Braves
Detroit Tigers
New York Giants
St. Louis Browns

14 letters
Cincinnati Reds
Minnesota Twins
New York Yankees

15 letters
Brooklyn Dodgers
Chicago White Sox
Milwaukee Braves
Toronto Blue Jays

16 letters
Baltimore Orioles
California Angels
Cleveland Indians

Kansas City Royals
Oakland Athletics
St. Louis Cardinals

17 letters
Los Angeles Dodgers
Pittsburgh Pirates

18 letters
San Francisco Giants
Washington Senators

20 letters
Philadelphia Phillies

Cricketing Terms and Expressions

3 letters
bye
cut
l.b.w.
run
ton

4 letters
bail
duck
hook
over

5 letters
bosie
cover
gully
mid-on
slips
sweep

6 letters
beamer
bowler
crease
googly
howzat! (how's

that!)
leg bye
long on
maiden
mid-off
no-ball
scorer
seamer
umpire
wicket
yorker

7 letters
batsman
bouncer
century
cow-shot
fielder
fine leg
flipper
innings
late cut
leg slip
leg spin
long hop
long leg
long off

off spin
shooter
striker
stumped

8 letters
body-line
boundary
chinaman
hat-trick
how's that!
    (howzat!)
longstop
short leg
third man

9 letters
batswoman
hit wicket
in-swinger
leg glance
mid-wicket
overthrow
square cut
squareleg
sticky dog
test match

10 letters
all-rounder
golden duck
non-striker
out-swinger
silly mid-on
silly point
top-spinner
twelfth man

11 letters
daisy-cutter
sight-screen
silly mid-off

12 letters
sticky wicket
stonewalling
wicketkeeper

13 letters
deep square leg

14 letters
leg-side fielder
offside fielder

15 letters
leg before wicket (l.b.w.)

16 letters
leg-theory bowling

Golf Terms

3 letters
ace
bye
par
pin
tee

4 letters
baff
fore!
iron
trap

5 letters
bogey
divot
dormy
eagle
green
rough
wedge

6 letters
birdie
bisque
bunker
caddie
driver
putter
sclaff
tee off

7 letters
blaster
brassie
fairway
midiron
niblick
upswing

8 letters
dead ball
handicap

sand shot
wood shot

9 letters
albatross
backswing
downswing
flagstick
hole in one

10 letters
dog-leg hole
dubbed shot
forecaddie
lofted shot
mashie iron

11 letters
driving iron
hanging ball
spot putting
water hazard

12 letters
hole-high ball
pitch and putt
recovery shot

13 letters
follow-through
rub of the green

14 letters
nineteenth hole

17 letters
addressing the ball

Rugby Positions and Roles

4 letters
lock [forward]
prop [forward]
wing [three-quarter]

6 letters
center
hooker
jumper
winger

7 letters
back row
blocker

flanker
fly-half
forward

8 letters
attacker
defender
front row
full-back
half-back
tight end

9 letters
loose head [prop]

scrum half
second row
tight head [prop]
try scorer

11 letters
ball carrier
number eight
wing forward

12 letters
loose forward
stand-off half
three-quarter

Rugby Positions and Roles *(continued)*

14 letters
back-row forward

15 letters
front-row forward

16 letters
second-row forward

20 letters
left wing three-quarter

21 letters
right wing three-quar-
ter

22 letters
left center three-quar-
ter

23 letters
right center three-
quarter

Boxing Weight Divisions

9 letters
flyweight

11 letters
heavyweight
lightweight

12 letters
bantamweight

middleweight
welterweight

13 letters
cruiserweight
featherweight

14 letters
light flyweight

16 letters
light heavyweight

17 letters
junior lightweight
light middleweight
light welterweight

Fencing Terms

4 letters
épée
foil
mask

5 letters
blade
coupé
feint
guard
lunge
parry
piste
saber
touch

6 letters
flèche
remise
touché

7 letters
cutover
en garde [on guard]
riposte

8 letters
foil grip

9 letters
foil guard

10 letters
foil button
supination

11 letters
corps à corps

13 letters
counterattack
running attack

14 letters
counter-riposte
electrical foil

MISCELLANEOUS

Cooking Terms

6 letters
baking
curing
frying

7 letters
boiling
smoking
stewing

8 letters
braising
broiling
coddling
currying
grilling
pickling
poaching
roasting
steaming
toasting

9 letters
sautéeing
simmering

10 letters
barbecuing
deep-frying
marinating
parboiling
scrambling
stir-frying

11 letters
casseroling
pot-roasting

12 letters
charbroiling
fricasseeing
oven-roasting
spit-roasting

Herbs

3 letters
rue

4 letters
dill
mint
sage

5 letters
anise
basil
thyme

6 letters
borage
chives
fennel
lovage
savory
sesame
sorrel

7 letters
bay leaf
chervil
chicory
comfrey
oregano
parsley
pot-herb
saffron

8 letters
angelica
bergamot
camomile
lavender
marjoram
rosemary
tarragon

9 letters
fenugreek
lemon mint
spearmint

10 letters
peppermint
sweet cicely

Spices

4 letters
mace

5 letters
chili
cumin

6 letters
capers
cassia
cloves
garlic
ginger
nutmeg

7 letters
curcuma
ginseng
mustard
paprika
pimento
vanilla

8 letters
allspice
cardamom
cinnamon
turmeric

Spices *(continued)*

9 letters
coriander

10 letters
five spices

11 letters
black pepper
garam masala
green pepper
white pepper

12 letters
caraway seeds

13 letters
cayenne pepper

14 letters
juniper berries

Cheeses

3 letters
Oka

4 letters
Brie
Edam
feta

5 letters
Colby
Derby
Gouda
grana
quark

6 letters
Cantal
chèvre
Dunlop
Romano
Samsoe
Tilsit
tvorog

7 letters
Boursin
Chaumes
Cheddar

Gervais
gjetost
Gruyère
Livarot
ricotta
Stilton
Windsor

8 letters
Beaufort
Bel Paese
blue brie
Cheshire
Churnton
  (*trademark*)
Emmental
halloumi
Liptauer
Monterey
Parmesan
pecorino
Reggiano
taleggio
vacherin
Vignotte

9 letters
Cambozola

Camembert
Ilchester
Leicester
Limburger
Port Salut
provolone
Reblochon
Roquefort
Sage Derby
Saint Agur
Tillamook
Wiltshire

10 letters
blue cheese
blue vinney
Caerphilly
curd cheese
Danish blue
Dolcelatte
Gloucester
Gorgonzola
Jarlesburg
Lancashire
mascarpone
mozzarella
Neufchâtel
stracchino

Windsor Red

11 letters
cream cheese
Liederkranz
Swiss cheese
Wensleydale

12 letters
fromage frais
Monterey Jack
Red Leicester
Sainte Honoré

13 letters
cottage cheese
Saint Nectaire
Tomme de
  Savoie

15 letters
Ami du
  Chambertin

16 letters
double
  Gloucester

Types of Pasta

4 letters
pipe

5 letters
penne

6 letters
bigoli
ditali
risoni
rotini

7 letters
capelli
fusilli
lasagne
lumache
noodles

ravioli
rotelle

8 letters
bucatini
ditalini
ditaloni
farfalle
fettucce
fidelini
gramigna
linguine
macaroni
rigatoni
stelline
taglioni
trenette

9 letters
agnolotti
annellini
manicotti
spaghetti
tuffoloni

10 letters
cannelloni
conchiglie
cravattine
farfalline
fettuccine
tagliolini
tortellini
tortelloni
vermicelli

11 letters
cappelletti
orecchiette
pappardelle
spaghettini
spaghettone
tagliatelle
tortiglioni

12 letters
paglia e fieno

Beans and Peas

6 letters
lentil

7 letters
pea bean
red bean

8 letters
chickpea
lima bean
mung bean
soya bean

split pea
sugar pea

9 letters
broad bean
flageolet
garden pea
horse bean
mangetout
petit pois
pinto bean

10 letters
adzuki bean
bean sprout
butter bean
French bean
kidney bean
runner bean
string bean
waxpod bean

11 letters
haricot bean

12 letters
sugar snap pea

13 letters
black-eyed bean
scarlet runner

Desserts

4 letters
fool
whip (gooseberry whip)

5 letters
jelly

6 letters
cajeta
junket
kissel
mousse
sorbet
sundae
trifle
yogurt

7 letters
baklava
cannoli
cobbler
compote
crumble
custard
granita
jam tart
pavlova

soufflé
spumoni
tapioca

8 letters
apple pie
fruit cup
ice cream
pandowdy
roly-poly
semolina
tiramisu
water ice

9 letters
bavaroise
entremets
fruit flan
tipsy-cake
Viennoise [pudding]

10 letters
banoffi pie
blancmange
Brown Betty
egg custard
fresh fruit

fruit salad
key lime pie
peach Melba
shoofly pie
zabaglione

11 letters
baked Alaska
banana split
Eve's pudding
plum pudding
rice pudding
spotted dick
stewed fruit
suet pudding
treacle tart

12 letters
Apfelstrudel
bread pudding
crème caramel

13 letters
crêpes Suzette
dairy ice cream
sponge pudding
summer pudding

14 letters
apple charlotte
cabinet pudding
charlotte russe
floating island
gooseberry whip
steamed pudding

16 letters
Christmas pudding
death by chocolate

17 letters
Black Forest gateau
Mississippi mud pie
upside-down pudding

18 letters
Knickerbocker Glory

Cakes

4 letters
baba

5 letters
scone
torte

6 letters
éclair
gateau
kuchen
muffin
parkin

7 letters
baklava
bannock
brownie
cruller
cupcake
hoecake
pancake
pavlova
rum cake
strudel
teacake
yule log

8 letters
doughnut
flapjack
meringue
pandowdy
plum cake
rock cake
seedcake

9 letters
angel cake
drop scone
fairy cake
fruit cake

Genoa cake
lardy-cake
madeleine
pound cake
queen cake
shortcake
Swiss roll
tipsy-cake

10 letters
almond cake
Battenburg
cheesecake
Dundee cake

Eccles cake	**11 letters**	**12 letters**	**14 letters**
frangipane	gingerbread	Bakewell tart	devil's food cake
koeksister	Madeira cake	Danish pastry	upside-down
ladyfinger	wedding cake	millefeuille	cake
marble cake			Victoria sponge
simnel cake			
sponge cake			

Wines and Varieties of Grapes

4 letters
Bual
Fino
Hock
Port
Rosé

5 letters
Byrrh
Crépy
Fitou
Gamay
Médoc
Mosel
Rioja
Syrah (Shiraz)
Tavel
Tokay

6 letters
Alsace
Bandol
Barolo
Barsac
Beaune
Cahors
Cassis
Chinon
Claret
Frangy
Graves
Kerner
Málaga
Malbec
Merlot
Muscat
Saumur
Sherry
Shiraz (Syrah)

Volnay

7 letters
Aligoté
Barbera
Campari
Chablis
Chianti
Cinsaut
Crémant
Falerno
Furmint
Gaillac
Madeira
Mammolo
Manseng
Margaux
Marsala
Martini
Meunier
Moselle
Orvieto
Pommard
Retsina
Verdejo
Vouvray

8 letters
Aleatico
Bordeaux
Brouilly
Burgundy
Carignan
Dolcetto
Dubonnet
Gigondas
Grenache
Marsanne
Mercurey

Montagny
Montilla
Muscadet
Nebbiolo
Pauillac
Pinotage
Riesling
Sancerre
Santenay
Sémillon
Sylvaner
Valençay
Verdelho
Verdello
Verduzzo
Vermouth
Vin Jaune
Viognier

9 letters
Blanc Fumé
Bourgueil
Champagne
Colombard
Côte-Rôtie
Fumé Blanc
Hermitage
Lambrusco
Meursault
Montlouis
Mourvedre
Pinot Gris
Pinot Noir
Sauternes
Trebbiano
Vernaccia
Zinfandel

Wines and Varieties of Grapes (continued)

10 letters
Barbaresco
Beaujolais
Bull's Blood
Chardonnay
Grignolino
Mandelaria
Manzanilla
Montrachet
Muscadelle
Pinot Blanc
Richebourg
Rivesaltes
Sangiovese
Verdicchio
Vermentino
Vinho Verde

11 letters
Aloxe-Corton
Amontillado
Chenin Blanc
Monbazillac
Pouilly-Fumé
Saint Julien
Tempranillo
Vin de Paille

12 letters

Côtes-du-Rhône
Romanée-Conti
Saint-Emilion
Saint Estephe
Valpolicella
Vosne-Romanée

13 letters
Cabernet Franc
Château d'Yquem
Château Lafite
Château Latour
Entre-Deux-Mers
Montepulciano
Müller-Thurgau
Pouilly-Fuissé
Tocai Friulano

14 letters
Château Margaux
Côtes-du-Ventoux
Gewürztraminer
Lacrima Christi
Malvasia Bianca
Sauvignon Blanc

15 letters
Côtes-de-Provence
Côtes-du-Vivarais

Crozes-Hermitage
Grüner Veltliner
Haut Poitou Wines
Morey-Saint-Denis

16 letters
Chambolle-Musigny
Château Haut-Brion
Gevrey-Chambertin
Savigny-lès-Beaune

17 letters
Cabernet Sauvignon
Corton-Charlemagne
Côtes-du-Roussillon
Nuits-Saint-Georges

18 letters
Blanquette de Limoux

19 letters
Chassagne-
  Montrachet

23 letters
Château Mouton-
  Rothschild

Champagne Measures

6 letters		**10 letters**	
magnum	= 2 bottles	methuselah	= 4 magnums
8 letters		salmanazar	= 6 magnums
jeroboam	= 2 magnums	**14 letters**	
rehoboam	= 3 magnums	nebuchadnezzar	= 10 magnums
9 letters			
balthazar	= 8 magnums		

Beers

3 letters
ale

4 letters
lite
mild

5 letters
lager
stout

6 letters
bitter
porter

7 letters
ice beer
keg beer
pale ale
real ale

8 letters
brown ale

9 letters
draft beer
strong ale

10 letters
canned beer

11 letters
bottled beer

14 letters
low-alcohol beer

15 letters
steam-brewed
  beer

Games

2 letters
it

3 letters
nim
swy
tag
taw
tig

4 letters
I spy
keno

5 letters
bingo
catch
craps
darts
jacks
lotto
piggy
potty
salvo
two-up
yacht

6 letters
beetle
crambo
fan-tan

ghosts
hazard
hoopla
quoits
tipcat

7 letters
boss out
conkers
curling
diabolo
hangman
jukskei
kickean
mah-jong
marbles
pinball
pyramid
ring taw
Yahtzee (*trademark*)

8 letters
bird cage
charades
dominoes
forfeits
leapfrog
liar dice
pachinko
pall-mall
red light (green light)

red rover
roulette
sardines
trap-ball

9 letters
Aunt Sally
bagatelle
chuck luck
hopscotch
paintball
poker dice
poison pot
Simon Says
tic-tac-toe

10 letters
cat's cradle
categories
dumb crambo
fivestones
green light (red light)
hit the spot
jackstraws
kick the can
mother may I
off the wall
prison base
quotations
spillikins
three holes

Games *(continued)*

11 letters
bumble-puppy
fox and geese
hide-and-seek
mumbletypeg
odds or evens
shovelboard
tick-tack-toe
tiddlywinks
word squares

12 letters
consequences
picking plums
pitch-and-toss

13 letters
eggs in the bush
increase pound
musical chairs
pass the parcel
postman's knock
spin the bottle

14 letters
blindman's bluff
ducks and drakes
follow-my-leader
fortifications
hunt the slipper
hunt the thimble
pig in the middle
shove-halfpenny

15 letters
Chinese whispers
murder in the dark
twenty questions

17 letters
cowboys and Indians
noughts and crosses

21 letters
grandmother's foot-
steps
pin the tail on the don-
key

Board Games

2 letters
go

4 letters
Clue *(trademark)*
kono
Life *(trademark)*
ludo
Risk *(trademark)*
wari

5 letters
chess
goose
halma
salta
shogi
Sorry! *(trademark)*
Taboo *(trademark)*

6 letters
Cluedo *(trademark)*
gobang
uckers
wei ch'i

7 letters
mahjong

mancala
merrill
pachisi
Reversi *(trademark)*
Yahtzee *(trademark)*

8 letters
checkers
cribbage
Monopoly *(trademark)*
Outburst *(trademark)*
peggotty
race game
Scrabble *(trademark)*
Stratego *(trademark)*

9 letters
Candy Land *(trade-mark)*
Parcheesi *(trademark)*
solitaire

10 letters
acey deucey
backgammon
Balderdash *(trademark)*
Battleship *(trademark)*

Mastermind *(trade-mark)*
Pictionary *(trademark)*

11 letters
fox and geese

12 letters
Chinese chess
steeplechase

13 letters
Scattergories *(trade-mark)*

14 letters
Trivial Pursuit *(trade-mark)*

15 letters
Chinese checkers

16 letters
Chutes and Ladders
(trademark)
snakes and ladders

Card Games

3 letters
loo
nap
Pam
Uno (*trademark*)
war

4 letters
brag
faro
ruff
skat
skin
snap
vint

5 letters
cheat
cinch
comet
gleek
monte
noddy
ombre
pedro
pitch
poker
rummy
scopa
whist

6 letters
banker
basset
belote
Boston
bridge
écarté
euchre
fan-tan
hearts
oh hell
piquet
quinze
red dog

7 letters
bezique
canasta
cassino
coon-can
high-low
lottery
muggins
old maid
pontoon
primero
reverse
setback
seven-up

8 letters
all fours
baccarat
Canfield
cribbage
Dom Pedro
gin rummy
imperial
Klondike
Michigan
patience
pinochle
Pope Joan
sixty-six
slapjack

9 letters
blackjack
forty-five
matrimony
Newmarket
Pelmanism
penny ante
quadrille
solitaire
thirty-one
tredrille
vingt-et-un

10 letters
Black Maria

blind poker
klaberjass
lansquenet
panguingue
twenty-five

11 letters
chemin de fer
crazy eights
five hundred
hand and foot
rouge et noir
Russian Bank
Sancho Pedro
speculation

12 letters
rubber bridge
Swedish rummy
whipper-ginny

13 letters
auction bridge
happy families

14 letters
California jack
snip-snap-snorum
spite and malice
spit in the ocean
strip Jack naked
three-card monte

15 letters
duplicate bridge

16 letters
beggar-my-neighbor

Fabrics and Fibers

3 letters

PVC (polyvinyl chloride)

4 letters

coir
cord
felt
hemp
jean
jute
lamé
silk
wool

5 letters

baize
chino
crepe
denim
drill
gauze
gunny
linen
Lycra (*trademark*)
moire
nylon
Orlon (*trademark*)
piqué
plaid
plush
rayon
satin
serge
sheer
suede
tabby
toile
tulle
tweed
twill

6 letters

alpaca
angora
burlap
calico
canvas
chintz
cotton
Dacron (*trademark*)
damask
duffel
faille
jersey
madras
melton
mohair
muslin
poplin
sateen
shoddy
tricot
velour
velvet
vicuña

7 letters

acetate
acrylic
brocade
buckram
bunting
cambric
challis
cheviot
chiffon
doeskin
flannel
gingham
hessian
hopsack
Malines
matting
nankeen

netting
organza
Paisley
stammel
ticking
viscose
webbing
worsted

8 letters

cashmere
chambray
chenille
corduroy
dungaree
gossamer
jacquard
Mackinaw
marocain
moleskin
organdie
sarsenet
tapestry
Terylene (*trademark*)
toweling

9 letters

astrakhan
camel hair
crimplene (*trademark*)
crinoline
gabardine
grenadine
haircloth
horsehair
huckaback
long cloth
oiled silk
polyester
sackcloth

sailcloth
sharkskin
stockinet
swansdown
tarpaulin
Tricotine
velveteen

10 letters

brocatelle
chinchilla
mackintosh
Marseilles
microfiber
mousseline

11 letters

Canton crepe
cheesecloth
flannelette
Harris tweed
herringbone
leatherette (*trademark*)
panne velvet

12 letters

crepe de Chine
Donegal tweed

13 letters

linsey-woolsey

14 letters

coconut matting
crepe-back satin
Georgette crepe

17 letters

polyvinyl chloride (PVC)

Sewing Techniques

6 letters

facing

7 letters

basting
binding
cutwork
darning
ruching
tucking

8 letters

appliqué
couching
laid work
mitering
pleating
quilting
ruffling
shirring
smocking

9 letters

drawn-work
faggoting
gathering
patchwork
whitework

10 letters

crocheting
embroidery
oversewing
scalloping

11 letters

fine-drawing
needlepoint
overcasting
overlocking

12 letters

topstitching

Sewing Stitches

4 letters

tack

9 letters

crow's foot
gros point
hemstitch
topstitch

10 letters

backstitch
French knot

lock stitch
overstitch
petit point
stay stitch
stem stitch
tent stitch
whipstitch

11 letters

blind stitch
chain stitch
cross stitch

needlepoint
satin stitch
tailor's tack

12 letters

kettle stitch

13 letters

blanket stitch
feather stitch
running stitch

15 letters

lazy daisy stitch

16 letters

buttonhole
   stitch
Florentine stitch

17 letters

herringbone
   stitch

Knitting Terms

4 letters

warp
yarn

5 letters

chain
graft

6 letters

argyle
Berlin [wool]

7 letters

bawneen [wool]
crochet
raschel
ribbing
worsted

8 letters

Fair Isle
increase
intarsia

9 letters

fingering [wool]
fisherman

10 letters

foundation
moss stitch
purl stitch
slip stitch

11 letters

cable stitch

plain stitch
shell stitch

12 letters

garter stitch

13 letters

trellis stitch

14 letters

double knitting
stocking stitch

Knots

3 letters
bow

4 letters
bend

5 letters
hitch

6 letters
prusik

7 letters
bowknot
bowline
cat's-paw

8 letters
loop knot
love knot
mesh knot
reef knot
slipknot
wall knot
wale knot

9 letters
half hitch
sheet bend
thumb knot
Turk's head
water knot

10 letters
clove hitch
granny knot
hawser bend
sheepshank
shroud-knot
square knot

11 letters
carrick bend
diamond knot
running knot
sailor's knot
timber hitch
weaver's knot
Windsor knot

12 letters
hangman's knot

harness hitch
Hercules knot
overhand knot
rolling hitch
surgeon's knot
true-love knot

13 letters
Matthew Walker

14 letters
Blackwall hitch
Englishman's tie
fisherman's bend
fisherman's knot
running bowline

17 letters
bowline on the bight
figure-of-eight knot

26 letters
round turn and two
  half hitches

Ceramics

4 letters
raku

5 letters
Adams
Dansk
Delft
Denby
Epoch
Lenox
Nikko
Sango
Spode

6 letters
bisque

Goebel
Harker
Lefton
Metlox
Mikasa
Minton
Oxford
Sèvres
Yamaka

7 letters
Bendigo
faience
Limoges
Pickard

8 letters
Coalport
flatware
Grindley
Haviland
maiolica (majolica)
Ming ware
Noritake
Seto ware
Sung ware
Syracuse
Tang ware
Ting ware
Toft ware
Wedgwood

9 letters

agateware
Arita ware
bone china
champlevé
cloisonné
creamware
fine china
Franconia
hard-paste
Imari ware
ironstone
Midwinter
porcelain
salt glaze
Spode ware
stoneware
Wentworth
Worcester

10 letters

Berlin ware
Castor ware
Crown Derby
Flintridge

hollowware
jasper ware
Kutani ware
queen's ware
stone china

11 letters

earthenware
Meissen ware
Nanking ware
Pfaltzgraff

12 letters

Dresden china
Fitz and Floyd
Kakiemon ware
Royal Doulton
Russel Wright
Talavera ware

13 letters

Chantilly ware
eggshell china
mezza-maiolica
Nabeshima ware

semi-porcelain
Vincennes ware

14 letters

Castleford ware
Ch'ing porcelain
fired porcelain
Rockingham ware
Royal Worcester

15 letters

Parian porcelain
porcelain enamel
Villeroy and Boch

16 letters

Chelsea porcelain
Satsuma porcelain

17 letters

Staffordshire ware

18 letters

soft-paste porcelain

Types and Styles of Furniture

5 letters

bombé

6 letters

boulle
Empire
inlaid
rustic
Shaker

7 letters

Bauhaus
Federal
Pilgrim
Regency

8 letters

bentwood
cabriole
Jacobean
Sheraton

9 letters

Classical
Queen Anne

10 letters

Adirondack
Louis Seize

11 letters

Chippendale

Duncan Phyfe
Hepplewhite
Louis Quinze
Louis Treize

12 letters

Neoclassical
reproduction
Scandinavian

13 letters

Early American
Gothic Revival
Louis Quatorze

Gemstones and Semiprecious Stones

4 letters
jade
onyx
opal
ruby

5 letters
agate
amber
topaz

6 letters
garnet
jasper
plasma
zircon

7 letters
cat's-eye
diamond
emerald

8 letters
amethyst

corundum
fire opal
hawk's-eye
hyacinth
sapphire
sardonyx

9 letters
almandine
caringorm
carbuncle
carnelian
moss agate

turquoise

10 letters
aquamarine
bloodstone
chalcedony
greenstone
tourmaline

11 letters
lapis lazuli

Colors

3 letters
dun
jet
red
tan

4 letters
blue
buff
cyan
ecru
fawn
gold
grey
iris
jade
navy
opal
pink
puce
rose
ruby
rust

5 letters
amber
azure
beige
black

brown
camel
coral
cream
ebony
green
hazel
ivory
khaki
lemon
mauve
ochre
olive
peach
pearl
raven
sable
sepia
tawny
topaz
umber
white

6 letters
auburn
bronze
cherry
claret
cobalt

copper
ginger
indigo
maroon
orange
purple
russet
salmon
silver
violet
yellow

7 letters
apricot
caramel
crimson
emerald
fuchsia
magenta
mustard
saffron
scarlet
sky blue

8 letters
burgundy
cerulean
chestnut
cinnamon

lavender
mahogany
mushroom
pea green
primrose
sapphire
sea green
viridian

9 letters
chocolate
lime green
royal blue
Titian red
turquoise
vermilion

10 letters
aquamarine
burnt ochre
burnt umber
powder blue

11 letters
bottle green
burnt sienna
ultramarine

Birthstones

(with dates)

4 letters			
ruby	July	emerald	May
opal	Oct.	**8 letters**	
		amethyst	Feb.
5 letters		sardonyx	Aug.
pearl	June	sapphire	Sept.
topaz	Nov.		
		9 letters	
6 letters		turquoise	Dec.
garnet	Jan.		
		10 letters	
7 letters		bloodstone	Mar.
diamond	Apr.		

Signs of the Zodiac

(with dates)

3 letters		7 letters	
Leo	July 23–Aug. 22	Scorpio	Oct. 24–Nov. 21
5 letters		**9 letters**	
Aries	Mar. 21–Apr. 19	Capricorn	Dec. 22–Jan. 19
Virgo	Aug. 23–Sept. 22	Aquarius	Jan. 20–Feb. 18
Libra	Sept. 23–Oct. 23		
		11 letters	
6 letters		Sagittarius	Nov. 22–Dec. 21
Taurus	Apr. 20–May 20		
Gemini	May 21–June 21		
Cancer	June 22–July 22		
Pisces	Feb. 19–Mar. 20		

Wedding Anniversaries

3 letters

tin	10th

4 letters

gold	50th
iron	6th
lace	13th
ruby	40th
silk	12th
wood	5th
wool	7th

5 letters

china	20th
coral	35th
fruit	4th
ivory	14th
linen	12th
paper	1st
pearl	30th
steel	11th

6 letters

bronze	8th
copper	7th
cotton	2nd
silver	25th
willow	9th

7 letters

crystal	15th
diamond	60th
emerald	55th
flowers	4th
leather	3rd
pottery	8th

8 letters

sapphire	45th

9 letters

aluminum	10th

Della

Tools

3 letters

awl
axe
hoe
ram
saw

4 letters

adze
file
fork
jack
rake
rasp
vice

5 letters

auger
bevel
clamp
drill
gavel
jemmy
knife
lever
miter
plane
punch
spade
swage
wedge

6 letters

beetle
chisel
clough
dibber
hammer
jigsaw
mallet
pliers
riddle
ripsaw
roller
sander
scribe
scythe
shears
shovel
sickle
trowel
wrench

7 letters

bradawl
crowbar
fretsaw
grinder
hacksaw
hand-axe
handsaw
mattock
nippers
pickaxe
pincers
scraper
spanner

8 letters

billhook
blowlamp
brace bit
chainsaw
tweezers

9 letters

blowtorch
burnisher
handspike

lawn mower
pitchfork
sandpaper
secateurs

10 letters

claw hammer
cultivator
perforator
spokeshave
wire cutter

11 letters

glass cutter
hammer drill
pruning hook
screwdriver

12 letters

edging shears
hedge clipper
sledgehammer
wire stripper

13 letters

soldering iron

Currencies of the World

(with countries)

2 letters

at	Laos
xu	Vietnam

3 letters

ban	Moldova, Romania
fen	China
jun	North Korea
kip	Laos
lek	Albania
leu (*pl.* lei)	Moldova, Romania
lev	Bulgaria
øre	Denmark, Norway
öre	Sweden
pul	Afghanistan
pya	Myanmar
sen	Cambodia, Indonesia, Japan, Malaysia
sol	Peru
som	Kyrgyzstan
sum	Uzbekistan
won	North Korea, South Korea
yen	Japan

4 letters

baht	Thailand
bani (*pl.* of ban)	
birr	Ethiopia
cedi	Ghana
cent	Antigua and Barbuda, Australia, The Bahamas, Barbados, Belau, Belize, Brunei, Canada, Cyprus, Dominica, Estonia, Ethiopia, Fiji, Grenada, Guyana, Jamaica, Kenya, Kiribati, Liberia, Malaysia, Malta, Marshall Islands, Mauritius, Micronesia, Namibia, Nauru, The Netherlands, New Zealand, Panama, St. Kitts and Nevis, St. Lucia, St. Vincent and the Grenadines, The Seychelles, Sierra Leone, Singapore, Solomon Islands, Somalia, South Africa, Sri Lanka, Suriname, Taiwan, Tanzania, Trinidad and Tobago, Tuvalu, Uganda, U.S., Zimbabwe
cént	Peru
chon	North Korea, South Korea
dong	Vietnam
dram	Armenia
euro	European Union
fils	Bahrain, Iraq, Jordan, Kuwait, United Arab Emirates, Yemen
jeon	South Korea
kina	Papua New Guinea
kobo	Nigeria
kuna (*pl.* kune)	Croatia
kyat	Myanmar
lari	Georgia
lats (*pl.* lati)	Latvia
leva (*pl.* of lev)	
lipa	Croatia
lira (*pl.* lire)	Italy, Malta, San Marino, turkey, Vatican City

Currencies of the World *(continued)*

loti	Lesotho	haler (halier)	Czech Republic,
luma	Armenia		Slovakia
lwei	Angola	khoum	Mauritania
para	Bosnia-Herzegovina,	kopek (copek, kopeck, copeck)	
	Macedonia, Yugoslavia		Belarus, Russia, Tajikistan
peso	Argentina, Chile, Colombia,	krona	Sweden
	Cuba, Dominican Republic,	króna	Iceland
	Guinea-Bissau, Mexico,	krone	Denmark, Norway
	Philippines, Uruguay	kroon	Estonia
pula	Botswana	kuruş (kurush)	Turkey
puli (*or* puls, *pl.* of pul)		laari	Maldives
punt	Republic of Ireland	leone	Sierra Leone
rand	South Africa	lepta (*pl.* of lepton)	
real	Brazil	litas (*pl.* litai)	Lithuania
rial	Iran, Oman, Yemen	manat	Azerbaijan, Turkenistan
riel	Cambodia	möngö	Mongola
sene	Samoa	naira	Nigeria
sent	Estonia	nakfa	Eritrea
sumy (*pl.* of sum)		ngwee	Zambia
taka	Bangladesh	paisa *pl.* paise)	Bangladesh, India,
tala	Samoa		Nepal, Pakistan
toea	Papua New Guinea	penni	Finland
vatu	Vanuatu	penny (*pl.* pence)	Republic of
yuan	China		Ireland, U.K.

5 letters

		pound	Cyprus, Egypt, Lebanon,
agora	Israel		Syria, U.K.
aurar (*pl.* of eyrir)		riyal	Qatar, Saudi Arabia
baiza	Oman	rupee	India, Mauritius, Nepal,
butut	The Gambia		Pakistan, Seychelles, Sri Lanka
colón	Costa Rica, El Salvador	senti (*pl.* of sent)	
denar	Macedonia	soles (*pl.* of sol)	
dinar	Algeria, Bahrain, Bosnia-	sucre	Ecuador
	Herzegovina, Iraq, Jordan,	tanga	Tajikistan
	Kuwait, Libya, Sudan, Tunisia,	tenge	Kazakhstan, Turkmenistan
	Yemen, Yogoslavia	tetri	
dobra	São Tomé and Principe	Georgia	
eyrir	Iceland	thebe	Botswana
franc	Andorra, Belgium, Burundi,	tolar	Slovenia
	Cameroon, Comoros,	tyiyn	Kyrgyzstan
	Democratic Republic of Congo,	zloty	Poland
	Djibouti, France, Gabon,		
	Guinea, Ivory Coast,	**6 letters**	
	Luxembourg, Madagascar, Mali,	agorot (*pl.* of agora)	
	Monaco, Niger, Rwanda,	balboa	Panama
	Switzerland	cauris	Guinea
gopik	Zerbaijan	centas (*pl.* -ai)	Lithuania
grosz	Poland	colóns (*pl.* of colón)	
		dalasi	The Gambia

dirham (dirhem)   Libya, Morocco,
    Qatar, United Arab Emirates
dollar   Australia, The Bahamas,
    Barbados, Belau, Belize, Brunei,
    Canada, Fiji, Guyana, Jamaica,
    Kiribati, Liberia, Malaysia,
    Marshall Islands, Micronesia,
    Nambibia, Nauru, New Zealand,
    Singapore, Solomon Islands,
    Taiwan, Trinidad and Tobago,
    Tuvalu, U.S., Zimbabwe
escudo   Cape Verde, Portugal
filler   Hungary
forint   Hungary
gourde   Haiti
groszy (*pl.* of grosz)
halala   Saudi Arabia
halier (haler, *pl.* haleru, halierov)
hryvna (*or* hryvnya)   Ukraine
kopeck (copeck, kopek, copek)
    Belarus, Russia, Tajikistan
koruna   Czech Republic, Slovakia
kroner (*pl.* of krone)
krónur (*pl.* of króna)
krooni (*pl.* of kroon)
kurush (kuruş)   Turkey
kwacha   Malawi, Zambia
kwanza   Angola
lepton   Greece
maloti (*pl.* of loti)
markka   Finland
pa'anga   Tonga
pennia (*or* -nis, *pl.* of penni)
peseta   Spain
pesewa   Ghana
qindar (qintar)   Albania
rouble   Belarus, Russia, Tajikstan
rupiah   Indonesia
satang   Thailand
seniti   Tonga
shekel (sheqel)   Israel
stotin   Slovenia
tugrik   Mongolia

7 letters

afghani   Afghanistan
bolívar   Venezuela
centavo   Argentina, Bolivia,
    Brazil, Cape Verde, Chile,
    Colombia, Cuba, Dominican
    Republic, Ecuador, El Salvador,
    Guatemala, Guinea-Bissau,
    Honduras, Mexico,
    Mozambique, Nicarague,
    Philippines, Portugal
centime   Algeria, Andorra,
    Belgium, Benin, Burkina Faso,
    Burundi, Cameroon, Central
    African Republic, Chad,
    Comoros, Congo, Democratic
    Republic of Congo, Côte
    d'Ivoire, Djibouti, Equatorial
    Guinea, France, Gabon, Guinea,
    Haiti, Liechtenstein,
    Luxembourg, Madagascar, Mali,
    Monaco, Morocco, Niger,
    Rwanda, Senegal, Switzerland,
    Togo, Vanuatu
cêntimo   São Tomé and Principe
céntimo   Andorra, Costa Rica,
    Paraguay, Spain, Venezuela
chetrum   Bhutan
cólones (*pl.* of colón)
drachma   Greece
guaraní   Paraguay
guilder   The Netherlands, Suriname
hryvnya (hryvna)   Ukraine
kopiyka   Ukraine
lempira   Honduras
lisente   Lesotho
metical   Mozambique
millime   Tunisia
ouguiya   Mauritania
pfennig   Germany
piastre   Egypt, Lebanon, Syria
quetzal   Guatemala
ringgit   Malaysia
rufiyaa   Maldives
santimi   Latvia
tambala   Malawi
tolarji (*pl.* of tolar)

8 letters

CFA franc   Benin, Burkina Faso,
    Central African Republic, Chad,
    Congo, Equatorial Guinea,
    Senegal, Togo
drachmae (*or* -as, *pl.* of drachma)
groschen   Austria
halierov (*pl.* of haler *or* halier)

Currencies of the World *(continued)*

ngultrum	Bhutan
pfennige *(pl.* of pfennig)	
qindarka *(pl.* of qindar)	
shilling	Kenya, Somalia, Tanzania, Uganda
stotinka *(pl.* -inki)	Bulgaria

9 letters

boliviano	Bolivia
centesimo *(pl.* -mi)	Italy, San Marino, Vatican City
centésimo	Panama, Uruguay
lilangeni	Swaziland
quetzales *(pl.* of quetzal)	
schilling	Austria

10 letters

córdoba oro	Nicaragua
emalangeni *(pl.* of lilangeni)	

11 letters

Deutschmark (Deutsche Mark)	Germany

12 letters

Deutsche Mark (Deutschmark)	Germany

19 letters

East Caribbean dollar	Antigua and Barbuda, Dominica, Grenada, St. Kitts and Nevis, St. Lucia, St. Vincent and the Grenadines

Economic Terms and Theories

2 letters
M1
M2
M3
M4

3 letters
GDP (gross domestic product)
GNP (gross national product)

4 letters
FIFO

5 letters
slump

7 letters
duopoly
Marxism
New Deal
slavery
statics

surplus

8 letters
fungible
Leninism
monopoly
property

9 letters
boom cycle
bust cycle
free trade
inelastic
liquidity
oligopoly
put option
recession

10 letters
added value
bear market
broad money
bull market
capitalism

depression
fiscal drag
free market
investment
monetarism
multiplier [effect]
protection
trade cycle
Trotskyism
value added

11 letters
colonialism
competition
consumerism
demand curve
imperialism
marginalism
materialism
narrow money
physiocracy
revisionism
stagflation
syndicalism

12 letters

econometrics
economic rent
fiscal policy
five-year plan
gold standard
Keynesianism
market forces
mercantilism
mixed economy
New Economics
productivity
public sector
surplus value
trade barrier

13 letters

demand economy
exchange value
futures market
neo-classicism
options market
private sector

14 letters

balanced budget
command economy
corporate state
economic growth
economic policy
macroeconomics

microeconomics
monetary policy
national income
windfall profit

15 letters

aggregate demand
division of labor
inflationary gap
positional goods
supply and demand
totalitarianism
velocity of money
wage-price spiral

16 letters

cost of production
deficit financing
economies of scale
institutionalism
retail price index
welfare economics

17 letters

means of production

18 letters

diminishing returns
economic classicism
elasticity of demand
labor theory of value

perfect competition

19 letters

economic equilibrium
supply-side economics

20 letters

gross domestic prod-
  uct (GDP)
gross national product
  (GNP)

21 letters

laissez-faire economics
quantity theory of
  money

22 letters

dialectical materialism
prices and incomes
  policy

23 letters

centrally planned
  economy
principle of accelera-
  tion

27 letters

marginal efficiency of
  capital

Financial Terms

3 letters
ISA
par
PEP

4 letters
agio

5 letters
MIRAS
snake
TESSA

6 letters
parity
shares
valuta

8 letters
agiotage
bank rate
rallying

9 letters
arbitrage
deflation

inflation
reflation
unit trust

11 letters
bimetallism
devaluation
Income Bonds
money market
sinking fund
stagflation

12 letters
depreciation
disinflation
exchange rate
gold standard
interest rate

13 letters
effective rate
financial year
revolving fund

14 letters
bill of exchange

strong currency
venture capital

15 letters
exchange premium
managed currency
personal pension

16 letters
equalization fund
floating currency

18 letters
inflationary spiral
minimum lending rate

19 letters
gilt-edged securities

21 letters
foreign exchange market

24 letters
capital-expenditure budget

Roman Numerals

1 letter

I	1
V	5
X	10
L	50
C	100
D	500
M	1000
V	5000
X	10,000
L	50,000
C	100,000
D	500,000
M	1,000,000

2 letters

II	2
IV	4
VI	6
IX	9
XI	11
XV	15
XX	20

3 letters

III	3
VII	7
XII	12
XIV	14
XVI	16
XIX	19

4 letters

VIII	8
XIII	13
XVII	17

5 letters

XVIII	18

APPENDIX: WORD GAMES

CONTENTS

Part One: *Fairly Easy*

1.	Double Meanings	385
2.	Removing a Letter	385
3.	Stinky Pinky	386
4.	Letters of Introduction	386
5.	Add Two Letters	387
6.	Palindromes	388
7.	Hidden Words	388
8.	Groups of Three	389
9.	Tops and Tails	389
10.	Awful Authors	390
11.	Three Letters	390
12.	Antonyms	391
13.	What's This Word?	391
14.	Only Connect (1)	392
15.	Only Connect (2)	393
16.	Briticisms	393
17.	Change a Letter	394
18.	Change Two Letters	394
19.	First Names	395

20.	Hidden Words (2)	395
21.	Homophones	396
22.	Homophonic Statements	397
23.	Think of a Word	398
24.	I Knew Him When...	398
25.	Synonyms	399
26.	Triple Meanings	399
27.	Anagrams	400
28.	Endings	401
29.	Fractured French	401
30.	Acronyms	402
31.	Hide and Seek	402
32.	Triple Anagrams	403
33.	Categories	403
34.	True or False?	404
35.	The Name Game	404
36.	Combinations	405
37.	Side by Side	405
38.	Miss World	406

Interlude: *Oxes and Bulls*

Part Two: *Fairly Difficult*

39.	Anagram Pairs	409
40.	Doublets	410
41.	Reversals	410
42.	Connections	411
43.	Spelling	412
44.	Meanings	413
45.	Vowel Play	413
46.	Dismissals	414
47.	Words Within Words	414
48.	Antonyms (2)	415
49.	Paired Homophones	415
50.	Old-fashioned Words	416
51.	Bookends	416
52.	Three in One	417
53.	Plurals	417
54.	Combinations (2)	418
55.	Foreign Words and Phrases	418

56.	Collective Nouns	419
57.	Word Row	420
58.	What's the Difference?	420
59.	The Storm Breaks	421
60.	Follow-On	421
61.	Contronyms	421
62.	Definitions	422
63.	Portmanteau Words	423
64.	Abbreviations	423
65.	Dictionary	424
66.	Humpty Dumpty	425
67.	Personal Anagrams	425
68.	Malapropisms	426
69.	Daft Definitions	426
70.	Mishmash	427
71.	Eponyms	428

Interlude: *A Nasty Cough*

Part Three: *Fiendish*

72.	Silent Letters	431	90.	Perverbs	442
73.	Hidden Word Squares	431	91.	Mishmash (2)	442
74.	Kangaroo Words	432	92.	Oxymorons	443
75.	Down Under	433	93.	Origins	443
76.	Derivations	433	94.	Cryptic Clues	444
77.	Hermans	434	95.	Uncommon Terms	445
78.	Letter Swaps	435	96.	Russian Dolls	446
79.	Associations	435	97.	Rebuses	447
80.	Heteronyms	436	98.	Vowels in Order	448
81.	Transadditions	437	99.	Overspecialized Words	448
82.	Tom Swifties	437	100.	French Eponyms	449
83.	Typewriter Words	438	101.	Crossed Lines	450
84.	Quotations	438	102.	Acronyms (2)	450
85.	Anagrammed Places	439	103.	What Is the Question?	450
86.	Devil's Dictionary	439	104.	Mnemonics	451
87.	Synonym Chains	440	105.	Consonants	452
88.	Spoonerisms	441	106.	Vowel Language	452
89.	Two-letter Words	441	107.	The Final Challenge	453

Answers

Part One
Fairly Easy

1. Double Meanings

Many words have more than one meaning. Try to identify the words described below.

Example
Which word means both "in good health" and "a hole in the ground from which water is obtained"?

Answer
Well.

1. Which word means the top of a mountain and also a very important conference?
2. Which word means to conceal and the skin of an animal?
3. Which word means a swelling on the skin and also to bubble with heat?
4. Which word means an unmarried woman and a failure to hit?
5. Which word means to enclose and to practice swordplay?
6. Which word means both healthy and suitable?
7. Which word means a type of marsh bird and part of a railroad track?
8. Which word means a fuss and a hinged part of an airplane wing?
9. Which word means depressed and the color of the sky?
10. Which word means stupid and more than 90 degrees?
11. Which word means to go forward and to lend (money).
12. Which word means a nickname for Mom's mom and a music award?

2. Removing a Letter

This game involves removing one letter from a word to make another word. Guess the first word, then remove a letter from it to get the second word, without rearranging any letters.

Example
Remove a letter from trash to get a place for your car.

Answer
Remove "b" from *garbage* to make *garage*.

1. Remove a letter from damp to get a thin fog.
2. Remove a letter from a transparent material to get a girl.
3. Remove a letter from a girl to get a donkey.
4. Remove a letter from a violinist to get a violin.
5. Remove a letter from the opposite of fresh to get a story.
6. Remove a letter from a cowboy's footwear to get the cries of a dissatisfied audience.

7. Remove a letter from yell to get a hypodermic injection.

8. Remove a letter from a figure of speech to get a pleasurable expression.

9. Remove a letter from solitary to get a number.

10. Remove a letter from a whitener to get a sandy area.

3. Stinky Pinky

Stinky pinkies (also called "stink pinks," "hanky pankies," and many other names) are pairs of rhyming words.

Try to think of suitable pairs to fit the following definitions.

Example
Which two rhyming words could mean "a girl from Switzerland"?

Answer
Swiss miss.

1. Which two rhyming words could mean "an amusing rabbit"?

2. Which two rhyming words could mean "a story told in a farm building"?

3. Which two rhyming words could mean "a bloodthirsty tale"?

4. Which two rhyming words could mean "a sweet-sounding stringed instrument"?

5. Which two rhyming words could mean "a friendly rustic"?

6. Which two rhyming words could mean "a drowned friar"?

7. Which two rhyming words could mean "a strange hypothesis"?

8. Which two rhyming words could mean "the result of misdirecting a hammer"?

9. Which two rhyming words could mean "an overweight feline"?

10. Which two rhyming words could mean "a more modest acrobat"?

11. Which two rhyming words could mean "a mysterious pair of pictures"?

12. Which two rhyming words could mean "a villainous clergyman"?

13. Which two rhyming words could mean "a more rapid heart"?

14. Which two rhyming words could mean "a broken date"?

15. Which two rhyming words could mean "a talkative pet rodent"?

16. Which two rhyming words could mean "a sightless orange peel"?

4. Letters of Introduction

All you have to do here is to add one or more letters to a word to make another word, without rearranging any letters.

Example
Add a letter to *pit* to make a unit of measurement.

Answer
Pint.

1. Add a letter to *and* to make part of the human body.
2. Add a letter to *ear* to make an animal.
3. Add a letter to *range* to make a fruit.
4. Add a letter to *cane* to make a boat.
5. Add a letter to *eagle* to make a dog.
6. Add a letter to *laughter* to make killing.
7. Add a letter to *tent* to make a fraction.
8. Add a letter to *aspirin* to make a word for hoping.
9. Add a letter to *gave* to make an auctioneer's hammer.
10. Add a letter to *ache* to make a hiding place.
11. Add a letter to *car* to make another mode of transportation.
12. Add a letter to *mite* to make a bishop's hat.
13. Add two letters to *dish* to make a vegetable.
14. Add two letters to *mine* to make a fur.
15. Add two letters to *fig* to make a dispute.
16. Add two letters to *coin* to make a long box.
17. Add two letters to *wren* to make a tool.
18. Add two letters to *and* to make an animal.
19. Add two letters to *end* to make a devil.
20. Add two letters to *an* to make a sound of complaint.

5. Add Two Letters

Here we give you two clues that lead to pairs of words, in which the second word can be made by adding two letters to the first word, without rearranging any letters.

Example
Devotee - lose consciousness.

Answer
Fan - faint.

1. Strong breeze - glass opening.
2. Number - frequently.
3. Portable shelter - renter of property.
4. Burrowing animal - annoy.
5. Saucy - skilled.
6. To present - to present.
7. Employ - do harm to.
8. Kind - accompanying person or thing.
9. Beneath - rob.
10. Steal - pulsate.

6. Palindromes

A palindrome is a word that reads the same backward as forward. So the names *Bob, Eve,* and *Otto* are all palindromes.

Try to identify palindromic words from the following clues.

Example
Part of the body.

Answer
Eye.

1. Midday.
2. A young dog.
3. Flat.
4. A word for addressing a lady.
5. An Eskimo canoe.
6. A system for detecting airplanes, ships, etc.
7. An action.
8. Pieces of music for one person.
9. Poetic form of "before."
10. An automobile driven at the Indy 500.
11. Doctrine.
12. Restorer.

7. Hidden Words

Can you see an animal hidden inside the sentence: "The parcel came later than the invoice?" If you look closely at "came later," you can find the word *camel.*

Try to find words for animals hidden in consecutive letters of the following sentences.

Example
Is that a new type of shampoo?

Answer
Newt.

1. I'll be around.
2. Do go and take a bath, please.
3. She was invited to a dinner.
4. They tried to grab bits of food from the buffet.
5. Remember the help I gave you last week.
6. He tried to be a very good person.
7. We kept the potion in a spherical flask.
8. Their minds wandered as they watched the vacation slides.
9. I'll go if Roger goes too.
10. You must learn to feel and think at the same time.

8. Groups of Three

What do nine threes add up to? The answer is usually 27, but here the
answer is nine plus six sixes: a total of 45.

In this puzzle, you are presented with nine groups of three letters. Try to
put them together in various sequences, without rearranging the letters, to
make six six-letter words and one nine-letter word.

Example

ERE	IEW	COH
INC	ORT	DEP
INS	ADH	REV

Answer

You can put INS, INC, and ERE together to make the nine-letter word
insincere. The six six-letter words could be *adhere, cohere, cohort, deport,
revere,* and *review*.

1. RAY	NZE	AST	4. ATA	AYS	DST
OCH	ADC	DRO	ONG	ESS	TOA
HMA	WSE	BRO	ABB	STR	OOL

2. ING	BLY	ACH	5. ATE	TSY	SOR
ATE	ARY	NIM	ROW	NCI	CUR
TAK	INA	BLE	LEG	CEN	ENU

3. PED	ICE	ISE	6. GEA	EER	NCE
ELO	OID	MAL	IAL	STA	DIN
NOT	NOV	DEV	RED	VEN	SPA

9. Tops and Tails

In this game, you simply have to think of a word that starts and ends
with a particular letter.

Example

Think of a word that starts with E and ends with H.

Answer

Each (or English or Elizabeth, etc.).

1. Think of a word that starts with T and ends with E.
2. Think of a word that starts with A and ends with D.
3. Think of a word that starts with V and ends with Y.
4. Think of a word that starts with Y and ends with T.
5. Think of a word that starts with G and ends with N.
6. Think of a word that starts with L and ends with H.
7. Think of a word that starts with C and ends with S.
8. Think of a word that starts with M and ends with C.
9. Think of a word that starts with F and ends with O.
10. Think of a word that starts with C and ends with A.

10. Awful Authors

In this game, you have to think of a suitable punning surname for the author of an imaginary book. The most popular example used to be *The Broken Window* by Eva Brick (which is a pun on "heave a brick").

Can you complete the names for the authors of these imaginary books?

Example

The Cliff Tragedy by Eileen . . . who?

Answer

Eileen Dover.

1. *The Miser* by Penny . . . who?
2. *Lumberjacks* by Tim . . .
3. *Carpeting the House* by Walter . . .
4. *Politeness* by Hugo . . .
5. *What's for Breakfast?* by Hammond . . .
6. *Continental Breakfast* by Roland . . .
7. *Native American Weaponry* by Tom A. . . . .
8. *Oiling Baseball Mitts* by Lynn C. . . . .
9. *Easy Money* by Robin . . .
10. *Campfire Recipes* by Chris P. . . . .
11. *Chemistry* by Tess . . .
12. *Counterfeit Antiques* by Fay . . .
13. *Successful Books* by Bess . . .
14. *Foreseeing the Future* by Horace . . .
15. *French Windows* by Pattie . . .
16. *Alcohol and Gambling* by Rex . . .
17. *Personal Religious Belief* by Mike . . .
18. *Pleasing the Public* by Lois Carmen . . .
19. *Traveling Light* by Freda . . .
20. *The Perfect Marriage* by Ruth . . . and Patrick . . .

11. Three Letters

You are presented below with sequences of three letters. The aim of the game is to think of a word that starts with the first letter of the group and includes the other two letters, in the order given. If finding one word is too easy, think of as many words as possible that include these letters.

Example

F - D - L.

Answer

Fiddle, floodlight, fondle, friendly, fundamental, etc.

1. C - V - T.   6. B - N - S.
2. S - W - D.   7. A - H - P.
3. D - C - T.   8. J - C - R.
4. T - N - C.   9. R - R - R.
5. P - L - M.   10. Z - I - A.

12. Antonyms

Antonyms are words that mean the opposite of another word—or virtually the opposite. Thus *hot* is an antonym of *cold*, and *help* is the opposite of *hinder*. Find antonyms for the words below. The answers must be single words, not phrases, but hyphenated combinations are acceptable.

Example
Find at least ten antonyms for *clumsy*.

Answer
Adroit, agile, deft, dexterous, graceful, limber, lissom, lithe, nimble, sprightly, spry.

1. Find at least six antonyms for *discordant*.
2. Find at least seven antonyms for *health*.
3. Find at least eight antonyms for *accidental*.
4. Find at least nine antonyms for *amiable*.
5. Find at least ten antonyms for *unconventional*.
6. Find at least eleven antonyms for *uncertainly*.
7. Find at least twelve antonyms for *taciturn*.
8. Find at least fourteen antonyms for *honesty*.
9. Find at least twenty antonyms for *intolerant*.
10. Find at least thirty antonyms for *transitory*.

13. What's This Word?

Can you identify these words from the clues provided?

Example
This four-letter word starts with G and ends with M, and it means a tiny organism that causes a disease.

Answer
Germ.

1. This seven-letter word starts with A and ends with Y, and means a college or school.
2. This seven-letter word starts with D and ends with E, and means to refuse.

3. This nine-letter word starts with M and ends with E, and means to hypnotize.

4. This eight-letter word starts with W and ends with F, and means a person transformed into a canine beast.

5. This thirteen-letter word starts with T and ends with S, and means a large carnivorous dinosaur.

6. This ten-letter word starts with R and ends with P, and means those who look at the contents of a newspaper or magazine.

7. This nine-letter word starts with D and ends with N, and means a ten-event athletic contest.

8. This ten-letter word starts with P and ends with S, and means ominous or pompous.

9. This twelve-letter word starts with E and ends with A, and means a spectacular production.

10. This eight-letter word starts with S and ends with Y, and means a tactical plan of action.

14. Only Connect (1)

In all these puzzles, you have to add one word to another word to construct a third word.

Example

Add a word for "gone by" to a word for "spoken" to get a word meaning "rural" or "bucolic."

Answer

Pastoral (*past* plus *oral*).

1. Add a vehicle to a domestic animal to make a floor covering.

2. Add a rodent to a woman to get a word that means "slightly" or "somewhat."

3. Add a negative word to a piece of furniture to get a word meaning "remarkable" or "eminent."

4. Add an insect to an animal to get an annoyance.

5. Add an insect to the edge of a garment to get a patriotic hymn.

6. Add an Italian citizen to a nervous spasm to get a loving or sentimental word.

7. Add a word for "plump" to a supporter to get a word meaning "mortally."

8. Add an abbreviated road to a distance to get a word meaning "unusual" or "alien."

9. Add a certain wizard's domain to a number to get a colorless gas.

10. Add visible combustion to a corporal's initials to get Spanish music.

15. Only Connect (2)

In the following examples, add three words together to make another word.

Example
Add a plate to a number and a pig's house to get a word meaning "untruthfulness."

Answer
Dishonesty (dish-one-sty).

1. Add a sum of money to an indefinite article and a word connected with the mind to get a word meaning "basic."
2. Add a male person to me and a medical success to get cosmetic treatment for the hands and fingernails.
3. Add something nocturnal to the opposite of "out" and a strong wind to get a tuneful bird.
4. Add eider feathers to "to perceive aurally" and Senator Kennedy to get a word for "depressed."
5. Add a honeyed drink to a bird and a biblical ship to get a songbird.
6. Add thin fog to two forms of myself to get a word meaning "to do something at the wrong moment."
7. Add a small bed to 2,000 pounds and a sphere to get a piece of absorbent fluff.
8. Add "to repair" to me and hypocrisy to get a beggar.
9. Add a taxi to a limb and a male sheep to get a telegraph message.
10. Add grain to an old word for "formerly" and any person to get the indispensable part of a foundation.

16. Briticisms

George Bernard Shaw said that "England and America are two countries divided by a common language." Americans and the British often use different words to describe the same things. For example, Americans use the word *suspenders* for what the British call *braces*.

Which American words are represented by the following Briticisms?

Example
Candyfloss.

Answer
Cotton candy.

1. Aubergine.
2. Banger.
3. Bumbag.
4. Clothes peg.
5. Courgette.
6. Draughts.
7. Drawing pin.
8. Jump leads.
9. Nappy.
10. Noughts and crosses.
11. Roundabout.
12. Sleeping partner.
13. Windscreen.
14. Worryguts.

17. Change a Letter

Often one word can be changed into another word simply by altering one of its letters. For example, *word* itself can be changed into *worm, cord, ward,* and several other words.

Try forming new words by changing just one letter in each of the cases below.

Example

Change one letter in *beat* to make a vegetable.

Answer

Bean (or beet).

1. Change one letter in *cat* to make another animal.
2. Change one letter in *sick* to make something to wear.
3. Change one letter in *coal* to make a young horse.
4. Change one letter in *moral* to make a painting on a wall.
5. Change one letter in *fiddle* to make a puzzle.
6. Change one letter in *fluke* to make a musical instrument.
7. Change one letter in *coat* to make a bird.
8. Change one letter in *keen* to make part of a boat.
9. Change one letter in *pints* to make trousers or underwear.
10. Change one letter in *force* to make someone's strong point.

18. Change Two Letters

Below we give you pairs of clues that lead to pairs of words that differ simply by having two letters different from one another.

Example

Human being - deadly substance.

Answer

Person - poison.

1. Root vegetable - ketchup ingredient.
2. Discovery - angling.
3. Keyboard instrument - factory.
4. Steady - lacking capacity.
5. Fortified building - wheel on furniture.
6. Day of the week - day of the week.
7. Muslim ruler's position - try to equal or excel.
8. Stringed instrument - toothed fastener.
9. Eat - assimilate.
10. Insane - poured.

19. First Names

People's first names (or given names, or Christian names) often sound like other words. For example, "Hazel" sounds like a tree or a nut, while "Bill" sounds like an invoice or a bird's beak.

Try to find the names that fit the following clues: puns or lateral thinking may help you to find the answers.

Example
What is a good name for a car mechanic?

Answer
Jack (or perhaps Andy).

1. What is a good name for a noble-looking man?
2. What is a good name for a woman who likes the beach?
3. What is a good name for a man who likes to garden?
4. What is a good name for a man who likes extremes?
5. What is a good name for a man who cannot say "Ah!"?
6. What is a good name for a woman who enjoys courtroom litigation?
7. What is a good name for a woman who sets fire to her electricity bill?
8. What is a good name for a woman who climbs walls?
9. What is a good name for a man who remodels bathrooms?
10. What is a good name for a woman who has ten dollars?

20. Hidden Words (2)

We have already encountered Hidden Words (see section 7). Try to find a word hidden in consecutive letters of each of these sentences.

Example
Find a three-letter tree hidden in this sentence: "Noel might help if you ask him."

Answer
Elm.

1. Find a five-letter game hidden in this sentence: "Are these peaches sweet?"
2. Find a five-letter country in this sentence: "I find I always distrust people."
3. Find a five-letter country in this sentence: "Invest your capital yearly."
4. Find a four-letter fish in this sentence: "I hate you, so leave me alone."
5. Find a seven-letter jewel in this sentence: "I am proud I am on deck 12 hours a day."
6. Find a six-letter word that means "less difficult" in this sentence: "The animal was not a male as I erroneously stated."
7. Find a six-letter lasso in this sentence: "Have you done the malaria test yet?"
8. Find a six-letter spread in this sentence: "Leon's stew was great, but Terry's cake was awful."

9. Find an eight-letter word that means "in unison" in this sentence: "He went to the mall to get her a handbag."

10. Find an eleven-letter swap in this sentence: "That painter changed his style in 1906."

21. Homophones

An old joke tells of a customer asking the assistant at a store: "Do you keep stationery?" and she replies: "No, I wriggle around a bit." The assistant clearly thought the customer meant the word "stationary" (motionless), not the word "stationery" (writing paper). There are many pairs of words like this, which sound the same but are spelled differently. They are called homophones.

Identify the pairs of homophones from the following clues.

Example
One word means a place for keeping airplanes; the other word means a shaped piece of wood, plastic, etc., on which you can hang clothes.

Answer
Hangar/hanger.

1. One word means simple; the other means a flying machine.
2. One word means expected; the other means condensed vapor.
3. One word means nautical; the other means something central to the body.
4. One word means connections; the other means a wild cat.
5. One word means an occasion; the other means a common herb.
6. One word means flesh; the other means to encounter.
7. One word means permitted; the other means audible.
8. One word means hospital clients; the other means forbearance.
9. One word is a primate; the other means an undercover fighter.
10. One word means matured; the other means gripe.
11. One means excluded; the other means a poet.
12. One word means a certain Sabbath; the other means an ice cream treat.
13. One word means pursued; the other means pure.
14. One word means a woolly South American animal; the other means a Tibetan monk.

Triple Homophones

Identify these three words that sound the same but are spelled differently.

Example
One word means a sheep; the second means a tree; the third means yourself.

Answer
Ewe/yew/you.

1. One word means yes; the second means a part of the body; the third means me.

2. One word means a passageway; the second means "I will"; the third means an island.

3. One word means fresh; the second means an animal; the third means "was aware of."

4. One word means part of the mouth; the second means an artist's board; the third is a portable platform.

5. One word means to quote; the second means something seen; the third means a a specific place.

6. One word means a disease; the second means "traveled through the air"; the third is part of a chimney.

9. One word means a vegetable; the second is a measure of weight for gems; the third indicates where to insert something omitted.

10. The first word means precipitation; the second and third mean something that may be long or short.

Quadruple Homophones

Identify these four words that sound the same but are spelled differently.

1. One word is a poetic contraction; the second signals an alternative; the third propels a boat; the fourth is a source of minerals.

2. One word means correct; the second means a ceremony; the third means a builder; the fourth means to form letters.

3. One means an invisible gas; the second is a poetic contraction; the third means before; the fourth is a beneficiary.

22. Homophonic Statements

Here are groups of words arranged into seemingly nonsensical sentences. Can you "homophonically translate" each sentence into a statement that makes sense?

Example
Weir lion two ewe.

Answer
We're lying to you.

1. Lettuce bee franc.

2. Weave build hymn four wry bred.

3. Eye no ewe Kant serf.

4. Hour made war blue genes.

5. For pea ems tee thyme.

23. Think of a Word

Example

How many four-letter words can you name for kinds of fish?

Answer

Bass, carp, char, chub, dace, hake, tuna, etc.

1. How many three-letter words can you name for parts of your body?
2. How many three-letter words can you name for animals?
3. How many three-letter words can you name for trees or shrubs?
4. How many four-letter words can you name for games or sports?
5. How many five-letter words can you name for fruit?
6. How many six-letter words can you name for things to eat?
7. How many words can you name for kinds of beds?
8. How many words can you name for kinds of boats?

24. I Knew Him When . . .

This is a silly punning game, based on the surnames of famous people. People commonly say things like: "I knew her before she was famous" or "I knew him when he was a baby." The game suggests that the speaker knew someone famous when he or she was less known or accomplished—in other words, smaller or less developed.

Identify the celebrities below from the punning clues to their surnames.

Example

I knew that Elizabethan explorer when he was just a duckling.

Answer

Francis Drake.

1. I knew that U.S. president when he was just a seedling.
2. I knew that witty British writer when he was just a little excited.
3. I knew that Civil War general when he was just a loan application.
4. I knew that comedienne and writer when she was just a pennant.
5. I knew that English navigator when he was just a dishwasher.
6. I knew that jazz singer when she was just a weekend break.
7. I knew that American political writer when he was just a dull ache.
8. I knew that great American actress when she was just a faint mist.
9. I knew that "Rebel Without a Cause" when he was just a teacher.
10. I knew that American writer when he was just a barrel-maker's apprentice.
11. I knew that cookbook writer when she was just a backyard gardener.
12. I knew that civil rights leader when he was just a prince.
13. I knew that American poet when he was just an ounce.

14. I knew that anthem writer when he was just a burglar's bobby pin.
15. I knew that country singer when he was just a bunny.
16. I knew that temperance leader when she was just a province.

25. Synonyms

Synonyms are words that mean the same (or roughly the same) as other words. For example, *sick, ill,* and *indisposed* are all synonyms of *unwell.* But *indisposed* is also a synonym of *reluctant* or *disinclined,* as in sentences such as "The teacher was indisposed to believe his pupil's excuses for lateness." Thus one word can be a synonym for two or more different-meaning words.

Try to think of one synonym for both of the words in the following pairs.

Example
Financial institution, mound of earth.

Answer
Bank.

1. Traverse, angry.
2. Unplanned, opportunity.
3. Departs, tree parts.
4. Limb, stage.
5. Stay, tolerate.
6. Man of the hour, submarine sandwich.
7. Caress, seizure.
8. Pale, brightness.
9. Remarkable, leaving work in protest.
10. Assume, convey.

26. Triple Meanings

Some words have three different meanings. Identify these particular words from the following clues.

Example
Which word means the bottom of a river, somewhere to plant flowers, and a place to sleep?

Answer
Bed.

1. Which word means a musical instrument, a container for oil, and part of the ear?
2. Which word means a golf-course, the loops of a chain, and devices for fastening the cuff of a shirt sleeve?
3. Which word means a pretext, an advancing mass of air, and the side of a house facing the street?

4. Which word means to indicate with a finger, a reason, and a score in a game?

5. Which word means acceptable, to penalize, and sheer?

6. Which word means an appearance, a melody, and something that is all around us?

7. Which word means strange, occasional, and not even?

8. Which word means to tolerate, to be upright, and an open-air store?

9. Which word means pugilists, baggy underwear, and dogs?

10. Which word means to smile, the breadth of a ship, and a long piece of wood?

27. Anagrams

An anagram, says the *Oxford Essential Dictionary*, is "a word or phrase formed by transposing the letters of another word or phrase." Can you transpose these words or phrases to make new words or phrases?

Example

Rearrange the letters of the word *rail* to make a dishonest person.

Answer

Liar.

1. Rearrange the letters of the word *eat* to make something to drink.

2. Rearrange *brush* to make a bush.

3. Rearrange *lemon* to make another fruit.

4. Rearrange *skate* to make a poet.

5. Rearrange *wand* to make a time of day.

6. Rearrange *Alice* to make another woman's name.

7. Rearrange *Dorothea* to make another woman's name.

8. Rearrange *supersonic* to make a part of an orchestra.

9. Rearrange *lowest* to make absorbent cloth.

10. Rearrange *spectrum* to make some British muffins.

11. Which food might you make out of *stale lamb*?

12. What do you have to be if you want to *listen*?

13. Which word describes *lithe acts*?

14. Which part of a newspaper may be an *adroit lie*?

15. In two words, where can you find a *schoolmaster*?

16. In two words, what is worn by *a stripteaser*?

17. Which part of the body is a ten-letter word in which the last five letters are an anagram of the first five letters?

18. Make two other words from the letters of *idolatry*.

19. Make three other words from the letters of *gallery*.

20. Make four other words from the letters of *players*.

21. Make four other words from the letters of *inlets*.

22. Make four other words from the letters of *maneless*.

23. What quality might characterize a *prime dunce*?

24. Which adjective might describe a *problem in Chinese*?

25. In three words, what characterizes *the nudist colony*?

26. Which German opera asserts the fact that *a kinder love's rare*?

28. Endings

The challenge here is to think of a word that ends with a particular sequence
of letters. If possible, try to think of *three* words for each group of letters.

Example
Which words end with *-ild?*

Answer
Build, child, mild.

1. Which words end with *-ife?*
2. Which words end with *-ny?*
3. Which words end with *-gle?*
4. Which words end with *-per?*
5. Which words end with *-ove?*
6. Which words end with *-ise?*
7. Which words end with *-cle?*

8. Which words end with *-ur?*
9. Which words end with *-dly?*
10. Which words end with -*dous?*
11. Which words end with *-shion?*
12. Which words end with *-gry?*

29. Fractured French

F. S. Pearson's book *Fractured French* (1951) popularized the idea of translat-
ing French phrases into English, using a mixture of imagination and puns.

Try to identify French words or phrases from the English translations
given here.

Example
On the wagon.

Answer
À la carte.

1. Mother-in-law.
2. Lawnmower.
3. Father of twins.
4. Let the cat in.
5. For God's sake, take Blanche home.
6. There are mice in the river.
7. Antiwar opposition.
8. I honestly believe I am going to be sick.

30. Acronyms

Acronyms are words formed from the initial letters (or first few letters) of
the words in a phrase, like *WASP* (White Anglo-Saxon Protestant) or
Benelux (Belgium, Netherlands, and Luxembourg). They are usually pronounced as single words, not as strings of letters.

Which phrases are normally represented by the following acronyms?

Example
DINK.

Answer
Double income, no kids.

1. VAT.
2. Radar.
3. MOMA.
4. NIMBY.
5. AWOL.
6. WYSIWYG.
7. PIN.
8. RAM.
9. ZIP (as in *zip code*).
10. Scuba.

31. Hide and Seek

Many words contain other words inside them. So *lady* contains the words
lad and *ad*, while *pontificate* contains *on, if,* and *ate*.

Search for the words hidden inside the words below.

Example
Find a bird inside the word *eternal*.

Answer
Tern.

1. Find an animal inside the word *illustrate*.
2. Find a word meaning to endure inside *elastic*.
3. Find a bird inside *hyphenction*.
4. Find an animal inside *benevolent*.
5. Find an animal inside *grasping*.
6. Find an animal inside *bathing*.
7. Find a vehicle inside *grievance*.
8. Find an animal inside *boating*.
9. Find two animals inside *bullion*.
10. Find a short sleep inside *snapshot*.
11. Find a part of the body inside *bearable*.

12. Find a woman's name inside *lemonade*.
13. Find five pronouns inside *ushers*?
14. Find the name of a Broadway musical inside *inevitable*.
15. Find a debt inside *capricious*.

32. Triple Anagrams

Each of the words below is an anagram of at least three other words. Try to find three anagrams by rearranging the letters.

Example
Large.

Answer
Glare, lager, regal.

1. Name.
2. Redraw.
3. Rose.
4. Spare.
5. Tied.

6. Merit.
7. Saps.
8. Ranged.
9. Stare.
10. Recap.

33. Categories

"Categories" is a game in which you try to think of words that start with a specified letter and that fit a particular category. Combinations of more than one word are acceptable, so *miniature golf* would qualify as a sport beginning with the letter M.

Example
Name five animals starting with the letter A.

Answer
Aardvark, alligator, antelope, ape, armadillo.

1. Name five birds starting with the letter C.
2. Name five occupations starting with the letter D.
3. Name five trees starting with the letter S.
4. Name five items of clothing starting with the letter G.
5. Name five musical instruments starting with the letter F.
6. Name five things to eat starting with the letter H.
7. Name five items found in a kitchen starting with the letter C.
8. Name five sports starting with the letter S.
9. Name five cities starting with the letter T.
10. Name five parts of an automobile starting with the letter W.

34. True or False?

Are these statements about words true or false?

Example

A *flexor* is a muscle in the human body.

Answer

True (it is a muscle that helps parts of the body to bend).

1. The word *engender* means the sex of a chicken.
2. A *dhoti* is a Chinese boat.
3. A *refectory* is a place where people eat.
4. *Chitterlings* are small birds.
5. *Pelota* is a Mexican food.
6. A *solecism* is an error or mistake.
7. The *obverse* is the "tail" side of a coin.
8. A *dingo* is a common pet in Australia.
9. A *muu-muu* is a garland of flowers worn in the Pacific islands.
10. *Obnubilate* means to brighten or illuminate.

35. The Name Game

The clues lead to first names (or Christian names) of people.

Example

Which man's name is stylish or fashionable?

Answer

Tony.

1. Which woman's name is a month?
2. Which man's name is honest?
3. Which woman's name is a small orange?
4. Which man's name is the sheltered side of a boat?
5. Which woman's name is a flower?
6. Which man's name is an herb?
7. Which woman's name is happiness?
8. Which man's name is German currency?
9. Which woman's name is a song?
10. Which man's name is a legal document?
11. Which woman's name is an Italian city?
12. Which women's names are palindromes (that is, they spell the same backward)?

36. Combinations

Add a single word after each of these three words to make three compound terms or phrases.

Example
Paper, dough, bell.

Answer
The word is *boy* which, when added after these three words, makes the combinations *paper boy, doughboy,* and *bellboy.*

1. Day, night, moon.
2. Nut, brief, suit.
3. Laundry, hand, paper.
4. Work, clothes, pommel.
5. Bee, goal, house.

6. Typing, motor, swimming.
7. High, path, water.
8. Horse, human, rat.
9. Vending, sewing, washing.
10. Ice, tie, wind.

37. Side by Side

Alphabetical order often creates amusing partnerships. For instance, in the *Oxford Essential Dictionary*, the entry for *ravenous* is followed directly by the entry for *ravine.* Taken together, as "ravenous ravine," the compound term could be defined as "a hungry gorge."

Identify the word pairs that satisfy the following definitions, keeping in mind that each pair of words appears in alphabetic sequence in the *Oxford Essential Dictionary*.

Example
A tool used by a small bird.

Answer
Wren wrench.

1. Despotic rule by a dinosaur.
2. An undead reptile.
3. Playground equipment for a pig.
4. A pin made of copper and tin.
5. A sleepy male descendant.
6. An avaricious Athenian.
7. No lemon peel.
8. A coloring stick fad.
9. A goldfish who likes merry-go-rounds.
10. Evil basketry twigs.
11. The bubbling sound of a small fish.
12. A perspiring resident of Stockholm.

38. Miss World

In beauty contests, winners are often named "Miss (something)"—for example, Miss World or Miss America. Developing this idea, we might say that a good title for a careless typist would be "Miss Print" (a pun of 'misprint').

Try to think of suitable "Miss" names for the following professions or types of people.

Example
A doubtful philanthropist.

Answer
Miss Giving (a pun of "misgiving").

1. An ineffective jurist.
2. An inept manager.
3. An accident-prone person.
4. A hairdresser having an affair.
5. Someone who hates people.
6. An inaccurate lexicographer (dictionary writer).
7. A hapless explorer.
8. A rascally boss.
9. A deceptive tour director.
10. A prehistoric person.

INTERLUDE

Oxes and Bulls

You have probably heard of Noel Coward's musical comedy *Bitter Sweet* and his song "Poor Little Rich Girl." Each of these titles seems to contradict itself. How can something be both bitter and sweet? How can a girl be rich and poor at the same time?

Self-contradictory phrases like this are known as *oxymorons*, which are the subject of a puzzle later in this book (see section 92). The word *oxymoron* itself is contradictory in origin, coming from two Latin words (*oxus* and *moros*) that mean "sharp" and "dull." Together they describe something that may appear incongruous but which paradoxically suggests a deeper meaning.

As an example of an oxymoron, the *Oxford Essential Dictionary* chooses Tennyson's line "Faith unfaithful kept him falsely true." Literature is full of oxymorons, often used as a poetic device. Was it Spenser who wrote about "proud humility?" Wordsworth talked of "peopled solitude," while Milton's *Paradise Lost* spoke of "darkness visible." In *Romeo and Juliet*, Shakespeare's Juliet called parting "such sweet sorrow," while Romeo talked of "heavy lightness, serious vanity!" Hamlet was the first but certainly not the last person to say: "I must be cruel only to be kind."

How often do we use the phrase "cruel to be kind" without realizing its incongruity? But this is the case with many sayings in everyday use: phrases such as "an open secret," "a living death," and "a deafening silence." We say that something is done "accidentally on purpose," or we exclaim "Good grief!" (or even "Now then!" and "Never again!"). The phrase "Not to mention" invariably introduces a mention of what we promised not to mention. We may go to a store to purchase paper tablecloths, plastic silverware, white chocolate, nondairy creamer, or fresh frozen peas. We may buy a live recording of Simon and Garfunkel's "Sound of Silence." At a restaurant, we might order a dry martini or jumbo shrimp.

Sometimes the contradictions are hidden in the origins of words. Thus we may talk of a typed manuscript without remembering that "manuscript" originally meant something written by hand. We might send our manuscript to a weekly journal, unaware that "journal" originally meant a daily publication or record.

Some single words join together two contrasting ideas: ballpoint, bridegroom, spendthrift, extraordinary, pianoforte (which combines Italian words for "soft" and "loud"), and preposterous (which combines Latin words for "before" and "after").

Oxymorons seem to be particularly prevalent in the armed forces, where military doublethink leads to such phrases as "clean bomb," "friendly fire," and "war game." Even the phrases "holy war," "tactical nuclear weapon," and "conventional weapons" appear self-contradictory to antimilitarists.

Often the contradiction is in the eye of the beholder, who sees a paradox where others see nothing unusual. According to your views, you may feel there is something incongruous in talking about a benevolent dictator, happy marriage, painless childbirth, safe sex, the United Nations, or background music.

Although they may seem to embody contradictions, oxymorons are generally acceptable because they express some truth, which is neither black nor white but a mixture of the two. Yet there are other sayings that are not only self-contradictory but also manifestly nonsensical, such as "If Mozart were alive, he'd turn over in his grave" or the jury foreman declaring: "We find the man who stole the car not guilty." Such an expression is usually called an "Irish bull," which Coleridge defined as "a mental juxtaposition of incongruous ideas, with a sensation, but without the sense, of connection."

A classic example of an Irish bull is credited to Dublin politician Sir Boyle Roche (1743-1807), who asserted, "Half of the lies our opponents tell about us are not true." An article in *The Spectator* for 1898 quoted the following conversation between two Irishwomen: "Did you ever see so thin a woman as that before?" "Thin! I seen a woman down in Wexford as thin as two of her put together!"

Irish bulls are in no way limited to the boundaries of Ireland. The Welsh have been credited with such sayings as: "You'll die before I do, if you live long enough," and "He's a happily married man, and his wife is too." In New Jersey, the police department announced a radical change in policy in these words: "From now on, we shall offer police jobs to qualified women regardless of sex." In the Marx Brothers movie *A Night at the Opera*, Chico explained that Harpo had insomnia and was trying to sleep it off. When the Finnish athlete Paavo Nurmi was asked the secret for setting a world record for the mile, he said: "You start out at full speed, gradually increasing pace."

Other classic Irish bulls include the following: "I'd give my right arm to be ambidextrous"; "I used to be indecisive—now I'm not so sure"; "If you don't receive this letter, write and let me know"; and "If ten cows were lying down in a field and one of them was standing up, that one would be the bull."

One man particularly notable for using Irish bulls was the movie producer Samuel Goldwyn (a founder of Metro-Goldwyn-Mayer). He created so many of these nonsequiturs that they have been called *Goldwynisms*. Perhaps his most famous saying is "Include me out," which has entered the language as a serious phrase. Some of his other remarks include: "A verbal contract isn't worth the paper it's written on"; "Let's have some new clichés"; "My wife's hands are very beautiful: I'm going to have a bust made of them"; and "In two words: im-possible!"

Part Two
Fairly Difficult

39. Anagram Pairs

Here are clues for making two-word phrases in which the second word is an anagram of the first word.

Example
A distant heavenly body.

Answer
Remote meteor.

1. A house made of sun-dried bricks.
2. Untrained conflict.
3. Domesticated partner.
4. Pieces of a belt.
5. Tiny sheep.
6. Cursed order.
7. Serious citrus fruit.
8. Large tree.
9. Angry nobleman.
10. What husbands should hear.
11. Safe liberation.
12. Illness at the beach.
13. Unelevated bird.
14. Undeveloped gift.
15. Injured emcee.
16. Ennui in the bunkhouse.
17. An unctuous smirk.
18. Wall hangings for the *Folies-Bergère*.
19. Anonymous agents.
20. Courageous Baltic person.
21. The feeling of other Baltic people.
22. Lasting beauty.
23. Nautical colleagues.
24. Loaded antelope.
25. Extremely fast drumming.
26. Frivolous amorous behavior.
27. Competitive gardener's pastime.
28. A feline on conditional release.
29. Silent female felines.

40. Doublets

Doublets is a game that was invented by Lewis Carroll, who described it in these words: "Two words are proposed, of the same length; and the puzzle consists in linking these together by interposing other words, each of which shall differ from the next word in *one letter only*. As an example, the word "head" may be changed into "tail" by interposing the words "heal, teal, tell, tall." Thus Carroll changed "head" into "tail" in five moves:

> HEAD
> HEAL
> TEAL
> TELL
> TALL
> TAIL

Try to make the following transformations in the specified number of moves.

1. Change CAT into DOG in three moves.
2. Change BOY into MAN in three moves.
3. Change HARD into EASY in five moves.
4. Change EAST into WEST in three moves.
5. Change ONE into TWO in eight moves.
6. Change OAK to YEW in three moves.
7. Change POST into BEAM in four moves.
8. Change RICH into POOR in six moves.
9. Change GRASS into GREEN in seven moves.
10. Change TREE into WOOD in eight moves.
11. Change HATE into LOVE in three moves.
12. Change BLACK into WHITE in seven moves.

41. Reversals

Many words make other words if they are turned back-to-front. Thus *now* becomes *won* when it is reversed, and *lived* becomes *devil*.

Try to find pairs of such reversible words from the clues below.

Example
Reverse a weight to make a negative.

Answer
Ton - not.

1. Reverse a portion to make an ambush.
2. Reverse rodents to make a heavenly body.
3. Reverse an insect to make a sharp taste.
4. Reverse a word for "married" to make condensed vapor.

5. Reverse a vegetable to make the base of a boat.

6. Reverse a storage compartment to make a prize.

7. Reverse an animal to make a deity.

8. Reverse dry stalks of grain to make hard growths on the skin.

9. Reverse a marsh bird to make a deceitful person.

10. Reverse a quick swallow to make a stopper.

11. Reverse a living being to make a thin plate or layer.

12. Reverse a potato or dahlia to make a word meaning "disprove."

42. Connections

This game involves a search for two combinations that have one word in common. Thus *dinner roll* and *roll call* both include the word *roll*.

Example
Which word could connect *hot* and *glass*?

Answer
Plate (which makes *hotplate* and *plate glass*).

1. Which word could connect *soap* and *office*?

2. Which word could connect *safe* and *slip*?

3. Which word could connect *ear* and *master*?

4. Which word could connect *food* and *gang*?

5. Which word could connect *punching* and *pipes*?

6. Which word could connect *farm* and *boat*?

7. Which word could connect *cable* and *sick*?

8. Which word could connect *funny* and *marrow*?

9. Which word could connect *tooth* and *pocket*?

10. Which word could connect *open* and *keeper*?

11. Which word could connect *April* and *hardy*?

12. Which word could connect *grand* and *forte*?

13. Which word could connect *jet* and *rat*?

14. Which word could connect *French* and *room*?

15. Which word could connect *birth* and *bed*?

16. Which word could connect *Elton* and *Wayne*?

43. Spelling

Pick out the correct spelling from these sets, in which only one of the words is spelled correctly.

Example
Etiquet, etiquette, etickette.

Answer
Etiquette.

1. Dilapidated, dillapidated, dilaperdated.
2. Recieve, receive, receve.
3. Allowance, allowence, alowance.
4. Maintainance, maintenence, maintenance.
5. Occasionally, occassionally, ocasionally.
6. Gaurantee, garantee, guarantee.
7. Rondayvous, rendezvous, rendayvoo.
8. Accommodation, accomodation, acommodation.
9. Necessary, nessessary, necessery.
10. Immediatly, imediately, immediately.
11. Aspidestra, asspidestra, aspidistra.
12. Embarassment, embarrassment, embarrasment.
13. Diptheria, diphtheria, diftheeria.
14. Hypocondriac, hypercondriach, hypochondriac.
15. Resussitate, resuscitate, risuscitate.
16. Inaccesable, inacessible, inaccessible.
17. Chiwahwah, chiwahwer, chihuahua.
18. Sacriligious, sacrilegious, sacreligious.
19. Vetinerary, vetrinery, veterinary.
20. Parallelogram, parallelergram, parallellogram.
21. Occurrance, occurrence, occurence.
22. Perseverance, persiveerence, perserverence.
23. Endevor, indeavor, endeavor.
24. Finesse, fanesse, finnesse.
25. Embarassed, embarrassed, imbarrassed.
26. Millennium, milennium, millenium.
27. Exstacy, extasie, ecstasy.
28. Logrithim, logarithm, logrhythm.
29. Abberijini, aborigine, aboriginie.
30. Qwestionair, questionair, questionnaire.

44. Meanings

There is a story of a child who discovered the word "mellifluous" and liked the sound of it. He thought it meant something like "horrible," so he went around applying the word "mellifluous" to everybody and everything that he hated. Only later did he discover that "mellifluous" actually means "as sweet as honey"! We often assume we know the meanings of particular words but our assumptions may be wrong.

Define the senses of the following words as precisely as possible.

Example
What is a *curmudgeon*?

Answer
A bad-tempered or miserly person.

1. What does *parsimony* mean?
2. What does *caries* mean?
3. What is *detritus*?
4. What does *fetid* mean?
5. What is *nepotism*?
6. What does *sardonic* mean?
7. What is a *peccadillo*?
8. What does *jejune* mean?
9. What is an *exegesis*?
10. What is an *oubliette*?
11. What is a *claque*?
12. What does *nubile* mean?
13. What does *C-note* mean?
14. What does *inchoate* mean?
15. What does *inspissated* mean?

45. Vowel Play

In this game, we have deleted the vowels (A, E, I, O, and U) from some words and left the consonants. Try to reconstruct the words from the consonants and the clues to each word's meaning.

Example
STTN = stopping place.

Answer
Station.

1. LRL = a tree or shrub.
2. MTRC = very rapid.
3. PLL = a Spanish dish of rice and seafood.
4. RVG = to devastate.
5. HWDH = a seat on an elephant.
6. NGT = a chewy candy.
7. THR = one or the other.

8. VNTD = evening.
9. TMBRN = musical instrument.
10. RFC = an opening.
11. SPS = to adopt.
12. PTRYX = a kiwi.
13. TCST = a banished person.
14. DR = a duck.
15. NT = to join.
16. VK = to draw forth.

17. TD = to surpass.
18. NQ = like no other.
19. GR = enthusiastic.
20. SLY = without difficulty.
21. NNPRL = unrivaled; peerless.
22. SH = a tree.
23. BT = to subside.
24. VCD = green pear-shaped fruit.
25. K = a bird.

46. Dismissals

It is difficult to get rid of some people. Yet you can at least think of suitable words for disposing of people who have particular professions or trades. For example, a wine merchant can be *deported* (with an obvious pun on the word *port*), while musicians can be disbanded or disconcerted.

Find appropriate words for getting rid of the people below.

Example
How do you get rid of podiatrists?

Answer
Defeat them.

1. How do you get rid of gamblers?
2. How do you get rid of cowboys?
3. How do you get rid of clerks?
4. How do you get rid of electricians?
5. How do you get rid of Superman?
6. How do you get rid of jockeys?
7. How do you get rid of tailors?
8. How do you get rid of crossword compilers?
9. How do you get rid of painters?
10. How do you get rid of lingerie salesmen?

47. Words Within Words

Words Within Words is an old but still popular game, in which players make as many words as they can out of the letters of a word. The word chosen is often something like *Constantinople,* but such a long word makes the game easy since it can generate a large number of other words. In the problems below, the source words contain only nine letters. Make as many words as possible of more than three letters. Each letter of the source word can be used only once to make another word. Words with a capital, plurals, hyphenated terms, and verbs ending in 's' are not allowed.

Example
Practical.

Answer
Altar, apart, arctic, aria, aril, capital, carp, cart, circa, clap, clip, crap, laic, lair, liar, lira, pair, part, partial, pica, racial, rail, rial, tail, tapir, tiara, trail, trap, trial, trip.

1. Tactfully (target: 20 words).
2. Declivity (target: 30 words).
3. Untwisted (target: 40 words).
4. Overreach (target: 50 words).
5. Veritable (target: 60 words).
6. Impressed (target: 70 words).
7. Sublimate (target: 140 words).
8. Breakdown (target: 150 words).

48. Antonyms (2)

We have already explained (see section 12) that an antonym is a word that means the opposite of another word. Thus *high* is the opposite of *low*, and *good* is the opposite of *bad*. Because many words have more than one sense, a word is sometimes the opposite of more than one other word.

Identify the single words that mean the opposite of each pair of words below.

Example
Normal and even.

Answer
Odd (as in "It was an odd experience" and "Seven is an odd number").

1. Sweet and wet.
2. Easy and weak.
3. Cooked and experienced.
4. Generous and sober.
5. Impractical and foolish.
6. Unimportant and joking.
7. Exclusion and denial.
8. Alive and punctual.
9. Fruitful and modest.
10. Inexperienced and unflavored.

49. Paired Homophones

Try to solve these clues to paired homophones; that is, words that sound the same but have different spellings (see Homophones, section 21).

Example
A lazy hero.

Answer
Idle idol.

1. An equine with a sore throat.
2. A postman.
3. A certain amount of money.

4. A line of people waiting to play billiards.

5. Peels fruit.

6. Nautical equipment at bargain prices.

7. A monk who is a short-order cook.

8. Cornflakes in installments.

9. A large sea mammal's cry.

10. The restraint of marriage.

50. Old-fashioned Words

Some words sound old-fashioned but they stay in the language because they are still used in special contexts or for particular purposes.

The words below are often labeled as *archaic* in dictionaries. What do they mean?

Example
Pard.

Answer
A leopard.

1. Anent.

2. Palfrey.

3. Trig (as an adjective).

4. Megrim (as an illness of humans).

5. Ancient (as a noun).

6. Sans (as a preposition).

7. Tucket.

8. Mage.

9. Uranography.

10. Quidnunc.

51. Bookends

Here is a challenge. For each letter of the alphabet, write down a word that begins and ends with that letter. So the word for "A" could be *area* (or *alpha, antonomasia, arena, aria, asthma* . . .) and the word for "B" might be *bob* or *blob*. If two or more people want to play this competitively, award points for each letter used: the winner is the person whose list of words contains the highest total number of letters.

If this is too easy, try making a list of such words that are proper names, such as *America, Beelzebub* . . . (Note: do not expect to come up with such words for all 26 letters.)

52. Three in One

This puzzle is similar to Words Within Words (see section 47), but in reverse. For instance, the letters from the word *version* could be used to make many words, including *rose*, *over*, and *sin*. What is particularly distinct about these three words is that, as a group, they use all the letters of *version*. To reverse this process, consider this example: which word can be made out of the letters in the three words *moor*, *root*, and *tow?* The answer (or, at least, one answer) is *tomorrow*.

In the puzzles below, try to find the eight-letter words that can be made from the letters of the sets of three words. (Keep in mind that each letter in the answer word can appear more than once in the group of three words.)

Example
Soon, sun, toil.

Answer
Solution.

1. Riot, rite, tone.
2. Agent, gnat, stage.
3. Filth, hot, tool.
4. Gone, nuts, rote.
5. Lids, new, rind.
6. Rim, sty, tin.
7. Lies, stone, tonsil.
8. Quir, tone, unit.
9. Emit, lime, stern.
10. Ale, lake, link.

53. Plurals

Is it *media* or *mediums*? Is it *tomatoes* or *tomatos* or *tomato's*?
Try to determine the correct plurals for the following words.

Example
Ox.

Answer
Oxen.

1. Louse.
2. Mother-in-law.
3. Index.
4. Teaspoonful.
5. Crisis.
6. Phenomenon.
7. Court-martial.
8. Incognito.
9. Opus.
10. Moose.
11. Radius.
12. Armful.
13. Addendum.
14. Stigma.

54. Combinations (2)

We have already encountered Combinations (see section 36). But can you add a single word *before* each of these three words to make three compound terms or phrases?

Example

Day, load, up.

Answer

Pay (which makes *payday, payload,* and *pay up*).

1. Lime, sand, silver.
2. Bone, pocket, flask.
3. Bowl, nail, painting.
4. Looking, morning, riddance.
5. Dutchman, fish, saucer.
6. Knowledge, practitioner, strike.
7. Bed, glazing, parking.
8. Bread, circuit, story.
9. Packed, sandwich, session.
10. Mail, out, sheep.
11. Bag, instrument, tunnel.
12. Trust, storm, wave.
13. Iron, boat, roller.
14. Fall, mill, pipe.
15. Case, maker, store.
16. Lance, hand, way.
17. Examine, roads, word.
18. Dog, hat, secret.
19. House, moon, back.
20. Splitting, line, show.
21. Fight, frog, terrier.
22. Paddle, house, wood.
23. Pool, phone, bomb.
24. Call, gut, nap.

55. Foreign Words and Phrases

Try to answer these questions about the English use of words and phrases that come from other languages.

Example

What is a *bête noire*?

Answer

Someone or something that you particularly hate or fear.

1. What is a *chaise longue*?
2. What is the meaning of *en famille*?
3. What was the former policy of racial segregation in South Africa?
4. What is the French word we use in English for a slaughterhouse?
5. What is a *bon mot*?
6. What is the meaning of *mea culpa*?
7. Where would you find a *flèche*?
8. What is the meaning of *ab ovo*?
9. What is the *mot juste*?
10. How should you play a piece of music that is marked *con amore*?

11. What does it mean if something is *sui generis*?
12. How does someone regard you if they look at you *de haut en bas*?
13. What is a *memento mori*?
14. When would you eat an *hors d'oeuvre*?
15. What is the meaning of *caveat emptor*?
16. What is a *tabula rasa*?
17. What is the meaning of *noblesse oblige*?
18. What is a *pons asinorum*?

56. Collective Nouns

Most people know that a group of wolves is called a *pack*, and a number of elephants is a *herd*. But what animals belong to a *murmuration* or *shrewdness*? These and other such terms are provided in the list below. Try to match each term in the list to the animals that form that group.

Example
Partridges.

Answer
A covey.

business	leap	rookery
cloud	mob	shrewdness
clowder	murmuration	skulk
exaltation	muster	string
kindle	pride	unkindness

1. Apes.
2. Cats.
3. Ferrets.
4. Flies.
5. Foxes.
6. Kangaroos.
7. Kittens.
8. Larks.
9. Leopards.
10. Lions.
11. Peacocks.
12. Penguins.
13. Racehorses.
14. Ravens.
15. Starlings.

57. Word Row

The two words "word row" constitute a palindrome—that is to say, it reads the same forward and backward.

Try to solve the following clues, which each lead to a palindromic phrase of two words.

Example
Always odd.

Answer
Never even.

1. The insane first man.
2. Prevent blemishes.
3. Without male offspring.
4. A strange coiffure.
5. Avoid moving your head.
6. A burglar's implement.
7. Observe umpires.
8. Uninteresting poet.
9. Nervous puddings.
10. Student's error.
11. Sinful smell.
12. Deer laughter.
13. Small number of us.
14. Take that back, Mr. President!
15. First appearance on television.
16. Saucepan lid.
17. Diaper-rash ointment.
18. Aging cats.
19. Clean church seats.
20. A make of car.

58. What's the Difference?

Some words are easily confused with other words, as is evident from the occurrence of malapropisms (see section 68). Try to sort out these pairs of words.

Example
What is the difference between a *boarder* and a *border?*

Answer
A *boarder* is a lodger at someone else's house; a *border* is the edge of something.

1. What is the difference between a *calendar* and a *colander?*
2. What is the difference between an *aviary* and an *apiary?*
3. What is the difference between a *cassock* and a *hassock?*
4. What is the difference between *principal* and *principle?*
5. What is the difference between an *allusion* and an *illusion?*
6. What is the difference between an *entomologist* and an *etymologist?*
7. What is the difference between *imply* and *infer?*
8. What is the difference between *eligible* and *illegible?*
9. What is the difference between a *carat* and a *caret?*
10. What is the difference between *oscillating* and *osculating?*

11. What is the difference between a *philatelist* and *philanthropist*?
12. What is the difference between *punctual* and *punctilious*?
13. What is the difference between a *palate* and a *palette*?
14. What is the difference between *discreet* and *discrete*?

59. The Storm Breaks

This extract from Shakespeare's *The Tempest* contains 29 words. But how many other words (of at least two letters) can you find composed of consecutive letters by working through the passage? You can start with *Ben* (a man's name) and continue with *en* (a unit of measurement used in printing), *no, fear,* etc.

Be not afeard: the isle is full of noises,
Sounds and sweet airs, that give delight, and hurt not.
Sometimes a thousand twangling instruments
Will hum about mine ears.

60. Follow-On

In this game, the challenge is to move from one word to another by means of compound terms or two-word phrases.

Example
Move from *shoe* to *shift* in no more than seven steps.

Answer
Shoe-tree: tree frog: frog man: manhole: hole up: upswing: swing shift.

1. Move from *sand* to *work* in no more than eight steps.
2. Move from *low* to *writer* in no more than five steps.
3. Move from *rattle* to *ladder* in no more than five steps.
4. Move from *Italian* to *lift* in no more than six steps.
5. Move from *good* to *power* in no more than nine steps.
6. Move from *motor* to *paper* in no more than seven steps.
7. Move from *adobe* to *handle* in no more than five steps.
8. Move from *live* to *school* in no more than eight steps.

61. Contronyms

Contronyms—also known as "autantonyms" or "Janus words"—are words that have two opposite meanings, according to the context in which they occur. For example, *with* can mean "alongside" in "Come with me" but "against" or "in opposition to" in "Hannibal fought with the Romans." And remember the pharmacist who unwisely advertises that he "dispenses with accuracy"!

Can you identify these contradictory words?

1. To spray with powder or to remove particles from.
2. Add to or remove from.
3. To open or to shut.
4. Move gracefully or move clumsily.
5. To stick together or to split apart.
6. A duty to notice things or a failure to notice things.
7. Remaining or departed.
8. Moving quickly or not moving.
9. Very enthusiastic about something or very annoyed at it.
10. Very pale or very red.
11. Acceptance and approval or disapproval and punishment.
12. A two-word phrase meaning a small leap or a massive leap.
13. A two-word phrase meaning to stop something or to start something.
14. A three-word phrase meaning "to like more" or "to like less."

62. Definitions

Which word is being described in the dictionary definitions quoted here?

Example
A network of interconnecting rabbit burrows.

Answer
Warren.

1. A light portable device for protection against rain, strong sun, etc., consisting of a usually circular canopy of cloth mounted by means of a collapsible metal frame on a central stick.
2. Each of five children born at one birth.
3. A wine merchant.
4. A device, sometimes of canvas stretched on an oblong frame, for carrying an injured person on.
5. A domesticated carnivorous mammal, *Canis familiaris*, usually having a long snout and nonretractile claws, and occurring in many different breeds kept as pets or for work or sport.
6. A flat ring or strip of soft material for sealing a joint between two metal surfaces.
7. A boat with twin parallel hulls.
8. The liver, gizzard, neck, etc., of a bird, usually removed and kept separate when the bird is prepared for cooking.
9. A Russian vehicle with a team of three horses abreast.
10. Women's trousers cut to resemble a skirt.
11. A dye that turns red under acid conditions and blue under alkaline conditions.
12. The action of throwing a person out of a window.

63. Portmanteau Words

Portmanteau words (also known as "blends") were so named by Lewis Carroll, who took the name from the kind of traveling bag called a portmanteau—which divides into two compartments. Portmanteau words blend together two words to make a new word: like *cheeseburger*, which is a blend of *cheese* and *hamburger*.

Try to determine which two words are blended together to create the following portmanteau words.

Example
Brunch.

Answer
Breakfast + lunch.

1. Motel.
2. Smog.
3. Telethon.
4. Oxbridge.
5. Simulcast.

6. Franglais.
7. Liger.
8. Avionics.
9. Tangelo.
10. Spanglish.

64. Abbreviations

Shakespeare said that "brevity is the soul of wit," which may explain why people are so eager to abbreviate words, so that "prisoner of war" becomes *POW* and "as soon as possible" becomes *ASAP*.
Try to solve the questions below about various abbreviations.

1. What is a *VIP*?
2. What is a *UFO*?
3. Which state is *NE*?
4. When talking about noise, what do the letters *dB* stand for?
5. What is *SOP*?
6. At the end of an invitation, what would the letters *RSVP* stand for?
7. As a measurement of speed, what does *kn* signify?
8. On a document, what does *PTO* tell you to do?
9. Which two countries are abbreviated as *UAE* and *VI*?
10. What is a *PR person*?
11. What is a *PAC*?
12. On a grave, what does *RIP* stand for?
13. Give the full name for the drug known as *LSD*.
14. At a live performance, what would *SRO* mean?

65. Dictionary

This is an old game known as "Dictionary," "The Dictionary Game," or "Fictionary." Players are presented with three definitions of a word—one true, the other two false—and try to choose the correct definition.

Example
Is a *kazoo*: (a) a dance, (b) a musical instrument, or (c) a bird?

Answer
It is a musical instrument that the player blows or hums into, making a sound like comb-and-paper.

1. Is an *ampersand*: (a) a symbol for the word "and," (b) a prehistoric animal resembling a dinosaur, or (c) sand used in electrical experiments?

2. Does *verso* mean: (a) a Russian measure of length, (b) a left-hand page of a book, or (c) a short poem?

3. A *lustrum* is a period of: (a) five years, (b) twenty years, or (c) a thousand years?

4. Is *bourride*: (a) a bumpy journey, (b) a beetle, or (c) a fish stew?

5. Is a *termagant*: (a) a medicine for curing indigestion, (b) a sea bird with large wings, or (c) a quarrelsome woman?

6. Is a *polymath*: (a) a very knowledgeable person, (b) a compound found in many proteins, or (c) a shellfish?

7. Does *cervine* mean: (a) pertaining to the neck, (b) a kind of sausage, or (c) of or like a deer?

8. Is *candytuft*: (a) a dialect word for a squirrel, (b) a plant with white, pink, or purple flowers, or (c) a kind of Scottish toffee?

9. Is a *rebec*: (a) the payment of a debt, (b) a musical instrument, or (c) a variety of pelican?

10. Does *largo* mean: (a) a brown patch on the skin, (b) an Italian food, or (c) a slow tempo in music?

11. Is *zebu*: (a) a Hungarian dance, (b) a Rumanian coin, or (c) an Indian ox?

12. Is a *hogan*: (a) a Navajo Indian hut, (b) a swimming pool, or (c) a Greek dancer?

13. Is an *accipiter*: (a) a meter for measuring electric currents, (b) someone who writes official letters for monarchs, or (c) a hawk?

14. Does *fianchetto* mean: (a) a move in the game of chess, (b) a kind of pasta, or (c) a long boat used on Italian rivers?

15. Does *boustrophedon* describe: (a) a prehistoric animal, (b) a Greek form of poetry, or (c) writing that goes alternately from right to left and left to right?

66. Humpty Dumpty

1. Fifteen six-letter words have fallen apart, leaving the three-letter segments below. Can you put them together again to restore the complete words? For example, ABO and UND can be put together to make *abound*.

ABO	ARE	ATE	BEW	DEB	GLE
GRI	HAP	HTY	IFT	ION	ISE
ISH	LAT	LOT	MIG	NOW	OWN
PEN	PIN	SLY	TAN	THR	THY
TRO	UGH	UND	UPL	WOR	ZEA

2. Can you do the same with these four-letter segments: putting them in pairs to make 15 eight-letter words?

ACED	AINE	AIRP	ACAL	BOLA
BTED	CONF	GANG	GGLY	IBLE
INDE	LANE	LATE	MATE	MATE
MIGR	PALA	PARA	PEAR	REAP
RENE	RIAL	RNAL	SQUI	TANG
TIAL	UNTR	WORR	YING	ZODI

67. Personal Anagrams

It is unkind to upset people, but the italicized clues here are "upset" (that is, jumbled) versions of famous people's names.

Example

Which American movie actor might have been a *costumier*?

Answer

Tom Cruise.

1. Which Dutch scholar was never a *masseur*?
2. Which British actor displays *genuine class*?
3. Which U.S. president was not normally a *vote loser*?
4. Which TV personality has probably learned to *enjoy L.A.*?
5. Which legendary rock performer now enjoys a *silvery sleep*?
6. Which Dutch painter could assert: "*I paint modern*"?
7. Which jazz trumpeter was possibly not as *dim as Elvis*?
8. Which jazz saxophonist played *gluey tenors*?
9. Which jazz entertainer made music that tinkled like *waterfalls*?
10. Which civil rights leader stood firm at the *line marking truth*?

68. Malapropisms

A *malapropism* is the mistaken use of one word for another. It is named after Mrs. Malaprop, a character in Sheridan's play *The Rivals* (1775), who was fond of using malapropos (i.e., inappropriate) statements such as "*Illiterate* him, I say, quite from your memory" (meaning "obliterate") or "My *affluence* over my niece is very small" (for "influence").

Can you substitute the correct terms for the malapropos italicized words in these sentences?

Example
The muscles around the stomach are known as the *abominable* muscles.

Answer
Abdominal ("abominable" means "detestable").

1. The *prospectus* resumed his search for gold.
2. After a long air flight, it is reassuring to get your feet back onto *terra-cotta*.
3. I couldn't change his decision: it was a *Fiat accompli*.
4. I can assert the truth of it, without fear of *contraception*.
5. The facts you have presented are *irreverent* to this case.
6. If you swallow poison, you should take an *anecdote*.
7. I was *prostate* with grief.
8. She ate with a *veracious* appetite.
9. The garden was brightened by the border of red *saliva*.
10. Each angle in an *equatorial* triangle is 60 degrees.
11. He was on the horns of an *enema*.
12. The doctor told him he had *very close veins*.

69. Daft Definitions

Daft definitions redefine words in an unexpected way, often wittily but also using puns and other forms of wordplay. For example, Ambrose Bierce defined *demure* as "grave and modest-mannered, like a particularly unscrupulous woman" but it might also be punningly defined as "what French people call the wall."

Create some silly new definitions for the following words (the answers are only suggestions; there will be many other possibilities).

Example
Accidental.

Answer
Knocking someone's teeth out with an axe.

1. Archaeologist.	14. Illegal.
2. Backbiter.	15. Knapsack.
3. Bacteria.	16. Myth.
4. Barbecue.	17. Optimistic.
5. Buoyant.	18. Precarious.
6. Flowchart.	19. Mischief.
7. Denial.	20. Shepherd.
8. Disarm.	21. Moraine.
9. Silverware.	22. Stalemate.
10. Emulate.	23. Tartrate.
11. Hamlet.	24. Travelogue.
12. Handmaiden.	25. Firecracker.
13. Hug.	26. Will.

70. Mishmash

Like Doublets, this is a game devised by Lewis Carroll. The aim is to think of words that contain a specified series of letters.

Which words include the following series of letters somewhere in the middle (i.e., surrounded by other letters)?

Example
EPE.

Answer
Sleeper (or independent, repeal, leper, tepee, etc.).

1. DGE.	12. CHOIN.
2. SSI.	13. EWH.
3. SEW.	14. GHG.
4. PD.	15. LJ.
5. THO.	16. HYX.
6. THQ.	17. DQ.
7. YEN.	18. FFB.
8. CD.	19. TCHPH.
9. NGU.	20. THP.
10. RSTU.	21. ZK.
11. RGR.	22. ESWE.

71. Eponyms

Eponyms are words derived from people's names, and usually applied to discoveries, inventions, places, etc. They include such words as *Freudian*, *Marxism*, and *ampere*—the last meaning a unit of electric current, derived from the name of the French scientist André Marie Ampère. When we make a snack from a filling inside two slices of bread, we call it a *sandwich*—after the fourth Earl of Sandwich, who supposedly ordered a slice of meat between two pieces of bread to eat while he was gambling. Try to identify eponyms from the following clues:

1. What was the surname of the 20th-century German scientist whose name is used for a device that detects and measures radioactivity?

2. Which 19th-century American cabinetmaker gave his name to a railroad car?

3. Which 20th-century English writer's middle name is used for a short piece of verse?

4. What word meaning the action of removing offensive words or passages from a book is derived from the name of a 19th-century Scottish doctor?

5. Which Scandinavian god gave his name to a day of the week?

6. What popular dance of the 1930s was named for a celebrated American pilot?

7. Which 16th-century English horse dealer gave his name to a take-it-or-leave-it attitude?

8. What word that describes the speed of sound is named for a 19th-century Austrian scientist?

9. Which genus of bacteria is named after a 19th-century American veterinarian?

10. What 19th-century French aerialist gave his surname to the one-piece, skin-tight garment worn by dancers?

11. What seemingly never-ending surface is named for a 19th-century German mathematician?

12. Which musical instruments are named after: (a) the March King; (b) a 19th-century Belgian instrument-maker?

INTERLUDE
A Nasty Cough

How do you spell the word *fish*? The conventional answer is F-I-S-H but a more inventive possibility is GH-O-TI—that is, GH as it is pronounced in *tough*, O as it sounds in *women*, and TI as pronounced in *motion*. This observation is sometimes attributed to George Bernard Shaw, but, whoever devised it, it is well enough known to have been parodied by James Joyce in his anarchic book *Finnegans Wake*: "Gee each owe tea eye smells fish"

The fact that *tough* is pronounced "tuff" is the sort of thing that makes the English language such a minefield for foreigners trying to learn it. Even if they learn this particular pronunciation, it provides no help when trying to pronounce other words ending in -OUGH, like *bough*, *cough*, *thorough*, and *through*. In fact the letters -OUGH can be pronounced in at least six different ways.

For a competition in England in 1989, Noel Petty provided appropriate rhymes to help learners with pronouncing the dreaded -OUGH words:

> To speak our tongue without a fluff
>
> Is, for a foreigner, quite tough.
>
> It's most depressing, for although
>
> You may be feeling ever so
>
> Delighted that you've found out how
>
> The English speak a word like plough,
>
> That doesn't give you too much clue
>
> About the right way to say through,
>
> Which leaves you none too clear about
>
> The proper way to deal with drought.
>
> At this stage some like you have thought
>
> It wise to give up, and abort
>
> The mission. But don't be put off,
>
> You're near the bottom of the trough,
>
> And nobody is going to kick up
>
> Much fuss about a minor hiccough.

The multiple pronunciations of *-ough* are only an extreme example of the fact that many groups of English letters are pronounced in several different ways. For example, the letters OU sound different in *sound*, *soul*, *soup*, *pour*, and *touch*. The complexities of English spelling are well illustrated in this poem by an unidentified writer called simply "T.S.W."

Easy English for Beginners

I take it you already know

Of *tough* and *bough* and *cough* and *dough*?

Others may stumble, but not you,
On *hiccough, thorough, lough [lake],* and *through.*
Well done! And now you wish, perhaps,
To learn of less familiar traps?
Beware of *heard,* a dreadful word,
That looks like *beard* and sounds like *bird.*
And *dead:* it's said like *bed,* not *bead—*
For goodness' sake don't call it 'deed'!
Watch out for *meat* and *great* and *threat,*
(They rhyme with *suite* and *straight* and *debt.*)
A *moth* is not a moth in *mother,*
Nor *both* in *bother, broth* in *brother,*
And *here* is not a match for *there,*
Nor *dear* and *fear* for *bear* and *pear.*
And then there's *dose* and *rose* and *lose—*
Just look them up—and *goose* and *choose,*
And *cork* and *work,* and *card* and *ward,*
And *font* and *front,* and *word* and *sword,*
And *do* and *go,* and *thwart* and *cart—*
Come, come, I've hardly made a start!
A dreadful language? Man alive,
I'd mastered it when I was five!

Another peculiarity of English pronunciation is the number of words that contain unpronounced letters. Which leads on naturally to . . .

PART THREE

Fiendish

72. Silent Letters

Many English words include letters that are not sounded in normal speech. Thus the B in *debt* and *lamb* is silent, as is the K in *knife,* and the P in *psalm.*

For how many letters of the alphabet can you think of a word in which that letter is silent?

73. Hidden Word Squares

The origins of many word games are hidden in the mists of history: nobody can tell who invented them. However, we know that the game of Hidden Word Squares was devised by Hubert Phillips, author of numerous puzzle books.

Readers are presented with a short piece of nonsense verse. A word is hidden in each line of the poem. If these words are found and placed in order, they make up a word square (in which the words across are the same as the words down). The example is borrowed from Hubert Phillips himself.

Example

What gives a cynic ample food for thought?
To have repeated when the tempest howls,
This doom eternal, which descends unsought;
You can't stop Reynard's slaughter of your fowls.

Answer

The first line conceals the word *camp* (in "cynic ample"); the second line conceals the word *aver* (in "have repeated"); and so on. The hidden words make the following word square:

C	A	M	P
A	V	E	R
M	E	T	E
P	R	E	Y

1. Marianne stood on the train,
   Wringing her hands with glee:
   Soon she would arrive in town,
   A go-go dancer she would be.
2. The moon shone on the village inn,
   But no pal could Nellie see.
   She climbed upon a nag so fair:
   A novel setting for a love story.

3. Getting rid of visitors is not easy,
   Especially when they come as a surprise.
   I sleep uneasily, fearing their arrival,
   Thus I'm made edgy, with bleary eyes.

4. Why call an elephant Jumbo?
   Are all the elephants fat?
   Most have an ear that is floppy,
   But none the less dear, so that's that!

5. Writing verses (O men!) is quite simple,
   And poets are not mad, every one.
   You will like it once you have tried it,
   And sonnets are easily done.

6. The skipper at sea gave the order:
   A butter pat for all of the crews.
   The butter tub at last became empty,
   So margarine was the best able seamen could use.

74. Kangaroo Words

Every schoolchild knows that kangaroos carry their babies in their pouches.
Fewer people know about kangaroo words, which carry their own baby
words with the same meanings.

For example, the kangaroo word *illuminated* contains the synonym *lit*
among its letters. Similarly *exists* hides the word *is*, and *deceased* includes
dead.

Try to find synonyms hidden in the following words.

Example
Revolution.

Answer
Ruin.

1. Amicable.
2. Appropriate (adjective).
3. Salvage (verb).
4. Hostelry.
5. Encourage.
6. Recline.
7. Before.
8. Instructor.
9. Separate (verb).
10. Catacomb.
11. Indolent.
12. Precipitation.
13. Deliberate (verb).
14. Observe.
15. Transgression.
16. Unsightly.
17. Destruction.
18. Masculine.
19. Umpteenth.
20. Because.

Can you find *two* synonyms inside these kangaroo words?

21. Alone.   24. Falsities.
22. Container.   25. Perambulate.
23. Frangible.   26. Expurgated.

75. Down Under

After kangaroo words, it seems appropriate to consider Australia. Most English-speakers know of the song *Waltzing Matilda*, which includes such Australian words as *swagman* (a tramp) and *Matilda* (the bundle carried by a tramp or bushman).

What are the meanings of these slang words used by Australians?

Example
Pommy (noun).

Answer
A British person, especially a recent immigrant to Australia.

 1. Arvo (noun).
 2. Cruel (verb).
 3. Furphy (noun).
 4. Go the knuckle.
 5. Nong (noun).
 6. Come the raw prawn.
 7. Woop woop (noun).
 8. Lair (noun—as a type of person).
 9. Do a Melba.
10. Droob (noun).
11. Rattle your dags.
12. She's apples.

76. Derivations

English words are derived from many different sources. The word *derivation* itself comes from Latin, originally meaning "from a river or stream."

Do you know—or can you guess—the derivations of the following words?

 1. Which word used in card games is an alteration of the word *triumph*?
 2. Which two months of the year are named after Roman emperors?
 3. Which word for putting on clothes comes from the phrase *to do on*?
 4. Which country got its name from the explorer Amerigo Vespucci?
 5. Which game was named from the tool with which it was originally made?

6. Which word for a cook comes from the French word for *chief*?

7. Which word for a space traveler comes from two Greek words meaning "star" and "sailor"?

8. What kind of certificate comes from an ancient Greek word meaning "a letter folded in two"?

77. Hermans

"Hermans" are sentences that use a pun on a person's name, modeled on the sentence: " 'She's my woman,' said Herman." Hermans can include more complicated examples, such as: " 'What comes after H?' said I, Jay, Kay, Ella, and Emma."

Suggest appropriate female names for the speakers of these sentences.

Example
'Bless this meal,' said . . .

Answer
Grace.

1. "Can you see I've been dieting?" said . . .
2. "Is that a horse I hear?" asked . . .
3. "Everything in the garden is lovely," said . . .
4. "I'm an egotist," said . . .
5. "I only just got up," said . . .
6. "I'm shrinking!" said . . .
7. "Sing do, re, mi, fa, sol, ti, do," said . . .
8. "My house in London has two lavatories," said . . .
9. "The answer is blowin' in the wind," said . . .
10. "Let us all run briskly forth," said . . .

Now suggest suitable *male* first names for the speakers of these sentences:

11. "I am the winner," said . . .
12. "I cannot tell a lie," said . . .
13. "That can't be a window," said . . .
14. "I've finished the excavation," said . . .
15. "On your knees!" shouted . . .
16. "I'm only joking," said . . .
17. "Do you like my telescope?" said . . .
18. "What's 2 plus 2?" said . . .
19. "How does that famous soliloquy start?" asked . . .
20. "Over and out," said . . .

78. Letter Swaps

Here are pairs of words in which two adjacent letters can be swapped to change one word into the other. Thus *shape* can be changed into *phase* by interchanging the first and fourth letters, and a *crooner* can be turned into a *coroner* by swapping the second and third letters.

Try to identify these letter swaps from the pairs of clues. Preceding each pair of clues is the first letter of the first word in the answer.

Example
R: to wander - limestone that is polished for buildings and sculptures.

Answer
Ramble - marble.

A: appropriate - a gentle touch.
B: a large pillow - a crustacean.
C: talk - preservation.
D: peril - a male goose.
E: anticipated - excluded.
G: entrance - escape.
H: listen - long for.
L: being the boss - a business.
M: of a marriage - of an army.
N: of a nucleus - obscure.
O: takes too far - excessive intake.
P: wall covering - book of psalms.
R: being upright - being sure.
S: holy - afraid.
T: horn sound - Dorothy's dog.
U: the passing of waste fluids - destruction.
W: loquacious - noisy.

79. Associations

Almost every word is associated in some way with several other words—for example, because they occur together in idioms or familiar phrases, or because they have similar meanings. In this game, we give you a set of five words, phrases, or names that are associated in some way with a mystery word. For example, if the mystery word is *rain*, the clues might include: *forest*, *acid*, *Spain*, *singin'*, and *Iran*—because *rain* occurs in the compound terms *rain forest* and *acid rain*; "the *rain* in Spain stays mainly in the plain" is from well-known song lyrics; *Singin' in the Rain* is the title of a song and movie; and *Iran* is an anagram of *rain*.

Guess the mystery words from these sets of five associated words.

Example
Sleep, truth, eye, Tchaikovsky, beast.

Answer
Beauty (which is connected with *sleep* in the phrase *beauty sleep*; with *truth* because the poet Keats said: "Beauty is truth, truth beauty"; with *eye* because "beauty is in the eye of the beholder"; with Tchaikovsky because he wrote *The Sleeping Beauty*; and with *beast* through *Beauty and the Beast*).

1. Foolish, Ezra, flesh, number, weight.
2. Island, Teresa, parade, less west, eggs.
3. Way, lost, sauce, James Dean, effect.
4. Want, sweat, land, haste, paper.
5. Nurture, a tuner, boy, vacuum, mother.
6. Slippers, Tuesday, forty, gentry, Kenny Rogers.
7. Lie, original, wages, seven, multitude.
8. Neck, shell, voice, dove, mock.

80. Heteronyms

Heteronyms (also called homographs or homonyms) are pairs of words that are spelled the same but have different pronunciations, such as *row* meaning an argument (which is pronounced to rhyme with "how") and *row* meaning to propel a boat with oars (which is pronounced to rhyme with "hoe").

From the definitions below, try to identify each pair of heteronyms.

Example
To exist; conveying electric power.

Answer
Live (pronounced to rhyme with "give" and "five").

1. To plant seeds; a female pig.
2. A period of time; tiny.
3. To say "no"; rubbish.
4. To rip; liquid sadness.
5. A voice; a fish.
6. Achieves; deer.
7. Abandon; lots of sand.
8. Conduit; embroiderer.
9. Imply; very friendly.
10. Disabled person; legally unacceptable.
11. Japanese drink; benefit.
12. Amazed; Christian love.

81. Transadditions

Transadditions are sequences of words made by starting with a short word and adding one letter at a time to make a new word each time. The letters can be rearranged at each move to make the new word.

Example

Make a string of six transadditions starting with the word *is*.

Answer

Is - sip - pies - spire - priest - striped - spirited.

1. Make a string of six transadditions starting with the word *he*.
2. Make a string of five transadditions starting with the word *en*.
3. Make a string of nine transadditions starting with the word *I*.
4. Make a string of eight transadditions starting with the word *O*.
5. Make a string of six transadditions starting with the word *re*.
6. Make a string of six transadditions starting with the word *lo*.
7. Make a string of six transadditions starting with the word *in*.
8. Make a string of at least ten transadditions starting with the word *a*.

82. Tom Swifties

Tom Swifties are sentences in which the last word or two summarizes the preceding statement with an outrageous pun. For example: " 'Who has stolen the apples?' asked Tom *fruitlessly*." The final word is often an adverb but it can be another part of speech or part of a punning phrase, as in: " 'My bicycle is melting,' she *spoke softly*."

Try to finish the following sentences with a suitably awful punning word or words.

Example

"I am a geologist," he said . . .

Answer

Stonily.

1. "I love camping," said Tom . . .
2. "Will you marry me?" he asked . . .
3. "He is dead and buried," she said . . .
4. "Go to the back of the ship," said Tom . . .
5. "I'm dying," he . . .
6. "This car needs to warm up," he . . .
7. "Turn down your headlights," he . . .
8. "Who turned off the heat?" she asked . . .
9. "I used to be a pilot," she . . .
10. "I have just returned from the Far East," said Tom . . .
11. "You will go to prison for six months," said the judge . . .

12. "I have eaten all of the cupcakes," Tom . . .

13. "I've just struck oil!" Tom . . .

14. "I think it's funny that I've got mumps," laughed Tom . . .

15. "That's a big shark," said Tom . . .

16. "I dropped the advertisements in the mud," said Tom . . .

17. "My hair has fallen out," said the damsel . . .

18. "I have eaten all the French bread," said Tom . . .

19. "I have an appointment at noon, so can we please get on with this operation?" the surgeon . . .

20. "I went too near the lion's cage," said Tom . . .

83. Typewriter Words

The top row of a typewriter or computer keyboard consists of the letters QWERTYUIOP. What is the longest word that you can type on this top row? The target is a word of ten letters.

84. Quotations

How often do we misquote famous sayings? We all know the quotation "One small step for man; one giant leap for mankind," but what Neil Armstrong said when he stepped onto the moon was "That's one small step for *a* man . . ."

The following well-known quotations are not the actual words written or spoken by the people who originated them. What were the original words?

Example

Water, water, everywhere, and not a drop to drink.

Answer

Water, water, everywhere, nor any drop to drink. - S. T. Coleridge's *Rime of the Ancient Mariner.*

1. Come up and see me sometime.

2. Laugh, and the world laughs with you; cry, and you cry alone.

3. To gild the lily.

4. Fresh fields, and pastures new.

5. A little knowledge is a dangerous thing.

6. Play it again, Sam.

7. Music hath charms to soothe the savage beast.

8. Money is the root of all evil.

9. Ask me no questions and I'll tell you no lies.

10. History repeats itself.

85. Anagrammed Places

Rearrange the letters of these words to make the names of countries or cities.

Example
Diagnose.

Answer
San Diego.

1. Ancestral.	14. Salvages.
2. More.	15. Oration.
3. Mail.	16. Erect.
4. Roved.	17. Hordes.
5. Pure.	18. Planes.
6. Caption.	19. Laity.
7. Aspire.	20. Also.
8. Pairs.	21. Chain.
9. Solo.	22. Serial.
10. Rumba.	23. Penalties.
11. Ordeul.	24. Regalia.
12. Rain.	25. Resoaping.
13. Hasten.	26. Zeus.

86. Devil's Dictionary

American journalist Ambrose Bierce (1842–1914?) composed a *Devil's Dictionary*, in which he defined words in a satirical or ironic way. For example, his definition of *peace* was: "in international affairs, a period of cheating between two periods of fighting."

Some of Bierce's definitions are given below. Try to guess which words they define.

Example
A person whom we know well enough to borrow from, but not well enough to lend to.

Answer
Acquaintance.

1. A period of 365 disappointments.
2. One who abstains from strong drink, sometimes totally, sometimes tolerably totally.
3. A physician's name for the rheumatism of a rich patient.
4. A person who talks when you wish him to listen.
5. A place where horses, ponies, and elephants are permitted to see men, women, and children acting the fool.

6. A person who is always interfering in disputes in which he has no personal interest.

7. A prestidigitator, who puts metal into your mouth and pulls coins out of your pocket.

8. The seamy side of love.

9. A dead sinner revised and edited.

10. A force alleged to control affairs, principally quoted by erring human beings to excuse their failures.

11. A day set apart and consecrated to gluttony, drunkenness, maudlin sentiment, gift-taking, public dullness, and domestic behavior.

12. One skilled in circumvention of the law.

13. An instrument for smashing the human thumb.

14. One to whom the interests of a part seem superior to those of the whole.

15. A means of livelihood affected by the more degraded portion of our criminal classes.

16. One who, professing virtues that he does not respect, secures the advantage of seeming to be what he despises.

17. The most acceptable hypocrisy.

18. One of the processes by which A acquires property for B.

19. Waking up early on a cold morning to find that it's Sunday.

20. The fundamental element and special glory of popular literature; all that is mortal of a departed truth; a jellyfish withering on the shore of the sea of thought; the cackle surviving the egg; a desiccated epigram.

87. Synonym Chains

Synonyms are words with the same meanings as one another. Right? Right. So, in a string of synonyms, the first word should mean the same as the last. Right? Not necessarily.

Dmitri Borgmann devised Synonym Chains, in which a series of synonyms leads from a word to its opposite. So Borgmann suggested that one can move from *black* to *white* with this chain of synonyms: black - dark - obscure - hidden - concealed - snug - comfortable - easy - simple - pure - white. In fact the transformation can be achieved in a smaller number of changes: black - dark - shadowy - gray - pallid - white.

See if you can progress from one word to its opposite, in as few steps as possible, for the following pairs of words.

1. Good - bad.

2. Terrible - excellent.

3. Wise - foolish.

4. Victory - defeat.

5. Absent - present.

6. Brave - cowardly.

88. Spoonerisms

Spoonerisms are phrases or compound terms in which the initial letters or sounds of the words (or root words) change places. These wordplays are named for English clergyman and educator William A. Spooner (1844–1930), who was supposedly guilty of creating many spoonerisms. He is said to have told a student: "You have tasted a whole worm" instead of "You have wasted a whole term."

In this game, solve the clues to words or phrases that can be turned into other words or phrases by using spoonerisms.

Example

Change *my abode* into *a tall rodent*.

Answer

My house – high mouse.

1. Change *awful tugboats* into *passionate embraces*.
2. Change *mountaineering tutors* into *scavenging insects*.
3. Change *toe coverings* into *a lack of animals' hindmost parts*.
4. Change *a pretty insect* into *what it does*.
5. Change *a comfortable corner* into *an inquisitive chef*.
6. Change *a fault-finding spouse* into *a threatening dagger*.
7. Change *a conflagration* into *a purchaser of fruit*.
8. Change *a lengthy stream* into *an erroneous bodily organ*.
9. Change *an ornithologist* into *Mrs. Malaprop*.
10. Change *a bass melody* into *farewell*.

89. Two-letter Words

People who play such games as Scrabble (*trademark*) often find two-letter words useful. Try to identify the two-letter words from the definitions below.

Example

Therefore.

Answer

So.

1. Self and others.
2. Interjection expressing hesitation.
3. Greek letter π.
4. Indian fig tree.
5. Expression of surprise or desire.
6. A unit of print measure.
7. Attracted to both sexes.

8. Informal father.

9. Kind of modern art.

10. Expression of mild disappointment.

11. Bone or mouth.

12. Hawaiian hawk.

13. Expression of pain.

14. Three-toed sloth.

90. Perverbs

We all know some proverbs, such as 'A rolling stone gathers no moss' or 'Too many cooks spoil the broth.' Proverbs may provide useful pieces of advice for us all, but they often turn into irritating clichés. Then we may be tempted to change them around, to pervert their meaning by unexpectedly changing the ending. W. C. Fields is said to have changed 'If at first you don't succeed, try, try, try again' to: 'If at first you don't succeed, give up.' Try to provide new endings for the following beginnings of well-known proverbs.

1. Half a loaf is better than . . .

2. The pen is mightier than . . .

3. People who live in glass houses shouldn't . . .

4. A woman's work is never . . .

5. Cast your bread upon the waters . . .

6. The best form of defense is . . .

7. He who hesitates is . . .

8. A penny saved is . . .

9. See no evil, hear no evil . . .

10. Early to bed and early to rise . . .

91. Mishmash (2)

We have already encountered Mishmash earlier in this book (see section 70). The questions here are similar, but they depend on adding the same letters before and after a 'nucleus' to make a word.

Example

Add the same two letters before and after RISCO to make a word.

Answer

Periscope.

1. Add the same letter before and after the letters MEB to make a word.

2. Add the same two letters before and after the letters RMI to make a word.

3. Add the same two letters before and after the letters LIGHT to make a word.

4. Add the same two letters before and after LUVI to make a word.

5. Add the same three letters before and after ERTAINM to make a word.

6. Add the same three letters before and after ERGRO to make a word.

7. Add the same three letters before and after IZAT to make a word.

8. Add the same three letters before and after ENTIALN to make a word.

9. Add the same three letters before and after ACHA to make a word.

10. Add the same three letters before and after AU to make a word.

92. Oxymorons

Oxymorons are phrases that appear to contain two contradictory ideas. For instance, in Shakespeare's *Romeo and Juliet*, Juliet says that 'parting is such sweet sorrow,' but we might ask how sorrow can be sweet. Other examples of oxymorons are 'an open secret,' 'plastic glasses,' and 'a deafening silence.'

Can you arrange the 40 words below into pairs to make 20 two-word phrases that are oxymorons? To start off, *baby* can be paired with *grand* to make the oxymoronic piano: a *baby grand*.

awful	baby	bitter	cable	chocolate
death	deliberate	difference	dry	fiction
gas	good	grand	health	heavyweight
ice	idiot	ill	inside	jumbo
light	link	liquid	live	living
missing	mistake	order	out	random
recording	same	savant	science	shrimp
student	sweet	teacher	white	wireless

93. Origins

The science of investigating word origins is called *etymology*. This suggests that etymological results should be true, because *etymology* derives from the Greek word *etumos,* which means "true." Yet it is not always possible to trace the true derivation of words, and etymologists often disagree on the origins of particular words. However, there is good evidence for the accuracy of the origins suggested below. Can you identify the words whose probable origins are described here?

Example

Which dog got its name from not being afraid to get its feet wet?

Answer

The *poodle*, from German *Pudelhund,* a hound that splashes in the water.

1. Which excuse would suggest that the accused was not at the scene of the crime?

2. Which empty orchestra might help the barroom singers of today?

3. Which lizard turned out to be much bigger than the average lizard?

4. Which group of stars started as the Milky Way?

5. Which breed of cat, goat, and rabbit is named from a Turkish delight?

6. Which form of voting depends on a little ball?

7. Which 'divine wind' might be deadly in battle?

8. Which word marks the death of a king and the end of a board game?

9. Which word suggests that half a headache is worse than a whole headache?

10. Which word sees red when accused of being tiny?

11. Which kind of book is a collection of pressed flowers?

12. Which servant was particularly in charge of the wine cellar?

13. Which hat provides the best shade?

14. Which metal comes from a Mediterranean island?

15. Which precious stone might help on the morning after?

16. Which disease was originally thought to be caused by bad air?

17. Which word connects a modern racetrack with a plowed field?

18. Which piece of paper bears the mark of the jester?

94. Cryptic Clues

Cryptic crosswords employ clues that are enigmatic, often necessitating lateral thinking. Try to solve these 26 cryptic clues, each of which is preceded by the first letter of the answer. The numbers of letters in the solution words are given in parentheses after each clue.

Example

R. Comment about the score (6).

Answer

Remark (which means "to comment"; 're mark' could mean "about the score").

A. A bit of advice for aching caryatids (5, 6).

B. To live with a golfer's warning earlier (6).

C. Keeps aloft (7, 2, 3, 3).

D. The beadiest disease (8).

E. Read about spirited hearing aid (7).

F. Anne and Sinatra and haricot and pole (6, 3, 5).

G. A pig for 21 shillings (6).

H. This boundary sounds funny (4).

 I. Die of cold (3, 4).

J. This female gardener holds plants (10).

K. Mixing a pink gin makes you a VIP (7).

L. Someone beaten in a close-run race (5).

M. A periodical full of shots?(8).

N. How to hide the seat of your pants (15).

O. An opening alternatively supposing it's frozen (7).

P. Sailors on a tilting vessel? (9, 4).

Q. Shake! We're Friends! (7).

R. Do a turn in a domed building (7).

S. Sitting tenants? (9).

T. Mental work inappropriate for Henry VIII (8).

U. An American period is common practice (5).

V. Don't upset the silver cat: it'll go straight up (9).

W. Draw back (4).

X. Two tens squeeze three-quarters of nothing (5).

Y. Shout loudly like a coward in pain (6).

Z. An animal made of brass without end (5).

95. Uncommon Terms

Here are 20 uncommon terms. Try to match them with the definitions below. For example, the word *accoucheur* should be matched with the definition "a male midwife."

Terms

accoucheur, anosmia, atrabilious, Barmecide, batter, demirep, devil's darning needle, ecru, gelada, haplology, inhume, liger, narthex, nulliparous, paramnesia, serein, tret, versant, vexillology, zugzwang.

Definitions

An antechamber in a church.

A male midwife.

An allowance of extra weight formerly made to purchasers of some goods for waste in transportation.

The omission of sounds when these are repeated in a word.

The loss of the sense of smell.

Relating to a woman who has never borne a child.

A dragonfly or damselfly.

A giver of benefits that are illusory or disappointing.

A wall with a sloping face.

A brownish gregarious baboon with a bare red patch on its chest.

A fine rain falling in tropical climates from a cloudless sky.

The offspring of a lion and a tigress.

The color of unbleached linen.

To bury.

An illusory feeling of having already experienced a present situation (= *deja vu*).

Melancholy; ill-tempered.

The extent of land sloping in one direction.

A woman of doubtful sexual reputation.

In the game of chess, an obligation to move even when this must be disadvantageous.

The study of flags.

96. Russian Dolls

These puzzles are like 'Only Connect' (see sections 14 and 15) but they involve putting one word *inside* another word to make a third word. As with the wooden Russian dolls called *matryoshki*, you find one nested inside another.

Example

Put a woman into a young fox or lion to make an angel.

Answer

Her + cub = cherub (put the word *her* inside the word *cub* and you get c-*her*-ub, that is *cherub*.

1. Put an insect into desserts to make underwear.
2. Put a word for "always" inside a trout to get overheated.
3. Put a word for "representing" inside an insect to make a word meaning "earlier."
4. Put a word for "exists" into your artistic inspiration to make a word meaning "ill-treat."
5. Put the sixteenth letter of the Greek alphabet inside cigar residue to become "like a monkey."
6. Put a seasoning inside a word for "each" to make a collection of psalms.
7. Put a heavenly being into a game to become eternal.
8. Put a word for "on" inside a mongrel to make a line on a map.
9. Put males into a doctrine to make an apartment building.
10. Put a silicate mineral inside a word for "talented" to become "friendly."
11. Put a large vase into a gratuity to make a vegetable.
12. Put a conjunction inside a male admirer to make a headband.
13. Put a negative inside a number to make a projecting piece of wood.
14. Put a word meaning "perform" into miraculous food to get the Virgin Mary.
15. Put a song inside a fishy man to make a ship conveying merchandise.
16. Put a coarse word into alcoholic withdrawal symptoms to make dry periods.

97. Rebuses

Rebuses are groups of letters, numbers, pictures, etc., that represent words or phrases. *IOU* is a kind of rebus, representing the phrase 'I owe you.'

In the following questions, you will be asked to either create or decipher a rebus.

Example

Which two letters, followed by a number, sound like a word for a person of any kind?

Answer

N E 1 ('anyone').

1. Which two letters of the alphabet sound like: (a) jealousy, (b) a climbing plant, (c) a literary composition, (d) a number?

2. How many women's names (first names) can you create out of groups of two or three letters?

3. If you wonder if someone is all right, what four letters might you use to find out?

4. Which sets of three letters of the alphabet, when spoken aloud, sound like words that mean respectively: (a) a flower; (b) a being; (c) an opponent; (d) vigor?

5. If 'B 9' sounds like *benign*, can you think of: (a) a letter and a number that sound like 'earlier'; (b) two letters and a number that sound like 'to diverge'; (c) a letter, a number, another letter, and another number that sound like 'to lessen your guilt?'

6. Solve this rhyming puzzle from *A New Collection of Enigmas* (1810):

> To nothing add ten, with three-fifths of two score,
> And let them be join'd by five hundred more;
> These rightly combin'd, will give you the name
> Of a city that's high in the annals of fame.

7. Decipher these rebuses:

       C C C C C C C
       & E E E
       ALL 4 1 & 1 4 ALL
       D &
       G B O
       WAR AND PEA
       M Y E C
       B X
       E W D & E D D
       THE SAND

8. Devise a rebus to represent the phrase 'Long time, no see.'

9. Which popular song from 1941 could be symbolized simply by the letter 'X?'

10. Try to uncover a phrase symbolized by each of these single-letter rebuses: A, D, V, R.

98. Vowels in Order

A favorite question of word-gamers is to ask which words include all five vowels (AEIOU) in alphabetical order. The best-known words are *abstemious* and *facetious* (plus *abstemiously, abstemiousness, facetiously,* and *facetiousness*).

Now try to think of words that include all five vowels in different orders.

Example
AEOIU.

Answer
Pandemonium, praseodymium.

1. AIEOU.	17. IOUAE.
2. AIOUE.	18. IOUEA.
3. AOUIE.	19. IUEAO.
4. AUIOE.	20. OAIUE.
5. AUOIE.	21. OAUIE.
6. EAIOU.	22. OEAUI.
7. EAOIU.	23. OUAIE.
8. EAOUI.	24. OUEAI.
9. EAUIO.	25. OUEIA.
10. EIUAO.	26. OUIAE.
11. EOUAI.	27. UAIOE.
12. EUAIO.	28. UEAIO.
13. EUIAO.	29. UEIOA.
14. EUOIA.	30. UOAIE.
15. IAOUE.	31. UOIAE.
16. IOEUA.	32. UOIEA.

99. Overspecialized Words

Some words have such specialized meanings that it is difficult to imagine the words ever being used. Many such terms are not included in reference books like the *Oxford Essential Dictionary* but most of them are included in the large *Oxford English Dictionary,* which attempts to be as inclusive as possible.

Here are some definitions for words of this type. Try to match them with the words below.

Definitions
1. An eagle without beak or feet.
2. The quality or condition of being bread.
3. The worship of bread.
4. The practice among certain peoples of naming a parent from his or her child.

5. Of the day before yesterday.

6. The first person one meets after leaving home on some special occasion.

7. Having less than four syllables.

8. Cow's urine, as a remedy.

9. A sacrifice of a thousand oxen.

10. A disease that leaves yellowish patches on the skin.

11. A practitioner of evil magic.

12. Someone whose hair was never cut.

13. Having the shape or form of a mulberry.

14. A place in which frogs are kept.

15. A government by the wind.

16. A small swivel-gun, especially one mounted on the back of a camel.

17. Struggling blindfolded.

18. Feeding on onions.

19. The act of cutting off, with a saw, the extreme parts of the body, when putrefied.

20. Walking equally in opposite directions.

Words

abatagati, acersecomic, acroteriasm, alerion, all-flower-water, ambilevous, amphisbaenous, andabatarian, anemocracy, artolatry, cepivorous, chiliomb, moriform, nudiustertian, oligosyllabic, paneity, qualtagh, ranarium, teknonymy, xanthelasma, zumbooruk.

100. French Eponyms

A good number of English words are derived from the names of French people. Can you identify these words that derive from French proper names?

1. A system of writing and printing for the blind.

2. A device for executions.

3. Deliberate cruelty.

4. Extreme patriotism or masculine pride.

5. An outline portrait.

6. A method of sterilizing milk by heating it.

7. A poisonous narcotic alkaloid.

8. A hairstyle.

101. Crossed Lines

The telephone rings. You pick it up and someone asks: 'May I speak to Mr. Pack, please?' The line is bad, and you ask the caller to spell the name. If the caller is sensible, he says something like: 'P as in *Peter*, A as in *apple*, C as in *cat*, and K as in *king*.' However, if he is less than sensible, the caller may give you misleading words as guides to the pronunciation, saying something like: 'P as in *Phil*, A as in *are* , C as in *curt*, and K as in *knot*.' For how many letters of the alphabet can you find similarly misleading terms that could confuse someone completely about spelling?

102. Acronyms (2)

Here is another batch of acronyms—harder than the previous set (in section 30). Try to spell out their meanings.

1. UNICEF.
2. UNESCO.
3. LASER.
4. QANTAS (the Australian airline).
5. DIN (applied to electrical connections, film speeds, etc.).
6. FIAT (as the name for a make of car).

103. What Is the Question?

Most quizzes give you a series of questions and expect you to supply the answers. However, here we provide the answers and ask you to think of appropriate questions. There may be several possible questions (the sillier the better!).

Example
Sagebrush.

Answer (i.e., the question)
What do you use to groom a wise man?

1. Go to blazes.
2. Castanets.
3. Superb.
4. Beethoven's fifth.
5. Sam Spade.
6. Fantastic!
7. Pathetic!
8. 'Oh, that this too too solid flesh would melt.'
9. Barbed wire.

10. The nuclear family.
11. Sweet dreams.
12. Et tu, Brute.
13. Get rich quick.
14. Poetic license.
15. A bundle of nerves.
16. On the rampage.
17. A flash in the pan.
18. All hands on deck.

104. Mnemonics

When you want to remember the number of days in a particular month, how often have you found yourself muttering under your breath: 'Thirty days have September, April, June, and November . . .?' This is a mnemonic: a device to assist the memory. Ingenious humans devise sequences of letters or words, sometimes in rhyme, to help them recall information. Thus politicians used 'BOMFOG' to remind them of the first letters of the words in a useful phrase for speeches: 'The brotherhood of man under the fatherhood of God.'

Can you say what the following mnemonics are designed to help us remember?

1. Divorced, beheaded, died; Divorced, beheaded, survived.

2. Every good boy deserves favor.

3. Rescue our young goose before it's vanished (or Richard of York gave battle in vain).

4. My vet examined my jumpy spaniel using normal procedures.

5. WASPLEG (or PEG'S LAW).

6. HOMES (or Sergeant Major hates eating onions).

7. 'Why are jaguars mad, Mother?' asked Johnny very hesitantly. 'They probably tasted Father's peanut butter logs. Jaguars generally hate greasy and chewy homemade cookies,' Mother replied. 'The woodchucks hate consuming his recipes, too!' exclaimed kind Johnny. 'Never feed critters really bad cookies!'

8. When will his stupid head remember just how easy each endeavor remains? Having had help eclipsing every reasoning, harassing hazy egotist methods, elaborately jumbling clear concise junctures, with a great grand gravity giving wit vexation.

105. Consonants

According to the *Oxford American Dictionary and Language Guide*, consonants are letters that represent speech sounds 'in which the breath is at least partly obstructed, and which to form a syllable must be combined with a vowel.' You might therefore not expect many words to include several consonants together. This quiz concerns the exceptions to the rule: words that contain an unexpectedly high number of consonants.

Example
Which nine-letter word contains four T's?

Answer
Statuette.

1. Which ten-letter word contains five consecutive consonants?
2. Which word of more than six letters contains six consecutive consonants?
3. Which word contains seven consecutive consonants (including the letter Y as a consonant)?
4. Which word contains eight consonants and only one vowel?
5. In which thirteen-letter word are the consonants arranged in alphabetical order?
6. Which eight-letter word contains five S's?
7. Which seven-letter word contains four G's?
8. Which eight-letter word contains four D's?
9. Which eight-letter hyphenated word contains four F's?
10. Which eight-letter word contains four G's?
11. Which eight-letter hyphenated word contains four L's?
12. Which eight-letter word contains four N's?
13. Which eight-letter word contains four R's?
14. Which ten-letter word contains four K's?
15. Which ten-letter word contains four Z's?
16. Which fourteen-letter word contains four P's?

106. Vowel Language

In the alphabet, vowels are heavily outnumbered by consonants. There are only five vowels (A, E, I, O, and U)—or six if you include Y, whereas there are twenty-one (or twenty) consonants. Yet some words seem to have more than their fair share of vowels.

Try to answer these questions about several such words.

1. Which word contains five consecutive vowels?
2. Which six-letter word contains four E's?
3. Which six-letter word contains four O's?

4. Which six-letter word contains four U's?
5. Which seven-letter word contains four E's?
6. Which eight-letter word contains four A's?
7. Which nine-letter word contains five E's?
8. Which ten-letter word contains four A's?
9. Which ten-letter word contains four I's?
10. Which ten-letter word contains four U's?
11. Which fourteen-letter word contains six I's?

107. The Final Challenge

This section contains a miscellany of difficult questions and puzzles. If you can answer these (especially after dealing with all the preceding sections in the book), you can claim to be a champion at wordplay.

But beware! The answers to many of these questions depend on outrageous puns or other forms of lateral thinking.

1. Which country contains a beautiful garden?
2. How many countries can you think of whose names contain words for animals?
3. If a *dromedary* is a camel with one hump, and a *Bactrian camel* has two humps, what do you call a camel with no humps?
4. Who was the coarsest ancient philosopher?
5. Which sturdy shrub might remind you of a comedy team?
6. Which color suggests an excellent sailor?
7. What state of ill health could two women create?
8. Which nut sounds like a sneeze?
9. Why are pianos hard to unlock?
10. Who wrote a *sympho*?
11. What would you say if Fido ran off?
12. What kind of cheese is made in reverse?
13. How do you pronounce VOLIX?
14. Where is a *diamond* square in shape?
15. Which countries contain pieces of cloth?
16. Which state is round at the ends and high in the middle?
17. Remove three consecutive letters from a large biblical character's name to make his birthplace.
18. In what part of the furniture could you keep a gun?
19. Which words read the same upside down if written in capital letters?
20. What does the abbreviation *DDT* stand for?
21. Why is Winnie the Pooh like Attila the Hun?
22. In which tool does the French precede the English?

23. Which word for a numeral has the same number of letters as the number it represents?

24. Which number has a number two less than itself right at its heart?

25. Which number has a number which is one less than itself at its heart?

26. Which words starting and ending with 'S' stay exactly the same in the plural?

27. How many numbers can you find in the word PIONEER?

28. Which prehistoric creature might remind you of being watched by Anne, Charlotte, and Emily?

29. In which Beatles song did a thousand get all mixed up?

30. Which word is defined in the *Oxford American Dictionary and Language Guide* as "a nymph who lives in a tree and dies when it dies"?

31. G. K. Chesterton and his friends formed a club called 'The IDK Club.' What did they answer when people asked what it stood for?

32. Add one letter to a one-syllable word to make it a three-syllable word.

33. Which word means "American" in Britain but "European" in the United States?

34. Which two contradictory words both mean "to defeat"?

35. If the letters of the alphabet are given scores (A = 1, B = 2, C = 3, etc.), which seven-letter words would achieve a score of at least 130?

ANSWERS

Part One

1. Double Meanings

1. summit.
2. hide.
3. boil.
4. miss.
5. fence.
6. fit.
7. rail.
8. flap.
9. blue.
10. obtuse.
11. advance.
12. Grammy.

2. Removing a Letter

1. moist - mist.
2. glass - lass.
3. lass - ass.
4. fiddler - fiddle.
5. stale - tale.
6. boots - boos.
7. shout - shot.
8. simile - smile.
9. lone - one.
10. bleach - beach.

3. Stinky Pinky

1. funny bunny.
2. barn yarn.
3. gory story.
4. mellow cello.
5. pleasant peasant.
6. sunk monk.
7. eerie theory.
8. numb thumb.
9. fat cat or flabby tabby.
10. humbler tumbler.
11. cryptic diptych.
12. sinister minister.
13. quicker ticker.
14. missed tryst.
15. verbal gerbil.
16. blind rind.

4. Letters of Introduction

1. hand.
2. bear.
3. orange.
4. canoe.
5. beagle.
6. slaughter.
7. tenth.
8. aspiring.
9. gavel.
10. cache.
11. cart.
12. miter.
13. radish.
14. ermine.
15. fight.
16. coffin.
17. wrench.
18. panda.
19. fiend.
20. moan.

5. Add Two Letters

1. wind - window.
2. ten - often.
3. tent - tenant.
4. mole - molest.
5. pert - expert.
6. offer - proffer.
7. use - abuse.
8. sort - escort.
9. under - plunder.
10. rob - throb.

6. Palindromes

1. noon.
2. pup.
3. level.
4. madam.
5. kayak.
6. radar.
7. deed.
8. solos.
9. ere.
10. racecar.
11. tenet.
12. reviver.

7. Hidden Words

1. bear.
2. dog.
3. toad.
4. rabbit.
5. pig.
6. beaver.
7. calf.
8. swan.
9. frog.
10. eland.

8. Groups of Three

1. broadcast; asthma, astray, bronze, brooch, browse, drowse.
2. inanimate; aching, bleach, bleary, nimble, nimbly, taking.
3. developed; device, devise, devoid, malice, notice, novice.
4. toadstool; abbess, essays, oolong, strata, stress, strong.
5. enunciate; censor, curate, cursor, curtsy, legate, sorrow.
6. vengeance; geared, spared, stance, stared, veneer, venial.

9. Tops and Tails

(Many more answers are possible.)

1. table, thrive, tickle, time, trade, tumble.
2. acid, addicted, aid, arachnid, asteroid, avoid.
3. vacancy, valley, vary, very, Vichy, visually.
4. yacht, yeast, yellowest, yet, yogurt, youngest.
5. gain, gibbon, gin, given, grimalkin, grin.
6. lash, lavish, Lilith, Lindbergh, loincloth, lungfish.
7. coldness, compendious, cosmos, coterminous, crisis, curvaceous.
8. magic, maniac, manioc, mosaic, music, mystic.
9. fandango, Fargo, Figaro, faro, folio, forego.
10. camera, chihuahua, chimera, cholera, cornea, cupola.

10. Awful Authors

(Many more answers are possible.)

1. Penny Pincher.
2. Tim Burr.
3. Walter Wall.
4. Hugo First.
5. Hammond Eggs.
6. Roland Butter.
7. Tom A. Hawk.
8. Lynn C. Doyle.
9. Robin Banks.
10. Chris P. Trout.
11. Tess Tube.
12. Fay Kingham.
13. Bess Sellers.
14. Horace Scope.
15. Pattie O'Dors.

16. Rex Holmes.
17. Mike Reed.
18. Lois Carmen Denominator.
19. Freda Wanda Atwill.
20. Ruth Fitzpatrick and Patrick Fitzruth.

11. Three Letters
(Many more answers are possible.)
1. caveat, cavity, cavort, chauvinist, civility, covet.
2. sawdust, screwdriver, seaweed, showdown, shrewd, slowdown.
3. dactyl, decent, decimate, disinfectant, doctor, document.
4. tannic, technical, tincture, tonic, tunic, turbulence.
5. palm, parliament, pilgrim, plume, preliminary, puzzlement.
6. bandstand, boneless, bonus, brainstem, brainstorm, bunkhouse.
7. anchorperson, anthropology, arachnophobia, archbishop, archetype, arthropod.
8. jackrabbit, jockstrap, jocular, judiciary, juicier, juncture.
9. rarer, recorder, refrigerate, remarry, reorder, rumormonger.
10. ziggurat, Zimbabwe, zinnia, zirconia, zodiac, zoological.

12. Antonyms
(Many more answers are possible.)
1. dulcet, euphonious, harmonious, mellifluous, melodious, musical, sweet, tuneful.
2. affliction, ailment, disease, disorder, frailty, illness, infirmity, malady, sickness, unhealthiness.
3. calculated, conscious, considered, contrived, deliberate, designed, intentional, planned, prearranged, premeditated, willful.
4. aloof, antagonistic, chilly, disagreeable, haughty, hostile, inhospitable, sour, standoffish, supercilious, surly, uncongenial, unfriendly, unsociable.
5. conforming, conservative, conventional, formal, normal, orthodox, punctilious, reactionary, routine, square, straight, straitlaced, traditional.
6. absolutely, certainly, clearly, conclusively, decidedly, decisively, definitely, indisputably, indubitably, obviously, plainly, positively, surely, undoubtedly, unequivocally, unquestionably.
7. chatty, effusive, fluent, gabby, garrulous, gossipy, long-winded, loquacious, prolix, rambling, talkative, unreserved, verbose, voluble, wordy.
8. cheating, deceit, deception, dishonesty, distortion, double-dealing, equivocation, evasion, evasiveness, falsehood, falseness, falsity, inaccu-

racy, lying, mendacity, misrepresentation, perjury, prevarication, untrustworthiness, untruthfulness.

9. broad-minded, charitable, compassionate, easygoing, forbearing, forgiving, generous, humane, indulgent, kind, kindhearted, lenient, liberal, long-suffering, magnanimous, merciful, moderate, open-minded, patient, permissive, sympathetic, tolerant, understanding.

10. abiding, boundless, changeless, constant, deathless, durable, endless, enduring, eternal, everlasting, immortal, immutable, imperishable, indestructible, infinite, invariable, lasting, limitless, long-lived, never-ending, perennial, permanent, perpetual, persistent, persisting, stable, timeless, unceasing, unchangeable, unchanging, undying, unending.

13. What's This Word?

1. academy.
2. decline.
3. mesmerize.
4. werewolf.
5. tyrannosaurus.
6. readership.
7. decathlon.
8. portentous.
9. extravaganza.
10. strategy.

14. Only Connect (1)

1. carpet (car-pet).
2. rather (rat-her).
3. notable (no-table).
4. bugbear (bug-bear).
5. anthem (ant-hem).
6. romantic (Roman-tic).
7. fatally (fat-ally).
8. strange (St-range).
9. ozone (Oz-one).
10. flamenco (flame-NCO).

15. Only Connect (2)

1. fundamental (fund-a-mental).
2. manicure (man-I-cure).
3. nightingale (night-in-gale).
4. downhearted (down-hear-Ted).
5. meadowlark (mead-owl-ark).
6. mistime (mist-I-me).
7. cottonball (cot-ton-ball).
8. mendicant (mend-I-cant).
9. cablegram (cab-leg-ram).
10. cornerstone (corn-erst-one).

16. Briticisms

1. eggplant.
2. sausage.
3. fanny pack.
4. clothespin.
5. zucchini.
6. checkers.
7. thumbtack.
8. jumper cables.
9. diaper.
10. tic-tac-toe.
11. traffic circle.
12. silent partner.
13. windshield.
14. worrywart.

17. Change a Letter

1. bat or rat.
2. sock.
3. foal.
4. mural.
5. riddle.
6. flute.
7. coot or chat.
8. keel.
9. pants.
10. forte.

18. Change Two Letters

1. potato - tomato.
2. finding - fishing.
3. piano - plant.
4. stable - unable.
5. castle - castor.
6. Sunday - Monday.
7. emirate - emulate.
8. zither - zipper.
9. ingest - digest.
10. demented - decanted.

19. First Names

1. Earl.
2. Shelly (or Sandy).
3. Bud.
4. Max.
5. Noah.
6. Sue.
7. Bernadette.
8. Ivy.
9. John.
10. Millicent.

20. Hidden Words (2)

1. chess.
2. India.
3. Italy.
4. sole.
5. diamond.
6. easier.
7. lariat.
8. butter.
9. together.
10. interchange.

21. Homophones

1. plain/plane.
2. due/dew.
3. naval/navel.
4. links/lynx.
5. time/thyme.
6. meat/meet.
7. allowed/aloud.
8. patients/patience.
9. gorilla/guerrilla.
10. grown/groan.
11. barred/bard.
12. Sunday/sundae.
13. chased/chaste.
14. llama/lama.

Triple Homophones

1. aye/eye/I.
2. aisle/I'll/isle.
3. new/gnu/knew.
4. palate/palette/pallet.
5. cite/sight/site.
6. flu/flew/flue.
7. carrot/carat/caret.
8. rain/reign/rein.

Quadruple Homophones

1. o'er/or/oar/ore.
2. right/rite/wright/write.
3. air/e'er/ere/heir.

22. Homophonic Statements

1. Let us be frank.
2. We've hilled him for rye bread.
3. I know you can't surf.
4. Our maid wore blue jeans.
5. Four PM's tea time.

23. Think of a Word

(Many more answers are possible.)

1. arm, ear, eye, gut, hip, jaw, lap, leg, lid, lip, rib, toe.
2. ape, bat, cat, cow, cub, doe, dog, elk, emu, ewe, fox, gnu, hog, man, pig, ram, rat, sow, yak.
3. ash, bay, box, elm, fig, fir, gum, oak, tea, yew.
4. dice, faro, golf, judo, keno, polo, pool, Risk.
5. agave, apple, grape, guava, lemon, mango, melon, peach, prune.
6. almond, bonbon, burger, canape, cheese, cookie, cutlet, éclair, ginger, greens, hot dog, mousse, muffin, noodle, paella, quiche.
7. bunk bed, chaise longue, cot, couch, cradle, crib, daybed, futon, hammock.
8. barge, cabin cruiser, canoe, catamaran, cruiser, dinghy, ferry, gondola, gunboat, houseboat, kayak, launch, lifeboat, lightship, motorboat, powerboat, tugboat.

24. I Knew Him When . . .

1. George Bush.
2. Oscar Wilde.
3. Ulysses S. Grant.
4. Fannie Flagg.
5. Captain James Cook.
6. Billie Holiday.
7. Thomas Paine.
8. Helen Hayes.
9. James Dean.
10. James Fennimore Cooper.
11. Fannie Farmer.
12. Martin Luther King, Jr.
13. Ezra Pound.
14. Francis Scott Key.
15. Eddie Rabbit.
16. Carrie Nation.

25. Synonyms

1. cross (as in 'Why did the chicken cross the road?' and 'I was cross at his bad manners').
2. chance (as in 'They had a chance meeting on the street' and 'They finally gave me a chance').
3. leaves (as in 'Noon is when she leaves' and 'It's time to rake the leaves').
4. leg (as in 'She broke her leg' and 'He was overtaken in the last leg of the race').
5. abide (as in 'She will abide here for a while' and 'I can't abide his vanity').
6. hero (as in 'Superman was the hero who saved them' and 'I would like a bite of your turkey hero').
7. stroke (as in 'I gently stroked the cat' and 'He had a stroke that paralyzed his right arm').
8. light (as in 'The dress was light blue' and 'I could almost read by the light of the moon').
9. striking (as in 'It was a striking display of gymnastics' and 'The workers were striking for better pay').
10. take (as in 'She should take full responsibility for the mishap' and 'Will this train take me to Boston?').

26. Triple Meanings

1. drum.
2. links.
3. front.
4. point.
5. fine.
6. air.
7. odd.
8. stand.
9. boxers.
10. beam.

27. Anagrams

1. tea.
2. shrub.
3. melon.
4. Keats.
5. dawn.
6. Celia.
7. Theodora.
8. percussion.
9. towels.
10. crumpets.
11. meatballs.
12. silent.
13. athletics.
14. editorial.
15. the classroom.
16. sparse attire.
17. intestines.
18. adroitly, dilatory.
19. allergy, largely, regally.
20. parleys, parsley, replays, sparely.
21. enlist, listen, silent, tinsel.
22. lameness, maleness, nameless, salesmen.
23. imprudence.
24. incomprehensible.
25. no untidy clothes.
26. *Der Rosenkavalier.*

28. Endings

(Many more answers are possible.)

1. fife, knife, life, wife, rife, strife.
2. any, canny, deny, grainy, many, rainy, tyranny.
3. angle, bangle, mangle, single, struggle, wiggle.
4. caper, hamper, juniper, super, temper, whimper.
5. above, cove, glove, love, move, stove.
6. arise, cruise, demise, premise, promise, surmise.
7. barnacle, bicycle, chicle, icicle, manacle, vehicle.
8. amour, augur, detour, lemur, occur, sulfur.
9. coldly, dastardly, friendly, hardly, kindly, lordly.
10. hazardous, horrendous, stupendous, tremendous (these four are the only common words ending with -*dous*).
11. cushion, fashion, pincushion (these three are the only common words ending with -*shion*).
12. angry, hungry (these two are the only common words ending with -*gry*).

29. Fractured French

1. *mal de mer.*
2. *coup de grâce.*
3. *pas de deux.*
4. *entrechat.*
5. *carte blanche.*
6. *mise en scène.*
7. *pièce de résistance.*
8. *honi soit qui mal y pense.*

30. Acronyms

1. value added tax.
2. radio detecting and ranging.
3. Museum of Modern Art.
4. not in my back yard.
5. absent without leave.
6. what you see is what you get.
7. personal identification number.
8. random access memory.
9. Zone Improvement Plan.
10. self-contained underwater breathing apparatus.

31. Hide and Seek

1. rat.
2. last.
3. hen.
4. vole.
5. asp.
6. bat.
7. van.
8. boa.
9. bull and lion.
10. nap.
11. ear.
12. Mona.
13. us, she, he, her, hers.
14. *Evita*.
15. IOU.

32. Triple Anagrams

(Other answers are possible.)

1. amen, mane, mean.
2. drawer, reward, warred.
3. ores, roes, sore.
4. pares, pears, spear.
5. diet, edit, tide.
6. miter, remit, timer.
7. asps, pass, spas.
8. danger, gander, garden.
9. aster, rates, tears.
10. caper, crape, pacer.

33. Categories

(Many more answers are possible.)

1. canary, chicken, cockatiel, condor, crow.
2. dentist, detective, disc jockey, draftsman, dressmaker.

3. sassafras, sequoia, spruce, sumac, sycamore.
4. galoshes, girdle, glove, gown, gym shorts.
5. fiddle, fife, flugelhorn, flute, French horn.
6. ham, hamburger, honey, hotdog, hummus.
7. cleaver, colander, cookbook, countertop, cutlery.
8. sailing, skating, skiing, soccer, squash.
9. Tallahassee, Tampa, Tel Aviv, Toledo, Toronto.
10. wheel, whitewall tire, windshield, window, wiper blade.

34. True or False?

1. False (*engender* means "to cause or bring about").
2. False (a *dhoti* is a loincloth worn by Hindus).
3. True (a *refectory* is the dining room in a monastery, college, etc.).
4. False (*chitterlings* are hog intestines prepared as food).
5. False (*pelota* is a Spanish game in which the players wear wicker baskets on their hands to catch and throw a ball).
6. True (a *solecism* is a mistake made in speaking or writing—for example, in grammar).
7. False (the *obverse* is the 'head' of a coin).
8. False (a *dingo* is a wild Australian dog).
9. False (a *muu-muu* is a loose, brightly colored dress worn by Hawaiian women).
10. False (*obnubilate* means to darken or obscure).

35. The Name Game

1. April, May, or June (sometimes others).
2. Frank.
3. Clementine.
4. Lee.
5. Daisy, Heather, Iris, Ivy, Lily, Myrtle, Rose, Veronica, Viola, Violet, etc.
6. Basil.
7. Felicity or Joy.
8. Mark.
9. Carol.
10. Will.
11. Florence.
12. Anna, Eve, Hannah, etc.

36. Combinations

1. light.
2. case.
3. bag.
4. horse.
5. keeper.
6. pool.
7. way.
8. race.
9. machine.
10. breaker.

37. Side by Side

1. tyrannosaurus tyranny.
2. living lizard.
3. swine swing.
4. bronze brooch.
5. somnolent son.
6. greedy Greek.
7. zero zest.
8. crayon craze.
9. carousel carp.
10. wicked wicker.
11. guppy gurgle.
12. sweaty Swede.

38. Miss World

1. Miss Trial or Miss Judge.
2. Miss Management.
3. Miss Take.
4. Miss Tress.
5. Miss Anthrope.
6. Miss Spelling.
7. Miss Adventure.
8. Miss Chief.
9. Miss Leading.
10. Miss Inglink.

Part Two

39. Anagram Pairs

1. adobe abode.
2. raw war.
3. tame mate.
4. strap parts.
5. wee ewe.
6. damned demand.
7. solemn lemons.
8. ample maple.
9. enraged grandee.
10. wives' views.
11. secure rescue.
12. seaside disease.
13. low owl.
14. latent talent.
15. shot host.
16. bedroom boredom.
17. slime smile.
18. striptease tapestries.
19. nameless salesmen.
20. valiant Latvian.
21. Estonians' sensation.
22. persistent prettiness.

23. steamship shipmates.
24. laden eland.
25. supersonic percussion.
26. trifling flirting.
27. measuring geraniums.
28. paroled leopard.
29. noiseless lionesses.

40. Doublets
(Other answers are possible.)

1. CAT-COT-DOT-DOG or
   CAT-COT-COG-DOG.
2. BOY-BAY-MAY-MAN or BOY-
   BAY-BAN-MAN.
3. HARD-CARD-CART-CAST-
   EAST-EASY.
4. EAST-PAST-PEST-WEST or
   EAST-LAST-LEST-WEST.
5. ONE-OWE-EWE-EYE-DYE-
   DOE-TOE-TOO-TWO.
6. OAK-YAK-YAW-YEW.
7. SICK-SILK-SILL-WILL-
   WELL.
8. POST-PEST-BEST-BEAT-
   BEAM.
9. GRASS-CRASS-CRESS-
   TRESS-TREES-TREED-
   GREED-GREEN.
10. TREE-FREE-FLEE-FLED-
    FEED-FEND-FOND-FOOD-
    WOOD.
11. HATE-HAVE-LAVE-LOVE or
    HATE-HAVE-HOVE-LOVE.
12. BLACK-BLANK-BLINK-
    CLINK-CHINK-CHINE-
    WHINE-WHITE.

41. Reversals

1. part - trap.
2. rats - star.
3. gnat - tang.
4. wed - dew.
5. leek - keel.
6. drawer - reward.
7. dog - god.
8. straw - warts.
9. rail - liar.
10. gulp - plug.
11. animal - lamina.
12. tuber - rebut.

42. Connections

1. box.
2. deposit.
3. ring.
4. chain.
5. bag.
6. house.
7. car.
8. bone.
9. pick.
10. book.
11. fool.
12. piano.
13. set.
14. dressing.
15. day.
16. John.

43. Spelling

1. dilapidated.
2. receive.
3. allowance.
4. maintenance.
5. occasionally.
6. guarantee.
7. rendezvous.
8. accommodation.
9. necessary.
10. immediately.
11. aspidistra.
12. embarrassment.
13. diphtheria.
14. hypochondriac.
15. resuscitate.
16. inaccessible.
17. chihuahua.
18. sacrilegious.
19. veterinary.
20. parallelogram.
21. occurrence.
22. perseverance.
23. endeavor.
24. finesse.
25. embarrassed.
26. millennium.
27. ecstasy.
28. logarithm.
29. aborigine.
30. questionnaire.

44. Meanings

1. meanness; stinginess; being very careful (or too careful) with money.
2. decay, especially of teeth.
3. debris, especially gravel or sand caused by erosion.
4. stinking; smelling very unpleasant.
5. favoritism toward relatives or friends when you are handing out jobs or privileges.
6. grimly humorous or mocking; cynical.
7. a small offense; a minor sin.
8. unsatisfying; shallow or simplistic; childish or puerile.
9. an explanation or interpretation of something written, especially scripture.
10. a dungeon that can be reached only through a trapdoor.
11. a group of people paid to applaud in an opera house or theater.
12. marriageable or sexually attractive.
13. a hundred dollar bill.
14. incoherent or confused; not yet fully formed; undeveloped.
15. thick or thickened; dense.

45. Vowel Play

1. laurel.
2. meteoric.
3. paella.
4. ravage.
5. howdah.
6. nougat.
7. either.
8. eventide.
9. tambourine.
10. orifice.
11. espouse.
12. apteryx.
13. outcast.
14. eider.
15. unite.
16. cvoke.
17. outdo.
18. unique.
19. eager.
20. easily.
21. nonpareil.
22. ash.
23. abate.
24. avocado.
25. auk or kea.

46. Dismissals

1. Discard them.
2. Derange them.
3. Defile them.
4. Defuse or degenerate them.
5. Dismantle him.
6. Dismount them.
7. Decrease, deplete, depress, or dispatch them.
8. Dissolve them.
9. Discolor them.
10. Debrief them.

47. Words Within Words

(Many more answers are possible.)

1. ally, calf, call, caul, clay, cull, cult, faculty, fall, fatty, fault, faulty, flat, flatly, flay, full, fully, lacy, tact, tactful, talc, tall, tally, taut, tautly.

2. cite, cited, city, civet, civil, deity, delict, devil, dice, dicey, diet, dive, edict, edit, elicit, evict, evil, iced, icily, idle, idly, ivied, levity, levy, lice, lied, live, lived, livid, tide, tidily, tidy, tied, tilde, tile, tiled, veil, veld, veldt, vice, vide, vied, vile, yeti, yield.

3. dent, dentist, diet, dine, dint, dune, dust, edit, isn't, nest, news, newt, nude, send, sent, sewn, side, sine, sinew, site, stew, stud, student, suit, suite, suited, swine, tend, tent, test, tide, tied, tint, tune, tuned, twin, twine, twined, twist, twisted, twit, unit, unite, unset, untwist, unwise,

used, wend, went, west, wetsuit, wide, widen, widest, wind, wine, wined, wise.

4. acer, ache, acre, arch, archer, care, career, carer, carve, carver, cave, caver, cere, char, cheer, chore, chorea, cohere, core, corer, cove, cover, crave, each, echo, ever, hare, have, havoc, hear, hearer, heave, here, hero, hoar, hoer, hove, hover, hoverer, ocher, orach, orache, orca, over, overhear, race, racer, rare, rave, raver, reach, rear, recover, roach, roar, rove, rover, veer.

5. abet, able, albeit, alert, alive, alter, bail, bait, bale, bare, bate, bear, beat, beater, beaver, beer, beet, belt, berate, beta, bevel, bier, bile, bite, biter, bleat, brave, earl, eater, elite, elver, ever, evert, evil, late, later, lave, leave, leer, lever, liar, liberate, liter, live, liver, rail, rale, rate, rave, real, rebel, reel, relate, relative, retail, reveal, revel, revet, rite, rival, table, tail, tale, teal, tear, tier, tire, trail, travel, treble, tree, trial, tribal, tribe, vale, veal, veer, veil, verb, verbal, viable, vile, vital.

6. deem, deep, deer, deism, demise, depress, desire, despise, dime, dire, disperse, diss, dress, drip, eider, emir, empire, empress, espied, idem, impede, impress, mere, mess, messed, messier, mire, miser, miss, missed, peed, peer, perm, permed, pied, pier, premise, preside, press, pressed, pride, pried, prim, prime, prise, prism, reed, remiss, reside, ride, rime, ripe, rise, seed, seep, seer, semi, series, side, simp, simper, simpered, sire, sired, sped, speed, sperm, spider, spied, spired, spree.

7. abet, able, abuse, abut, aisle, albeit, album, alum, amble, amulet, amuse, autism, bail, bait, bale, balm, base, basil, baste, bate, beam, beast, beat, beau, beaut, belt, best, bestial, beta, bias, bile, bite, blame, blase, blast, bleat, blest, blue, bluest, built, bust, bustle, east, email, emit, etui, iamb, ileum, imbue, isle, islet, item, lamb, lame, last, late, least, lest, lieu, limb, lime, list, litmus, lust, lute, mail, male, mall, malt, mast, mate, maul, meal, meat, melt, mesa, metal, mile, mist, mite, mule, muse, must, mutable, mute, sable, sale, salt, salute, same, sate, sauté, seal, seam, seat, sebum, simulate, site, slab, slam, slat, slate, slim, slime, slue, slum, slut, smelt, smile, smite, smut, stab, stabile, stable, stale, steal, steam, stem, stile, stub, stumble, sublet, sublime, submit, subtle, suet, suit, suitable, suite, table, tail, tale, tame, teal, team, tile, time, tuba, tube, tumble, turn, umbel, usable, utile.

8. abed, abode, adobe, adore, adorn, aeon, anew, anode, awed, awned, awoke, awoken, bade, bake, baked, baker, band, bane, bank, banked, banker, bard, bare, bared, bark, barked, barn, baron, bawd, bead, beak, bean, bear, beard, bend, boar, board, bode, bond, bone, boned, boner, bonk, bonked, bore, bored, born, borne, bowed, bower, brad, brake, braked, bran, brand, brawn, bread, break, bred, brew, broad, broaden, broke, broken, brow, brown, browned, dank, dare, dark, darken, darn, dawn, dean, dear, debar, debark, doer, done, dower, down, downer, drab, drake, drank, draw, drawn, drew, drone, drown, earn, endow, knead, knew, knob, know, knower, naked, near, node, oaken, onward, owed, owned, owner, radon, rake, raked, rank, ranked, read, redo, redone, rend, road, roan, robe, robed, rode, rowan, rowed, wade, wad-

er, wake, waked, waken, waker, wand, wander, wane, waned, ward, warden, ware, warn, warned, weak, wean, wear, wend, woke, woken, wonder, word, wore, work, worked, worn, wreak, wren.

48. Antonyms (2)

1. Dry (as in 'dry white wine' and 'a dry day').
2. Tough (as in 'a tough problem' and 'a tough gangster').
3. Raw (as in 'cashews should not be eaten raw' and 'a raw recruit').
4. Tight (as in 'he's a bit tight with his money' and 'I drank too much and got rather tight').
5. Sensible (as in 'sensible shoes' and 'a sensible woman').
6. Serious (as in 'a serious illness' and 'you can't be serious!').
7. Admission (as in 'he was allowed admission to the zoo' and 'It was an admission of guilt').
8. Late (as in 'the late lamented cat' and 'she is often late for work').
9. Vain (as in 'a vain attempt' and 'he's so vain').
10. Seasoned (as in 'she is a seasoned professional' and 'the chicken is seasoned with paprika').

49. Paired Homophones

1. Hoarse horse.
2. Mail male.
3. Some sum.
4. Cue queue.
5. Pares pears.
6. Sail sale.
7. Friar fryer.
8. Serial cereal.
9. Whale wail.
10. Bridal bridle.

50. Old-fashioned Words

1. Concerning; about.
2. A horse for ordinary riding.
3. Trim, spruce, smart.
4. Migraine.
5. A standard-bearer; a banner or flag.
6. Without.
7. A trumpet fanfare.
8. A magician; a wise or learned person.
9. The branch of astronomy concerned with describing and mapping the stars.
10. A gossip.

51. Bookends

Here is one possible list (although it lacks words for some letters):

aroma, bib, chronic, devastated, extempore, fluff, going, health, illuminati, kayak, loyal, minimum, nitrogen, onto, primp, rubber, suppress, tenement, willow, xerox, yesterday.

For proper names: Antarctica, Beelzebub, Cadillac, David, Elbe, Falstaff, Grieg, Heath, Iraqi, Kalmuck, Lowell, Muslim, Nicaraguan, Ohio, Philip, Roger, Silas, Taft, Urdu, Voroshilov, Woodrow, Xerox.

52. Three in One

1. interior.
2. stagnate.
3. foothill.
4. sturgeon.
5. swindler.
6. ministry.
7. insolent.
8. quotient.
9. minstrel.
10. alkaline.

53. Plurals

1. lice.
2. mothers-in-law.
3. indexes or indices.
4. teaspoonfuls.
5. crises.
6. phenomena.
7. courts-martial.
8. incognitos.
9. opuses or opera.
10. moose.
11. radii or radiuses.
12. armfuls.
13. addenda.
14. stigmas or stigmata.

54. Combinations (2)

1. quick.
2. hip.
3. finger.
4. good.
5. flying.
6. general.
7. double.
8. short.
9. jam.
10. blaκ.
11. wind.
12. brain.
13. steam.
14. wind.
15. book.
16. free.
17. cross.
18. top.
19. full.
20. side.
21. bull.
22. dog.
23. car.
24. cat.

55. Foreign Words and Phrases

1. A sofalike chair with a backrest at only one end (the French phrase literally means "long chair").

2. In the family, with one's family, or at home.

3. Apartheid (the Afrikaans word literally means "apartness" or "separation").

4. Abattoir.

5. A joke or witty saying (the French phrase literally means "a good word").

6. I am wrong, I am guilty, or I am to blame (the Latin phrase literally means "my fault").

7. On a church: it is a slender spire.

8. From the beginning (the Latin phrase literally means "from the egg").

9. Exactly the right word to describe something; the most appropriate expression.

10. Tenderly, lovingly (the Italian phrase means "with love").

11. Unique or special (the Latin phrase literally means "of its own kind").

12. Superciliously, contemptuously, in a superior manner (the French phrase literally means "from high to low," suggesting that you are being scrutinized disapprovingly).

13. Something (like a skull) that reminds us that we all have to die.

14. Usually at the start of a meal, although occasionally in the middle of a meal. It is an appetizer. (The French phrase literally means "outside the work.")

15. "Let the buyer beware," which describes the principle that if people shop imprudently, they should not complain if they are dissatisfied with the things they buy.

16. A mind unaffected by preconceived ideas (the Latin phrase means "a clean slate").

17. Being noble or having privileges entails responsibility—usually to be courteous, thoughtful, or generous toward other people (the French expression literally means "nobility obliges").

18. Something difficult to consider or deal with—for example, a difficult proposition in philosophy or a stumbling block (the Latin phrase literally means "bridge of asses").

56. Collective Nouns

1. shrewdness.
2. clowder.
3. business.
4. cloud.
5. skulk.
6. mob.
7. kindle.
8. exaltation.
9. leap.
10. pride.
11. muster.
12. rookery.
13. string.
14. unkindness.
15. murmuration.

57. Word Row

1. mad Adam.
2. stop spots.
3. no son.
4. odd do.
5. don't nod.
6. loot tool.
7. see referees.
8. drab bard.
9. stressed desserts.
10. pupil's slip-up.
11. amoral aroma.
12. elk cackle.
13. we few.
14. retract, Carter.
15. tube debut.
16. pot top.
17. redness ender.
18. senile felines.
19. swept pews.
20. a Toyota.

58. What's the Difference?

1. A *calendar* is a list of dates of the year. A *colander* is a sieve or strainer.

2. You keep birds in an *aviary*. You keep bees in an *apiary*.

3. A *cassock* is a full-length garment worn by a clergyman or a member of a choir. A *hassock* is a thick cushion used as a footstool or to kneel on.

4. *Principal* is an adjective meaning "most important, chief" or a noun meaning "the head of a college, school, etc." *Principle* is a noun meaning "a fundamental law or truth."

5. An *allusion* is a reference to something, usually an indirect or passing reference—although it can be significant, as when you continually make allusions to the devil when in the presence of a clergyman. An *illusion* is something that you imagine you see: a deceptive or faulty perception. It can also mean a mistaken idea, as in 'It is an illusion to believe that all clergymen are as pure as the driven snow.'

6. An *entomologist* studies insects. An *etymologist* studies words and their origins.

7. To *imply* is to suggest something indirectly. To *infer* is to deduce or conclude something from facts or reasoning.

8. *Eligible* means suitable for or entitled to some position or situation, especially suitable as a partner in marriage ('an eligible bachelor'). *Illegible* means unreadable.

9. A *carat* is a unit of weight (0.2 grams) for precious stones. A *caret* is a sign like an inverted letter 'v,' indicating where something should be inserted in a piece of written or printed text.

10. *Oscillating* means moving or swinging back and forth. *Osculating* means kissing.

11. A *philatelist* collects postage stamps. A *philanthropist* is someone who is benevolent or charitable.

12. *Punctual* means keeping to an agreed time or habitually being neither early nor late. *Punctilious* means formal or precise in behavior or manners.

13. The *palate* is the roof of the mouth and also means the sense of taste. A *palette* is the board on which a painter mixes colors.

14. *Discreet* means tactful or prudent, especially in not revealing information that is secret or private. *Discrete* means individual, separate, or distinct, as in 'Sociology looks at people as groups, not as discrete individuals.'

59. The Storm Breaks

(Other answers are possible.)

Ben, en, no, fear, ear, he, is, lei, leis, lo, no, is, so, sand, sands, we, wee, eta, ha, hat, at, ed, deli, light, tan, an, no, so, some, me, met, time, times, me, mesa, sat, at, thou, ho, us, sand, an, and, wan, wangling, angling, ling, gin, in, strum, rum, rumen, me, men, swill, ill, um, bout, out, in, near, nears.

60. Follow-On

1. sand flea: fleabag: bagpipe: pipe dream: dreamboat: boat race: racecourse: coursework.

2. lowfat: fat cat: catbird: birdsong: songwriter.

3. rattlesnake: snakeskin: skintight: tightrope: rope ladder.

4. Italian ice: ice cream: cream cheese: cheese fondue: fondue fork: forklift.

5. good-night: nightlight: lighthouse: housefly: fly paper: paperback: backdoor: doorman: manpower.

6. motormouth: mouthwatering: watering can: can-do: do without: without end: endpaper.

7. adobe brick: bricklayer: layer cake: cake pan: panhandle.

8. live wire: wiretap: tap dance: dance hall: hallmark: markup: upgrade: grade school.

61. Contronyms

1. dust (The airplane dusted the fields; Have you dusted this room?).
2. trim (She trimmed the dress with lace; Trim the pie crust around the edge).
3. draw (curtains).
4. trip (She tripped across the fields; He tripped over the carpet).
5. cleave ('Shall a man cleave unto his wife?' — *Genesis* 2; You can cleave the log in two with an ax).
6. oversight (She has oversight of the entire program; My failure to check the meter was simply an oversight).
7. left (There is one cookie left; She has just left on a vacation).
8. fast (A fast horse runs; A fast color does not run).
9. mad (He's mad about chocolate; They were mad at me for being late).
10. livid (The accident victim was a livid color; He was livid with anger).
11. sanction (The king gave his sanction; They imposed sanctions on the warring parties).
12. quantum leap (In physics, this means a sudden change in an atom or molecule; in general use it means a huge change).
13. wind up (Let's wind up this meeting; The clock starts when I wind it up).
14. think better of (I think better of him after he saved the cat; I have thought better of telling my boss he's a fool).

62. Definitions

1. umbrella.
2. quintuplet.
3. vintner.
4. stretcher.
5. dog.
6. gasket.
7. catamaran.
8. giblets.
9. troika.
10. culottes.
11. litmus.
12. defenestration.

63. *Portmanteau Words*
1. motor + hotel.
2. smoke + fog.
3. television + marathon.
4. Oxford + Cambridge.
5. simultaneous + broadcast.
6. Francais + Anglais.
7. lion + tiger (actually the result of mating a male lion with a tigress).
8. aviation + electronics.
9. tangerine + pomelo (grapefruit).
10. Spanish + English.

64. *Abbreviations*
1. very important person.
2. unidentified flying object.
3. Nebraska.
4. decibels.
5. standard operating procedure.
6. répondez s'il vous plaît (i.e., please reply).
7. knots.
8. please turn over.
9. United Arab Emirates and Virgin Islands.
10. a public relations expert.
11. political action committee.
12. requiescat in pace (Latin for "rest in peace").
13. lysergic acid diethylamide.
14. standing room only.

65. *Dictionary*
1. An *ampersand* is the symbol &, signifying the word "and." It is a corruption of the phrase 'and per se and,' which means "*&* by itself is *and.*"
2. The *verso* is the left-hand page of a book (the right-hand page is called the *recto*).
3. A *lustrum* is a period of five years.
4. *Bourride* is a fish stew similar to bouillabaisse.
5. A *termagant* is a quarrelsome woman. The word is a corruption of the name of a domineering character in the old morality plays.
6. A *polymath* is a very knowledgeable person.

7. *Cervine* means "of or like a deer."

8. *Candytuft* is a plant.

9. A *rebec* is a stringed musical instrument, popular in medieval times, played with a bow.

10. *Largo* designates a slow tempo in music.

11. The *zebu* is an Indian ox.

12. A *hogan* is a Navajo Indian hut.

13. An *accipiter* is a hawk of the genus *Accipiter*.

14. A *fianchetto* is a move in the game of chess, involving the bishop.

15. *Boustrophedon* describes writing that goes alternately from right to left and left to right. The word comes from two Greek words, which together mean "ox turning"—as this form of writing takes the same course as an ox does when pulling a plow.

66. Humpty Dumpty

1. abound, beware, debate, grisly, happen, latish, mighty, nowise, pinion, tangle, thrown, trough, uplift, worthy, zealot.

2. airplane, conflate, gangrene, indebted, material, maternal, migraine, palatial, parabola, reappear, squiggly, tangible, untraced, worrying, zodiacal.

67. Personal Anagrams

1. Erasmus.

2. Alec Guinness.

3. Roosevelt.

4. Jay Leno.

5. Elvis Presley.

6. Piet Mondrian.

7. Miles Davis.

8. Lester Young.

9. Fats Waller.

10. Martin Luther King (Jr.).

68. Malapropisms

1. prospector (a prospector is a person who explores a region in search of something precious, usually gold; a prospectus is a brochure advertising a project, commercial enterprise, etc.).

2. terra firma (terra firma means solid ground or dry land; terra-cotta is unglazed earthenware).

3. fait accompli (a fait accompli is something that has been done and cannot be altered; a Fiat is a make of car).

4. contradiction (contradiction means denying the truth of something; contraception is the intentional prevention of pregnancy).

5. irrelevant (irrelevant means not applicable or pertinent; irreverent means disrespectful or sacrilegious).

6. antidote (an antidote is a medicine that counteracts a poison; an anecdote is a short account or story).

7. prostrate (prostrate means lying down; prostate is a gland in male bodies).

8. voracious (voracious means greedy or ravenous; veracious means truthful).

9. salvia (salvia is a flowering plant; saliva is a liquid secreted in the mouth).

10. equilateral (equilateral means having all sides equal; equatorial means of or near the equator).

11. dilemma (someone on the horns of a dilemma is faced with equally unattractive alternatives; an enema is an injection of liquid into the rectum).

12. varicose veins (varicose veins are veins that are swollen, a condition that has nothing to do with their being 'very close' together).

69. Daft Definitions

1. Someone whose career is in ruins.
2. A mosquito.
3. The rear entrance to a cafeteria.
4. A line of people waiting for a haircut.
5. A young male ant.
6. A table of rivers.
7. The longest river in Egypt.
8. The opposite of dat arm.
9. Clothing for the Lone Ranger's horse.
10. A dead emu.
11. A small pig.
12. A manicurist.
13. A roundabout way of showing affection.
14. A sick bird of prey.
15. A sleeping bag.
16. A female moth.
17. Misty-eyed.
18. (Of a tooth) not yet decayed.

19. A female tribal leader.
20. Someone who hangs out with a crook.
21. A wet forecast.
22. Your former spouse.
23. The cost for a small pastry.
24. A dugout canoe.
25. A saltine dipped in Tabasco sauce.
26. A dead giveaway.

70. Mishmash
(Other answers are possible.)
1. badger, budget, codger, hedgehog, lodger, midget.
2. fission, fussiness, mission, passion, passionate.
3. elsewhere, unsewn, housewares.
4. snapdragon, lapdog.
5. without, hothouse.
6. earthquake.
7. hyena, doyens.
8. anecdote.
9. tongue, language, linguist.
10. overstuff, understudy.
11. evergreen, overgrown.
12. echoing.
13. somewhat, somewhere.
14. thoroughgoing.
15. killjoy.
16. asphyxia.
17. headquarters.
18. offbeat.
19. catchphrase.
20. toothpaste.
21. blitzkrieg.
22. minesweeper.

71. Eponyms

1. Geiger (Johannes Hans Wilhelm Geiger)—after whom was named the *Geiger counter*.

2. Pullman (the *Pullman car* was designed by George Mortimer Pullman).

3. Clerihew (devised by Edmund Clerihew Bentley, who also wrote the detective novel *Trent's Last Case*). Clerihews are short comic (often nonsensical) poems about famous people, such as:

   Sir Christopher Wren
   Said 'I am going to dine with some men.
   If anybody calls,
   Say I am designing St Paul's.'

4. Bowdlerize (from Thomas Bowdler).

5. Woden (or Odin or Wotan), whose name is preserved in Wednesday.

6. The Lindy (named after Charles A. Lindbergh, nicknamed 'Lucky Lindy, ' the first aviator to fly solo nonstop across the Atlantic).

7. Thomas Hobson, a stable owner who, when he rented out horses, insisted that his customers take the horse nearest the stable door. Thus *Hobson's choice* came to mean the choice of taking what is offered—or nothing at all.

8. Mach, as in *Mach 1, Mach 2* (named after Ernst Mach, who defined the speed of objects in relation to the speed of sound).

9. *Salmonella* (from Daniel Elmer Salmon).

10. Jules Léotard.

11. Möbius strip (from August Ferdinand Möbius).

12. (a) Sousaphone (after the 19th- and 20th-century American band-leader and composer John Philip Sousa); (b) saxophone (after Adolphe Sax).

Part Three

72. Silent Letters

There are various possibilities for most letters of the alphabet. Here are some suggestions:

   A: board, coat. B: bomb, doubt. C: muscle, scene. D: djinn. E: euca-lyptus, groove. G: campaign, gnat, sign. H: heir, honor, hour. I: friend, fruit. J: marijuana. K: knife, knock. L: almond, calf, salmon. M: mnemonic. N: damn, solemn. P: pneumatic, psalm, receipt. R: forecas-tle. S: island, viscount. T: castle, Tchaikovsky. U: circuit, plaque. W: write, wrong. X: tableaux; Y: Yugoslavia, Yukon; Z: rendezvous.

   It is difficult to find examples of silent pronunciations for F, O, Q, or V, but perhaps *you* can manage these as well!

73. Hidden Word Squares

1. A R I A
   R I N G
   I N T O
   A G O G

2. H O N E
   O P A L
   N A G S
   E L S E

3. G R I D
   R I S E
   I S L E
   D E E D

4. L A N E
   A R E A
   N E A R
   E A R S

5. O M E N
   M A D E
   E D I T
   N E T S

6. R A T S
   A B U T
   T U B A
   S T A B

74. Kangaroo Words

1. amiable.
2. apt.
3. save.
4. hotel.
5. urge.
6. lie.
7. ere.
8. tutor.
9. part.
10. tomb.
11. idle.
12. rain.
13. debate.
14. see.
15. sin.
16. ugly.
17. ruin.
18. male.
19. nth.
20. as.
21. lone, one.
22. can, tin.
23. fragile, frail.
24. falsies, lies.
25. amble, ramble.
26. pure, purged.

75. Down Under

1. Afternoon.
2. To spoil or thwart.
3. A rumor; a false or absurd story.
4. To fight or punch.
5. A foolish or stupid person.
6. To attempt to deceive.
7. A remote outback town or district.
8. A man or youth who dresses flashily or shows off.
9. To return from retirement or make several farewell appearances (as the Australian opera singer Nellie Melba did).

10. A hopeless-looking ineffectual person.
11. To hurry up.
12. Everything is fine.

76. Derivations
1. Trump.
2. July (from *Julius* Caesar) and August (from *Augustus* Caesar).
3. Don.
4. America.
5. Jigsaw puzzle.
6. Chef.
7. Astronaut.
8. Diploma.

77. Hermans
1. Lena.
2. Winnie.
3. Flora.
4. Mimi.
5. Rose.
6. Violet.
7. Nola.
8. Lulu.
9. Gail.
10. Sally.
11. Victor.
12. Frank.
13. Isadore.
14. Doug.
15. Neil.
16. Josh.
17. Seymour.
18. Adam.
19. Toby.
20. Roger.

78. Letter Swaps
A: apt - pat.
B: bolster - lobster.
C: conversation - conservation.
D: danger - gander.
E: expected - excepted.
G: gateway - getaway.
H: harken - hanker.
L: leadership - dealership.
M: marital - martial.
N: nuclear - unclear.
O: overdoes - overdose.
P: plaster - psalter.
R: rectitude - certitude.
S: sacred - scared.
T: toot - Toto.
U: urination - ruination.
W: wordy - rowdy.

79. Associations

1. Pound ("penny wise, *pound* <u>foolish</u>" is a familiar proverb; <u>Ezra</u> *Pound* was an influential 20th-century poet; Shylock demanded his '*pound* of <u>flesh</u>' in Shakespeare's *Merchant of Venice*; the symbol for "<u>number</u>" (#) is the same symbol used to designate *pound*; a *pound* is a measure of <u>weight</u>).

2. Easter (*Easter* <u>Island</u> is off the coast of South America; <u>Teresa</u> is an anagram of *Easter*; *Easter* <u>Parade</u> is the title of a song and a movie; "<u>less west</u>" is a punning clue for "more east," or *easter*; <u>eggs</u> are traditionally colored at *Easter* time).

3. Cause (it occurs in the compound *cause<u>way</u>* and in the phrase <u>lost</u> *cause*; <u>sauce</u> is an anagram of *cause*; <u>James Dean</u> starred in the movie *Rebel Without a Cause*; effect is used in the phrase *cause and <u>effect</u>*).

4. Waste ('*Waste* not, <u>want</u> not,' says the proverb; <u>sweat</u> is an anagram of *waste*; T. S. Eliot's most famous poem was called *The Waste <u>Land</u>*; '<u>Haste</u> makes *waste*' says another proverb; you should recycle your *waste<u>paper</u>*).

5. Nature (a familiar dichotomy is '*nature* versus <u>nuture</u>'; rearrange the letters of <u>a tuner</u> and you get *nature*; *Nature* <u>Boy</u> is the title of a popular song; we are told that '*Nature* abhors a <u>vacuum</u>'; we have all heard of <u>Mother</u> *Nature*).

6. Ruby (in *The Wizard of Oz*, Dorothy wore the enchanted *ruby* <u>slippers</u>; *Ruby* <u>Tuesday</u> was a hit record for the Rolling Stones in 1967; a *ruby* wedding anniversary; *Ruby* <u>Gentry</u> was a 1952 movie starring Jennifer Jones; singer <u>Kenny Rogers</u> had a hit in 1969 with *Ruby*).

7. Sin (a popular song says 'It's a *sin* to tell a <u>lie</u>'; many Christians believe in the doctrine of <u>Original</u> *Sin*; 'The <u>wages</u> of *sin* is death,' said St. Paul; there are said to be <u>seven</u> deadly *sins*; the proverb says that 'Charity covers a <u>multitude</u> of *sins*').

8. Turtle (there are *turtle<u>neck</u>* shirts; 'The <u>voice</u> of the *turtle* is heard in our land,' says the Song of Solomon in the Bible; the *turtle<u>dove</u>* is a bird; the <u>Mock</u> *Turtle* appears in Lewis Carroll's *Alice in Wonderland*).

80. Heteronyms

1. sow (pronounced to rhyme with 'go' and 'cow').
2. minute (pronounced <u>min</u>-nit and my-<u>newt</u>).
3. refuse (pronounced ri-<u>fyooz</u> and <u>ref</u>-yoos).
4. tear (pronounced to rhyme with 'bare' and 'fear').
5. bass (pronounced to rhyme with 'case' and 'pass').
6. does (pronounced to rhyme with 'fuzz' and 'nose').
7. desert (pronounced di-<u>zert</u> and <u>dez</u>-ert).
8. sewer (pronounced to rhyme with 'newer' and 'lower').
9. intimate (pronounced <u>in</u>-ti-mate and <u>in</u>-ti-mut).

10. invalid (pronounced <u>in</u>-vi-lid and in-<u>val</u>-id).
11. sake (pronounced to rhyme with 'jockey' and 'cake').
12. agape (pronounced a-<u>gayp</u> and ah-<u>gah</u>-pay).

81. Transadditions
(Many other answers are possible.)
1. he - she - hers - share - hearts - shatter - theaters.
2. en - ten - nest - scent - ascent - ascents.
3. I - is - sir - sari - rains - arisen - nastier - straiten - transient - itinerants.
4. O - to - hot - shot - short - throes - torches - crochets - crotchets; or O
   - no - ton - note - tenor - orient - retinol - relation - relations.
5. re - era - pear - taper - depart - trapped - strapped.
6. lo - sol - lost - stole - hostel - holster - hostlers.
7. in - win - wing - swing - swinge - swinger - swingers.
8. a - at - tan - rant - train - retain - certain - reaction - cremation -
   importance - emancipator; or a - at - tea - sate - tears - astern - nastier
   - entrains - transient - stentorian - transection; or a - at - rat - rate -
   irate - attire - nitrate - interact - intricate - recitation - ratiocinate -
   reactivation.

82. Tom Swifties
1. intently or tentatively.
2. engagingly.
3. gravely.
4. sternly.
5. croaked.
6. choked.
7. beamed.
8. icily or coldly.
9. explained.
10. disorientedly.
11. with conviction.
12. scoffed.
13. gushed.
14. infectiously.
15. superficially.
16. admiringly.
17. in distress.
18. painfully.
19. cut in sharply.
20. offhandedly.

83. Typewriter Words

Some of the words that you can type on the top row of the keyboard are: *pepper, perpetuity, poetry, proprietor, purity, quire, repertoire,* and *torture.* Of these, *perpetuity, proprietor,* and *repertoire* are the longest, all containing ten letters. But perhaps the most interesting word that can be typed on the top row is another ten-letter word: *typewriter!*

84. Quotations

1. Why don't you come up sometime, and see me? - Mae West to Cary Grant in the 1933 movie *She Done Him Wrong.*

2. Laugh, and the world laughs with you; weep, and you weep alone. - in Ella Wheeler Wilcox's poem *Solitude.*

3. To gild refined gold, to paint the lily. - in Shakespeare's *King John,* Act 4.

4. Fresh woods, and pastures new. - in Milton's poem *Lycidas.*

5. A little learning is a dangerous thing. - in Alexander Pope's *Essay on Criticism.*

6. If she can stand it, I can. Play it! - Humphrey Bogart in the 1942 movie *Casablanca,* in which Ingrid Bergman had earlier said 'Play it, Sam. Play *As Time Goes By.'*

7. Music has charms to soothe a savage breast. - in Congreve's *The Mourning Bride,* Act 1.

8. The love of money is the root of all evil. - in the *Bible,* I Timothy, 6:10 (King James version).

9. Ask me no questions and I'll tell you no fibs. - in Oliver Goldsmith's *She Stoops to Conquer,* Act 3.

10. History, we know, is apt to repeat itself. - in George Eliot's *Janet's Repentance* in *Scenes of Clerical Life.*

85. Anagrammed Places

1. Lancaster.
2. Rome.
3. Lima or Mali.
4. Dover.
5. Peru.
6. Pontiac.
7. Persia.
8. Paris.
9. Oslo.
10. Burma.
11. Laredo.
12. Iran.
13. Athens.
14. Las Vegas.
15. Ontario.
16. Crete.
17. Rhodes.
18. Naples.
19. Italy.
20. Laos.
21. China.
22. Israel.

23. Palestine.   25. Singapore.
24. Algeria.   26. Suez.

86. Devil's Dictionary
1. year.   11. Christmas.
2. teetotaler.   12. lawyer.
3. gout.   13. hammer.
4. bore.   14. patriot.
5. circus.   15. politics.
6. judge.   16. hypocrite.
7. dentist.   17. politeness.
8. jealousy.   18. labor.
9. saint.   19. relief.
10. destiny.   20. platitude.

87. Synonym Chains
(Many answers are possible.)
1. good - moral - innocent - simple - stupid - incompetent - bad.
2. terrible - formidable - excellent.
3. wise - prudent - frugal - mean - trifling - foolish.
4. victory - win - rout - defeat.
5. absent - out - disclosed - visible - existing - present.
6. brave - intrepid - reckless - negligent - slovenly - vile - dastardly - cowardly.

88. Spoonerisms
1. horrid tugs - torrid hugs.
2. rock coaches - cockroaches.
3. toenails - no tails.
4. butterfly - flutter by.
5. cozy nook - nosy cook.
6. nagging wife - wagging knife.
7. big fire - fig buyer.
8. long river - wrong liver.
9. bird watcher - word botcher.
10. low song - so long.

89. Two-letter words

1. us or we.	8. pa.
2. er or um.	9. op.
3. pi.	10. aw.
4. bo.	11. os.
5. oh or ah.	12. io.
6. em or en.	13. ow.
7. bi.	14. ai.

90. Perverbs

There are no 'correct' answers to this section, but here are some possible perverted changes to the proverbs.

1. Half a loaf is better than a quarter of a loaf.
2. The pen is mightier than a stubby bit of pencil.
3. People who live in glass houses shouldn't undress with the light on.
4. A woman's work is never fun.
5. Cast your bread upon the waters and it gets all soggy.
6. The best form of defense is running away.
7. He who hesitates is . . . er, what was that again?
8. A penny saved is not much of a nest egg.
9. See no evil, hear no evil, have no fun at all.
10. Early to bed and early to rise, and your girl goes out with other guys.

91. Mishmash (2)

1. ameba.	6. underground.
2. termite.	7. ionization.
3. enlighten.	8. essentialness.
4. alluvial.	9. bleachable.
5. entertainment.	10. bedaubed.

92. Oxymorons

awful good	inside out
baby grand	jumbo shrimp
bitter sweet	light heavyweight
deliberate mistake	liquid gas
dry ice	live recording
idiot savant	living death
ill health	missing link

random order student teacher
same difference white chocolate
science fiction wireless cable

93. Origins

1. *Alibi*, which is Latin for "elsewhere"—from the plea that a defendant was somewhere else at the time when a crime was committed. The word is now a noun but it was originally used as an adverb: 18th-century law reports refer to defendants trying to prove that 'they were alibi.'

2. *Karaoke*, which is Japanese for "empty orchestra." *Karaoke* is a form of entertainment in which individuals or groups sing popular songs to prerecorded soundtracks.

3. The *alligator*, which the Spaniards called *el lagarto* ("the lizard") when explorers first encountered it. In fact *lagarto* derives from the Latin word *lacertus* (meaning "the muscles of the upper arm"), perhaps because all lizards were originally thought to be as long as a person's forearm. It must have shocked the explorers to discover the alligator, which is much longer than anyone's forearm. However, it is no cause for crying *crocodile tears*, which were named from the belief that crocodiles pretended to cry so as to attract their victims.

4. *Galaxy*, which comes ultimately from the Greek *gala, galaktos*, meaning "milk." 'The Galaxy' originally referred to the Milky Way and came to be applied to other groups of stars.

5. The *Angora cat, Angora goat,* and *Angora rabbit* all get their names from *Angora*, the old form of *Ankara*, the capital of Turkey. All three types of animal are distinguished by their long hair: the mohair the merrier!

6. *Ballot*, from Italian *ballotta*, meaning "a small ball, " named from the old-fashioned method of voting by dropping different colored balls (in ancient Greece, shards of pottery were used) into a jar. White balls favored the candidate; black balls expressed disapproval: hence the expression 'to *blackball*.'

7. *Kamikaze*, which comes from the Japanese. The *kamikazes* were Japanese suicide pilots who, during World War II, deliberately crashed their aircraft into enemy targets. The word *kamikaze* is Japanese for "divine wind" and it dates back to the divinely inspired (or expired?) gale that destroyed Mongol ships attacking Japan in 1281.

8. *Checkmate*, in the game of chess, describing the end of a game because the king cannot move without being taken. The word *checkmate* comes from Persian *shah mat* or *sah mat* "the king is defeated or helpless." Although the queen is the most powerful piece in chess, the king decides the game's outcome: a situation implied because the word *chess* derives ultimately from *s(h)ah* "the king."

9. *Migraine*, an extremely painful headache, deriving ultimately from a shortening of Greek *hemikrania* "half the cranium." It was so named

because migraines were originally thought to affect only one side of the head.

10. *Miniature*, which sounds as if it comes from the Latin *minor* (small) or *minimus* (smallest). But the root is actually *minium*, which was a red lead or vermilion. Red lead was used to illuminate manuscripts with decorative paintings. Because these *miniatures* were usually small, they were confused with *minor* and *minimus*. Thus *miniature* came to mean "very small."

11. An *anthology*, which comes from a Greek word meaning "flower collection."

12. The *butler*, whose title derives ultimately from the Old French *bouteille* meaning "bottle."

13. The broad-brimmed *sombrero*, a Spanish word that comes from *sombra* "shade"—which is connected with the word *sombre* (from the Latin *sub* "under" + *umbra* "shade").

14. *Copper*, which derives from the Latin *cyprium aes* "metal of Cyprus"— so named because Cyprus was a noted source of this metal.

15. The *amethyst*, which was thought to prevent drunkenness. It comes from Greek *amethustos*, which means "not wine."

16. *Malaria*, an Italian word that comes from *mala aria* "bad air." Before the mosquito was declared guilty of causing the disease, malaria was believed to arise from the bad air emanating from marshy places.

17. *Furlong*, a distance of one-eighth of a mile, is now used primarily to describe the length of horse races. Originally the word meant "furrow-long"—that is, the usual length of a furrow plowed in a common field.

18. *Foolscap*, a paper that used to have a watermark of a jester's cap— hence the name.

94. Cryptic Clues

A. agony column (a caryatid is a statue that holds up a column).

B. before (*be* meaning "to live" + *fore* a golfer's warning = *before* which means "earlier").

C. castles in the air (keeps = castles).

D. diabetes (anagram of *beadiest*).

E. eardrum (anagram of *read* + *rum*, which is a spirit).

F. franks and beans (Anne and Sinatra are two famous *Franks*, and haricot and pole are two types of *beans*).

G. guinea (a guinea pig; a *guinea* is an old English coin worth 21 shillings).

H. ha-ha (a word for a sunken fence or wall).

I. ice cube (a *die* is a cube, best known in the plural *dice*).

J. jardiniere (a *jardinière* is a pot for plants; the original French word meant a female gardener).

K. kingpin (anagram of *pink gin*; 'kingpin' is a 'very important person,' or VIP).

L. loser (*cLOSE-Run*).

M. magazine (a *magazine* is a publication and also a container for bullets).

N. notwithstanding.

O. orifice (an opening, made up from *or* = alternatively + *if* = supposing + *ice*, which is frozen).

P. passenger list (a *list* is the tilt of a ship).

Q. Quakers (also known as the Society of Friends).

R. rotunda (anagram of *do a turn*).

S. squatters.

T. thinking (*thin* + *king*).

U. usage (*US* + *age*).

V. verticals (anagram of *silver cat*).

W. ward (*draw* spelled backward).

X. Xerox (*X* = ten, surrounding *ero*, which is three-quarters of *zero*).

Y. yellow (*yell ow!*).

Z. zebra (anagram of *brazen*, without the final *n*).

95. Uncommon Terms

accoucheur = a male midwife.

anosmia = the loss of the sense of smell.

atrabilious = melancholy; ill-tempered.

Barmecide = a giver of benefits that are illusory or disappointing.

batter = a wall with a sloping face.

demirep = a woman of doubtful sexual reputation.

devil's darning needle = a dragonfly or damselfly.

ecru = the color of unbleached linen.

gelada = a brownish gregarious baboon with a bare red patch on its chest.

haplology = the omission of sounds when these are repeated in a word.

inhume = to bury.

liger = the offspring of a lion and a tigress.

narthex = an antechamber in a church.

nulliparous = relating to a woman who has never borne a child.

paramnesia = an illusory feeling of having already experienced a present situation (= *déjà vu*).

serein = a fine rain falling in tropical climates from a cloudless sky.

tret = an allowance of extra weight formerly made to purchasers of some goods for waste in transportation.

versant = the extent of land sloping in one direction.

vexillology = the study of flags.

zugzwang = in the game of chess, an obligation to move even when this must be disadvantageous.

96. Russian Dolls

1. ant + pies = panties.
2. ever + fish = feverish.
3. for + bee = before.
4. is + muse = misuse.
5. pi + ash = apish.
6. salt + per = psalter.
7. angel + chess = changeless.
8. onto + cur = contour.
9. men + tenet = tenement.
10. mica + able = amicable.
11. urn + tip = turnip.
12. and + beau = bandeau.
13. no + ten = tenon.
14. do + manna = Madonna.
15. chant + merman = merchant-man.
16. rough + DTs = droughts.

97. Rebuses

1. (a) N V (envy); (b) I V (ivy); (c) S A (essay); (d) A T (eighty).
2. Some possibilities are K T (Katie), L C (Elsie), L N (Ellen), M L E (Emily), L N R (Eleanor).
3. R U O K (Are you okay?)
4. (a) P N E (peony); (b) N T T (entity); (c) N M E (enemy); (d) N R G (energy).
5. (a) B 4 (before); (b) D V 8 (deviate); (c) X 10 U 8 (extenuate).
6. OXFORD (0 + the Roman numeral X for *ten* + three-fifths of *FORty* + the Roman numeral D for 500).
7. The Seven Seas; Andes; all for one and one for all; damper sand (D + ampersand); bingo (B in GO); to make a long story short (*War and Peace* shortened); appendectomy (append E C to M Y); beaten (B - the Roman numeral for ten); wined and dined (W in E D and D in E D); head in the sand.
8. Possibilities are E NT U RY and E P O H (*century* and *epoch* without the 'C').
9. *Deep in the Heart of Texas* (which is the location of the letter 'X' in the word 'Texas').
10. Possible answers (there may be thousands of others):

A = the second of JAnuary (or the sixth of FebruAry, or the second of MArch . . .)

D = dauntless aunt (i.e., *daunt* less *aunt*).

V = the center of graVity.

R = the bitteR end.

98. Vowels in Order

1. ambidextrous, calciferous.
2. anxiousness, grandiloquent, variousness.
3. jalousie, tambourine.
4. auctioned, cauliflower, cautioned.
5. authorize.
6. mendacious, nefarious, precarious, tenacious, veracious.
7. crematorium, pelargonium.
8. pedagoguism.
9. exhaustion.
10. gesticulatory.
11. encouraging, expostulating.
12. deputation, education, equation, mensuration, peculation, permutation, persuasion, regulation, reputation, speculation.
13. elucidator, elucidatory, enunciator.
14. eulogia, euphoria, pneumonia, sequoia.
15. dialogue.
16. incommensurably.
17. discourage, importunate, inoculate, inosculate.
18. thiourea.
19. vituperator.
20. odalisque, portraiture.
21. boatbuilder.
22. overhauling.
23. fountained, ossuaries, outpatient.
24. counterclaim, countermanding, countermarching, countervail, housemaid, outreaching.
25. volumetrically.
26. communicate.
27. mustachioed, ultraviolet, unsanctioned.
28. numeration, ulceration.
29. questionary.
30. unsportsmanlike.
31. subordinate, uncopiable, unmotivated, unsociable.
32. subcontinental, uncomplimentary, unnoticeably.

99. Overspecialized Words

1. An eagle without beak or feet = alerion.
2. The quality or condition of being bread = paneity.
3. The worship of bread = artolatry.
4. The practice among certain peoples of naming a parent from his or her child = teknonymy.
5. Of the day before yesterday = nudiustertian.
6. The first person one meets after leaving home on some special occasion = qualtagh.
7. Having less than four syllables = oligosyllabic.
8. Cow's urine, as a remedy = all-flower-water.
9. A sacrifice of a thousand oxen = chiliomb.
10. A disease that leaves yellowish patches on the skin = xanthelasma.
11. A practitioner of evil magic = abatagati.
12. Someone whose hair was never cut = acersecomic.
13. Having the shape or form of a mulberry = moriform.
14. A place in which frogs are kept = ranarium.
15. A government by the wind = anemocracy.
16. A small swivel-gun, especially one mounted on the back of a camel = zumbooruk.
17. Struggling blindfolded = andabatarian.
18. Feeding on onions = cepivorous.
19. The act of cutting off, with a saw, the extreme parts of the body, when putrefied = acroteriasm.
20. Walking equally in opposite directions = amphisbaenous.

100. French Eponyms

1. Braille — from Louis Braille (1809–52).
2. Guillotine — from Joseph Ignace Guillotin (1738–1814).
3. Sadism — from the Marquis de Sade (1740–1814).
4. Chauvinism — from Nicolas Chauvin, a soldier who idolized Napoleon.
5. Silhouette — from Étienne de Silhouette (1709–67).
6. Pasteurization — after Louis Pasteur (1822–95).
7. Nicotine — from Jean Nicot (?1530–1600), who introduced tobacco to France.
8. Pompadour — from Madame de Pompadour (1721–64), mistress of King Louis XV.

101. Crossed Lines

It is difficult to find suitable words that start with F, N, and R. Possible misleading words for the other letters are: aesthetic, bdellium, cue, djinn, eye, gnosticism, hour, Iwo Jima, jai alai, knee, llano (with Spanish pronunciation 'yahno'), mnemonic, Ouija, pneumonia, Quito, see, Tchaikovsky, urn, volkslied, why, xylophone, you, and Zhou Enlai.

102. Acronyms (2)

1. United Nations International Children's Emergency Fund (now United Nations Emergency Fund).
2. United Nations Educational, Scientific, and Cultural Organization.
3. Light amplification by stimulated emission of radiation.
4. Queensland and Northern Territory Aerial Services.
5. Deutsche Industrie-Norm (or Das ist Norm).
6. Fabbrica Italiana Automobili Torino.

103. What is the Question?

1. What do firemen do?
2. How do Spanish fishermen work?
3. Which herb is best for flavoring soup?
4. Johann is third in line, but where is Ludwig?
5. Has Sam received his salary?
6. What is Berlioz's symphony like?
7. What is Tchaikovsky's 6th Symphony like?
8. What did Hamlet say at Weight Watchers?
9. What do you call a sarcastic telegram?
10. What is the most explosive sociological unit?
11. What does Henry Sweet do at night?
12. How many chocolates did you have, Caesar?
13. How do you order someone to fetch Richard in a hurry?
14. What do sonnet writers have to renew annually?
15. What does a neurologist take to the laundry room?
16. Where in a magazine would you find information about male sheep?
17. What do you get when you put a photographer in a skillet?
18. What is the result when each cardplayer wants to deal first?

104. Mnemonics

1. The fate of King Henry VIII's six wives.

2. In music, the notes on each line of the staff of the treble clef: E, G, B, D, F.

3. The colors of the spectrum (red, orange, yellow, green, blue, indigo, violet).

4. The planets, moving out from the sun: Mercury, Venus, Earth, Mars, Jupiter, Saturn, Uranus, Neptune, Pluto.

5. The Seven Deadly Sins: wrath, avarice, sloth, pride, lust, envy, gluttony.

6. The Great Lakes: Huron, Ontario, Michigan, Erie, and Superior. The sentence beginning 'Sergeant Major . . .' gives the lakes in their correct order from west to east.

7. The presidents of the United States from 1789 to 2000: Washington, Adams, Jefferson, Madison, Monroe, Adams, Jackson, Van Buren, Harrison, Tyler, Polk, Taylor, Fillmore, Pierce, Buchanan, Lincoln, Johnson, Grant, Hayes, Garfield, Arthur, Cleveland, Harrison, Cleveland, McKinley, Roosevelt, Taft, Wilson, Harding, Coolidge, Hoover, Roosevelt, Truman, Eisenhower, Kennedy, Johnson, Nixon, Ford, Carter, Reagan, Bush, Clinton.

8. The monarchs of England from 1066 to 1901: William, William, Henry, Stephen, Henry, Richard, John, Henry, Edward, Edward, Edward, Richard, Henry, Henry, Henry, Edward, Edward, Richard, Henry, Henry, Edward, Mary, Elizabeth, James, Charles, Charles, James, William, Anne, George, George, George, George, William, Victoria.

105. Consonants

(Other answers are possible.)

1. witchcraft.
2. catchphrase.
3. rhythms or strychnine.
4. strengths.
5. baccalaureate.
6. assesses.
7. gagging.
8. doddered.
9. riff-raff.
10. giggling.
11. pell-mell.
12. nonunion.
13. referrer.
14. knickknack.
15. razzmatazz.
16. whippersnapper.

106. *Vowel Language*
(Other answers are possible.)

1. queueing.
2. teepee.
3. voodoo.
4. muumuu.
5. referee.
6. maharaja.
7. beekeeper.
8. amalgamate.
9. visibility.
10. tumultuous.
11. indivisibility.

107. *The Final Challenge*
(Other answers are possible.)

1. Sweden (Eden).
2. Botswana (swan), Romania (man), Iceland (eland), Morocco (roc), Turkey, Guinea.
3. Humphrey ('hump-free').
4. Socrates (anagram of *coarsest*)
5. A hardy laurel ('Laurel and Hardy').
6. Ultramarine.
7. Malady (*ma - lady*).
8. Cashew.
9. Because the keys are inside.
10. Schubert (he wrote the *Unfinished Symphony*).
11. Doggone!
12. Edam (the word *made* in reverse).
13. Volume nine.
14. On a baseball field.
15. Nicaragua, Paraguay (which both contain *rag*)
16. Ohio.
17. Remove 'OLI' from *Goliath* to make *Gath*.
18. Upholstery (which contains *holster*)
19. NOON and SWIMS are two.
20. Dichlorodiphenyltrichloroethane.
21. Because they have the same middle name.
22. Lathe, in which *la* (the French for "the") precedes *the*.
23. Four.
24. SeVen (V is the Roman numeral for five).
25. FIVe (IV is the Roman numeral for four).
26. Series, species.
27. At least five: pi, one, 1, 10, and 0.

28. The brontosaurus ('The Brontës saw us').
29. *Twist and Shout* ('and shout' is an anagram of *thousand*).
30. Hamadryad.
31. 'I Don't Know.'
32. came – cameo; ides – ideas; lien – alien; rode – rodeo; smile – simile; whine – wahine.
33. Transatlantic.
34. Best and worst.
35. *Zymurgy* (135), *tryouts* (138).